Harvard Semitic Monographs

Volume 3

The Theodotionic Revision of the Book of Exodus

A Contribution to the Study of the Early History of the Transmission of the Old Testament in Greek

Kevin G. O'Connell, S.J.

Harvard University Press

Cambridge, Massachusetts

1972

Library of Congress card number 76-160026

SBN 674-87785-3

To my Father and Mother

PREFACE

The following study was prepared as a doctoral dissertation at Harvard University in 1965-67 under the direction of Professor Frank M. Cross, Jr. Prior to publication, the author has had the benefit of critical suggestions from Professor John Strugnell of Harvard and Msgr. Patrick W. Skehan of Catholic University. While their comments have always been taken into account, they are in no way responsible for the final expressions of opinion on specific points.

This book is not meant to provide the last word on the Palestinian revisions of the Septuagint in the first centuries B.C. and A.D. Rather it attempts, by rigorous investigation and careful attention to methodology, to provide a firm basis of information and evaluation from which further investigation can safely advance.

At this time I need only express my thanks to all who have helped make this book a reality: the Danforth Foundation, which supported my research and writing of the original dissertation through a Kent Fellowship; Miss Carol Cross, who has twice carefully typed the entire manuscript; Mr. Charles Przybylek and Mr. James D. Redington, S.J., who spent many weary hours helping me proofread the original manuscript; and especially my Jesuit brethren and my students, who found so many ways to help me stay human in the face of so much detailed and often random data.

Kevin G. O'Connell, S.J.
Cambridge, Massachusetts
August 1970

CONTENTS

ABBREVIATIONS

B	Vaticanus
BDB	F. Brown, S. R. Driver and C. A. Briggs, eds., *A Hebrew and English Lexicon of the Old Testament*, corrected reprint of 1907 ed. (Oxford, 1966)
B-McL	A. E. Brooke and N. McLean, with H. St. J. Thackeray for Vols. II and III, eds., *The Old Testament in Greek*: Vol. I, *The Octateuch*; Vol. II, *The Later Historical Books*; Vol. III, Part 1, *Esther, Judith, Tobit* (London, 1906-1940).
DA	D. Barthélemy, *Les devanciers d'Aquila* (Leiden, 1963)
Field	F. Field, ed., *Origenis Hexaplorum quae supersunt*, 2 vols. (Oxford, 1875)
H-R	E. Hatch and H. A. Redpath, *A Concordance to the Septuagint*, 3 vols. in 2 (Graz, Austria, 1954; photomechanical reprint of the 1897 Oxford ed.)
HTR	*Harvard Theological Review*
JBL	*Journal of Biblical Literature*
JQR	*Jewish Quarterly Review*
Lagarde	P. de Lagarde, *Bibliothecae Syriacae a Paulo de Lagarde collectae quae ad philologiam sacram pertinent*, ed. A. Rahlfs (Göttingen, 1892)
LXX	Septuagint
Mandelkern	S. Mandelkern, *Veteris Testamenti Concordantiae Hebraicae atque Chaldaicae*, 5th expanded and rev. ed. (Jerusalem—Tel-Aviv, 1962)
MT	Masoretic Text
OG	Old Greek
OT	Old Testament
PS	Peshitto
RB	*Revue Biblique*
RT	J. Reider, *An Index to Aquila*, completed and revised by N. Turner (Leiden, 1966)
$	Syro-hexapla
SP	Samaritan Pentateuch
TLZ	*Theologische Literaturzeitung*
TO	Targum Onkelus
VT	*Vetus Testamentum*
Ziegler	J. Ziegler, ed., *Septuaginta: Vetus Testamentum Graecum Auctoritate Societatis Litterarum Gottingensis editum*, Vols. XII-XVI (Göttingen, 1939-1965)

INTRODUCTION

Theodotion of Ephesus was a Gentile convert to Judaism who lived in the second century A.D. Traditionally, the hexaplaric readings marked with θ' (and hence coming from Origen's sixth column) have been attributed to an edition of the Greek Old Testament prepared by him sometime in the third quarter of the second century.[1] While it was recognized that some parts of Theodotion's version antedated the second century, and hence Theodotion himself, it was generally felt that the work as a whole owed its existence and character to the second century proselyte.[2]

---

[1]See, e.g., Field, pp. xxxviii-xlii; H. B. Swete, *An Introduction to the Old Testament in Greek*, rev. ed. (Cambridge, 1914), pp. 42-49; O. Eissfeldt, *The Old Testament: An Introduction*, tr. P. R. Ackroyd (New York and Evanston, 1965), p. 716.

[2]"Such unstability of the sacred text [i.e., in Greek] called for editorial intervention. On the other hand, the stabilization of the Hebrew text and its translation by Aquila facilitated the task by furnishing the future editor of the Septuagint with a standard of correctness. Theodotion of Ephesus, a Gentile converted to the Jewish faith, was the first, so far as we know, who undertook the task of revision, probably between 161-169. Since this *Theodotionis editio*, although filling up the lacunae of the current text (so in Job, Jeremiah) and cutting some expansions not found in the Hebrew (so in Daniel), was a revision of existing manuscripts, it is quite natural that 'Theodotionic' readings may appear long before his time, so in the New Testament and Josephus." E. J. Bickerman, "Some Notes on the Transmission of the Septuagint," *Alexander Marx Jubilee Volume* (New York, 1950), p. 173. B. J. Roberts, in *The Old Testament Text and Versions* (Cardiff, 1951), pp. 123-126, also gave the traditional view that Theodotion's revision of the LXX was made some fifty or sixty years after Aquila, but still in the second century A.D. He noted, however, that some, including Kahle and Orlinsky, have raised doubts about this position.

While this has been the dominant evaluation of Theodotion, a few scholarly voices have been raised in dissent. Thus, in 1936, H. M. Orlinsky stated:

> That chronology did not enter into the columnar make-up of the Hexapla is evident from the fact that the Septuagint of col. (v) antedated cols. (ii), (iii) and (iv), and that Theodotion in col. (vi) flourished prior to Symmachus in col. (iv) and almost certainly even to Aquila in col. (iii). [In a footnote to that sentence, he added:] There is absolutely no evidence other than that based upon the column order of the Hexapla that Aquila antedated Theodotion. All evidence extant definitely points to the priority of Theodotion to Aquila.[3]

Similar opinions have been expressed by F. Kenyon[4] and by P. Kahle.[5] While Theodotion's version has generally been considered a

---

[3]H. M. Orlinsky, "The Columnar Order of the Hexapla," *JQR* n.s. 27 (1936-1937), 142-143.

[4]"Since 'Theodotionic' readings are found in works earlier than the date of Theodotion (in the New Testament, Barnabas, Clement, Hermas, to say nothing of Irenaeus and Tertullian, who were his younger contemporaries), it would appear that Theodotion took over, with or without revision, an earlier translation which has otherwise disappeared except in these few quotations." *The Chester Beatty Biblical Papyri*, fasc. vii, *Ezekiel, Daniel, Esther* (London, 1937), p. x.

[5]After quoting the above statement of Kenyon, Kahle added: "As a matter of fact there can be no doubt that we must see in the text revised by Theodotion an 'earlier translation,' which clearly differed from the text later to become as 'Septuagint' the standard text of the Christian Church, and which was well-known and widely used in earlier times. The quotations from Daniel in writings of the first Christian century show that Theodotion could not have altered substantially the text of the older translation when he adapted it to the authoritative Hebrew text....This old form of the Greek Bible must have been held in high esteem. It was widely quoted in its unrevised form during the first Christian century; after its revision by Theodotion, the text of Daniel was taken over by the Church." *The Cairo Genizah*, 2nd ed. (Oxford, 1959), p. 253; see also pp. 195-196.

revision of the LXX text rather than a fresh translation,[6] Kahle argued that it contains an originally independent translation of the Hebrew text.

In 1952, a Greek scroll of the Minor Prophets was discovered in the Wâdî Khabrâ. D. Barthélemy recognized almost immediately that the scroll represented a systematic revision of the LXX into conformity with a Hebrew text that was directly related to the present MT, though not identical with it.[7] Since the scroll can be dated to approximately the late first century B.C. or the early first century A.D., the revision itself must be at least that early.[8] Barthélemy further suggested that this early revision was known and used by Aquila in his further revision to the present MT sometime in the early second century A.D.

Barthélemy's suggestions were criticized by Kahle,[9] but he has now provided fairly substantial evidence to support them.[10] Barthélemy argued that this new revision (which he called both "R" and ΚΑΙΓΕ, from its systematic use of Greek καιγε to represent MT *gm*) was to be identified with various other elements in the manuscript traditions of the

---

[6]"Theodotion seems to have produced a free revision of the LXX rather than an independent version." Swete, *Introduction*, p. 43. "In contrast to that of Aquila, [Theodotion's translation] laid stress upon an intelligible Greek, but otherwise is less a fresh translation than a revision of 𝔊 undertaken with as great a dependence as possible upon 𝔐." Eissfeldt, *Introduction*, p. 716. See also the quotation from Bickerman given above in fn. 2.

[7]D. Barthélemy, "Redécouverte d'un chaînon manquant de l'histoire de la Septante," *RB* 60 (1953), 18-29.

[8]Barthélemy first dated the scroll to the end of the first century A.D. (*ibid.*, p. 19), but C. H. Roberts argued for a date fifty to a hundred years earlier (between 50 B.C. and 50 A.D.). This oral opinion was quoted with approval by P. Kahle, *Opera Minora* (Leiden, 1956), p. 113. It was also accepted by F. M. Cross, Jr., *The Ancient Library of Qumran and Modern Biblical Studies*, rev. ed. (Garden City, N.Y., 1961), p. 171, fn. 13. Barthelemy has since allowed a date in the middle of the first century A.D. for the scroll. See *DA*, pp. 167-168.

[9]*Opera Minora*, pp. 113-127.

[10]*DA*, esp. pp. 1-88.

LXX. Foremost among these is the majority recension for large segments of the Greek Books of Kingdoms (Samuel-Kings), namely 2 Sam. 11:2- 1 Kings 2:11 and 1 Kings 22- 2 Kings.[11] H. St.J. Thackeray had recognized earlier the special nature of these sections, which he labeled βγ and γδ, respectively.[12] Barthélemy discussed the first section (βγ) extensively, and showed that it and his Minor Prophets scroll formed part of a single unified revision of the LXX.[13] He pointed out that the other section (γδ) also belonged to this KAIΓE revision.[14]

Another member of the KAIΓE recension, according to Barthélemy, is the material attributed to Theodotion for most of the OT, but not that found in the βγ section of Samuel-Kings or in the Minor Prophets.[15] This was not proven by Barthélemy and deserves further investigation. The purpose of the present study is to test the proposed identification by an extensive independent examination of the Theodotionic material in a book of the OT whose Theodotionic version has not previously been analyzed in detail.

I have chosen Theodotion's version of Exodus as the subject of investigation for three reasons: it has not received detailed study; it is in a part of the OT not primarily considered by Barthélemy in the elaboration of his theory; and it is attested in a fairly large number of preserved Theodotionic readings for Exodus. While this investigation concerns only Exodus directly, I hope that it will prove applicable to the Pentateuch as a whole.

---

[11] J. D. Shenkel has accumulated substantial evidence suggesting that the first KAIΓE segment actually begins at 2 Sam. 10:1, rather than at 11:2, as originally suggested by Thackeray. Shenkel's discussion is included as Appendix B of *Chronology and Recensional Development in the Greek Text of Kings* (Cambridge, 1968), pp. 117-20.

[12] H. St.J. Thackeray, *The Septuagint and Jewish Worship: A Study in Origins* (London, 1921), pp. 16-28, 114-115.

[13] *DA*, pp. 91-143, 179-202.

[14] *DA*, pp. 142-143.

[15] *DA*, pp. 46-47, 128-136, 253-260. Thackeray, *Septuagint*, pp. 24-25, had already pointed out similarities between the majority recension of βδ (=βγ and γδ) in Samuel-Kings and the Theodotionic material generally.

Throughout the book the terms, Theodotion and Theodotionic, refer to the man (or men) mainly responsible for the unified version taken up into Origen's sixth column and labeled θ' in hexaplaric witnesses. Since this study confirms Barthélemy's suggestion that the version, at least in Exodus, is prior to Aquila and forms part of the larger ΚΑΙΓΕ recension, Theodotion of Ephesus cannot have been its author, although he may well have adopted it for his own use later. The name Theodotion has been retained for the first century author because it fits the *siglum* θ', but it is not claimed that he actually bore that name.

Through a detailed investigation into the Theodotionic material in Exodus, this study seeks to demonstrate that the Theodotionic readings in Exodus come from a careful and generally consistent revision of an already partially revised form of the OG to a Hebrew text virtually identical with the present MT. It intends to show that this Theodotionic recension of Exodus was presupposed by Aquila, was further refined by him, and must therefore be dated in the first century A.D. or earlier. The study further demonstrates that this Theodotionic recension of Exodus is related to Barthélemy's ΚΑΙΓΕ recension and is to be regarded as an integral part of that recension. The detailed discussion of all the Theodotionic readings in this extended section of the Pentateuch will serve as a firm base for future inferences or comparisons. It may also reveal inadequacies in previous evaluations of Theodotion's work, while giving a solid foundation to the new insights that have recently been emerging.

The first two chapters provide selected but detailed evidence as to the nature of the Theodotionic material in Exodus, with some attention being given to its relationship both to the Theodotionic material elsewhere in the OT and to Barthélemy's ΚΑΙΓΕ recension. Subsequent chapters establish the virtual identity between the Theodotionic material in Exodus and the present MT, the dependence of this material on a slightly revised form of the OG, and Aquila's use of the same material in the preparation of his version of Exodus. The relationship of Theodotion in Exodus to the ΚΑΙΓΕ recension in general is also examined.

The MT is cited from Kittel's standard edition.[16] Greek textual

---

[16] R. Kittel *et al.*, eds., *Biblia Hebraica*, 11th ed., emended printing of 7th ed., a rev. and expanded version of 3d ed. (Stuttgart, n.d.).

readings are based on B-McL and Ziegler, supplemented where necessary by Rahlf's handbook edition for the text[17] and by Field for hexaplaric variants. Readings from the Syrohexapla ($\mathfrak{S}$) for Genesis through 2 Kings are cited directly from Lagarde. Elsewhere they are cited from Ziegler or Field, and checked against Ceriani's photolithographic edition of the Ambrosian codex.[18] In general, the *sigla* of these editions are used to designate the various manuscripts, versions, and patristic citations quoted therefrom.[19]

Hebrew, Syriac, and occasional Arabic readings are transliterated (unvocalized) according to a uniform set of equivalents.[20] The plural

---

[17] A. Rahlfs, ed., *Septuaginta Id est Vetus Testamentum graece iuxta LXX interpretes*, 7th ed., 2 vols. (Stuttgart, 1962).

[18] A. M. Ceriani, ed., *Codex Syro-Hexaplaris Ambrosianus photolithographice editus* (Milan, 1874).

[19] The principal versions quoted from B-McL are denoted as follows:

$\mathfrak{A}$ = Armenian.

$\mathfrak{B}$ = Bohairic ($\mathfrak{B}^{l}$ = Lagarde's edition; $\mathfrak{B}^{w}$ = Wilkin's edition).

$\mathfrak{C}$ = Sahidic ($\mathfrak{C}^{c}$ = Ciasca's edition; $\mathfrak{C}^{m}$ = Maspero's edition).

$\mathfrak{E}$ = Ethiopic ($\mathfrak{E}^{c}$ = Dillmann's codex C; $\mathfrak{E}^{f}$ = his codex F).

$\mathfrak{L}$ = Old Latin ($\mathfrak{L}^{b}$ = Belsheim's edition of the Vienna palimpsest; $\mathfrak{L}^{r}$ = Robert's edition of the Lyons Octateuch; $\mathfrak{L}^{v}$ = Extracts given by Vercellone, *Variae Lectiones*; $\mathfrak{L}^{w}$ = Ranke's edition of the Würzburg palimpsest).

$\mathfrak{P}$ = Palestinian Aramaic.

$\mathfrak{S}$ = Syrohexapla (for Genesis-2 Kings, quoted directly from Lagarde's edition; $\mathfrak{S}$-ap-barh = quotations from $\mathfrak{S}$ in the *Auṣar Rāzē* of Barhebraeus; $\mathfrak{S}^{m}$ = readings supplied by A. Masius from a manuscript in his possession, but now lost).

[20] Transliteration equivalents:

Translit.	*Heb.*	*Syr.*	*Arab.*	*Translit.*	*Heb.*	*Syr.*	*Arab.*
ʾ	א	ܐ	ا	ḍ			ض
b	ב	ܒ	ب	h	ה	ܗ	ه
g	ג	ܓ		w	ו	ܘ	و
j			ج	z	ז	ܙ	ز
d	ד	ܕ	د	ẓ			ظ
ḏ			ذ	ḥ	ח	ܚ	ح

mark in Syriac is represented by the diaresis ("), typed over a letter whose form is appropriate, for example, ÿ, ẅ, m̈, ẗ. Thus it does not always appear over the same letter in the transliteration as in the original script. Where it is necessary to give the vocalization of a particular form, it is cited in the appropriate alphabet. Greek citations are given in Greek, but without accents, breathings, or iota subscripts.[21] Hexaplaric signs normally are given in Greek (for example, θ', α', σ'), even when they are preserved in Syriac (for example, ܬ, ܐ, ܣ). The Syriac sign ܥ is cited as ʿ', rather than as ε', however. The asterisk, obelus, and metobelus are always represented by ※, ÷, and ⋎, respectively.

The Theodotionic material under investigation in this book is preserved in Greek or in Syriac translation. The bulk of the material is taken from B-McL or from Lagarde's *S*. A relatively few additional readings occur in Field's first volume and are cited on his authority. The investigation is restricted to these readings, since they alone are readily accessible and since they constitute an extensive sample of the entire Theodotionic version for Exodus.

There are approximately 400 separate Theodotionic readings (Greek and/or Syriac) in the collection of material defined above. These

Translit.	*Heb.*	*Syr.*	*Arab.*	*Translit.*	*Heb.*	*Syr.*	*Arab.*
ḫ			خ	p	פ	ܦ	
ṭ	ט	ܛ	ط	f			ف
y	י	ܝ	ي	ṣ	צ	ܨ	ص
k	כ	ܟ	ك	q	ק	ܩ	ق
l	ל	ܠ	ل	r	ר	ܪ	ر
m	מ	ܡ	م	ś	שׂ		
n	נ	ܢ	ن	š	שׁ	ܫ	ش
s	ס	ܣ	س	t	ת	ܬ	ت
ʿ	ע	ܥ	ع	ṯ			ث
ǵ			غ				

[21]Accents, breathings, and iota subscripts are similarly omitted in the hexaplaric readings and textual variants listed in B-McL. Their insertion into the Greek citations of this study would serve no purpose and would lead to unnecessary problems of interpretation.

readings vary in length from a single word (sometimes only a conjunction or a preposition) to several consecutive verses. About 350 readings are under six words in length, while the remaining fifty are longer. The 400 readings include equivalents for slightly less than 1,600 distinct Hebrew items in the present MT for Exodus.[22] Since the MT of Exodus contains roughly 26,000 separate items,[23] this collection of Theodotionic material covers about 6.2% of the entire book of Exodus.

The material is spread throughout Exodus, although there are concentrations of material in various chapters. The readings are preserved in a number of sources, of which *S̸* is by far the most important. Fairly often, but by no means always, the Greek equivalent of the Syriac reading attributed to Theodotion survives unlabeled in the text or margin of one or more Greek manuscripts. Often this Greek equivalent can be identified with some certainty, but equally often one can only suspect or suggest that a particular Greek reading is the one intended by the Syriac translation. In a few cases, both Greek and Syriac versions are attributed to Theodotion, thus providing some check on the evaluation of the other Syriac citations. Most of the Greek citations are found in the margins of one or more of a few Greek witnesses, F^bM*b*jsvzc_2, of which v is perhaps the most important. These same witnesses also frequently have variants from Aquila or Symmachus, as well as readings attributed to Origen's corrected OG column (o'), and readings attributed to γ' ("the three") or οι λ̥ (either "the rest" or perhaps "Lucian"). Although the latter citations may plausibly be interpreted as subsuming ϑ', at least where no separate Theodotionic citation is preserved, this interpretation is not certain. Therefore these readings have not been included in the collection of Theodotionic material under discussion.

---

[22]This total includes the definite article (about 120 times), the conjunction *w*- (about 160 times), the independent accusative marker (about 70 times), pronominal suffixes (about 140 times), independent personal pronouns (about 30 times), prepositions (at least 145 times), nouns, adjectives, and verbs (close to 900 times), as well as various other conjunctions and particles.

[23]This estimate is very rough, based upon the approximate average of 400 items per page and a total of 65 pages for the Hebrew text of Exodus in Kittel, *Biblia Hebraica*.

I Eight Selected Passages from the Theodotionic Version

In this chapter, eight relatively short passages chosen from various parts of Exodus are subjected to detailed analysis. In each case parallel columns contain the readings from the MT, OG, and 𝔖, along with whatever additional continuous citations are appropriate. Separate items in the set of columns are numbered for easy reference. A series of notes follows, containing textual variants, further manuscript evidence, necessary vocalizations, and other information for those numbers where this is called for. Detailed comments on each numbered set of readings from the columns are provided. The comments are concerned with all aspects of the Theodotionic readings. The discussion of each passage is concluded by an evaluation that summarizes the results of the investigations found in that set of comments.

Exodus 2:14

	MT	*OG*	𝔖^{txt}	θ'(*in* v^{mg})	α'(*in* v^{mg})	σ'(*in* v^{mg})
1.	wy'mr	ο δε ειπεν	hw dyn 'mr			
2.	my śmk	τις σε κατεστησεν	mnw 'qymk			
3.	l'yš śr	αρχοντα	※lgbr'↙ ryšn'			
4.	wšpṭ	και δικαστην	wdyn'			
5.	ʿlynw	εφ ημων	ʿlyn			
6.	hlhrgny	μη ανελειν με	'w lmqṭl ly	η ανελειν με	μητι του αποκτειναι με	μητι αποκτειναι με
7.	'th	συ	{ 'mr	συ	συ	συ
8.	'mr	θελεις	'nt }	λεγεις	λεγεις	λεγεις

	MT	OG	S̸^{txt}	θ'(*in v^{mg}*)	α'(*in v^{mg}*)	σ'(*in v^{mg}*)
9.	k'šr	ον τροπον	bhw zn' d-	ον τροπον	καθα	ον τροπον
10.	hrgt	ανειλες εχθες	qṭlt	ανειλες	απεκτεινας	απεκτεινας
11.	't hmṣry	τον αιγυπ- τιον	lmṣry' ∸'tmly↙	τον αιγυπ- τιον	συν τον αιγυπτιον	τον αιγυπ- τιον
12.	wyyr'	εφοβηθη δε	dḥl dyn			
13.	mšh	μωυσης	mwš'			
14.	wy'mr	και ειπεν	w'mr			
15.	'kn	ει ουτως	'n hkn'			
16.	nwd'	εμφανες γεγονεν	glyt' hwt			
17.	hdbr	το ρημα τουτο	mlt' ∸hd'↙			

Notes

1. nE̸ add αυτω after OG ειπεν. Cp. *lh* in the Peshitto and *lw* in 4Q Ex^{a} (called to my attention by Prof. Cross).

3. xA̸-codd insert εις ανδρα before OG αρχοντα (so also A̸-ed, but with ·※· for εις).

6. μη is replaced by η in AF*Mceg-jrsvxz-c_2E̸S̸, Cyr; and by *si* in A̸.

8. λεγεις is added in 64^{mg}.

10-11. εχθες is found before OG τον αιγυπτιον only in B*lru, while B^{ab}bdfhnpqxd_2 have χθες in that position. AFMacegijkmostvwyzb_2c_2 B̸C̸^{m}E̸L̸^{r}S̸(under ∸), Cyr$\frac{1}{2}$-codd$\frac{1}{2}$, put εχθες (χθες in Acegjkmsvwyz) after OG τον αιγυπτιον. a_2 has τη χθες before OG ανειλες, while A̸ has *heri occidisti* for that verb.

13. μωσης is found for OG μωυσης in efnpxc_2d_2.

Commentary

6. The reading attributed to Theodotion is identical with that found in about half of the Greek manuscripts collated by B-McL.[1] Both

---

[1]On the variants μη/η for MT *h*-, see the Notes for item 6. There is no evidence for a Hebrew variant *'*m lhrgny* as the basis for Greek μη

Aquila and Symmachus replace μη or η with a different interrogative pronoun, μητι. In addition, they both substitute αποκτειναι for OG ανελειν to represent MT *hrg*, while Aquila also inserts του to represent the MT preposition *l*-.

OG αποκτεινειν represents the majority of the occurrences of MT *hrg*. It is used only a relatively small number of times for other MT verbs, notably the Hiphil of *mwt*. OG αναιρειν, however, is used indiscriminately for occurrences of MT *hrg*, *nkh* (Hiphil), *pg*ʿ, *mwt* (Hiphil), etc.[2] The substitutions made by Aquila and Symmachus both here and in item 10 were presumably motivated by a desire for lexical consistency. Theodotion did not perceive the need for this particular change.

7. All three versions agree with the OG.

8. All three versions replace OG θελεις with λεγεις, a more literal reflection of MT *ʾmr*. The same revision is found in $\cancel{S}^{txt}$ and in 64^{mg}.

9. While Theodotion and Symmachus both reproduce the OG reading unchanged, Aquila replaces it with καθα. This is probably an attempt at greater literalism: *k*-*ʾšr*= καθ᾽α.

10-11. Theodotion once again accepts the readings of the OG, but rejects the plus εχθες/χθες. The plus, which is not supported by the present MT, is found at slightly different places in the various Greek witnesses. It could be an inner-Greek expansion, or it could reflect an original *ʾtml* that dropped out by haplography before *ʾt hmṣry* in the Hebrew texts underlying the MT and the Samaritan Pentateuch. The Peshitto has the plus, however.

Aquila and Symmachus also omit the plus, and agree on replacing OG ανειλες with απεκτεινας to represent MT *hrgt* (see the comment under item 6, *supra*). In addition, Aquila inserts the adverb συν to reflect the

---

ανελειν με. The particle *ʾm* is used in indirect questions only four times in Exodus, and nowhere is it translated by μη. The relevant examples are Exod. 22:7 (LXX v.8) and 22:10 (LXX v.11), where OG η μην μη... twice translates MT *ʾm lʾ*..., and Exod. 16:4 and 17:7, where MT *ʾm lʾ* is twice used to complete a question introduced by the particle *h*-. Each time MT *h*-...*ʾm lʾ* is translated by OG ει...η ου. No statistics are available for the OG treatment of the MT interrogative particle *h*-.

2. For these and other evaluations of OG usage, see H-R.

Hebrew accusative particle *'t* explicitly. This peculiarity has long been recognized as a characteristic of Aquila's revision.

Evaluation

The version attributed to Theodotion is almost identical with the OG. Apart from the replacement of θελεις by λεγεις and the omission of εχθες/χθες, both shared by Aquila and Symmachus, Theodotion reproduces the text of the OG or, in item 6, the text of a large number of LXX witnesses. At the same time, Theodotion's version clearly reflects the Hebrew text found in the present MT.

The versions of Aquila and Symmachus share three differences from the OG against Theodotion, two in item 6 and one in item 10, while Aquila alone has three other such changes, in items 6, 9, and 11. All six changes are lexical or stylistic, and clearly presuppose the same Hebrew text. While Aquila and Symmachus could be dependent on the OG directly or only indirectly through Theodotion's version, the latter is clearly based directly on the dominant Greek tradition.

Exodus 32:25

	MT	*OG*	$\mathcal{S}^{txt}$	θ'	α'	σ'
1.	wyr'	και ιδων	wḥz'	και ειδεν	ειδεν δε	ειδεν δε (ḥz' dyn)
2.	mšh	μωυσης	mwš'	μωυσης	μωυσης	μωυσης (mwš')
3.	't h'm	τον λαον	l'm'	τον λαον	τον λαον	τον λαον (l'm')
4.	ky	οτι	d-	οτι	οτι	οτι (d-)
5.	pr' hw'	διεσκε- δασται	'tplhdw	διεσκεδασ- μενος εστιν	αποπετασ- μενος αυτος	γεγυμνωται ('rṭly)
6.	ky pr'h	διεσκεδα- δεν γαρ αυτους	plhd 'nwn gyr	οτι διεσ- κεδασεν αυτον	οτι απ- επετασεν αυτον	προεδωκεν γαρ αυτον
7.	'hrn	ααρων	'hrwn	ααρων	ααρων	ααρων
8.	lšmṣh	επιχαρμα	lḥdwt'	επιχαρμα	εις ονομα ρυπου	εις κακωνυ- μιαν
9.	bqmyhm	τοις υπεναν- τιοις	lhnwn dlqwbl'	τοις ανθεσ- τηκοσιν	εν ανθεσ- τηκοσιν	τοις ανθεσ- τηκοσιν

MT	*OG*	$\cancel{S}^{txt}$	ϑ'	α'	σ'
	αυτων	dylhwn	αυτων	αυτων	αυτοις

Notes

The ϑ', α', and σ' readings are taken from s^{mg}v^{mg}z^{mg}, Part of the σ' reading (items 1-5) is also found in $\cancel{S}^{mg}$, and the Syriac readings are given in parentheses beneath the Greek.

1. ειδεν is found for OG ιδων in x$\cancel{A}\cancel{L}^{rw}\cancel{S}^{txt}$.

2. μωσης is found for μωυσης in kmn and in the α' and σ' versions of v^{mg}.

5. In the ϑ' and α' versions of s^{mg}, εστιν and αυτος, respectively, are missing. εξεκαλυφθη is added in i^{mg}.

6. αυτον is added in z^{mg} (at αυτους of z^{txt}).

9. In the ϑ' version, αυτων is found only in z^{mg}, while s^{mg} has αυτον and v^{mg} apparently has αυτοις.

Commentary

1. Theodotion replaces the OG participle with the finite aorist, so as to reflect the Hebrew converted imperfect more exactly. This change is shared by Aquila and Symmachus, and is also found in x$\cancel{A}\cancel{L}^{rw}\cancel{S}$. The substitution of δε for OG και by Aquila and Symmachus is unusual, especially in Aquila's version (where OG δε is regularly replaced by και to reflect the Hebrew conjunction *w*-). It may be a secondary scribal change in Aquila's version. In any case, Theodotion's reading is a correction of the OG toward the present MT.

2. All three versions retain the OG reading. The variations between μωυσης and μωσης must be seen as merely scribal variation.

3-4. The OG readings are again retained in all three versions. Note that Aquila does not bother to insert the adverb συν to reflect the Hebrew *nota accusativi* (compare item 11 of the previous reading).

5. The OG reading is replaced differently in all three versions. The Hebrew verb *pr'* only occurs three times in the book of Exodus, twice in this verse (items 5 and 6) and once in Exod. 5:4. In the latter place, MT *tpry'w* is translated διαστρεφετε (with the variants διαστρεφεται in A, αποστρεφετε in p, and *auertistis* in $\cancel{L}^{r}$). The following set of readings is found in M^{mg}v^{mg}z^{mg}: α' αποπεταζετε σ' αποτρεπετε ϑ' διασκεδαζετε. Conflicting readings are given by c$_2^{mg}$: σ' αποστρεφετε ϑ'

διασωζετε. The major correspondences of MT *pr‘* in Exodus may be outlined as follows:

	Exod. 5:4	*Exod. 32:25 (item 5)*	*Exod. 32:25 (item 6)*
MT	tpry‘w	pr‘ hw’	pr‘(h)
OG	διαστρεφετε	διεσκεδασται	διεσκεδασεν
ϑ'	διασκεδαζετε (διασωζετε)	διεσκεδασμενος εστιν (om s^{mg})	διεσκεδασεν
α'	αποπεταζετε	αποπετασμενος αυτος (om s^{mg})	απεπετασεν
σ'	αποτρεπετε (αποστρεφετε)	γεγυμνωται	προεδωκεν

It is clear that Theodotion has accepted the OG verb used in this verse (διασκεδαζειν, "to scatter, disperse"), and has substituted it for the different OG verb in Exod. 5:4. The reading attributed to Theodotion by c_2^{mg} in Exod. 5:4 is corrupt or secondary. In item 6 of the present verse, Theodotion simply adopts the OG reading. In item 5, however, he modifies the finite form into a periphrastic construction that more exactly represents the supposed Hebrew construction. The omission of εστιν by s^{mg} is secondary.

In each case, Aquila replaces the previous reading (whether the OG or Theodotion's revision) with the corresponding form of the verb αποπεταζειν ("to spread out"). Presumably he judged it to be a more accurate translation of Hebrew *pr‘*. In reproducing the periphrastic construction of item 5 in the present verse, moreover, Aquila uses αυτος (a more exact reflection of Mt *hw’* than Theodotion's εστιν). The omission of αυτος in s^{mg} is secondary.

The various readings used by Symmachus for the three occurrences of MT *pr‘* in Exodus are not characterized either by consistency or by accuracy of meaning.

Both Theodotion and Aquila have introduced lexical consistency into the treatment of MT *pr‘* in Exodus. Theodotion's choice is based directly on the OG, however, while that of Aquila is independent. Both Theodotion and Aquila also introduced Greek periphrastic constructions to represent MT *pr‘ hw’*. Aquila's version is even more exactly literal than Theodotion's.

6. Certain aspects of this reading have already been discussed in connection with the preceding item. In addition, Theodotion and Aquila, but not Symmachus, replace OG γαρ with οτι to represent MT *ky* more exactly. All three versions substitute αυτον for OG αυτους to represent more accurately the third person, masculine, singular suffix on MT *pr'h*.

7. All three versions retain the OG reading, which accurately represents MT *'hrn* by ααρων.

8. Theodotion retains OG επιχαρμα to represent the Hebrew *hapax*, *l-šmṣh*, even though the OG expression fails to provide an explicit reflection of the Hebrew preposition. Aquila's strange reading may simply be a valiant effort to paraphrase an obscure term. It might also reflect a corruption **l-šm ṣ'h*, or the like.[3] The noun used by Symmachus is a *hapax* (a related adjective also occurs only once). Both Aquila and Symmachus agree (against the OG and Theodotion) in reflecting MT *l-* by εις, and in relating the noun *šmṣh* to Hebrew *šm* ("name").

9. Here all three versions agree in replacing OG υπεναντιοις with ανθεστηκοσιν to represent the Qal participle plural of *qwm* in MT *b-qmyhm*. OG υπεναντιος is used to represent MT *qwm* only here and in Exod. 15:7 (where no variants are cited by B-McL). Elsewhere it stands for MT *'yb* (eleven times), *ṣr* (ten times), and *śn'* (three times).[4] The revision common to Aquila, Symmachus, and Theodotion avoids the rare correspondence.

In addition, Aquila substitutes εν for τοις to reflect the Hebrew preposition *b-* more accurately. In Theodotion's version, the variants αυτον in s^{mg} and apparently αυτοις in v^{mg} for αυτων in z^{mg} (which equals OG αυτων, also preserved by Aquila) are presumably secondary. The substitution of αυτοις for αυτων by Symmachus removes a grammatical

---

[3]Compare the following equivalents: OG τον ρυπον for MT *ṣ't* (construct of *ṣ'h*) in Isa. 4:4; α' ρυπον (in 86^{mg}) for MT *ṣ'* (OG paraphrases freely) in Isa. 30:22; σ'θ' τον ρυπον σου (in b^{mg}ȿ$^{m\ mg}$, and without θ' in ȿ-ap-Barh), but α' το εξελθον σου (in M^{mg}*b*^{mg}ȿ$^{m\ mg}$), in place of OG την ασχημοσυνην σου to represent MT *ṣ'tk* in Deut. 23:14 (LXX v. 13); and, according to H-R, θ' (τον) ρυπον or a related form in a replacement for OG την δε εξοδον αυτου to represent MT *mṣ'tw* in Prov. 30:12.

[4]See H-R, p. 1407b, c.

roughness that neither Theodotion nor Aquila attempted to avoid.

Evaluation

The version attributed to Theodotion is again closely related to the OG (item 8; also items 5, 6; cf. items 2-4). Its author must have known the OG directly, and not merely indirectly through Aquila or Symmachus (items 5, 6, 8; also items 1, 9). The differences from the OG found in items 1, 5, 6, and 9 of Theodotion's version all serve to reflect the Hebrew structure or vocabulary more exactly.

There is no reason why Aquila's version cannot be understood as a further revision of Theodotion (items 5, 6, 8, 9). It could also be seen as an independent revision of the OG, however. The version attributed to Symmachus is less easily classified. Only twice, in items 1 and 9, do all three versions agree on a common reading not found in the OG.

Exodus 5:16

	MT	*OG*	$\mathcal{S}^{txt}$	ϑ'	α'	σ'
1.	tbn	αχυρον	tbn'			
2.	'yn ntn	ου διδοται	l' mtyhb			
3.	l'bdyk	τοις οικεταις σου	l'b̸d̸yk			
4.	wlbnym	και την πλινθον	wlbn̸'			
5.	'mrym lnw	ημιν λεγουσιν	'mryn ln			
6.	'św	ποιειν	lm'bd			
7.	whnh	και ιδου	wh'	και ιδου	και ιδου	και
8.	'bdyk	οι παιδες σου	'b̸d̸' dylk	οι δουλοι σου	δουλοι σου	οι δουλοι σου
9.	mkym	μεμαστιγωνται	kly'yn	μεμαστιγωνται	πεπληγμενοι	μεμαστιγωμενοι
10.	wḥṭ't	αδικησεις ουν	m'wl 'nt hkyl	και η αμαρτια	και αμαρτια	και αμαρτιαν
11.	'mk	τον λαον σου	b'm' dylk	εις τον λαον σου	λαω σου	εχεις

Notes

The ϑ', α' and σ' readings are taken from $j^{mg}v^{mg}z^{mg}$.

5. ημιν λεγουσιν is found only in ABafioqru and perhaps in ɃɆ, while λεγουσιν ημιν (υμιν dlp) is found in FMb-eghj-npstv-c_2ȺȽ^{r}Ꞩ.

6. ποιετε is found for OG ποιειν in bw.

10-11. The MT vocalization is וְחָטָאת עַמֶּךָ.

Commentary

7. Theodotion and Aquila both preserve the OG reading, which reflects the MT exactly. The reason for the omission of OG ιδου by Symmachus is not clear.

8. All three versions agree in substituting δουλοι for OG παιδες, perhaps in order to reflect MT *ʿbdy(k)* more literally. Both correspondences are frequent in the OG, however, and a similar ambiguity seems to remain in the three versions. A detailed examination of the usage of the three versions in this matter is not possible here. The variant common to Theodotion, Aquila, and Symmachus is apparently reflected in Ꞩ. Aquila also omits the OG article οι, retained by Theodotion and Symmachus, since there is no Hebrew article to support it.

9. Theodotion accepts the OG form, which does translate the Hebrew accurately. Symmachus substitutes a participle of the same verb for the finite form found in the OG and Theodotion. Aquila introduces a participle derived from the different verb πλησσειν, perhaps in order to provide a more literal or more consistent reflection of Hebrew *mkym*. A rapid check of the seventeen instances in which derivatives of πλησσειν are attributed to Aquila by H-R (of which one, Ps. 3:8, is not supported by Field) revealed that fourteen are used where the MT has some derivative of the root *nkh*. The two exceptions are 1 Kings 14:14 (MT *krt*) and Job 33:16 (where the form *yḥtm* may come from *ḥtt*). A more detailed investigation of Aquila's treatment of MT *nkh* is not needed here. Note, however, that Aquila is said by 86^{mg} to have replaced OG ατιμασαντων in Ezek. 28:24 with μαστιγουντων to represent MT *ḥšʾṭym*. This may provide a clue as to the reason why Aquila wanted to avoid using μαστιγουν to represent Hebrew *nkh*.[5]

---

[5]Note also α'σ' μαστιξ (86^{mg}) for MT *šyṭ* (שִׁיט) in Isa. 28:15 and α' μαστιγες (86^{mg}) for MT *šwṭ* (שׁוֹט) in Isa. 28:18. The OG equivalent is καταιγις each time.

10-11. The Hebrew forms, as vocalized, do not fit easily into the framework of normal Biblical Hebrew. The form *ḥṭ’t* is vocalized as a Qal verb, second person singular, feminine, while *‘mk* is taken as "your people." The Qal of *ḥṭ’* (with the meanings "to commit an error, to sin against") does not normally govern a direct object, although an object introduced by *l-* may be used. The OG apparently overlooked that difficulty, and took *‘mk* as the object of *ḥṭ’t*.

Theodotion and Aquila both reject this interpretation, and agree on taking *ḥṭ’t* as a noun ("sin") in construct with *‘mk*. Aquila further refines Theodotion's version by removing two excessive articles and the preposition εις, which did not correspond to anything in the Hebrew. The latter change brought with it the replacement of λαον with λαω.

Symmachus accepts this new interpretation of *ḥṭ’t*, but couples it with a different understanding of *‘mk*. He takes it to be the preposition *‘m* with the second person singular suffix. The resultant combination he then translates freely as "you have (the) sin."

Theodotion and Aquila thus share a common approach to this difficult Hebrew phrase. It is easy to see why Aquila would refine the reading found in Theodotion so as to reflect the Hebrew more exactly. There is no reason, however, why Theodotion would revise Aquila's reading to get that now attributed to Theodotion. Hence it is at least probable that Theodotion's reading was later revised and adopted by Aquila. The precise affinities of the version found in Symmachus are again not clear.

Evaluation

Theodotion clearly shares OG readings in items 7 and 9, but makes those adjustments that seem necessary to reflect the MT more accurately in items 8, 10, and 11. Aquila shares the item 7 OG reading with Theodotion, replaces the item 9 OG reading retained by Theodotion so as to achieve lexical consistency, and further refines readings introduced by Theodotion in items 8, 10, and 11. This passage thus provides a particularly convincing example of Aquila's dependence upon Theodotion, rather than on the OG directly, and of his further reworking of Theodotion's revision. Symmachus' version is related to those of Theodotion and Aquila in items 8, 10, and possibly 9, but has its own peculiarities in items 7, 10, and 11.

MT Exodus 8:25 (LXX v. 29)

	MT(v.25)	*OG(v.29)*	S^{txt}*(v.25)*	ϑ'*(in* v^{mg}*)*	α'*(in* v^{mg}*)*	σ'*(in* v^{mg}*)*
1.	wy'mr	ειπεν δε	'mr dyn	και ειπεν	και ειπεν	ειπεν δε
2.	mšh	μωυσης	mwš'	μωσης	μωσης	μωσης
3.	hnh	οδε	h'	ιδου	ιδου	ως αν
4.	'nky	εγω	'n'	εγω ειμι	εγω ειμι	
5.	ywṣ'	εξελευ-σομαι	npq 'n'	εκπορευ-ομαι	εξερχομαι	εξελϑω
6.	m'mk	απο σου	mn lwtk	απο σου	παρα σου	παρα σου
7.	wh'trty	και ευξο-μαι	w'zl'	και ευξο-μαι	και ικε-τευσω	ευξομαι
8.	'l YHWH	προς τον ϑεον	lwt 'lh'	προς ...	προς $\overline{κυ}$	προς ...

Notes

Only the first part of the verse is treated here.

2. OG μωυσης is replaced by μωσης in amnxc$_2$.

3. OG οδε is found only in ABailoqrtuvxa$_2$b$_2$. It is replaced by ωδε in bcdfhnpsyz; by οτι in Or-gr; and by ιδου in egjkmc$_2$, 77, ɃɆⱣS. It is omitted by wȺ. Items 3 and 4 are both omitted by 71.

8. OG τον ϑεον is replaced by *Dominum Deum* in Ᵽ.

Commentary

1. Theodotion and Aquila agree in replacing OG δε with και to reflect the Hebrew conjunction *w-* more accurately. Symmachus retains the OG reading.

2. All three versions agree with amnxc$_2$ in having μωσης for OG μωυσης, but this change in spelling is probably not significant (cf., e.g., item 2 of the second reading).

3. Theodotion and Aquila agree in substituting ιδου for OG οδε (or its minority variant ωδε) to represent MT *hnh*. This revision has also found its way into egjkmc$_2$, 77, ɃɆⱣS. The variant found in Symmachus is part of a free rephrasing of the entire clause (items 3-6).

4. Theodotion and Aquila share an interesting revision that has already been discussed by Barthelemy, though not in connection with this verse.[6] OG εγω is expanded to εγω ειμι, so that MT *'nky* may be

[6] *DA*, pp. 69-78. Compare the earlier discussion of its use by

differentiated from *ʾny* (for which εγω alone would be retained). This revisional feature is particularly noteworthy because it is regularly followed by a finite verb in the first person singular (in this case Theodotion's εκπορευομαι and Aquila's εξερχομαι, both replacements for OG εξελευσομαι).

The form *ʾnky* occurs twenty-two times in the MT for Exodus.[7] Three times (3:6; 20:2, 5), the OG translates it by the phrase εγω ειμι. In each of these cases, *ʾnky* refers to God, and is the subject of a nominal sentence in which he identifies himself as "the god of your father" (3:6) or as "YHWH your god" (20:2, 5). In all three instances, εγω ειμι is firmly established in the textual tradition.

Three more times (3:11; 4:23; 8:25 [LXX v.29]), Aquila and Theodotion are both credited with the reading εγω ειμι to reflect MT *ʾnky*. The most complex of these is Exod. 3:11, where *ʾnky* occurs in Moses' question: *my ʾnky* plus a clause introduced by *ky*. The various renditions are:

$A^{*vid}F^{*}Mdefijlqrtuvyzb_2c_2^{a?}$:	τις		ειμι	οτι
74, $B̸^{vid}E̸^{vid}$:	τις	εγω		οτι
$A^{a}BF^{a}abghmnoswxa_2A̸C̸^{m}L̸^{r}$:	τις	ειμι	εγω	οτι
ck:	τις	εγω	ειμι	οτι
S̸:	*mnw*	※α′θ′ ʾnʾ	ʾyty	d-.

Most probably, ειμι alone was the original Greek reading, while ειμι εγω was an early expansion. One or the other of these readings was then revised to εγω ειμι (a revision found in both Theodotion and Aquila, according to S̸, and adopted by the hexaplaric manuscripts ck). The variant found in 74, $B̸^{vid}E̸^{vid}$ is not important. The purpose of the revision common to Aquila and Theodotion, as already noted, seems to have been to provide a distinction in Greek between Hebrew *ʾnky* and Hebrew *ʾny*.

The next instance of εγω ειμι attributed to Theodotion and Aquila

---

Aquila in Ilmari Soisalon-Soininen, *Der Charakter der asterisierten Zusätze in der Septuaginta* (Helsinki, 1959), pp. 50-51, where he refers to H. St.J. Thackeray's earlier remarks in *The Septuagint in Jewish Worship* (London, 1921), p. 23.

[7] Exod. 3:6, 11, 12, 13; 4:10 *bis*, 11, 12, 15, 23; 7:17, 27; 8:24, 25; 17:9; 19:9; 20:2, 5; 23:20; 32:18; 34:10, 11.

is in Exod. 4:23, where MT *ʾnky* occurs in the phrase *hnh ʾnky hrg*. The Greek textual evidence may be summarized as follows: ορα (om 𝔄) ουν (γουν p, Or-gr-codd; om 71, 𝔄) εγω (om 𝔏ʳ, Cyr; + ειμι ckx; + *sum ergo* 𝔄) αποκτενω (αποκτεννω B; αποκτεινω dhta$_2$; απεκτεινα p; *qui occidam* 𝔄; om 𝔏ʳ); while 𝔖 has: *ḥzy hkyl ʾnʾ* ※α'θ' *ʾytyꭙ qṭl ʾnʾ*. The construction *qṭl ʾnʾ* (participle followed by personal pronoun subject) is commonly used as a present continuous tense in Syriac.[8] Here it undoubtedly represents αποκτενω, with the result that 𝔖 is identical with ckx. The version cited from 𝔄 (*sum ergo qui occidam*) is presumably a reflection of this same Greek reading.

In Exod. 4:23, then, Theodotion and Aquila are given responsibility for the expanded form εγω ειμι to represent Hebrew *ʾnky*. In ckx𝔖, at least, this form is followed by the finite, first person verb αποκτενω (*qṭl ʾnʾ*). While this construction is not explicitly attributed to either Theodotion or Aquila, it is reasonable to suppose that they both accepted it. In items 4-5 of the present verse, in fact, such a construction is attributed in different forms to both Theodotion and Aquila. And in this latter case, the revised form εγω ειμι is found only in the versions of Theodotion and Aquila, while Symmachus omits all reflection of the Hebrew pronoun.

In Exod. 32:18, a verse that will be discussed shortly, there is the single instance in Exodus in which the revision εγω ειμι is found in Theodotion but not in Aquila. MT *ʾnky šmʿ* is translated by OG εγω ακουω (no Greek variants). This is accurately reflected by 𝔖^{txt} *ʾnʾ šmʿ ʾnʾ*, a reading that is retained in the Aquila and Symmachus versions found in 𝔖^{mg}. In the Theodotion version of 𝔖^{mg}, however, the expanded reading *ʾnʾ ʾyty dšmʿ ʾnʾ* appears. In all probability, the Greek predecessor of this reading is simply εγω ειμι ακουω. Be that as it may, this is the only instance in Exodus in which Aquila does not share this expansion with Theodotion, as opposed to three instances in which it is attributed to both Theodotion and Aquila.[9]

---

[8]T. H. Robinson, *Paradigms and Exercises in Syriac Grammar*, rev. by L. H. Brockington, 4th rev. ed. (Oxford, 1962), p. 60.

[9]Note that Barthélemy (*DA*, p. 74) overlooks the readings of Exod. 3:11 and Exod. 8:25 (LXX v.29), and thus is able to discount the importance of the only other agreement between Aquila and Theodotion on this point in the Pentateuch (Exod. 4:23).

There are no citations from either Theodotion or Aquila that overlap any of the other occurrences of MT *ʾnky* in Exodus. In Exod. 23:20, however, a citation by Phil-gr adds ειμι to OG εγω (for MT *ʾnky*) according to some codices.[10] Apparently the verb αποστελλω was left unchanged. This is the only other trace of this distinctive revision in the textual evidence collated for Exodus by B-McL.

We might note in passing the one instance in Exodus in which a Theodotion reading is cited for MT *ʾny*. In Exod. 31:6, the following evidence is pertinent:

MT *wʾny hnh ntty* . . .

LXX ϰαι (+ ιδου cegjm) εγω (om efgjx; + α'σ'ιδου s^{mg}Ӕ^{txt} [om α'σ']; α'σ'ϑ' ※ ϰαι εγω ιδου v^{mg}) δεδωϰα (εδωϰα Bagho; εϰδεδωϰα x) . . .

$ *wʾnʾ* ※α'ϑ' *hʾx yhbt(h)* . . .

The evidence is decisive. All three versions retained OG εγω to represent MT *ʾny*.

5. In the preceding discussion, reference has been made to the significance of the finite, first person verb forms used after εγω ειμι by both Theodotion and Aquila. Both versions replace the future tense of the OG with verbs in the present tense. This reflects the verbal use of the Hebrew participle (*ywṣʾ*), rather than the imperfect (which would be implied by a Greek future). Both verbs chosen are commonly found in the OG to represent forms of Hebrew *yṣʾ*. A brief examination of the usage of both εξερχεσθαι and εϰπορευεσθαι by Theodotion and Aquila in the Pentateuch and the historical books (an investigation based on the incomplete listings in H-R, where the present verse is not mentioned for either Aquila or Theodotion) failed to reveal any clear pattern of usage for either version.[11] The inconclusive results of the investigation of

---

[10] B-McL notes that many codices omit the entire citation, while OG εγω is itself omitted the other time that Phil-gr cites this verse.

[11] The H-R citations that were supported by B-McL include: Exod. 21:7 *bis*; Num. 1:20; Deut. 23:14 (LXX v.13); Josh. 8:14; 15:9; Judg. 4:14; 14:14 *bis*; 2 Kings 11:9. A slight tendency toward lexical consistency on the part of both Theodotion and Aquila is discussed under item 6 of the fifth reading (Exod. 21:7-8a), but it is not pertinent for the changes under discussion in the present example.

these readings made it inadvisable to extend the survey of usage to the remaining books of the Old Testament. It need not be assumed, nor would it be possible to prove, that all lexical changes in Theodotion (or in Aquila) are motivated by a desire for perfect consistency. The different reading chosen by Symmachus is conditioned by the new construction introduced in item 3.

6. The OG phrase is retained by Theodotion, while Aquila and Symmachus agree in replacing OG απο with παρα to represent the composite Hebrew preposition *m-ʿm*. The change may have been motivated by a desire to distinguish in Greek between the Hebrew prepositions *mn/m-* and *m-ʿm*, by restricting απο and εκ for the former, and by introducing παρα for the latter. The present state of the material does not make it feasible to test this hypothesis in detail, nor does the present study, which is concerned primarily with Theodotion, require such an investigation.

7. The OG reading is accepted by Theodotion and, with a minor change due to the different syntax in items 3-6, by Symmachus. The substitution of ικετευσω by Aquila is interesting. In Exodus, OG ευχεσθαι represents the Hiphil of *ʿtr* five times and the Qal twice.[12] In Exod. 10:17, the Hiphil of *ʿtr* is represented by OG προσευχεσθαι. There are no other occurrences of MT *ʿtr* (Qal or Hiphil) or of OG ευχεσθαι and προσευχεσθαι in the book of Exodus.[13] Elsewhere, OG ευχεσθαι is used for MT *ʿtr* only in Job 22:27 (Hiphil); 33:26 (Qal). It stands for MT *ndr/nzr* and their derivatives thirty-five times, for MT *htpll* eight times, and for other MT forms eleven times. OG προσευχεσθαι is elsewhere used almost always to represent MT *htpll*.[14] There are no instances listed by H-R in which OG ικετευειν represented MT *ʿtr*, nor are any Aquila uses of ικετευειν cited (not even the present one). While it can be suggested that Aquila wished to restrict OG ευχεσθαι and προσευχεσθαι to MT *ndr/nzr* and MT *htpll*, and thus introduced a new equation (ικετευειν = *ʿtr*) in the present verse, no further evidence can be provided at present.[15] In any case, only Aquila departs radically from the OG

---

[12] Hiphil: Exod. 8:4, 5, 24, 25 (LXX vv. 8, 9, 28, 29); 9:28; Qal: Exod. 8:26 (LXX v.30); 10:18.

[13] These statements are based on Mandelkern and H-R, respectively.

[14] These figures are based on the listings in H-R.

[15] Note, however, that Aquila introduces ικετικος to represent MT *nʿtr* in Prov. 27:6 (cited from Nobil. by Field).

reading in the item under discussion.

8. All three versions accept the OG preposition προς to represent MT *'l*. While Aquila replaces OG τον θεον with $\overline{\kappa\upsilon}$ to reflect MT *YHWH*, the relevant readings from Theodotion and Symmachus have not been preserved. A conflation of the OG reading and Aquila's variant is found in 𝔓. The treatment of the Hebrew tetragrammaton by Theodotion, Aquila, and Symmachus is considered in chapter three.

Evaluation

In the first part of Exod. 8:25 (LXX v.29), Theodotion and Aquila share three readings against the OG (items 1, 3, 4). In item 2, only a minor change in spelling distinguishes the form shared by Theodotion, Aquila, and Symmachus from that found in the OG. In items 6 and 7, the OG form is retained by Theodotion, but is changed by Aquila. In item 5, Theodotion and Aquila have different revisions of the OG verb, while the reading in item 8 is inconclusive. It is at least highly probable that Aquila here knew the OG through Theodotion's revision, and that Aquila further revised that revision. Symmachus seems to have an independent reworking of the OG (items 1, 3-5, 7, 8; also item 2), with one revision (item 6) common to Aquila and Symmachus against the OG and Theodotion.

Exodus 21:7-8a

	MT	*OG*	𝔖*txt*	θ'	α'	σ'
	(v.7)					
1.	wky	εαν δε	'n dyn		και οταν (w'mty d-)	
2.	ymkr 'yš	τις αποδωται	nzbn 'nš		πωληση ανηρ (nzbn gbr')	
3.	't btw	την εαυτου θυγατερα	brt' dylh		την θυγατερα (lbrt' dylh)	
4.	l'mh	οικετιν	l'mt'		εις οικετιν (brt byt')	
5.	l' tṣ'	ουκ απελευσεται	l' tpwq	ουκ εξελευσεται (l' tpwq)	ουκ εξελευσεται (l' tpwq)	ου προσλευσεται (l' tpwq)

	MT	*OG*	$\mathcal{S}^{txt}$	ϑ'	α'	σ'
6.	kṣ't	ωσπερ αποτρε- χουσιν	'yk m' dnpqn	ωσπερ εκπορευ- ονται ('ykn' dnpqyn)	ως εξοδος ('yk mpqt')	προσελ- ευσιν (mpqt')
7.	hʿbdym (v.8)	αι δουλαι	'm̈ht'	οι δουλοι (ʿbd̈')	των δουλων (dʿbd̈')	δουλικην ('mhyt')
8.	'm	εαν	'n	ει ('n)	εαν ('n dyn)	ει ('n)
9.	rʿh	μη ευαρεσ- τηση	l' tšpr	πονηρα εστιν (byst' 'ytyh)	κακισθη (ttmkk)	μη αρεσκη (l' tšpr)
10.	bʿyny		※' 'bʿyn'↙	εν οφθαλ- μοις (bʿyn')	εν οφθαλ- μοις (bʿyn')	εν οφθαλ- μοις (bʿyn')
11.	'dnyh	τω κυριω αυτης	dmr' ※ dylh↙	$\overline{\kappa\upsilon}$ αυτης (dmr' dylh)	$\overline{\kappa\upsilon}$ αυτης (dmr' dylh)	τω $\overline{\kappa\omega}$ αυτης (dmr' dylh)
12.	'šr	ην	hy d-	ην (hy d-)	ος (hw d-)	η (hy d-)
13.	l'	αυτω	l'	ου (l')	ου (l')	μη (l')
14.	yʿdh	καθωμολο- γησατο	'štwdy lh	καθωμολο- γησατο αυτην ('štwdyh)	καθωμολο- γησατο αυτην ('štwdyh)	καθωμολο- γημενη ('ttwdyt)
15.	whpdh	απολυτρω- σει αυτην	nprqyh			

Notes

The ϑ', α' and σ' readings are taken from $j^{mg}s^{mg}v^{mg}z^{mg}\mathcal{S}^{mg}$. The α' reading is without any name in j^{mg}, which only gives items 1-4, and in s^{mg}. The Syriac forms are given in parentheses under the Greek forms for each item under θ′, α′, and σ′.

1-3. The anonymous variant εαν τις πωληση την θυγατερα αυτου is found in $F^{b\ mg}$.

2. OG τις αποδωται is replaced by αποδωται τις in ack^{mg}A̸$S̸^{txt}$ and by αποδω τις in $k^{txt}m$.

3. OG την εαυτου θυγατερα is replaced by την θυγατερα αυτου (εαυτου c) in acfikm$A̸^{vid}S̸^{vid}$.

4. εις is inserted before OG οικετιν (οικετιδα F^a) in $F^{a?b?}$.

6. προσελευσιν is replaced by προελευσιν in the σ′ reading of v^{mg} z^{mg}.

8. δε is added after OG εαν in AF^abejptwxa_2b_2B̸$C̸^m$E̸. A space of two or three letters follows εαν in o.

10. The phrase εν οφθαλμοις is added in $F^{b\ mg}$ackA̸$S̸^{txt}$ (under ※‘ ′). εν alone is added in qu.

11. ουν is added after αυτης in the θ′ reading of s^{mg}.

12. OG ην is replaced by η in $Bfb_2^{a?}$$E̸^{vid}$ and is omitted by aA̸$C̸^m$. ος is replaced by ο in the nameless version of s^{mg} that is otherwise identical with the α′ version of $v^{mg}z^{mg}$.

13. OG αυτω is found only in BnquxE̸ and perhaps in i*. It is omitted in $fi^{a?}r$. It is replaced by *cui* in A̸$C̸^m$, by εαυτω in $F^{a?}$, by αυτος in bw, and by ου in $AF^*M^{txt}acdehj^{txt}klmops^{txt}tv^{txt}y\text{-}b_2$$B̸^{vid}$ $S̸^{txt}$.

14. OG καθωμολογησατο is replaced by *desponsata est* in A̸ and by *confessus est dare eam* in $C̸^m$. After OG καθωμολογησατο, the following additions are made: αυτω in Aacm; εαυτω in k; αυτην in $F^*dhi^{a?}loprs^{txt}$ $tv^{txt}y\text{-}b_2$$B̸^{vid}S̸^{txt}$; εαυτην in f; and αυτη εν οφθαλμοις in ej^{txt}.

Commentary

1-4. Only Aquila's version is preserved by name for this part of the verse. The anonymous version in $F^{b\ mg}$ might reflect Theodotion's revision, but there is no way to prove this.

5. Theodotion and Aquila agree on a revision of the OG reading, while a further variant is found in Symmachus. In S̸, the Syriac forms attributed to all three versions, as well as that found in the text, are identical.

6. Theodotion revises the OG, but without attempting to reflect the syntax of the Hebrew. The revisions made by Theodotion in items 5

and 6 of this verse, as well as in item 5 of the previous reading (Exod. 8:25 [LXX v.29]), establish a certain lexical consistency that was not present in the OG. Each occurrence of MT *yṣ'* is marked by a Greek verb containing the preposition εκ:

	Exod. 8:25 (LXX v.29)	*Exod. 21:7 (item 5)*	*Exod. 21:7 (item 6)*
MT	*ywṣ'*	*tṣ'*	*k-ṣ't*
OG	εξελευσομαι	απελευσεται	ωσπερ αποτρεχουσιν
ϑ'	εκπορευομαι	εξελευσεται	ωσπερ εκπορευονται

A similar consistency marks the different readings found in Aquila (εξερχομαι . . . εξελευσεται . . . ως εξοδος), but not those used by Symmachus (εξελθω . . . προσελευσεται . . . προ(σ)ελευσιν).

Aquila's reading for this item, ως εξοδος, exactly reflects the syntax of MT *k-ṣ't*. While Aquila could have known either the OG reading or Theodotion's revision, Theodotion could not have used Aquila's variant as the basis for his own revision. Theodotion's closeness to the OG demands a relationship of direct dependence on the OG. The variant found in Symmachus approximates the MT structure, but fails to provide any reflection of MT *k-*. The noun προσελευσιν is consistent with the verb προσελευσεται used by Symmachus in item 5. The reading προελευσιν in $v^{mg}z^{mg}$ is either a scribal error for προσελευσιν, or perhaps the original Symmachus reading (from which προσελευσιν could be derived under the influence of the preceding verb). Ꞩ has not preserved any distinction between the nouns found in Aquila and in Symmachus.

7. Theodotion replaces OG αι δουλαι with οι δουλοι, to reflect more exactly the masculine noun *h'bdym*. Aquila's variant, των δουλων, is demanded by the change in syntax found in item 6. It represents the Hebrew structure more precisely. Symmachus' variant, δουλικην, provides a less literal rendition of the Hebrew.

8. Aquila and the OG both have εαν, followed in item 9 by a subjunctive verb. The expansion δε, found in a number of OG manuscripts and in the α' reading of Ꞩ, is clearly secondary. Theodotion and Symmachus share the variant ει, followed in item 9 by the indicative and the subjunctive, respectively. This item need not mean that Aquila here knew the OG independently of Theodotion. This interpretation is not impossible, but it is at least as possible that Theodotion replaced OG εαν μη ευαρεστηση with ει πονηρα εστιν, and that this in turn was

rejected by Aquila in favor of εαν κακισθη. The agreement between Aquila and the OG on the use of εαν and the subjunctive would then be coincidental.

9. The Samaritan Pentateuch has *rʿh hyʾ* where the MT merely has *rʿh*. Theodotion's πονηρα εστιν is almost certainly a reflection of this longer reading proper to the Palestinian Hebrew text. A similar expansion is found in the Peshitto (*snyʾ hy*). It was to provide explicit reflection of the Hebrew pronoun used predicatively that Theodotion replaced OG εαν μη ευαρεστηση with ει πονηρα εστιν. The use of εστιν for the Hebrew pronoun is not unusual. Theodotion uses it four times in Exodus to represent MT *hwʾ*.[16] Because his Hebrew text contained *rʿh hyʾ*, Theodotion treats *rʿh* as an adjective. The OG, which presumably translated a text without *hyʾ*, takes *rʿh* as a verb. Aquila, revising to the present MT (also without *hyʾ*), similarly takes *rʿh* as a verb and translates it with a single Greek verb. Symmachus agrees with the OG against Aquila (and Theodotion) in using μη plus a verb with positive content to translate the simple Hebrew verb with negative content.

This is the first time Theodotion has been found to agree with a Hebrew text different from the present MT. Chapter three shows that there are very few instances of this in Theodotion's version of Exodus.

In the OG generally, both πονηρος and κακος (and related words) are most often used to represent derivatives of Hebrew *rʿʿ*. An investigation of the Aquila and Theodotion usages noted in H-R failed to reveal any clear pattern of correspondence for Aquila in the Pentateuch, while no instances of κακος or related words are attributed to Theodotion in the Pentateuch. The verb κακιζεσθαι only occurs once in the OG (4 Macc. 12:2) and in the present verse in Aquila. If, as suggested, Aquila had Theodotion's reading before him and rejected it, this was not primarily for lexical reasons but for stylistic ones. He wanted a one-word Greek equivalent, a verb, to reflect the MT verb *rʿh*.

10. The three versions agree in inserting the same reflection of the MT plus *bʿyny*. This addition is also found in F$^{b\ mg}$ackA, under ※ '' in S^{txt}, and out of place (after item 14) in ej^{txt}. The preposition εν alone is inserted in qu. Since the object of the phrase *bʿyny* here is not Yahweh but the girl's owner (*ʾdnyh*), this example is not really

---

[16] Exod. 29:14; 31:14; 32:9, 25.

covered by the KAIΓE characteristic isolated by Shenkel, though it is related to that characteristic.[17]

11. In spite of the insertion just discussed, Symmachus retains the OG reading unchanged (cf. ack). Theodotion and Aquila both replace OG τω κυριω with $\overline{\kappa\upsilon}$, thereby both smoothing the syntax and removing the Greek article that had no counterpart in the MT. The addition of ουν after αυτης in the version of Theodotion found in s^{mg} is certainly due to secondary scribal error and may be disregarded.

12. The presumed OG reading is retained by Theodotion, while a minor variant (not reflected as different by $) is found in Symmachus and also in $Bfb_2^{a?}$Ɇ^{vid}. A further variant, reflecting a different judgment on the antecedent of MT *ʾšr*, is found in Aquila. The reading ο, found in the nameless version of s^{mg} that otherwise agrees with Aquila's version as contained in $v^{mg}z^{mg}$^{mg}, is presumably due to scribal error.

13. OG αυτω is found in a relatively small number of witnesses (BnquxɆ, possibly i*, and out of place in Aacm). Related variants are found in $F^{a?}$ (and out of place in k), in ȺȻ^{m}, and in bw. These readings are based on a Hebrew variant **lw/*lh* (לה*/לו*), or on a misunderstanding of MT *lʾ*. The correct interpretation of MT *lʾ* is reflected in ου of the majority of Greek manuscripts. This reading is accepted by both Theodotion and Aquila. A further variant, based on this same interpretation, is found in Symmachus.

14. Theodotion and Aquila both retain OG καθωμολογησατο, along

---

[17] J. D. Shenkel, *Chronology and Recensional Development in the Greek Text of Kings* (Cambridge, 1968), pp. 13-17. The equation εν οφθαλμοις = *bʿyny* has significance as a characteristic of the KAIΓE recension primarily where *bʿyny* refers to *YHWH*, since this is when the OG in Samuel-Kings regularly avoided the literal translation as excessively anthropomorphic. In general, it can be said that the KAIΓE revision used εν οφθαλμοις exclusively to translate MT *bʿyny* (the few exceptions would be due to inadvertence), while the OG did so only in certain circumstances and not always even then. The present case would fall under those circumstances in which even the OG might reasonably be expected to use the literal translation. Hence its presence in Theodotion (and in Aquila and Symmachus) does not prove that the KAIΓE revision is here in evidence, but merely that the KAIΓE revision could be here.

with the added αυτην (found in F*dhi[a?]loprs[txt]tv[txt]y-b_2𝔅[vid]ℭ[m], and presumably reflected in 𝔖[txt]), to represent MT *y'dh* (verb plus third singular, feminine suffix). A variant is found in Symmachus.

Evaluation

Theodotion and Aquila agree against the OG five times (items 5, 10, 11, 13, 14), joined by Symmachus only in item 10. In two of these agreements (items 13, 14), the reading shared by Theodotion and Aquila is found in a large number of Greek witnesses, and may have been present in the Greek textual tradition presupposed by Theodotion and Aquila. Only in item 11 does Symmachus agree with the OG against the other two versions. In item 12 Theodotion agrees with the majority Greek reading against Aquila, while Symmachus has the variant found only in Bfb_2[a?]𝔈[vid]. Twice, items 6 and 7, Theodotion is clearly closer to the OG than either Aquila or Symmachus. Aquila agrees with the OG against Theodotion and Symmachus in item 8, but it is a minor point. And in item 9 all three versions differ from each other and from the OG. In this case, Theodotion agrees with the Palestinian reading preserved in the Samaritan Pentateuch against the present MT.

On the whole, Theodotion's version again may be understood as a revision of the OG towards a Hebrew text. It is related to Aquila's version, but does not seem to be dependent on it. Symmachus' version is relatively independent of Aquila's and Theodotion's and is loosely related to the OG.

Exodus 19:13

	MT	*OG*	𝔖*txt*	ϑ'	α'	σ'
1.	l' tg'	ουχ αφεται	l' tgšwp			
2.	bw	αυτου	bh			
3.	yd	χειρ	'yd'			
4.	ky sqwl	εν γαρ λιθοις	bk'p' gyr			
5.	ysql	λιθοβοληθησεται	ntrgm			
6.	'w	η	'w			
7.	yrh	βολιδι	bg'r'	τοξευομενος	ροιζησει	βελεσιν

	MT	*OG*	$\not S^{txt}$	θ'	α'	σ'
8.	yyrh	κατατοξευ- θησεται	ntkšṭ			
9.	'm bhmh	εαν τε κτηνος	w'n b'yr'			
10.	'm 'yš	εαν τε ανθρωπος	w'n br 'nš'			
11.	l' yḥyh	ου ζησεται	l' n'ḥ'			
12.		οταν αι φωναι	'mty dyn d-q̈l'			
13.		και αι σαλ- πιγγες	w‹šypwr̈'			
14.			n'zlwn			
15.		και η νεφελη απελθη	-wt'zl 'nn'			
16.		απο του ορους	mn ṭwr'‹			
17.	bmšk			εν τη απελευσει (bm'zlt')	εν ελ- κυσμω (bngd')	οταν αφελκυσθη ('mty dn'br)
18.	hybl			του ιωβηλ (dywbl)	του παρα- φεροντος (dhw dm'br)	ο σαλπιγμος (ywbb')
19.	hmh	εκεινοι	hnwn	αυτοι	αυτοι	αυτοι
20.	y'lw	αναβη- σονται	nsqwn	αναβη- σονται	αναβη- σονται	αναβαινετω- σαν
21.	bhr	επι το ορος	'l ṭwr'	εις το ορος	εν ορει	εις το ορος

Notes

7. These θ', α', and σ' readings are taken from $M^{mg} j^{mg} s^{mg} v^{mg} z^{mg}$. There is no name on the θ' reading in s^{mg}. For OG βολιδι, m has εν βολιδι, a_2 has βολιδα, and F*A$\not S$ have βολισιν.

9-10. κτηνος and ανθρωπος are interchanged in bfijnsvzd_2, Cyr-cod.

12. δε is inserted after OG οταν in abcfhijnptwxd_2A$\not S$, Cyr-ed.

13. Lagarde's B for $\not S$ has *wšypwr̈'*‹ for *w‹šypwr̈'*.

14. παυσονται is added to the OG reading by 71.

17-18. These ϑ', α' and σ' readings are taken from v^{mg}S̸^{mg}. The ϑ' reading is also found without name in b^{mg}.

18. *dywbb* is found for *dywbl* in the ϑ' reading of Lagarde's B^{l} for S̸.

19-21. These ϑ', α', and σ' readings are taken from v^{mg}.

21. OG επι is replaced by εις in bh.

Commentary

7. All three versions replace OG βολιδι with new readings. Theodotion's choice, τοξευομενος, is related to OG κατατοξευθησεται (to represent MT *yyrh*) in item 8. Hence it is a reasonable choice to reflect the cognate infinitive absolute *yrh*. Related nouns, τοξοται and τοξων (to represent two occurrences of the Hiphil participle of *yrh*), are attributed to Theodotion by j^{mg} in 1 Sam. 31:3, while the verb τοξευσει (to reflect the Hiphil imperfect of *yrh*) is attributed to σ'ϑ' by 86^{mg} in Isa. 37:33. In all three cases, different readings are found in the OG.

The only other Theodotionic equivalents for MT *yrh* come from Nobil. (as cited by Field). In Ps. 11:2 (LXX 10:2), σ'ϑ' are credited with του κατατοξευσαι (also found in the OG) for MT *lyrwt*. In Ps. 64:8 (LXX 63:8), finally, Theodotion has κατατοξευσει αυτους to represent the Hiphil converted imperfect with third person, plural suffix (*wyrm*, following the MT vocalization וַיֹּרֵם). The OG variant και υψωθησεται presupposes a different evaluation of the same consonantal form (וַיָּרָם*).

While the OG used a variety of equivalents for MT *yrh* (in the Qal, Niphal, and Hiphil), the relatively consistent usage found in Theodotion agrees with the standard pattern of correspondences in the ΚΑΙΓΕ sections of Samuel-Kings.[18] Further parallels are found in the OG for Chronicles

[18] 2 Sam. 11:20: MT *yrw*] B^{ab}bgoc_2e_2 πληγησεσθε] AB*MN rell. τοξευσουσιν (τοξευουσιν Aac*efmnswxa_2). 2 Sam. 11:24: MT *wyr'w hmwr'ym* (Qere ignores the two alephs)] boc_2e_2 και κατεβαρυνθη τα βελη] ABMN rell. και ετοξευσαν οι τοξευοντες (-σαντες i). 2 Kings 13:17: MT *yrh wywr*] Bdefmpqstw om.] Nbg-jnoruxyzc_2e_2C̸^{m}E̸ τοξευσαν και ετοξευσεν] v ροιζησον] AA̸^{vid}S̸(under ※α') ροιζησον και εροιζησεν. 2 Kings 19:32: MT *ywrh*] ABN omnes τοξευσει (-σεις t*; -σης g). These are the only instances of *yrh* I (Qal or Hiphil) in the ΚΑΙΓΕ sections of Samuel-Kings.

and elsewhere.[19] The KAIΓE recension and Theodotion are thus in agreement in leveling through one set of OG equivalents for MT *yrh* so as to achieve lexical consistency.

The evidence is less clear for Aquila's variant ροιζησει, a verbal noun introduced to represent the MT infinitive absolute. This new reading was probably chosen with a view to a different pattern of lexical consistency (presuming, of course, a similar change in item 8 that has not been preserved), a pattern that is totally independent of OG usage. The verb ροιζειν and its derivatives are never used by the OG to represent MT *yrh*. It is used by the OG only in Song of Sol. 4:15, where it represents MT *nzl*.

Three times, all where the OG either failed to provide any reflection of MT *yrh* or is no longer extant, a form of ροιζειν is found in a very few witnesses:

Gen.31:51: MT *yryty*] OG om.] ao εστησα] cc_2 εστησας] Ⱥ *statuimus*] km ερυζησα] x εροιζησα. (The attribution of this reading to Aquila by Field is based on inference alone.)

2 Kings 13:17: MT *yrh*] Bdefmpqstw om.] Nbg-jnoruxyzc_2e_2Ȼ^{m}Ɇ τοξευσον] AvȺ^{vid} ροιζησον] S̸^{txt}(under ※α') *'šb*.

2 Kings 13:17: MT *wywr*] Bdefmpqstw om.] Nbg-jnoruxyzc_2e_2Ȼ^{m}Ɇ και ετοξευσεν] AȺ^{vid} και εροιζησεν] S̸^{txt}(under ※α') *w'šb* (*w'yšb* B^{1}).

In addition to the two readings of Aquila found in S̸^{txt} of 2 Kings 13:17 (presumably representing the forms of ροιζειν found in A), the following four readings attributed to Aquila should be noted:

Exod. 19:13: α' ροιζησει for MT *yrh* (inf. abs.) in $M^{mg}j^{mg}s^{mg}v^{mg}z^{mg}$; ϑ' and σ' variants also cited.

Isa. 37:33: α' ροιζησει for MT *ywrh* in 86^{mg}; σ'ϑ' variant also cited.

---

[19] 1 Chron. 10:3; MT *hmwrym*] OG οι τοξοται. 1 Chron. 10:3: MT *hywrym*] OG των τοξων. 2 Chron. 35:23: MT *wyrw hyrym*] OG και ετοξευσαν οι τοξοται. To these should be added: OG κατατοξευθησεται for MT *yyrh* in Exod. 19:13, OG του κατατοξευσαι for MT *lyrwt* in Ps. 11:2 (LXX 10:2) and again in Ps. 64:5 (LXX 63:5), and OG κατατοξευσουσιν αυτον for MT *yrhw* in Ps. 64:5 (LXX 63:5).

Ps. 64:8 (LXX 63:8): α' και ροιζησει for MT *wyrm* in Nobil. as cited by Field; ϑ' and σ' variants also cited from Nobil., while a conflicting α'σ' reading from $\not{S}$ (*nznwq hkyl*) is said by Field to be equivalent to the σ' variant ακοντισει ουν cited from Nobil.

1 Sam. 31:3: α' ροιζουντες for MT *(h)mwrym* in $j^{mg}z^{mg}$, with a ϑ' variant in j^{mg}.

To this last should be added the $\underset{\circ}{\lambda}$ reading απο των ροιζουντων, with σ' and ϑ' variants also cited, for MT *mhmwrym* in 1 Sam. 31:3 (all variants found in j^{mg}).

The foregoing series of readings suggests that Aquila rejected all OG equivalents for MT *yrh*, and introduced a new equivalent, ροιζειν. Three times this reading is found without name in one or two manuscripts, in two of which the α' attribution of $\not{S}$ is reasonably invoked. Four more times this variant is attributed to Aquila and once to $\underset{\circ}{\lambda}$ (with σ' and ϑ' variants also given).

Once again, then, Theodotion and Aquila both manifest tendencies toward lexical consistency in their respective representations of the MT. But Theodotion has a pattern of usage that is characteristic of the ΚΑΙΓΕ recension in Samuel-Kings and that is found occasionally in the OG elsewhere, while Aquila introduces a completely new pattern.

Symmachus' variant, βελεσιν, is an independent and fairly unimportant revision of the OG. It does not represent any consistent pattern of usage either in the OG or in Symmachus' version.

12-16. These items, partially under ÷ in $\not{S}^{txt}$, seem to represent an ancient variant for the MT phrase given in items 17-18 (which is not otherwise reflected in the OG or in $\not{S}^{txt}$). This ancient variant has apparently undergone secondary expansion.

17. All three versions agree in reflecting the present MT. The structure of the divergent OG passage is retained by Symmachus (cf. OG οταν in item 12), while Theodotion and Aquila both represent MT *b-* with εν. Theodotion's τη απελευσει is probably a revision of the OG verb απελθη (item 13). The noun better reflects the MT infinitive construct.

The OG uses απερχεσθαι to represent MT *mšk* only four times.[20] The

[20] Exod. 12:21; Judg. 4:6; Job 21:33; Ecclus. 14:19.

most common OG equivalent for MT *mšk* is ελκυειν/ελκειν, used eight or nine times,[21] together with its compounds εξελκυειν (Gen. 37:28) and συνελκειν (Ps. 28:3 [LXX 27:3]).

The verb ελκυειν/ελκειν or its Syriac equivalent *ngd* to represent MT *mšk*, is variously attributed to Aquila (six times),[22] to Symmachus (four times),[23] to Theodotion (twice),[24] and to οι λ̥ (twice).[25] An anonymous reading, εν ελκυσμω αυτου for MT *bmškw* (where the OG had εν τω ελκυσαι αυτον, and Symmachus had *kd ngdh*, which presumably represents *ελκυσας αυτον or the like) is cited from Chrysostom by Field for Ps. 10:9 (LXX 9:30). The following compounds are also used by the versions to represent MT *mšk*: ανελκυειν by Symmachus in Jer. 38:13 (LXX 45:13); εξελκυειν by Aquila in Ezek. 32:20. In addition, the Niphal of *mšk* is reflected by Theodotion's εφελκυσθαι or α'σ'θ' αφελκυσθαι in Isa. 13:22.

With the exception of απερχεσθαι, no other equivalent is used more than twice by the OG to represent MT *mšk*. Individual instances of different equivalents are found three times in Symmachus,[26] and once each in Aquila[27] and Theodotion.[28] Equivalents for the noun *mšk* need not be discussed here.

It is clear that Theodotion's τη απελευσει does not conform to any standard pattern of correspondence. Presumably it was influenced by OG απελθη in item 15 of this verse and OG απελθοντες in Exod. 12:21 (representing the only other occurrence of *mšk* in Exodus).

---

[21] Deut. 21:3; Judg. 5:14; Neh. 9:30 (Esdras B 19.30 - this is not OG in the strict sense, however. Cf. fn. 33); Job 8:18; Ps. 10:9 (LXX 9:30); Eccles. 2:3; Song of Sol. 1:4; Jer. 31:3 (LXX 38:3); 38:13 (LXX 45:13).

[22] Judg. 4:7; Ps. 28:3 (LXX 27:3); 36:11 (LXX 35:11); Job 40:25 (LXX v.20); Song of Sol. 1:4; Eccles. 2:3.

[23] Isa. 5:18; Ps. 10:9 (LXX 9:30); Job 40:25 (LXX v.20); Song of Sol. 1:4.

[24] Job 40:25 (LXX v.20); Eccles. 2:3.

[25] Hos. 11:4; Amos 9:13.

[26] αθροιζειν In Judg. 4:7; διδασκειν in Judg. 5:14; παροικιζειν in Ezek. 12:25.

[27] Syriac *mtyḥ'* to represent the Hebrew Pual participle in Prov.13:12.

[28] επισπασθαι in Judg. 5:14.

Aquila's variant, ελκυσμω, conforms to the more common pattern of usage in the OG generally, and is presumably due to a desire for lexical consistency. The article, found in Theodotion but not supported by the Hebrew text, is omitted by Aquila.

The variant found in Symmachus is less rigidly patterned on the Hebrew structure, but it also agrees with the more regular lexical pattern discussed above.

18. The most frequent OG equivalent for MT *ywbl/ybl* is αφεσις. At no place does the OG have any one of the readings found in this item. Here and in Lev. 25:10, Theodotion used the transliteration ιωβηλ. In Num. 36:4, however, Theodotion retained OG η αφεσις for MT *hybl* (according to the ϑ'ο' citation of v^{mg}), while Symmachus adopted the transliteration ο ιωβηλ (according to b^{mg}). The transliteration ιωβηλ is also found in the text or margin of one or more manuscripts fourteen times for MT *ywbl/ybl*,[29] and four times for the plural of the same word.[30] It is not possible to conclude that all or many of the occurrences of ιωβηλ without any explicit attribution must have come from Theodotion's revision. This is a distinct possibility, however. In any event, Theodotion here clearly revises to reflect the present MT in a way that is not unexpected, but that is independent of OG usage. The variant *dywbb* (for *dywbl*) in B^1 of $ is undoubtedly due to scribal error under the influence of the similar Syriac word, *ywbb*ʾ, found in Symmachus' version.

Aquila's variant, του παραφεροντος, is consistent with the readings attributed to Aquila in Lev. 25:10 (παραφερων for MT *ywbl*) and in Num. 36:4 (ο παραφερων for MT *hybl*). This correspondence is not otherwise attested in the OG or in any of the variants found in B-McL and Ziegler. The word is presumably an attempt at a literal translation of the Hebrew noun *ywbl/ybl*, taken as the Qal active participle of the verb **ybl* (which only occurs in the Hiphil and Hophal in biblical Hebrew). While παραφερειν is never used for the Hiphil or Hophal of *ybl* in the OG, φερειν is so used three times,[31] αναφερειν once,[32] and αποφερειν four

---

[29]Lev. 25:10, 11, 12, 13, 15, 28, 30, 31, 33, 40, 50, 52; 27:17; Josh. 6:5 (LXX v.4).

[30]Josh. 6:4, 6, 8 (LXX v.7), 13.

[31]Ps. 68:30 (LXX 67:30); 76:12 (LXX 75:12); Zeph. 3:10.

[32]Isa. 18:7.

times.[33]

In Job 10:19, moreover, α'θ' replace OG απαλλαγη with απηνεχθειν (αποφερειν) to represent MT *'wbl* (Hophal of *ybl*), according to Field. Aquila's reading in the present verse, then, is apparently due to a regular attempt at an etymological translation of the Hebrew noun *ywbl/ybl*.

Symmachus' reading, ο σαλπιγμος, is not otherwise attested in the OG, but is related to αι σαλπιγγες of the different OG version (item 13). Symmachus does not seem to have used it elsewhere to represent MT *ywbl/ybl*.[34]

19. All three versions agree in replacing OG εκεινοι with the non-demonstrative αυτοι to represent MT *hmh*.[35]

20. Theodotion and Aquila both retain the OG reading, while Symmachus modifies it slightly.

21. Theodotion and Symmachus both replace OG επι with εις (also found in bh) This change fits the meaning, but does not conform to the more usual correspondence of εν for MT *b-*. The inconsistency is corrected by Aquila, who also omits the OG article retained by Theodotion and Symmachus, but not supported by a consonantally separate element in the MT.

Evaluation

In item 20, Aquila and Theodotion both agree with the OG, while

---

[33]Hos. 10:6; Ps. 45:15 (LXX 44:15), 16 (LXX 44:16); Job 21:32. In Esdras B 5:14, αποφερειν corresponds to the Haphel of *ybl* in Ezra 5:14. As R. Klein has shown, however, Esdras B represents a revision of the OG to the developing Palestinian Hebrew text or else a new translation of that text. The OG version of the Egyptian Hebrew text is retained in Esdras A. In the latter, 6:17 (18) corresponds to Ezra 5:14, and there απηρεισατο (from απερειδειν) apparently represents the Aramaic form. For Klein's demonstration that Esdras A represents the OG and that Esdras B is a revision to or at least a reflection of the developed, Palestinian proto-MT, see his "Studies in the Greek Texts of the Chronicler" (Th.D. diss., Harvard University, 1966), pp. 309-311, 321-323.

[34]Cf. σ' ο ιωβηλ in Num. 36:4 and σ' *ddkr'* in Josh. 6:5 (LXX v.4).

[35]Cf. α', σ', and θ' αυτοι for MT *hm* in Exod. 5:7, where it = OG, and in Exod. 7:11, where the OG does not represent MT *hm*.

Symmachus has a revised reading. In item 19, all three versions agree on a revision of the OG that reflects the MT more exactly. In item 21, Theodotion and Symmachus share a minor revision of the OG, while Aquila revises still further to provide a more exact and literal reflection of the MT phrase.

In items 17-18, all three versions represent the present MT, as against the divergent OG passage in items 12-16. In item 17, Theodotion and Aquila agree, in contrast to Symmachus, in representing the Hebrew prepositional structure with a similar Greek structure. Aquila also omits the unsupported article found in Theodotion. Theodotion's noun in item 17 is perhaps due to OG usage in Exodus, and almost never elsewhere, while Aquila's variant conforms to the more regular OG usage outside Exodus. Aquila's variant is thus presumably due to a desire for general lexical consistency. The same could be said for the verb found in Symmachus. Theodotion and Aquila have readings in item 18 that are consistent with their respective usages elsewhere, both independent of OG patterns, while Symmachus' variant is unparalleled.

In item 7, Theodotion agrees with KAIΓE usage, itself based on one OG pattern of correspondences, for his revision of the OG, while Aquila departs from the OG but establishes a pattern that he follows elsewhere. Once again Symmachus' variant is unparalleled and of little immediate importance.

The variants preserved for Exod. 19:13, then, do not contradict the preliminary evaluations that have already been advanced. They tend to support the suggestions that Theodotion is directly dependent on the OG; that Theodotion revises toward the present MT; that Aquila is somehow dependent on, or at least related to, Theodotion's revision in his own further revisional activity; that Theodotion cannot have depended on Aquila for his familiarity with the OG; and that Symmachus does not exhibit the same tendencies as do Theodotion and Aquila.

Exodus 32:18

	MT	*OG*	$\mathcal{S}^{txt}$	ϑ'(*in* $\mathcal{S}^{mg}$)	α'(*in* $\mathcal{S}^{mg}$)	σ'(*in* $\mathcal{S}^{mg}$)
1.	wy'mr	και λεγει	w'mr			
2.	'yn	ουκ εστιν	l' 'ytwhy	l' 'ytwhy	l' 'ytwhy	l' 'ytyh
3.	qwl	φωνη	ql'	ql' dqrb'	ql'	g't'

	MT	*OG*	S^{txt}	ϑ'(*in* S^{mg})	α'(*in* S^{mg})	σ'(*in* S^{mg})
4.	‘nwt	εξαρχοντων	dhnwn	dm‘nyn	dhlyn	dhnwn
			dm‘nyn		dm‘nyn	dpqdyn
5.	gbwrh	κατ ισχυν	bḥyl’	bḥyl’	bḥyl’	gnbrwt’
6.	w’yn	ουδε	’p l’	wl’ ’ytwhy	wl’ ’ytwhy	wl’
7.	qwl	φωνη	ql’	ql’	ql’	g‘t’
8.	‘nwt	εξαρχοντων	dhnwn	dm‘nynyt’	dhnwn	dpqd’
			dm‘nyn		dm‘nyn	
9.	ḥlwšh	τροπης	bzkwt’	dzkwt’	mn zkwt’	zkwt’
10.	qwl	αλλα φωνην	’l’ bql’	ql’	’l’ ql’	’l’ ql’
11.	‘nwt	εξαρχοντων	dhnwn	dhnyn	dm‘nyn’	dmb’šnwt’
		οινου	m‘ḥyn’	dm‘nyn		
			dhmr’			
12.	’nky	εγω	’n’	’n’ ’yty d-	’n’	’n’
13.	šm‘	ακουω	šm‘ ’n’	šm‘ ’n’	šm‘ ’n’	šm‘ ’n’

Notes

1. *dixit* is found for OG λεγει in $BC^{m}L^{rwz}S^{txt}$. μωυσης is added in F^{a}dfknptx(μωσης kn)A-edE(*ei Moses*)L^{rwz}.

4. The MT vocalization is: עֱנוֹת.

4-5. OG εξαρχοντων κατ ισχυν is replaced by *de principibus cum uirtute* in L^{r}, by *de principu cum uirtute* in L^{w}, and by κατισχυωντων αρχοντων in x.

5. Lagarde says of *bḥyl’* in the ϑ' and α' versions: "...bis *bḥyl’* edidi, quibus locis C *bnḥl’* videre in B sibi visus erat."[36]

7. For OG φωνη, x has φωνης and a has φωνην.

8. The MT vocalization is עֱנוֹת.

8-9. OG εξαρχοντων τροπης is replaced by *de principum* (*-pium* L^{r}) *fugae* in L^{rw} and by *principū fug*[*ient*]*ium* in L^{z}.

9. OG τροπης is replaced by *pugnae* in B^{1}.

10. For OG φωνην, gjm have φωνη (+ην gj) and z^{mg} has φωνης.

11. The MT vocalization is: עַנּוֹת. OG εξαρχοντων is replaced by *principatus* in L^{rw}. OG οινου is replaced by *ex uino* in L^{z} and by *uini ludentiu* in L^{w}.

---

[36] I have substituted transliterations for the Syriac script used by Lagarde.

Commentary

2. Theodotion and Aquila both retain the Syriac form of the OG reading found in $\mathcal{S}^{txt}$, while a minor variant (due to the new subject introduced in item 3) is found in Symmachus. Presumably all three versions actually preserved OG εστιν.

3. Aquila retains $\mathcal{S}^{txt}$ *ql'*, which represents OG φωνη. The latter is most frequently found as a translation for MT *qwl* throughout the LXX.

Theodotion has an expanded Syriac reading, *ql' dqrb'*, that is not reflected in any Greek witnesses. This is probably a secondary expansion in the Theodotionic text presumably based on MT *qwl mlḥmh* (OG φωνη πολεμου, $\mathcal{S}^{txt}$ *ql' dqrb'*) in the previous verse. At all events, it is a departure from the OG, independent of the MT, and not known or followed by Aquila. This is the second such reading that we have encountered in the version attributed to Theodotion, and it is not paralleled in items 7 and 10.

Symmachus rejects OG φωνη ($\mathcal{S}^{txt}$ *ql'*) here and in item 7, but not in item 10. The new Syriac form, *g't'*, might represent Greek βοη (so Field), but need not do so. This change is contrary to OG usage, and does not seem to be part of any recognizable pattern.

4. The various Syriac forms found here and in items 8 and 11 give rise to serious problems of evaluation and interpretation. Hebrew *'nh* is divided into four distinct roots by Brown-Driver-Briggs[37] and Lisowski,[38] while Mandelkern, apparently followed by H-R, compresses all the occurrences into two groups.[39] Syriac *'n'*, in its various forms, includes all four meanings assigned to Hebrew *'nh* by BDB and Lisowski.

It is Hebrew *'nh* IV (to sing) that is of concern in the present verse. While OG αποκρινεσθαι is regularly used for *'nh* I (to answer),

---

[37] BDB. The four roots are: (1) to answer, respond; (2) to be occupied, busied with; (3) to be bowed down, afflicted; (4) to sing.

[38] G. Lisowsky, *Konkordanz zum hebräischen Alten Testament* (Stuttgart, 1958). He reverses BDB's II and III, and he includes in IV one citation assigned to *'wn* by BDB (Isa. 13:22, where the text is obscure).

[39] Mandelkern's I includes BDB's I and IV; his II includes BDB's II and III.

it is used only two or three times for *ʿnh* IV.[40] OG εξαρχειν is used for ten of the remaining twelve occurrences of *ʿnh* IV,[41] while OG φθεγγεσθαι is found for the last two.[42] Apart from the present verse the following hexaplaric variants for MT *ʿnh* IV have been preserved:

Aquila: και κατελεγεν (M^{mg}, without name in $v^{mg}z^{mg}$ and only the verb in $F^{b\ mg}$), *mʿnyʾ hwt*($\cancel{S}^{mg}$) for MT *wtʿn* in Exod. 15:21.

κατaλεξατε (α'σ' citation in $M^{mg}g^{txt}v^{mg}$, without name in $k^{mg}z^{mg}$; cf. s^{mg}) for MT *ʿnw* in Num. 21:17.

lmʿnyw ($\cancel{S}^{mg}$, for which Field suggests "του εξαρχειν") for MT *lʿnwt* in Ps. 88:1 (LXX 87:1).[43]

καταλεξατε (cited from Euseb. by Field) for MT *ʿnw* in Ps. 147:7 (LXX 146:7).

καταλεξουσιν (86^{mg}) or *npnʾ* ($\cancel{S}^{mg}$, which Field and Ziegler interpret as "αποκριθησεται," cf. $\cancel{S}^{txt}$ *npnwn* for OG αποκριθησονται) for MT *yʿnh* in Jer. 25:30 (LXX 32:16).

και καταλεξουσιν (86^{mg}) for MT *wʿnw* in Jer. 51:14 (LXX 28:14).

Symmachus: *mʿnyʾ hwt dyn* ($\cancel{S}^{mg}$) for MT *wtʿn* in Exod. 15:21.

καταλεξατε (α'σ' citation--cf. Aquila list) for MT *ʿnw* in Num. 21:17.

κατελεγον ($b^{mg}j^{mg}m^{mg}z^{mg}$) for MT *yʿnw* in 1 Sam. 21:12 (LXX v.11).

καταλεξατε (cited from Euseb. by Field) for MT *ʿnw* in Ps. 147:7 (LXX 146:7).

εξαρξει (86^{mg}), *nʿnʾ* ($\cancel{S}^{mg}$) for MT *yʿnh* in Jer. 25:30 (LXX 32:16).

wnʿnwn ($\cancel{S}^{mg}$, for which Field suggests "και εξαρξουσιν") for MT *wʿnw* in Jer. 51:14 (LXX 28:14).

---

[40] Jer. 25:30 (LXX 32:16); Ps. 88:1 (LXX 87:1). In Esdras B 3:11 (= Ezra 3:11), αποκρινεσθαι also represents MT *ʿnh* IV, but more probably the original OG equivalent is φωνειν of Esdras A 5:58. See the comments in fn. 33.

[41] Exod. 15:21; 32:18 *ter*; Num. 21:17; 1 Sam. 18:7; 21:12 (LXX v.11); 29:5; Isa. 27:2; Ps. 147:7 (LXX 146:7).

[42] Jer. 51:14 (LXX 28:14); Ps. 119:172 (LXX 118:172).

[43] The various Syriac readings for Jeremiah and Psalms have been taken from A. M. Ceriani, ed., *Codex Syro-Hexaplaris Ambrosianus photolithographice editus* (Milan, 1874).

Theodotion: said by $\mathcal{S}^{mg}$ to agree with ο′ ("*ʾyk šbʿyn*"), where $\mathcal{S}^{txt}$ had *mšrʾ hwt* ... *dyn* and the OG had εξηρχεν δε to represent MT *wtʿn*, in Exod. 15:21.

No occurrences of καταλεγειν are attributed to Theodotion by H-R, and none have been discovered in the course of this study. Aquila and Symmachus each have one further occurrence of καταλεγειν, where the MT does not have *ʿnh*.[44]

For the three occurrences of *ʿnwt* (two vocalized Qal and one vocalized Piel) in this verse, the OG had αξαρχοντων ("of ones beginning, taking the lead, teaching, ruling") each time, followed in the third occurrence by the expansion οινου. These forms are possibly reflected by the Syriac readings found in $\mathcal{S}^{txt}$:[45] *dhnwn dmʿnyn* (Aphel participle, "of those leading or teaching singing" or "of those raising a shout") for the first two, and *dhnwn dmʿnyn*ʾ ⸆*dhmrʾ*⸌ ("of those singers, song-leaders, ⸆of wine⸌") for the third. The reason for a different Syriac form in item 11, where the OG form remains the same, is not clear.

Very similar (and in one case identical) Syriac forms are attributed to Aquila by $\mathcal{S}^{mg}$, while related but different forms are attributed to Theodotion:

Aquila: *dhlyn dmʿnyn*, "of these leading, teaching singing," or "of these raising a shout."

dhnwn dmʿnyn, "of those leading or teaching singing," or "of those raising a shout."

*dmʿnyn*ʾ, "of singers," or "of song-leaders."

Theodotion: *dmʿnyn*, "of singing-leaders," or "of singing-teachers," or "of shout-raisers."

*dmʿnynyt*ʾ, "of (fem.) singers," or "of (fem.) song-leaders."

dhnyn dmʿnyn, "of those (fem.!) leading or teaching singing," or "of those (fem.!) raising a shout."

---

[44] Judg. 5:11: MT *mḥṣṣym*] OG ανακρουομενων] α′ καταλεγοντων σ′ συμπινωντων ο′ ευφραινομενων (z^{mg}). Ps. 145:6 (LXX 144:6): MT *ʾsprnh*] OG διηγησονται] α′ διηγησομαι αυτας, θ′ διηγησομαι αυτην, σ′ καταλεξω αυτην (all from Nobil. as cited by Field).

[45] Compare Greek εξαρξει and Syriac *nʿnʾ*, attributed to Symmachus by 86^{mg} and $\mathcal{S}^{mg}$, respectively, in Jer. 25:30 (LXX 32:16).

It is possible to argue that Aquila and Theodotion both employed various forms more or less closely related to the OG readings reflected by $\mathfrak{S}^{txt}$ (if, indeed, those readings are reflected by $\mathfrak{S}^{txt}$). The Syriac evidence would seem to indicate that Aquila is much closer to the OG than is Theodotion. However, the normal choice of Aquila for MT *ʿnh* IV is καταλεγειν (five times). And once Greek κατελεγεν and Syriac *mʿnyʾ hwt* are both attributed to Aquila (Exod. 15:21). In addition, *lmʿnyw* is also attributed to Aquila once, where Field's suggested equivalent, του εξαρχειν, may well be misleading. If Aquila is faithful to his normal pattern here, then it is impossible to decide what type of readings Theodotion has. Those in items 8 and 11 seem to reflect the feminine plural ending of the Hebrew infinitives construct. Theodotion does not seem to have followed any pattern in treating MT *ʿnh* IV. The only other time that his reading is cited (Exod. 15:21), he is said by $\mathfrak{S}^{mg}$ to agree with the reading of $\mathfrak{S}^{txt}$. There OG εξηρχεν δε (for MT *wtʿn*) is presumably reflected by Syriac *m̆šry̆ʾ hwt ... dyn* ("she then began").

Since, however, the Pael and Aphel of *ʿnʾ* do not provide particularly adequate representations of καταλεγειν ("to recount, tell at length and in order; to repeat; to conclude by enumeration"), even Aquila's readings must remain in doubt. These readings illustrate only too well the difficulties encountered in the evaluation of hexaplaric variants preserved only in Syriac.

Symmachus' variants distinguish clearly between the first two occurrences of MT *ʿnwt*, both pointed as Qal, and the third, pointed as Piel. The first two are translated as "commanders" or the like, while the third is interpreted as "iniquity" or "harm." These variants are not at all related to those of the OG, Aquila, and Theodotion, but the third has an interesting parallel in the Samaritan Pentateuch.[46]

In summary, the various readings in item 4 and in items 8 and 11 do not allow a more exact evaluation of Theodotion's relation to the OG or to Aquila, but they do show that Theodotion's Hebrew text did not

---

[46]B.K. Waltke has noted in "Prolegomena to the Samaritan Pentateuch" (Ph.D. diss., Harvard University, 1965), pp. 197-198, that the majority of Samaritan manuscripts and translations replace the third *ʿnwt* with *ʿwnwt* (עֲוֹנוֹת, "iniquities"). He cited the Arabic translation *d̲nwb* (ذنوب , "sins, offenses, crimes").

differ from the MT.

5. According to Lagarde's editing,[47] Theodotion and Aquila both share the reading found in $\mathcal{S}^{txt}$, which presumably represents OG κατ ισχυν. Symmachus introduces a variant, *gnbrwt'*, whose Greek equivalent is not preserved.

6. Theodotion and Aquila both replace OG ουδε ($\mathcal{S}^{txt}$ *'p l'*) with *wl' 'ytwhy* to represent MT *w'yn*. This undoubtedly represents και ουκ εστιν (cf. item 2), and provides a uniform translation of MT *'yn* on its two occurrences in this verse. Symmachus, however, omits *'ytwhy*, thus translating accurately but not retaining consistency in the choice of equivalents.

7. Theodotion and Aquila retain the reading of $\mathcal{S}^{txt}$, which reflects OG φωνη, while Symmachus exhibits the same variant he had in item 3. Apart from the secondary expansion in Theodotion's earlier reading, all versions are consistent with their respective usages in item 3.

8. These readings have already been discussed in connection with item 4. Note that Aquila's Syriac reading here is identical with that found in $\mathcal{S}^{txt}$.

9. OG τροπης means "of turning" (i.e., "of the turning about" of the enemy, hence, "of routing" the enemy, or "of putting" him "to flight"). This is only a very free rendition of MT *ḥlwšh*, "(of) weakness, prostration." Syriac *zkwt'* means "victory," so that $\mathcal{S}^{txt}$ *bzkwt'* could be understood as a reasonable reflection of OG τροπης (since a *rout* of the enemy represents a *victory* for the one causing the rout). The slightly different readings found in the three versions may be due to different Greek, or Syriac, constructions demanded by the readings in item 8. It is hard to believe that Aquila would introduce a Greek preposition (Syriac *mn*) where the Hebrew and the OG had none, so the phrase *mn zkwt'* may be a paraphrase of his Greek variant. Hebrew *ḥlwšh* occurs only here in the Hebrew Bible, while no patterns are evident in the treatment of the related verb (*ḥlš*: Exod. 17:13; Isa. 14:12; Job 14:10) and noun (*ḥlš*: Joel 4:10). No pertinent conclusions can be drawn from the Syriac readings in this item.

---

[47] *bnḥl'*, "in the torrent," would not make any sense at all. If a genuine reading, it is probably due to secondary, inner-Syriac scribal error (ܒܢܚܠܐ for ܒܚܝܠܐ).

10. All three versions agree in omitting the Syriac preposition found before *ql'* in $\mathcal{S}^{txt}$. If $\mathcal{S}^{txt}$ *bql'* represents OG φωνην, then the forms without the preposition could represent the nominative φωνη (as in m, and with an expansion in gj). In choice of words, Theodotion and Aquila agree with their usage in items 3 and 7, as well as with OG usage in all three items. Symmachus, however, fails to retain his new reading found in the other two items. Theodotion alone rejects *'l'* (= OG αλλα), which has no support in the Hebrew text. Since Aquila and Symmachus retain the OG word, even though it is not supported by the MT, Theodotion's omission must have taken place after, or independently of, Aquila's revision. This latter, as already noted, frequently appears to have known the OG only through Theodotion's revision. Thus the present reading might provide a first slight trace of a second revisional stage in the Theodotionic material, a stage that is posterior to Aquila and for this reason is appropriately assigned to the time and the scholarly activity of traditional Theodotion.[48] It is important to note that this variant is closer to the MT than is the common reading of the OG, Aquila, and Symmachus. Chapter six isolates all the readings that might show evidence of a second Theodotionic revision to the MT independently of Aquila to see whether or not such a revision is supported, or even strongly suggested, by the readings still extant.

11. These readings have been discussed in connection with item 4. Note that the OG expansion, οινου, is under the obelus in $\mathcal{S}^{txt}$ and is omitted by all three versions.

12. Aquila and Symmachus retain $\mathcal{S}^{txt}$ *'n'* (= OG εγω) to represent MT *'nky*. Only Theodotion here uses the distinctive expansion *'n' 'yty d-* (reflecting εγω ειμι) that has already been discussed in connection with item 4 of the fourth reading (Exod. 8:25 [LXX v.29]). As in item 10 of this verse, a Theodotionic revision is not accepted by Aquila. This time, however, it can plausibly be argued that either Aquila or a subsequent scribe omitted the Theodotionic expansion ειμι, which certainly conflicts with Greek style. This reading is some sixteen chapters later than the last of the three instances in Exodus where Aquila is said

[48]Note that the omission could also be due to a simple haplography by a Syriac scribe: *-'* <*'l'*> *ql'*. This was suggested to me by Professor Strugnell.

to agree with Theodotion on this point.[49] Thus Aquila could easily have overlooked the peculiar reading before, or not have been bothered by it, and then could have decided not to retain it in the present verse.

13. All three versions agree with $\mathcal{S}^{txt}$ in accurately reflecting OG ακουω. The latter, in turn, is a good equivalent for the Hebrew participle used as a finite verb. Note that Theodotion retains the finite verb form after the expanded *'n' 'yty d-*. This is a characteristic feature of the ΚΑΙΓΕ expansion εγω ειμι to represent MT *'nky*.

Evaluation

Because all three variants are preserved only in Syriac, their detailed evaluation is difficult and many points remain obscure. Since much of the Theodotionic material in Exodus exists also or only in Syriac, some first-hand experience of the problems such readings raise is important.

Twice (item 13 and, with a minor Syriac change, item 2) all three versions agree with the OG. In items 5 and 7 Theodotion and Aquila agree with the OG (as reflected in $\mathcal{S}^{txt}$), while Symmachus introduces variants. In item 3 Aquila accepts the OG reading, while Theodotion adds to the OG reading an expansion not based on the Hebrew text. This expansion may be secondary in the Theodotionic tradition. Symmachus again has a variant. In item 6 Theodotion and Aquila share a revision of the OG that introduces consistency into the OG usage, while a different variant is found in Symmachus. In item 12 Aquila and Symmachus agree with the OG, while Theodotion introduces a characteristic expansion. In item 10 Aquila and Symmachus share a minor revision of the $\mathcal{S}^{txt}$ reflection of the OG reading. Theodotion accepts this revision, but also omits an OG word, retained by Aquila and Symmachus, that is not supported by the MT. In item 9 all three versions have minor variants for the $\mathcal{S}^{txt}$ reflection of the OG reading. Three times (items 4, 8, 11) the variants are difficult to interpret, but Aquila and Theodotion appear to be related to each other and to $\mathcal{S}^{txt}$, which may or may not represent the OG, while Symmachus introduces different variants. All three omit an OG expansion in item 11 that is retained under obelus in $\mathcal{S}^{txt}$. Aquila's Syriac readings in these three items are much closer to those in $\mathcal{S}^{txt}$ than are Theodotion's, but

---

[49] Exod. 3:11; 4:23; 8:25 (LXX v.29).

patterns of usage elsewhere make it at least possible that Aquila does not agree with the various OG readings in these three items.

Thus, while all three versions have a few features in common, Theodotion and Aquila are more closely related to each other and to the OG than Symmachus is to any one of them. Theodotion has suffered one secondary expansion and preserves two revisions of the OG that are not found in Aquila. At least one of these (item 10) may point to a secondary revision of the Theodotionic material independent of Aquila's revisional activity. At best, this difficult set of variants complicates the tentative conclusions reached in the earlier analyses.

MT Exodus 38:1-2 (LXX 38:22)

	MT (v.1)	*OG (v. 22)*	*F^b ckA̸E̸^c (v. 1)*	*S̸^txt (v. 1)*
1.	wy'ś	ουτος εποιησεν	και εποιησεν	w'bd
2.	't mzbḥ	το θυσιαστηριον	το θυσιαστηριον	lmdbḥ'
3.	h'lh		(του ολοκαυτωματος F^bE̸^c)	
4.		το χαλκουν	(το χαλκουν ckA̸)	dnḥš'
5.		εκ των πυρειων	εκ των πυρειων	‑mn pyr̈m'
6.		των χαλκων	των χαλκων	dnḥš'
7.		α ησαν	α ησαν	hlyn d'yt hww
8.		τοις ανδρασιν	τοις ανδρασιν	bgbr̈'
9.		τοις κατασταστασιασασι	τοις κατασταστασιασασιν	hnwn dšgšw
10.		μετα της κορε συναγωγης	μετα της κορε συναγωγης	'm knwšt' dqwrḥ‹
11.	'ṣy šṭym		εκ ξυλων ασηπτων	※θ' mn qyÿ' l' m̈blṭ'
12.	ḥmš 'mwt		πεντε πηχεων	ḥmš 'm̈'
13.	'rkw		μηκος αυτου	'wrk' dylh
14.	wḥmš 'mwt		και πεντε πηχεων	wḥmš 'm̈'
15.	rḥbw		ευρος αυτου	pty' dylh
16.	rbw'		τετραγωνον	ṭṭrgwnwn
17.	wšlš 'mwt		και τριων πηχεων	wdtlt 'm̈'
18.	qmtw		υψος αυτου	rwm' dylh
	(v. 2)		*(v. 2)*	*(v. 2)*
19.	wy'ś		εποιησεν	'bd
20.	qrntyw		τα κερατα αυτου	lqr̈nt' dylh

	MT (v. 2)	*F*^{b}*ckȺɆ*^{c} *(v. 2)*	*S̸*^{txt} *(v. 2)*
21.	ʿl ʾrbʿ	επι των τεσσαρων	ʿl ʾrbʿ
22.	pntyw	γωνιων αυτου	g̈wnwtʾ dylh
23.	mmnw	εξ αυτου	mnh
24.	hyw	εγενοντο	ʾytyhyn hwy
25.	qrntyw	τα κερατα αυτου	qr̈ntʾ dylh
26.	wyṣp ʾtw	και εκαλυψεν αυτω	wḥpyh
27.	nḥšt	χαλκω	bnḥšʾܐ

Notes

In chapters 36-39 of Exodus, the OG text-form departs radically in order and content from that found in the MT. A small group of witnesses (F^{b}GckmȺɆ^{c}S̸) reproduces, with some gaps, a text-form that conforms closely to the MT. In many cases, however, the divergent portions of the OG version are also retained by one or more of these witnesses (usually under ÷ in G and S̸), but rearranged according to the order of the MT. In the present passage, where only F^{b}ckȺɆ^{c}S̸ are extant among the witnesses to the revised text form, F^{b}Ɇ^{c} omit the OG material not supported by the MT (and mainly under ÷ in S̸), while k omits the material absent from the OG but demanded by the present MT. The Syriac equivalent of this latter material is attributed as a whole to Theodotion by S̸^{txt} (and is under ※). Notes on particular items follow:

1. In S̸^{txt}, Lagarde's B has ÷ before *wʿbd*, rather than before *mn* of item 5.

3-4. F^{b}Ɇ^{c} substitute του ολοκαυτωματος for OG το χαλκουν (retained by ckȺS̸).

5. In his edition of S̸, Lagarde follows his F in placing ÷ before *mn*, although his B puts it before *wʿbd* of item 1.

5-10. F^{b}Ɇ^{c} omit this entire section (as well as item 4).

7. OG ησαν is found only in Babdhn-rtux (cf. ck). It is replaced by ην in AFMefgijlsvwy-b_2, Cyr.

8. εν is inserted before τοις ανδρασιν by dnpta_2 and by k. Ⱥ has *in manibus virorum*.

11-27. This entire section is omitted by k, and also by the OG.

13. F^{b} omits αυτου.

15. F^{b} omits αυτου.

17. και is found in F^bȺɆ^c; it is replaced by εκ in c.

18. F^b inserts το before υψος αυτου.

19. F^bɆ^c insert και before εποιησεν; Ⱥ adds *et* after εποιησεν.

20. F^b omits αυτου.

22. F^b omits αυτου.

23-25. This section is omitted by c (homeoteleuton--from αυτου to αυτου).

24. Since ck are lacking here, while F^b has εγενοντο, B-McL's "ησαν" must be a reconstruction (based presumably on ȺɆ^{c}Ꞩ).

25. The αυτου of this phrase has been added between the lines in F^b.

26. αυτω, found only in c, is corrected to αυτο (presumably on the basis of Ɇ^{c}Ꞩ) by B-McL. F^bȺ-codd substitute αυτα for αυτω.

Commentary

The following comments deal only with the section that is attributed to Theodotion by Ꞩ^{txt}. Note also that only F^bɆ^c represent MT *h‘lh* of item 3 and omit the OG section (items 4-10) not supported by the MT.

11-27. This entire passage is attributed to Theodotion by Ꞩ^{txt}. There are fifteen such attributions in Ꞩ^{txt} for MT Exod. 36:8-39:43, ranging in length from a single word to six verses (37:10-15), together with two α'θ' attributions and three σ'θ' attributions. In addition, there are four attributions in the text that do not mention Theodotion explicitly (one α'σ', one σ', and two γ'). The preponderance of Theodotionic attributions that have been taken into the text of Ꞩ and that have generally been adopted by those few witnesses that follow the MT text-type for these chapters suggests strongly that the Theodotionic version was the first to revise to the (proto-)MT. It has already been suggested that Aquila and Symmachus are both later than the Theodotionic version.[50]

11. The Syriac phrase attributed to Theodotion accurately reflects the Greek phrase in F^bc (=ȺɆ^c). The OG always uses the same equivalents for MT ‘*ṣy šṭym*, often with the preposition εκ. Similar usages are attributed to Theodotion eight times in Exodus, along with an additional

---

[50]Note the curious fact that k omits ten of the twenty Theodotionic insertions given by Ꞩ^{txt} for these chapters, and three of the four labeled insertions that do not mention Theodotion explicitly as well.

citation for *šṭym* alone.[51] Other equivalents for MT *šṭym* are attributed to Aquila and Symmachus in Exodus and elsewhere.[52]

A comparison of the various readings given in the preceding two footnotes reveals that Theodotion's treatment of *šṭym* throughout Exodus is in complete agreement with OG usage, while Aquila and Symmachus both favor different equivalents.

12-18. The Syriac readings attributed to Theodotion adequately reflect the Greek version drawn from F[b] and c. F[b] omits αυτου in items 13 and 15, and inserts το before υψος in item 18 (this last would not be represented in the Syriac); c has εκ for και in item 17. In every detail, the Syriac readings and the Greek they represent are fully consistent

---

[51] The following equivalents for MT *ʿṣy šṭym* are attributed to Theodotion: *mn qȳsʾ lʾ ħblṭʾ* in Exod. 25:23 (LXX v.22); 37:1 (LXX 38:1), 4 (LXX 38:4), 10 (LXX 38:9), 15 (LXX 38:11); 38:1 (LXX 38:22); ξυλα ασηπτα in Exod. 35:7; *qȳsʾ lʾ ħblṭʾ* in Exod. 38:6 (LXX 38:24). In addition, *lʾ ħblṭʾ* is attributed to Theodotion for MT *šṭym* in Exod. 26:37.

[52] E.g., Aquila: *dsṭym* in Exod. 25:23 (LXX v.22); 26:37; and σεττιμ in Deut. 10:3. Symmachus: ακανθινα in Exod. 35:7; *kwbħyʾ* in Exod. 26:37; ακανθηνον or *kwbnȳʾ* in Exod. 25:23 (LXX v.22). Contrast Aquila's use of ασιπτων τεθεωμενων for MT *(ʿṣy) gpr* in Gen. 6:4.

In Isa. 41:19, MT *šṭh* is apparently represented by OG και πυξον. Symmachus substitutes και ακαπνον ξυλον, while Theodotion has ακανθαν.

MT *šṭym* occurs as a common noun twenty-six times in Exodus and once in Deuteronomy. Never does the OG provide any other equivalent than ασηπτα.

MT *hšṭym* also occurs as a proper name or in a description of a place five times:

Num. 25:1: OG σαττειν, with variants.
Josh. 2:1: OG σαττειν, with variants.
Josh. 3:1: OG σαττειν, with variants.
Joel 4:18: OG των σχοινων; α'σ'θ'των ακανθων.
Mich. 6:5: OG των σχοινων; οι λ' or π' σεττιμ.

The name *byt hšṭh* in Judg. 7:22 is represented by βηθσεεδτα in B, with numerous spelling variants. M[mg] attributes the variant οικου ασεττα to Aquila, and various partially conflated forms are in a number of minuscules.

with regular OG usage and reflect the MT exactly.[53]

---

[53]The OG uses both πλατος and ευρος to represent MT *rḥb*, and both Greek words would be represented by Syriac *pty'*. The three readings cited for Theodotion are all in Syriac: Exod. 37:1 (LXX 38:1), 10 (LXX 38:9); 38:1 (LXX 38:22). The last two times, only (το) ευρος is found in the few Greek witnesses that insert the plus. In Exod. 37:1 (LXX 38:1), however, only F^b has το ευρος, while ck have το πλατος (as do $AF^{b\ mg}$wy, 118, in an insertion of this plus into the OG text-form).

The following variations in the treatment of MT *rḥb* are found in Exodus:

Exod. 25:10 (LXX v.9): OG το πλατος] $M^{mg}s^{mg}v^{mg}z^{mg}$ ευρος.

Exod. 27:1: OG το ευρος] 25 το πλατος] q το πλατος...το ευρος.

Exod. 27:12: OG το δε ευρος] $F^{b\ mg}$ κλιτ.. πλατος.

Exod. 27:13: OG και ευρος] $F^{b\ mg}$ και το κλιτ..πλατ..(το κλιτ del. al. m.).

Exod. 30:2: OG το ευρος] h το πλατος.

Exod. 37:6 (LXX 38:5): OG om.] Gckm το πλατος] F^b το ευρος.

In 1 Kings 6:20 (LXX v.19), OG πλατος (pr το $bhoc_2e_2$, Thdt) is attributed to ο', α'θ', and σ' by j^{mg}. In Ezek. 40:5, OG το προτειχισμα (+ το A'') πλατος, for MT *'t rḥb hbnyn*, is matched by α'σ' το πλατος της οικοδομης in 87^{mg}, 91^{mg}. In Ezek. 41:1 (LXX v.2), the OG omits the third occurrence of MT *rḥb* in the verse, and α' inserts πλατος (Q^{txt}). Note that the OG represented the first *rḥb* by το πλατος and the second by το ευρος. Similarly, σ' inserts πλατους for MT *rḥb* in Ezek. 41:12 (the insertion is a doublet to OG πλατος, but the OG version follows a different text-form for this verse). In Ezek. 42:20, Field argues that a revision to the MT (where the OG differed considerably, and had ευρος), in which πλατος represents MT *rḥb*, is to be attributed to Aquila. This suggestion is ignored by Ziegler.

In Isa. 51:9, MT *rhb* (with *h*, not *ḥ*!), in a phrase omitted by the OG, is represented by πλατος in θ' ($Q^{mg}$$\mathcal{S}^{mg}$, 86^{mg}) and in some witnesses. Another reading (αλοζονειαν) is found in many witnesses and is attributed to α' by 86^{mg}, Eus, while ορμημα is attributed to α' by 86^{mg}, Eus, Tht. Presumably Theodotion either misread MT *rhb* as *rḥb*, or else had the latter minor variant in his Hebrew text.

19. The Syriac reading attributed to Theodotion and its Greek counterpart in c both omit any representation of MT *w*-. The other witnesses, F^{b}Ɇ^{c} and Ⱥ, all provide such representation (out of place in Ⱥ). This minor divergence is not very significant. Presumably Theodotion had MT *wyʿś* before him, and omitted the conjunction by simple oversight.[54]

20-22. The Syriac readings attributed to Theodotion accurately reflect the Greek readings found in c (= ȺɆ^{c}), while F^{b} omits αυτου in items 20 and 22. The Theodotionic readings conform to OG usage and represent the present MT exactly.

23-25. Since these items are omitted by haplography in c, the Greek of F^{b} is quoted. The Syriac readings attributed to Theodotion apparently represent these Greek readings accurately. Even εγενοντο in item 24 is acceptable, both as an equivalent for Syriac *ʾytyhyn hwy* and as a translation of MT *hyw*. There is no need to reconstruct ησαν, as B-McL does, though such a Greek reading for Theodotion is not impossible.

In Isa. 59:14, MT *brḥwb* is represented by OG εν ταις οδοις αυτων. According to 86^{mg}, α' had εν πλατει (παντι cod), while Eus credits σ' with εν πλατεια.

In Zach. 2:8 (LXX v.4), MT *przwt* is represented by OG κατακαρπως, while 86^{mg} cites σ' ατειχιστως ϑ' εις πλατος.

These are the only hexaplaric occurrences of πλατος cited by H-R, while only one occurrence of ευρος is given: Theodotion, in Exod. 37:10 (*sic!* H-R's 37:11 is wrong). It has been noted that this citation is actually found in Syriac, where the equivalent could equally well represent πλατος.

This survey shows that the versions apparently preferred to use πλατος for MT *rḥb*, while the OG used both πλατος and ευρος. There is no way of evaluating the Theodotionic readings in Exodus, however, since they are found in Syriac (which is ambiguous on this point).

[54] Out of 160 instances in which a Theodotionic reading overlaps the conjunction *w*- in the present MT of Exodus, only four occurrences of *w*- are not reflected at all in Theodotion (Exod. 1:19; 13:13; 24:6; 38:2 [LXX v.22]). Two are translated by δε (Exod. 15:21; 32:31), one by Syriac *l*- (Exod. 40:30 [LXX v.26], in a Syriac idiom), and one by Syriac *ʾp* (presumably reflecting και, in Exod. 22:26 [LXX v.27]). The remaining 152 occurrences are represented by και (or Syriac *w*-) in Theodotion.

Both equivalents are common in the OG and are found in all three versions.[55] Thus Theodotion's version for items 23-25 once again reflects the present MT exactly.

26. The Syriac conjunction and verb represent Greek και εκαλυψεν, as in F^bc (= Ⱥ$Ɇ^c$), but the Syriac suffix would seem to demand an αυτο or the like, rather than αυτω of c or αυτα of F^bȺ-codd. Presumably $Ɇ^c$ agrees with the Syriac. As B-McL suggests, αυτω in c may be a scribal corruption for αυτο, which would agree with the antecedent το θυσιαστηριον (item 2), with the Syriac suffix, and with MT *'tw*.

The verb εκαλυψεν (Syriac *ḥpy*) is interesting. OG καλυπτειν regularly represents MT *ksh* (Niphal, Piel, Pual). It does so some eighteen times in Exodus alone,[56] and only represents MT *ṣph* (Piel) in Exod. 27:2. This latter verse is parallel to the present verse (not found in the OG), and the usage there seems to have influenced Theodotion here. A few verses further along, in Exod. 38:6 (LXX 38:24), MT *wṣph* (not represented in the OG) is again rendered *wḥpy* by Theodotion in Ꞩ. The Greek original of this reading, και εκαλυψεν, is preserved in ck (= Ⱥ$Ɇ^c$), while F^b has

[55]See, for example, θ' γενεσθαι (86^{mg}, as cited by Field) for MT *hywt* (OG εσται) in Exod. 8:18 (LXX v.22); α' και εγενετο (c_2^{mg}) for MT *wyhy* (OG και εγενετο) in Exod. 14:20 (where σ' had και ην in $v^{mg}z^{mg}$, but not in $M^{mg}c_2^{mg}$); α' εγενετο ($M^{mg}s^{mg}v^{mg}$, and without name in j^{mg}) and σ' εγενετο ($j^{mg}s^{mg}v^{mg}$) for MT *hyth* (cf. OG γεγονεν, though the phrase differs greatly from the MT) in Gen. 18:12; α'σ' γενωμεθα εις εξουδενωσιν (j^{mg} v^{mg}) for MT *nhyh lbwz* (OG καταγελασθωμεν) in Gen. 38:23. On the use of ειναι, see, for example, α' ουκ ην ($j^{mg}v^{mg}$) for MT *l' hyth* (OG μη ειναι) in Gen. 38:22; α' και εσται (v^{mg}, and without name in $j^{mg}s^{mg}$) and σ' εσται δε (M^{mg}) for MT *whyh* (OG εσται δε) in Gen. 27:40; α'θ' και εσωνται (b^{mg}) for MT *wyhyw* (cf. OG εναντι κυριου) in Num. 31:3.

Most of the Theodotionic equivalents for MT *hyh* and *hyw* in Exodus are found only in Syriac (Exod. 4:9; 7:19; 37:14 [LXX 38:10]; 39:9 [LXX 36:16]; 40:10 [LXX v.9]). A detailed investigation of the material is beyond the scope of this study, but it is clear that the evidence for Theodotion's usage in Exodus is ambiguous. There is no clear evidence that Theodotion, any more than the OG, systematically employed either γενεσθαι or ειναι to represent the Hebrew verb *hyh*.

[56]See H-R, *s.v.*

the variant και περιεχαλκωσεν. The only other trace of καλυπτειν for MT *ṣph* is found in Exod. 38:28 (LXX 39:6), where OG και κατεχρυσωσεν represents MT *wṣph*. This reading is retained by Gckm𝔄𝔈^{c}𝔖^{txt} (*wʾdhb*), but F^{b} substitutes και εκαλυψεν. In Exodus generally, the most common OG equivalent for MT *ṣph* (Piel) is καταχρυσουν (thirteen times), together with χρυσουν (three times, and once for the Pual).[57] The other OG equivalents in Exodus are not important.

This dominant OG pattern of equivalence has been followed by Theodotion three times, twice where the OG did not represent MT *ṣph* at all.[58]

Thus Theodotion has more than one equivalent for MT *ṣph* (Piel), just as did the OG before him. Both words he employs, moreover, find parallels in OG usage in Exodus. No variants from Aquila or Symmachus have been preserved in Exodus.[59] Theodotion's reading in this item, therefore, which has not been preserved unchanged by either c or F^{b}, again reflects the present MT exactly.

27. Syriac *bnḥšʾ* adequately translates Greek χαλκω, found in F^{b}c

---

[57]See H-R, *s.v.*

[58]Exod. 37:4 (LXX 38:4): MT *wyṣp* I OG om. I F^{b}G(under ※)ckm𝔄𝔈^{c} και κατεχρυσωσεν I ϑ' in 𝔖^{txt} *wqrm*.

Exod. 37:11 (LXX 38:11): MT *wyṣp* I OG om. I F^{b}G(under ※)c𝔄𝔈^{c} και κατεχρυσωσεν I ϑ' in 𝔖^{txt} *wqrm(h)*.

Exod. 37:15 (LXX 38:11): MT *wyṣp* I OG (also under ÷ in G𝔖, and a doublet in F^{b}c𝔄𝔈) και κατεχρυσωσεν (Syriac *wqrm*) I F^{b}G(under ※)c𝔄𝔈^{c} και κατεχρυσωσεν I ϑ' in 𝔖^{txt} *wqrm*.

[59]The only other hexaplaric variants I have found are in 1 Kings 6:20. In the sixth chapter, OG περιεχειν is used to represent MT *ṣph* (Piel) some eight times (according to H-R). Elsewhere that word has various other Hebrew correspondents, but never *ṣph*. In 1 Kings 6:20, MT *wyṣphw* is represented by OG και περιεσχεν αυτον. This same reading is attributed to ο' by j^{mg}, while σ' and α'ϑ' are credited with the variant και περιεπειλησεν αυτο by j^{mg} (cf. 𝔖^{txt}*wqrmh*).

In 1 Kings 6:21 (LXX v.20), MT *wyṣp* (not represented in the OG) is reflected by και περιεπιλησεν in Aj^{mg} (-πειλ-, under ※)x𝔄𝔖^{txt} (*wqrmh*, under ※). Further along in the same verse, however, OG και περιεσχεν αυτον (to represent MT *wyṣphw*) appears in 𝔖^{txt} as *wʾḥdh*. This set of readings finds no parallels anywhere in Exodus.

(= ȺȻ[c]), and this reading is an exact translation of MT *nḥšt*.

Evaluation

Theodotion's version, preserved in Ş^{txt}, and more or less accurately reflected by F[b]cȺȻ[c], is an accurate translation of the present MT. The only deviation from the MT, in item 19, is of minor importance and probably does not point to a variation in Theodotion's Hebrew *Vorlage*. At no point does Theodotion's fresh translation conflict with OG usage. The juxtaposition of Theodotion's new translation and the divergent OG version (under ÷ in Ş^{txt}) is undoubtedly due to Origen's editorial practices, and did not characterize Theodotion's version of Exodus. Finally, it is at least probable that the version of Theodotion was original with him, since there is no evidence of prior Greek versions that attempted to reflect the divergent Hebrew order and content for chapters 36-39. This is in sharp contrast to the situation found in Exod. 28:22-30 (LXX vv.22-26).

II A Special Case--MT Exodus 28:22-30 (LXX vv.22-26)

This chapter deals with a six-verse reading in which Theodotion took over an earlier revision of the OG and adapted it further toward the present MT. The procedure followed is similar to that used in chapter one.

	MT (v. 22)	*OG (v. 22)*	S^{txt} *(v. 22)*
1.	w‘śyt	και ποιησεις	wt‘bd
2.	‘l hḥšn	επι το λογιον	‘l pdt’
3.	šršt	κροσους	ḥẅt’
4.	gblt	συνπεπλεγμενους	g̈dyl’
5.	m‘śh ‘bt	εργον αλυσιδωτον	‘bd’ šš̈lny’
6.	zhb ṭhwr	εκ χρυσιου καθαρου	ddhb’ dky’
	(v. 23)	*OG* *LXX*^{2} *(*$F^{a?}$*Mcdegjkmnpstvz A̸E̸*^{c}*)*	*(v. 23)*
7.	w‘śyt	(+ ※ svz) και ποιησεις	※ϑ′ wt‘bd
8.	‘l hḥsn	επι του λογιου	‘lyh dpdt’
9.	šty ṭb‘wt zhb	δυο δακτυλιους χρυσους	tr̈tyn ‘z̈qt’ ddhb’
10.	wntt	και δωσεις	wttl
11.	’t šty hṭb‘wt	τους δυο δακτυλιους	’nyn ltr̈tyḥyn ‘z̈qt’
12.	‘l šny qṣwt hḥšn	επι των δυο ακρων του λογιου	‘l tr̈yhwn r̈šyh dpdt’
	(v. 24)		*(v. 24)*
13.	wntth	και δωσεις	wttl
14.	’t šty ‘btt hzhb	τα δυο αλυσιδωτα τα χρυσα	’nyn ltr̈tyhyn šš̈lt’ ddhb’
15.	‘l šty hṭb‘t	επι τοις δυσι δακτυλιοις	‘l tr̈tyhyn ‘z̈qt’
16.	’l qṣwt hḥšn	προς τα ακρα του λογιου	lwt r̈yšyh dpdt’

	MT (v. 25)	OG	LXX²	S^{txt} (v. 25)
17.	w't šty qṣwt		και τα δυο ακρα	wltr̈yhwn r̈yš'
18.	šty h'btt		των δυο αλυσεων	dtr̈tyhyn šš̆lt'
19.	ttn		δωσεις	ttl
20.	'l šty hmšbṣwt		επι των δυο συσφιγκτων	'l tr̈tyhyn ḥÿṣt'
21.	wntth		και δωσεις	wttl
22.	'l ktpwt h'pd		επι τους ωμους της επωμιδος	'l ktꝑth dkbynt'
23.	'l mwl pnyw		επι το μετωπον του προσωπου αυτου	lwqbl byt 'ÿn' dprṣwp' dylh
	(v. 26)			(v. 26)
24.	w'śyt		και ποιησεις	wt'bd
25.	šty ṭb'wt zhb		δυο δακτυλιους χρυσους	tr̈tyn 'z̈qt' ddhb'
26.	wśmt 'tm		και θησεις αυτους	wttl 'nyn
27.	'l šny qṣwt hḥšn		επι τα δυο ακρα του λογιου	'l tr̈yn r̈yšyh dpdt'
28.	'l śptw		επι του χειλους αυτου	'l spt' dylh
29.	'šr 'l 'br h'pd		ο εστιν εις το μερος της επωμιδος	hw d'ytwhy mn lqwblh dkbynt'
30.	byth		εσωθεν	mn lgw
	(v. 27)			(v. 27)
31.	w'śyt		και ποιησεις	wt'bd
32.	šty ṭb'wt zhb		δυο δακτυλιους χρυσους	tr̈tyn 'zq̈t' ddhb'
33.	wntth 'tm		και δωσεις αυτους	wttl 'nyn
34.	'l šty ktpwt h'pwd		επι τους δυο ωμους της επωμιδος	'l tr̈tyn ktꝑth dkbynt'
35.	mlmṭh		κατωθεν	mn ltḥt
36.	mmwl pnyw		εκ του κατα προσωπον	mn lwqbl prṣwp'
37.	l'mt mḥbrtw		κατα την συμβολην αυτων	šlm'yt wrmy' d'kḥd' dylh
38.	mm'l lḥšb h'pwd		επανω του μηχανωματος της επωμιδος	l'l mn mtqnwt' dkbynt'
	(v. 28)			(v. 28)
39.	wyrksw		και συσφιγξουσιν	wnḥwṣwnh
40.	't hḥšn		το λογιον	lpdt'
41.	mṭb'tw		εκ του δακτυλιου αυτου	mn 'zqt' dylh

	MT (v. 28)	*OG*	*LXX*[2]	*S*^{txt} *(v. 28)*
42.	’l ṭb‘t h’pd		εις τον δακτυλιον της επωμιδος	l‘zqt’ dkbynt’
43.	bptyl tklt		εν κλωσματι υακινθινω	bpšl’ dtklt’
44.	lhywt		ινα η	lmhw’
45.	‘l ḥšb h’pwd		επι του μηχανωματος της επωμιδος	‘l mtqnwt’ dkbynt’
46.	wl’ yzḥ hḥšn		και ου μη αποσπασης το λογιον	wl’ thw’ mtplṭ’ pdt’
47.	m‘l h’pwd		απο της επωμιδος (+ ⋎ svz)	mn kbynt’ (+ ⋎ C)
	(v. 29)		*OG (v. 23)*	*(v. 29)*
48.	wnś’ ’hrn		και λημψεται ααρων	wnhw’ nsb ’hrwn
49.	’t šmwt		τα ονοματα	lšm̈h’
50.	bny yśr’l		των υιων ισραηλ	dbn̈y’ d’ysr’yl
51.	bḥšn hmšpṭ		επι του λογιου της κρισεως	‘l pdt’ ddyn’
52.	‘l lbw		επι του στηθους	‘l ḥdy’ ※‘´ dylh⋎
53.	bb’w ’l hqdš		εισιοντι εις το αγιον	m’ d‘’l lbyt qwdš’
54.	lzkrn		μνημοσυνον	dwkrn’
55.	lpny YHWH		εναντι του θεου	qdm ’lh’
56.	tmyd			bkl zbn
			(v. 24)	
57.			και θησεις	÷wtsym
58.			επι το λογιον της κρισεως	‘l pdt’ ddyn’
59.			τους κροσους	lḥẅṭ’
60.			τα αλυσιδωτα	dšš̈lt’
61.			επ αμφοτερων των κλιτων του λογιου	‘l tr̈yhwn sṭr̈yh dpdt’
62.			επιθησεις	tsym
			(v. 25)	
63.			και τας δυο ασπιδισκας	wltr̈tyhyn mẅḥdt’
64.			επιθησεις	tsym
65.			επ αμφοτερους τους ωμους της επωμιδος	‘l tr̈tyhyn ktp̈th dkbynt’
66.			κατα προσωπον	lwqbl prṣwp’

	MT (v. 29)	*OG (v. 25)*	S̸^{txt} *(v. 29)*
67.			mn ltḥt˂
68.			※σ'θ' bkl zbn˂
	(v. 30)	*(v. 26)*	*(v. 30)*
69.	wntt	και επιθησεις	wtsym
70.	’l ḥšn hmšpṭ	επι το λογιον της κρισεως	‘l pdt’ ddyn’
71.	’t h’wrym	την δηλωσιν	lglyn’
72.	w’t htmym	και την αληθειαν	wlšrr’
73.	whyw	και εσται	wthw’
74.	‘l lb ’hrn	επι του στηθους ααρων	‘l ḥdyh d’hrwn
75.	bb’w	οταν εισπορευηται	’mty d‘’l
76.		εις το αγιον	lbyt qwdš’
77.	lpny YHWH	εναντιον κυριου	qdm mry’
78.	wnś’ ’hrn	και οισει ααρων	wnyt’ ’hrwn
79.	’t mšpṭ	τας κρισεις	ldyn̈’
80.	bny yśr’l	των υιων ισραηλ	dbn̈y’ d’ysr’yl
81.	‘l lbw	επι του στηθους	‘l ḥdy’ ※α'σ' dylh˂
82.	lpny YHWH	εναντιον κυριου	qdm mry’
83.	tmyd	δια παντος	bkl zbn

Notes

In Exodus 28, MT vv. 23-28 (items 7-47) are not found in the OG (i.e., in ABF*abfhiloqruwxya$_2$b$_2$B̸E̸^{f}L̸^{r}). A translation of this material is inserted between v. 22 and LXX v. 23 (= MT v.29) in a later hand (F$^{a?}$) in the margin of F and in McdegjkmnpstvzA̸E̸^{c}S̸. The passage is under ※ in svz and under ※ θ' in S̸ (the metobelus is found only in Lagarde's C). In the preceding chart, those manuscripts that contain the insertion have been labeled LXX^2.[1]

---

[1]This insertion is found in the Lucianic witnesses (dgnpt). Since it is prior to the first-century Theodotionic version, as is demonstrated below, the insertion must itself date from the first century A.D. or earlier. Therefore it cannot come from the later Lucianic revision, but must be regarded as a genuine fragment of the Proto-Lucianic Recension in Exodus; hence LXX^2 = LXX^L (or, better, LXX^{P-L}). See the discussion of

A widely variant and much shorter form of the same material is found in LXX vv. 24-25 (items 57-66, with the addition of item 67 in Ꞩ and ckȺ). It is thus between the OG equivalents of MT vv. 29 and 30. This variant text, which is only omitted by F$^{?\ \mathrm{vid}}$Ɇ^{c}Ł^{r} and is found under ⸓ in Ꞩ, presumably belongs to the oldest phase of the OG tradition.

The preceding columns begin with v. 22 and end with MT v.30 (= LXX v.26), where the OG and the MT are in substantial agreement. The number of columns varies with the needs of the material being presented. Material that is not immediately relevant to the study of Theodotion is not normally discussed in the comments. Notes on particular items follow:

1-6. This verse is omitted by c (homeoarcton--compare items 1-2 with items 7-8, noting the variant in c for item 8).

2-4. For OG επι-συνπεπλεγμενους, Ł^{r} has *emeritionem criniculas conplectentes* and Ⱥ has *cistam unam plexam fimbriis*.

2. OG επι is omitted by n.

3. κροσους is found only in AB(F*)hns(v*)z-b_2, while κροσσους is found in F^{b}Mabd-gi-mo-rtuv^{b}wxy; οι λ̥ αλυσεις is found in M^{mg}s^{mg}z^{mg} and without name in v^{mg}, while α'σ' s̈šlt'· ϑ' nẙpt' is found in Ꞩ^{mg}.

5. αλυσιδωτον is replaced by αλυσιδωτου in Bch and by *catenae* in Ł^{r}; βροχωτον is found in F$^{b\ mg}$, while σ' βροχωτον ο εβραιος εσσην is found in j^{mg}.

6. OG εκ is omitted by AF*MaegjnqsuvyzꞨ.

8. το λογιον is found for του λογιου in c; the entire phrase is omitted by Ɇ^{c}.

10. *pones* is found for δωσεις in Ⱥ.

11. τας is found for τους in d; δυο is omitted by km; *aureos* is added after δακτυλιους by Ⱥ.

12. δυο is omitted by m.

13-16. This verse is omitted by p (homeoteleuton--compare item 16 with item 12).

13. *pones* is found for δωσεις in Ⱥ.

14. The second τα is omitted by ms.

15. τοις δυσι δακτυλιοις is replaced by τους δυο δακτυλιους in F$^{a?}$

---

the Proto-Lucianic Recension in Samuel by F. M. Cross, Jr., in "The History of the Biblical Text in the Light of Discoveries in the Judean Desert," *HTR* 57 (1964), 292-297.

ckm; δυσι is omitted by g.

16. προς τα ακρα is replaced by επι το ακρον in egjsvz.

16-17. του λογιου-ακρα is omitted by c (homeoteleuton--ακρα to ακρα).

18. δυο is omitted by d; αλυσεων is replaced by αλυσιδωτων in M.

19. και is inserted before δωσεις in s.

20. συσφιγκτων is replaced by σφιγκτων in m; α' *ḥyyṣt*ʾ· σ' *ḥyyṣt* (*ḥyṣt* in B) *ʾkḥdʾ* is found in S̸^{mg}.

22. της επωμιδος is replaced by των επομιδων in c and by του εφουδ in F^{b}.

23. αυτου is replaced by αυτης in F$^{a?}$ckm; while ο'θ' του προσωπου αυτης α' εναντιον προσωπου αυτου σ' κατα προσωπον αυτου is found in v^{mg}.

26. θησεις is replaced by δωσεις in F$^{a?}$ckmA̸S̸ and by ποιησεις in j; ο'θ' και δωσεις αυτους is found in s^{mg}v^{mg}z^{mg}; α'σ' και θησεις αυτους is found in v^{mg}.

28-37. επι-αυτων is omitted by p (perhaps homeoarcton--from <u>επι</u> to <u>επανω</u>).

28. αυτου is omitted by A̸.

29. μερος is replaced by αντικρυς in F$^{a?}$cA̸, by αντικρυ in m, and by μερος αντικρυ in k; της επωμιδος is replaced by του εφουδ in F^{b}. The following marginal variants are found: α' ο προς περαν του επενδυματος in v^{mg}z^{mg} and without name in s^{mg}; ο'θ' ο εστιν εις το αντικρυς της επωμιδος in v^{mg} and without ο' in z^{mg}; σ' ο εστιν εις το αντικρυς του επενδυματος in v^{mg}z^{mg} and with εκτος for εις το in s^{mg}.

29-30. ο'θ' αντικρυς της επωμιδος εσωθεν is found in s^{mg}.

30. α' οικονδε is found in v^{mg}z^{mg} and without name in s^{mg}; ο'θ'σ' εσωθεν is found in v^{mg} and without σ' in s^{mg}.

32. δυο is preceded by ετερους in m; it is omitted by egjsvz.

34. της επωμιδος is replaced by του εφουδ in F^{b}.

36-37. ο'θ' εκ του κατα προσωπον συμφωνως κατα την συμβολην αυτου α' απο εναντιον προσωπου αυτου συμφωνως επι συμβολη αυτου σ' εκ του κατα προσωπον συμφωνως κατα την συμβολην αυτου is found in v^{mg}.

36. προσωπον is replaced by προσωπου in n; αυτ<u>..</u> is added by F^{b}.

37. κατα is replaced by συμφωνως κατα in F$^{a?b}$ and by συμφωνως και in ckmA̸, while z^{mg} adds συμφωνως and s^{mg} adds συμφωνος before (or at) κατα. την συμβολην is replaced by την συμβουλην in ds and by τη συμβολη in n$^{a?}$. αυτων is omitted by c and is replaced by αυτου in F$^{a?}$dkmtA̸E̸$^{c\ vid}$.

38. μηχανωματος is replaced by μηχανηματος in $F^{a?}$degkp and by αναλαγματος in F^{b}; while α′ διαζωσματος σ′ του κατασκευασματος is found in v^{mg}, α′ *d̄hmyn*ʾ˙ σ′ *dtwqn*ʾ is found in $S̸^{mg}$, and διαζωσματα κατασκευασματα is found in z^{mg}. της επωμιδος is replaced by του εφουδ in F^{b}.

39. και συσφιγξουσιν is replaced by και συνσφιγγιουσιν in $F^{a?}$ and by κατασυσφιξουσι in d.

41. MT vocalization: מִטַּבְּעֹתָו. εκ is replaced by επι in e; δακτυλιου is replaced by δακτυλου in $F^{a?}$; αυτου is omitted by $F^{a?\ vid}$; εκ του δακτυλιου is replaced by *ex annulis* in $A̸E̸^{c}$.

42. MT vocalization: טַבְּעֹת. τον is replaced by το in m; τον δακτυλιον is replaced by *annulos* in $A̸E̸^{c}$; της επωμιδος is replaced by του εφουδ in F^{b}.

43. τω is inserted before κλωσματι by $F^{a?}$ckm and again after κλωσματι by $F^{a?}$ck; υακινθινω is replaced by υακινθω in c.

44. ινα η is omitted by $F^{a?}$m; η is omitted by sz.

45. μηχανωματος is replaced by μηχανηματος in $F^{a?}$cek; α′ διαζωσματος σ′ κατασκευασματος is found in s^{mg}. της επωμιδος is replaced by του εφουδ in F^{b}.

46-47. και-επωμιδος is omitted by m (homeoteleuton--επωμιδος to επωμιδος).

46. αποσπασης is replaced by αποσπασθη in ck$A̸E̸^{c}$ and by αποσπασ.. in $F^{a?}$; while the following is found in $s^{mg}v^{mg}$ and without names in z^{mg}: α′ο′ (om ο′ v^{mg}) και ου σαλευθησεται σ′ και μη αποκλινηται (αποκλινητε z^{mg}) ο′θ′ (om ο′ s^{mg}) ου μη αποσπασθη.

47. της επωμιδος is replaced by του εφουδ in F^{b}. In his edition of S̸, Lagarde simply notes: "ܐ addidit C."

48. λημφεται is replaced by ληψη in 16.

49. τα ονοματα is replaced by *nomen* in A̸-ed.

50. των is omitted by m; ισραηλ is omitted by f.

51. του λογιου is replaced by το λογιον in Ay*; της κρισεως is replaced by των κρισεων in e; της is replaced by του in d.

52-58. τπι-κρισεως is omitted by s (homeoteleuton--της κρισεως to της κρισεως).

52-53. α′ επι καρδιας αυτου εν τω εισερχεσξαι αυτον (αυτο s^{mg}) is found in $s^{mg}v^{mg}$; ο′ επι του στηθους αυτου εισιοντι αυτω is found in v^{mg}.

52. του στηθους is replaced by καρδιαν αυτου in F^{b}, while αυτου is added after στηθους in ckm$A̸B̸^{1}$. The similar addition (attributed to ‘′)

in $\mathcal{S}^{txt}$ appears with a plural vocalization in Lagarde's B.

53. εισιοντι is replaced by εισιων in dfnpt$\mathcal{L}$ and by εισιον in i; while αυτω is inserted after εισιοντι in cm.

54. εις is inserted before μνημοσυνον by $F^{a?}$m; μνημοσυνον is replaced by *memoriae causa* in $\mathcal{L}^r$ and by *in memoriam aeternam* in $\mathcal{A}$.

55. εναντι is replaced by εναντιον in acegjlmnqruxb$_2$, Cyr-cod; κυριου is inserted before του θεου by Cyr; του is omitted by b'f and is added over an erasure by w^a.

56. δια παντος is added by F^bcegjkm$\mathcal{E}^c\mathcal{S}^{txt}$.

57-66. This material is omitted by $F^{?\ vid}\mathcal{E}^c\mathcal{L}^r$. Together with item 67 (only found in ck$\mathcal{A}\mathcal{S}$), it is placed under ÷ by $\mathcal{S}$.

57. θησεις is replaced by θησει in a$_2$.

59. τους κροσους is omitted by a$_2$; κροσους (found only in ABF*Mms xzb$_2$) is replaced by κροσσους in F^ba-gi-ln-rt-wy and by λογους in h.

60. τα αλυσιδωτα is preceded by και in r, replaced by τους αλυσιδωτους in k, and omitted in b'.

61. του λογιου is replaced by το λογιον in af.

62. After επιθησεις, c adds επ αμφοτερους τους ωμους της επομιδος επιθησεις, while $\mathcal{B}^w$ adds *et pones ea super utraque latera rationalis*.

63-64. και-επιθησεις is omitted by a (homeoteleuton--επιθησεις to επιθησεις).

63. ασπιδισκας is replaced by ασπιδας in f.

64. επιθησεις is omitted by cm.

65. αμφοτερους is replaced by αμφοτερων in fn; τους-επωμιδος is omitted by c; τους ωμους is replaced by του σωματος in n.

66. κατα προσωπον is omitted by $\mathcal{B}^w$; κατα is omitted by s.

67. κατωθεν is added by ck$\mathcal{A}\mathcal{S}$.

69. και is omitted by c; επιθησεις is replaced by επιθη in m and by *pones* in $\mathcal{L}^r$.

70. επι is omitted by c; της κρισεως is replaced by των κρισεων in Phil.

71-72. την δηλωσιν-αληθειαν is replaced by *lucentia et signacula* in $\mathcal{E}^c$; οι λ̥ τους φωτισμους και τας τελειοτητας is found in $s^{mg}v^{mg}$ and without name in $k^{mg}z^{mg}$; α'σ'θ' *lnwhr' wlšwmly'* is found in $\mathcal{S}^{mg}$.

73. και is omitted by 16, $\mathcal{L}^r$; εσται is replaced by *erint* in $\mathcal{E}^c\mathcal{L}^r$.

74. επι του στηθους is replaced by εις το στηθος in e and by επι την καρδιαν in $F^b\mathcal{E}^c$; α' της (om v^{mg}) καρδιας is found in $s^{mg}v^{mg}$ and

without name in z^{mg}; ααρων is omitted by 130* and is replaced by αυτου in 130^{b}.

75-78. οταν-ααρων is omitted by L̸^{r} (homeoteleuton--ααρων to ααρων).

75. εισπορευηται is replaced by εισπορευεται in bckmnsa$_2$ and by εισερχηται in Phil.

76. εις το αγιον is transposed after κυριου of item 77 in f, is replaced by *in sancta* in A̸, and is omitted by k.

77. εναντιον is found only in Bcknor, Phil; it is replaced by εναντι in AFMabd-jlmpqs-b$_2$, Cyr.

78. οισει is replaced by ϑησει in qu and by εισοισει in F$^{a?b?\ mg}$ kmra$_2$E̸, Cyr.

79. τας κρισεις is replaced by *judicium* in E̸.

80. εναντι is inserted before των by a$_2$.

81. επι του στηϑους is transposed after κυριου of item 82 by 73, Cyr$\frac{1}{2}$(+ αυτου); it is replaced by επι την καρδιαν in F^{b}; αυτου is added after στηϑους by cmA̸B̸.

82. εναντιον is found only in Bcfk-nrxb$_2$; it is replaced by εναντι in AFMabdeg-jopqs-wyza$_2$, Cyr.

Supplement

The passage in MT Exod. 28:22-28 is parallel to MT Exod. 39:15-21 (LXX 36:22-29). The latter passage is found in the OG and is retained substantially unchanged by F^{b}GckmA̸E̸^{c}S̸ in their revised text-form. The Hebrew passage in MT 39:16-21 seems to have served as the basis for the insertion into the MT of 28:23-28. The OG translation found in LXX 36:23-29 was not used as the basis for the later Greek reflection of MT Exod. 28:23-28, however. This last assertion will not be proven here, but a comparison of the foregoing charts with those given below will demonstrate its validity.

For easy reference in the discussions of MT Exod. 28:22-30 (LXX vv. 22-26), MT Exod. 39:15-21 (LXX 36:22-29) is given below in columns, followed by textual notes. These columns are arranged in items corresponding to the items found in the preceding charts, but each item number is preceded by p (for parallel). Apart from necessary changes in the tense and person of the various verbs (chapter 28 contains instructions, while chapter 39 relates the accomplishment of the instructions), the two

Hebrew texts are substantially identical. The only other divergences are in items 3, 8-9, 14, 16, 21, 26, and possibly 33, together with thirteen differences in the use of *plene* or defective writings. A table relating to this last point and a brief discussion are found at the conclusion of this section.

	MT (39:15)	*OG (36:22)*	*F^b GckmA̸E̸^c (39:15)*	*S̸^txt (39:15)*
p1.	wyʿsw	και εποιησαν	και εποιησαν	wʿbdw
p2.	ʿl hḥšn	επι το λογιον	επι το λογιον	ʿl pdtʾ
p3.	šršrt	κροσους	κροσσους	ḥẅṭʾ
p4.	gblt	συνπεπλεγμενους	συνπεπλεγμενους	mʿr̈zlʾ
p5.	mʿśh ʿbt	εργον εμπλοκιου	εργον ενπλοκιου	ʿbdʾ dgdwlʾ
p6.	zhb ṭhwr	εκ χρυσιου καθαρου	εκ χρυσιου καθαρου	mn dhbʾ dkyʾ
	(39:16)	*(36:23)*	*(39:16)*	*(39:16)*
p7.	wyʿśw	και εποιησαν	και εποιησαν	wʿbdw
p8.	šty mšbṣt zhb	δυο ασπιδισκας χρυσας	δυο ασπιδισκας χρυσας	tr̈tyn skr̈ʾ ddhbʾ
p9.	wšty ṭbʿt zhb	και δυο δακτυ- λιους χρυσους	και δυο δακτυ- λιους χρυσους	wtr̈tyn ʿz̈qtʾ ddhbʾ
		(36:24)		
p10.	wytnw	και επεθηκαν	και επεθηκαν	wsmw
p11.	ʾt šty hṭbʿt	τους δυο δακτυ- λιους τους χρυσους	τους δυο δακτυ- λιους (+ ₜ G) τους χρυσους (+ ˠ G)	ltr̈tytyn ʿz̈qtʾ ₜddḧbʾˠ
p12.	ʿl šny qṣwt hḥšn	επ αμφοτερας τας αρχας του λογιου	επ αμφοτερας τας αρχας του λογιου	ʿl tr̈yhwn r̈yšyh dpdtʾ
	(39:17)	*(36:25)*	*(39:17)*	*(39:17)*
p13.	wytnw	και επεθηκαν	και επεθηκαν	wsmw
p14.	šty hʿbtt hzhb	τα εμπλοκια εκ χρυσιου	τα εμπλοκια εκ χρυσιου	ʾnyn lg̈dyltʾ dmn dhbʾ
p15.	ʿl šty hṭbʿt	επι τους δακτυλιους	επι τους δυο δακτυλιους	ʿl tr̈tyhyn ʿz̈qtʾ
p16.	ʿl qṣwt hḥšn	επ αμφοτερων των μερων του λογιου	επ αμφοτερων των μερων του λογιου	ʿl tr̈yn gbÿh dpdtʾ

	MT (39:18)	*OG (36:25)*	*F^{b}GckmȺɆ^{c} (39:18)*	*$\mathcal{S}^{txt}$ (39:18)*
p17.	w'ṭ šty	και εις τας δυο	και εις τας δυο	wbtr̈tyhwn dbꝗ'
	qṣwt	συμβολας	συμβολας	
p18.	šty h'btt	τα δυο εμπλοκια	τα δυο εμπλοκια	ltr̈tyhyn
				ǥdylt'
		(36:26)		
p19.	ntnw	και επεθηκαν	και επεθηκαν	wsmw
p20.	ʻl šty	επι τας δυο	επι τας δυο	ʻl tr̈tyhyn
	hmšbṣt	ασπιδισκας	ασπιδισκας	skr̈'
p21.	wytnm	και επεθηκαν	και εθηκαν αυτας	wsmw 'nyn
p22.	ʻl ktpt	επι τους ωμους	επι τους ωμους	ʻl ktꝑth
	h'pd	της επωμιδος	της επωμιδος	dkbynt'
p23.	'l mwl	εξ εναντιας κατα	εξ εναντιας κατα	mn lwqbl
	pnyw	προσωπον	προσωπον αυτου	prṣwp' dylh
	(39:19)	*(36:27)*	*(39:19)*	*(39:19)*
p24.	wyʻśw	και εποιησαν	και εποιησαν	wʻbdw
p25.	šty ṭbʻt	δυο δακτυλιους	δυο δακτυλιους	tr̈tyn ʻz̈qt'
	zhb	χρυσους	χρυσους	ddhb'
p26.	wyśymw	και επεθηκαν	και επεθηκαν	wsmw
p27.	ʻl šny	επι τα δυο	επι τα δυο	ʻl tr̈tyn
	qṣwt hḥšn	πτερυγια επ	πτερυγια (+ ⸆ G)	kĦpt' ʻl
		ακρου του λογιου	επ ακρου (+ ↙ G)	ryš' dpdt'
			του λογειου	
p28.	ʻl śptw	και επι το ακρον	επι το ακρον	ʻl ryš'
p29.	'šr 'l ʻbr	του οπισθιου της	του οπισθιου της	hw dbstrh
	h'pd	επωμιδος	επωμιδος	dkbynt'
p30.	byth	εσωθεν	εσωθεν	mn lgw
	(39:20)	*(36:28)*	*(39:20)*	*(39:20)*
p31.	wyʻśw	και εποιησαν	και εποιησαν	wʻbdw
p32.	šty ṭbʻt	δυο δακτυλιους	δυο δακτυλιους	tr̈tyn ʻz̈qt'
	zhb	χρυσους	χρυσους	ddhb'
p33.	wytnm	και επεθηκαν	και εθηκαν αυτους	wsmw 'nyn
p34.	ʻl šty	επ αμφοτερους	επ εμφοτερους	ʻl tr̈tyhyn
	ktpt h'pd	τους ωμους της	τους ωμους της	ktꝑth dkbynt'
		επωμιδος	επωμιδος	
p35.	mlmṭh	κατωθεν αυτου	κατωθεν	mn ltḥt

	MT (39:20)	*OG (36:28)*	*F^bGckmȺĘ^c (39:20)*	*Ꞩ^{txt} (39:20)*
p36.	mmwl pnyw	κατα προσωπον	κατα προσωπον	lwqbl prṣwp'
			αυτου	dylh
p37.	l‘mt	κατα την	κατα την	lwqbl dbq'
	mḥbrtw	συμβολην	συμβολην αυτου	dylh
p38.	mm‘l lḥšb	ανωθεν της	ανωθεν της	l‘l mn zqwr'
	h'pd	συνυφης της	συνυφης της	dkbynt'
		επωμιδος	επωμιδος	
	(39:21)	*(36:29)*	*(39:21)*	*(39:21)*
p39.	wyrksw	και συνεσφιγξεν	και συνεσφιγξεν	wḥṣw
p40.	't hḥšn	το λογιον	το λογειον	lpdt'
p41.	mṭb‘tyw	απο των δακτυ-	απο των δακτυ-	mn ‘žqt'
		λιων των επ αυτου	λιων των επ αυτου	d‘lyh
p42.	'l ṭb‘t	εις τους δακτυ-	εις τους δακτυ-	b‘žqt'
	h'pd	λιους της	λιους της	dkbynt'
		επωμιδος	επωμιδος	
p43.	bptyl tklt	συνεχομενους εκ	συνεχομενους εκ	d'ḥydn mn
		της υακινθου	της υακινθου	tklt'
p44.	lhyt	συνπεπλεγμενους	συνπεπλεγμενους	dmgdln
p45.	‘l ḥšb	εις το υφασμα	εις το υφασμα	bzqwrh
	h'pd	της επωμιδος	της επωμιδος	dkbynt'
p46.	wl' yzḥ	ινα μη χαλαται	ινα μη χαλαται	'ykn' dl'
	hḥšn	το λογιον	το λογιον	ttršl pdt'
p47.	m‘l h'pd	απο της επωμιδος	απο της επωμιδος	mnh dkbynt'
p48*.	k'šr ṣwh	καθα συνεταξεν	καθα συνεταξεν	'ykn' dpqd
	YHWH 't mšh	κυριος τω μωυση	κυριος τω μωση	mry' lmwš'

Notes to the Supplement

p1-p10. F^b is defective up to <u>...</u>αν (for επεθηκαν).

p1. OG εποιησαν is replaced by εποιησεν in y.

p2. OG επι is replaced by εις in fi and is omitted in Ƀ.

p3. OG κροσους is only found in Bafh*ora$_2$b$_2$; it is replaced by κροσσους in AMbdegh^{b}ijlnpqs-wyz and followed by χρυσους in fi.

p4. Ⱥ adds *super duos annulos* after συνπεπλεγμενους.

p5. OG εμπλοκιου is replaced by εμπλοκιον in b$_2$, by εκπλοκιου in q, by *tortile* in Ꝉ^r, and by <u>...</u>*tum* in Ꝉ^z. For *dgdwl'* of Ꞩ^{txt}, Ꞩ^{mg} has α'σ' *gdyl'* · θ' *dššlt'*.

p6. OG εκ is omitted by n$L^{z\ vid}$; OG καθαρου is omitted by a.

p8. OG ασπιδισκας is replaced by ασπιδας in g*n and by ασπιδικας in g^a; while α'σ' σφιγκτηρας is found in M^{mg}, and α' *ḥšṣt'* · σ' *ḥyṣt 'kḥd'* · θ' *ḥšwṣt'* is found in S^{mg}, all for ασπιδισκας (Syriac *skš'*).

p9. OG και-χρυσους is omitted by L^r and the same phrase is omitted by A-cod; OG και is omitted by af; OG χρυσους is replaced by χρυσας in n.

p9-p11. OG χρυσους-δακτυλιους is omitted by 1.

p10-p11. OG και-χρυσους is omitted by jn$L^{z\ vid}$.

p11. OG τους δυο-χρυσους is replaced by αυτους in p; επι is inserted before τους δυο by G*c; δυο is omitted by yL^r and by m; τους χρυσους is omitted by k. The form *ltštytyn* occurs in Lagarde's edition of S; presumably it is a mistake for *ltštyhyn* (cf. item p15) or *ltštyn* (cf. item p9).

p13-p14. OG και-χρυσιου is omitted by b_2.

p13. OG επεθηκαν is replaced by επεθηκεν in egjsz.

p14. OG τα εμπλοκια is replaced by το εμπλοκιον in begjnsvzL^r; OG εκ χρυσιου is replaced by του χρυσου in 128; the same phrase is omitted by A; καθαρου is inserted after χρυσιου in dhnpt; M^{mg} has α'σ' αλυσεις θ' χαλαστα for OG εμπλοκια.

p15. δυο is inserted before OG δακτυλιους in AMbd-gijlnprstvwza_2b_2 B$E^f L^r$; δυο is omitted by F^bm.

p16. OG επ is found only in Bahoqru; it is replaced by εξ in AMbd-gijlnpstvwy-$b_2E^fL^r$.

p17. OG συμβολας is replaced by συμπλοκας in a_2.

p18. δυο is omitted by a_2 and by c.

p19. OG και is omitted by dnptL^r and is shifted after επεθηκαν in 76; OG επεθηκαν is replaced by επεθηκεν in b_2B.

p20. OG και is omitted by b'; ασπιδισκας is replaced by ασπιδας in c.

p21. OG επεθηκαν is replaced by επεθηκεν in egjz* and is omitted in w; εθηκαν is replaced by επεθηκαν in F^bkm; αυτας is replaced by αυτα in k and is omitted by F^b.

p22. επι is omitted by F^b; OG τους-επωμιδος is replaced by της επωμιδος τους ωμους in n and by τας δυο επωμιδας των ωμων in b'; δυο is inserted before ωμους in quwBL^r.

p23. OG εξ εναντιας is omitted by b_2; after OG προσωπον AMdegjlp-zb$_2$Ƀ add αυτου and a_2 adds αυτων; αυτου is omitted by Ⱥ.

p24-p30. The entire verse is omitted by Ɇ^{c}.

p25. OG χρυσους is replaced by χρυσηους in n and is omitted in Ł^{r}.

p27-p33. OG επι-επεθηκαν is omitted by a_2Ɇ^{f}.

p27-p48*. F^{b} is defective after επι τα.

p27. OG επ is replaced by απ in Md-gil-prstv-zɃŁ^{r}; επ ακρου is omitted by k; ακρου is replaced by ακρον in c.

p28. OG και is omitted by AMbdfgi-npstv-zb$_2$Ƀ^{1}Ł^{r}; OG το ακρον is replaced by *duas summitates* in Ƀ^{1}.

p28-p29. OG επι-οπισθιου is replaced by *in cacumine posteriore* in Ł^{r}.

p29. OG οπισθιου is replaced by λογιου in r.

p31. OG εποιησαν is replaced by εποιησεν in o; similarly εποιησαν is replaced by εποιησε in c.

p32. OG χρυσους is omitted by yŁ^{r}.

p33. OG επεθηκαν is replaced by επεθηκεν in 16; εθηκαν is replaced by επεθηκαν in km and by επεθηκεν in c; αυτους is omitted in Ⱥ.

p34. επι is inserted after OG αμφοτερους in a_2; OG της is replaced by αυτης in q.

p35-p38. OG κατωθεν-επωμιδος is omitted by B (homeoteleuton--from της επωμιδος to της επωμιδος).

p35. OG αυτου is replaced by εαυτου in g. For *ltḥt* of Ꞩ^{txt}, Ꞩ^{mg} has *lgw*.

p36. το is inserted before OG προσωπον in 32; κατα προσωπον αυτου is omitted by k (homeoarcton--from κατα to κατα).

p37-p38. OG κατα-ανωθεν is replaced *secundū commissuram superiorem* in Ł^{r}.

p37. OG κατα is omitted by a_2; OG την is omitted by f; αυτου is omitted by Ⱥ.

p38. OG ανωθεν is replaced by απανωθεν in w and by επανωθεν in 118; OG συνυφης is replaced by συναφης in f and also in m, by συναφειας in n^{b}, and by υφης in la_2.

p39. OG συνεσφιγξεν is replaced by συνεσφιξεν in b'u and by συνεσφιξαν in *b*Ƀ; similarly συνεσφιγξεν is replaced by *constrinxerunt* in Ⱥ.

p41. OG απο is replaced by εκ in n; OG δακτυλιων is replaced by επωμιδων in w; OG των επ is replaced by τω επ in b; OG αυτου is replaced by αυτους in aqu and also in m, and by αυτοις in f; των επ αυτου is replaced by *eius* in A̸E̸^{c}.

p42. δακτυλιους is replaced by δακτυλους in k.

p43-p45. OG συνεχομενης-επωμιδος is omitted by d.

p43. OG συνεχομενους is replaced by συνεχομενης in 71; OG της is replaced by του in w.

p45. OG εις is replaced by επι in fiB̸^{w}.

p46-p47. OG ινα-επωμιδος is omitted in B*w.

p46. OG χαλαται is replaced by χαλα in 25.

p47. απο is replaced by επι in c.

p48*. OG μωυση is replaced by μωυσει in qru and by μωση in n; μωση is replaced by μωσει in m and by μωυση in ck.

Orthography of the Parallel Hebrew Passages

In the following table, words that might be subject to variations in the use of *plene* or defective spellings have been listed in accordance with their spelling in MT Exod. 28:22-28.[2] Where necessary, other spelling variations found in MT Exod. 39:15-21 have been indicated in parentheses. After each word, the table indicates whether it occurs written *plene* (x) or defectively (-) in the two parallel passages. There are no variations in usage in items 1 through 6, which correspond to the verse found in all Greek witnesses to both parallels. In the remaining verses, however, the MT of Exodus 28 has twenty-one *plene* writings, while the MT of Exodus 39 has only ten, of which one is not present in Exodus 28. This divergence in orthographic practice may reflect the later origin of MT Exod. 28:23-28. The scribe who composed it on the basis of MT Exod. 39:16-21 apparently used a fuller orthography in his own new composition, while he retained the more defective orthography when simply copying the older passage.

---

[2]The word *ḥšn*, which occurs seven times in this passage, is not listed because it is never found *plene* in its twenty-four occurrences in the MT. Similarly, *l ʿmt* is not included in the list. The word *gblt* is included, however, since it only occurs in these parallels and a writing *gblwt* is theoretically possible.

Comparative Table (x = *plene*; - = defective).

	Item No.	*Word*	*Exod. 28*	*Exod. 39*
1)	item 3	šrš(r)t[3]	-	-
2)	item 4	gblt	-	-
3)	item 5	ʿbt	-	-
4)	item 6	ṭhwr	x	x
5)	item 8	(mšbṣt)[4]		-
6)	item 9	ṭbʿwt	x	-
7)	item 11	hṭbʿwt	x	-
8)	item 12	qṣwt	x	x
9)	item 14	(h)ʿbtt[5]	-	-
10)	item 15	hṭbʿt	-	-
11)	item 16	qṣwt	x	x
12)	item 17	qṣwt	x	x
13)	item 18	hʿbtt	-	-
14)	item 20	hmšbṣwt	x	-
15)	item 22	ktpwt	x	-
16)	item 22	hʾpd	-	-
17)	item 23	mwl	x	x
18)	item 23	pnyw	x	x
19)	item 25	ṭbʿwt	x	-
20)	item 27	qṣwt	x	x
21)	item 29	hʾpd	-	-
22)	item 32	ṭbʿwt	x	-
23)	item 34	ktpwt	x	-
24)	item 34	hʾpwd	x	-
25)	item 36	mmwl	x	x
26)	item 36	pnyw	x	x
27)	item 38	hʾpwd	x	-

[3]The form *šršt* occurs only in Exod. 28:22; elsewhere *šršr(w)t* is standard.

[4]Item 8 differs in the two parallels; the word *mšbṣt* is not found in Exod. 28:23, but only in Exod. 39:16.

[5]The article is inserted (and *ʾt* before *šty* is omitted) in Exod. 39:17.

	Item No.	Word	Exod. 28	Exod. 39
28)	item 41	mṭb'tw[6]	-	-
29)	item 41	mṭb'tw	-	x
30)	item 42	ṭb't	-	-
31)	item 42	h'pd	-	-
32)	item 43	bptyl	x	x
33)	item 44	lhywt	x	-
34)	item 45	h'pwd	x	-
35)	item 47	h'pwd	x	-

Commentary

The following discussions concern MT Exod. 28:22-30 (LXX vv.22-26). The parallel passage in MT Exod. 39:15-21 (LXX 36:22-29) is referred to only when it is important for the understanding of particular Theodotionic readings.

1-6. The OG and the MT reflect the same text-form in this verse. The minor variants within the OG tradition need not detain us here. The only hexaplaric variants in this verse concern item 3.

3. MT *šršt*, a *hapax*, is presumably an error for *šršrt* ("chains," cf. item p3, above). The latter occurs seven times in the MT.[7] In 1 Kings 7:17, MT *šršrwt* does not seem to be reflected in the OG (v.5) or in any Greek witnesses. The other six occurrences have the following equivalents:

Exod. 28:14 (1): MT *šršrt*] OG κροσωτα/κροσσωτα] $\mathcal{S}^{txt}$ *ḥwṭ'*] $F^{b\ mg}$ αλυσειδ...] M^{mg} α'σ' αλυσεις εν αλλω βιβλιω ευρον α'σ' συσφιγκτα θ' χαλαστα] $\mathcal{S}^{mg}$ α'σ' *"ššlt'*· θ' *nypt'*] b^{mg} α'σ' αλυσις] $v^{mg}z^{mg}$ σ' συσφιγμα. (The readings συσφιγκτα and συσφιγμα are possibly misplaced variants for MT *(h)mšbṣt* in the same verse or for MT *mšbṣt* in v. 13. See the discussion of equivalents for MT *mšbṣwt* and related words in item 20 of the present passage.)

Exod. 28:14 (2): MT *'t šršrt*] OG τα κροσωτα/κροσσωτα] $\mathcal{S}^{txt}$ *'mn lḥwṭ'*.

---

[6]There are two possibilities for *plene* writing in this one word: *mṭb'(W)t(Y)w*. The first is indicated by number 28 and the second by number 29.

[7]Exod. 28:14 *bis*; 39:15; 1 Kings 7:17; 2 Chron. 3:5, 16 *bis*.

Exod. 39:15: MT *šršrt*] OG κροσους/κροσσους] Ś^{txt} *hwt'*.

2 Chron. 3:5: MT *wšršrwt*] OG και χαλαστα] be_2 και αλυσεις.

2 Chron. 3:16 (1): MT *šršrwt*] OG σερσερωθ (σενσερωθ A; σερωθ i)] be_2 αλυσιδωτα] g σεραλυσιδωτασερωθ.

2 Chron. 3:16 (2): MT *bšršrwt*] OG επι των χαλαστων] be_2 επι των αλυσεων.

As indicated in the note to item 3 in the foregoing charts, the equivalents for MT *šršt* in the present verse are: OG κροσους/κροσσους] $M^{mg}s^{mg}z^{mg}$ (and without name in v^{mg}) οι λ̥ αλυσεις] Ś^{mg} α'σ' *ššlt'*· θ' *nypt'*.

Since αλυσεις and *ššlt'* both mean "chains," while *nypt'* and χαλαστα mean "loosely-hanging (chains)" and "relaxed (things)," respectively, the Syriac readings attributed to Theodotion and to Aquila and Symmachus in the present item and the Greek-Syriac readings (α'σ' αλυσεις or αλυσις, *ššlt'*; θ' χαλαστα, *nypt'*) of Exod. 28:14 are in agreement. The divergent Aquila and Symmachus readings--α'σ' συσφιγκτα, σ' συσφιγμα--from Exod. 28:14 are presumably to be related to some other Hebrew word. The οι λ̥ attribution of $M^{mg}s^{mg}z^{mg}$ for αλυσεις in the present item must be understood to refer properly only to α'σ' (as in Ś^{mg}). Thus the three versions and the OG equate the unique *šršt* with the better attested *šršrt*, or else their Hebrew texts had the latter, more correct form.

Theodotion's word (χαλαστα) is used for MT *šršrwt* by the OG in 2 Chron. 3:5 and once in 2 Chron. 3:16. Both times the word used here by Aquila and Symmachus appears in be_2. The other time that MT *šršrwt* occurs in 2 Chron. 3:16, the OG has a transliteration. A form related to that used here by Aquila and Symmachus is found in be_2 and is inserted into the middle of the OG transliteration in g.

In Exodus, the OG had interpreted MT *šršrt* and *šršt* to mean "tassels" or "fringe," rather than "chains." Theodotion rejects the OG choices in favor of the more accurate equivalent used twice by the OG, or at least by the majority Greek recension, in 2 Chronicles. Aquila and Symmachus, however, share a different correspondent that is accurate, but not based on OG usage. Traces of this same revision are found in be_2 of 2 Chronicles.

Theodotion also uses χαλαστα at least once to represent MT *'btt*

(Exod. 39:17 [LXX 36:25]).[8] Elsewhere in Exodus, Theodotion uses Syriac *šš̌lt'* (presumably representing αλυσεις or αλυσιδωτα) for MT *'btt* twice (MT Exod. 28:24, 25--items 14 and 18 of the present passage) and for MT *'bt* once (Exod. 28:14). He uses the singular *dššlt'* for MT *'bt* in Exod. 39:15 (LXX 36:22). Compare these readings with OG αλυσιδωτον (-του Bch), $\mathfrak{S}^{txt}$ *ššlny'*, for MT *'bt* in item 5 of this passage. The readings will be discussed under item 14.

The reading τα χαλαστα is cited only once more by H-R, in Symmachus at Isa. 3:19. There it stands for MT *hnṭypwt* (OG και το καθεμα, θ' τα καθεματα, α' κροκυφαντους).

In summary, the OG translation of the MT was not really accurate. Theodotion introduces one revision, and Aquila and Symmachus another. Both revisions are accurate, and find parallels in the Greek witnesses to Chronicles.

7-47. This entire section, amounting to six verses in the MT, is omitted by a large number of Greek witnesses, including those that most frequently preserve the original OG, Bhiloqruw. A translation of this passage is found in an equally large number of witnesses, under ※ in svz. This series of witnesses I have labeled LXX^2 and have placed in a separate column in the charts at the beginning of this section. The material corresponding to this section in $\mathfrak{S}^{txt}$ has been attributed as a whole to Theodotion. Scattered readings from all three versions appear in the margins of some Greek witnesses and of $\mathfrak{S}$. The Syriac passage is the longest continuous segment attributed to Theodotion in Exodus. It is in basic agreement with the earlier revision of the OG represented by LXX^2, but it includes certain further modifications of that revision. Its importance for the understanding of the Theodotionic revision of Exodus is obvious.

Where the Syriac reading attributed to Theodotion corresponds exactly to the Greek reading found in the LXX^2 column, and where this in turn represents the MT accurately and in conformity with normal OG usage, no special comments are made, unless, of course, variants from Aquila or Symmachus are also preserved.

---

[8]It is suggested under item 14, in the discussion of the various equivalents for MT *'btt*, that Theodotionic χαλαστα is misplaced and was meant to represent a different MT word.

12. OG treatment of MT קָצָה, its plural *qṣwt*, and the related קָצֶה, is extremely inconsistent. For קָצָה, which occurs only six times,[9] the OG uses το ακρον only twice, both in Exod. 37:8 (LXX 38:7). For *qṣwt*, which occurs thirty times,[10] the OG uses τα ακρα only in Isa. 40:28; 41:5, 9; Jer. 49:36 (LXX 25:16); and the singular only in Ps. 19:7 (LXX 18:7).[11] MT קָצֶה occurs thirty-two times in the Pentateuch alone.[12] Only seven times is it represented by ακρον in the OG,[13] and twice by the plural of the same word.[14] It was not thought necessary to check the treatment of MT קָצֶה outside the Pentateuch, where a similar situation would presumably prevail.

The other equivalents used most frequently by the OT for all three Hebrew words are το κλιτος/τα κλιτη and το μερος/τα μερη.[15] In the

---

[9]Exod. 25:19 (LXX v.18) *bis*; 26:4; 36:11; 37:8 (LXX 38:7) *bis*.

[10]Exod. 25:18 (LXX v.17), 19 (LXX v.18); 27:4; 28:7, 23, 24, 25, 26; 37:7 (LXX 38:6), 8 (LXX 38:7); 38:5 (LXX 38:24); 39:4 (LXX 36:11), 16 (LXX 36:24), 17 (LXX 36:25), 18 (LXX 36:25), 19 (LXX 36:27); Judg. 18:2; 1 Kings 6:24 (LXX v.23); 12:31; 13:33; 2 Kings 17:32; Isa. 40:28; 41:5, 9; Jer. 49:36 (LXX 25:16); Ezek. 15:4; Pss. 19:7 (LXX 18:7); 65:9 (LXX 64:9); Job 26:14; 28:24. In Exod. 37:8; 38:5; 39:4; Ps. 65:9, the form is spelled and/or vocalized as if it were the plural of **qṣwh*.

[11]The OG phrase πτερυγια επ ακρου in LXX Exod. 36:27, which corresponds to MT *qṣwt* in MT Exod. 39:19, probably should not be allowed to enter this discussion.

[12]Gen. 8:3; 19:4; 23:9; 47:2, 21 *bis*; Exod. 13:20; 16:35; 19:12; 26:5, 28 *bis*; 36:12, 33 *bis*; Num. 11:1; 20:16; 22:36, 41; 23:13; 33:6, 37; 34:3; Deut. 4:32 *bis*; 13:8 (LXX v.7) *bis*; 14:28 (LXX v.27); 28:49, 64 *bis*; 30:4.

[13]Deut. 4:32 *bis*; 13:8 (LXX v.7) *bis*; 28:64 *bis*; 30:4. Note that the first three sets are all the idiom *mqṣh* ... *w'd qṣh*, while the last (MT *bqṣh* in Deut. 30:4) is actually treated by the OG as if the same idiom were present in its *Vorlage* (OG απ ακρου ... εως ακρου, with the second phrase omitted only in Gcdgoqxa$_2$, Phil-cod).

[14]Gen. 47:21 *bis*, where the Hebrew idiom *mqṣh* ... *w'd qṣhw*, mentioned in the preceding note, is again found.

[15]το κλιτος = קָצָה in Exod. 25:19 (LXX v.18) *bis*.
το κλιτος = קָצֶה in Exod. 26:28 *bis* and in F[b]ckm𝔄𝔈[c]𝔖 for Exod.

parallel to the present reading, however, the OG equivalent for MT *qṣwt* is τας αρχας, with αμφοτερας (rather than δυο) used for MT *šny* (item p12).[16]

In the present passage, MT *qṣwt* is represented four times by τα ακρα in the group of witnesses I have labelled LXX² (items 12, 16, 17, 27; and in item 16, egjsvz replace τα ακρα with το ακρον).[17] All four belong to the passage that is attributed to Theodotion by S̸. This usage has some support in the OG, as we have seen above, but it is not the regular pattern. The only other traces of this usage that I have been able to discover are:

36:23 *bis* (where the OG provides no equivalent).

τα κλιτη = *qṣwt* in Exod. 25:18 (LXX v.17), 19 (LXX v.18); 27:4. Cf. LXX Exod. 28:24 (item 61 of the present passage), and F^b for Exod. 37:7 and 38:5.

το μερος = קָצָה in Exod. 26:4 and in F^{b}ckmA̸E̸^{c}S̸ for Exod. 36:11 (where the OG provides no equivalent).

το μερος = קְצֵה in Gen. 23:9 (majority of manuscripts; μερις in Ay); Exod. 16:35; 26:5; Num. 11:1; 20:16; 22:36, 41; 23:13; 33:6; 34:3; and in F^{b}GkmA̸E̸^{c}S̸ for Exod. 36:12 (where the OG provides no equivalent).

τα μερη = *qṣwt* in Exod. 28:7; 38:5 (LXX 38:24); 39:4 (LXX 36:11), 17 (LXX 36:25); Job 26:14 (?); in GckmA̸E̸^{c}S̸ for Exod. 37:7 (LXX 38:6) and in GckmE̸^{c}S̸ for Exod. 37:8 (LXX 38:7), where the OG provides no equivalent either time.

το μερος = *qṣwt* in 1 Kings 6:24 (LXX v.23) *bis*; 12:31: 13:33; in various witnesses for Judges 18:2 and in $borc_2e_2$ for 2 Kings 17:32, where no OG equivalent can be identified either time.

OG ακρον, κλιτος, and μερος all have a variety of other equivalents in the MT. It is not necessary to enumerate or discuss them here.

[16]No other instances of OG αρχη to represent MT קָצָה are noted in H-R. Two instances of its use for MT קְצֵה (Judges 7:11, 17) and one instance of its use for MT *qṣ* (2 Sam. 14:26) are cited. Otherwise, OG αρχη has a variety of equivalents, of which MT *rʾš* and related words are perhaps the most frequent.

[17]No such consistency is found in the OG of the parallel passage, however. Cf. items p12, p16, p17, and p27.

Exod. 25:18 (LXX v.17): σ' των ακρων (M^{mg});

Exod. 37:8 (LXX 38:7): $G^{b\ mg}$ $Ⱥ^{vid}$ $Ꞩ^{mg}$ ακρων (ħs');

Ezek. 15:4: σ' *ħyš' dylh* ($Ꞩ^{mg}$), σ'θ' *summitates eius* (Hi);

and possibly 1 Kings 6:24 (LXX v.23): α'σ' *tmn mn ryš'* ($Ꞩ^{mg}$).

Contrast the following readings of Aquila (again where the MT has a form of *qṣwt*):

Isa. 40:28: α' "τελευταια" (Chr.--as cited in small type by Ziegler);

Isa. 41:5: α' τελευταια (86^{mg});

Isa. 41:9: α' τελευταιων (86^{mg});

Ezek. 15:4: α' *novissima eius* (Hi);

Ps. 19:7 (LXX 18:7): α' *šwlm' dylhwn* ($Ꞩ^{mg}$).

Finally, there is σ' περατων (86^{mg}) for MT *qṣwt* in Isa. 41:9.

The evidence is far too slender to permit any more than a suggestion that Theodotion tended to use ακρα rather than any of the other OG equivalents to represent MT *qṣwt*. While Symmachus used this and other equivalents, Aquila showed a preference for τελευταια, which is not used in this way in the OG.[18]

---

[18]One might note that Theodotion also has ακρον in at least the following places: Judg. 7:11 (MT *qṣh*); Isa. 37:24 (MT *qṣ*; α' τελευταιον, σ' ακρον); 56:11 (MT *qṣh*; α' τελευταιον, σ' ακρον). Aquila has it in Isa. 57:5 (MT *s'py-*; σ' or σ'θ' εξοχαι); Jer. 50:26 (LXX 27:26; MT *qṣ*; the α' citation with ακρον in 86^{mg} may conflict with α' *šwlm'* in $Ꞩ^{mg}$; σ' συμπαντες); Ezek. 17:3 (MT *ṣmrt*; σ' εγκαρδιον, θ' καυλος); 31:3 (MT *ṣmrt*), 14 (MT *ṣmrt*; σ' καρδιαι, θ' καυλος or *kħmt'*).

In Gen. 47:31, MT *r'š* is represented by OG το ακρον. According to v^{mg}, σ' has το ακρον, θ' agrees with ο', and α' has κεφαλη. This set of attributions is reversed by c_2^{mg}, which credits α' with το ακρον and σ' with κεφαλη. Presumably v^{mg} is to be preferred.

Other occurrences of ακρον in Symmachus come in Exod. 16:35 (MT *qṣh*; σ' ακρα in Field is based on a Latin citation in Procop.); 25:18 (LXX v.17; MT *qṣwt*; σ' ακρα); Josh. 15:21 (MT *qṣh*; θ' τελος, α' τελευταιον); 1 Sam. 15:27 (MT *knp*); 24:5 (MT *knp*); Job 37:3 (MT *knpwt*; σ' ακρα, θ' πτερυγες); 38:13 (MT *knpwt*; σ' ακρα); Isa. 37:24 (MT *qṣ*; see θ' list); 56:11 (MT *qṣh*; see θ' list); Jer. 25:31 (LXX 32:17: MT *qṣh*; σ' ακρα, α' *šwlm'*); Ezek. 5:3 (MT *knpym*; σ' ακρον του ιματιου or κρασπεδα; α' πτερυγια); 7:2 (MT *knpwt*; σ' ακρα); 17:22 (MT *r'š*; θ' κεφαλη); Dan. 11:45 (MT

14. The Syriac phrase attributed to Theodotion corresponds to the Greek found in the LXX^2 column. The word *'nyn* merely provides explicit representation for the first τα. The presence or absence of the second τα (omitted by ms) is not indicated by the Syriac form, but its presence is more probable. The treatment of MT *'btt* here and in item 18 requires some discussion. There is no general consistency in the OG treatment of MT עֲבֹת, which occurs six times in the singular, of its feminine and masculine plurals, which occur six times and twelve times, respectively, and of the related adjective עָבֹת, which occurs four times.[19]

---

qṣ; θ' μερος; α' *finis*); Zach. 4:7 (MT *r'šh*; σ' ακρος, θ' πρωτος, α' προτευων).

In the foregoing lists, all forms have been cited in the nominative case without articles or suffixes.

[19]The various readings are:

עֲבֹת: Exod. 28:14, MT *'bt*, OG πλοκης.
Exod. 28:22, MT *'bt*, OG αλυσιδωτον.
Exod. 39:15 (LXX 36:22), MT *'bt*, OG εμπλοκιου.
Ps. 129:4 (LXX 128:4), MT *'bwt*, OG αυχενας.
Isa. 5:18, MT *(wk)'bwt*, OG ζυγου ιμαντι.
Job 39:10, MT *'btw*, OG ζυγον αυτου.

עֲבֹתֹת: Exod. 28:14, MT *h'btt*, OG τα πεπλεγμενα.
MT Exod. 28:24, MT *'btt*, OG om., LXX^2 αλυσιδωτα.
MT Exod. 28:25, MT *h'btt*, OG om., LXX^2 αλυσεων.
--cf. LXX Exod. 28:24, OG τα αλυσιδωτα.
Exod. 39:17 (LXX 36:25), MT *h'btt*, OG τα εμπλοκια.
Exod. 39:18 (LXX 36:25), MT *h'btt*, OG εμπλοκια.
Hos. 11:4, MT *(b)'btwt*, OG δεσμοις.

עֲבֹתִים: Judg. 15:13, MT *'btym*, OG καλωδιοις.
Judg. 15:14, MT *h'btym*, OG τα καλωδια.
Judg. 16:11, MT *(b)'btym*, OG καλωδιοις.
Judg. 16:12, MT *'btym*, OG καλωδια.
Ps. 2:3, MT *'btymw*, OG τον ζυγον αυτων.
Ps. 118:27 (LXX 117:27), MT *(b)'btym*, OG τοις πυκαζουσιν.
Ezek. 3:25, MT *'bwtym*, OG δεσμοι.
Ezek. 4:8, MT *'bwtym*, OG δεσμους.

In items 14 and 18 of the present passage, Theodotion has *ššlt'* to represent MT *(h)'btt* each time. This presumably reflects αλυσιδωτα in item 14 and αλυσιδωτων in item 18. The latter has been replaced by αλυσεων in all Greek witnesses except M. In Exod. 28:14, Theodotion has *dššlt'* for MT *'bt*, while he has the singular *dššlt'* for MT *'bt* in Exod. 39:15 (LXX 36:22). A comparison of the OG readings listed in footnote 19 will reveal that this usage is supported only by the OG reading in Exod. 28:22, to which the OG reading in LXX Exod. 28:24 should probably be added. These readings are found in items 5 and 60 of the present passage, where the Syriac equivalents (*ššlny'* for αλυσιδωτον and *dššlt'* for τα αλυσιδωτα) support the interpretation of the Theodotionic readings found only in Syriac.

A different equivalent, χαλαστα, is attributed to Theodotion by M^mg in item p14 of Exod. 39:17 (LXX 36:25) for MT *'btt*. Since the α'σ' reading of M^mg, αλυσεις, is also unexpected, it is likely that the entire citation is misplaced. Perhaps it should be associated with OG κροσσους in LXX Exod. 36:22, which stands for MT *šršrt* in MT Exod. 39:15. This would bring both variants into conformity with the patterns discussed above under item 3 of the present passage.

No other Theodotionic equivalents for MT *'bt* and related Hebrew words are found in Exodus. The citations found in Isaiah, Psalms, and Ezekiel are not related to those in Exodus.[20]

Ezek. 19:11, MT *'btym*, OG στελεχων.

Ezek. 31:3, MT *'btym*, OG νεφελων.

Ezek. 31:10, MT *'bwtym*, OG νεφελων.

Ezek. 31:14, MT *'btym*, OG νεφελων.

עָבֹת : Lev. 23:40, MT *'bt*, OG δασεις.

Neh. 8:15, MT *'bt*, OG δασεος.

Ezek. 6:13, MT *'bth*, OG δασειας (om B).

Ezek. 20:28, MT *'bt*, OG κατασκιον.

[20]Other Theodotionic citations include; θ' κλοιους for MT *'bwt* in Ps. 129:4 (LXX 128:4), a citation drawn from Theodoret by Field; α'σ'θ' βροχω for MT *(wk)'bwt* in Isa. 5;18; α'θ' δασεων, θ' *'byṭt'* for MT *'btym* in Ezek. 19:11; α'θ' δασεων for MT *'btym* in Ezek. 31;3; θ' *sbys'* for MT *'bwtym* in Ezek. 31:10; both θ' and ε' are said to agree with ο' in Ps. 118:27 (LXX 117:27), where OG τοις πυκαζουσιν represents MT *(b)'btym*,

Only three citations from Aquila and Symmachus for MT *ʿbt* and related words are found in Exodus: σʹ βροχωτον for MT *ʿbt* in Exod. 28:22; αʹσʹ *gdylʾ* for MT *ʿbt* in Exod. 39:15 (LXX 36:22); and αʹσʹ αλυσεις for MT *hʿbtt* in Exod. 39:17 (LXX 36:25). The difficulties associated with this citation have already been mentioned. Neither these citations in Exodus nor the citations found elsewhere in the OT are treated here.[21]

No patterns of correspondence for MT *ʿbt*, *ʿbtt*, and *ʿbtym*, that are valid throughout the entire OT, can be established for the OG or for any of the versions. The readings attributed to Theodotion in the present item and in item 18 are paralleled by two other Theodotionic readings and at least one OG reading in Exodus, while the conflicting Theodotionic reading in Exod. 39:17 (LXX 36:25) may be attached to the wrong word. This minor subpattern is confined to the book of Exodus, and has not left any trace in Aquila or Symmachus.

15. The Syriac reading attributed to Theodotion could represent either the Greek dative of most manuscripts or the Greek accusative of $F^{a?}$ckm. Compare the similar replacement of του λογιου with το λογιον in c for item 8.

16-17. The treatment of MT *qṣwt* has already been discussed in connection with item 12.

16. The variant found in egjsvz might presuppose a slightly different Hebrew *Vorlage: ʿl qṣt hḥšn*. For the different preposition, compare the variant in the parallel, item p16.

---

according to Field's citation from Vat. In addition, αʹσʹθʹ accept OG δασειας (not found in B, Co, Hi^{test}) for MT *ʿbth* in Ezek. 6:13, and θʹ αλσωδες is found for MT *ʿbt* (adj.) in Ezek. 20:28.

[21]Other citations from Aquila and Symmachus include: αʹ, σʹ βροχους, αʹσʹ *šrbwqytʾ* for MT *ʿbwt* in Ps. 129:4 (LXX 128:4), citations given by Field; σʹ, αʹσʹθʹ βροχω for MT *(wk)ʿbwt* in Isa. 5:18; αʹσʹ *ḥnqʾ dylhwn* for MT *ʿbtymw* in Ps. 2:3, citation given by Field; αʹ πιμελεσιν, *(b)ḥblʾ*, σʹ πυκασματα for MT *(b)ʿbtym* in Ps. 118;27 (LXX 117:27), citations given by Field; σʹ βροχοι for MT *ʿbwtym* in Ezek. 3:25; αʹθʹ δασεων, σʹ συμφυτων for MT *ʿbtym* in Ezek. 19:11; αʹθʹ δασεων, σʹ πυκαζοντων (ποικ- cod) for MT *ʿbtym* in Ezek. 31:3; σʹ των πυκαζοντων for MT *ʿbwtym* in Ezek. 31:10; σʹ πυκασματα for MT *ʿbtym* in Ezek. 31:14; αʹσʹθʹ δασειας for MT *ʿbth* in Ezek. 6:13; αʹσʹ δασυ for MT *ʿbt* (adj.) in Ezek. 20:28.

18. Syriac *ššlt'* could represent either αλυσιδωτων of M or αλυσεων of the remaining Greek witnesses. While either word would satisfy the general pattern discussed under item 14, the variant in M might be due to a desire for even greater consistency in the choice of correspondents for MT *'btt*. If the substitution of αλυσιδωτων for LXX^2 αλυσεων were due to Theodotion, a suggestion that cannot be proven, then this item would be an example of Theodotion's further revision of the already revised Greek text that was available to him.[22]

20. In addition to the Theodotionic reading of ܣ^{txt} (*ḥyṣt'*), an identical reading from Aquila and a different one from Symmachus (*ḥyṣt 'kḥd'*) are cited by ܣ^{mg} for MT *hmšbṣwt*. The Syriac form *ḥyṣt'* could represent σφιγκτων (found in m), while the compound *ḥyṣt 'kḥd'* would presumably represent συσφιγκτων (found in the other Greek witnesses to this verse). Other possible equivalents are σφιγκτηρων and συσφιγκτηρων, respectively.

The Hebrew noun *mšbṣwt* occurs four times in Exod. 28, four times in Exod. 39, and once in Ps. 45:14. The related noun *tšbṣ* occurs only once (Exod. 28:4), the verb *šbṣ* occurs once each in the Piel (Exod. 28:39) and in the Pual participle (Exod. 28:20), and the noun *šbṣ* also occurs only once (2 Sam. 1:9). These thirteen words, eleven of which are in Exod. 28 and Exod. 39, have the following OG correspondences:

Exod. 28:11, MT *mšbṣwt*, OG om.

Exod. 28:13, MT *mšbṣt*, OG ασπιδισκας (ܣ *mlḥdt'*).

Exod. 28:14, MT *hmšbṣt*, OG τας ασπιδισκας (ܣ *mlḥdt'*).

Exod. 28:25, MT *šty hmšbṣwt*, OG om.; cf. OG τας δυο ασπιδισκας (ܣ [*w*]*ltrtyhyn mlḥdt'*) in LXX Ex 28:25 (ܣ 28:29, under ÷).

Exod. 39:6 (LXX 36:13), MT *mšbṣt*, OG και περισεσιαλωμενους (also in G group; ܣ *wḥdyrn*).

Exod. 39:13 (LXX 36:20), MT *mšbṣt*, OG και συνδεδεμενα (also in G group; ܣ *wqby'n*).

Exod. 39:16 (LXX 36:23), MT *mšbṣt*, OG ασπιδισκας (also in G group; ܣ *skr'*).

Exod. 39:18 (LXX 36:26), MT *šty hmšbṣt*, OG τας δυο ασπιδισκας (also in G group; ܣ *trtyhyn skr'*).

Isa. 45:14 (LXX 44:14), MT *mmšbṣwt*, OG εν κροσσωτοις (ܣ *kd bḥlṣt'*).

---

[22]See the concluding remarks concerning item 37.

Exod. 28:4, MT *tšbṣ*, OG κοσυμβωτον (𝔖 *dqwsumbṭwn*, out of place).

Exod. 28:39 (LXX v.35), MT *wšbṣt* (Piel, perfect, 2 m.s.), OG και οι κοσυμβοι (κοσυμβωτοι B; 𝔖 *wqwsumbw*, without a plural sign in Lagarde's B).

Exod. 28:20, MT *mšbṣym zhb* (Pual part.), OG περικεκαλυμμενα (περικεκλωσμενα dnpta$_2$) χρυσιω (+ και AF*Mbdilnp-b$_2$ĚĽ^r; + *et sint* 𝔅^1) συνδεδεμενα εν χρυσιω (𝔖 *dmksyn bdhb' ⌐d'syrn 'kḥd' bdhb'*⌐).

2 Sam. 1:9, MT *hšbṣ* (noun), OG σκοτος δεινος.[23]

In Exod. 28:11, the MT plus is reflected only in cmy$^{b?}$𝔄𝔖^{txt} and in the margin of jsvz (with σ' prefixed to the entire citation in v^{mg}), and the following variants are given for MT *mšbṣwt*:

cj^{mg}m𝔄 και συνεσφραγισμενους.

z^{mg} και συνεσφισμενους.

s^{mg}v^{mg}y$^{b?}$𝔖^{txt} και συνεσφιγμενους (𝔖 *wḥzyqn 'kḥd'*).

The following hexaplaric readings and related marginal variants have been preserved:

Exod. 28:11 (MT *mšbṣwt*), θ' και συνεσφιγμενους (z^{mg}) *vs* θ' και συνεσφραγισμενους (s^{mg}v^{mg}), σ' *m'tdt'* (𝔖^{mg}, this does not support the apparent σ' citation, συνεσφιγμενους, of v^{mg}), α' εσφιγμενους, *mḥzqt'* (s^{mg}v^{mg}𝔖^{mg}).

Exod. 28:13 (MT *mšbṣt*), α' σφιγκτηρας (s^{mg}v^{mg}), α'σ' σφιγκτηρας (M^{mg}), F$^{b\ mg}$ σφιγ...μ..τ..

Exod. 28:14 (MT *hmšbṣt*), α' σφιγκτηρας (z^{mg}, also without name and out of place in k^{mg}).

MT Exod. 28:25 (MT *hmšbṣwt*), LXX^2 συσφιγκτων (σφιγκτων m), θ' *ḥyṣt'* (𝔖^{txt}), α' *ḥyṣt'*· σ' *ḥyṣt 'kḥd'* (𝔖^{mg}).

Exod. 39:6 (LXX 36:13; MT *mšbṣt*), οι λ̥ συνεσφιγμενους (M^{mg}s^{mg}v^{mg}z^{mg}; also found replacing an earlier word, OG συνπεπορπημενους, in e).

Exod. 39:16 (LXX 36:23; MT *mšbṣt*), α'σ' σφιγκτηρας (M^{mg}), α' *ḥyṣt'*· σ' *ḥyṣt 'kḥd'*· θ' *ḥywṣt'* (𝔖^{mg}).

Ps. 45:14 (LXX 44:14; MT *mmšbṣwt*), αλλος δια συσφιγκτηρων (Chrysost.),

---

[23]Minor variants within the OG text tradition are generally not noted in the list.

σ' *kd byd ḥyṣ'* (Syr^{mg})--Field equates the two readings.[24]

Exod. 28:4 (MT *tšbṣ*), α'σ' συσφιγκτον (M^{mg}), F$^{b\ mg}$ σφιγκτον, Syr^{mg} *ḥyṣt'*.

Exod. 28:39 (LXX v.35; MT *wšbṣt*, Piel), α' και συσφιγξεις, *wtḥyṣyh* (*b*^{mg}Syr^{mg}), F^{b} και συσφιγξεις, E^{c} *et facies*, οι λ̥ αι συσφιγξεις (M^{mg}j^{mg}s^{mg}v^{mg}z^{mg}).

2 Sam. 1:9 (MT *hšbṣ*, noun), α' ο σφιγκτηρ (j^{mg}).

Apart from Theodotion's συνεσφραγισμενους in Exod. 28:11, which is probably a corruption for συνεσφιγμενους, and Symmachus' *M'tdt'* in the same verse, all the reading attributed to the three versions come from the verbs σφιγγειν and συσφιγγειν and nouns related to them. These are normally represented by Syriac *ḥwṣ* and derivatives, also by Syriac *ḥzq*. There does not seem to be any exact pattern governing the precise form chosen in each version for each case, nor can a precise one-to-one correspondence be established between the Syriac forms and the various Greek alternatives attested.

This general pattern of correspondence common to all three versions has no basis in OG usage, as is evident from the list of OG equivalents given above. The only OG occurrences of these two verbs according to H-R are the following:

συσφιγγειν : MT *rks* in Exod. 36:29 (MT 39:21).
MT *'pd* in Lev. 8:8 (MT v.7).
MT *qpṣ* in Deut. 15:7.
MT *šns* (Piel) in 1 Kings 18:46.
σφιγγειν : MT *ṣwr* in 2 Kings 12:10 (MT v.11).
MT *tmk* (Niphal) in Prov. 5:22.

The related Greek nouns are not listed as occurring anywhere in the OG.

All three versions share a common approach to MT *mšbṣwt* and related words, although the precise details cannot be predicted a priori for any given instance. The Syriac readings attributed to Theodotion, Aquila, and Symmachus in this item are consistent with this common approach. Aquila or Theodotion, or both, could reflect σφιγκτων here, although σφιγκτηρων is also possible. Symmachus presumably reflects συσφιγκτων.

---

[24]Field's citation has *ḥš'*, while Ceriani's photo-lithographic edition has the correct *ḥyṣ'*.

22. According to Mandelkern, MT *ktp* occurs forty-nine times in the singular and eighteen times in the plural. Among the OG equivalents for MT *ktp* listed by H-R, the most common is ωμος, twenty-one times, together with ωμια, eleven times.[25] The only other frequent OG equivalent is νωτον/νωτος, occurring twenty times, eight in Joshua and seven in Ezekiel.[26] The other OG equivalents listed by H-R occur infrequently.[27]

The treatment of MT *ktpwt* in items 22 and 34 is thus in agreement with the most consistent usage of the OG. Both translations are of

---

[25] OG ωμος--Exod. 28:12 *bis*; 36:14 (MT 39:7), 26 (MT 39:18), 28 (MT 39:20); Num. 7:9; Deut. 33:12; Judg. 16:3; 1 Sam. 17:6; 1 Kings 7:34; 2 Chron. 35:3; Job 31:22; Isa. 46:7; 49:22; Ezek. 12:6, 7, 12; 24:4; 25:9; 29:18; 34:21.

OG ωμια--1 Kings 6:8; 7:30 *bis*, 34, 39 *ter*; 2 Kings 11:11 *bis* (this is not strictly OG, but the readings common to boc_2e_2 and the majority or ΚΑΙΓΕ recension--as well as α'--can tentatively be attributed to the no longer extant OG); 2 Chron. 23:10 *bis*.

OG ωμια occurs only one additional time, in 1 Kings 7:2, where it represents MT *krtwt*, but where the OG *Vorlage* may well have contained a plural form of *ktp*.

OG ωμος occurs twice to represent MT *ṣd* (Isa. 60:4; 66:12) and thirteen times for MT *škm* (Gen. 21:14; 24:15, 45; 49:15; Exod. 12:34; Joel 4:5; Judg. 9:48; 1 Sam. 10:9; Job 31:36; Isa. 9:6 [MT v.5]; 10:27; 14:25; 22:22), while seven times the equivalent is problematic (Exod. 28:25 [MT v.29], item 65 of this passage; Joel 9:4; Job 31:20; Mal. 2:3; Isa. 10:27 *bis*; Jer. 38[31]:21).

[26] Exod. 37:12 (MT 38:14), 13 (MT 38:15); Num. 34:11; Josh. 15:8, 10, 11; 18:12, 13, 16, 18, 19; Neh. 9:29; Zach. 7:11; Ezek. 40:18, 40 *bis*, 41, 44 *bis*; 46:19. Three times the incorrect νοτος occurs in many manuscripts (Josh. 15:8; 18:13, 16).

[27] They are: γωνια in 2 Chron. 4:10; επωμις in Exod. 28:7 ($F^{b\ mg}$ has ωμοι); 36:11 (MT 39:4); Ezek. 41:2; πλιτος in Exod. 27:14, 15; Ezek. 47:1, 2; and οροφωμα in Ezek. 41:26. The H-R citations total only sixty-one, while sixty-seven MT occurrences are listed by Mandelkern. The remaining six are: 1 Chron. 15:15 (MT *bktpm*, OG κατα την γραφην); Isa. 11:14 (MT *bktp*, OG εν πλοιοις); 30:6 (MT *ʿl ktp*, OG om.); Ezek. 29:7 (MT *kl ktp*, OG πασα χειρ); plus items 22 and 34 of the present passage.

course attributed to Theodotion by $\mathcal{S}^{txt}$. The only other Theodotionic equivalents for MT *ktp* in Exodus are also in Syriac. In Exod. 27:14, MT *lktp* is represented by OG τω κλιτει τω ενι ($\mathcal{S}^{txt}$ *lsṭr' ḥd*), while $\mathcal{S}^{mg}$ has α'σ'θ' *dktp' ḥd'* (compare α'σ' τη ωμια in $M^{mg}v^{mg}z^{mg}$ and without σ' in s^{mg}). And in Exod. 27:15, MT *wlktk* is represented by OG και το κλιτος ($\mathcal{S}^{txt}$ *wsṭr'*), while $\mathcal{S}^{mg}$ has σ'θ' *wlktp'*. Both of these readings are also in conformity with the majority OG usage. While a detailed study of the rest of the OT would produce further exeamples from Theodotion, as well as from Aquila and Symmachus, the evidence from Exodus is sufficient for the present purpose.[28]

According to Mandelkern, the Hebrew noun *'pwd/'pd* occurs forty-nine times in the MT, twenty-nine of these in Exodus alone; **'pdh* occurs three times in the construct or with a suffix, twice in Exodus and once in Isaiah. The noun *'pdn* occurs once, in Dan. 11:45, and the verb *'pd* occurs twice, in Exod. 29:5 and Lev. 8:7. Only *'p(w)d* and the related feminine form **'pdh* are of concern here. Two Greek equivalents account for most of the MT occurrences that are reflected either in the OG or in supplementary expansions of the OG toward the expanded MT. They are επωμις, occurring twenty-two times for *'pwd/'pd* in the OG, once for **'pdh* in the OG, and eight times for *'pwd/'pd* in supplementary expansions of the OG, and εφωδ/εφουδ, occurring twelve times in the OG and twice in supplementary expansions of the OG for MT *'pwd/'pd*.[29]

---

[28]See, for example, α' εν ωμια σ'θ' δια των ωμων for MT *bktp* (OG εν πλοιοις) in Isa. 11:14; θ' επι ωμων for MT *'l ktp* (OG om.) in Isa. 30:6; α' παντα ωμον for MT *kl ktp* (OG πασα χειρ) in Ezek. 29:7; and note also α' ωμον ενα for MT *škm 'ḥd* (OG σικιμα εξαιρετον) in Gen. 48:22; α' επ (or επι του) ωμου αυτου for MT *'l škmw* (OG επι του ωμου αυτου) in Isa. 9:5 (LXX v.6); and α'σ'θ' επι του ωμου αυτου for MT *'l škmw* (OG αυτω) in Isa. 22:22.

[29]In the OG, επωμις = *'p(w)d* in Exod. 25:7 (LXX v.6); 28:4, 6, 12, 15; 29:5 *bis*; 35:9 (LXX v.8), 27; 39:2 (LXX 36:9), 7 (LXX 36:14), 8 (LXX 36:15), 18 (LXX 36:26), 19 (LXX 36:27), 20(LXX 36:28) *bis*, 21 (LXX 36:29) *ter*, 22 (LXX 36:30); Lev. 8:7 *bis*; and it = **'pdh* in Exod. 28:8.

In various supplements to the OG, επωμις = *'p(w)d* in LXX^2 for MT Exod. 28:25, 26, 27 *bis*, 28 *ter* (items 22, 29, 34, 38, 42, 45, and 47 of the present passage; compare LXX Exod. 28:25, item 65 of this passage,

The form επωμις is the most frequent OG equivalent for MT *'p(w)d*. It, or its Syriac equivalent *kbynt'*, is attributed to Theodotion twelve times; ten occurrences are in Exodus, seven of these in the present passage.[30] The form εφωδ is also attributed to Theodotion twice, and its Syriac and Latin equivalents once, to represent MT *'p(w)d*.[31] This latter usage may be secondary in the Theodotionic tradition. That there was a late tendency to insert the transliteration εφουδ to represent MT *'p(w)d* is amply demonstrated by the fact that εφουδ occurs sixteen times in the text or margin of F^b in Exodus in place of other equivalents of the Hebrew word.[32] The presence of εφωδ in Theodotion, contrary to his normal tendency, may be due to a similar secondary revision. The use of επωμις by Theodotion is clearly in conformity with the most frequent

---

where επωμις occurs in the shorter and divergent OG text); in Abcoxc$_2$ (under ⁜)e$_2$*A**S* for 1 Sam. 21:10 (LXX v.9).

In the OG, εφωδ/εφουδ = *'p(w)d* in Judg. 8:27 (εφωθ Bor); 17:5; 18:14, 18, 20; 1 Sam. 2:18, 28; 14:3; 22:18; 23:6, 9; 30:7.

In supplements to the OG, εφουδ = *'p(w)d* in AMNb(εφουθ b')cefhi*j kptvxyb$_2$, 131, *AEL*^{r}*S* for Judg. 18:17; in Abcoxc$_2$e$_2$*A* for 1 Sam. 30:7.

The remaining five occurrences of MT *'p(w)d* and their treatment by the OG are:

Exod. 28:31 (LXX v.27): MT *'t m'yl h'pwd*, OG υποδυτην ποδηρη.

Exod. 29:5: MT *w't m'yl h'pd*, OG τον ποδηρη.

2 Sam. 6:14: MT *'pwd bd*, OG στολην εξαλλον.

1 Chron. 15:27: MT *'pwd bd*, OG στολη βυσσινη.

Hos. 3:4: MT *w'yn 'pwd*, OG ουδε ιερατειας.

The OG treatment of MT *'pdtw* in Exod. 36:11 (MT 39:5) is obscure. The pertinent phrase seems to be εργον υφαντον (for MT *wḥšb 'pdtw*), which was retained unchanged in the revised text of F^bGckm(υφαντου)*AE*^{c}*S*. In Isa. 30:22, MT *w't 'pdt mskt zhbk* is represented only by και τα περικεχρυσωμενα (with τα ειδωλα understood from the previous phrase) in the OG.

[30]Exod. 28;6, 25 (MT), 26 (MT), 27 (MT) *bis*, 28 (MT) *ter*; 29:5; 39:22 (LXX 36:30); Lev. 8:7; 1 Sam. 21:10 (LXX v.9).

[31]εφωδ in Exod. 39;2 (LXX 36:9), according to Montef. as cited by Field, and in 1 Sam. 2:18; Syriac *'pwd'* (Latin *epod*) in Hos. 3:4.

[32]Exod. 25:7 (LXX v.6); 28:4, 6, 12, 15, 25 (MT), 26 (MT), 27 (MT) *bis*, 28 (MT) *ter*, 31 (LXX v.27); 29:5 *ter*.

pattern in the OG.

Aquila introduces a new equivalent, επενδυμα, to represent MT *ʾp(w)d*. He is credited with its use eleven times, once also under the Syriac form *dlʿl mn lbwšʾ*, and a similar Syriac phrase, *ddlʿl mn lbwšʾ*, is attributed to him once.[33] The related forms ενδυμα and επενδυτης each occur once in Aquila for MT *ʾp(w)d*, while conflations or double readings involving επωμις occur twice.[34] Aquila is credited with the Syriac reading *lbwšʾ* for MT *ʾpwd* in Hos. 3:4. This may represent ενδυμα. Thus, apart from the two problematic citations in which επωμις seems to have been added to or substituted for the more normal reading, Aquila's treatment of MT *ʾp(w)d* is fairly consistent, with only minor deviations from his regular equivalent επενδυμα. This equivalent, however, is original with Aquila. It is not supported by either the OG usage or the readings attributed to Theodotion.[35]

The readings attributed to Symmachus for MT *ʾp(w)d* are diverse, and need not be discussed in detail here.[36] They do not fit into any one

---

[33] επενδυμα--Exod. 28:4, 26 (MT), 31 (LXX v.27); 29:5 (also in Syriac as *dlʿl mn lbwšʾ*); 39:2 (LXX 36:9), an α'σ' citation from Montef. by Field; Lev. 8:7; 1 Sam. 2:18; 21:10 (LXX v.9); 22:18; 2 Sam. 6:14; 1 Chron. 15:27 (also found out of place in one manuscript).

ddlʿl mn lbwšʾ--Exod. 39:22 (LXX 36:30).

[34] 1 Sam. 23:9: α' το ενδυμα (j^{mg}); 1 Sam. 14:3: α' επενδυτην (z^{mg}); 1 Sam. 30:7: α'σ' την επωμιδα (j^{mg}), α' το επενδυμα (j^{mg}), α' την επωμιδα (z^{mg}); Judg. 17:5: α' ενδυμα (b^{mg}), α' επωμιδα ενδυμα (z^{mg}), α' επομιδα (M^{mg}).

[35] The α'σ'θ' reading επενδυμα in Exod. 25:7 (LXX v.6), cited from 85 by Montef. according to Field, has been omitted in this discussion, because 85 = B-McL's z, and no such reading is here cited from z by B-McL.

[36] Symmachus has the following equivalents--Exod. 28:26 (MT): σ' του επενδυματος ($s^{mg}v^{mg}z^{mg}$); Exod. 29:5: σ' του επενδυματος ($j^{mg}s^{mg}z^{mg}$), σ' *dlʿl mn lbwšʾ* ($\mathcal{S}^{mg}$), σ' του υπενδυματος (v^{mg}); Exod. 39:2 (LXX 36:9): α'σ' το επενδυμα (cited from Montef. by Field); Exod. 39:22 (LXX 36:30): σ' *dlʿl mn lbwšʾ* ($\mathcal{S}^{mg}$); Lev. 8:7: σ'θ' της επωμιδος (M^{mg}); Judg. 17:5: σ' επωμιδα προσωπ...ενδυμα ιερατικον (b^{mg}), σ' ενδυμα ειρατικον ($M^{mg}z^{mg}$); 1 Sam. 2:18: σ' εφουδ ($M^{mg}z^{mg}$); 1 Sam. 21:10 (LXX v.9): σ' εφουδ (j^{mg}); 1 Sam. 30:7: α'σ' την επωμιδα (j^{mg}); 2 Sam. 6:14: σ' υποδυτην (j^{mg}); 1

pattern, but sometimes agree with either Theodotion or Aquila.

Thus the readings attributed to Theodotion by $\mathcal{S}$ (and also found in LXX[2]) to represent MT *ʾp(w)d* in items 22, 29, 34, 38, 42, 45, and 47 are consistent with his regular usage. This, in turn, is based upon the most frequent practice of the OG. The Greek variant found in c for the present item is secondary, while the reading of F^b also falls into a regular pattern. Aquila's fairly consistent usage is independent of the OG and of Theodotion, as well as of the second OG pattern consistently used by F^b, while Symmachus is eclectic in his treatment of MT *ʾp(w)d*.

23. The phrase *ʾl mwl pny-* occurs eight times in the MT, five times followed by a noun and three times by the third masculine singular suffix; the related form *mmwl pnyw* occurs twice.[37] The word *mwl* occurs twenty-five more times in various phrases, including *ʾl mwl* six times, *mmwl* six times, and *mmly* once.[38] Only the two longer phrases will be discussed in detail here, since the OG treatment of the others is too varied to be helpful.

Of the eight occurrences of the phrase *ʾl mwl pny-*, three are translated by OG κατα προσωπον.[39] Note also the similar OG reading in LXX Exod. 28:25 (item 66 of the present passage), which presumably reflected the equivalent of item 23 *ʾl mwl pny-* in the different OG *Vorlage*.

Three times the OG equivalent is a longer phrase, but one that includes κατα προσωπον:

Chron. 15:27: σʹ επωμιδα (b^{mg} and out of place in z^{mg}); Hos. 3:4: σʹθʹ *epod* (cited from Jerome, *Epist. 29 ad Marcellam*, 6, by Field and Ziegler).

[37]MT *ʾl mwl pnyw* is in Exod. 28:25; 39:18; Lev. 8:9. MT *ʾl mwl pny* + noun is in Exod. 26:9; 28:37; Num. 8:2, 3; 2 Sam. 11:15. MT *mmwl pnyw* is in Exod. 28:27; 39:20.

[38]MT *ʾl mwl* is in Exod. 34:3; Josh. 8:33 *bis*; 9:1; 22:11; 1 Sam. 17:30. MT *mmwl* is in Lev. 5:8; 2 Sam. 5:23; 1 Kings 7:39; 1 Chron. 14:14; 2 Chron. 4:10; Mic. 2:8. MT *mmly* is in Num. 22:5. MT *mwl* is in Exod. 18:19; Deut. 2:19; 3:29; 4:46; 11:30; 34:6; Josh. 18;18; 19:46; 1 Sam. 14:5 *bis*; 1 Kings 7;5.

Note also MT מֹל, as opposed to the normal מוּל, in Deut. 1:1, and possibly MT לְמוּאל in Neh. 12:38.

[39]Exod. 26:9; 28:37 (LXX v.33); Lev. 8:9.

Exod. 39:18 (LXX 36:26): OG εξ (om b_2) εναντιας (om b_2) κατα προσωπον I F^bGckm$A$$E^c$$S$ εξ εναντιας κατα προσωπον.

Num. 8:2: OG εκ (+ του ενος dpt$A$) μερους κατα (om S^1) προσωπον (om S^1).

Num. 8:3: OG εκ του ενος μερους (om 1) κατα προσωπον.

In each case, the apparent OG reading may be a conflation of ancient variants. Traces of the original separation may be preserved in b_2 of Exod. 39:18 (LXX 36:26) and in S^1 of Num. 8:2, although these readings are probably better understood as the result of secondary omissions.

In 2 Sam. 11:15, the OG equivalent for MT *ʾl mwl pny* is not extant, although it may be preserved in the variant εις of the proto-Lucianic witnesses boc_2e_2 (joined by L). The reading of the majority recension, εξ εναντιας, is to be attributed to the ΚΑΙΓΕ recension.[40]

In item 23 the manuscripts that include a reflection of MT Exod. 28:23-28 represent MT *ʾl mwl pny-* by επι το μετωπον του προσωπου. The attribution of a Syriac equivalent of this reading to Theodotion by S^{txt} is confirmed by the partial reading of v^{mg}, ο'θ' του προσωπου. The representation of the suffix is discussed below. The reading επι το μετωπον for MT *ʾl mwl* is entirely without parallel. The word μετωπον occurs eight times in the OG, four times in Theodotion, once in Aquila, twice in Symmachus, and once in οι λ̥. Apart from the present case and one usage in Symmachus, the Greek word always represents MT *mṣḥ*.[41] The usage found in LXX^2 and attributed to Theodotion by S^{txt} in the present case remains unique.[42]

---

[40]Cf. *DA*, pp. 91-126, esp. pp. 125-126; and Cross, "The History of the Biblical Text," *HTR* 57 (1964), 282-283, 292-296.

[41]It = MT *mṣḥ* in the OG for Exod. 28:34 (MT v.38) *bis*; 1 Sam. 17:49 *bis*; 2 Chron. 26:19, 20; Isa. 48:4; Ezek. 9:4; in Theodotion for Ezek. 3:8 *bis*, 9; and in both Aquila and Symmachus for Ezek. 3:7. It = MT *pʾh* in Symmachus for Jer. 9:26 (MT v.25); and it = MT *mwl* in the present item, where it is found in LXX^2 and is attributed to Theodotion by S^{txt}. No other instances of μετωπον are listed by H-R. RT also lists an οι λ̥ usage of μετωπον to represent MT *mṣḥ* in Jer. 3:3. The citation, based on S^{mg}, is found in both Ziegler and Field (who gives the Syriac reading, *hnwn dšrkʾ byt ʿynʾ*).

[42]It does allow the explicit representation of MT *ʾl* by επι. This

Symmachus has the normal equivalent κατα προσωπον. This equivalent is attributed to α'θ' in Exod. 28:37 (LXX v.33), where it was already present in the OG. Before Aquila's usage is discussed, the treatment of MT *mmwl pnyw* requires brief consideration. In Exod. 39:20 (LXX 36:28; item p36), the OG had κατα προσωπον for MT *mmwl pnyw*. This is repeated, with the addition of αυτου, in the revised witnesses Gcm𝔄𝔈^{c}𝔖. In MT Exod. 28:27, item 36, there is no OG equivalent for MT *mmwl pnyw*, but LXX^2 has εκ του κατα προσωπον, with fragmentary αυτ.. only added by F^{b}. This reading is attributed to Theodotion by 𝔖^{txt}, and is also attributed to both ο'θ' and σ' by v^{mg}. The Aquila reading of v^{mg} is discussed below. In this last case, an attempt has been made to represent the Hebrew preposition *m-* by introducing Greek εκ (του). In the OG reading for Exod. 39:20 (LXX 36:28), however, *mmwl* has simply been reflected by κατα. This is adequate, but less exact.

In the present item, Aquila represents MT *ʾl mwl pnyw* with εναντιον προσωπου αυτου. Similarly, in item 36 he uses απο εναντιον προσωπου αυτου for MT *mmwl pnyw*. In Deut. 2:9; 4:46 he uses εναντιον for MT *mwl*, while in 2 Sam. 5:23 he uses εξ εναντιας for MT *mmwl*. Apart from the α'θ' reading of Exod. 28:37 (LXX v.33),[43] Aquila is consistent in his introduction of εναντιον to represent MT *mwl*. The one divergent citation could be explained as an OG-Theodotionic reading that Aquila inadvertently left unchanged.

Aquila's usage is not entirely without parallel. The long OG reading in LXX Exod. 36:26 (MT 39:18), εξ εναντιας κατα προσωπον for MT *ʾl mwl pny(w)*, has already been mentioned. In 2 Sam. 11:15, the majority Greek recension stems from the ΚΑΙΓΕ revision. It has εξ εναντιας for MT *ʾl mwl pny* (where boc$_2$e$_2$𝔏 had εις). In 1 Sam. 17:30, MT *ʾl mwl* is not

---

is unusual because Theodotion regularly uses προς (Syriac *lwt*) or even εις (Syriac *l-*) to represent MT *ʾl*, and uses επι for MT *ʿl*. Furthermore, Syriac *lwqbl* is unexpected as the equivalent of επι, which is normally represented by Syriac *ʿl*. Presumably this troublesome reading was present in the Greek text available to Theodotion and was left unchanged by him. (The *Vorlage* of that Greek text may have had *ʿl* where the present MT has *ʾl*.) In 1 Sam. 17:30, Theodotion apparently represented MT *ʾl mwl* by εις τοπον (according to the θ'λ̥ attribution of m^{txt}).

[43] α'θ' κατα προσωπον for MT *ʾl mwl pny*.

reflected in the OG. Some witnesses (Acdjlpqtxz^{txt}Ɓ^{l}Ȼ^{w}Ɫ^{v}) have εις εναντιον (αιν- A), while others (bghioz^{mg}$a_2c_2e_2$Ⱥ, Chr^{vid}) have εις μερος and still others (efmsw, with the entire citation under ϑ' λ ※ in m) have εις τοπον.

In 2 Chron. 4:10, OG κατεναντι apparently represents MT *(m)mwl*.[44] In Mic. 2:8, OG κατεναντι also represents MT *mmwl*. In 2 Sam. 5:23, MT *mmwl* was translated by OG πλησιον. This was replaced by εξ εναντιας in deflmp-twz*(cf. α' εξ εναντιας of z^{mg}), while j^{mg} has κατεναντιον. Finally, in Num. 22:5, MT *mmly* is reflected by OG εχομενος μου, but s^{mg} adds απεναντι.

Thus Aquila's characteristic revision is based on a single OG usage, together with one instance in the KAIΓE revision of 2 Samuel. Related usages occur in the OG twice, and a few scattered parallels appear in minority witnesses. Theodotion's usage in the present item is unusual in its treatment of MT *mwl*, and also in the use of επι to represent MT *'l*. Elsewhere Theodotion follows general OG usage in reflecting MT *'l mwl pny-* by κατα προσωπον. Symmachus is faithful to this usage even in the present item. In footnote 42, it was suggested that Theodotion here simply retained the reading already present in the LXX^2 Greek text available to him. Compare, for example, items 26, 29, 37, and 46 for indications that Theodotion's revision was based upon such a previous Greek text.

The use of προσωπον for MT *pny-* in all three versions needs no comment, but it should be noted that only Theodotion retains the LXX^2 article του. Since it is not supported by a Hebrew article, του is omitted by both Symmachus and Aquila. Theodotion uses αυτης, also found in F$^{a?}$ ckm, to represent the Hebrew suffix, because he has της επωμιδος as the antecedent. Aquila and Symmachus use αυτου, however, since Aquila and possibly Symmachus presumably had του επενδυματος as the antecedent.[45] The αυτου of the remaining Greek witnesses is incorrect, since they retain της επωμιδος.[46]

---

[44] For MT *mmwl ngbh*, the following Greek evidence is given in B-McL: ως (εως dpqtz; om bne$_2$Ɓ) προς ανατολας κατεναντι (εκ [om b] του μερους του προς νοτον [νωτον b'] be$_2$; om Ɓ).

[45] See the discussion under item 22.

[46] Possibly Theodotion, followed by F$^{a?}$ckm, replaced αυτου of LXX^2

26. According to Ꞩ^{txt} and s^{mg}v^{mg}z^{mg}, Theodotion uses και δωσεις to represent MT *wśmt*. This reading is also found in F$^{a?}$ckmȺ. Aquila and Symmachus substitute the more accurate και θησεις, also found in Mdegnps^{txt}tv^{txt}z^{txt}ȺɆ^{c}, while j has the aberrant reading και ποιησεις.

The overwhelming practice of the OG is to use διδοναι to represent MT *ntn*. This occurs 431 times in the Pentateuch alone, of which fifty-four are in Exodus. In the Pentateuch, OG διδοναι represents MT *śym* only seven times in Exodus and once in Numbers, and it is used only rarely for other Hebrew words. The use of OG τιθεναι is less specialized. It represents MT *ntn* twenty-seven times, MT *śym* thirty times, and has other equivalents at least fourteen times in the Pentateuch.

In item 26 Theodotion's δωσεις is unexpected and inaccurate. The o'θ' attribution of s^{mg}v^{mg}z^{mg} might imply that Theodotion merely retained the reading he found in other manuscripts, but the distribution of variants appears to argue against this. Since διδοναι is used correctly for MT *ntn* five times in this short passage attributed to Theodotion (items 10, 13, 19, 21, 33), while MT *śym* does not occur again, Theodotion may have inadvertently written δωσεις here rather than θησεις. Note that a similar error has taken place in j, where the verb of item 24 is repeated here.[47]

Three further Theodotionic equivalents for MT *śym* are given by Ꞩ in Exodus. Twice, once joined by Aquila and Symmachus, Theodotion apparently uses a form of τιθεναι, presumably και εθηκε(ν), to represent MT *wyśm* where no OG equivalent was given.[48] In Exod. 24:6, however, Symmachus and Theodotion are said by Ꞩ^{mg} to agree with Ꞩ^{txt}, which reflects OG ενεχεεν for MT *(w)yśm*. Only Aquila has the more accurate εθηκεν.

---

with the more correct αυτης. This was replaced by αυτου in the versions of Aquila and Symmachus, once they had replaced της επωμιδος with a masculine antecedent.

[47]At least two other explanations are also possible, albeit unlikely: that the correction made by Aquila and Symmachus subsequently spread into most other witnesses; that the Hebrew text used by Theodotion had the variant *wntt* for MT *wśmt*.

[48]Exod. 40:28 (LXX v.25): GcȺɆ^{c} και εθηκεν, F$^{b\ mg}$ και εθηκε, θ' in Ꞩ^{txt} *wsm*. Exod. 40:30 (LXX v.26): GckȺɆ^{c} και εποιησεν, Ꞩ^{txt} *w'bd*, F$^{b\ mg}$ και εθηκε, α'σ'θ' in Ꞩ^{mg} *wsm*.

There is no need to gather other readings for Aquila and Symmachus from Exodus, or for all three versions from elsewhere in the Pentateuch and beyond. The readings analyzed above show that Theodotion was less consistent in his treatment of MT *śym* than was Aquila. This inconsistency is not unknown to the OG, but particularly in the case of διδοναι it occurs only infrequently. Aquila's systematization reflects one of the patterns found in the OG, and avoids the inaccurate use of διδοναι for MT *śym*. All three versions agree in retaining LXX^{2} αυτους to represent MT *ʾtm*.

27. The use of ακρα for MT *qṣwt* has been treated under item 12.

28. Note the different equivalent for MT *śptw* in item p28.

29. The correspondences for each Hebrew word in this item should be treated separately. MT *ʾšr* is reflected by ο εστιν in all the Greek witnesses grouped as LXX^{2}. Both Theodotion and Symmachus retain the same reading. Aquila omits the word εστιν, regarding the relative ο as an adequate reflection of MT *ʾšr*. This concern for exactness and word-for-word correspondence is characteristic of Aquila. Other cases in which Theodotion uses a relative and the verb "to be" for MT *ʾšr* include Exod. 25:26 (LXX v.25); 37:13 (LXX 38:10).

The Hebrew phrase *ʾl ʿbr* causes more difficulty. The translation εις το μερος is found in most of the witnesses to this passage (Mdegjnp s^{txt}tv^{txt}z^{txt}Ɇ^{c}). The variant εις το αντικρυς is found in F$^{a?}$cȺ and with a minor change in m. A conflation of the two readings, εις το μερος αντικρυ, is found in k. The reading εις το αντικρυς is also attributed to ο'θ' by v^{mg} and partially by s^{mg}, to θ' by z^{mg}, and to σ' by v^{mg}z^{mg}. A further variant, εκτος αντικρυς, which may be due to scribal corruption, is attributed to σ' by s^{mg}.

The situation is further complicated by the reading, *mn lqwblh*, found in the Theodotionic passage of Ꞩ^{txt}. Because ckm most frequently reflect the reading found in Ꞩ^{txt} and also because of the Theodotionic citations listed above, one would expect that Syriac *mn lqwblh* is meant to represent Greek εις το αντικρυς. The correspondence is inexact at best, however, while the Syriac preposition *mn* calls to mind the adverbial preposition εκτος found in the aberrant reading attributed to Symmachus by s^{mg} alone.

The word αντικρυς is never found in the OG, nor does it occur elsewhere in any version to translate MT *ʿbr*. It is used by Theodotion in a joint citation with Symmachus in Isa. 57:2 to represent MT *nkḥ*. Elsewhere αντικρυς occurs in S[c.a] of Neh. 12:9 (Esdras B 22:8) to represent MT *lngd*. It is attributed to Symmachus for MT *lnkḥ* in Gen. 30:38, and for MT *ngd* or its compounds eight times.[49] Finally, Symmachus has την αντικρυ for MT *lngd* in Ps. 17:25 (MT 18:25). Thus there is no parallel for the reading, εις το αντικρυς, shared by Theodotion and Symmachus here. The variant, εις το μερος, is equally unusual.[50] It was presumably present in the text available to Theodotion, but was rejected by him.

Aquila replaces εις το αντικρυς (or εις το μερος) with προς περαν. The preposition προς is more frequently used even by Theodotion to represent MT *ʾl* in Exodus.[51] It is also frequent in the OG. More significant is Aquila's use of περαν to represent MT *ʿbr*. This is the regular OG equivalent for MT *ʿbr* and related forms, and is never used in the OG to represent any other Hebrew words.[52] A detailed discussion of Aquila's acceptance of this practice is not attempted here.[53] Excepting as noted below, I have found no evidence of the use of περαν in any of the versions to represent anything other than MT *ʿbr* or a word apparently derived from *ʿbr*. Finally, Theodotion and Aquila, the latter joined by

---

[49] Symmachus uses αντικρυς for MT *ngd* in Pss. 30:20 (MT 31:20); 38:6 (MT 39:6); 43:16 (MT 44:16); 51:11 (MT 52:11); for MT *lngd* in Pss. 35:2 (MT 36:2); 89:8 (MT 90:8); and for MT *kngd* in Gen. 2:18, 20. In Gen. 2:20, αντικρυς is also attributed to Aquila, but this may be erroneous.

[50] In Exod. 32:15, MT *ʿbryhm* is represented by OG των μερων αυτων. In Jer. 48:28 (LXX 31:28), MT *bʿbry* (OG εν πετραις) is represented by εν μερεσι in Aquila (86[mg], which also attributes περαν to Symmachus).

[51] Theodotion has προς or its Syriac equivalent *lwt* for MT *ʾl* in Exod. 1:19 (taken from Nobil. by Field); 6:13; 8:25 (LXX v.29); 28:24 (MT); 32:9. Contrary equivalents are Syriac *lwqbl* (= επι?) in item 23 and Syriad *l-* (= εις) in item 42 of the present passage.

[52] H-R cite some eighty-four occurrences of OG περαν or περα, all representing MT עֵבֶר, עֲבַר, compound phrases containing one or the other, or מַעֲבָר.

[53] The only exceptions I have found in Aquila are α'σ' περαν for MT *bqṣh* in Isa. 7;18 (OG κυριευει μερους; θ' εν μερει) and the citations for Jer. 48;28 (LXX 31:28), given in footnote 50, where the scribe may perhaps have reversed the α' and σ' attributions.

Symmachus, have their respective equivalents for MT *hʾpd*; these were discussed under item 22.

The various readings in this item raise many problems, some of which have only been alluded to in the preceding discussion. In spite of the obscurities, Theodotion and Symmachus can be said to share a new rendition of MT *ʾsr ʾl ʿbr* that is accurate and intelligible, even if it does not fit into any pattern of usage attested elsewhere. Aquila's variant conforms to the normal pattern of correspondence for MT *ʿbr* in the OG. It is not necessary to decide whether either of these variants, or even the older reading found in many of the Greek witnesses, actually provides the correct translation of what remains a difficult Hebrew phrase. The Syriac version of Theodotion's reading may simply be a free rendition and interpretation of the correct Greek phrase, or it may spring from a scribal corruption similar to that found in the Symmachus reading of s^{mg}.[54]

30. According to H-R, εσωθεν is used occasionally by the OG for various expressions involving MT *byt* (*bbyt*, *byth*, *mbyt*, and *mbyth*), as well as for compounds of MT *pnym*. The same can be said of εσω and εσωτερον, although they have other equivalents as well.

The form *hbyth* occurs eighteen times in the MT.[55] The only OG equivalents and later variants are εις (τον) οικον and εις (την) οικιαν. Once, in 1 Kings 13:15, where the OG has no reflection of MT *hbyth*, Ax$\not{A}$ add εις την οικιαν and $\not{S}^{txt}$ has ※σʹθʹ *lbytʾ*↙.

The form *byth* in construct with a following noun occurs six times in the MT.[56] In Gen. 44:14, the OG has προς with no variants. In Gen. 28:2 and 47:14, the OG has εις τον οικον. The only variant is προς in s^{mg} for Gen. 47:14. In Exod. 8:20 (LXX v.24), the OG reading is εις τους οικους, again with no variants. In Gen. 43:17, most witnesses and both οʹ and θʹ of v^{mg} have εις τον οικον, Aegjln and σʹ of v^{mg} have εις την οικιαν, and αʹ of v^{mg} has οικονδε. And in Gen. 43:24 ($\not{S}$ v.23), the clause

---

[54]Note that the OG for the parallel passage (item p29) is totally different from all the variants found here.

[55]Gen. 19:10; 24:32; 39:11; 43:16, 26; Exod. 9:19; Josh. 2:18; Judg. 19:15, 18; 1 Sam. 6:7; 2 Sam. 13:7; 14:31; 17:20; 1 Kings 13:7, 15; 17:23; 2 Kings 4:32; 9:6.

[56]Gen. 28:2; 43:17, 24; 44:14; 47:14; Exod. 8:20.

containing Hebrew *byth* is omitted by the OG. It is added by acmxb$_2$A, which have εις τον οικον, and under ※ in S, which has *lbyt' dyn*, presumably representing οικονδε.

The form *mbyth* (absolute) occurs only in 1 Kings 6:15. It is not reflected in the OG, but Adefjmnptv(out of place)w-zA insert εσωθεν and S inserts ※α'σ'θ' *mn lgw*⋎ (which equals εσωθεν).

The absolute forms *byth* and *wbyth* occur six times and twice, respectively, in the MT.[57] Three times there is no evidence of εσω or εσωθεν.[58] In 2 Sam. 5:9, OG και τον οικον αυτου for MT *wbyth* is replaced by και εσω in Symmachus (j^{mg}z^{mg}). In Ezek. 44:17, MT *wbyth* is not reflected in the OG. A''-239'-403 *O*-62' Arab add και εσω (εσω under ※ in *O*), *L*''-613 add και εσωτερον, while Q^{txt} has α'θ' [※] και <※> εσω. MT *byth* is represented by OG εσω in 2 Chron. 4:4 and by OG εσωθεν in Exod. 39:19 (LXX 36:27; item p30), with no variants either time. This last citation is parallel to the present reading, where MT *byth*, not reflected in the OG, is represented by εσωθεν in LXX^2. This form is attributed to ο'θ'σ' by v^{mg} and to ο'θ' by s^{mg}, while its Syriac equivalent (*mn lgw*) is attributed to Theodotion by S^{txt}. The characteristic variant οικονδε is attributed to Aquila by v^{mg}z^{mg} and is found without name in s^{mg}.

The reading εσωθεν is thus consistent with one usage of the OG, although Theodotion also uses phrases involving οικος or οικια. While Aquila tends to use οικονδε, so that the Greek suffix -δε reflects the Hebrew suffix *-h*, he too uses εσωθεν for *mbyth*; here οικονδε would clearly be incorrect. All three versions also use εσωθεν for related Hebrew phrases, for example, θ' and α' εσωθεν for *mbyt* in 1 Kings 6:16 (LXX v.17) and α'σ' εσωθεν for *byt* in Ezek. 1:27, while εσω and εσωτερον are also used in various ways.

---

[57]MT *byth* (absolute) is in Exod. 28:26; 39:17; 1 Kings 7:25; Isa. 14:17; Ps. 68:7; 2 Chron. 4:4. MT *wbyth* (absolute) is in 2 Sam. 5:9; Ezek. 44:17.

[58]1 Kings 7:25 (LXX v.13): OG εις (επι a$_2$) τον οικον (τοιχον iE), M^{mg}boc$_2$e$_2$ εις το ενδον (om εις το b'); Isa. 14:17: OG om., 88 *L*'''-46-233 449' εις τας οικιας αυτων (εαυτων *lI*'-96*-46), σ' εις οικιαν (Eus); Ps. 68:7 (LXX 67:7): OG and θ' and ε' εν οικω, σ' οικιαν, α' οικονδε(the α', σ', and ε' readings are all cited from Euseb. and the θ' reading from Colb. by Field).

34. MT *ktpwt* and MT *h'pwd* have been discussed in connection with item 22.

35. The use of κατωθεν (Syriac *mn ltḥt*) to represent MT *mlmṭh* is in full agreement with standard OG usage.[59]

36. The equivalents for MT *mmwl pnyw* in item 36 (LXX^2, οʹθʹ, σʹ εκ του κατα προσωπον, Syriac *mn lwqbl prṣwp'*, and αʹ απο εναντιον προσωπου αυτου) have been discussed in connection with the equivalents for MT *'l mwl pnyw* in item 23. Note that the suffix on *pnyw* is only reflected by Aquila, and fragmentarily by F^b, while Aquila alone omits the superfluous article του, found in LXX^2, οʹθʹ, and σʹ.

The variations in Theodotion's treatment of MT *'l mwl* in item 23 and MT *mmwl* in the present item, together with αʹθʹ κατα προσωπον (= OG) for MT *'l mwl pny* in Exod. 28:37 (LXX v.33) and θʹλ̥ εις τοπον ετερον for MT *'l mwl 'ḥr* in 1 Sam. 17:30, make it very difficult to find any consistent pattern or general tendency. Presumably Theodotion did not have any standard approach to this relatively rare phrase, and generally left unchanged whatever equivalent was present in the Greek text he was revising.

37. The phrase *l'mt mḥbrtw* occurs only twice in the MT, in the present item and in its parallel (item p37) from Exod. 39:20 (LXX 36:28). In the latter place, the OG has κατα την συμβολην, to which GckmɆ^{c}Ꞩ, but

---

[59]The Hebrew expression *mlmṭh* occurs six times in the MT, all in Exodus: 26:24; 27:5; 28:27; 36:29; 38:4; 39:20. In Exod. 26:24 and 27:5, the OG has κατωθεν (Syriac *mn ltḥt*, which is also attributed to σʹ by Ꞩ^{mg}). In Exod. 39:20 (LXX 36:28; item p35), the OG has κατωθεν αυτου, but GckmȺɆ^{c}Ꞩ simply have κατωθεν (*mn ltḥt*). In Exod. 36:29, which is not reflected in the OG, F^{b}GckmȺɆ^{c} have κατωθεν and Ꞩ has *mn ltḥt* (the entire passage is under ※). In Exod. 38:4 (LXX 38:24), where the OG has υπο αυτο for MT *mlmṭh* and κατωθεν for the MT preposition *tḥt*, ckȺꞨ reverse the two, so that κατωθεν (*mn ltḥt*) represents MT *mlmṭh*. And in the present item, which is not reflected in the OG, κατωθεν (*mn ltḥt*) is found in LXX^2 and is attributed to Theodotion by Ꞩ to represent MT *mlmṭh*. Thus, the only OG exception to this usage was later revised into conformity.

Elsewhere OG κατωθεν occurs only four times: with an unknown correspondent in Exod. 36:32 (MT 39:24), and representing MT *tḥt*, *mtḥt*, and *tḥtwn*, respectively, in Deut. 33:13; Isa. 14:9; and Ezek. 4:7.

not A̸, add αυτου. The noun συμβολη represents MT *mḥbrt* in the OG or in whatever witnesses reflect the Hebrew word in all eight of its occurrences.[60] The phrase *l'mt*, in construct or with a suffix, occurs some thirty times in the MT, while *ml'mt*, *l'mwt*, and *'mt* each occur once.[61] A variety of equivalents are attested, of which only the following are directly pertinent to the present discussion:

κατα is found in LXX[2] for the present item; in the OG for Exod. 39:20 (LXX 36:28); and in the OG for Ezek. 40:18. Perhaps σ' *'kwt(hyn)* for Ezek. 1:20 or σ' *'yk d-* for Ezek. 48:18 also represent Greek κατα.

καθως is found in the OG for 1 Chron. 24:31 *bis*.

κατεναντι is found in the OG for 1 Chron. 26:16; in the OG for Ezek. 3:8 *bis*; in F^b for Exod. 38:18 (LXX 37:16); in be_2 for 1 Chron. 24:31; in be_2 for 1 Chron. 25:8; in be_2A̸ for 1 Chron. 26:12; in *L''* for Ezek. 45:6; in *L''*$^{-46}$-613 for Ezek. 48:18. Perhaps θ' *lwqbl* for Ezek. 48:18 also represents Greek κατεναντι.

συμφωνως is found in the received text for Eccles. 7:14, while a variant has συμφωνον;[62] α' συμφωνως is found in 86^{mg} for Ezek. 3:8; 11:22.

Of the four equivalents cited above, only the first and fourth are found in the readings under discussion here. The second and third are at least superficially related to the first, and have been cited for the sake of comparison.

---

[60]Exod. 26:4, 5; 28:27 (MT); 36:11 (MT) *bis*, 12 (MT), 17 (MT); 39:20 (LXX 36:28). Note that the Syriac equivalents in S̸ are varied.

[61]See Mandelkern, p. 897.

[62]The received text represents MT *gm 't zh l'mt zh 'śh h'lhym* by καιγε συν τουτω συμφωνως τουτο εποιησεν ο θεος, while the variant καιγε τουτο συμφωνον τουτω εποιησεν ο θεος is found in some witnesses. There are replacements of τουτω by τουτο, and vice versa, in both readings. Presumably the first reading is to be attributed to Aquila and the second to Theodotion. These readings are taken from Field, who also cites the following version of Symmachus from Nobil., Hieron., S̸^{mg}: και γαρ τουτο αναλογον τουτου εποιησεν ο θεος.

The Hebrew phrase *l‘mt mḥbrtw* is translated κατα την συμβολην αυτων (αυτου dtⱻ$^{c\ vid}$) by Mdegjnps^{txt}tv^{txt}z^{txt}Ɇ^{c} in item 37. This reading, in general conformity with the OG reading for item p37, is thus found in most of the witnesses that make up LXX^{2}. The translation of *l‘mt* by κατα has some OG parallels, quoted above, while the representation of *mḥbrt* by συμβολη is standard.

The variant συμφωνως or συμφωνος is found in z^{mg} or s^{mg}, respectively, to represent *l‘mt*, as in Eccles. 7:14 and in two Aquila readings for Ezekiel. The conflate reading συμφωνως κατα την συμβολην αυτου is found in F$^{a?b}$ and is attributed to both ο′θ′ and σ′ by v^{mg}. A corrupt form of this reading, with και for κατα, is found in ckmȺ (αυτου is omitted by c) and in the Theodotionic version of S̸^{txt}. A similar replacement of και by κατα is found in d for item 39.

Aquila modifies the conflate reading by replacing κατα, or και, with επι. He also puts the noun in the dative case, after επι, and omits the unsupported article. Compare τη συμβολη of n$^{a?}$, where the dative case is also used, but where the article is retained.

In summary, an original "short" reading is expanded or conflated by Theodotion and Symmachus, with subsequent corruption in some witnesses. The insertion of συμφωνως is clearly intended to provide a more exact or accurate representation of MT *l‘mt*. This item shows again that Theodotion was not responsible for the original composition of the Greek passage corresponding to MT Exod. 28:23-28, but that he revised a text into which a representation of this passage had already been inserted (compare especially items 29 and 46). Aquila further revised the version common to Theodotion and Symmachus, perhaps in its subsequently corrupted form. The reason for Aquila's introduction of επι to replace κατα or και is not clear, but the omission of the article is consistent with Aquila's general practice. The replacement of αυτων with αυτου, common to all three versions and also found in F$^{a?}$dkmtȺɆ$^{c\ vid}$, to represent the singular suffix, is presumably due to Theodotion's revisional efforts.

38. The use of επανω (του) to represent MT *mm‘l l-* is an adequate equivalent that has parallels in OG usage.[63] The treatment of MT *h’pwd*

[63] See H-R listings under επανω (= MT *mm‘l l-* seven times), and compare the listings under επανωθεν, ανωθεν, υπερανω, and υπερανωθεν. The various hexaplaric uses of επανω and επανωθεν noted by H-R provide further parallels.

has been discussed in connection with item 22.

The noun *ḥšb* (חֵשֶׁב), found here and in item 45, occurs eight times in the MT -- seven times in Exodus and once in Leviticus -- and is always used in construct with *hʾpwd* or *ʾpdtw*.[64] The only OG equivalents are υφασμα in Exod. 28:8 and in Exod. 39:21 (LXX 36:29; item p45), συνυφη in Exod. 39:20 (LXX 36:28; item p38), and ποιησις in Lev. 8:7.[65]

In the present item, Syriac *mtqnwtʾ* is attributed to Theodotion in S̸^{txt}. This could represent either του μηχανωματος of Mcjmnstv^{txt}z^{txt} or του μηχανηματος of F$^{a?}$degkp as a translation for MT *ḥšb*. Similarly, in item 45, Syriac *mtqnwtʾ*, again attributed to Theodotion in S̸^{txt}, could also represent either του μηχανωματος of Mdgjmnps^{txt}tvz or του μηχανηματος of F$^{a?}$cek as a translation for MT *ḥšb*. In Lev. 8:7, M^{mg} has σ'θ' τω μηχανωματι, and s^{mg} has τω μηχανηματι to represent MT *bḥšb*. These are the only occurrences of μηχανωμα cited in H-R. The word μηχανημα also occurs in Symmachus for Pss. 66:5 (LXX 65:5); 77:13 (LXX 76:13). It represents a form of MT *ʿlylh* each time. In Ps. 9:12, μηχανημα is attributed to αλλος and μηχανη to Symmachus, again to represent a form of MT *ʿlylh*.[66]

While Symmachus agrees with Theodotion in using μηχανωμα for MT *ḥšb* in Lev. 8:7, in the present item and in item 45 he uses κατασκευασμα (Syriac *twqnʾ*) to represent MT *ḥšb*.[67] No other hexaplaric occurrences of this latter word are noted in H-R.

Aquila substitutes a new word, διαζωσμα (Syriac *hmynʾ*) as his equivalent for MT *ḥšb* in the present item, in item 45 and also in Lev. 8:7.[68]

---

[64] Exod. 28:8, 27, 28; 29:5; 39:5, 20, 21; Lev. 8:7.

[65] In Exod. 29:5, the OG presupposed a variant text (perhaps *ḥšn bʾpd* for MT *bḥšb hʾpd*), and no revision is preserved. In Exod. 39:5 (LXX 36:11), OG εργον υφαντον εις αλληλα συνπεπλεγμενα apparently represents MT *wḥšb ʾpdtw* (GS̸ omits συνπεπλεγμενα, as do cmȺɆ^{c}, and put εις αλληλα under ÷).

[66] The variants for Psalms are cited from Field. Presumably μηχανωμα and μηχανημα are to be regarded as identical, since either one could be an itacistic corruption for the other.

[67] Item 38: MT *(l)ḥšb*, v^{mg} σ' του κατασκευασματος, S̸^{mg} σ' *dtwqnʾ*. Item 45: MT *ḥšb*, s^{mg} σ' κατασκευασματος.

[68] Item 38: MT *(l)ḥšb*, v^{mg} α' διαζωσματος, S̸^{mg} α' *dhmynʾ*. Item 45: MT *ḥšb*, s^{mg} α' διαζωσματος. Lev. 8:7: MT *bḥšb*, M^{mg} α' εν τω διαζωσματι.

No other occurrences of this word are noted in H-R. In the present item, a corrupt conflation of the readings from Aquila and Symmachus is found in z^{mg} (διαζωσματα κατασκευασματα).

No hexaplaric variants for the other five occurrences of MT *ḥšb* have been noted in B-McL. In the three cases where variants are given, Theodotion and Aquila have their respective equivalents each time. Twice Symmachus also has his own equivalent, but once he retains that of Theodotion. Each variant is a tentative rendition of a rare Hebrew word, but not one of them is based on attested OG usage.[69] The variant αναλαγμα is found in F^{b} for the present item. No occurrences are cited for this word in H-R, nor is it used elsewhere for the Hebrew noun *ḥšb*.

39. The Hebrew verb *rks* occurs only here and in item p39 of Exod. 39:21 (LXX 36:29). In the latter instance, the OG uses συσφιγγειν (Syriac *ḥ-ṣ*), with only minor variants attested. The reading και συσφιγξουσιν (Syriac *wnḥwṣwnh*) of the present item is consistent with the single OG usage, and its acceptance by Theodotion is not surprising. The minor variants of $F^{a?}$ and of d are due to scribal corruption.

41-42. The Hebrew forms *mṭb'tw* and *ṭb't* are consonantally ambiguous. They could be vocalized either as singular or as plural, although the writing of the possessive suffix with only *-w* would imply a singular form for the first word. The vocalization of the present MT is plural (מִטַּבְּעֹתָו and טַבְּעֹת), a tradition reflected in both Targum Onkelos and the Peshitto. Only ȺɆ^{c} interpret the consonantal forms as plural. The other witnesses, including Theodotion according to S̸^{txt}, follow the more obvious implications of the consonantal script and treat the forms as singular. The minor variants of $F^{a?}$, δακτυλου for δακτυλιου, and of m, το for τον, are insignificant. The omission of αυτου by $F^{a?vid}$ is also of no real importance, since it is probably simple haplography (homeoteleuton). The treatment of MT *h'pd* has been discussed in item 22.

The parallel passage, items p41-p42 of Exod. 39:21 (LXX 36:29), is of interest for the light it sheds on the MT vocalization and its acceptance by ȺɆ^{c}. There MT *mṭb'tyw 'l ṭb't h'pd* must be vocalized as plural, since the suffix *-yw* is only used on plural nouns. The MT vocalization

---

[69] Note the interesting reading in 2 Chron. 26:15: MT *ḥšbnwt mḥšbt ḥwšb*, OG μηχανας μεμηχανευμενας λογιστου. It provides two analogies for the usage adopted by Theodotion.

and all Greek witnesses take the two nouns as plural. A glance at the readings for this passage[70] reveals that *all* the witnesses except ȺɆ^{c} translate the suffix on *mṭbʿtyw* by the paraphrase των επ αυτου, with minor variants. This paraphrase is not found in any witness to the passage from Exodus 28. This is not surprising, since LXX^{2} obviously is independent of the OG parallel in its approach to the present items. The use of the singular for *mṭbʿtw* and *ṭbʿt* and also the translation of the preposition *m-* by εκ in item 41, but by απο in the OG for item p41, make this independence quite clear. In ȺɆ^{c} the effects of a secondary comparison of the parallels are no less clear. In the present items, ȺɆ^{c} insert the plural forms from the parallel passage. In the parallel, they reject the periphrastic treatment of the suffix in favor of the simple *eius* (= αυτου) found in the present items. Whether ȺɆ^{c} depend upon otherwise unattested readings of Aquila for these changes need not be decided here.

Theodotion is clearly following a consonantal text that agrees with the present MT exactly. He does not appear to be aware of the tradition preserved in the vocalization of the MT and presumably based on the parallel passage in Exod. 39:21 (LXX 36:29), where all witnesses, and the consonantal Hebrew text in one case, interpret the forms as plural. Only ȺɆ^{c} preserve evidence of a secondary comparison of the two passages and a mutual correction of each by the other. The person(s) responsible for this latter revisional activity must remain unidentified.

43. The Hebrew word *tklt* occurs some forty-nine times in the MT, and its normal OG equivalent is υακινθος or υακινθινος.[71] A preliminary

---

[70]MT מִטַּבְּעֹתָיו אֶל טַבְּעֹת הָאֵפֹד I OG απο (εκ n) των δακτυλιων (επωμιδων w) των (τω b) επ αυτου (αυτους aqu; αυτοις f) εις τους δακτυλιους της επωμιδος I GckmȺɆ^{c} απο των δακτυλιων των επ αυτου (αυτους m; *eius* for των επ αυτου ȺɆ^{c}) εις τους δακτυλιους (δακτυλους k) της επωμιδος I $ *mn ʿšqtʾ dʿlyh bʿšqtʾ dkbyntʾ*.

[71]H-R lists twelve instances in which OG υακινθινος represents MT *tklt* and thirty-one instances in which OG υακινθος does so: OG υακινθινος in Exod. 26:4; 28:27 (MT v.31); 36:30 (MT 39:22), 40 (MT 39:31); Num. 4:6, 9, 11, 12; 15:38; Esther 8:15 (only S^{2}); Exek. 23:6; Ecclus. 6:3; OG υακινθος in Exod. 25:4; 26:1, 31, 36; 27:16; 28:5, 8, 15, 29 (MT v.33),

investigation of the hexaplaric usages of θακινθος and υακινθινος listed in H-R revealed that the latter word, not attested in Aquila or Symmachus, is used by Theodotion only for MT *tklt*; υακινθος is similarly reserved for MT *tklt* by Aquila and Theodotion. Symmachus, however, uses υακινθος to represent both MT *tklt* and MT *tršyš*.[72]

The Hebrew word *ptyl* occurs only eleven times in the MT, but its treatment by the OG is much more varied.[73] Twice, in Gen. 38:18, 25, the OG equivalent is ορμισκος. In Exod. 39:3 (LXX 36:10) the OG has τριχες, while in Num. 19:15 the OT equivalent seems to be καταδεδεται. In Ezek. 40:3 the OG equivalent is σπαρτιον. In none of these five instances is there any evidence of a variant κλωσμα, nor does the Hebrew phrase *ptyl tklt* occur in any of them. Five of the remaining six occurrences of *ptyl* involve that phrase. The sole exception, Judg. 16:9, has the phrase *ptyl hnʿrt*. There the equivalents for *ptyl* are στρεμμα in Befijqrsuza$_2$, κλωσμα in AGMabchkmxyb$_2$𝔄, το κλωσμα (...το διαφθειρομενον) in dptv, το σπαρτιον (...το διαφθειρομενον) in glnow, and apparently στιππυον in $M^{mg}k^{mg}$.[74]

---

33 (MT v.37), 35:6, 23, 25; 36:9 (MT 39:2), 10 (MT 39:3), 12 (MT 39:5), 15 (MT 39:8), 29 (MT 39:21), 32 (MT 39:24), 37 (MT 39:29), 37:3 (MT 36:35), 5 (MT 36:37), 16 (MT 38:18); 39:13 (MT 39:1); 2 Chron. 2:7 (MT v.6, not in Bhc$_2$), 14 (MT v.13); 3:14; Jer. 10:9; Ezek. 27:7, 24; Ecclus. 45:10.

The only other MT equivalent for these two OG words that is cited in H-R is *thš*; it is represented by υακινθινος thirteen times, of which two are doubtful, and by υακινθος once. The only other OG equivalent for MT *tklt* noted in H-R is ολοπορφυρος in Num. 4:7; the same word also represents MT *ʾrgmn* in Num. 4:13. The other five occurrences of MT *tklt* are not clearly reflected in the OG.

[72]Symmachus uses υακινθος to represent MT *tršyš* in Exod. 28:20; Song of Sol. 5:14; Ezek. 1:16; 10:9. These readings are drawn primarily from Field.

[73]MT *ptyl* is found in Gen. 38:18, 25; Exod. 28:28, 37 (LXX v.33); 39:3 (LXX 36:10), 21 (LXX 36:29), 31 (LXX 36:40); Num. 15:38; 19:15; Judg. 16:9; Ezek. 40:3.

[74]The various equivalents for the entire MT phrase *ptyl hnʿrt* are: Befijqrsuza$_2$ στρεμμα στιππυου (στυππιου efisa$_2$)] AGMabchkmxyb$_2$𝔄 κλωσμα

The five occurrences of the phrase *ptyl tklt* are accompanied by more frequent use of κλωσμα to represent *ptyl*. In Num. 15:38, MT *ptyl tklt* is simply represented by OG κλωσμα υακινθινον. In Exod. 39:31 (LXX 36:40), where the OG equivalent is λωμα υακινθινον, the variant κλωσμα υακινθινον occurs in o. In Exod. 28:37 (LXX v.33), MT *ʿl ptyl tklt* is represented by OG επι υακινθου κεκλωσμενης. This is revised to επι κεκλωσμενου υακινθινου (-θου m), Syriac *ʿl pšl' dtklt'*, by ckm$\mathcal{S}$. Here it is the related participle κεκλωσμενης (-μενου) that represents *ptyl*. The phrase *bptyl tklt* occurs in the present item and in item p43 of Exod. 39:21 (LXX 36:29). In the latter, the OG equivalent is συνεχομενους εκ της υακινθου (with no variants preserved). In the present item, however, where the OG does not reflect the passage, LXX[2] has εν (+ τω $F^{a?}$ckm) κλωσματι (+ τω $F^{a?}$ck) υακινθινω (-θω c). This is reflected in Syriac *bpšl' dtklt'*, attributed to Theodotion by $\mathcal{S}^{txt}$. The Syriac version cannot reflect either the presence or the absence of the articles added by $F^{a?}$c k(m). The variant υακινθω in c is presumably secondary.

Thus the reading attributed to Theodotion in this item finds some support in OG usage elsewhere, although it is independent of OG usage in the parallel passage found in Exod. 36:29 (MT 39:21). Tendencies to extend the usage of κλωσμα for *ptyl* further than the OG had done have been noted in one witness for Exod. 39:31 (LXX 36:40) and many witnesses for Judg. 16:9. According to H-R, OG κλωσμα is never used for any other MT expressions, but Symmachus uses it in Jer. 52:21 to represent MT *ḥwṭ*. In Gen. 38:18, 25, Symmachus twice uses το περιτραχηλον (-λιον) or Syriac *dlwt qdl'* to represent MT *ptyl*, while Aquila introduces στρεπτος in Gen. 38:18. The use of υακινθινος to represent MT *tklt* is in conformity with one pattern of OG usage, as was noted above.

44. MT *lhywt* is adequately represented by ινα η, found in most of the witnesses that reflect this passage. The Syriac reading attributed to Theodotion, *lmhw'*, undoubtedly represents ινα η. The omission of η by sz and of ινα η by $F^{a?}$m is clearly secondary. The OG equivalent in item p44 of Exod. 36:29 (MT 39:21), συνπεπλεγμενους, is unexpected and

---

(στιππυον $M^{mg}k^{mg}$) του αποτιναγματος ⌶ dptv το (+ το t) κλωσμα του αποτιναγματος το διαφθειρομενον ⌶ glnow το σπαρτιον (+ απο l) του αποτιναγματος το διαφθειρομενον ⌶ $\mathcal{S}$ *bpšl' hy dmtyḥ* ⌶ $\mathcal{L}^{r}$ *spartum* ⌶ $\mathcal{E}$ *filum*.

may point to a different Hebrew expression in the OG *Vorlage* for that passage.

45. The various equivalents for MT *ḥšb* have been discussed in connection with item 38. The treatment of MT *h'pwd* has been considered under item 22.

46. MT *wl' yzḥ* is represented by και ου μη αποσπασης in Mdegjnp $s^{txt}tv^{txt}z^{txt}$, but by και ου μη αποσπασθη in ckAE^{c}. The latter variant is represented by Theodotion's Syriac reading in $𝔖^{txt}$, *wl' thw' mtplṭ'*. Similarly, ου μη αποσπασθη is attributed to ο'θ' by v^{mg} and to θ' by s^{mg}, and is found without names in z^{mg}. The defective reading of $F^{a?}$, και ου μη αποσπασ.., could reflect either alternative.

Both Aquila and Symmachus reduce the negative ου μη to one of its component parts and introduce new verbs to represent MT *yzḥ*. The readings are found in $s^{mg}v^{mg}z^{mg}$: α' (α'ο' s^{mg}; om z^{mg}) και ου σαλευθησεται σ' (om z^{mg}) και μη αποκλινηται (-ητε z^{mg}). The form αποκλινητε of z^{mg} is presumably a scribal error. The α'ο' attribution of s^{mg} is an error for α'. Compare the ο'θ' attribution of v^{mg}.

The Hebrew word *yzḥ* is presumably the Niphal of **zḥḥ* (to remove, be removed). The only other occurrence of the form is in item p46 of Exod. 39:21 (LXX 36:29). There MT *wl' yzḥ* is translated by ινα μη χαλαται, with no significant variants. No other forms of the verb **zḥḥ* are attested in the MT.

In this item, either the translation found in most witnesses presupposes a variant *tzḥ*, that is, second person singular of the Qal, or else it is a free translation. The clause as a whole functions as a negative purpose clause. Compare OG ινα μη in the parallel. This nuance, or the related nuance of prohibition, is preserved in the translation found in most witnesses to LXX^{2} (ου μη and the aorist subjunctive). Theodotion simply replaces the second person active verb with the third person passive of the same verb, retaining the construction with ου μη and the aorist subjunctive. The verb αποσπαν (to tear or drag away from) is perhaps too strong for the context. It occurs about ten times in the OG, with a variety of equivalents. The use of αποσπαν to represent the MT Hithpael of *prd* in Job 41:9 is attributed to Theodotion by 𝔖 according to Field. Aquila uses αποσπαν twice, in Num. 11:25 to represent the MT verb *'ṣl* and in Isa. 41:9 to represent the related MT noun *'ṣyl*. No instances of αποσπαν are attributed to Symmachus in H-R.

Aquila removes the verb αποσπαν, which he presumably wishes to reserve for MT *'ṣl*. He replaces it with σαλευειν, which is used often in the OG--but not in Genesis through Joshua--with a variety of equivalents. Aquila also omits μη and puts the verb in the future passive indicative. This is a more literal rendition of the Hebrew, but it loses the nuance of negative purpose or prohibition.

Symmachus' revision introduces a third verb, αποκλινειν, that is found very infrequently in the OG, and only here in Symmachus. Symmachus also simplifies the negative ου μη, but retains μη rather than ου. His construction of μη and the present subjunctive passive serves to reflect the nuance of negative purpose or prohibition that characterizes the Hebrew expression.

Theodotion thus revises the Greek version of LXX^2 only enough to reflect the person of the Hebrew verb more accurately. This revision is also found in ckA̸E̸^{c}. Both Aquila and Symmachus revise the Greek more extensively but independently of each other. Aquila's desire for literalness causes him to lose the true meaning of the Hebrew clause.

47. The representation of the composite Hebrew preposition *m-ʿl* by Greek απο (as in the OG for item p47) apparently was acceptable to Theodotion. At least there is no evidence that he changed it in any way.[75] The treatment of MT *h'pwd* has been discussed under item 22. The addition of ⋎ by svz and by Lagarde's C (in S̸) marks the completion of this six-verse passage not found in the OG and attributed to Theodotion by S̸^{txt}. The various investigations made above have suggested that Theodotion found this passage in the Greek text he was revising, and that he adopted it with various minor precisions and small corrections (compare especially items 29, 37, and 46). The few variants preserved from Aquila and Symmachus reveal that more extensive revisions and adaptations were undertaken by them. The exact extent of their work in this section cannot be recovered from the scanty evidence that has been preserved.

48-56. The MT and the OG are in substantial agreement for this verse.

56. MT *tmyd* is not represented by the OG. Only F^{b}cegjkmE̸^{c}S̸ insert δια παντος (*bkl zbn*). In item 68, the same insertion is attributed to σ'θ' by S̸. The intervening material (items 57-67) is not found in the MT,

---

[75]Note that this is in tension with the *tendency* of Barthélemy's ΚΑΙΓΕ recension to replace απο, επανω, etc., with επανωθεν or απανωθεν as the translation for MT *m-ʿl*. See *DA*, pp. 54-59.

and is under ÷ in Ꞩ. Hence the σ'θ' reading of item 68 in Ꞩ is to be equated with the reading found in F^{b}cegjkmꞨ^{c} and (as a doublet) in Ꞩ for item 56. It is an accurate reflection of MT *tmyd*. Compare, for example, item 83, where MT *tmyd* is reflected by OG δια παντος, Syriac *bkl zbn*.

57-67. This material, not supported by the present MT, is a shorter and divergent equivalent to MT vv. 23-28 (items 7-47). It is placed under ÷ in Ꞩ^{txt} and is omitted by F$^{?\ vid}$Ɇ^{c}Ł^{r}.

68. This σ'θ' reading of Ꞩ is a misplaced equivalent for MT *tmyd*. See the discussion under item 56.

69-83. In this verse, the MT and the OG are once again in substantial agreement. The only variants concerning Theodotion are found in items 71-72.

71-72. The cultic terms *ʾwrym* and *tmym* occur together five times in the MT, while *ʾwrym* occurs alone two, or possibly three, more times. The regular OG equivalents seem to have been δηλωσις or δηλοι for *ʾwrym* and αληθεια for *tmym*.[76]

---

76 Exod. 28:30 (LXX v.26): MT *ʾt hʾwrym wʾt htmym*, OG την δηλωσιν και την αληθειαν.

Lev. 8:8: MT *ʾt hʾwrym wʾt htmym*, OG την δηλωσιν και την αληθειαν.

Deut. 33:8: MT *tmyk wʾwryk*, OG δηλους (την δηλωσιν Cyr-ed) και (+ την Cyr) αληθειαν. Note that the OG transposes the two terms.

R. Klein, "Studies in the Greek Texts of the Chronicler" (Th.D. diss., Harvard University, 1966), pp. 309-311, 321-323, shows that LXX Esdras A represents the OG version of Ezra-Nehemiah, but in a text family different from that represented by the MT, while LXX Esdras B represents a revision to, or an independent translation of, the developing (Palestinian) Hebrew text. Thus Esdras B cannot be cited as the OG for the following two readings.

Ezra 2:63: MT *lʾwrym wltmym*; Neh. 7:65: MT *lʾwrym wtmym*; Esdras A 5.40 (= OG): ενδεδυμενος (*doctus in* Ł^{v}) την δηλωσιν και την αληθειαν. (The passage Esdras A 5:7-46 is parallel to both Ezra 2:1-70 and Neh. 7:6-73.)

Num. 27:21: MT *hʾwrym*, OG των δηλων (τον δηλον 1).

1 Sam. 28:6: MT *bʾwrym*, OG εν (om a$_{2}$) τοις δηλοις, j^{mg} σ' δια των δηλων.

Finally, in Isa. 24:15, MT *bʾrym* has been vocalized בָּאֻרִים. There is no equivalent in the OG or in any version.

In the present case, the variant τους φωτισμους και τας τελειοτητας is attributed to οι λ̥ by $s^{mg}v^{mg}$ and is found without names in $k^{mg}z^{mg}$. In $\mathfrak{S}^{mg}$, the reading *lnwhrʾ wlšwmlyʾ* is attributed to α'σ'θ'. The only difference between the two seems to be that the Greek nouns are plural, while the Syriac nouns are singular. This may be an error on the part of the Syriac translator, however. The reading of $\mathfrak{L}^{c}$, *lucentia et signacula*, may be derived from the Greek οι λ̥ variant.

In Lev. 8:8, j^{mg} attributes τους φωτισμους και τελειωσεις to α'θ'. The same reading, with the addition of τας before τελειωσεις, is found in M^{mg}. A related reading, τους φωτισμους και τους τελειους, is found in $s^{mg}z^{mg}$ and as a doublet before the OG reading in g.

In Deut. 33:8, φωτισμους is found in $F^{b\ mg}$ as a variant to OG δηλους.

In the revision of the OG, or the independent later translation of the proto-MT, found in Esdras B, these familiar variants again appear:

Esdras B 2:63: τοις φωτιζουσιν και τοις (ταις be_2) τελειοις (τελειωσεσι be_2).

Esdras B 17:65 (Neh. 7:65): (+των αδηλων c^a) φωτισων (τοις φωτισμοις και ταις τελειωσεσιν be_2).

Finally, in 1 Sam. 28:6, j^{mg} has α' εν φωτισμοις and z^{mg} has α' τοις φωτισμοις for MT *bʾwrym*.

While detailed investigation of these readings and of related variants would probably reveal more than one stage in the deliberate revision of Greek terms for MT *ʾwrym* and *tmym*, it is sufficient to note here that Aquila and Theodotion both agree on the rejection of OG δηλωσις (or δηλοι) and αληθεια as equivalents for the two Hebrew terms. In the present case they are joined by Symmachus, while in 1 Sam. 28:6 Symmachus' revision does not involve the rejection of δηλοι as an equivalent for MT *ʾwrym*.

Evaluation

Theodotion's revision in items 7-47 was based upon a Greek text that already contained a reflection of MT Exod. 28:23-28. His changes in the text were not extensive and were generally motivated by a desire for greater accuracy or for more consistency in translational equivalents. This is particularly clear in items 29, 37, and 46; items 18, 20, 23, and 26 remain uncertain. For the most part, readings retained by Theodotion were apparently felt by him to be satisfactory reflections of the Hebrew text that did not depart from acceptable OG usage. Occasional inadvertence on his part is not impossible (for example, item 23). In no case was it necessary to conclude that Theodotion's Hebrew text differed from the present MT.

Only scattered readings from Aquila and Symmachus have been preserved for this passage, in items 20, 23, 26, 29-30, 36-37, 38, 45, and 46. In general, these readings have tended to depart more radically from the earlier Greek text or from Theodotion's revision. Item 20 is uncertain, but Theodotion and Aquila, followed by m, may agree on a revision of LXX^2, while Symmachus retains the earlier reading. In items 23, 38, and 45, Aquila and Symmachus have different revisions of LXX^2 readings retained by Theodotion. In item 23, there is also a Theodotionic revision of LXX^2 that was apparently revised again -- independently of LXX^2, but in agreement with it -- by Aquila and Symmachus. In item 46, Aquila and Symmachus have different major revisions, while Theodotion has only a minor revision of LXX^2. In items 30 and 36, Aquila revises or replaces LXX^2 readings retained by both Theodotion and Symmachus. In items 29 and 37, Symmachus and Theodotion share revisions of LXX^2, while Aquila introduces several further changes. In item 29, Symmachus and Aquila also share a replacement of a word that is common to LXX^2 and Theodotion. In item 26, Aquila and Symmachus agree with LXX^2 against what seems to be an accidental variant in Theodotion. The restoration by Aquila and Symmachus may be independent of LXX^2, even though agreeing with it.

Aquila's revisions are often consistent with patterns introduced by him elsewhere as well (items 23, 29-30, 36, 38, and 45; perhaps also items 37 and 46). As in the earlier readings studied, Aquila seems here to have known and used Theodotion's revision as the basis for his own work (item 37; possibly also items 20 and 46). To some extent, Symmachus occupies an intermediate position between Theodotion and Aquila (items 29-30, 36-37).

Apart from the problematic reading in item 26 and possibly also the treatment of the suffix in item 23, there is no evidence that the readings attributed to Theodotion were posterior to Aquila and/or Symmachus, or that Aquila and Symmachus knew only a Greek text that had not been revised by Theodotion.

III The Relationship Between the Theodotionic Material and the Present MT in Exodus

In most cases, the Theodotionic readings preserved in Exodus agree exactly with the present MT. The definite article and the independent accusative marker are sometimes not reflected explicitly in Greek Theodotionic readings, and still less often in Syriac translations of these readings. All other aspects of the Hebrew text normally have distinct reflections in Theodotion's version. The previous two chapters amply illustrate and substantiate these generalizations.

This chapter is concerned with all readings that disagree with the MT and that seem to reflect a different Hebrew text, all readings that actually or apparently disagree with the MT for any other reason, and all readings that might raise problems about dependence on the MT. Instances of genuine disagreement with the MT are not too numerous. Those that can be attributed to variant Hebrew readings are so few as to be negligible, and most of these involve very minor differences, most frequently the presence or absence of the Hebrew conjunction *w*-. Almost all of the other readings are found to be consonant with the present MT. In no way do they imply or prove the existence of variants in Theodotion's Hebrew text. The problem readings that remain are too few in number or in kind to alter the picture. The Hebrew text presupposed by the extant Theodotionic material in Exodus is virtually identical with the present MT. While in some few instances Theodotion agrees with the Samaritan Pentateuch and/or the Peshitto against the MT, no consistent pattern of agreement against the MT can be established.

In the following lists, the format is adapted to the demands of the various types of reading. Each major witness is cited separately. The readings are introduced by the appropriate abbreviations or symbols[1] and

---

[1]The Samaritan Pentateuch (SP) is cited from A. von Gall, ed., *Der*

are separated from each other by a vertical line (|). The hexaplaric variants are introduced by the familiar abbreviations (ϑ′, α′ϑ′, α′σ′ϑ′), and the textual evidence is given in parentheses at the end of the reading.[2] Variants within a given reading are cited in parentheses at the appropriate place within the reading, followed by the supporting evidence. Unimportant variants are not always cited. When it is necessary to cite variants within longer variants or expansions, brackets are used within the parentheses. When MT variants are cited from Kennicott[3] or DeRossi,[4] they are preceded by "var." or by "or," and the supporting manuscripts are not listed. The same procedure is followed for variants within the other readings for which the textual evidence is not given.

Throughout the chapter, the significant items are numbered consecutively for ease in reference. Each item contains the appropriate readings from MT, SP, OG, Ꞩ, ϑ′, α′, σ′, and PS. The readings from TO are added only in the first section. The discussions are as brief as possible, and concern only those aspects of the Theodotionic readings that differ from the MT or that appear to do so.

---

hebräische Pentateuch der Samaritaner, 5 vols. in 1 (Berlin, 1966; a photomechanical reprint of the 1914-1918 Giessen edition). When von Gall's textual evidence for SP variants is given, his symbols are employed. The Peshitto (PS) is cited from W. E. Barnes, *et al.*, eds., *Pentateuchus syriace post Samuelem Lee* (London, 1914). The Targum Onkelos (TO) is cited from A. Sperber, ed., *The Bible in Aramaic Based on Old Manuscripts and Printed Texts*, Vol. I: *The Pentateuch According to Targum Onkelos* (Leiden, 1959). When Sperber's textual support for variants is given, his symbols are employed.

[2]When hexaplaric readings are quoted from Greek manuscripts, only the symbols are given (vz, jsvz, Mjv, and the like). When the readings are quoted from Ꞩ, textual and marginal citations are distinguished as Ꞩ^{txt} and Ꞩ^{mg}, respectively.

[3]B. Kennicott, ed., *Vetus Testamentum Hebraicum cum variis lectionibus*, Vol. I (Oxford, 1776).

[4]J. B. DeRossi, ed., *Variae lectiones Veteris Testamenti*, Vol. I (Amsterdam, 1969; a reprint of the 1784 Parma edition).

Theodotionic Expansions as Compared with the MT

1. Exod. 5:7: MT *šlšm*] SP *šlšwm*] OG και τριτην ημεραν (+ και το της σημερον AMdj^{mg}n[ημερου]pqtuv^{txt}z^{mg}a$_2$b$_2$c$_2$)] S̸ *wd-bywm'⋖ tlyty'*] θ' και της τριτης (jvz)] α' τριτην (jvz)] σ' και προτερον (jvz-- σ' variant includes part of preceding phrase as well)] PS *w'yk dmntml*] TO *wmdqmwhy*.

2. Exod. 12:7: MT *'l* (var. *w'l*) *hbtym*] SP (+ *w-* int.lin. E) *'l hbtym*] OG (+ και bcdk-nptwzd$_2$, Chr) εν (επι abwx) τοις (τους b'; των x) οικοις (οικους b'; οικων x)] S̸^{txt} *bt'*] α'σ'θ' *w'l* (S̸^{mg})] PS *w'l bt'*] TO *'l bty'*.

3. Exod. 13:13: MT *tpdh w'rptw*] SP *tpdnw w'rptw*] OG αλλαξης (απολυτρω[σης] F^{b}; + λυτρω ac) λυτρωση (εξαγορασης F^{b}) αυτο] S̸^{txt} *tḥlpywhy tprqywhy*] θ' *tprqywhy tpswq ḥsh* (S̸^{mg}; cf. θ' νωτοκοπησεις [-σης c$_2$; + αυτο j] in Mjvzc$_2$)] α' *tprwq tqṭw' qdlh* (S̸^{mg}; cf. α' τενοντωσεις [-νεντ- z; -σης c$_2$] in Mjvzc$_2$)] σ' *tprqywhy tqṭlywhy* (S̸^{mg}; cf. σ' αποκτενεις in Mjvzc$_2$)] σαμ. παραδωσης (c$_2$)] PS *tprqywhy tqṭlywhy*] TO *tprwq wtqpyh*. The Greek readings for θ', α', σ', and σαμ. refer to the second MT verb, and in one case also to its suffix.

4. Exod. 21:8: MT *'m r'h*] SP *'m r'h hy'*] OG εαν (+ δε AF^{a}bejptwx a$_2$b$_2$B̸C̸^{m}E̸) μη (om w) ευαρεστηση (ευαρεστειη n; ευαρεστη qu; αρεστη η w; αρεστη εστιν F$^{b?}$)] S̸^{txt} *'n l' tšpr*] θ' ει πονηρα εστιν (jsvz)] θ' *'n byst' 'ytyh* (S̸^{mg})] α' εαν κακισθη (vz; cf. s^{mg})] α' *'n dyn ttmkk* (S̸^{mg})] σ' ει μη αρεσκη (jsvz)] σ' *'n l' tšpr* (S̸^{mg})] PS *'n sny' hy*] TO *'m byšt*.

5. Exod. 25:20 (LXX v.19): MT *knpym*] SP = MT] OG τας πτερυγας (+ αυτων acmA̸B̸, Or-lat)] S̸^{txt} *gp'* ※σ'θ' *dylhwn*⋖] PS *gpyhwn*] TO *gdpyhwn*.

6. Exod. 26:13: MT *yhyh*] SP = MT] OG (+ και abcmA̸, Or-lat) εσται (om hk)] S̸^{txt} ※θ' *w⋖nhw'*] PS *nhw'*] TO *yhy*.

7. Exod. 27:14: MT *lktp*] SP = MT] OG τω κλιτει τω ενι] S̸^{txt} *lsṭr' ḥd*] α'σ'θ' *dktp' ḥd'* (S̸^{mg})] α'σ' τη ωμια (Mvz; also α' in s)] L̸^{r} *lateri unius*] n om.] PS *dsṭr'*] TO *l'br'*.

8. Exod. 28:6: MT *tklt*] SP = MT] OG om.] ckmA̸E̸^{c} και υακινθου] S̸ *wywqnt'*] θ' και υακινθου (vz; cf. j^{mg}s^{mg})] F^{b} εξ υακινθου] PS *tklt'*] TO *tkl'*.

9. Exod. 28:6: MT *twl't* (var. *wtwl't*; also *tl't*, *wtl't*, and *twl'*) *šny*

(var. *hšny*) | SP *wtwl*ʿ*t šny* | OG om. | F^{b}ckm𝔄𝔈^{c} και κοκκινου νενησμενου (κεκλωσμενου m; om 𝔈^{c}) | 𝔖^{txt} *wzḥwryt*ʾ *d*ʿ*zyl*ʾ | ϑʹ και κοκκινου νενησμενου (vz; cf. j^{mg}s^{mg}; cf. also ϑʹ *mšḥlp*ʾ in 𝔖^{mg}) | σʹ *wzḥwryt*ʾ *trynt ṣwb*ʿʾ (𝔖^{mg}) | αʹ *wtwl*ʿ*t*ʾ *mšḥlpt*ʾ (𝔖^{mg}) | PS *wṣwb*ʿʾ *dzḥwryt*ʾ | TO *wṣb*ʿ (*ṣb*ʿ JBFab) *zhwry*.

10. Exod. 28:11: MT *mšbṣwt* | SP = MT | OG om. | cj^{mg}m𝔄 και συνεσφραγισμενους | s^{mg}y$^{b?}$ και συνεσφιγμενους | 𝔖^{txt} *wḥzyqn* ʾ*kḥd*ʾ | z^{mg} και συνεσφισμενους | ϑʹ και συνεσφραγισμενους (sv) | ϑʹ και συνεσφιγμενους (z) | σʹ και συνεσφιγμενους (v^{vid}) | αʹ εσφιγμενους (sv) | αʹ *mḥšqt*ʾ (𝔖^{mg}) | σʹ *m*ʿ*tdt*ʾ (𝔖^{mg}; but *m*ʿ*tdt*ʾ in B) | PS *wmšḥn* | TO *mrmṣn*.

11. Exod. 32:2: MT *bnykm* | SP = MT | OG om. | F^{b}ckm𝔄𝔏^{r} και (+ των F^{b}) υιων υμων (om k𝔄; m𝔏^{r} omit the following OG phrase) | ϑʹ *wdbny*ʾ *dylkwn* (𝔖^{txt}) | PS *wdbnykwn* | TO *bnykwn*.

12. Exod. 32:18: MT *qwl* ʿ*nwt gbwrh* | SP = MT | OG φωνη εξαρχοντων κατ ισχυν | 𝔖^{txt} *ql*ʾ *dhnwn dm*ʿ*nyn bḥyl*ʾ | ϑʹ *ql*ʾ *dqrb*ʾ *dm*ʿ*nyn bḥyl*ʾ (𝔖^{mg}; *bnḥl*ʾ was read by C in B) | αʹ *ql*ʾ *dhlyn dm*ʿ*nyn bḥyl*ʾ (𝔖^{mg}; *bnḥl*ʾ was read by C in B) | σʹ *g*ʿ*t*ʾ *dhnwn dpqdyn gnbrwt*ʾ (𝔖^{mg}) | PS *ql*ʾ *dmmll*ʾ *dgnbr*ʾ | TO *ql gybryn dnṣḥyn bqrb*ʾ.

13. Exod. 35:11 (LXX v.10): MT ʾ*t* (var. *w*ʾ*t*) ʾ*hlw* | SP *w*ʾ*t* ʾ*hlw* | OG και τα (om egj) παραρυματα (+ αυτης F^{b}ckm𝔄) | 𝔖^{txt} *wlzqwry ṣbt*ʾ ※ ʿʹ *dylh*↙ | αʹσʹϑʹ *wltksyt*ʾ *dylh* (𝔖^{mg}) | οι λ̥ και την σκεπην αυτης (Msv; cf. z^{mg}) | F$^{b\ mg}$ και τας τενδ... | PS *wprsh* | TO *yt* (*wyt* cdl) *prsyh*.

14. Exod. 35:11 (LXX v.10): MT ʾ*t* (var. *w*ʾ*t*) *qrsyw* | SP *w*ʾ*t qrsyw* | OG και τα διατονια (+ αυτης F^{b}cm𝔄) | 𝔖^{txt} *wltwlb*ʾ ※ *g*ʹ *dylh*↙ | v^{mg} και τα διατονια | σʹϑʹ και τας περονας αυτης (v) | αʹ και τους κρικους αυτης (v) | σʹϑʹ ʿ*b*ʾ (𝔖^{mg}) | αʹσʹϑʹ *wlqwlqs*ʾ *dylh* (𝔖^{mg}) | αʹ κρικους (Msvz; cf. *b*^{mg}) | σʹ περονας (Msvz) | F$^{b\ mg}$ και τα κρικ... | PS *wprpwhy* | TO (+ *yt* 𝔅Q; + *wyt* l) *pwrpwhy*.

15. Exod. 35:11 (LXX v.10): MT ʾ*t* (var. *w*ʾ*t*) *bryḥ*- (with plural vocalization; var. *bryḥy*-) | SP *w*ʾ*t bryḥy*- | OG και τους μοχλους | 𝔖 *wlmwkl*ʾ | σʹϑʹ και τους μοχλους (v) | PS *wmwkl*- | TO (+ *yt* 𝔅Q) ʿ*brw*- (*w*ʿ*brw*- l).

16. Exod. 35:11 (LXX v.10): MT ʾ*t* (var. *w*ʾ*t*) ʿ*mdyw* (var. ʿ*mwdyw*) | SP *w*ʾ*t* ʿ*mdyw* (var. ʿ*mwdyw*) | OG και τους στυλους (*vectes earum* 𝔈^{c}; + αυτης F^{b}cm𝔄) | 𝔖 ⸗*wl*ʿ*mwd*ʾ↙ ※ *g*ʹ *dylh*↙ | ϑʹ ※ και τους στυλους (v) | αʹ τους στυλους αυτης (v) | σʹ και τους πασσαλους αυτης

(v) ⁅ PS *w'ḥwdwhy* ⁅ TO (+ *yt* ǤQ) *'mwdwhy* (*w'mwdwhy* 1). For the omission of αυτης in ϑ', see no. 31 below.

17. Exod. 35:12 (LXX v.11): MT *'t* (var. *w't*) *h'rn* (var. *h'rwn*) ⁅ SP *'t h'rwn* ⁅ OG και την κιβωτον του (om F[b?]k) μαρτυριου (om F[b?]k) ⁅ Ꞩ *wlq'bwt'* ÷*dshdwt'* (+ ↙ B) ⁅ ϑ' και την κιβωτον (v) ⁅ σ' την κιβωτον (v) ⁅ α' συν το γλωσσοκομον (v) ⁅ PS *wqbwt'* ⁅ TO *yt 'rwn'*.

18. Exod. 35:35: MT *btwl't* (var. *wbtwl't*; also *btl't* and *wbtl't*) *hšny* ⁅ SP *wbtwl't hšny* ⁅ OG (+ και εν ckmȺɆ[c]) τω κοκκινω (+ τω αλλοιουμενω cmȺɆ[c]) ⁅ Ꞩ[txt] ※ ϑ' ...*w*↙*bzḥwryt'* ※ *dmštgny'*↙ ⁅ ϑ' και εν τω κοκκινω τω αλλοιουμενω (svz) ⁅ α' εν σκωληκος τω διαφορω (svz) ⁅ σ' και του κοκκινου του διβαφου (svz) ⁅ PS (out of place) *wbṣwb'' dzḥwryt'* ⁅ TO *bṣb'* (*wbṣb'* kl) *zhwry*.

19. Exod. 37:14 (LXX 38:10): MT *hyw* (var. *yhyw*) ⁅ SP = MT ⁅ OG om. ⁅ G(under ※)cȺɆ[c] και εγενοντο ⁅ ϑ' *whwy* (Ꞩ[txt]) ⁅ PS *hwy* ⁅ TO *hw'h* (*hww* an).

20. Exod. 37:14 (LXX 38:10): MT *btym* (var. *lbtym*) *lbdym* ⁅ SP = MT ⁅ OG ευρεις (+ τοις διωστηρσιν b) ...τοις διωστηρσιν((λοστοις η μοχλοις F[b]) ⁅ G(under ※)cȺɆ[c] εις θηκας τοις (om Ⱥ) αναφορευσιν (om Ⱥ), with a rough equivalent of the OG version retained earlier as a doublet in G(under ÷)cȺ ⁅ ϑ' *ltyq'* *lqwp'* (Ꞩ[txt], with an equivalent of the OG version retained earlier under ÷: *ptyt'*...*bḥšq'*) ⁅ F[b] (ενδοθεν) των αναφορων ⁅ PS *dwkt' lqwp'* ⁅ TO *'tr' l'ryḥy'*.

21. Exod. 37:25 (MT): MT *'mh* ⁅ SP = MT ⁅ OG om. ⁅ ckȺ πεντε πηχεων ⁅ Ꞩ[txt](under ※) *wdḥmš 'm'* ⁅ α'σ'ϑ' *wd'mt'* (Ꞩ[txt]) ⁅ F[b]Ɇ[c] πηχεος ⁅ PS *'m'* ⁅ TO *'mt'*.

22. Exod. 39:33 (LXX 39:14): MT *'t h'hl* ⁅ SP = MT ⁅ OG και την σκηνην (σκεπην ckmȺɆ[c]) ⁅ ϑ' *wlstr'* (Ꞩ[txt]) ⁅ PS *mškn'* ⁅ TO *yt mškn'*[(2)].

23. Exod. 39:33 (LXX 39:14): MT *qršyw* ⁅ SP = MT ⁅ OG om. ⁅ cmȺ και σανιδας αυτης ⁅ ϑ' *wdp'* *dylh* (Ꞩ[txt]) ⁅ Ɇ[c] *et circulos eius* ⁅ PS *wdpwhy* ⁅ TO *dpwhy*. One additional noun has been inserted into the list of Ɇ[c] (preceded by *et*), and two additional nouns have been inserted into the list of PS (each preceded by *w-*).

Seventeen of the foregoing twenty-three Theodotionic expansions involve the conjunction και (nos. 8-10, 14-18) or its Syriac equivalent *w-* (nos. 1, 2, 6, 11, 13, 19, 21-23). Eight times (nos. 2, 9, 13-18) some

MT manuscripts have the conjunction *w*-, although it is not printed in the text of BH^3. Two more Theodotionic expansions involve the insertion of a possessive pronoun (no. 5) or an accusative pronominal suffix (no. 3), while the remaining four concern the addition of the forms εστιν (no. 4), *ḥd'* (no. 7), *dqrb'* (no. 12), and *l*- (no. 20). According to Kennicott, the last of these is supported by four MT manuscripts.

The following chart synopsizes the support for these expansions in the various witnesses. The following symbols are used: x = the presence of the plus; - = the absence of the plus; 0 = the witness does not reflect the phrase or verse in which the plus occurs, or its reading is not attested. A parenthesis around one of these symbols means that the interpretation is only probable. When a few manuscripts differ from most manuscripts within a witness, the symbol for the majority is given first, followed by the symbol for the minority in parentheses. The seventeen instances of the conjunction και/*w*- are listed first, followed by the other six items.

Item	*MT*	*SP*	*PS*	*TO*	*OG*	*S*^{txt}	α'	σ'	*Plus in* ϑ'
1.	-	-	x	x	x	x	-	(x)	και
2.	- (x)	- (x)	x	-	- (x)	-	x	x	*w*-
6.	-	-	-	-	- (x)	(= ϑ')	0	0	*w*-
8.	-	-	-	-	0 (x)	x	0	0	και
9.	- (x)	x	x	x (-)	0 (x)	x	x	x	και
10.	-	-	x	-	0 (x)	x	(-)	(x)	και
11.	-	-	x	-	0 (x)	(= ϑ')	0	0	*w*-
13.	- (x)	x	x	- (x)	x	x	x	x	*w*-
14.	- (x)	x	x	- (x)	x	x	x	x	και/*w*-
15.	- (x)	x	x	- (x)	x	x	0	x	και
16.	- (x)	x	x	- (x)	x	x (under ÷)	(-)	x	και
17.	- (x)	-	x	-	x	x	(-)	(-)	και
18.	- (x)	x	x	- (x)	- (x)	(= ϑ')	-	x	και/*w*-
19.	-	-	-	-	0 (x)	(= ϑ')	0	0	*w*-
21.	-	-	-	-	0 (-)	x (under ※)	x	x	*w*-
22.	-	-	-	-	x	(= ϑ')	0	0	*w*-
23.	-	-	x	-	0 (x)	(= ϑ')	0	0	*w*-
3.	-	x	x	-	-	x	-	x	acc. suffix (on first verb)

Item	*MT*	*SP*	*PS*	*TO*	*OG*	*$\mathfrak{S}^{txt}$*	α′	σ′	*Plus in* ϑ′
4.	-	x	x	-	- (x)	-	-	-	εστιν/*ʾytyh*
5.	-	-	x	x	- (x)	(= σ′ϑ′)	0	x	*dylhwn*
7.	-	-	-	-	x	x	x	x	*ḥdʾ*
12.	-	-	-	(x ?)	-	-	-	-	*dqrbʾ*
20.	- (x)	-	-	-	- (x)	(= ϑ′)	0	0	*l-*

Only four instances of the expansion και/*w-* are not supported by one or more of the major witnesses (SP, PS, TO, OG) or by variants within the MT tradition: items 6, 8, 19, 21. The last of these is in a joint α′σ′ϑ′ citation, and the expansion may be due to the Syriac scribe. $\mathfrak{S}^{txt}$ also has the unsupported conjunction against the other hexaplaric witnesses (ck$\mathfrak{A}$), while the second α′σ′ϑ′ *wdʾmtʾ* in $\mathfrak{S}^{mg}$ for the same verse correctly has *w-* to represent the conjunction in MT *wʾmh*. There is no need to discuss the seventeen και/*w-* expansions in Theodotion at length. In view of the general instability of the conjunction *w-* in the transmission and/or translation of Biblical texts, these expansions are of little importance. Even if all of them were supported by Theodotion's Hebrew text, this would not mean that it differed significantly from the MT.[5]

The other six Theodotionic expansions, with the possible exception of item 12, are also supported either by variants within the MT tradition (item 20) or by at least one of the major witnesses (items 3 and 4 by SP and PS, item 5 by PS and TO, item 7 by OG, and item 12 apparently by TO). Each of these expansions must be discussed briefly.

The expansion *dqrbʾ* in item 12 is presumably due to the phrase *qwl mlḥmh* in the MT for the preceding verse (Exod. 32:17). This expansion was discussed in the seventh reading of chapter one, where it was argued that the expansion is secondary in the Theodotionic material. The possible agreement between this plus and *bqrbʾ* in TO need not mean that Theodotion's Hebrew text, or any other Hebrew text, actually had such an expansion in Exod. 32:18.

The expansion *l-* (= *εις) in item 20 may reflect the longer *lbtym*

---

[5]Note that Theodotion represents MT *w-* over 150 times (see Appendix B, *s.v.*), and fails to reflect it only three times (items 24b, 28, 32, in the following section).

found in four of Kennicott's manuscripts. It could also be a translational expansion in Theodotion, due to his earlier translation of MT *lbtym lbdym* by εις θηκας τοις αναφορευσιν in Exod. 30:4.

In item 7, the expansion *ḥdʾ* (common to α'σ'θ') is related to the OG plus ενι ($\$^{txt}$ *ḥd*). According to $\$^{mg}$, α'σ'θ' replaced OG τω κλιτει ($\$^{txt}$ *lsṭrʾ*) with a new form *dktpʾ* (perhaps = τη ωμια, attributed to α'σ' by $M^{mg}v^{mg}z^{mg}$), but failed to omit the subsequent OG plus. Instead they presumably replaced OG τω ενι with the appropriate feminine form. While it is not impossible that the originator of the reading common to α'σ'θ', presumably Theodotion, had an expanded Hebrew text, the absence of the expansion in all the independent witnesses suggests rather that the OG plus was simply not seen to be superfluous. The presence of the longer MT phrase *wlktp hšnyt*[6] in the following verse (Exod. 27:15) might have made the OG plus in v. 14 less evidently superfluous to Theodotion.

Theodotion's εστιν/*ʾytyh* in item 4 reflects an expansion equivalent to that found in SP (*hyʾ*) and reflected in PS (*hy*).[7] The OG does not reflect the expansion, while Aquila and Symmachus make no effort to represent it.

In item 3, Theodotion and Symmachus agree with SP, PS, and $\$$ in supplying a pronominal object for MT *tpdh*(2). This expansion is not unexpected, because it makes explicit what the MT and the OG necessarily implied.[8] Aquila omits the object, in conformity with the present MT.

Finally, in item 5, σ'θ' agree with PS and TO in supplying a possessive suffix for MT *knpym*. This would involve at most the insertion of *h*

---

[6]OG και το κλιτος το δευτερον] $\$^{txt}$ *wsṭrʾ hw trynʾ*] α'σ'θ' *wlktpʾ trynytʾ* ($\$^{mg}$).

[7]Since it occurs in SP, this plus may properly be called "Palestinian."

[8]See the further discussion of this reading under item 28 below, where it is suggested that θ', PS, $\$^{txt}$, and σ' may have misdivided MT *tpdh wʿrptw* as *tpdhw ʿrptw, while SP would have an independent expansion of the MT. In this case, there would be no quantitative difference between Theodotion's Hebrew text and the MT here. Aquila followed the MT word-division, but he failed to note the omission of any reflection of the MT conjunction.

before the final *m* in *knpym*.[9] Once again the expansion only makes explicit what the MT had already implied.

It is at least possible that all six of these longer readings were supported by Theodotion's Hebrew text, though this is less likely for items 7 and 12. Even if these six minor expansions and the seventeen και/*w*- expansions were all present in the Hebrew text used by Theodotion, that text would still be virtually identical with the present MT. Neither in number nor in kind are these twenty-three longer readings of any real significance.

Theodotionic Omissions as Compared with the MT

24. (a, b). Exod. 1:19: MT *ʾlhn hmyldt* (הַמְיַלְּדֹת) *wyldw* ‖ SP = MT ‖ OG προς αυτας τας μαιας και ετικτον ‖ $ *lwthyn ḥyt' wyldn hwy* θ' προς αυτας τικτουσι (Nobil.--cited by Field) ‖ σ' τας μαιας τικτουσιν (Nobil.--cited by Field) ‖ ℒ *obstetrices pariunt* ‖ PS *ʿlyhyn ḥyt' yldH.*

25. Exod. 3:14: MT *ʾhyh ʾšr* (om 244) *ʾhyh* ‖ SP = MT ‖ OG εγω ειμι ο ων ‖ $ *ʾnʾ ʾyty hw dʾytwhy* ‖ α'θ' εσομαι εσομαι (64--cited by Field) ‖ Graeco-Ven. εσ. ος εσ. (cited by Field) ‖ PS *ʾhyh ʾšr ʾhyh.*

26 (a, b). Exod. 5:3: MT *bdbr ʾw bḥrb* ‖ SP = MT ‖ OG θανατος η φονος (φοβος A*vid m) ‖ $txt *mwtʾ ʾw qṭlʾ* ‖ θ' *mwtʾ ʾw sypʾ* ($mg) ‖ α' λοιμου σ' η μαχαιρα θ' η ρομφαια (*b*) ‖ α'σ' λοιμος η μαχαιρα (Mv; cf. zmg) ‖ α'σ' λιμος η μαχαιρα (F^I; σ' for α'σ' in F?) ‖ α' *bmwtʾ ʾw bsypʾ* ($mg) ‖ PS *bḥrbʾ ʾw bmwtʾ.*

27. Exod. 12:42: MT *hwʾ hlylh hzh* ‖ SP = MT ‖ OG εκεινη (αυτη m; om 71) η νυξ αυτη (om m) ‖ $txt *hw llyʾ hw* ‖ θ' *hw lllyʾ* ($mg) ‖ α'σ' *hnʾ llyʾ hnʾ* ($mg) ‖ PS *hw llyʾ hnʾ.*

28. Exod. 13:13: See the variants listed under item 3.

29. Exod. 28:27 (MT): MT *mmwl pnyw* ‖ SP = MT ‖ OG om. ‖ Fa?Mcdegjkm nstvtxt zAℒc εκ του κατα προσωπον (-που n; + αυτ.. Fb) ‖ θ' *mn lwqbl prṣwpʾ* ($txt) ‖ ο'θ' and σ' εκ του κατα προσωπον (v) ‖ α' απο εναντιον προσωπου αυτου (v) ‖ PS *mn lwqbl ʾpyh.*

---

[9]The expansion could also mean that the ending *-ym* was taken as equivalent to *-yhm*, perhaps with the assimilation of the *h* to the preceding semi-vowel *y* (**-eyhem* > **-eyyem*, or the like).

30. Exod. 31:13: MT *(w)bynykm* ‖ SP *(w)bynkm* ‖ OG εν υμιν ‖ $ *(w)bkwn* ‖ σ'θ' υμιν (130--a one-word reading cited by Field) ‖ n υμιν ‖ Iren. *uobis* ‖ Thdt. τοις υιοις ισραηλ ‖ PS *(w)lkwn.*

31. Exod. 35:11 (LXX v.10): See the variants listed under item 16.

32. Exod. 38:2 (LXX 38:22): MT *wyʿś* ‖ SP = MT ‖ OG om. ‖ F^b cA$^c και (after εποιησεν A; om c) εποιησεν ‖ θ' *ʿbd* ($^txt) ‖ PS *wʿbd.*

Two of the nine numbers listed above include two items each, which can be denoted by a and b: 24a. MT *hmyldt*; 24b. MT *w-*; 26a. MT *b(dbr)*; 26b. MT *b(ḥrb)*. Of the eleven Theodotionic omissions included in the list, three concern the conjunction *w-* (nos. 24b, 28, 32), two the pronominal suffix on a noun (nos. 29, 31), two the preposition *b-* (nos. 26a, 26b), two the pronouns *ʾšr* (no. 25) and *hzh* (no. 27), one the noun *hmyldt* (no. 24a), and the remaining one possibly the preposition *byn-* (no. 30). Number 30 should probably be ruled out of consideration here, since the one-word citation could also be interpreted as an agreement with a single OG word. Theodotion would be expected to replace OG εν with another preposition better suited to represent MT *byn*. He uses Syriac *bmṣʿt* once in Exod. 11:7 and twice in Exod. 31:17, and Syriac *bynt* twice in Exod. 40:30 (LXX v.26) for this purpose. Either or both of these might represent Greek ανα μεσον or a similar phrase. Apart from no. 30, where the short reading of n was a factor, instances in which an apparent omission occurs at the beginning or the end of a Theodotionic citation are not listed, since the word or words in question may simply not have been included by the scribe who made the particular citation. All omissions that come in the middle of longer citations are included.

The failure to represent the suffixes on MT *pnyw* (no. 29) and MT *ʿmdyw* (no. 31) is probably due to carelessness or inadvertence. In each case the suffix was not represented in the Greek text that Theodotion was presumably revising, and he simply failed to note the omission. In no. 29 Aquila supplied αυτου, while in no. 31 Aquila and Symmachus both supplied αυτης. Each time both SP and PS preserve the MT suffix. It is virtually certain that the two suffixes were also present in Theodotion's Hebrew text, though not in his Greek original.

The two omissions in no. 26 are somewhat more problematic. Either the OG translation for the last part of Exod. 5:3 was rather free, or else it reflected a variant Hebrew text. While there is some confusion in the hexaplaric readings that have been preserved, it is clear that

Theodotion differed from the OG on only one point, the use of ρομφαια (*syp'*) rather than OG φονος to represent MT *(b)ḥrb*. He apparently made no attempt to reflect the two MT prepositions, which are also present in SP and in the somewhat different version of PS, or to replace OG θανατος with a more accurate translation for MT *(b)dbr*. According to $\mathcal{S}^{mg}$, but not $F^{I\ mg}M^{mg}V^{mg}$, Aquila introduced a reflection of the two prepositions into his version. While Theodotion's Hebrew text may have differed from the MT here, it is equally possible, if not more likely, that he either failed to note the full extent of the discrepancy between the OG and the MT or for some reason decided against revising the last part of the verse completely.

The omission of any representation for MT *'šr* in no. 25, in a reading attributed to α'θ', is suspect. It is unlikely that *'šr* was missing from Theodotion's Hebrew text, although haplography, from the second aleph to the third, is not impossible. Kennicott's MT manuscript 244 has actually suffered such a haplography. More probably the omission is a secondary scribal error, perhaps by the scribe who copied the reading into manuscript 64. A haplography in an abbreviated text like that of Graeco-Ven. would be very easy (εσ. ος εσ.).

The reading from which no. 27 was taken is corrupt (see no. 37 below), and the omission of any reflection for MT *hzh* may also be a secondary scribal error. Although no other witnesses, except the hexaplaric m, omit the word, a haplography in Theodotion's Hebrew text from the final letter of *hlylh* to the final letter of *hzh* is not impossible.

A noun and the following conjunction are omitted in no. 24. Both words are in SP and are reflected in the OG. The conjunction is omitted by PS and also by σ' and Ɇ. These last two omit the OG phrase that immediately precedes the OG noun omitted by Theodotion. The two items must be discussed separately. The omission of the conjunction may have characterized Theodotion's Hebrew text. Compare PS, Ɇ, and σ'; note also the change from aorist to present tense by θ', σ', and Ɇ. The noun and its article were probably lost by haplography in the Greek text (προς αυτας τας μαιας). A similar but less obvious type of haplography may be involved in the omission of OG προς αυτας or of some other phrase corresponding to MT *'lhn* in σ' and Ɇ.

In nos. 28 and 32, Theodotion fails to reflect MT *w*-. In each case it is possible that his Hebrew text did not contain the conjunction. In no. 28, where the OG did not reflect the conjunction and where all three versions make extensive changes without inserting a reflection for MT *w*-, this seems quite likely. Indeed it is not impossible that PS, $\not{S}^{txt}$, ϑ', and σ' simply divided MT *tpdh w'rptw* as **tpdhw 'rptw*. SP *tpdnw w'rptw* could be an independent expansion of either Hebrew form. Aquila followed the MT division and omitted the unsupported suffix, but he failed to insert a translation of the MT conjunction.

In no. 32, it is more likely that Theodotion's Hebrew text had *wy'ś*, and that either he neglected to translate the conjunction or a subsequent scribe omitted it by mistake. The conjunction is present in SP and PS, as well as F^bȺɆ^c, and even c and ϑ' have the verb in the past tense.

The eleven Theodotionic omissions listed above are not very impressive in view of the approximately 1600 Hebrew items covered by the extant Theodotionic material in Exodus. One (no. 30) is doubtful, three (nos. 24a, 25, 27) are probably due to secondary scribal error, two (nos. 29, 31) do not point to a different Hebrew text, two (nos. 26a, 26b) are problematic but relatively minor, and the remaining three (nos. 24b, 28, 32) concern only the absence of the MT conjunction *w*-.

Textual Corruptions Within the Theodotionic Material

33. Exod. 5:4: MT *tpry'w*] SP *tprydw*] OG διαστρεφετε] Ꞩ *mdwdyn 'ntwn*] ϑ' διασκεδαζετε (Mvz)] ϑ' διασωζετε (c_2)] α' αποπεταζετε (Mvz)] σ' αποτρεπετε (Mvz)] σ' αποστρεφετε (c_2)] PS *mbṭlyn 'ntwn*.

These variants have been discussed in chapter one, in connection with the second reading (Exod. 32:25), where Theodotion's διασκεδαζετε and Aquila's αποπεταζετε were shown to be part of their respective consistent patterns of translation for MT *pr'* in Exodus. The Theodotionic variant διασωζετε is presumably secondary, especially since both readings in c_2^{mg} differ from those attested elsewhere. There is no evident relation between any of these variants and SP *tprydw*. In Exod. 32:25, SP has *pr'* twice, in agreement with the MT.

34. Exod. 5:17: MT *hm ylkw wqššw*] SP *hm ylkw wyqššw*] OG αυτοι πορευεσθωσαν και συναγαγετωσαν] $\not{S}^{txt}$ (no ※ or ⋎) α'ϑ' *hnwn n'zlwn wnknšwn*] ϑ' αυτοι πορευεσθωσαν (πορευθεντες j) και καλαμασθωσαν (jvz)] α' αυτοι πορευεσθωσαν (jvz)] σ' αυτοι απερχομενοι

καλαμασθωσαν (jvz) I α'σ'θ' καλαμασθωσαν (Mv; cf. $j^{mg}z^{mg}c_2^{mg}$) I PS *hnwn n'zlwn nqšwn*.

The substitution of πορευθεντες for πορευεσθωσαν in the θ' reading of j^{mg} is clearly secondary, perhaps influenced by the participial construction found in Symmachus. Note that the conjunction και is retained after πορευθεντες, resulting in an awkward grammatical construction. There is no way to tell whether any or all of the Greek versions were based upon SP *wyqššw* rather than upon MT *wqššw*.

35. Exod. 7:24: MT *lštt mmymy hy'r* I SP *lštwt mmymy hy'r* I OG πιειν υδωρ απο (εκ $Fcegj^{txt}v^{txt}z^{txt}$) του ποταμου (ρειθρου F^b) I $\text{\$}^{txt}$ *lmšt' mỹ' mn nhr'* I θ' πιειν (om c_2--part of a longer haplography) εκ του υδατος του ποταμου (vzc_2) I θ' *lmšt' mỹ' mn dnhr'* ($\text{\$}^{mg}$) I σ' πιειν εκ του υδατος του ποταμου ($jvzc_2$) I σ' *lmšt' mn mỹ' dnhr'* ($\text{\$}^{mg}$) I α' πιειν εκ του υδατος του ποταμου ($jvzc_2$) I α' *mn mỹ' mỹ' dḥdy' lmšt'* ($\text{\$}^{mg}$) I PS *lmšt' mn mỹ' dnhr'*.

While differences in order and vocabulary between the three versions have been preserved in $\text{\$}^{mg}$, a single form, which is apparently that of Symmachus, has been attributed to all three in the Greek witnesses. According to \$, Theodotion's reading followed the format of the OG, Symmachus reflected the MT structure, and Aquila inexplicably shifted the verb to the end of the sentence. Aquila also introduced lexical changes: Syriac *ḥdy'* for MT *y'r* (cf. ρειθρου of F^b) and a double Syriac reading, *mỹ' mỹ'*, to represent the reduplicated *mymy* of the MT. If \$ is correct, Theodotion simply failed to rearrange the OG version. This does not necessarily mean that his Hebrew text followed an order different from that common to the MT, SP, and PS. If the Greek witnesses are correct, however, and if the Syriac variations are secondary, then Theodotion and the other two versions shared a common revision of the OG to reflect the order of the Hebrew text more accurately. Of the two alternatives, the first is more likely.

36. Exod. 12:26: MT *lkm* I SP = MT I OG om. I acegjkmxA̸, Or-gr$\frac{1}{2}$ υμιν I α'σ' *lkwn* ($\text{\$}^{txt}$) I θ' *ln* ($\text{\$}^{mg}$) I PS om.

The Theodotionic variant represents *ημιν, a simple itacistic corruption of the correct reading υμιν (= α'σ' *lkwn*). The corruption of the Theodotionic reading took place in Greek, so that the Hebrew reading on which it was originally based was identical with that found in the MT and SP. There is no reason to posit a hypothetical variant **lnw* in Theodotion's Hebrew text.

37. Exod. 12:42: MT *lyhwh šmrym* I SP = MT I OG προφυλακη (προσφυλακη d; προς φυλακην m; + εστιν dnptx$\not{L}^{z\ vid}$) κυριω (τω $\overline{κω}$ Fdlnptvxz c_2; $\overline{κυ}$ cefgj$\not{B}^{vid}\not{E}^{vid}\not{L}^{z}$; om a) I $\not{S}^{txt}$ *mṭrt' lmry'* I bkw κυριω προφυλακη I θ' *dmṭrt'...lpypy dnṭwrt'* ($\not{S}^{mg}$) I α'σ' *lpypy dmṭrt'* ($\not{S}^{mg}$) I α' παρατηρησεων (vz) I α' παρατηρησεως (c_2) I σ' παρατετηρημενη (vz) I σ' παρατετηρημενον (c_2) I $F^{b\ mg}$ φυλαγματων I PS *lmry' nṭyr' hw'*.

Two equivalents of MT *šmrym* have been preserved as doublets in the Theodotionic reading of $\not{S}^{mg}$. The first, *dmṭrt'*, is out of place at the beginning of the longer citation. It is identical with the Syriac form attributed to α'σ' by $\not{S}^{mg}$, and is closely related to the reading of $\not{S}^{txt}$. It is probably to be regarded as an erroneous repetition of the α'σ' term (which was given just before the θ' reading in $\not{S}^{mg}$). The second form, *dnṭwrt'*, is presumably Theodotion's own equivalent. Its Greek original is uncertain, but it surely represents MT *šmrym*. The fact that all the Syriac forms and most of the Greek ones are singular does not mean that a singular variant was present in the Hebrew texts available to Theodotion, Aquila, or Symmachus. Discrepancies in number are discussed separately below (see especially no. 103). They are frequently due to translational practices or to the demands of proper usage in the two target languages, Greek and Syriac.

38. Exod. 22:27 (LXX v.28): MT *l' tqll* I SP = MT I OG ου κακολογησεις I $\not{S}^{txt}$ *l' t'mr byš'yt* I α'σ'θ' ουκ ατιμασεις (jvz) I α'σ'θ' ου καταμασεις (s) I α' *l' tlwṭ* · σ' *l' tšwṭ* · θ' *'yk šb'yn* ($\not{S}^{mg}$) I PS *l' tṣḥ'*.

The α'σ'θ' reading of s^{mg} is clearly a corruption of that found in $j^{mg}v^{mg}z^{mg}$. The latter accurately represents MT *l' tqll*. $\not{S}^{mg}$ seems to imply that the three versions originally had separate readings, one of which survived and was attributed to all three in the Greek witnesses. However, since $\not{S}^{txt}$ also uses *l' t'mr byš'yt* to represent MT/SP *l' t'r* later in the same verse, where the OG has the corresponding phrase ουκ ερεις κακως (ου κακως ερεις in Bkmo), the readings of $\not{S}^{mg}$ may well have been misplaced. Note that PS has *tlwṭ* for MT *t'r*, a form identical with that attributed to α' by $\mathcal{S}^{mg}$. If this suggestion is correct, then Theodotion retained OG ουκ ερεις κακως (= $\mathcal{S}^{txt}$ *l' t'mr byš'yt*$^{(2)}$), to represent MT *l' t'r*, while Aquila and Symmachus each had new equivalents for the same Hebrew phrase. In either case, the readings attributed to Theodotion do not suggest that his Hebrew text departed from the MT here.

39. Exod. 28:26 (MT): MT *'l ʿbr* ‖ SP *ʿl ʿbr* (*ḥbr* ABD^4-INPQW^{2}ꞴꞴꞴꞴ ηκ) ‖ OG om. ‖ Mdegjns^{txt}tv^{txt}z^{txt}Ꞵ^c εις το μερος ‖ F$^{a?}$ckmꞴ εις το (+ μερος k) αντικρυς (-κρυ km) ‖ ο'θ' εις το αντικρυς (v) ‖ ο'θ' αντικρυς (s) ‖ θ' εις το αντικρυς (z) ‖ θ' *mn lqwblh* ($\mathcal{S}^{txt}$) ‖ σ' εις το αντικρυς (vz) ‖ σ' εκτος αντικρυς (s) ‖ α' προς περαν (vz; cf. s^{mg}) ‖ PS *dʿl spth.*

Theodotion and Symmachus presumably originally shared the reading εις το αντικρυς, a revision of the earlier expansion εις το μερος. The θ' reading of $\mathcal{S}^{mg}$ either agrees with the σ' reading of s^{mg}--and both are to be regarded as a secondary scribal corruption of the correct reading--or is a free rendition of the Greek version attributed to Theodotion. The former alternative appears to be more likely. The phrase εις το αντικρυς presumably represents MT *'l ʿbr*, rather than either variant Hebrew reading preserved in SP.

40. Exod. 28:27 (MT): MT *lʿmt mḥbrtw* ‖ SP = MT ‖ OG om. ‖ F$^{a?}$Mcdegj kmns^{txt}tv^{txt}z^{txt}ꞴꞴ^c (+ συμφωνως F$^{a?}$F^{b}ckmz^{mg}Ꞵ; + συμφωνος s^{mg}) κατα (και ckmꞴ) την (τη n$^{a?}$) συμβολην (συμβουλην ds; συμβολη n$^{a?}$) αυτων (αυτου F$^{a?}$dkmtꞴꞴ^c ^{vid}; om c) ‖ ο'θ' and σ' συμφωνως κατα την συμβολην αυτου (v) ‖ θ' *šlm'yt wrmy' d'kḥd' dylh* ($\mathcal{S}^{txt}$) ‖ α' συμφωνως επι συμβολη αυτου (v) ‖ PS *lwqbl dbqh.*

The corruption και *(w-)* for κατα is found in ckmꞴ and in the Theodotionic version of $\mathcal{S}^{txt}$. The correct reading is attributed to Theodotion and Symmachus by v^{mg}, and is found in the remaining Greek manuscripts that have this verse. Theodotion's expansion of the earlier reading by the insertion of συμφωνως before κατα was presumably an attempt to render the phrase *lʿmt* more exactly. The secondary corruption was due to scribal error in the subsequent transmission of the Greek text. Once again, there is no need to suppose that Theodotion's Hebrew text differed from the present MT.

41. Exod. 32:25: MT *pr' hw'* I SP *prw' hw'* I OG διεσκεδασται I $\mathcal{S}^{txt}$ *d'tplhdw* I ϑ' διεσκεδασμενος εστιν (vz) I ϑ' διεσκεδασμενος (s) I α' αποπετασμενος αυτος (vz) I α' αποπετασμενος (s) I σ' γεγυμνωται (svz) I σ' *d'rṭly* ($\mathcal{S}^{mg}$) I i^{mg} εξεκαλυφθη I PS *dhtw lhwn.*

The revisions attributed to ϑ' and α' by v^{mg}z^{mg} clearly reflect the MT phrase *pr' hw'* or its *plene* form in SP. The omission of εστιν and αυτος in the ϑ' and α' versions of s^{mg} is puzzling. While this could represent a subsequent revision to a shorter Hebrew text, it is more likely that it is due to later scribal simplification. This simplification would be independent of any Hebrew text. The Greek verb εστιν is a perfectly acceptable equivalent for the Hebrew pronoun used predicatively.

42. Exod. 33:5: MT *mh* I SP = MT I OG α I $\mathcal{S}^{txt}$ *hlyn d-* I ϑ' *mṭl d-* ($\mathcal{S}^{mg}$) I α' *mn'* ($\mathcal{S}^{mg}$) I σ' *'yk šb'yn* ($\mathcal{S}^{mg}$) I PS *mn'*.

The OG reading is plural, while the MT is singular. The variant attributed to Aquila by $\mathcal{S}^{mg}$ is singular. Its Greek original might be the interrogative pronoun ο or perhaps even the expanded expression ο τι. The latter could easily be the source of the unexpected Theodotionic reading of $\mathcal{S}^{mg}$: *mṭl d-* = *οτι < ο τι. If so, it is possible that Aquila and Theodotion originally shared a common revision of the OG reading, or at least had similar revisions, but that Theodotion's reading suffered subsequent corruption or misinterpretation.

43. Exod. 35:11 (LXX v.10): MT *w't qršyw* I SP = MT I OG om. I F^{b}ckm s^{mg}v^{mg}(pr ※) z^{mg} ✗ και τας σανιδας αυτης (om k) I $\mathcal{S}^{txt}$ *wldpw* ※ σ' ϑ' *dylh*✗ I σ'ϑ' και τας σανιδας (v) I ϑ' και τας σανιδας αυτης (130--out of place--cited by Field) I α' και τας σανιδας... (v) I PS *wdptwhy.*

According to $\mathcal{S}^{txt}$, σ'ϑ' reflect the presence of the suffix on MT *qršyw*, but the σ'ϑ' reading of v^{mg} clearly lacks any pronominal form. It is likely that αυτης was simply omitted by haplography in v^{mg} (σανιδας αυτης). This suggestion is supported by the Theodotionic reading cited from manuscript 130 by Field, even though the latter reading is out of place. Even if Theodotion had failed to represent the suffix at all, it would not prove that his Hebrew text differed from the MT. It is almost certain that his text actually did contain the suffix.

44. Exod. 38:23 (LXX 37:21): MT *w'tw* (וְאִתּוֹ) I SP = MT I OG και I cm Ⱥ και μετα (+ τα c) ταυτα I ϑ' *wbtrkn* (Ꞩ^{txt}-- ܘܒܬܪܟܢ) I α'σ' *w'mh* (Ꞩ^{mg}) I F^{b}kɆ^{c} και μετ αυτου I PS *w'mh*.

The correct rendition of MT/SP *w'tw* is found in F^{b}kɆ^{c} (and in PS), and is attributed to α'σ' by Ꞩ^{mg}. The reading attributed to ϑ' by Ꞩ^{txt} obviously agrees with that found in mȺ and with a slight expansion in c. This reading is another scribal corruption: μετα (τα) ταυτα < *μεταυτα < μετ αυτου. The middle step is purely illustrative; the existence of such a form is highly unlikely. Presumably all three versions originally shared the reading και μετ αυτου to represent MT *w'tw*. The subsequent corruption occurred in the transmission of the Greek Theodotionic text. It does not point to a different Hebrew reading.

45. Exod. 40:5: MT *hptḥ* I SP = MT I OG επι (εις egjs^{txt}v^{txt}z^{txt}; *in* Ł^{z}; παρα s^{mg}z^{mg}; *ad* Ł^{rw}) την (της fi) θυραν (θυρας fi) I Ⱥ *in janua* I Ꞩ *'l tr''* I ο' επι την θυραν (v) I ϑ' της θυρας (v) I σ' της πυλης (v) I α' του ανοιγματος (v) I ϑ' επι (z) I PS *'l tr''*.

According to v^{mg}, all three versions omit the preposition that is not supported by the MT. The full readings are: MT *'t msk hptḥ*; ϑ' το επισπαστρον της θυρας I σ' το παρατανυσμα της πυλης I α' το παρατανυσμα του ανοιγματος. The various forms of the longer LXX reading need not be quoted in full here. The three hexaplaric readings clearly presuppose the present MT. The attribution of επι to ϑ' in z^{mg} is in contradiction with the ϑ' reading of v^{mg}. Since z^{txt} has εις rather than OG επι, perhaps the ϑ' of z^{mg} is an error for ο'. Compare the longer ο' reading of v^{mg}, and also v^{txt} εις for OG επι. If this suggestion is not correct, then the ϑ' attribution of z^{mg} must be regarded as out of place. The first alternative is more likely.

None of the readings considered thus far in this section necessarily implies a difference between Theodotion's Hebrew text and the present MT. Close inspection reveals that few, if any, lend any support at all to the possibility of variant Hebrew readings. The remainder of this section surveys the other corrupt or conflicting readings attributed to Theodotion in Exodus.

A few corrupt readings appeared in the items discussed in the first two sections of this chapter. The omission of one or two words in nos. 24a, 25, and 27 is probably due to secondary scribal error. There is no need to assume that Theodotion's Hebrew text was shorter than the MT in these cases. A further corruption is found in no. 10 above (Exod. 28:11), where και συνεσφιγμενους and και συνεσφραγισμενους are both attributed to ϑ' and are also found in the few witnesses that reflect the phrase. All the confusion presumably goes back to a single scribal error (συνεσφραγισ-μενους for συνεσφιγμενους; cf. also συνεσφισμενους in z^{mg}) in a copy of the Theodotionic text. In no. 14 above (Exod. 35:11 [LXX v.10]), the α'σ'ϑ' attribution of $\mathcal{S}^{mg}$ is the result of secondary conflation. The separate σ'ϑ' and α' attributions of v^{mg}, together with the shorter σ'ϑ' attribution of $\mathcal{S}^{mg}$, make the error obvious. A relatively unimportant itacistic spelling variant is found in no. 28 above (Exod. 13:13), where the ϑ' reading of c_2^{mg} is presumably secondary to that found in $M^{mg}j^{mg}$ $v^{mg}z^{mg}$.

Of the other variations or corruptions within the Theodotionic material, perhaps the most striking concerns the equivalents used to represent MT *yhwh*. While κυριος is the normal equivalent for the MT tetragrammaton in LXX manuscripts, evidence has begun to accumulate that this is a secondary, post-Christian usage. Just as Hebrew scribes at Qumran, and presumably elsewhere, sometimes wrote the tetragrammaton in archaic Hebrew script while the remainder of their text was in the more ordinary "Jewish" script,[10] so the early LXX scribes made arrangements in their Greek texts for the tetragrammaton to be written in Hebrew

---

[10]The archaic tetragrammaton occurs, for example, in 11Q Ps^a. See J. A. Sanders, *The Psalms Scroll of Qumrân Cave 11 (11Q Ps^a)* (Oxford, 1965), plates II-XVII, with clear examples in almost every column. It also occurs in the biblical quotations of the Habakkuk Commentary (col. 6, l. 14; col. 10, ll. 7 and 14; col. 11, l. 10) See M. Burrows, ed., *The Dead Sea Scrolls of St. Mark's Monastery*, Vol. I: *The Isaiah Manuscript and the Habakkuk Commentary* (New Haven, 1950), p. xxiii and the appropriate plates. On the term "Jewish," which can be divided into "Early Jewish" and "Late Jewish," see F. M. Cross, Jr., "The Development of the Jewish Scripts," in *The Bible and the Ancient Near East* (Garden City, N.Y., 1965), n.5 on pp. 246-247.

characters, according to either alphabet.[11] A similar situation prevails in the Greek Minor Prophets scroll from the first century A.D. discussed by Barthélemy.[12] Presumably the tetragrammaton, or its Graecization πιπι, was original in Theodotion's Greek text, as well as in the Greek texts available to him and in the Greek texts of Aquila and Symmachus.[13]

---

[11]For the most recent discussion of this question in the LXX, see R. W. Klein, "Studies in the Greek Texts of the Chronicler" (Th.D. diss., Harvard University, 1966), pp. 186-188, and the references given there. An earlier discussion, also supporting the priority of the tetragrammaton to κυριος in the LXX, is found in P. Kahle, *Opera Minora* (Leiden, 1956), pp. 115-116. Papyrus Fuad 266, a first century B.C. scroll of Deuteronomy, in which the tetragrammaton in Jewish script appears in place of κυριος, should have been published in *Etudes de Papyrologie* IX, 81-150. This publication is not yet available, but the introduction to the text appeared separately (and has been reviewed by this author in *JBL* 86 [1967], 476-477): F. Dunand, *Papyrus grecs bibliques (Papyrus F. Inv. 266), Volumina de la Genèse et du Deutéronome (Introduction)* (Le Caire, 1966). Dunand refers to the separate publication of the text in a footnote to the preface and discusses the tetragrammaton on pp. 39-50 of *Papyrus grecs*. She summarizes the other available evidence, with the exception of 4Q LXX Lev^b. The latter is a papyrus manuscript written in a hand similar to that of P.F.266, and hence to be dated to the first century B.C. It has IAΩ in place of κυριος. See P. W. Skehan, "The Qumran Manuscripts and Textual Criticism," *Volume du Congrès Strasbourg, 1956* (Leiden, 1957), p. 157. Greek IAΩ is an attempt to transliterate the Hebrew pronunciation of the tetragrammaton.

[12]In *DA*, plates 1 and 2 (after p. 168), there are several instances of the tetragrammaton written in a very corrupt form of the archaic Hebrew script. This practice was followed by both of the Greek scribes who worked on the scroll. In his transcription of the entire text of the scroll (*DA*, pp. 170-178), Barthelemy uses the abbreviation "tetr" to indicate the presence of the tetragrammaton each time it occurs. See also his brief comment in *DA*, p. 168.

[13]See F. C. Burkitt, ed., *Fragments of the Books of Kings According to the Translation of Aquila* (Cambridge, 1897), pp. 3-8, for examples of the Hebrew tetragrammaton in a Greek text of Aquila, and pp. 15-16, for a

Subsequent scribal activity eliminated all trace of this usage in later LXX manuscripts, normally replacing the tetragrammaton (or πιπι) with the appropriate form of κυριος.

Similar scribal reworking was partially effective in the texts of Aquila, Symmachus, and Theodotion. Evidence that this reworking was only partially effective is liberally scattered through the hexaplaric readings collected in B-McL, Ziegler, and Field. Only those instances that involve Theodotion in Exodus are listed here.

Most instructive is Exod. 32:9, where scribal activity has been only partially successful: MT *yhwh*] SP = MT] OG om.] cmp$^{b?}$, 128, A $\overline{\kappa\varsigma}$] $\mathcal{S}^{txt}$(under ※) *mry'*] σ'θ' $\overline{\kappa\varsigma}$ (svz)] σ'θ' *pypy* ($\mathcal{S}^{mg}$)] b_2 ο $\overline{\theta\varsigma}$] PS *mry'*. The Syriac *pypy* is simply an uncomprehending transliteration of Greek πιπι.

Elsewhere in Exodus, the following Theodotionic equivalents for MT *yhwy* have been preserved:

Exod. 4:24: σ'θ' *mry'* ($\mathcal{S}^{mg}$)] α' *'lh'* ($\mathcal{S}^{mg}$).

Exod. 8:6 (LXX v.10): α'σ'θ' *pypy* ($\mathcal{S}^{mg}$).

Exod. 8:22 (LXX v.26): α', σ', and θ' *mry'* ($\mathcal{S}^{mg}$).

Exod. 12:42: a) θ' *'yk šb'yn* ($\mathcal{S}^{mg}$; cf. $\mathcal{S}^{txt}$ *mry'*)] α' and σ' *pypy* ($\mathcal{S}^{mg}$)] α' πιπι (*b*).

b) θ' and α'σ' *pypy* ($\mathcal{S}^{mg}$)--see no. 37 above.

Exod. 12:48: α'θ' *mry'* ($\mathcal{S}^{txt}$).

Exod. 15:18: α', σ', and θ' *pypy* ($\mathcal{S}^{mg}$).

Exod. 19:18: θ' $\overline{\kappa\nu}$ (v)] α' $\overline{\kappa\varsigma}$ (v).

Exod. 22:10 (LXX v.11): α'σ'θ' *pypy* ($\mathcal{S}^{mg}$).

Exod. 29:18: α'θ' κυριω ("one Regius"--cited from Montef. by Field).

In all cases the Theodotionic reading is consonant with the present MT.

Conflicting attributions are relatively few. These three additional

---

brief discussion. See also C. Taylor, ed., *Hebrew-Greek Cairo Genizah Palimpsests from the Taylor-Schechter Collection* (Cambridge, 1900), pp. 6-11, for a fragment of the hexapla in which the tetragrammaton is represented by Greek πιπι in cols. 3-5. These columns contain the versions attributed to Aquila and Symmachus, as well as Origen's version of the LXX.

instances do not affect the evaluation of Theodotion's relation to the MT:

Exod. 1:8 (MT *ḥdš*): α′ αλλος σ′ δευτερος ϑ′ καινος (c_2) I α′ϑ′ καινος (j) I α′σ′ καινος (z) I α′σ′ϑ′ καινος (v) I οι λ̥ καινος (M) I *g′ ḥdt*ʾ ($\mathcal{S}^{mg}$).

Exod. 18:26 (MT *hqšh*): α′σ′ σκληρον ϑ′ (om s) δυσχερες (jsz) I α′σ′ϑ′ σκληρον δυσχερες (M).

Exod. 28:32, LXX v.28 (MT *tḥrʾ*): α′ϑ′... προσπλοκην σ′ ... σειρωτον (M) I α′ ... προσπλοκην (-πλοκης v; -πλοις s) σ′ϑ′ ... σειρωτον (svz).

Relatively minor changes in the form of a word, again not affecting the evaluation of Theodotion's relation to the MT, occur as follows:

Exod. 1:7 (MT *wyšrṣw*): ϑ′ εξειρπον (*b*) I α′ϑ′ εξειρποσαν (Mv) I ϑ′ *wršpyn hww* ($\mathcal{S}^{mg}$) I additional α′ and σ′ readings are also given.

Exod. 1:13 (MT *bprk*): σ′ εντρυφωντες ϑ′ εμπεγμω (M) I σ′ εντρυφωντες ϑ′ εμπαιγμοι (v) I α′ εντρυ... (64--acc. to Field) I α′ εντρυφηματι σ′ϑ′ εμπαιγματι (Montef., no source given --cited by Field) I cf. εντρυφωντες εμπαιγμων in c_2^{mg}.

Exod. 4:25 (MT *ʾth ly*; SP = MT): ϑ′ and σ′ συ μοι (vz) I οι λ̥ συ μοι (Mz; cf. v^{mg}) I α′ϑ′ *ʾyt ly* ($\mathcal{S}^{mg}$) I PS *ʾyt ly*. Syriac *ʾyt ly* seems to be a scribal error for *ʾnt ly* (i.e.,  for ).

Exod. 19:13 (MT *hywbl*): ϑ′ του ιωβηλ (v; cf. b^{mg}) I ϑ′ *dywbl* ($\mathcal{S}^{mg}$--but *dywbb* in Lagarde's B[1]) I σ′ *ywbbʾ* ($\mathcal{S}^{mg}$) I σ′ ο σαλπιγμος (v) I α′ του παραφεροντος (v) I α′ *dhw dmʿbr* ($\mathcal{S}^{mg}$).

Exod. 25:6 (MT *bśmym*): α′σ′ϑ′ *hlwmʾ* ($\mathcal{S}^{mg}$--but without the plural mark in Lagarde's B) I οι γ′ αρωματα (*b*).

Exod. 27:4 (MT *mkbr*): α′σ′ϑ′ *ʾyk dʿrblʾ* ($\mathcal{S}^{mg}$--no marker in the text) I σ′ϑ′ κοσκηνομ. (*b*) I οι λ̥ κοσκινωμα (M). The reading in $\mathcal{S}^{mg}$ can be understood as a descriptive translation of Greek κοσκινωμα.

Exod. 29:5 (MT *mʿyl*): ϑ′ επενδυτην (jsz) I ϑ′ *(wl)lʿl mn lbwšh* ($\mathcal{S}^{mg}$) I ϑ′ επιδυτην (v) I α′ and σ′ readings are also given.

Exod. 30:20 (MT *ʾšh*): α′ϑ′ πυρρον (Montef., no source given--as cited by Field, correcting to πυρον; cf. α′ϑ′ πυρον for MT *ʾšh* in Exod. 29:18, in "one Regius" according to Montef. as cited by Field).

Exod. 32:9 (MT *mšh*): σ'θ' μωυσην (sz) I σ'θ' μωσην (v).

Exod. 32:25 (*bqmyhm*): θ' τοις ανθεστηκοσιν αυτων (s[αυτον]v [αυτοις^{vid}]z) I α' εν ανθεστηκοσιν αυτων (svz) I σ' τοις ανθεστηκοσιν αυτοις (svz).

Twice secondary expansions are found in one of several witnesses to a particular Theodotionic reading: in Exod. 7:24, οι is inserted before κυκλω in z^{mg}, but not in v^{mg}c$_2$^{mg}; in Exod. 21:8, ουν is inserted after αυτης in s^{mg}, but not in j^{mg}v^{mg}z^{mg}S̸^{mg}. Both expansions are due to subsequent scribal error, and do not imply any difference in Hebrew *Vorlage*.

Neither the textual corruptions discussed in nos. 34-45 nor the other variations and corruptions within the Theodotionic material mentioned above provide clear examples of divergence between Theodotion's Hebrew text and the present MT.

Apparent Expansions in Theodotion as Compared with the MT

46. Exod. 25:23 (LXX v.22): MT *ʿṣy* I SP = MT I OG (+ εκ F*ntz^{mg}a$_2$) χρυσιου (... + και ξυλων b) I F$^{b\ mg}$acmA̸E̸^{c} εκ ξυλων I θ' *mn qy̌sʾ* (S̸^{txt}) I σ' *mn qy̌sʾ* (S̸^{mg}) I α' *dqysʾ* (S̸^{mg}) I PS *dqysʾ*.

47. Exod. 37:1 (LXX 38:1): MT *ʿṣy* I SP = MT I OG om. I F^{b}F$^{b\ mg}$G (under ※)ckmA̸E̸^{c} εκ ξυλων I θ' *mn qy̌sʾ* (S̸^{txt}) I PS *dqysʾ*.

48. Exod. 37:4 (LXX 38:4): MT *ʿṣy* I SP = MT I OG om. I F^{b}G(under ※) ckmA̸E̸^{c} εκ ξυλων I θ' *mn qy̌sʾ* (S̸^{txt}) I PS *dqysʾ*.

49. Exod. 37:10 (LXX 38:9): MT *ʿṣy* I SP = MT I OG εκ χρυσιου I F^{b}G (under ※)cA̸E̸^{c} εκ ξυλων I θ' *mn qy̌sʾ* (S̸^{txt}) I PS *dqysʾ*.

50. Exod. 37:15 (LXX 38:11): MT *ʿṣy* I SP = MT I OG om. I F^{b}G(under ※)cA̸E̸^{c} εκ ξυλων I θ' *mn qy̌sʾ* (S̸^{txt}) I PS *dqysʾ*.

51. Exod. 38:1 (LXX 38:22): MT *ʿṣy* I SP = MT I OG (εκ των πυρειων...) I F^{b}cA̸E̸^{c} εκ ξυλων I θ' *mn qy̌sʾ* (S̸^{txt}) I PS *dqysʾ*.

In each of the above cases, MT *ʿṣy (šṭym)* describes the material out of which an article, just named, is to be made. Only once, in Exod. 38:6 (LXX 38:24), is Theodotion said to translate MT *ʿṣy* in such a construction by *qy̌sʾ* alone (cf. ξυλα in c; but contrast εκ ξυλων in F^{b}A̸^{vid} E̸$^{c\ vid}$). The longer usage is also common in the OG for Exodus--eight or nine times in cc. 25-27 and ch. 30, according to H-R--and does not imply the presence of a longer reading in Theodotion's Hebrew text.

52. Exod. 20:24 (Ꞩ v.21): MT *ʾdmh* ‖ SP = MT ‖ OG εκ γης ‖ Ꞩ^{txt} *mn ʾrʿʾ* ‖ θʹ *mn ʾdmtʾ* (Ꞩ^{mg}) ‖ αʹ *dʾrʿʾ* (Ꞩ^{mg}) ‖ σʹ *bʾdmtʾ* (Ꞩ^{mg}) ‖ PS *dʾdmtʾ*.

53. Exod. 28:6: MT *zhb* ‖ SP = MT ‖ OG om. ‖ cj^{mg}kms^{mg}AE^{c} εκ χρυσιου (χρυσου m; + *puro* A) ‖ Ꞩ^{txt} ※ σʹ *mn*⸔ *dhbʾ* ‖ θʹ εκ χρυσιου (vz) ‖ F^{b} χρυσουν ‖ PS *ddhbʾ*.

These two examples are similar to those found in nos. 46-51 above. Neither of them points to a longer reading in Theodotion's Hebrew text.

54. Exod. 25:26 (LXX v.25): MT *ʾšr* ‖ SP = MT ‖ OG om. ‖ acmA α εστιν ‖ θʹ *hlyn dʾytyhyn* (Ꞩ^{txt}) ‖ PS om.

55. Exod. 28:26 (MT): MT *ʾšr* ‖ SP = MT ‖ OG om. ‖ F$^{a?}$Mcdegjkmns^{txt} tv^{txt}z^{txt}AE^{c} ο εστιν ‖ θʹ *hw dʾytwhy* (Ꞩ^{txt}) ‖ οʹθʹ ο εστιν (v) ‖ θʹ ο εστιν (z) ‖ σʹ ο εστιν (svz) ‖ αʹ ο (vz; cf. s^{mg}) ‖ PS *d-*.

56. Exod. 30:38: MT *ʾyš ʾšr* ‖ SP = MT ‖ OG (+ ανηρ F$^{c?}$cs^{mg}z^{mg}A; + ανηρ... m) ος (ως o; + *autem* B) αν (εαν k; om d; ... + ανηρ egj) ‖ Ꞩ^{txt} ※ αʹθʹ *gbrʾ*⸔*hw dʾn* ‖ αʹθʹ ※ ανηρ ος αν σʹ α̅ν̅ο̅ς̅ ος αν (v) ‖ PS *wgbrʾ d-*.

57. Exod. 37:13 (LXX 38:10): MT *ʾšr* ‖ SP = MT ‖ OG om. ‖ G(under ※) cAE^{c} α εστιν (*erant* A) ‖ θʹ *hlyn dʾytyhyn* (Ꞩ^{txt}) ‖ F^{b} εως ‖ PS om.

In no. 56, Theodotion retains OG ος αν to represent MT *ʾšr* before *yʿśh* (OG ποιηση). This is clearly a question of style, and does not point to any expansion in Theodotion's Hebrew text. In the other three instances (nos. 54, 55, 57), Theodotion uses a relative pronoun plus the verb εστιν or its Syriac equivalent to represent MT *ʾšr*. In each case the Hebrew has a nominal sentence, with no expressed verb or copula. Once again the apparent expansions are due to the demands of Greek style, and cannot be used to argue for expansions in Theodotion's Hebrew text. The same can be said about Theodotion's use of *lʾ ʾytwhy* and *wlʾ ʾytwhy* to represent MT *ʾyn* and *wʾyn* (OG ουκ εστιν and ουδε, respectively) in Exod. 32:18. Aquila agrees with Theodotion each time, but Symmachus has *lʾ ʾytyh* and *wlʾ*.

Theodotion's regular use of the "expansion" εγω ειμι to represent MT *ʾnky* was discussed in connection with the fourth reading, Exod. 8:25 (LXX v.29), in chapter one. This usage does not point to any expansion in Theodotion's Hebrew text, but only to the presence of *'nky* (as in MT and SP) rather than *'ny*.

58. Exod. 38:10 (LXX 37:8): MT *wwy h'mdym* I SP *wwy h'mwdym* I OG om. I ckA̸E̸^{c} και οι κοσμοι των στυλων I θ' *wšbt' d'ṭwd'* (S^{txt}) I α' *wšplyd' d'ṭwd'* (S^{mg}) I F^b και οι κρικοι (διατονια F$^{b?\ mg}$) αυτων I PS *wqwb'lhwn d'mwd'*.

59. Exod. 38:11 (LXX 37:9): MT *wwy h'mwdym* I SP = MT I OG om. I cA̸ E̸^{c} και οι κοσμοι των στυλων I θ' *wšbt' d'ṭwd'* (S^{txt}) I F^b και οι κρικοι αυτων I PS *wqwb'yhwn d'mwd'*.

60. Exod. 38:12 (LXX 37:10): MT *wwy h'mdym* I SP *wwy h'mwdym* I OG om. I cA̸E̸^{c} και οι κοσμοι των στυλων I θ' *wšbt' d'ṭwd'* (S^{txt}) I F^b και οι κρικοι αυτων (corr F$^{b?\ mg}$) I PS *wqwb'yhwn d'mwd'*.

The insertion of Syriac *w-* (= και) before the translation of MT *wwy* in each of these three instances is not to be regarded as an expansion. Rather the initial *w* of *wwy* was regarded as equivalent to or as doubling for the conjunction *w-*. While the OG uses other equivalents for MT *wwy* and *wwyhm*, they are regularly preceded by OG και (see, for example, Exod. 26:32, 37; 27:10, 11, 17; 36:36[LXX 37:4], 38[LXX 37:6]). This is also the usage of PS in nos. 58-60 and of Aquila in no. 58. There is no reason to assume an awkward and unlikely Hebrew reading, **wwwy*, in Theodotion's Hebrew text for these verses. In Exod. 38:28 (LXX 39:6), however, where the conjunction clearly would not fit, α'σ' *šplyd'* θ' *šbt'* in S^{mg} and κεφαλιδας in F^b replace OG εισ τας αγκυλας (S^{txt} *b'nqwl's*) as translations for MT *wwym*.

61. Exod. 29:14: MT *ḥṭ't hw'* I SP *ḥṭ't hy'* I OG αμαρτιας (αμαρτια c krvz) γαρ (χαριν f) εστιν (om f) I S *dḥṭh' gyr 'ytwhy* I ο' αμαρτιας γαρ εστιν (svz) I σ'θ' περι αμαρτιας εστιν (v) I α' περι αμαρτιας εστιν (s) I α' and θ' περι αμαρτιας (z) I α' αμαρτιας (?) εστιν (v) I PS *ḥṭh' hw*.

All three versions agree in replacing OG αμαρτιας γαρ with περι αμαρτιας to translate MT *ḥṭ't*. The Greek phrase is apparently used to express the meaning of the Hebrew noun more exactly. There is no firm evidence for supposing that there was an expanded Hebrew phrase (**'l ḥṭ't*, or the like) as the basis for the Greek phrase.

62. Exod. 25:33 (LXX v.32): MT *gbʿym mšqdym*$^{(2)}$ I SP = MT I OG om. I Ꞩ^{txt} *ʾgnʾ dmṭpsn gwzʾ*$^{(2)}$ I Ⱥ *craterae in nucis modum formatae* I ϑ′ *ʾgnʾ dʾyt ʿlyhyn dmwtʾ dlwzʾ* (Ꞩ^{mg}) I α′ *ʿrbʾ dʾyt ʿlyhyn dmwtʾ dlwzʾ* (Ꞩ^{mg}) I σ′ *ʾgnʾ mṭpst blwzʾ* (Ꞩ^{mg}) I PS *ʾsqpyn qbyʿyn*$^{(2)}$.

While the expanded Syriac phrases attributed to Aquila and Theodotion may represent similarly expanded Greek expressions, these latter would presumably be periphrastic attempts to translate the complex Hebrew phrase found in the MT and SP. There is no reason to assume that some sort of expanded Hebrew reading was present in the texts used by Aquila and Theodotion.

None of the apparent expansions discussed in this section proved on closer examination to provide any evidence for expansions in the Hebrew text used by Theodotion. All the instances are relatively minor, and are due to translational practices or to the desire for more accurate expression of the meaning of the Hebrew text.

Qualitative Differences between Theodotion's Version and the Present MT

63. Exod. 7:1: MT *rʾh nttyk ʾlhym lprʿh* I SP = MT I OG ιδου (+ εγω y) δεδωκα (διδωμι Phil; τεθεικα Eus$\frac{1}{2}$, Ath$\frac{1}{3}$vid, Chr, Cyr$\frac{1}{4}$, Thdt$\frac{1}{2}$, Nov, Hil$\frac{1}{2}$; τιθημι Thdt$\frac{1}{2}$; κατεστηκα Eus$\frac{1}{2}$) σε (σοι cf, Phil-cod$\frac{2}{4}$; + σημερον Eus$\frac{1}{2}$; + εις Ł^{r}, Hip, Ath$\frac{1}{2}$) θεον (om f; + τω dnpt, Eus$\frac{1}{2}$, Ath$\frac{2}{3}$, Thdt$\frac{1}{2}$; + του Ath$\frac{1}{3}$, Cyr$\frac{1}{4}$, Thdt$\frac{1}{2}$) φαραω (om f) I Ꞩ *hʾ yhbtk ʾlhʾ lprʿwn* I σ′θ′ ιδε κατεστησα σε θ̄ν̄ φαραω (v) I σ′ ιδε κατεστησα σε θ′ θ̄ν̄ φαραω (jz) I α′ ιδε δεδωκα σε θ̄ν̄ τω φαραω (jvz) I PS *ḥzy dyhbtk ʾlh lprʿwn.*

If the σ′θ′ citation of v^{mg} is correct, then Theodotion may have had **smtyk* or the like in his Hebrew text in place of MT *nttyk*. More probably the citations of j^{mg}z^{mg} are correct, with v^{mg} introducing a secondary conflation. The presence of κατεστησα in Symmachus is not surprising, since he frequently varies Greek expressions without apparent reference to the Hebrew. If κατεστησα is correctly attributed to Theodotion's version, it is also possible to suggest that the form was inadvertently introduced by him, or that it had found its way into his Greek text through earlier scribal inadvertence and was not recognized as inappropriate by him.

64. Exod. 8:22 (LXX v.26): MT *hn nzbḥ* I SP = MT I OG εαν (+ τε s)

γαρ (δε c_2𝔈; om i*) θυσωμεν (out of place egj; γαρ θυσωμεν out of place 25) I 𝔖^{txt} *'n gyr ndbḥ* I θ' *wdbḥynn* (𝔖^{mg}) I α' *'n dbḥyn ḥnn* (𝔖^{mg}) I σ' *'n dyn dbḥynn* (𝔖^{mg}) I PS *w'n dbḥynn*.

There is no immediately obvious reason why Theodotion should have replaced OG εαν γαρ with the simple conjunction *w-* to represent MT *hn*. Perhaps his Hebrew text had the minor expansion *whn*, similar to the expansion in PS *w'n*. Then if Theodotion inserted και to represent Hebrew *w-* and also omitted OG γαρ, he may inadvertently have forgotten to retain OG εαν in his new version. No matter what explanation is suggested, it would seem that Theodotion's Hebrew text differed in some small way (either *w-* or *whn* for MT *hn*) at this point.

65. Exod. 13:16: MT *wlṭwṭpt* I SP *wlṭṭpwt* I OG και (om d_2) ασαλευτον (σαλευτον a*) I 𝔖^{txt} *wmttzy'n'* I α'σ'θ' *wdmttzy'* (𝔖^{mg}) I α' και εισενεκτα (j) I α' και εισιν ακτα (z; cf. v^{mg}) I α' εις νακτα (M) I οι ο' ασαλευτον (j) I οι ℷ ασαλευτον (vz) I PS *wdwkrn'*.

The form attributed to α'σ'θ' by 𝔖^{mg} is the genitive of the active participle of *'ttzy'* (Ettaphal of *zw'*), "to be moved, agitated." The related adjective in 𝔖^{txt} means "movable." Both forms are reminiscent of a* σαλευτον ("tottering, shaken"), and are the opposite of OG ασαλευτον ("unmoved, unshaken"). The meaning of the Greek readings variously attributed to α' is uncertain (νακτα = "close-pressed, solid things," but ακτα and εισενεκτα remain enigmatic). While the Syriac form attributed to α'σ'θ' is singular and genitive, it would be precarious to suggest what Greek reading it might represent or to argue that a variant Hebrew reading was found in Theodotion's text. Even the apparent change from plural to singular, in agreement with the OG, is contradicted by the various Greek forms attributed to Aquila.

66. Exod. 16:16: MT *lpy 'klw* I SP = MT I OG εις τους καθηκοντας (+ παρ αυτω acmx𝔄) I 𝔖^{txt} *lhwn dzdqyn* ※ *lwth*⸔ I θ' *lm'kwlt' dylh* (𝔖^{mg}) I α' *lpwm' dm'kwlt' dylh* (𝔖^{mg}) I σ' *lwt mlt' dm'kwlt' dylh* (𝔖^{mg}) I 𝔏^{v} *in tauernaculis proportionibus* I $F^{b\ mg}$ εις το αρκουν αυτω I PS *mst m'klh*.

67. Exod. 16:21: MT *kpy 'klw* I SP *lpy 'klw* I OG το καθηκον αυτω I 𝔖^{txt} *hw m' dzdq lh* I θ' *bhlyn d'klyn lh* (𝔖^{mg}) I α' *'yk pwm'*

dm'kwlt' dylh ($\mathcal{S}^{mg}$) I σ' *'yk mlt' dm'kwlt' dylh* ($\mathcal{S}^{mg}$) I B om. I j^{mg} το αρκουν η ο δυνατον I $F^{b\ mg}$ το αρκουν I PS *mst m'klh*.

In no. 66, Theodotion's translation represents the MT fairly accurately, except that he provides no explicit reflection of MT *py* in *lpy*. In no. 67, however, Theodotion's translation is much less exact or literal. He again fails to translate MT *py* explicitly, and he also fails to reflect MT *k*- (or SP *l*-) exactly. Furthermore his reading is plural, although all other versions, including the OG, agree with the MT singular. Because of the idiomatic nature of the Hebrew expressions, there is no real doubt that Theodotion's Hebrew text contained MT *py* each time, but it is impossible to say whether it agreed with MT *kpy* or SP *lpy* in no. 67. The variants attributed to Aquila and Symmachus provide explicit representation for MT *py* each time, and also clearly agree with MT *kpy* against SP *lpy* in no. 67. These are the only two instances, apart from those noted in nos. 24-32 above and in no. 69 below, of apparent omissions due to translational practices that I have found in the Theodotionic material in Exodus. It is not clear why the Theodotionic phrase in no. 67 is such a free rendition of the Hebrew expression, but there is no firm evidence to support a widely variant reading in Theodotion's Hebrew text as the basis for his translation.

68. Exod. 22:3 (LXX v.4): MT *mšwr ʿd ḥmwr ʿd śh ḥyym* I SP *mšwr ʿd ḥmwr ʿd śh ʿd kl bhmh ḥyym* I OG απο τε (του djs; μοσχου και ackxA̸, Eus; om AFMeghlmnpquvza$_2$) ονου (βοος ονου $F^{b\ mg}$; + και μοσχου b^{mg}; + και Cyr-ed) εως (+ μοσχου και m) προβατου ζωντα (om 136, A̸E̸) I $\mathcal{S}^{txt}$ *mn* ※ϑ' *twr' wḥmr' ʿdm' lʿrb' kd ḥyyn* I PS *mn twr' wlḥmr' wʿdm' lnqy' kd ḥyyn*.

PS agrees with MT and SP in having a longer phrase than the OG, but it introduces the conjunction *w*- after its reflection of MT *mšwr*. The expansion of the OG attributed to ϑ' by $\mathcal{S}^{txt}$ agrees with PS in having the conjunction *w*- after the translation of MT *(m)šwr*. While $\mathcal{S}^{txt}$ retains no reflection of MT *ʿd*$^{(1)}$ between *w*- and *ḥmr'*, PS *(w)l*- may represent the MT preposition. Thus, if PS supposes a Hebrew *Vorlage* **mšwr wʿd ḥmwr*, then Theodotion could be understood as agreeing with it against the MT. The omission of any reflection of MT *ʿd*$^{(1)}$ in Theodotion (or at least in $\mathcal{S}^{txt}$), and in the few Greek witnesses that agree with $\mathcal{S}^{txt}$, could be due to inadvertence in editing on Origen's part or even to an error by Theodotion.

These witnesses, however, do not prove that Theodotion had no reflection of the preposition. If the foregoing suggestion is not adopted, then Theodotion could also be understood as implying a Hebrew variant **mšwr wḥmwr* (etc.). It is at least possible that Theodotion's Hebrew text here differed slightly from the present MT, with either *wʿd* or *w-* replacing MT *ʿd*(1).

69. Exod. 22:18 (LXX v.19): MT *mwt ywmt* ❙ SP = MT ❙ OG θανατω (om a_2 b_2ß) αποκτενειτε (αποκτενητε k; αποθανειται np) αυτους (αυτον b′ dfi$^{a?}$nrtß₤, Cyr-ed; om AFMegj^{txt}pqsu-xz𝔄) ❙ $\text{\S}^{txt}$ *bmwtʾ tqṭlwnyhy* ❙ θ′ αναθεματισθησεται (part of a longer reading cited by Montef. from Basilianus, according to Field; Holmes' scribe merely cites this word from the margin with no attribution, again according to Field) ❙ j^{mg} αναθεματισθησετε ❙ PS *mtqṭlw ntqṭl.*

There is no apparent reason for this rather free translation in Theodotion. It is passive, in agreement with MT *ywmt* against the OG, but fails to provide any explicit reflection of the MT infinitive absolute *mwt*, which the OG had represented by θανατω. Nevertheless, it is not necessary to assume that Theodotion's Hebrew text differed from the MT at this point.

70. Exod. 28:14: MT *mgblt tʿśh ʾtm* ❙ SP *mgblwt tʿśh ʾtm* ❙ OG καταμεμιγμενα (και τα μεμιγμενα dop; μεμιγμενα am; ποικιλμενα 32) εν (om el$ß^{vid}$) ανθεσιν (υακινθεσιν kn) ❙ $\text{\S}^{txt}$ *dmhlṭyn bhbbʾ* ❙ θ′ *gdyly ʾkḥdʾ nʿbd ʾnwn* ($\text{\S}^{mg}$) ❙ $F^{b\ mg}$ αντι εκ χρ...νημ.τ.. ❙ PS *ḥtʾmtʾ ʿbd ʾnyn.*

The Theodotionic version represents the MT very well, as opposed to the radically different OG reading. The only difference is in the use of Syriac *nʿbd* where the MT has *tʿśh*. The change from second person singular to either third person singular or first person plural may be a simple mistake, a translational variant, or even a reflection of a slightly different Hebrew reading. Even if the last possibility should be correct, the difference would be very slight, involving a single letter. SP and presumably PS agree with the MT on this point, making a Theodotionic Hebrew variant less likely.

71. Exod. 28:26 (MT): MT *wśmt ʾtm* ❙ SP = MT ❙ OG om. ❙ $F^{a?}$Mcdegjkmnp $s^{txt}v^{txt}z^{txt}$𝔄₤^{c} και θησεις (δωσεις $F^{a?}$ckm𝔄; ποιησεις j) αυτους ❙

ϑ' *wttl ʾnyn* ($\not{s}^{txt}$) I ο'ϑ' και δωσεις αυτους (svz) I α'σ' και ϑησεις αυτους (v) I PS *wsym ʾnwn.*

There is no apparent reason why Theodotion should have και δωσεις/ *wttl* to represent MT *wśmt*. The choice becomes even more unusual if the majority reading (και ϑησεις) is assumed to have been present in the Greek text available to Theodotion. Perhaps the Theodotionic variant is an inadvertent one, influenced by the four occurrences of δωσεις--each time reflecting a form of *ntn* in the MT--in the previous three verses and the further occurrence of δωσεις, again for a form of *ntn*, in the following verse.[14] It is also possible, but less likely, that MT *wśmt* was replaced by **wntt(h)* in Theodotion's Hebrew text, under the influence of the surrounding Hebrew usage.

72. Exod. 30:32: MT *(w)bmtkntw* I SP *(w)btkntw* I OG κατα την (το n) συνϑεσιν (συνεσιν w*; ειδος n) ταυτην (εαυτιν c; τουτο n; αυτου $k^{txt}m$) I $\not{s}$ *(w)ʾyk mrkbwtʾ hdʾ* I k^{mt} το ειδος τουτο I σ'ϑ' κατα την συνταξιν ταυτην (v) I α' κατα την συμμετριαν (v) I α' συμμετριαν (M; cf. z^{mg}) I PS *(w)bdmwth.*

The revision of the OG common to Theodotion and Symmachus retains OG ταυτην rather than any reflection of the MT suffix. Theodotion's concentration on a new noun to replace OG συνϑεσιν, presumably for lexical reasons, may have led to his presumably inadvertent retention of the OG demonstrative. The OG reading may be due to an early scribal error. It could also be a free rendition of the Hebrew of either MT or SP, as well as a witness to a different Hebrew reading. There is no way to prove that Theodotion's Hebrew text differed from the MT at this point.

73. Exod. 37:13 (LXX 38:10): MT *wyṣq lw* I SP *wyṣq* I OG και εχωνευσεν αυτη (αυτην eox; om b_2) I $F^bGc\not{A}\not{E}^c$ (+ ÷ G) ... και εχωνευσεν αυτη (αυτην c*) ... (+ ※ G) ... και εποιησεν (εχωνευσεν F^b) αυτη ... (+ ✓ G)--$F^b\not{E}^c$ omit the entire section that is under ÷ in G I $\not{s}^{txt}$ ÷ ... *wnsk lh* ... ✓ ※ ϑ'... *wʿbd lh* ... ✓ I PS *wḥšl lh.*

In Exod. 37:10-17, MT *wyʿś* occurs seven times, while *wyṣp*, *wyṣq*, and *wytn* each occur once. Because of the seven occurrences of και εποιησεν, each corresponding to MT *wyʿś*, in the immediate context, Theodotion

[14] See discussion of this point in chapter two.

may inadvertently have replaced OG και εχωνευσεν with και εποιησεν. This variant is similar to that discussed under no. 71. Here too it is possible, though unlikely, that the sequence of *wyʿś* phrases in the immediate context led to the replacement of MT *wyṣq* by **wyʿś* in Theodotion's Hebrew text. It is impossible to prove that this variant was actually present in Theodotion's Hebrew text.

74. Exod. 37:13 (LXX 38:10): MT *wytn* I SP = MT I OG om. I F^{b}G(under ※)cȺɆ^{c} και επεθηκεν (εθηκε F^{b}) I ϑʹ *wsm* (Ꞩ^{txt}) I PS *wyhb*.

The Theodotionic translation could point to a variant Hebrew reading (**wyśm*), but more probably it is a slightly free translation of MT *wytn*. Both SP and PS support the MT, while the OG has no reflection of the verb at all.

Of the twelve instances of apparent or real qualitative differences between Theodotion and the MT discussed above, no. 65 is of uncertain interpretation, and is attributed to all three versions. Numbers 66, 67, and 69 are apparent omissions that are probably due to translational practices. Numbers 64 and 68 involve the insertion of the conjunction *w-* and the apparent or real omission of a conjunction (MT *hn* in no. 64) or preposition (MT *ʿd* in no. 68). Number 72 involves the retention of OG ταυτην where the MT has only a pronominal suffix on the noun. In no. 70 Theodotion corrects to an MT phrase that differs substantially from the OG, but he fails to represent exactly the person, and possibly the number, of the MT verb. In nos. 63, 71, 73, and 74, Theodotion introduces a verb that does not reflect the MT verb exactly; of these, no. 63 may be the result of a conflation in attribution. In nos. 63, 71, and 73, the OG or the majority supplement to an OG minus has a more accurate translation of the MT verb.

Any or even all of these readings could point to variants in Theodotion's Hebrew text. Numbers 63, 64, 68, 70, 71, 73, and 74 may well do so, although some doubt remains in every case. All seven variants are relatively minor. Together with the probable variants pointed out in the previous sections of this investigation, they constitute an objectively insignificant part of the entire body of Theodotionic material preserved in Exodus.

Another apparent qualitative variant, ϑʹ *mwtʾ* (= OG θανατος) for MT *(b)dbr*, is found in no. 26 (Exod. 5:3). As pointed out in the discussion of Theodotion's failure to represent the two MT prepositions in that item, Theodotion retained the OG with only one change.[15] He made no real effort to revise the OG thoroughly, so that it might reflect the radically different MT. Theodotion's failure to revise the OG extensively might have been due to any number of reasons, and cannot be used to prove that his Hebrew text actually differed from the MT at that point.

Various discrepancies between singular and plural forms in the MT and Theodotion are considered next. Frequently these discrepancies are translational in nature and normally do not imply variants in the Hebrew text used by Theodotion.

75. Exod. 15:8: MT *nʿrmw*] SP = MT] OG διεστη] 𝔖 *ʾtpršw*] α′σ′θ′ εσωρευθη (Mjvz)] PS *ʾtʿrmw*.

The MT subject is *mym*, regularly represented in Greek by the singular το υδωρ (so here: OG διεστη το υδωρ = MT *nʿrmw mym*). The retention of singular number in the α′σ′θ′ revision is therefore completely normal and expected.

76. Exod. 32:1: MT *wyqhl*] SP = MT] OG και συνεστη (συνεστησαν cdk m)] 𝔖^{txt} *wqm*] α′θ′ και εκκλησιασθη (*b*)] α′θ′ *wʾtknšw* (𝔖^{mg})] σ′ *ʾyk šbʿyn* (𝔖^{mg})] PS *wʾtknšw*.

The MT subject is *hʿm* (OG ο λαος; 𝔖^{txt} *ʿmʾ*), which was treated as singular by the OG and 𝔖^{txt}, in agreement with MT and SP, as well as by α′θ′ according to *b*^{mg}. The plural form attributed to α′θ′ in 𝔖^{mg} is due to an interpretation of Syriac *ʿmʾ* (or of ο λαος) in a collective sense. Such an interpretation is found in PS (*wʾtknšw ʿmʾ*), and need not imply a variant Hebrew reading.

77. Exod. 32:6: MT *wyškymw*] SP *wyškmw*] OG και ορθρισας] 𝔖^{txt} *wkd qdm*] α′θ′ *wqdm*˙ σ′ *kd qdmw dyn* (𝔖^{mg})] PS *wqdmw*.

While Aquila and Theodotion replaced the OG participle with the corresponding finite verb in order to reflect the MT structure more exactly, they forgot to change from singular to plural number. That this omission was inadvertent may be seen from their treatment of the following verb in the same verse: MT *wyʿlw*] SP = MT] OG ανεβιβασεν (ανεβιβασαν g; ανηνεγκεν ck^{a})] 𝔖^{txt} *ʾsq*] α′σ′ *ʾsqw*˙ θ′ *wʾytyw* (𝔖^{mg})] PS *wʾsqw*.

---

[15]See pp. 119-120.

Only Symmachus, who replaced OG ορθρισας with a plural participle, has the correct plural number for both MT verbs. It is possible that α'θ' *wqdm* is the result of a simple scribal error: *ορθρισεν <*ορθρισαν. It is not necessary or desirable to postulate a singular form in Theodotion's Hebrew text.

These are the only instances of discrepancy in number for verbs that I have discovered in the Theodotionic material for Exodus. The first is translational. The second is a divergence within the evidence for Theodotion, and seems to be due to a secondary interpretation by a scribe or by the Syriac translator. The third is due to inadvertence, or perhaps to scribal error. In no case is there clear evidence for a different reading in Theodotion's Hebrew text.

78. Exod. 32:24: MT 3 m.s.suffix on *w'šlkhw* (antecedent *zhb*)] SP 3 m.s.suffix on *w'šlykhw* (antecedent *zhb*)] OG om. (antecedent χρυσια [χρυσα a_2; χρυσιω bc; χρυσιον $flnxz^{mg}b_2$AE^{vid}L^{rwz}; *aurum ibi* B])] cxBC^m αυτα (antecedent--see above, under OG)] S^{txt} ※ *'nwn*⌄ (antecedent *ddhb'*)] α'σ'θ' *'nwn* (S^{mg})] AL^{rw} *illud* (antecedent--see above, under OG)] PS 3 m.s.suffix on *w'rmyth* (antecedent *dhb'*).

79. Exod. 36:2: MT 3 m.s.suffix on *blbw* (antecedent *kl 'yš*)] SP = MT] OG om. (antecedent παντας τους εχοντας [παντας...εχοντας g; πασαν εχουσαν f; παντα τον (τους q*) εχοντα q])] cm αυτων (antecedent--see above, under OG)] S^{txt} ※α'θ' *dylhwn*⌄ (antecedent *wlklhwn hnwn d'yt lhwn*)] B *eius* (antecedent--see above, under OG)] S^{mg} *dylh*] PS 3 m.s.suffix on *blbh* (antecedent *wlkl gbr*).

In these items, the α'σ'θ' and α'θ' insertions agree in number with the antecedents as found in the OG, rather than with the MT suffixes or, consequently, with the MT antecedents. This is probably due to inadvertence, rather than to variants in Theodotion's or Aquila's Hebrew text. These are the only discrepancies in number in the representation of MT suffixes that I have discovered in the Theodotionic material for Exodus. The revisions of the two antecedents to agree in number with the MT and the similar revisions of the reflections of the two suffixes, attested in a few witnesses, are independent of or subsequent to the versions of Theodotion and Aquila.

80. Exod. 8:22: MT *ky tw'bt* (תּוֹעֲבַת) I SP *ky tw'bt* (*tw'bwt* HP) I OG τα γαρ βδελυγματα I $\mathcal{S}^{txt}$ *Ḥdydwt' gyr* I ϑ' *mṭl dlṭḤpwt'* ($\mathcal{S}^{mg}$) I σ' *ṭḤpwt' gyr* ($\mathcal{S}^{mg}$) I α' *mṭl dṭnpwt'* ($\mathcal{S}^{mg}$) I a_2 το γαρ βδελυγμα I 𝔄 *si abominationes* I PS *mṭl dmn ṭnpwt'*.

81. Exod. 8:22: MT *'t tw'bt* (תּוֹעֲבַת) I SP *'t tw'bt* (*tw'bwt* HP) I OG τα βδελυγματα I $\mathcal{S}^{txt}$ *ṭnḤwt'* I ϑ' *lṭnpḤt'* ($\mathcal{S}^{mg}$) I σ' *lṭḤpwt'* ($\mathcal{S}^{mg}$) I α' *lṭnpwt'* ($\mathcal{S}^{mg}$) I PS *dḤlt'*.

82. Exod. 9:32: MT *whksmt* (וְהַכֻּסֶּמֶת) I SP = MT I OG και η ολυρα I $\mathcal{S}^{txt}$ *wkḤnt'* I α'σ' *kḤnt'*· ϑ' *kḤnt'* ($\mathcal{S}^{mg}$) I α'σ' η ζεα (*b*) I PS *wkwḤt'*.

83. Exod. 13:16: MT *wlṭwṭpt* (וּלְטוֹטָפֹת) I SP *wlṭṭpwt* I OG και (om d_2) ασαλευτον (σαλευτον a*) I $\mathcal{S}^{txt}$ *wmttzy'n'* I α'σ'ϑ' *wdmttzy'* ($\mathcal{S}^{mg}$) I α' και ελσενεκτα (j) I α' και ελσιν ακτα (z; cf. v^{mg}) I α' εις νακτα (M) I οι ο' ασαλευτον (j) I οι λ̥ ασαλευτον (vz) I PS *wdwkrn'*. See no. 65 above for a discussion of the variants.

84. Exod. 28:28 (MT): MT *mṭb'tw* (מִטַּבְּעֹתָו) I SP = MT I OG om. I $F^{a?}$ Mcdegjkmnpstvz εκ (επι e) του δακτυλιου (δακτυλου $F^{a?}$) αυτου (om $F^{a?\ vid}$) I ϑ' *mn 'zqt' dylh* ($\mathcal{S}^{txt}$) I $\mathfrak{AE}^{c}$ *ex annulis eius* I PS *mn zqḤqth*.

85. Exod. 28:28 (MT): MT *'l ṭb't* (טַבַּעַת) *h'pd* I SP *'l ṭb't h'pwd* I OG om. I $F^{a?}$Mcdegjkmnpstvz εις τον (το m) δακτυλιον της επωμιδος I ϑ' *l'zqt' dkbynt'* ($\mathcal{S}^{txt}$) I $\mathfrak{AE}^{c}$ εις *annulos* της επωμιδος I PS *lzqḤqth dpdt'*.

86. Exod. 35:3: MT *hšbt* (הַשַּׁבָּת) I SP = MT I OG των σαββατων I $\mathcal{S}^{txt}$ *dšb'* I ϑ' *dšb'* ($\mathcal{S}^{mg}$) I α'σ' *dšbt'* ($\mathcal{S}^{mg}$) I h του σαββατου I PS *dšbt'*.

These seven items concern Hebrew words that end in *-t*. In the MT none have *-w-* before the final *-t*. In unpointed texts the first six could be taken as either singular or plural. The seventh should be singular, since the plural would be *hšbtt*, but the mistaken plural number of the OG form could easily have been overlooked by Theodotion. There is no need to discuss these seven items at any greater length. The first six are in perfect agreement with the unpointed MT, and hence cannot possibly imply variants in Theodotion's Hebrew text, while the seventh need not do so, since Theodotion simply retains the OG reading. Other problems raised by the α'σ'ϑ' variant in no. 83 were discussed earlier under no. 65.

Theodotion's diverse treatment of MT *ʿbt* (plural *ʿbtt*) and MT *qṭrt* may be summarized here, since these words fall into the same general class as those just treated:

Exod. 28:14: MT *ʿbt* (עֲבֹת) ‖ SP *ʿbwt* ‖ θ′ *dš̈šlt'* (𝔖^{mg}).

Exod. 39:15 (LXX 36:22): MT *ʿbt* (עֲבֹת) ‖ SP *ʿbwt* ‖ θ′ *dš̈šlt'* (𝔖^{mg}).

Exod. 28:24 (MT): MT *'t šty ʿbtt* ‖ SP *'t šty ʿbtwt* ‖ θ′ *'nyn ltr̈tyhyn ššl̈t'* (𝔖^{txt}).

Exod. 28:25 (MT): MT *šty hʿbtt* ‖ SP *šty hʿbtwt* ‖ θ′ *dtr̈tyhyn š̈šlt'* (𝔖^{txt}).

Exod. 39:17 (LXX 36:25): MT *(h)ʿbtt* ‖ SP *ʿbtwt* ‖ θ′ χαλαστα (M). The θ′ and α′σ′ variants of M^{mg} may be applied to the wrong word.[16]

Exod. 30:7: MT *qṭrt* (קְטֹרֶת) ‖ SP = MT ‖ θ′ and α′σ′ θυμιαμα (s [om α′]vz).

Exod. 31:8: MT *hqṭrt* (הַקְּטֹרֶת) ‖ SP = MT ‖ α′σ′θ′ του θυμιαματος (sv; cf. z^{mg}) ‖ θ′ *db̈sm'* (𝔖^{txt}).

Exod. 35:8 (LXX v.7): MT *wlqṭrt* (וְלִקְטֹרֶת) ‖ SP = MT ‖ θ′ and σ′ και εις το θυμιαμα (svz) ‖ θ′ *wlbsm'* (𝔖^{txt}).

Exod. 35:15 (LXX v.16): MT *hqṭrt* (הַקְּטֹרֶת) ‖ SP = MT ‖ θ′ *db̈sm'* (𝔖^{txt}).

While *ʿbt* is properly the singular and *ʿbtt* the plural, Theodotion may inadvertently have taken MT *ʿbt* in Exod. 28:14 as plural. The plural Syriac equivalents for MT *qṭrt* attributed to Theodotion in Exod. 31:8 and in Exod. 35:15 (LXX v.16) are probably translational; compare α′σ′θ′ του θυμιαματος alongside θ′ *db̈sm'* in Exod. 31:8. However, they could also represent an interpretation of MT *qṭrt* as plural. There is no need to postulate a variant Hebrew reading to account for any of these apparent discrepancies.

87. Exod. 34:19: MT *wkl mqnk* (מִקְנְךָ) ‖ SP *wkl mqnyk* ‖ OG om. ‖ ckm, 128 (out of place) και (om k) παντων των κτηνων σου (om k) ‖ 𝔖^{txt} ※θ′ *wdklhwn bʿÿr' dylk*↙ ‖ PS *wkl (bwkr̈') dbʿyrk*.

Here Theodotion's *Vorlage* agreed with the plural *mqnyk* of SP against the MT singular *mqnk*, or Theodotion may have taken the MT form as a

---

16 See p. 79.

defective writing of the plural. The treatment of *(w)kl* is, of course, dependent on the evaluation of the noun it modifies. At most, this item points to a minor variant in Theodotion's Hebrew text.

88. Exod. 35:29: MT *lkl hml'kh*] SP = MT] OG (ποιειν) παντα (om eghjs^{txt}v^{txt}z) τα (om F*) εργα] *𝔖 (wlm'bd) klhwn 'bd'*] θ' and σ' εις παντα τα εργα (v)] α' εις παν το εργον (sv)] PS *lkl 'bd*.

The OG represents MT *(l)kl hml'kh* with the plural παντα τα εργα, but has no equivalent for MT *l-* in *lkl* and also exhibits other divergences from the MT. Theodotion and Symmachus insert εις to represent MT *l-* and further revise the OG to bring it into reasonable conformity with the MT in form and content, but they fail to notice, or at least to change, the plural noun and modifiers for the more correct singular. There is no need to assume a plural noun in Theodotion's Hebrew text at this point, however.

89. Exod. 36:4: MT *'t kl ml'kt* (מְלֶאכֶת) *hqds*] SP = MT] OG (+ παντα bck) τα εργα του αγιου] 𝔖^{txt} ※σ'θ' *klhwn*↙*'bd' dqwds'*] PS *'bd' dqwds'*.

The same noun *ml'kh* is involved, but in the construct singular. The latter form is ambiguous in an unpointed text, and could be interpreted as plural; compare nos. 80-86 above. This is the interpretation of the OG, which has nothing to correspond to MT *kl*. Theodotion and Symmachus make good this lack, while retaining the plural number of the OG reading. Since the MT writing is ambiguous, there is no need to attribute inadvertence to Theodotion here. He merely adapted the OG reading to the demands of a consonantal text that agreed with the present MT.

90. Exod. 21:30: MT *kkl 'šr yušt 'lyw*] SP = MT] OG (+ και κατα παντα m; + κατα παντα acegj𝔄) οσα (ως a_2; ο n𝔈^{vid}; *quodcumque* 𝔏^{r}) εαν (αν AFMa-eghi*jlptw$a_2$$b_2$; om 𝔏^{r}) επιβαλωσιν (εβαλωσιν w; επιβαλλωσιν fm; επιβληθωσιν F; επιβαλη A; *aestimatum fuerit* 𝔏^{r}) αυτω (om 𝔏^{r})] 𝔖^{txt} ※α'θ' *'yk klhyn*↙*'ylyn d'n nrmwn 'lwhy*] PS *km' dš' lyn lh*.

The OG provides a rather free equivalent for the MT phrase: periphrastic, plural, and with no explicit reflection of MT *kkl*. Theodotion and Aquila provide a reflection of the omitted words that takes its number from the OG expression rather than from MT *ywšt*. There is no evidence that any changes have been introduced by Theodotion or Aquila into the OG phrase itself. The plural number of α'θ' *klhyn* (= παντα) is best attributed to inadvertence in revision. There is no basis for positing a plural verb form (in place of MT *ywšt*) in Theodotion's Hebrew text.

The use of plurals by all three versions to represent MT *'t kl 'šr bśdh* in Exod. 9:25 is perfectly acceptable, since the Hebrew phrase is not specified as to number.

91. Exod. 25:18 (LXX v.17): MT *mqšh* (מִקְשָׁה) I SP = MT I OG τορευτα (or τορνευτα; etc.) I $\mathcal{S}^{txt}$ *ngydy bṭwrnwn* I σ'θ' *ngydy bṭwrnws* ($\mathcal{S}^{mg}$) I α' ελατους (*b*) I α' *ršyš'* ($\mathcal{S}^{mg}$--with *dšyš'* in Lagarde's B, corrected by his C) I F$^{b\ mg}$ ελατα I PS *dnskt'*.

The word *mqšh* is in apposition to the plural *šnym krbym* (OG δυο χερουβειμ). It is not surprising that the OG used a plural form to reflect it, and that σ'θ' and α' all have plural variants. Once again, there is no need to posit a plural variant in Theodotion's Hebrew text. In Exod. 25:31 (LXX v.30), however, the noun to which MT *mqsh* is in apposition is singular, and so the readings of the OG and of all three versions are in the singular.

92. Exod. 35:22: MT *wkl 'yš 'šr hnyp* I SP *wkl 'šr hnyp* I OG και (om F^{b}nx, 71, $\mathcal{L}^{r}$) παντες (om F^{b}nx, 71, $\mathcal{L}^{rw}$; + οι ανδρες c$\mathcal{A}$) οσοι (*quodquod* $\mathcal{L}$; om F^{b}mnx, 71, $\mathcal{EL}^{r}$; + ηλθον a_2; + *erant* $\mathcal{A}$) ηνεγκαν (προσηνεγκαν 71; *ferebant* $\mathcal{A}$-codd) I $\mathcal{S}^{txt}$ *wklhwn* ※α'θ' *gbr'* ⋎ *hlyn d'ytyw* I PS *wkl gbr' d'prš*.

MT *'yš* is omitted by SP and OG, and was presumably not present in the OG *Vorlage*. The OG equivalent for the remainder of the MT phrase is plural. Theodotion and Aquila insert an equivalent for MT *'yš* that takes its number from the plural OG phrase into which it is inserted. There is no reason to suppose that Theodotion's or Aquila's Hebrew text had a plural noun and verb. Once again the discrepancy in number is due to simple inadvertence. Elsewhere Theodotion uses the singular forms ανηρ/*gbr'* (Exod. 16:16; 30:38; 35:23) and *'nš* (= *τις; Exod. 21:8, 23) to represent MT *'yš*.

93. Exod. 35:35: MT *wrqm* I SP = MT I OG και τα (om Backmnorx)

ποικιλτα (ποικιλτικα x)] Ꞩ^{txt} *wlḥptk*] θ' (+ ※ v) και ποικιλτα (svz)] PS *wṣyr*.

The OG reading for this verse is considerably shorter than the MT, and also follows a different order. In re-arranging and expanding the OG, Theodotion retained the OG plural noun, but without the article, to represent the MT singular *(w)rqm*. The resultant disagreement in number is due to simple inadvertence on Theodotion's part, and does not point to a variant Hebrew reading.

Instances in which Theodotion has a plural noun to represent an MT singular are found in nos. 87-93. With the possible exception of no. 87, where Theodotion may agree with SP *mqnyk* against MT *mqnk*, none of these readings provides solid evidence of a variant form in Theodotion's Hebrew text. Before those instances are discussed in which Theodotion has a singular noun to correspond to an MT plural, mention should be made of Exod. 36:5, where MT *lʾmr* (not represented in the OG) is reflected by σ' θ' *kd ʾmryn* (= λεγοντες of AckyȺ) in Ꞩ^{txt}. This is obviously only a translational variant, with no implications of a different Hebrew reading. The plural Syriac phrase *bhlyn dʾklyn lh*, apparently representing MT *kpy ʾklw*, has been discussed briefly under no. 67 above. As a rather free translation, it does not imply a plural variant in Theodotion's Hebrew text.

94. Exod. 4:13: MT *ʾdny* (אֲדֹנָי)] SP = MT] OG κυριε] Ꞩ *mryʾ*] α'θ' κε (Mvz)] PS *mry*.

95. Exod. 21:8: MT *ʾdnyh*] SP = MT] OG τω κυριω αυτης (εαυτης ik)] Ꞩ^{txt} *dmrʾ* ※ *dylh*↙] θ' κυ αυτης (jsvz)] α' κυ αυτης (vz; cf. s^{mg})] σ' τω κω αυτης (jsvz)] α', σ', and θ' *dmrʾ dylh* (Ꞩ^{mg})] PS *mrh*.

96. Exod. 21:36: MT *bʿlyw*] SP = MT] OG om.] acmȺ-codd (also out of place in egj, 25) ο κς αυτου (om Ⱥ-codd)] θ' *mrʾ dylh* (Ꞩ^{txt})] PS *mrh*.

In all three instances, the MT noun refers to a single individual: to Yahweh in no. 94, to a human master or owner in nos. 95 and 96. In no. 94, the unpointed form could be either singular or plural. In the other two cases the forms are plural, but they are used with singular Hebrew verbs: *yʿdh whpdh* and *ymšl* in no. 95; *yšmrnw* and *yšlm* in no. 96. It would be impossible to use the plural to translate any of these nouns into Greek without seriously distorting the meaning. Therefore Theodotion's use of singular nouns is to be expected. It does not point to singular forms in his Hebrew text.

Similarly, Theodotion uses the singulars θ̅ν̅ (Exod. 7:1) and *ʾlhʾ* (Exod. 8:6, 22 [LXX vv.10, 26]) to represent forms of Hebrew *ʾlhym* that refer to a single individual: Moses in Exod. 7:1; Yahweh in Exod. 8:6, 22. In Exod. 22:8, 19 (LXX vv.9, 20), however, the plural *ʾlhʾ* is twice used by all three versions to represent MT *ʾlhym*. In Exod. 22:19 (LXX v.20), the word refers to false gods, and so the OG also has the plural. In Exod. 22:8 (LXX v.9), the matter is more complicated. The OG version of the entire phrase is periphrastic, but uses a singular noun for "god." The MT uses a plural verb (יַרְשִׁיעֻן), but the SP form is ambiguous (*yršyʿnw*). The sentence is somewhat involved, and Theodotion, together with Aquila and Symmachus, may have failed to notice that MT *ʾlhym* properly refers to Yahweh rather than to "gods." In any case, the variations in the equivalents for MT *ʾlhym* do not point to variant Hebrew readings.

97. Exod. 33:15: MT *ʾm ʾyn pnyk hlkym* I SP = MT I OG ει μη αυτος συ (or συ αυτος) πορευη (or συμπορευη; etc.; + μεθ ημων AFMb-gi-lnop stvwy-$b_2d_2(\frac{1}{2})$, 130, ꞶꞴꞒ^{m}Ꝉ^{r}; etc.) I ꞩ^{txt} *ʾn ʾnt lʾ ʾzl ʾnt ʿmn* I αʹ *ʾn pṙṣwpʾ dylk lʾ ʾzlynʾ* σʹθʹ *ʾn prṣwpʾ dylk lʾ ʾzl* (ꞩ^{mg}) I PS *ʾn ʾnt lʾ ʾzl ʾnt ʿmn*.

The Hebrew noun *pnym* is plural, but Greek usage requires that it be translated by the singular προσωπον (Syriac *prṣwpʾ*). This Theodotion does here and in Exod. 28:25 (MT), 27 (MT), 37 (LXX v.33). In the last three cases, singular forms are also found in Aquila, Symmachus, and all other Greek witnesses. The use of the plural by Aquila in the present instance is due to his tendency toward excessive literalism.

In no. 97, Theodotion and Symmachus have had to put their equivalent of MT *hlkym* in the singular as well, since it must agree with *prṣwpʾ dylk*. Neither the present item nor the other three Theodotionic readings just mentioned point to variants in Theodotion's Hebrew text.

98. Exod. 25:30 (LXX v.29): MT *lḥm pnym* I SP = MT I OG αρτους (om l; + διπλοπροσωπους f; + διπροσωπους $i^{a?}$) ενωπιους (om b, Phil-arm) I ꞩ^{txt} *lḥṁʾ dqdm ʾp̈ʾ* I θʹ προθεσεως (M) I σʹ προθεσεως (F^{b}vz; cf. $j^{mg}k^{mg}s^{mg}$) I σʹ *dsymwt qdmʾ* (ꞩ^{mg}) I σʹ προσωπου (M)

I α' προσωπου (Mjsvz; cf. k^{mg}) I α' αρτους προσωπου (F^{b}) I PS *lḥm 'p'*.

Once again Theodotion and the other versions--with some confusion as to Symmachus' proper reading--use singular nouns to translate MT *pnym*. The use of προθεσεως rather than προσωπου by Theodotion is due to the special phrase *lḥm pnym*, and does not point to a Hebrew variant. The OG, PS, and the three versions all reflect the reading found in the MT and SP.

99. Exod. 28:30 (LXX v.26): MT *'t h'wrym* I SP = MT I OG την δηλωσιν I S^{txt} *lglyn'* I α'σ'θ' *lnwhr'* (S^{mg}) I οι λ̥ τους φωτισμους (sv; cf. $k^{mg}z^{mg}$) I L^{c} *lucentia* I PS *nhyr'*.

100. Exod. 28:30 (LXX v.26): MT *w't htmym* I SP = MT I OG και την αληθειαν I S^{txt} *wlšrr'* I α'σ'θ' *wlšwmly'* (S^{mg}) I οι λ̥ και τας τελειοτητας (sv; cf. $k^{mg}z^{mg}$) I L^{c} *et signacula* I PS *wšlm'*.

If the singular number of these α'σ'θ' readings is not due to the peculiarities of the Syriac translator, so that α'σ'θ' and οι λ̥ would be in agreement, it could probably be attributed to simple inadvertence due to the OG singulars. It is very unlikely that singular variants ever appeared in any Hebrew text at this point.

101. Exod. 29:36: MT *'l hkprym* I SP = MT I OG του καθαρισμου (εξιλασμου n) I S^{txt} *ddwky'* I α'σ'θ' εξιλασμου (Mjvz; cf. k^{mg}) I s^{mg} εξιλασμα I PS *'l ḥwsy'*.

While it is possible that a variant in the singular appeared in some Hebrew text, it is more probable that the singular number was retained through inadvertence when the OG reading was replaced.

102. Exod. 35:8 (LXX v.7): MT *wlqṭrt hsmym* I SP = MT I OG om. I cde $ghjmnps^{txt}ty^{b?}z^{txt}$, 133, A και (+ εις $cmy^{b?}$) το θυμιαμα της (om s) συνθεσεως (om s) I θ' και εις το θυμιαμα της συνθεσεως (svz) I θ' *wlbsm' drwkb'* (S^{txt}) I σ' και εις το θυμιαμα των ηδυσματων (svz) I F^{b} και θυμιαμα των ηδυσματων I PS *wl'ṭr' dbšm'*.

In this instance, the reading of deghjnpstz, 122, A may well have been present in Theodotion's Greek text. If so, he only revised it slightly (inserting εις to represent MT *l*-; cf. $cmy^{b?}$) and failed to notice that the equivalent for MT *smym* was singular. A plural variant is attributed to Symmachus. In Exod. 30:7, however, where the OG equivalent for MT *qṭrt smym* was less acceptable (θυμιαμα συνθετον [συνθεσεως blwx] λεπτον [λεπτης bwx]), Theodotion has θυμιαμα αρωματων (svz) and Aquila and Symmachus have θυμιαμα ηδυσματων (α'σ' in vz and σ' in s). As in a number of the other instances discussed above, Theodotion's divergence from the MT in no. 102 is to be attributed to inadvertence on his part rather than to any variation in the Hebrew text available to him.

The use of a singular by σ'θ' to represent MT *hšmym* in Exod. 24:10 raises no problem, since the OG regularly exhibits the same usage.

103. The plural noun *šmrym* occurs twice in the MT, both times in Exod. 12:42. In each instance the OG has a singular equivalent, presumably reflected in $\mathcal{S}^{txt}$. The first time Theodotion is said by $\mathcal{S}^{mg}$ to agree with $\mathcal{S}^{txt}$, while singular variants are attributed to Aquila and Symmachus. The second time a corrupt reading with two equivalents for MT *šmrym*, both singular and one out of place, is attributed to Theodotion. Singular and plural variants are attributed to Aquila, while two singular equivalents are attributed to Symmachus. The variants for this second occurrence of MT *šmrym* are listed above under no. 37. In both cases, the singular readings attributed to Theodotion are presumably due to inadvertence and the influence of the singular OG readings, rather than to variations in his Hebrew text.

In the discussion of Theodotionic singular nouns representing MT plurals (nos. 94-103), it was never found necessary to posit variants in Theodotion's Hebrew text, though this possibility could not be ruled out entirely in all cases. Once again, the possible differences are all very minor and their presence in Theodotion's Hebrew text would not cause it to differ significantly from the MT.

A few more apparent variants that are translational or of doubtful validity should be noted. In Exod. 4:25, Theodotion and Symmachus both have αιματων to represent MT *dmym*, but $\mathcal{S}^{mg}$ attributes the singular *ddmʾ* to α'θ'. The Syriac plural *myʾ* is used for the Greek singular υδωρ twice in Theodotion's version of Exod. 7:24, once to represent MT *mym* and once to represent MT *(m)mymy*. Problems connected with this last reading are discussed above under no. 35. In Exod. 8:2 (LXX v.6) and in Exod. 40:30 (LXX v.26), the Syriac plural alone is attributed to Theodotion to represent MT *mymy* and *mym*, respectively. The Greek singular της ολοκαυτωσεως and the Syriac plural *dyḳd' šlm'* are attributed to α'σ'θ' and to θ', respectively, for MT *h'lh* in Exod. 31:9, while the Syriac plural is attributed to σ'θ' for MT *h'lh* in Exod. 35:16 (LXX v.17). In Exod. 40:25 (LXX v.26), however, the Syriac singular (*lyqd' šlm'*) is attributed to θ' for MT *'t h'lh*, and in Exod. 29:42 the same Syriac form is attributed to α'θ' to represent MT *'lt* (עֹלַת).

In Exod. 7:11, 24, Theodotion and Symmachus both retain OG plurals to represent MT *mṣrym*, while Aquila substitutes the singular. In Exod. 3:9, where the OG again has the plural noun, Theodotion is said to agree with o', and the same plural is also attributed to Aquila and Symmachus. Twice in Exod. 8:22 (LXX v.26), however, Theodotion and Aquila both have the singular, while the OG and Symmachus have the plural, to represent the two occurrences of MT *mṣrym*. Similarly in Exod. 8:2 (LXX v.6), $\mathcal{S}^{txt}$ apparently attributes the singular of the OG to σ'θ', once again to represent MT *mṣrym*. Neither the Syriac variants nor the inconsistencies in Theodotion's treatment of MT *mṣrym* point to variant readings in Theodotion's Hebrew text.

104. Exod. 1:5: MT *yṣ'y yrk y'qb* ‖ SP = MT ‖ OG (+ αι oȻ; + αι εξελθουσαι i*md$_2$ȺɃ; + εξελθοντων akx; + των εξελθοντων c) εξ (om m) ιακωβ (om m) ‖ $\mathcal{S}^{txt}$ ※ *dhnwn dnpqw*⸔ *mn y'qwb* ‖ fi$^{a?}$r, Or-lat$\frac{1}{2}$ αι εξελθουσαι μετα (om f) ιακωβ (om f) εις (om Or-lat$\frac{1}{2}$) αιγυπτον (om Or-lat$\frac{1}{2}$) ‖ θ' αι εκ μηρου (ιακωβ) (64--according to sched. Bodl., as quoted by Field) ‖ θ' αι εκ μηρων (Sched. Bodl., as "falsely" cited by Holmes--according to Field) ‖ α'θ' εκ μηρων ιακωβ (64--cited by Montef.--quoted by Field) ‖ PS *dnpq mn ḥṣh dy'qwb*.

This evidence remains unreliable. If the singular is accurate, then Theodotion's translation reflects the MT more exactly. The use of the preposition εκ is merely translational. Even if the plural is more accurate, there is no need to posit a variant in Theodotion's Hebrew text.

Of the forty-two numbered instances discussed in this section and the other variants mentioned in passing, only eight could reasonably be regarded as evidence for variations from the MT in Theodotion's Hebrew text: nos. 63, 64, 68, 70, 71, 73, 74, and 87. Of all the readings investigated so far in this chapter, only thirty-three have been found that point with any degree of reliability toward variant Hebrew readings:

nos. 1-6, 8-11, 13-23, 24b, 25, 28, 32, 63, 64, 68, 70, 71, 73, 74, and 87. In relation to the more than 1600 Hebrew items covered by the extant Theodotionic material, thirty-three relatively minor variants comprise only two percent. Their relative unimportance is emphasized by the fact that at least twenty out of the thirty-three merely involve the presence or absence of the conjunction *w-* (nos. 1, 2, 6, 8-11, 13-19, 21-23, 24b, 28, 32).

Other Theodotionic Readings Possibly Reflecting a Different Hebrew Text

In an investigation of possible variations between Hebrew and Greek or Syriac readings, completeness is a relative thing. Among the items not included in this section are the cases in which a copulative verb is used to translate the Hebrew pronoun *hwʾ*, since this usage is completely acceptable and in no way indicative of a variant Hebrew form.[17] Few, if any, of the readings treated actually reflect a different Hebrew text.

105. Exod. 1:11: MT *ʾt ptm* I SP *ʾt pytwn* I OG την τε (om 132) πειθω (Bb'kqruwx, 132^{vid}, Ɇ; πειθωμ Mcvy*^{vid}z; πιθωμ As; etc.) I Ꞩ^{txt} *wlpytwm* I ϑ' *lpytwʾ* α'σ' *lpytw* (Ꞩ^{mg}) I PS *lpytwm.*

The various changes in the spelling of proper names are usually due to scribal error in transmission. No conclusions as to the Hebrew form available to Theodotion are possible.

106. Exod. 1:19: MT *bṭrm* I SP = MT I OG πριν η (om Phil) I Ꞩ *qdm d-* I Mabdhi*pstvwza$_2$d$_2$ προ του I ϑ' διοτι πριν (Nobil.--cited by Field) I σ' και πριν (Nobil.--cited by Field) I Ɇ *priusquam* I PS *wʿdlʾ.*

The Theodotionic variant is presumably translational, although a Hebrew reading **ky bṭrm* is not impossible.

107. Exod. 2:14: MT *hlhrgny* I SP = MT I Babdfk-qtuwyd$_2$ȺꞨȻ^{m}Ƚ^r μη (*si* Ⱥ) ανελειν με (after next word Ƚ^r) I AF*Mceg-jrsv^{txt}xz-c$_2$Ɇ, Cyr η ανελειν με I Ꞩ^{txt} *ʾw lmqṭl ly* I ϑ' η ανελειν με (v) I α' μητι του αποκτειναι με (v) I σ' μητι αποκτειναι με (v) I PS *lmqṭlny.*

While Theodotion's η might point to a Hebrew variant **ʾm (lhrgny)*, it is almost certain that Theodotion merely retained the reading present

[17] The relevant instances are Exod. 29:14; 31:14; 32:9, 25; as well as an *ʾyk šbʿyn* citation in Exod. 12:42.

in the Greek text he was revising.

108. Exod. 4:26: MT *wyrp mmnw* I SP *wyrp mmnh* I OG (om v.26 Bequc$_2$, Cyr-ed$\frac{1}{3}$) και απηλθεν απ (om coA) αυτου (αυτω d; αυτης 76, Cyr$\frac{1}{3}$; αυτων p, 107; om coA + ο [om 128] αγγελος [+ *Dni* Lr; + απ αυτου coA] M^{mg}bcdfhinoprtv^{txt}xz^{txt}, 76, 128, ALr) I Ș *w'zl mnh* I θ' και αφηκεν αυτον (vz) I σ' αφηκεν δε αυτον (vz) I PS *w'rpy mnh*.

Theodotion's concern here was to replace OG και απηλθεν with και αφηκεν to represent MT *wyrp*. In so doing, he also put the accusative pronoun in place of the OG prepositional phrase. The OG phrase reflected the MT phrase *mmnw* more exactly, but Theodotion apparently felt that his entire clause και αφηκεν αυτον ("and he left him alone") expressed the meaning of the Hebrew clause more exactly. It is unlikely that a different Hebrew expression is reflected in Theodotion's version.

109. Exod. 4:26: MT *'z 'mrh* I SP = MT I OG (om v.26 Bequc$_2$, Cyr-ed$\frac{1}{3}$) διοτι ειπεν I Ș *mṭl d'mrt* I θ' and σ' οτι ειπεν (vz) I PS *hydyn 'mrt*.

Presumably OG διοτι was felt to be inappropriate as a reflection of MT *'z*, perhaps because διοτι is too narrowly causal. The change was minor, but the word οτι is less restricted in its meaning and hence was less inappropriate. In any case, it is not necessary to suppose that Theodotion's Hebrew text had **ky*, or the like, rather than MT *'z*.

110. Exod. 5:16: MT *wḥṭ't ʿmk* I SP = MT I OG αδικησεις (μη αδικησης f; etc.) ουν (om A) τον (om a$_2$) λαον σου I Ș *mʿwl 'nt hkyl bʿm' dylk* I θ' και η αμαρτια εις τον λαον σου (jvz) I α' και αμαρτια λαω σου (jvz) I σ' και αμαρτιαν εχεις (jvz) I PS *wḥṭ' 'nt ʿl ʿmk*.

This set of variants was discussed under the third reading of chapter one, where it was shown that all three versions were striving to reflect the difficult phrase in the MT more accurately. There is no reason to suggest that Theodotion had a different Hebrew reading before him at this point.

111. Exod. 5:20: MT *wypgʿw 't mšh* I SP = MT I OG συνηντησαν (συνηντησε 1) δε (om m) μωυση (μωυσει qu; μωση nx; μωσει mc$_2$; μωυσην df; μωυσης 1) I Ș^{txt} *pgʿw dyn* ※σ'θ' *bšmwš'* I PS *wpgʿw bmwš'*.

Syriac *b*- (demanded by the Syriac idiom involving *pg*ʿ) presumably reflects the article *τω, inserted to represent MT *ʾt*, rather than the preposition *εν. Hence there is no reason for suggesting a different Hebrew reading (*bmšh* in place of MT *ʾt mšh*), especially since Hebrew *pg*ʿ is not normally construed with *b*- before a personal object.

112. Exod. 6:23: MT *ʿmyndb*] SP = MT] OG αμειναδαβ (etc.)] Ꞩ^{txt} *d ʿmyndb*] α'σ' *bh bdmwtʾ ʿmyndb*· ϑ' *ʿnmyddb* (Ꞩ^{mg})] PS *ʿmyndb*.

The peculiar form of the proper name attributed to Theodotion is undoubtedly due to secondary scribal error, either in Greek or in Syriac. It reveals nothing about the form of the name present in Theodotion's Hebrew text.

113. Exod. 7:19: MT *whyh*] SP *wyhy*] OG και εγενετο (γενησεται F^{b}dn pɃ; εσται y)] Ꞩ^{txt} *whwʾ*] ϑ' *hwʾ*· α'σ' *nhwʾ* (Ꞩ^{mg})] PS *wnhwʾ*.

The MT future tense (reflected by α'σ', by y, and by F^{b}dnpɃ) is more appropriate in the context, since the following verse proceeds to relate the fulfilment of Yahweh's command by Moses and Aaron. The OG past tense was retained by Theodotion, perhaps because he did not notice its inappropriateness, perhaps also because his Hebrew text had *wyhy* with the SP rather than *whyh* with the MT. Either inadvertence or the Hebrew variant would be a sufficient explanation for Theodotion's retention of the past tense.

114. Exod. 10:14: MT *lpnyw lʾ hyh kn ʾrbh kmhw*] SP = MT] OG προτερα αυτης (ταυτης acȺ) ου γεγονεν (ουκ εσται z^{mg}) τοιαυτη (om ackmx) ακρις (om Ƀ; + τοιαυτη ackmx)] Ꞩ^{txt} *qdmwhy lʾ hwʾ* ※ *dʾyk hnʾ*↙ *qmṣʾ ʾkwth*] α'ϑ' *ddmʾ lh* (Ꞩ^{mg}--marked as a variant for *dʾyk hnʾ*)] s προτερα αυτης τοιαυτη ου γεγονεν ακρις] f και ου γεγονεν ουδεποτε] PS *wʾkwth lʾ hwʾ qmṣʾ qdmwhy*.

While α'ϑ' *ddmʾ lh* is marked as a variant for the Ꞩ^{txt} equivalent of MT *kn*, it would more accurately represent MT *kmhw*. Perhaps it is misplaced in Ꞩ. Even if it is not misplaced, however, the Greek reading it reflects may well be an acceptable translation for MT *kn*. It is impossible to prove that Theodotion's Hebrew text differed from the MT at this point.

115. Exod. 12:21: MT *mškw wqḥw lkm ṣʾn*] SP *mškw qḥw* (*wqḥw* Q) *lkm ṣʾn*

I OG απελθοντες λαβετε υμιν (after εαυτοις 71; υμων 1; om Ɓ) εαυτοις (Bhi; after προβατον egj[-τα gj]; αυτοι b_2*; αυτοις AM dfk-oqrst$^{a?}$vxyzb$_2^{a?}$c$_2$, Cyr; om abcpt*wa$_2$Ɐ^{vid}Ɓ) προβατον (προβατα Aacdgj-npt-zc$_2$) I $\mathcal{S}^{txt}$ *zlw sbw ʾntwn lkwn ʿḤbʾ* I α'σ'θ' *ʾntwn lkwn* ($\mathcal{S}^{mg}$) I PS *bʿgl sbw lkwn ʿnʾ*.

While it is not clear which Greek phrase is reflected by α'σ'θ' *ʾntwn lkwn*, there is little doubt that it translates MT *lkm*.

116. Exod. 13:13: MT *tpdh bśh* I SP = MT I OG αλλαξεις (-ξης eho^{a}b$_2$, Phil-cod$\frac{1}{2}$) προβατω (-του am, Phil-codd; -των 1; -τον c$_2$) I $\mathcal{S}^{txt}$ *tḥlpywhy bʿrbʾ* I θ' *tprwq mn mrʿytʾ* ($\mathcal{S}^{mg}$) I α' *tprqywhy bbr mrʿytʾ* ($\mathcal{S}^{mg}$) I σ' *tprwq bhw drʿʾ* ($\mathcal{S}^{mg}$) I F$^{b\ mg}$ απολυτρω[σεις] I PS *bʾmrʾ tprqywhy*.

The Theodotionic phrase *mn mrʿytʾ* is unusual as an equivalent for MT *bśh*. It may be a somewhat unsuccessful Syriac attempt to translate a reasonable Greek equivalent, or it may represent a free rendition in Greek by Theodotion. The possibility of a Hebrew variant underlying this reading cannot be ruled out, but there is no other evidence to support such a variant. It is curious that the Syriac phrases attributed to Aquila and Symmachus are also strangely periphrastic.

117. Exod. 13:20: MT *bʾtm bqṣh hmdbr* I SP *bʾtm ʾšr bqṣh hmdbr* I OG εν οθομ (etc.) παρα την ερημον I $\mathcal{S}$ *bʾtm dlwt mdbrʾ* I α'σ'θ' εν ηθαν την ερημοτατην (M) I F$^{b\ mg}$ εν σημειω I PS *bʾtm dbšwpy mdbrʾ*.

The form of the proper name is unimportant here, since Greek scribal error can reasonably be invoked. The phrase την ερημοτατην is a free and rather imaginative translation for MT *bqṣh hmdbr*, but there is no doubt that the MT expression was present in Theodotion's Hebrew text. There is no evidence that Theodotion's text contained the expansion (*ʾšr*) found in SP, however.

118. Exod. 14:2: MT *py hḥyrt* I SP = MT I OG της επαυλεως (πολεως i*m) I $\mathcal{S}^{txt}$ *dyrʾ* I α'σ'θ' φιεθρω (M) I α'σ' *pyʾyrwt*˙ θ' *pʾyrwt* ($\mathcal{S}^{mg}$) I F$^{b\ mg}$ ακροτ... της χερωθ I PS *pwmh dḥrytʾ*.

119. Exod. 14:9: MT *py hḥyrt* I SP = MT I OG της επαυλεως I $\mathcal{S}^{txt}$ *dyrʾ* I α'θ' φιεθρων (M) I α'θ' *pʾyʾyrwt* ($\mathcal{S}^{mg}$) I σ' του στοματος της ιαρωθ (M) I σ' *pwmʾ dʾyrwt* ($\mathcal{S}^{mg}$) I PS *pwmh dḥrytʾ*.

In each case, scribal errors have affected the attempts to reproduce the Hebrew name. There is no reason to assume that a different form
was present either time in Theodotion's Hebrew text.

120. Exod. 15:23: MT *mrth* (מָרָתָה)] SP = MT] OG εις μερρα (or μερ-
     ραν; etc.; *Murra* ₵ᶜ)] 𝔖ᵗˣᵗ *lmwr'*] σ' *lmwrt·* θ' *'yk šbʿyn lmwr'*
     (𝔖ᵐᵍ)] PS *lmwrt*.

The Greek form used by Theodotion is uncertain, but there is no
reason to assume a variant in his Hebrew text.

121. Exod. 18:5: MT *ytrw*] SP = MT] OG ιοθορ (ιοθωρ ab'ijl; ιωθορ
     n; ιωθωρ qu, Cyr-cod)] 𝔖 *ytrwn*] θ' ιοθορ (v)] σ' ιοθορ
     (sv)] σ' ιοθωρ (jz)] α' ιεθρω (vz)] α' ιεθρο (js)] PS
     ytrwn.

Theodotion retained the OG form of the name. There is no reason to
assume that there was a variant in his Hebrew text. This is the last of
the proper names that require mention in this investigation of apparent
variants from the MT in Theodotion.

122. Exod. 18:18: MT *gm hʿm hzh*] SP = MT] OG και πας (om cx) ο (om
     t*) λαος (+ σου Aqu) ουτος (ουτως πας c; om B*[hab Bᵃᵇ ᵐᵍ]opa₂b₂
     𝔄𝔈)] 𝔖ᵗˣᵗ *wklh ʿm' hn'*] 𝔖ᵐᵍ *wlklh ʿm' hn'*] α'σ'θ' *wʿm' hn'*
     (𝔖ᵐᵍ)] PS *'p klh ʿm' hn'*.

While neither Theodotion nor Aquila uses καιγε here, there is no
need to say that their Hebrew texts had *w-* instead of MT *gm*. The revisor,
Theodotion, presumably failed to introduce καιγε because his attention
was taken up by the unsupported OG πας, which he omitted. Note also MT
wgm in Exod. 3:9, where Theodotion is said to agree with ο' (και εγω or
perhaps καγω), while Aquila introduces καιγε. In Exod. 7:11, however,
both Aquila and Theodotion are said to have καιγε to represent MT *gm*.
These are the only places in Exodus where the extant Theodotionic material
overlaps MT *gm* or *wgm*.

123. Exod. 19:18: MT *mpny 'šr yrd*] SP = MT] OG δια το καταβεβηκεναι
     ] 𝔖 *mtwl dnht*] θ' δια το καταβηναι (v)] α' απο προσωπου ου
     κατεβη (v)] PS *mṭl dnht*.

Theodotion only makes a minor revision in the OG reading, thereby
retaining a rather free rendition of the MT phrase. There is no reason

to suspect the existence of a variant in Theodotion's Hebrew text.

124. Exod. 21:7: MT *kṣ't h'bdym* ‖ SP = MT ‖ OG ωσπερ αποτρεχουσιν (αποτρεχουσαι 30) αι δουλαι ‖ $\mathcal{S}^{txt}$ *'yk m' dnpqn 'mht'* ‖ ϑ' ωσπερ εκπορευονται οι δουλοι (jsvz) ‖ ϑ' *'ykn' dnpqyn 'bd'* ($\mathcal{S}^{mg}$) ‖ α' ως εξοδος των δουλων (vz; cf. s^{mg}) ‖ α' *'yk mpqt' d'bd'* ($\mathcal{S}^{mg}$) ‖ σ' προσελευσιν (προελευσιν vz) δουλικην (jsvz) ‖ σ' *mpqt' 'mhyt'* ($\mathcal{S}^{mg}$) ‖ PS *'yk dnpqyn 'bd'*.

Theodotion again makes revisions in the OG reading but does not attempt to reflect the syntactic structure of the Hebrew phrase. There is no evidence of a variant in Theodotion's Hebrew text at this point.

125. Exod. 22:10 (LXX v.11): MT *šlḥ ydw* ‖ SP = MT ‖ OG αυτον (αυτ. F*; αυτος $F^{b}bklquwxb_2$; αυτω 16*) πεπονηρευσθαι (-ρευεσθαι dnp; -ρευται fl; + το 73) καθολου (καθ ολον $b_2^{a?\ vid}$; καθ ολης $M^{mg}d$ $fi^{a?}prt$; εφ ολης A; om bw) ‖ ac μετασχειν αυτον (αυτων c) καθολου ‖ $\mathcal{S}^{txt}$ *'štwtpₜkl klh* ‖ σ'ϑ' *mtḥ 'b'š* ($\mathcal{S}^{mg}$) ‖ σ' μετεσχηκεναι αυτον (s [αυτο] v) ‖ z^{mg} μετεσχηκεναι αυτων ‖ M^{mg} μετεσχηκεναι ‖ k^{mg} μετασχειν ‖ α' *šdr 'yd' dylh* ($\mathcal{S}^{mg}$) ‖ PS *'wšb 'ydh*.

The meaning of the Syriac σ'ϑ' reading, *mtḥ 'b'š*, is uncertain (*mtḥ* = to stretch out; *'b'š* = to do evil), as is its relation to the Greek σ' reading μετεσχηκεναι (αυτον). It may represent, somewhat inaccurately, a conflation of μετεσχηκεναι (or μετασχειν) with OG πεπονηρευσθαι. It might also reflect a free rendition of the Hebrew phrase up to the suffix. With the interpretation of the σ'ϑ' variant so uncertain, it would be unreasonable to suggest a different reading in Theodotion's Hebrew text.

126. Exod. 24:10: MT *wk'ṣm hšmym* ‖ SP = MT ‖ OG και ωσπερ (ως αν Phil-gr) ειδος (εργον Cyr-ed$\frac{2}{3}$) στερεωματος (-ματι p) του (om bcm pwx) ουρανου ‖ $\mathcal{S}^{txt}$ *w'yk m' dḥzt' drqy'' dšmy'* ‖ σ'ϑ' *'kwth dšmy'* ($\mathcal{S}^{mg}$) ‖ PS *w'yk krwm' dšmy'*.

There is no reason to suspect that σ'ϑ' *'kwth* reflects a Greek reading based on a Hebrew expression differing from MT *(w)k'ṣm*.

127. Exod. 28:21: MT *'l šmw* ‖ SP = MT ‖ OG κατα (κατ brw; om a_2) το (τα fhikn, Cyr; om brw) ονομα (ονοματα fhikn, Cyr; + αυτου c𝔄𝔅; + αυτων hn, Cyr) ‖ $\mathcal{S}$ *'yk šm'* ※'' *dylh* ‖ α'ϑ'σ'ο' κατα το ονομα αυτου (v) ‖ M^{mg} τας γενεσεις ‖ PS *'l šmh*.

All three versions retain the OG phrase, together with αυτου to represent the MT suffix. Although κατα is not the usual translation for MT *ʿl*, it was presumably felt to be acceptable and perhaps even necessary in a translation of the particular idiom *ʿl šmw*. There is no reason to posit a variant in Theodotion's Hebrew text.

128. Exod. 28:33 (LXX v.29): MT *ʿl šwlyw* ‖ SP = MT ‖ OG επι (υπο B* n, Cyr-ed) το λωμα (δωμα m; απολισμα n^mg; το ακρον η ποδ.. F^b mg) του υποδυτου (υποδηματος m; φελων.. F^b; *tunicae talaris* Ł^r) κατωθεν (κυκλοθεν A; there are also glosses on λωμα and υποδυτης in F^b mg) ‖ S^txt *ʿl špwlwhy dlbwš' mn ltḥt* ‖ σ'θ' *lwt rgl'* (S^mg) ‖ σ' προς ποδων (Msvz) ‖ α' αποληγμα (svz) ‖ α' αποπλεγμα (M) ‖ PS *ʿl špwlwhy*.

Probably σ'θ' *lwt rgl'* (= σ' προς ποδων) is meant to translate only the MT noun *šwly(w)*. It can be regarded as an acceptable descriptive translation, one that is based on a Hebrew text in agreement with the MT. If the σ'θ' phrase were meant to represent MT *ʿl šwly(w)*, however, then it would not seem to be an acceptable equivalent and might possibly be interpreted as reflecting a variant Hebrew reading. This alternative is highly unlikely.

129. Exod. 28:43 (LXX v.39): MT *ʿwlm lw* ‖ SP = MT ‖ OG αιωνιον (εις τον αιωνα msvz) αυτω (αυτων F^b s) ‖ S *dlʿlm lh* ‖ α'ο'(?)θ' αιωνιον αυτου (v) ‖ α' αιωνιον αυτ. (s) ‖ PS *lʿlm lh*.

It is not clear why Aquila and Theodotion have αυτου in place of OG αυτω to represent MT *lh*, but it is unlikely that their Hebrew texts differed from the MT at this point.

130. Exod. 31:5: MT *lml't* ‖ SP = MT ‖ OG om. ‖ c πληρωσεως ‖ m πληρωσαι ‖ θ' *dmwly'* (S^txt) ‖ PS *lmšlmw*.

Theodotion's use of the noun *dmwly'* (= πληρωσεως of c) to represent the MT expression (preposition plus the Piel infinitive construct of *ml'*) is perfectly acceptable. The variant in m represents an attempt at greater literalness. Even though a singular noun represents a Hebrew expression that is formally plural and the Hebrew preposition is not explicitly reflected, there is no reason to suppose that Theodotion's Hebrew text differed from the MT here.

131. Exod. 32:25: MT *lšmṣh* I SP *lšmṣw* I OG επιχαρμα I ﾠ$ *lḥdwtʾ* I θʹ επιχαρμα (svz) I αʹ εις ονομα ρυπου (svz) I σʹ εις κακωνυμιαν (svz) I PS *dnhwwn šmʾ sryʾ*.

These variants have been discussed in the second reading of chapter one. Theodotion retains the OG reading and does not provide any explicit reflection of the MT preposition. Presumably he found the OG reading to be an acceptable rendition of the difficult Hebrew phrase. There is no way to tell whether Theodotion had MT *lšmṣh* or SP *lšmṣw* in his Hebrew text.

132. Exod. 33:22: MT *bnqrt hṣwr* I SP *bnqyrwt hṣwr* I OG εις (ως n; + την x, Cyr-hier) οπην (σχισμ.. F^b mg; σχισμαδ... i^mg) της πετρας I $^txt *bhrwrʾ dšwʿʾ* I αʹσʹθʹ *qywlnʾ* ($^mg vid--Lagarde notes that Field corrected *bhwlnʾ* from *ʾwṣr ʾḤzʾ*; B-McL accept this emendation and translate *in rimam* I αʹ εν τω κολαματ... (*b*) I PS *bmʿrtʾ dṭrnʾ*.

The Syriac reading attributed to αʹσʹθʹ is obscure. The reading given by Lagarde might be a corrupt reflection of the Greek noun κολαματ..., whose meaning is also unknown. While this reading raises problems, it provides no additional information about Theodotion's Hebrew text.

133. Exod. 34:35: MT *ʿwr pny mšh* I SP = MT I OG om. I egjsz η οψις του προσωπου αυτου (om e) I m η οψις του χρωματος αυτου I cv^mg (under ※) η οψις του χρωτος του προσωπου αυτου I $^txt ※θʹ *ḥztʾ dxpgrʾ dprṣwpʾ dylh* I A *visus coloris vultus eius* I σʹ ο χρως του προσωπου μωσει (v) I αʹ δερμα προσωπου μωσει I PS *mškʾ dʾpwhy dmwšʾ*.

Apparently the θʹ variant *ḥztʾ* (= η οψις of cegjmsv^mg z) and the σʹ variant ο χρως for MT *ʿwr* have been conflated in cv^mg A$^txt. While *ḥztʾ*/ η οψις is not the most successful translation for MT *ʿwr*, it need not be taken to reflect a variant Hebrew reading. The inclusion of *d-* (= του) in the θʹ citation of $^txt is probably due to carelessness by the scribe or the author. It is unlikely that Theodotion was responsible for the conflation of the two variants.

134. Exod. 35:16 (LXX v.17): MT *ʾšr lw* I SP = MT I OG om. I ckms^mg v^mg z^mg AE^c το (του m) αυτου I σʹθʹ *dylh* ($^txt) I PS *dylh* (out of place).

Probably σ'θ' *dylh* of Ꞩ^{txt} is meant to represent το αυτου of cks^{mg} v^{mg}z^{mg}ȺɆ^{c}. If so, then it would reflect MT *ʾšr lw* exactly. Even if Theodotion and Symmachus omitted το, this would not justify the conclusion that Theodotion's Hebrew text had a variant from MT *ʾšr lw*. The apparent variant or omission can best be attributed to Syriac translation practices.

135. Exod. 39:1 (LXX 39:13): MT *wmn htklt* ‖ SP = MT ‖ OG και την καταλειφθεισαν (καταλιφθεισαν AB*; λειφθεισαν x) υακινθον ‖ σ'θ' *wtklt' hy dšrkt* (Ꞩ^{txt}) ‖ Ⱥ *et fimbrias ex hyacintho* ‖ Ɇ^{c} *ex hyacintho* ‖ PS *wmn tklt'*.

Theodotion and Symmachus share a Syriac phrase that accurately represents the OG expresion. The latter provides an interpretation of the slightly different MT. Apparently Theodotion felt no need to substitute a prepositional phrase for the OG noun and participle, so as to reflect the structure of the MT more exactly. There is, however, no reason to assume that Theodotion's Hebrew text varied from the MT here.

136. Exod. 40:30 (LXX v.26): MT *wbyn* ‖ SP = MT ‖ OG om. ‖ F^{b}G(under ※)cȺɆ^{c} και ανα μεσον ‖ θ' *lbynt* (Ꞩ^{txt}) ‖ PS *lbyt*.

The apparent Theodotionic variant *l(bynt)* must be due to Syriac idiom (compare PS *lbyt*) when the prepositions are used correlatively: MT *byn* ... *wbyn* and F^{b}G(under ※)cȺɆ^{c} ανα μεσον ... και ανα μεσον, but θ' (Ꞩ^{txt}) *bynt* ... *lbynt* and PS *byt* ... *lbyt*. If this explanation is correct, then Theodotion's apparent variant would be due to Syriac translational practices. In any case, it is unlikely that there was a variant in Theodotion's Hebrew text here.

With the possible exception of nos. 106, 107, 113, and 116, the readings listed under nos. 105-136 do not point toward variants in Theodotion's Hebrew text. Because of the difficulty of interpreting Syriac translations of Greek equivalents for Hebrew readings, some traces of Hebrew variants may have escaped notice; however, it is unlikely that any such omissions would significantly alter the results of these exhaustive investigations and analyses. Theodotion does not always restrict himself to a single Greek equivalent for a given Hebrew word, but in general these variations cannot be used to prove the existence of variant readings in Theodotion's Hebrew text. Since all investigations along these lines have been inconclusive, no attempt is made to list the various instances of lexical inconsistency.[18]

There are some fifteen places in which Theodotion is simply said to agree with ο′ (Syriac *ʾyk šbʿyn*). Even where these presumed readings differ from the MT, it can be said only that Theodotion failed to perceive the need for a revision. There is no certainty that his Hebrew text actually differed from the MT. In the interests of completeness the fifteen readings are given here:

137. Exod. 3:9: MT *wgm rʾyty ʾt hlḥṣ ʾšr mṣrym lḥṣym ʾtm* I SP = MT I OG καγω (Bafikmoqrsu; και εγω AFMb-eghj^{txt}lnptv^{txt}wxyz^{txt}a$_2$b$_2$c$_2$) εωρακα τον (την 32) θλιμμον (θλιψιν 32; + αυτων a$\mathcal{B}\mathcal{C}^{m}$) ον (ην 32) οι (om df) αιγυπτιοι θλιβουσιν (εκθλιβουσιν bw) αυτους I $\mathcal{S}$ *wʾnʾ ḥzyt lʾwlṣnʾ hw dmṣḥyʾ ʾlṣyn lhwn* I θ′ (ο′ j) ομοιως τοις ο′ (jvz) I σ′ και εωρακα την θλιψιν αυτων ην οι αιγυπτιοι θλιβουσιν αυτους (jvz) I α′ καιγε εωρακα συν τον αποθλιμμον ον οι αιγυπτιοι αποθλιβουσιν αυτους (jvz) I PS *wʾp ḥzyt ʾwlṣnʾ dmṣḥyʾ ʾlṣyn lhwn.*

---

[18] The following set of equivalents exemplifies this lexical inconsistency:

Exod. 28:37 (LXX v.33): MT and SP *hmṣnpt*$^{(1)}$ I OG της μιτρας I $\mathcal{S}$ *klylʾ* I α′θ′ της κινδαρεως (jsv).

Exod. 28:37 (LXX v.33): MT and SP *hmṣnpt*$^{(2)}$ I OG της μιτρας I $\mathcal{S}$ *dklylʾ* I α′θ′ της κινδαρεως (v).

Exod. 28:39 (LXX v.35): MT and SP *mṣnpt* I OG κινδαριν I $\mathcal{S}$ om. I α′σ′ μιτραν θ′ υφωμα (M).

Exod. 28:40 (LXX v.36): MT and SP *(w)mgbʿwt* I OG κινδαρεις I $\mathcal{S}$ *(w)mṣnptʾ* I α′σ′ μιτρας θ′ υφωματα (v).

If there were total consistency in the use of correspondents for Hebrew words, then one would have to say that MT *mṣnpt* was replaced by **mgbʿt* in the Hebrew texts of Theodotion, Aquila, and Symmachus for Exod. 28:39 (LXX v.35). Even the OG equivalents appear to lend support to this suggestion, but neither the MT nor the SP exhibit the desired readings. The proposed variant in Theodotion's Hebrew text for Exod. 28:39 (LXX v.35) has to remain conjectural, and the same would be true for similar proposals based on Theodotion's inconsistency in the treatment of other Hebrew terms as, for example, the verb *prṣ*, the noun *bdym*, and the noun *šny* in the expression *twlʿt šny*.

138. Exod. 12:11: MT *psḥ* | SP = MT | OG πασχα | S̸^{txt} *pṣḥ̈'* | θ' *'yk šbʿyn* (S̸^{mg}) | α' υπερβασις (Mjvz) | α' *mʿbrt'* (S̸^{mg}) | α' υπερβασιν (j) | α' και σ' φασιν (j) | σ' φασεχ (φασεκ v; φασιν jz) υπερμαχησις (Mjvz) | σ' *pṣḥ̈' msyʿwt tktwš'* (S̸^{mg}) | σ' φασεκ υπερμαχησης (c_2) | φιλον διαβατηριον (j) | PS *(mṭl d)pṣḥ̈'*.

139. Exod. 12:27: MT *psḥ hw'* | SP = MT | OG το πασχα τουτο (out of place a_2A̸; om n, Or-gr) | S̸^{txt} *hw pṣḥ̈' hn'* | α' *dmʿbrt' 'ytwhy*· σ' *pṣḥ̈' 'ytwhy*· θ' *'yk šbʿyn* (S̸^{mg}) | PS *hw dpṣḥ̈h*.

140. Exod. 12:42 (LXX vv.41-42): MT *lyl šmrym hw' lyhwh* | SP *lylh šmrym hw' lyhwh* | OG νυκτος (om A*y*c_2, Ath, Thdt; out of place Mvz; + νυκτα F$^{b?}$; + *[h]aec* E̸^{z}) προφυλακη (προφυλακης abx; προσφυλακη dp) εστιν (*erat* A̸; *enim erat* P̸) τω (om egjnprwB̸$^{l\ vid}$E̸^{vid}) κυριω (κ̅υ̅ egjnB̸$^{l\ vid}$E̸^{vid}) | S̸^{txt} *blly' dmṭrt' 'ytyh hwt drmy'* | θ' *'yk šbʿyn* (S̸^{mg}) | α' νυξ παρατηρησεως τω πιπι (*b*) | α' παρατηρησεων (M) | α' *lly' dmṭrt' 'ytwhy hw' lpypy* (S̸^{mg}) | σ' *lly' nṭyr' 'ytwhy lpypy* (S̸^{mg}) | σ' παρατετηρημενη (M) | F$^{b\ mg}$ νυκτα φυλαγματ[ων] | k^{mg} παρατηρησις | σαμ.' φυλαξεως εστι κ̅ω̅ (c_2^{mg}--marked for the next OG προφυλακη) | PS *lly' nṭyr hw' lmry'*.

141. Exod. 14:7: MT *wšlšm* (וְשָׁלִשִׁם) | SP *wšlšym* (or *wšlyšym*) | OG και τριστατας | S̸^{txt} *wtlytỹ' dqymyn* | α' *wtlytỹ'*· σ' *wtlt' tlt'*· θ' *bdmwt' dhnwn šbʿyn* (S̸^{mg}--followed by a gloss about *tlytỹ'*) | σ' ανα τρεις (Mv; cf. j^{mg}z^{mg}) | F$^{b\ mg}$ παλλικα... | PS *wgbr̈'*.

142. Exod. 15:16: MT *'ymth wpḥd* | SP *'ymh wpḥd* | BalsB̸ τρομος και φοβος | S̸^{txt} *rʿlt' wdḥlt'* | α' *twht' wdḥlt'*· θ' *'yk šbʿyn* (S̸^{mg}) | AFMb-km-rtvx-$b_2$$d_2$E̸P̸, Or-lat, Cyr, Luc φοβος και τρομος | w τρομος | PS *dḥlt' wzwʿt'*.

143. Exod. 15:21: MT *wtʿn* | SP = MT | OG εξηρχεν δε | S̸^{txt} *mšry' hwt ... dyn* | α' *mʿny' hwt*· σ' *mʿny' hwt dyn*· θ' *'yk šbʿyn* (S̸^{mg}) | α' και κατελεγεν (M; cf. j^{mg}z^{mg}) | F$^{b\ mg}$ κατελεγεν | PS *wmʿny' hwt*.

144. Exod. 18:1: MT *ytrw* | SP = MT | OG ιοθορ (ιοθωρ ab'gijl$^{a?}$; ιωθορ fn; ιωθωρ qu, Cyr-cod; ιαθωρ m; ιορθορ a_2; out of place in p) | S̸^{txt} *ytrwn* | α' *ytrw*· σ'θ' *'yk šbʿyn* (S̸^{mg}) | PS *ytrwn*.

145. Exod. 18:1: MT *ḥtn* | SP = MT | OG ο (οτι h) γαμβρος (πενθερος F$^{b\ mg}$dlp^{b}w^{b}) | S̸^{txt} *hw ḥmwhy* | α' *ḥtn'*· σ' *ḥmwhy*· θ' *'yk šbʿyn* (S̸^{mg}) | PS *ḥmwhy*.

146. Exod. 20:17 (S v.14): MT *byt rʿk* I SP *byt rʿk* ... *śdhw* I OG την οικιαν (οικειαν q) του πλησιον σου (αυτου for του--σου k, Theoph; om την--σου b'denpz*) ουδε (ουτε BFMh; ου f) τον αγρον αυτου (om ουτε--αυτου F[b?]) I S[txt] *byth dqryb' dylk wl' ḥql' dylh* I α' *dbyt' dḥbr' dylk·* σ'θ' *'yk šbʿyn* (S[mg]) I PS *byth dḥbrk*. Note that only acAS and PS restore or retain the order of clauses found in MT and SP.

147. Exod. 22:27 (LXX v.28): MT *l' t'r* I SP = MT I OG ουκ (ου Bkmo) ερεις κακως (ερεις after κακως Bkmo) I S[txt] *l' t'mr bys'yt*(2) I α' *l' tlwṭ·* σ' *l' tšwṭ·* θ' *'yk šbʿyn* (S[mg]) I PS *l' tlwṭ*. See the discussion under no. 38 above for the reasons for associating these variants from S[txt] with *l' t'mr byš'yt*(2) of S[txt] and not with *l' t'mr byš'yt*(1) (which corresponds to MT *l' tqll* and OG ου κακολογησεις) as marked.

148. Exod. 23:31: MT *plštym* I SP = MT I OG της (των 32, B; om h) φυλιστιειμ (φιλιστιειμ b'filnpa$_2$) I S[txt] *dplšt* I α'θ' *bdmwt' dhnwn šbʿyn·* σ' *dplšty'* (S[mg]--marker in text out of place) I F[b mg] των αλλοφυλων I PS *dplšty'*.

149. Exod. 24:6: MT *wyśm* I SP *wyśm* I OG ενεχεεν (ενεχθεν s; προσεχεεν ma$_2$; εχεεν 78; ενεχεν και προσεχεεν a[b mg]) I S[txt] *nsk* I σ'θ' *bdmwt' dhnwn šbʿyn* (S[mg]--there is no indication how far the agreement extends) I α' εθηκεν (z; cf. s[mg]) I PS *w'rmy*.

150. Exod. 25:31 (LXX v.30): MT *mqšh* I SP = MT I OG τορευτην (τορνευτην f, Cyr-ed; *tornatum* AEL[rv], Phil-arm; *in auro tornatili* B) I S[txt] *ngydt bṭwrnwn* I α' *ršyšt'·* σ'θ' *'yk šbʿyn* (S[mg]) I α' ελατην (b; cf. F[b mg]) I PS *dnskt'*.

151. Exod. 25:33 (LXX v.32): MT *wprḥ*(2) I SP = MT I OG om. (cf. OG και κρινον, S[txt] *wšwšnt'*(1), etc., which represent MT *wprḥ*(1)) I S[txt](under ※) *wšwšnt'*(2) I A *et lilium*(2) I α' *prʿ'·* σ' *hbb'·* θ' *'yk šbʿyn* (S[mg]) I PS *wšwšn'*(2).

152. Exod. 28:15; MT *ḥšb* (חֹשֶׁב) I SP = MT I OG (+ του f) ποικιλτου (ποικιλτουν 16, A[vid]B[vid]; *uario* L[r]; υφαντου Cyr) I S[txt] *dmptkn'* I α'σ' *dmtṭʿnn'* (*dmtṭknn'* C[corr])· θ' *bdmwt' dhnwn šbʿyn* (S[mg]) I α' λογιστικου (b) I PS *d'wmn'*.

In all of the above instances, excepting no. 151, the OG, or the version of the OG reflected in S[txt], does not differ radically from the MT, and it is not surprising that Theodotion chose simply to retain the

OG reading. In no. 151, however, the OG did not reflect the repetitious MT clause. Origen filled out his text by repeating the previous clause of the OG. Theodotion is said to agree with one word in this expansion, for which Aquila and Symmachus had variants. Quite possibly Theodotion filled out his own Greek text in the same way that Origen later did, by relying on the OG for the earlier occurrence of the MT clause. In any case, Theodotion's Hebrew text here agreed with the MT against the shorter OG.

Evaluation

The conclusions reached in this chapter are significant. There is a close agreement between Theodotion in Exodus and the present MT. Only about thirty-seven times--less than two and a half percent of the extant Theodotionic material in Exodus--are at all likely to point toward Hebrew variants. Over half of these items concern merely the presence or absence of the conjunction *w*-. Many of the other divergences are equally minor. Because Theodotion often agrees with the MT independently of other witnesses or after revising them, his dependence on the MT is almost certainly direct.

Barthélemy has suggested that the genuine Theodotionic material from the hexapla belongs to the recension exemplified by the ΚΑΙΓΕ material in the Minor Prophets and in Samuel-Kings.[19] In contrast to Theodotion in Exodus, the ΚΑΙΓΕ material in these other books does not reflect the present MT exactly. It is based on the proto-MT, a text that is related to the MT but that also differs significantly from it.[20] Since, as shall subsequently be shown, there is very little clear evidence for a secondary recension of the Theodotionic material in Exodus independently of or after its use by Aquila, one must conclude that the ΚΑΙΓΕ revisor(s) had access to the excellent text of the Pentateuch that is preserved in the Masoretic recension. Since the proto-MT elsewhere, especially in Samuel-Kings, was less satisfactory, however, the text was more fluid and there is evidence of greater recensional activity.

---

[19] *DA*, p. 47.

[20] See, for example, F. M. Cross, Jr., "The History of the Biblical Text in the Light of Discoveries in the Judean Desert," *HTR* 57 (1964), 282-283.

IV The Relationship Between the Theodotionic Material and the OG in Exodus

The assumption to be tested is that Theodotion used some form of the OG text as the basis for his revision toward the Hebrew text available to him. In general, Theodotionic readings were preserved when they differed from the OG or when their agreement with the OG was felt to be of special importance, for example, when Aquila and/or Symmachus differed significantly from the reading common to the OG and Theodotion. The Theodotionic material preserved in Exodus covers only a little more than six percent of the entire book. While over half of the 399 different Theodotionic readings in Exodus have no agreement with the OG at all and over two-fifths of the remainder have only minor agreements with the OG, it may be supposed that this high degree of divergence is due to the interests of those who preserved the readings rather than to the general character of the Theodotionic version. There are 111 Theodotionic readings in Exodus that have, or appear to have, some significant agreement with the OG or with a major strand of LXX manuscripts.

Theodotionic Readings that Have Little or No Agreement with the OG

There are 213 Theodotionic readings that have nothing or only the conjunction *και/w-* in common with the OG, and seventy-three further readings that have, or appear to have, some minor agreement with the OG. The first group needs no extensive discussion here; a brief description of the main types of reading it includes will suffice.

One hundred and twenty-two of the readings in the first group are simple expansions. In $\mathcal{S}^{txt}$ or in the margin of Greek hexaplaric manuscripts, Theodotion, sometimes in a joint citation with Aquila or Symmachus, is said to have a word or phrase not found in the OG. Most of these readings are under six words in length, but a few are longer.[1]

---

[1]For example, σ'θ' και ειπεν $\overline{\kappa\varsigma}$ προς μωυσην (μωσην v) εωρακα τον

Many of the expansions are only one or two words in length, while twenty-nine are simply pronouns reflecting Hebrew pronominal suffixes. Frequently, but by no means always, the Theodotionic expansion or a variant appears in a few LXX manuscripts. For the most part these are hexaplaric manuscripts or other manuscripts, often Lucianic, that have undergone hexaplaric influence.[2] In every case, as far as I can tell, Theodotion is the source for the new reading. There is no evidence that the surrounding material in Theodotion's text either agreed with the OG or differed from it.

Of the remaining ninety-one readings in the first group, sixty-eight are short variants that have nothing, except perhaps a definite article, in common with the OG. Nine more are short variants that share και/*w*- with the OG.[3] On a few occasions the Theodotionic variants also occur in manuscripts that have come under hexaplaric influence.[4] Finally there are fourteen short variants, two with και/*w*- in common with the OG, that

---

λαον τουτον και ιδου λαος σκληροτραχηλος εστιν (om s) in $s^{mg}v^{mg}$(pr ※) z^{mg} for Exod. 32:9. The passage, which reflects the MT exactly, is not found in the OG. It is found, with minor variants, in $cmp^{b?}b_2$, 128, A̸, and under ※ in S̸^{txt}. Other long Theodotionic readings that fill in OG gaps are found in Exod. 35:14-15 (LXX vv.16-17); 37:1 (LXX 38:1), 4-5 (LXX 38:4); 40:30 (LXX v.26); and elsewhere.

[2]For example, ackmxA̸ (and, with a change, 128) for Exod. 11:3; acd kmnptA̸B̸C̸^{m} for Exod. 21:6; M^{mg}cdmnptA̸E̸^{vid} (and a variant expansion in $A^{c\ mg}$ FM^{txt}abegjklqsu-b_2B̸L̸^{r}) for Exod. 29:28; cmquxA̸B̸^{1}C̸^{m} for Exod. 32:29; AckyA̸ for Exod. 36:5. Variants to Theodotionic pluses may be found, e.g., in acegjkmxA̸S̸ for Exod. 9:20; in ackmxA̸S̸ for Exod. 9:22; in acegjkmxA̸, Or-gr$\frac{1}{2}$ for Exod. 12:26; and in abcfimr and xA̸S̸ for Exod. 25:6.

[3]In Exod. 39:33 (LXX 39:14), the conjunction is not supported by the MT, but its presence in Theodotion and in the OG is not enough to prove any dependence of Theodotion on the OG. The example is item 22 of chapter three. The other eight instances of the conjunction are all supported by the MT.

[4]For example, in S̸, csv, and anwz for Exod. 22;9 (LXX v.10); in $F^{b\ mg}$acmA̸E̸^{c} for Exod. 25:23 (LXX v.22); as a doublet to the OG reading in MdnptL̸^{rv} for Exod. 25:29 (LXX v.28).

contain items not present in the OG.[5] All ninety-one variants are under five words in length. The Theodotionic version from which they came could have resembled the OG very closely or could have differed considerably from the OG. These readings provide no evidence supporting either alternative.

In addition to the 213 Theodotionic readings just summarized, there are seventy-three readings that appear to have some minor agreement or connection with the OG. Six short Theodotionic expansions have a proper name, the conjunction καιι/*w*-, or apparently the definite article in common with the OG. In all six cases the agreement could be due to coincidence. It does not prove that Theodotion had the OG as the basis of his revision. Seventeen Theodotionic variants share points of agreement with the OG. In every case the agreement between Theodotion's reading and the OG correspondent is very minor: a pronoun, a conjunction, a negative adverb, a preposition, a simple noun or adjective. Some of the Syriac agreements may not represent actual agreements in the respective Greek originals. Even if they do, all the agreements in these readings could be due to the demands of the Hebrew phrases being translated rather than to any direct dependence of Theodotion on the OG. There are seventeen additional Syriac variants, each under four words in length, many or all of which might agree with the OG. In some cases the interpretation of the Syriac readings remains uncertain, while in all cases the agreement could be due to coincidence rather than to direct dependence on the OG. Seven more short variants, five of which are in Syriac, have lexical similarities to the OG. In every case the similarity could be coincidental, since the Theodotionic readings are perfectly normal translations of the MT.

---

[5]In Exod. 35:11 (LXX v.10), the conjunction και/*w*-, common to Theodotion and the OG, is not supported by the MT (but see item 13 of chapter three). In Exod. 12:7, the Theodotionic expansion *w*- (= και) is not found in the MT or SP, but also appears in bcdk-nptwzd_2, Chr$\frac{1}{2}$, while the Theodotionic variant (the Syriac preposition *ʿl*) is found (as επι) in ab wx. This is item 2 of chapter three. In Exod. 34:20, variant reflections of the MT suffix are also found in AFMbdefgijlnoprstvyzb_2ABC^m and in a_2. Here the Theodotionic reading could be considered a simple variant to the expanded expression, as well as an expanded variant to the OG.

There are eleven short variants that contain items not present in the OG and that also have minor agreements with the OG. Five more variants containing items not found in the OG have lexical similarities to the OG. The corrupt Theodotionic reading found in Exod. 12:42 also has minor agreements or similarities with the OG. In all seventeen cases the agreements or similarities could have arisen independently in the translation of the various MT expressions and hence do not provide any firm evidence for genuine Theodotionic dependence on the OG. Finally there are nine short variants that omit items found in the OG and that also either agree partially with the OG or have lexical similarities with the OG. In no case is the agreement or similarity such as to prove Theodotionic dependence on the OG.

The 286 Theodotionic readings summarized in this section can be found in Appendix A. The subdivisions are arranged in the order followed above. No supporting textual evidence is included, nor are the corresponding MT or OG readings given. Two additional citations are listed as problematic. In Exod. 26:24 $\mathcal{S}^{mg}$ has α' *mtʾmynʾ* σ' *mn ltḥtʾ* ϑ' as variants for $\mathcal{S}^{txt}$ *šqyn mn ltḥt* (= OG εξ ισου κατωθεν) to represent MT *tʾmym mlmṭh*. Since no reading is attributed to Theodotion, this citation adds nothing. The enigmatic ϑ' επι of Exod. 40:5 is discussed under item 45 of chapter three. As an erroneous or misplaced citation, it tells nothing about Theodotion's relation to the OG.

The remaining one hundred and eleven Theodotionic readings are mentioned at the end of Appendix A. They are all discussed, at least briefly, in the next section and provide the basis for any evaluation of Theodotion's relation to the OG.

Theodotionic Readings that Have or May Have Significant Agreements with the OG

For ease in reference, the various readings discussed under different headings in this section are numbered consecutively.

Theodotionic Variants that Partially Agree with the OG

1. Exod. 5:3: ϑ' *npgʿ bn mwtʾ ʾw sypʾ* ($\mathcal{S}^{mg}$; cf. ϑ' η ρομφαια in *b*) I OG συναντηση (-σει AFMb'ginopa$_2$) ημιν θανατος η φονος I $\mathcal{S}^{txt}$ *nʾrwʿ ln mwtʾ ʾw qṭlʾ* I MT *ypgʿnw bdbr ʾw bḥrb*.

Additional textual evidence for this reading is given under item 26 of chapter three. The Theodotionic variant retains the structure of the OG, against that common to MT, SP, and PS. The latter is reflected by Aquila according to $\mathcal{S}^{mg}$, but not according to F^{I}Mv. It is unlikely that this similarity between Theodotion and the OG is due to chance, or that Theodotion's Hebrew text differed from the MT here. There is little doubt that Theodotion simply failed to correct the OG expressions thoroughly, perhaps through inadvertence.

2. Exod. 6:1: θ' *bʾydʾ ʾḥydtʾ nšdr ʾnwn wbʾydʾ ʾḥydtʾ* ($\mathcal{S}^{mg}$)] OG εν ... χειρι κραταια εξαποστελει αυτους και εν βραχιονι υψηλω] $\mathcal{S}^{txt}$ *bʾydʾ ... ʾḥdtʾ nšdr ʾnwn wbdrʿʾ rmʾ*] MT *byd ḥzqh yšlḥm wbyd ḥzqh.*

If $\mathcal{S}^{mg}$ and $\mathcal{S}^{txt}$ are faithful to their Greek originals, Theodotion revised the OG only enough to reflect the MT exactly. He used the OG equivalent for the first *byd ḥzqh* to reflect the second occurrence of the phrase as well, while retaining the OG verb and object. He also omitted OG γαρ, and presumably inserted *οτι or the like before εν χειρι$^{(1)}$ to reflect MT *ky* more accurately. More extensive changes are found in both Aquila and Symmachus, also according to $\mathcal{S}^{mg}$. The partial agreement between Theodotion and the OG is probably due to dependence by the former on the latter rather than to simple coincidence.

3. Exod. 7:1: σ'θ' ιδε κατεστησα σε θυ̅ φαραω (v)] σ' ιδε κατεστησα σε θ' θυ̅ φαραω (jz)] OG ιδου δεδωκα σε θεον (+ τω dnpt) φαραω] MT *rʾh nttyk ʾlhym lprʿh.*

This variant is discussed under item 63 of chapter three. If v^{mg} is correct, then Theodotion and Symmachus both differed from the OG rather strikingly, and the agreement of all three on the last two words would be rather unimportant. If, however, $j^{mg}z^{mg}$ are correct, Theodotion's agreement for the last two words would be contrasted with Aquila's expansion (θυ̅ τω φαραω) and would not necessarily imply a Theodotionic variant from the OG for the first three words. In either case the agreement between Theodotion and the OG for the last two words could easily be coincidental, since θεον φαραω, with or without the intervening article to represent MT *l-* explicitly, is the most obvious translation for MT *ʾlhym lprʿh.*

4. Exod. 14:2: θ' *qdmwhy tšrwn* ($\mathcal{S}^{mg}$)] OG ενωπιον αυτων στρατοπεδευσεις] $\mathcal{S}^{txt}$ *qdmyhwn tšrʾ*] MT *nkḥw tḥnw.*

According to $\mathfrak{S}$, Theodotion's variant reading differs from the OT only in the number of the pronoun, singular for plural, and of the verb, plural for singular. In each case Theodotion's variant reflects the MT more exactly. The general similarity between the two Syriac readings could be coincidental, but a relationship of dependence is more likely. Both Aquila and Symmachus have variant equivalents for the MT preposition as well.

5. Exod. 15:18: θ' *pypy dmmlk* ($\mathfrak{S}^{mg}$) I OG κυριος βασιλευων I $\mathfrak{S}^{txt}$ *mryʾ hw dmmlk* I MT *yhwh ymlk*.

Apparently Theodotion agrees with the OG in having a participle to represent the Hebrew imperfect *ymlk*. His Syriac form or that of $\mathfrak{S}^{txt}$ could also represent the finite present tense (βασιλευει), found in Phil-codd$\frac{1}{2}$ and reflected in $\mathfrak{A}$-codd, but this is less likely. Both Aquila and Symmachus are credited with the Syriac imperfect *nmlk* (presumably reflecting *βασιλευσει or the like) by $\mathfrak{S}^{mg}$. The latter is the more frequent and expected translation for the Hebrew form. The apparent agreement on the less usual participle points to a dependence by Theodotion on the OG here.

6. Exod. 19:18: θ' δια το καταβηναι επ αυτο $\overline{\kappa\nu}$ (v) I OG δια το καταβεβηκεναι τον (om o) θεον ($\overline{\kappa\nu}$ F; τον θεον after αυτο [αυτον x; αυτου ak, Eus] Ba[inserts $\overline{\kappa\nu}$ before τον $\overline{\vartheta\nu}$]kmrx, Eus) επ αυτο (αυτω bdep, Phil-codd; αυτου akqu, Eus; αυτον x, Cyr$\frac{1}{4}$; $\overline{\kappa\nu}$ επ αυτο M^{mg} s^{mg}) I MT *mpny ʾšr yrd ʿlyw yhwh*, compare SP *mpny ʾšr yrd yhwh ʿlyw*.

Theodotion's structural agreement and lexical similarity with the OG in the first part of the variant, where the translation is free rather than literal, is almost certainly due to direct dependence by Theodotion on the OG. The various changes introduced by Theodotion are intended to reflect the MT more accurately. Note that the change in order is also found in Bakmrx, Eus, and in $M^{mg}s^{mg}$. This is probably due to hexaplaric influence, even in Br.[6] The different order of the OG was also found in

---

[6]It is also possible that Br represent the original OG reading, that most LXX manuscripts have a Proto-Lucianic revision to the Palestinian Hebrew text exemplified in SP, and that akmx have a further hexaplaric revision back to the present MT.

the Palestinian text tradition represented by SP. Aquila's variant for this phrase is much more literal: α' απο προσωπου ου κατεβη επ αυτου κς (v).

7. Exod. 20:25 (Ꞩ v.22): θ' οτι την ρομφαιαν σου επιβεβληκας επ αυτο (js[αυτον]vz; cf. θ' *mṭl dlsyp' dylk 'rmyt 'lwhy* in Ꞩ^{mg})] OG το γαρ ενχειριδιον σου (μου A; om Fejlqru₵^{m}Ɇ^{f}, Phil-arm) επιβεβληκας επ αυτο] Ꞩ^{txt} *br 'yd' gyr* ※ *dylk*⸔ *'rmyt 'lwhy*] MT *ky ḥrbk hnpt 'lyh.*

The agreement between Theodotion and the OG on the verb επιβεβληκας--both Aquila and Symmachus have variants--is probably not due to chance. The substitution of ρομφαια for ενχειριδιον to represent MT *ḥrb* is related to the similar substitution of ρομφαια (for OG φονος) in Exod. 5:3 (item 1 of this section). The other minor change, οτι for OG γαρ, is meant to reflect MT *ky* more literally. The partial agreement between Theodotion's variant and the OG is best understood as the result of genuine dependence by the former on the latter.

8. Exod. 22:18 (LXX v.19): θ' παν κοιμωμενον μετα κτηνους αναθεματισθησεται (cited from Basil. by Montef. according to Field, while only the final verb is said to have been cited by Holmes' scribe)] OG παν (πας 76, 136; παντα F^{b}acdfi$^{a?}$kmnprstvxz) κοιμωμενον (-μενος 76, 136) μετα κτηνους (*pecore omni* Ɓ) θανατω (om a_2b_2Ɓ) αποκτενειτε (αποθανειται np) αυτους (αυτον b'dfi$^{a?}$nrtƁɆꞨ, Cyr-ed; om AFMegj^{txt}pqsu-xzȺ; αναθεματισθησετε αυτους j^{mg}] MT *kl škb 'm bhmh mwt ywmt.*

The agreement between Theodotion and the OG, if correctly reported, extends over four consecutive words. While this agreement is probably due to dependence on the OG, the possibility of coincidence cannot be ruled out. The Theodotionic variant for OG θανατω αποκτενειτε (αυτους) is unusual, but not pertinent to the present investigation. See item 69 of chapter three.

9. Exod. 27:14: α'σ'θ' *dktp' ḥd'* (Ꞩ^{mg}; cf. α'σ' τη ωμια in Ms[om σ'] vz)] OG τω κλιτει τω ενι] Ꞩ^{txt} *lsṭr' ḥd*] MT *lktp.*

If Theodotion did not have an expanded Hebrew text before him, then the expansion in his variant would probably be due to the similar expansion in the OG. The uncertainty about the interpretation of this variant means that it cannot be included among those that tend to prove Theodotionic dependence on the OG, although such dependence would obviously explain the expansion.

10. Exod. 27:15: σ'θ' *wlktpʾ trynytʾ* (Ѕ^mg) ‖ OG και το κλιτος το δευτερον ‖ Ѕ^txt *wsṭrʾ hw trynʾ* ‖ MT *wlktp hšnyt*.

The partial agreement of Theodotion and Symmachus with the OG could easily be due to their having translated the same Hebrew phrase, and cannot be taken as proof for Theodotionic dependence on the OG.

11. Exod. 28:3: α'σ'θ' π̅ν̅ς σοφιας (v) ‖ OG πνευματος αισθησεως ‖ MT *rwḥ ḥkmh*.

Once again the partial agreement of Theodotion, Aquila, and Symmachus with the OG could easily be coincidental since all versions obviously presuppose the phrase found in the MT. It need not imply genuine Theodotionic dependence on the OG.

12. Exod. 28:37 (LXX v.33): α'θ' κατα προσωπον της κινδαρεως (v) ‖ OG κατα προσωπον της μιτρας ‖ MT *ʾl mwl pny hmṣnpt*.

The agreement of Theodotion and Aquila with the OG, especially on the use of κατα to represent MT *ʾl mwl*, is probably due to dependence by Theodotion on the OG, and by Aquila on Theodotion, rather than to coincidence.

13. Exod. 28:43 (LXX v.39): α'ο'(?)θ' αιωνιον αυτου (v) ‖ OG αιωνιον (εις τον αιωνα nsv^txt z) αυτω (αυτων F^b s) ‖ MT *ʿwlm lw*.

The partial agreement with the OG might be due to dependence on the OG, but it could just as easily be coincidental. There is no obvious reason why Theodotion or Aquila would deliberately replace OG αυτω with αυτου. The change could be accidental.

14. Exod. 29:26: σ'θ' *dšwmlyʾ* (Ѕ^mg) ‖ OG της τελειωσεως ‖ Ѕ^txt *dšwmlyʾ* ‖ MT *hmlʾym*.

The similarity between the σ'θ' reading of Ѕ^mg and the reflection of the OG found in Ѕ^txt may mean that Theodotion had the OG reading before him and simply replaced it with the more accurate plural of the same noun. It is, however, just as possible that the resemblance is coincidental. The plural of τελειωσις would be a reasonable choice as a translation for the Hebrew noun *mlʾym*.

15. Exod. 29:20: θ' *w'l ṭrp' d'dn' dbḥy' dylh* (ܣ txt) I OG και επι τους λοβους των ωτων των υιων αυτου I ܣ txt (under ÷) *w'l ṭrp' d'dn' dbḥy' dylh* I MT *w'l tnwk 'zn bnyw*.

The Theodotionic and OG readings coincide, except that Theodotion has singular nouns in place of the OG plurals where the MT nouns are singular. The OG phrase is in a different position in the verse than is the MT equivalent. The Theodotionic variant is inserted into ܣ txt at the place corresponding to the MT position. The same change is found in cmA. While the partial agreement between Theodotion and the OG may well be due to dependence of the former on the latter, an independent translation of the MT phrase would probably have the same degree of resemblance to the OG.

16. Exod. 30:32: σ'θ' κατα την συνταξιν ταυτην (v) I OG κατα την συνθεσιν ταυτην I MT *(w)bmtkntw*.

The retention of OG ταυτην to represent the MT and SP suffix points to a genuine dependence of Theodotion and Symmachus on the OG at this point. It is rather unlikely that the similarity was accidental, or that Theodotion and the OG shared a Hebrew text that had a demonstrative in place of the MT/SP suffix. This reading was treated under item 72 of chapter three.

17. Exod. 33:5: θ' *mṭl d' 'bd lk* (ܣ mg) I OG α ποιησω σοι I ܣ txt *hlyn d' 'bd lk* I MT *mh ' 'śh lk*.

The variants in this reading are discussed under item 42 of chapter three. The partial agreement between Theodotion and the OG could be due either to dependence of the former on the latter or to independent translations of the same Hebrew phrase (*' 'śh lk*).

18. Exod. 35:29: θ' του ενεγκαι εις παντα τα εργα (v) I OG εισελθοντας (εισελθοντα B*ar; εισελθοντες F*fix; εισελθειν eghjsv^{txt}z; εισελθοντων 1; εισηλθον του B$^{a?b}$; εισελθων γαρ a_2) ποιειν παντα (om eghjsv^{txt}z) τα εργα I MT *lhby' lkl hml'kh*.

The discrepancy between Theodotion's plural and the MT singular is discussed under item 88 of chapter three, where it is suggested that the plural may have been retained inadvertently from the OG. If this suggestion is correct, then the reading obviously reveals Theodotionic dependence on the OG at this point.

19. Exod. 36:1: α'σ'θ' *lmdʿ lmʿbd* (Syr^{mg}) ‖ OG (+ του qu) συνιεναι (om b; + ωστε bcmqu; + και nL^{r}) ποιειν ‖ Syr^{txt} *lmstklw* (+ ※ Lagarde) *ʾyk*⤙ *dlmʿbd* (*ʾyk d*⤙ Lagarde) ‖ MT *ldʿt lʿśt*.

The agreement of α'σ'θ' and the OG on ποιειν/*lmʿbd* to represent MT *lʿśt* could be coincidental or the result of genuine dependence by Theodotion on the OG. There is no way to decide between the two alternatives.

While all nineteen items considered above may owe their partial agreements with the OG to the dependence of Theodotion on the OG, this is most likely in nos. 1, 6, and 16. It is reasonably likely in nos. 2, 4, 5, 7, 8, 12, and 18. The remaining items (nos. 3, 9-11, 13-15, 17, 19) are inconclusive; their agreements with the OG are relatively minor.

There are eight longer Theodotionic readings that partially agree with the OG and that should also be discussed.

20. Exod. 1:19: θ' οτι ζωογονουσιν αυται διοτι πριν εισελθειν προς αυτας τικτουσι (Nobil., acc. to Field) ‖ OG τικτουσιν γαρ πριν η εισελθειν προς αυτας τας μαιας και ετικτον ‖ MT *ky ḥywt hnh bṭrm tbwʾ ʾlhn hmyldt wyldw*.

The Theodotionic failure to reflect MT *hmyldt* and the following conjunction is discussed under item 24 (a,b) in chapter three, while the apparent expansion διοτι πριν is noted under item 106 in the same chapter. The partial agreements of Theodotion and the OG are suggestive, but they do not prove that Theodotion was dependent on the OG here.

21. Exod. 5:7: θ' καθαπερ εχθες και της τριτης αυτοι πορευεσθωσαν (πορευθεντες j) και καλαμασθωσαν εαυτοις αχυρον (jvz) ‖ OG καθαπερ εχθες (χθες B^{b}cdfghlmnpx) και (+ την x) τριτην ημεραν (+ και το της σημερον AMdj^{mg}n[ημερου]pqtuv^{txt}z^{mg}a$_2$b$_2$c$_2$) αυτοι πορευεσθωσαν και συναγαγετωσαν εαυτοις (+ τα aioqrsu) αχυρα ‖ Syr^{txt} *ʾyk mʾ dʾtmly wd* ÷*bywmʾ*⤙ *tlytyʾ* α'θ' *hnwn nʾzlwn wnknšwn lhwn tbnʾ* (no ※ or ⤙) ‖ MT *ktml šlšm hm ylkw wqššw lhm tbn*.

Aspects of this reading are discussed under items 1 and 34 of chapter three. The general agreement of this Theodotionic variant with the OG is extensive, especially if πορευθεντες of j^{mg} is secondary within the Theodotionic textual tradition. The replacement of OG τριτην ημεραν with της τριτης was to remove ημεραν, which did not represent a separate noun in the Hebrew text. The substitution of καλαμασθωσαν for OG συναγαγετωσαν may have been intended to achieve lexical consistency, while the singular αχυρον is a more literal translation of MT *tbn* than is the OG plural. The structural and lexical agreements with the OG are too many to be attributed to mere chance. They testify to a genuine dependence of Theodotion on the OG.

22. Exod. 5:16--see the third reading in chapter one.

Theodotion agrees with the OG more closely than do Aquila or Symmachus. Particularly significant is the use of μεμαστιγωνται by both Theodotion and the OG to represent the MT participle *mkym*. This variant points rather clearly to a direct dependence of Theodotion on the OG, even when he also introduces extensive changes into the OG text.

23. Exod. 7:24: θ' και ωρυξαν παντες οι αιγυπτιοι (+ οι z) κυκλω του ποταμου υδωρ εις το πιειν οτι ουκ ηδυναντο πιειν (om οτι--πιειν(2) c_2) εκ του υδατος του ποταμου vzc_2; cf. θ' *my̆' lmšt' mṭl dl' mṣyn hww lmšt' my̆' mn dnhr'* in $\mathcal{S}^{mg}$)] OG ωρυξαν δε παντες οι αιγυπτιοι κυκλω του ποταμου ωστε πιειν υδωρ (before ωστε kx; before πιειν(1) bwA̸; + απο [εκ 30] του ποταμου B*h, 30) οτι ουκ ηδυναντο πιειν υδωρ απο (εκ Fcegj^{txt}v^{txt}z^{txt}) του ποταμου] MT *wyḥprw kl mṣrym sbybt hy'r mym lštwt ky l' yklw lštt mmymy hy'r.*

The conflict between the Greek and Syriac versions attributed to Theodotion for the last part of this reading is discussed under item 35 of chapter three. The entire Theodotionic reading is closely related to the OG, with only those changes that were necessary to reflect the MT more exactly: θ' και for OG δε; θ' υδωρ εις το πιειν for OG ωστε πιειν υδωρ; θ' εκ του υδατος του ποταμου for OG υδωρ απο του ποταμου (but note θ' *my̆' mn dnhr'* in $\mathcal{S}^{mg}$). The general agreement in vocabulary between Theodotion and the OG at this point is a good indication that Theodotion based his version on the text of the OG.

24. Exod. 8:22 (LXX v.26): θ' *mṭl dlṭn̈pwt' dmṣryn ndbḥ lmry' 'lh' dyln wdbḥynn lṭnpwt' dmṣryn qdm 'y̆n' dylhwn wl' rgmyn ln* ($\mathcal{S}^{mg}$)] OG τα γαρ βδελυγματα των αιγυπτιων (+ ου bfmsw, Cyr-cod) θυσομεν (θυσωμεν AMbcdf-ilmnqrtvwza$_2$b$_2$A̸, Cyr-cod, Phil-cod; + ημεις fir) κυριω (after τω x; om acE̸, Phil$\frac{1}{2}$) τω θεω ημων εαν (+ τε s) γαρ (δε c_2 E̸; om i*) θυσωμεν τα βδελυγματα των αιγυπτιων εναντιον αυτων λιθοβοληθησομεθα] $\mathcal{S}^{txt}$ *n̈dydwt' gyr dmṣ̈ry' ndbḥ lmry' 'lh' dyln 'n gyr*

ndbḥ ṭnpwt' dmṣry' qdmyhwn mtrgmynn I MT *ky tw'bt* (תּוֹעֲבַת) *mṣrym nzbḥ lyhwh 'lhynw hn nzbḥ 't tw'bt* (תּוֹעֲבַת) *mṣrym l'ynyhm wl' ysqlnw.*

The strange Theodotionic *w-* for MT *hn* is discussed in item 64 of chapter three, while other aspects of this reading are included in items 80-81 of the same chapter. Apart from the features discussed there, Theodotion's reading reflects the MT better than the OG does. There are various similarities between Theodotion's reading and the OG, including perhaps agreement on the nouns used to represent MT *tw'bt* twice. The most significant agreement is between ϑ' *qdm 'yn' dylhwn* and OG εναντιον αυτων (𝔖[txt] *qdmyhwn*), where Theodotion simply inserted *των οφθαλμων or the like into the OG phrase so as to reflect MT *'yny-* explicitly. Aquila has a different reading, Syriac *l'yn' dylhwn*, that is less closely related to the OG. Most probably the partial agreement between Theodotion's reading and the OG is again best explained as the result of direct dependence by Theodotion on the OG.

25. Exod. 8:25 (LXX v.29)--see the fourth reading in chapter one.
26. Exod. 32:18--see the seventh reading in chapter one.
27. Exod. 32:25--see the second reading in chapter one.

In item 25, Theodotion's agreement with the OG includes especially the verb ευξομαι as a translation for MT *(w)h'trty*. His variants are all intended to reflect the MT more accurately or with greater consistency: ϑ' και for OG δε; ϑ' ιδου for OG οδε; and ϑ' εγω ειμι εκπορευομαι for OG εγω εξελευσομαι. Probably the partial agreement between the two versions points to Theodotionic dependence on the OG, although the accidental convergence of independent translations is not impossible either.

The Theodotionic expansion, *dqrb'*, in item 26 is discussed under item 12 of chapter three. The fact that the Theodotionic reading is in Syriac makes it difficult to determine the extent of its agreement with the OG. Probably here the agreement between Theodotion and the OG is less significant, so that it could be due either to direct dependence of Theodotion on the OG or to the fact that Theodotion and the OG both translate the same Hebrew text.

Aspects of item 27 are discussed under items 41 and 131 of chapter three. Theodotion has some variants from the OG that reflect the MT more accurately: ϑ' ειδεν for OG ιδων; ϑ' οτι for OG γαρ; ϑ' διεσκεδασμενος εστιν for OG διεσκεδασται; θ' αυτον for OG αυτους; and θ' ανθεστηκοσιν for OG υπεναντιοις. He also has certain striking agreements or lexical similarities with the OG:

θ' διεσκεδασμενος εστιν, OG διεσκεδασται, MT *prʿ hwʾ*.

θ' διεσκεδασεν, OG *idem*, MT *prʿ-*.

θ' επιχαρμα, OG *idem*, MT *lšmṣh*.

These make it virtually certain that Theodotion used the OG as the basis for his own version at this point.

Items 21-23 and 27 exhibit strong resemblances to the OG; they almost certainly point to direct dependence by Theodotion on the OG. Items 24 and 25 have resemblances that are less striking but that also provide proof of such dependence. Items 20 and 26 are inconclusive. The six long readings, items 21-25 and 27, and ten short readings, items 1, 2, 4-8, 12, 16, and 18, that point with more or less certainty to direct Theodotionic dependence on the OG constitute a firm first step in the attempt to show that Theodotion's relationship to the OG is characterized by such dependence.

Theodotionic Variants that Partially Agree with the Majority of LXX Manuscripts Against B and Related Manuscripts

28. Exod. 9:8: α'σ'θ' *sbw lkwn* (Ꞩ^{mg})] OG λαβετε (λαβε g) υμεις (υμιν AM*b*degjlptvwyzb_2c_2ꞴE; υμιν αυτοις a_2)] Ꞩ^{txt} *sbw ʾntwn*] MT *qḥw lkm*.

Syriac *ʾntwn* of Ꞩ^{txt} reflects OG υμεις (found in Bab'cfhikmnoqrsux AP), while α'σ'θ' *lkwn* represents the variant υμιν. Since the latter is found in a large number of LXX manuscripts, it may have been present in the OG manuscript used by Theodotion. The agreement on λαβετε υμιν as a translation for MT *qḥw lkm* is not particularly striking, and this Theodotionic variant cannot be used to prove a genuine dependence by Theodotion on either strand of LXX witnesses.

29. Exod. 18:5: θ' και ηλθεν ιοθορ γαμβρος μωυσει (v)] OG και εξηλθεν (Bfioqru; ηλθεν AFM rell AB^{vid}EL^{z}Ꞩ, Cyr, Thdt) ιοθορ (ιοθωρ ab' ijl; ιωθορ n; ιωθωρ qu, Cyr-cod) ο γαμβρος μωυση (μωση aknx)] MT *wybʾ ytrw ḥtn mšh*.

Theodotion agrees almost exactly with the Greek version found in all but a few LXX manuscripts. While the variant εξηλθεν may be the OG reading, it could also have been introduced secondarily into a forerunner of Bfioqru. The change from OT μωυση to θ' μωυσει is a very common itacism. The omission of the article before γαμβρος could be deliberate, although Theodotion does not consistently omit articles that have no correspondent in the Hebrew text. The agreement on ιοθορ to represent MT *ytrw* is particularly significant. This reading probably points to Theodotion's dependence on the OG text available to him. It is less likely that the agreement with the OG arose independently.

30. Exod. 21:18: α'σ'θ' *wnmḥ*' *'nš* (Ṡmg)] OG και (om 18) παταξωσιν (Bbmqu; καταπαταξη c; παταξη afb₂Ɇ; παταξη τις AFᴵM rell Ꜳ (+ *ex eis*)Ȼᵐⱡʳ, Eus, Cyr, Spec(+ *ex his*); παταξη ο εις F*; παταξη ανηρ Fᵇ; *percusserit unus eorum* Ƀ)] Ṡtxt *wnmḥwn*] MT *whkh 'yš*.

In this variant, α'σ'θ' reflect the reading found in almost all LXX manuscripts, και παταξη τις.[7] This in turn reflects the MT expression fairly well, but represents MT *'yš* with τις rather than with ανηρ which is found only in Fᵇ. Barthélemy has argued that a distinctive feature of the ΚΑΙΓΕ group is the systematic replacement of OG εκαστος with ανηρ to reflect MT *'yš*, even where MT *'yš* is used idiomatically to mean "each."[8] This distinctive usage is normally retained by Aquila.[9]

In Exod. 21: 33, α'θ' are again said by Ṡtxt to have inserted *'nš* (= τις of ac) to reflect MT *'yš* on its second occurrence in the verse. The first MT *'yš* in the verse was already represented by τις in the OG. Since Theodotion elsewhere uses ανηρ/*gbr*' to represent MT *'yš* in Exodus,[10]

---

[7]In Ṡ, Syriac *gbr*' is regularly used to represent Greek ανηρ, while Syriac *'nš* corresponds to Greek τις. No evidence of contrary correspondences has been found in Ṡ for Exodus.

[8]*DA*, pp. 48-54.

[9]*Ibid.*, p. 52.

[10]Exod. 16:16: θ' and α' *gbr*' (Ṡmg), OG εκαστος, Ṡtxt and σ' (Ṡmg) *kl ḥd*; Exod. 30-38: α'θ' ανηρ (v), α'θ' *gbr*' (Ṡtxt), OG om., Fᶜ?cmsᵐᵍzᵐᵍ Ꜳ ανηρ, σ' α̅ν̅ο̅ς (v); Exod. 35:22: α'θ' *gbr̈*' (Ṡtxt), OG om., cꜲ οι ανδρες; Exod. 35:23: α' and σ' and θ' ανηρ (svz), α'θ' *gbr*' (Ṡtxt), OG om., ckꜲ ανηρ. The plural number in α'θ' for Exod. 35:22 is probably due to the plural number in the shorter OG phrase, και παντες οσοι, into which the reflection of MT *'yš* was inserted. See item 92 in chapter three. Thus,

his use of *ʾnš* (= τις) on two occasions must be explained.

In Exod. 21:18 Theodotion apparently retained the Greek reading present in his OG manuscript without change. Aquila presumably derived the reading from Theodotion, while Symmachus' affinities remain unclear. Perhaps Theodotion did not notice that τις, rather than ανηρ, represented MT *ʾyš*, or perhaps this usage did not meet with his disapproval. In Exod. 21:33, Theodotion's choice of *ʾnš* (= τις) to represent the second MT *ʾyš* was probably influenced by OG τις for the first MT *ʾyš*. In each case, but in different ways, Theodotion's failure to follow usage normal to him and to KAIΓE is best explained as a failure to modify the usage already present in his text of the OG. In Exod. 21:18, moreover, this usage was not present in the original OG (if Bbmquš^{txt} preserve the OG reading), but was presumably introduced in an early revision of the original παταξωσιν. This reading thus provides good evidence for genuine Theodotionic dependence on a form of the OG that had already undergone revision toward the Hebrew text. The Theodotionic expansion in Exod. 21:33, as well as the plural α'θ' expansion (*gbrʾ*) in Exod. 35:22 (discussed in fn. 10), may provide supporting though not decisive evidence for Theodotionic dependence on the OG, since they may be conditioned by OG usage in their respective contexts.

31. Exod. 22:27 (LXX v.28): σ'θ' *lryšnʾ* (š^{mg}) I OG αρχοντας (Bacovz A-coddC^{m}, Phil, Eus, Thdt$\frac{1}{7}$, Did; αρχοντα AFMbd-np-uwxa_2b_2A-edBE, Acta$^{23.5}$, Chr, Cyr, Thdt$\frac{6}{7}$, Cyp, Vg) I š^{txt} *(w)lryšnʾ* I MT *(w)nśyʾ*.

The plural form may be the original OG or a secondary development in Bacovz, but the singular was almost certainly present in the OG text available to Theodotion. Since agreement on the translation for a single MT word could be coincidental, especially when the equivalent is not unexpected, this reading cannot be used to prove Theodotionic dependence on any form of the OG.

32. Exod. 29:1: θ' εις το αγιασαι (*b*; cf. α'θ' *lmqdšw* in š^{mg}) I OG αγιασεις (BchoquxB^{w}; *et sanctificabis* A; αγιασας r; αγιασαι AFM rell B^{l}C^{m}EL^{r}, Cyr) I MT *lqdš*.

---

if it is not a secondary error by the hexaplaric collator or a subsequent scribe, the plural number of this reading may point to Theodotion's dependence on the OG once again. See the remarks made under item 18 of this section.

Theodotion's variant is an expansion of that found in most LXX manuscripts, so as to reflect the MT preposition *l*-. Since αγιαζειν is the expected equivalent for MT *qdš*, the agreement between Theodotion and the LXX manuscripts does not prove direct dependence by Theodotion on the major strand of OG witnesses.

33. Exod. 32:4: α'θ' *w'mrw* (S^{mg}) I OG και ειπεν (ειπαν AF$^{a?}$Mabcgi-lo rsvwyzb_2, Cyr-ed; ειπον F^{b}n; *dixerunt* C^{m}E^{f}; *dicunt* A) I S^{txt} *w'mrw* I MT *wy'mrw*.

The singular reading is found only in BF*^{vid}defhmpqtua_2BE^{c}L^{z}. The plural form attributed to α'θ' by S^{mg} could represent either ειπαν, found in most LXX witnesses, or the variant ειπον, found in F^{b}n. No matter which form Theodotion had, he could have chosen it independently of the LXX witnesses as the appropriate rendition of the MT plural. This reading cannot be used to prove a dependence of Theodotion on any Greek version.

34. Exod. 32:27: α'σ'θ' διελθετε (v) I OG και (om fA) διελθατε (διελθετε F$^{a?}$Ma-hjmnp-uwz) I MT *'brw*.

The OG form διελθατε is found only in ABF*^{vid}iklov^{txt}xya_2b_2, while Theodotion, together with Aquila and Symmachus, has the form found in the remaining LXX witnesses. This agreement for an isolated verb proves nothing, but it suggests once again that Theodotion based his version on the form of the OG text that was available to him, a form that differed to some extent from the original OG.

35. Exod. 32:31: θ'α'ο' επεστρεψεν δε μωσης (v) I OG (+ και egjns^{txt} v^{txt}z^{txt}, 25, L$^{z\ vid}$) υπεστρεψεν (επεστρεψεν AFMbcdklmprs^{mg}twyz^{mg} a_2b_2; απεστρεψεν n[-ψε]x; απεστραφη egjs^{txt}v^{txt}z^{txt}, 32; ανεστραφη 25) δε (om egjnsvz, 25, L^{z}) μωυσης (μωσης kmn) I MT *wyšb mšh*.

With the possible exception of the *'yk šb'yn* citation in Exod. 15:21 (item 143 in chapter three), this is the only time that Theodotion uses δε to represent MT *w*-. Elsewhere in Exodus Theodotion regularly uses και to represent MT *w*-, frequently where the OG has δε. Aquila also normally avoids using δε to represent MT *w*-, although Symmachus exhibits no such tendency.[11] The retention of δε by Theodotion and Aquila here is most

[11]One exception to this pattern in Aquila occurs in Exod. 32:25 (the

probably due to inadvertence. It points to their dependence on some form of the OG text. The Theodotionic verb επεστρεψεν is found in most LXX manuscripts, while the presumed original OG reading υπεστρεψεν appears only in Bafhioqu. The change in spelling of the proper name may be scribal, since both forms are sometimes attributed to Theodotion elsewhere in Exodus.[12] This reading points rather strongly toward genuine dependence by Theodotion on the revision of the OG found in most LXX manuscripts.

36. Exod. 34:22: α'θ' *wʿʾdʾ* (Sᵐᵍ) I OG και αρχην (BahrCᵐ; αρχη u; εορτη i*; εορτην AFMb-giᵃj-ps[+ και εορτην]tv-b₂ABELʳʷ; + ... εορτην h) I Sᵗˣᵗ *wryšʾ* I MT *wḥg*(2).

The presumed OG reading αρχην survives in only a few manuscripts and in Sᵗˣᵗ. It is identical with the OG equivalent found in virtually all LXX witnesses for MT *bkwry* later in the same verse: OG αρχην, Sᵗˣᵗ *ryšʾ*. The variant εορτην/*ʿʾdʾ*, found in most LXX manuscripts and attributed to α'θ' by Sᵐᵍ, is identical with the OG equivalent found for the earlier occurrence of MT *(w)ḥg* in the verse: OG εορτην, Sᵗˣᵗ *(w)ʿʾdʾ*. The correct replacement of αρχην with εορτην to represent the second MT *(w)ḥg*, found in most LXX manuscripts, was undoubtedly present in the OG text available to Theodotion. The agreement between Theodotion and the majority of LXX manuscripts on this point is not sufficient to prove that Theodotion was dependent on a form of the OG text here, however, since an independent translation of the MT might reasonably be expected to adopt the same equivalent for the Hebrew noun *ḥg*.

Of the nine short readings considered thus far, only items 29, 30, and 35 point with any degree of certainty to genuine Theodotionic dependence on a revised form of the OG. The others may reflect such dependence, but they cannot be used to prove it. There are two longer readings that include some agreement of Theodotion with the majority of LXX manuscripts against B and related manuscripts.

---

second reading of chapter one), where Theodotion and the OG both have και, while Aquila and Symmachus both have δε.

[12] In Exod. 32;9, both σ'θ' μωυσην (sz) and σ'θ' μωσην (v) are found. Note also θ' μωσης (v) in Exod. 8;25 (LXX v.29); θ' μωυσει (v) in Exod. 18:5; θ' μωυσης (svz) in Exod. 32:25. Similar variations occur in the forms attributed to Aquila and Symmachus.

37. Exod. 2:14--see the first reading in chapter one.

38. Exod. 21:7-8--see the fifth reading in chapter one.

In item 37, Theodotion replaces OG θελεις with λεγεις, to represent MT *ʾmr*, and has no trace of the OG expansion εχθες/χθες, that occurs in different positions in the various LXX witnesses. He shares η with AF*Mceg-jrsv^{txt}xz-c$_2$Ɇ, Cyr, rather than μη of Babdfk-qtuwyd$_2$ɃȻ^{m}Ƚ^r, to represent the MT interrogative *h*-. For the rest of this reading Theodotion is in complete agreement with the OG, even on the use of ανελειν and ανειλες to translate MT *(h)lhrg*- and *hrgt*, respectively, and on the use of ον τροπον to translate MT *kʾšr*. The substantial agreement between Theodotion and the OG (or in one case a large number of LXX manuscripts) in item 37 shows rather clearly that at this point Theodotion based his version on the form of the OG available to him.

In item 38, the Theodotionic variant πονηρα εστιν is discussed under item 4 of chapter three. In the first part of the reading, Theodotion has several differences from the OG, but shares the construction ωσπερ plus present tense to represent MT *k*- plus infinitive construct. In the last part of the reading, Theodotion shares ου καθωμολογησατο with AF*Macdehj^{txt}klmops^{txt}tv^{txt}y-b$_2$Ƀ against OG αυτω καθωμολογησατο (found only in BnquxɆ), and adds αυτην with F*dhi$^{a?}$loprs^{txt}tv^{txt}y-b$_2$Ƀ^{vid}, all to represent MT *lʾ yʿdh*. In spite of his variants, these agreements and other minor ones show clearly that Theodotion once again based his version on the form of the OG available to him, a form that had already undergone some revision toward the Hebrew text, and that he then revised it still further to reflect the Hebrew text more exactly. These two long readings thus lend strong support to the argument that Theodotion's version is a deliberate revision of the already partially revised OG.

Theodotionic Readings that Partially Agree with the OG or the Shortened OG and that Also Expand the OG

39. Exod. 7:11: θʹ καιγε αυτοι οι επαοιδοι των αιγυπτιων εν ταις φαρμακειαις (!) αυτων ωσαυτως (vz; cf. j^{mg}; the B-McL citation has -κειας, presumably a misprint, while Field has -κειαις) ‖ OG και οι επαοιδοι των αιγυπτιων ταις φαρμακιαις αυτων ωσαυτως ‖ MT *gm hm ḥrṭmy mṣrym blhṭyhm kn*.

Theodotion uses καιγε rather than OG και to represent MT *gm*. He also uses αυτοι and εν to reflect MT *hm* and the MT preposition *b*-, neither of which is reflected explicitly in the OG. Otherwise he agrees exactly with the OG, except for the insignificant and very common itacism, ει for ι, in φαρμακειαις. This extensive agreement between Theodotion and the OG is a reliable indication of Theodotion's direct dependence on the OG at this point. Aquila, on the contrary, differs almost totally from the OG while sharing καιγε αυτοι and εν with Theodotion.

40. Exod. 8:3 (LXX v.7): ϑ' οι επαοιδοι εν ταις φαρμακειαις αυτων (85--cited from Montef. by Field)] OG και (om Ɇ) οι επαοιδοι των (om M1yɆ^{f}S̸) αιγυπτιων (om M1yɆ^{f}S̸; + εν AB^{ab}amoqu) ταις φαρμακιαις (επαοιδαις AM^{mg}qu[-διαις qu]) αυτων] MT *hḥrṭmym blṭyhm*.

This citation may be a misplaced partial quotation of the reading found in the previous item, since ms 85 is B-McL's z and this reading is not given by B-McL at LXX Exod. 8:7. If it is a correct reading, then Theodotion omits those elements in the OG reading that are not supported by the MT. Otherwise his agreement with the OG is similar to that discussed in the previous item, though less extensive, and would again point to genuine Theodotionic dependence on the OG.

41. Exod. 28:1: ϑ' εις ιερατευειν αυτον μοι (vz)] OG ιερατευειν (+ αυτον cm) μοι (εμοι egjsv^{txt})] MT *lkhnw ly*.

Theodotion's reading reflects the MT expression more exactly, by providing εις and αυτον to represent the preposition and the suffix on MT *lkhnw*. The partial agreement between Theodotion and the OG could have come about in the course of independent translations of the same Hebrew phrase and need not imply any dependence of Theodotion on the OG at this point.

42. Exod. 28:5: ϑ' και το κοκκινον το διαφορον (v; compare s^{mg}z^{mg} and also α'ϑ' *mšḥlptʾ* in S̸^{mg})] OG και το κοκκινον] MT *wʾt twlʿt hšny*.

Theodotion's longer reading includes the shorter OG reading, but this could be due either to the fact that both versions are translating the same Hebrew noun (*twlʿt*) or to a relationship of dependence between Theodotion and the OG. Since, however, only *twlʿt (h)šny* as a whole means "scarlet," while the first noun literally means "worm" (compare α' σκωληκος, here and elsewhere), Theodotion's retention of κοκκινον ("scarlet") to represent *twlʿt* and his inconsistent efforts to provide a further translation for *šny* make it more reasonable to attribute his agreement with the OG to dependence rather than to coincidence.[13]

43. Exod. 28:6: θ' και ποιησουσιν την επωμιδα εκ χρυσιου και υακινθου και πορφυρας και κοκκινου νενησμενου και βυσσου κεκλωσμενης (vz; compare j^mg s^mg; cf. also θ' *mšḥlpʾ* in 𝔰^mg] OG και ποιησουσιν την επωμιδα εκ βυσσου κεκλωσμενης] MT *wʿśw ʾt hʾpd zhb tklt wʾrgmn twlʿt šny wšš mšzr*.

The agreement between the OG and part of the longer Theodotionic reading could easily be due to coincidence, since the words in question--with the possible exception of κεκλωσμενης--are those we would expect to find in any translation of the Hebrew text. There is no need to say that Theodotion actually depended on the OG at this point, although he presumably did.

44. Exod. 28:16: α'σ'θ' σπιθαμης το μηκος αυτου (v; cf. α'θ' *dylh* in 𝔰^txt)] OG σπιθαμης το μηκος] MT *zrt ʾrkw*.

Once again the agreement between α'σ'θ' and the OG could be due to a dependence of Theodotion on the OG, but it could also be the result of accidental convergence by independent translations of the same Hebrew phrase.

45. Exod. 28:21: α'θ'σ'ο' κατα το ονομα αυτου (v)] OG κατα το ονομα] MT *ʿl šmw*.

In this case the agreement between Theodotion and the OG is significant, because κατα is not the normal equivalent of MT *ʿl*. Theodotion simply added αυτου to provide explicit reflection of the MT suffix.

46. Exod. 29:14: σ'θ' περι αμαρτιας εστιν (v; compare θ' περι αμαρτιας in z)] OG αμαρτιας γαρ εστιν] MT *ḥṭʾt hwʾ*.

---

[13]Compare the other Theodotionic equivalents for MT *šny* (שָׁנִי) in Exodus: νενησμενου or *mšḥlpʾ* (should = *διαφορου or the like) in Exod. 28:6; *dmštgnynytʾ* in Exod. 28:33 (LXX v.29); αλλοιουμενον (should = **mšgnytʾ* or the like) or *ṣbyʿtʾ* in Exod. 35:23; τω αλλοιουμενω (= **dmšt-gnyʾ*) in Exod. 35:35; *ʿzyltʾ* (= *το νενησμενον) in Exod. 39:1 (LXX 39:13). In every case except Exod. 28:33 (LXX v.29), where no equivalent is preserved, Theodotion uses κοκκινον/*zḥwrytʾ* to represent MT *twlʿt*.

The partial agreement between the OG and the Theodotionic variant may well be coincidental. This reading is also considered under item 61 of chapter three.

47. Exod. 29:16: ο'θ'σ'α' το αιμ[α] αυτου (v)] OG το αιμα] MT *'t dmw*.

The partial agreement between Theodotion and the OG is not unusual here, and cannot be used to prove direct dependence by Theodotion on the OG.

48. Exod. 29:22: σ'θ' το στεαρ και το κερκιον (v)] OG το στεαρ αυτου] MT *ḥḥlb wh'lyh*.

The use of το στεαρ to represent MT *ḥḥlb* is not surprising, and so once again the partial agreement between Theodotion and the OG cannot be used to prove direct dependence of the one on the other.

49. Exod. 30:38: α'θ' ※ ανηρ ος αν (v; cf. α'θ' *gbr'* in S^txt)] OG ος αν] MT *'yš 'šr*.

Theodotion and Aquila share the use of αν after the relative with the OG, while also providing an explicit reflection of MT *'yš*. This partial agreement with the OG is not expected, since the use of αν in a relative clause is not common in Theodotion. It provides further small but firm evidence for Theodotionic dependence on the OG. This reading is also found under item 56 of chapter three.

50. Exod. 31:6: α'σ'θ' ※ και εγω ιδου (v; cf. α'θ' *h'* in S^txt)] OG και εγω] MT *w'ny hnh*.

The use of και εγω to represent MT *w'ny* is not unusual, and so the agreement between the OG and part of Theodotion's reading does not prove that he was dependent on the OG here.

51. Exod. 32:8: σ'θ' μοσχον χωνευτον (v)] OG μοσχον] MT *ʿgl mskh*.

Similarly, Theodotion's use of μοσχον to represent MT *ʿgl* does not prove his dependence on the OG.

52. Exod. 35:7-8 (LXX v.7): θ' και ξυλα ασηπτα (+ ※ v) και ελαιον εις το φως και αρωματα εις το ελαιον της χρισεως και εις το θυμιαμα της συνθεσεως (svz; cf. θ' *wmšḥh lnhyr' whrwm' lmšḥ' dmšyḥwt' wlbsm' drwkb'* in S^txt)] OG και ξυλα ασηπτα] MT *wʿṣy šṭym wšmn lm'wr wbśmym lšmn hmšḥh wlqṭrt hsmym*.

The agreement of Theodotion with OG και ξυλα ασηπτα to represent MT *w'ṣy šṭym* is not unexpected, and does not prove that Theodotion used the OG as the base into which he inserted his expansion to represent MT v.8.

The Theodotionic expansion is also found in cmy[b?], and without the third εις in ϗ. The entire MT phrase is also reflected in dhpt, but with Theodotion's εις το before ελαιον(2) replaced by και and his third εις omitted. The variant in F[b mg] agrees with dhpt on these points. The last part of the expansion also occurs in egjnsz, 133, in agreement with dhpt on both variants from Theodotion. The variant form of the expansion found in dhpt could have been present in the OG text available to Theodotion, so that he simply made two minor changes demanded by the MT. It is also possible that dhpt are dependent on Theodotion through the hexapla here and have suffered secondary corruption. The shorter reading in egjn sz, 133, is due to haplography in the dhpt text: <u>και ελαιον</u> ... <u>και ελαιον</u>.

53. Exod. 35:11 (LXX v.10): θ' ※ και τους στυλους και τας βασεις αυτης (v)] OG και τους στυλους] MT *'t 'mdyw w't 'dnyw.*

The presence of και(1) and the absence of any translation for the suffix on MT *'mdyw* are discussed under items 16 and 31, respectively, of chapter three. While neither one alone proves that Theodotion was using the OG here, taken together they make it likely that he was dependent on the OG at this point and that he added a translation for MT *w't 'dnyw* without noticing the other discrepancies between the OG and the Hebrew text.

54. Exod. 35:23: θ' (+ ※ v) και πας ανηρ ω ευρεθη παρ αυτω υακινθος και πορφυρα και κοκκινον αλλοιουμενον και βυσσος και αιγεια και δερματα κριων (svz; cf. θ' *ṣby't'* for αλλοιουμενον in ܣ[mg]) and α'σ' θ' πεπυρωμενα (v)] OG (= Bafhinqrux, 71) και παρ (παντι n) ω (ο n) ευρεθη βυσσος (+ παρ αυτων n; + εν αυτω 71) και (om f) δερματα (om f) υακινθινα (om f) και δερματα κριων ηρυθροδανωμενα ηνεγκαν (om r)] MT *wkl 'yš 'šr nmṣ' 'tw tklt w'rgmn wtwl't šny wšš w'zym w'rt 'ylm m'dmym w'rt tḥšym hby'w.*

Because of the peculiar problems in this verse, the OG and the MT have been cited for the entire verse, even though the Theodotionic readings do not cover the last Hebrew words. The SP is in substantial agreement with the MT and need not be quoted separately. The majority of LXX manuscripts depart from the OG in various significant ways. Their readings and those of ܣ and PS are cited in full prior to discussion of this item:

FMdegjlps^{txt}tv^{txt}z^{txt}a_2b_2ܒ: και πας (παντι dpt) ω (+ εαν a_2) ευρεθη (+ παρ αυτω F*d[αυτου]lpta_2b_2ܒ) βυσσος (om F*la_2b_2ܒ; + παρ αυτω F$^{a?}$Megj) και (om F*Mla_2b_2ܒ) δερματα κριων ηρυθροδανωμενα (+ ηνεγκαν Megjsvz) και δερματα (om p; + ηνεγκαν F[om F$^{b?}$]) υακινθινα ηνεγκαν (om FMegjsvz).

83 has doublets for the first part of the verse, apparently: και παρ ω ευρεθη βυσσος παρ αυτω και πας ω ευρεθη παρ αυτω (etc.).

Abowy: και πας ω ευρεθη παρ αυτω υακινυος και πορφυρα και κοκκινον και βυσσος και δερματα υακινθινα και δερματα κριων ηρυθροδανωμενα (ηρυθοδαν- A; + και δερματα αιγια A[αγια A*]y) ηνεγκαν.

ckmAE^{c}: και (om m) πας (om m) ανηρ (om mE^{c}) ω (ο m) ευρεθη παρ (vid A; om E^{c}) αυτω (vid A; αυτοις m; om E^{c}) υακινθος και πορφυρα και κοκκινον αλλοιουμενον (om k) και βυσσος και αιγια (c; αιγες m; τριχες αιγιαι kAE^{c}) και δερματα κριων ηρυθροδανωμενα και δερματα υακινθινα ηνεγκαν (*et attulit* E^{c}; *ferebant* A).

ܣ^{txt}: *wkl* ※ α'θ' *gbrʾ*⌄ *hw dʾštkḥ lwth* ※σ' *tkltʾ w*⌄*ʾrgwnʾ* (⌄ before *w-* B) *wzhwrytʾ mšgnytʾ wbwṣʾ* ※σ' *wsʿrʾ dʿzʾ*⌄ (⌄ before *dʿzʾ* B) *wmšk*ʾ *sʿypʾ ddkrʾ wmškʾ ʾwʾdntynʾ ʾytyw*.

PS: *wkl gbrʾ dʾštkḥ lh tkltʾ wʾrgwnʾ wṣwbʿʾ dzhwrytʾ wbwṣʾ wsʿrʾ dʿzʾ wmškʾ ddkrʾ dʾspynyqʾ wmškʾ dssgwnʾ ʾytyw*.

The OG for this verse is quite short. It has no equivalents for MT *kl ʾyš*, for MT *tklt wʾrgmn wtwlʿt šny w-*, and for MT *wʿzym*. All three phrases are found in SP and PS, as well as MT. The OG represents MT *ʾšr (nmṣʾ) ʾtw* by παρ ω (ευρεθη) and puts the translation of MT *wʿrt tḥšm* before that of MT *wʿrt ʾylm mʾdmym*.

Most LXX manuscripts replace OG παρ with πας to represent MT *kl* (compare παντι of dnpt), and many then insert παρ αυτω to reflect MT *ʾtw*. One large group, FMdegjlpstvza_2b_2ܒ, restores the MT order in the two και δερματα phrases. In some of these manuscripts, F and Megjsvz, OG ηνεγκαν (= MT *hbyʾw*) is shifted out of place. A smaller group of manuscripts, Abowy, inserts a reflection of MT *tklt wʾrgmn wtwlʿt šny w-* in which κοκκινον alone represents MT *twlʿt šny*. A clumsy reflection of MT *wʿzym* is found out of place in Ay.

The hexaplaric manuscripts, ckmA̸E̸ᶜS̸, restore the MT order for the και δερματα phrases and insert the Abowy reflection of MT *tklt wʾrgmn wtwlʿt sny w-*. All but k add αλλοιουμενον (Syriac *mšgnytʾ*) after κοκκινον to represent MT *šny* separately from MT *twlʿt*. All insert different attempts to reflect MT *wʿzym*. The one in S̸^{txt} is attributed to σʹ. Compare also αʹ και αιγεια and σʹ και τριχες in their respective variants in svz. Only ckA̸S̸ insert ανηρ, attributed to αʹθʹ by S̸^{txt} and also found in αʹ and σʹ of svz, to represent MT *ʾyš*.

The basic reading found in FMdegjlpstvza$_2$b$_2$B̸ is probably the proto-Lucianic or Palestinian revision. It may well have been the form of OG text available to Theodotion at this point. The extensive agreements between the two suggest strongly that Theodotion used this form of the OG, with παρ αυτω in its proper place and without the omission of βυσσος, and that he inserted reflections for the remaining MT words. He also replaced ηρυθροδανωμενα with πεπυρωμενα to represent MT *mʾdmym* more literally.

The text of Abowy agrees with the OG against proto-Lucian and has a reflection of MT *tklt wʾrgmn wtwlʿt šny w-* that is one word shorter than Theodotion's. This omission also occurs in k. It is possible that this shorter form of the expansion was also present in Theodotion's Greek text, but the textual evidence makes this doubtful. The expansion in Abowy is more probably due to hexaplaric influence, although the omission of αλλοιουμενον is puzzling.

While some ambiguities in the textual history of this verse remain unsolved, Theodotionic dependence on a revised form of the OG at this point is almost certain.

55. Exod. 35:35: θʹ (+ ※ v) και ποικιλτα εν τη υακινθω και εν τη πορφυρα και εν τω κοκκινω τω αλλοιουμενω (+ ⋎ v) και τη βυσσω (svz; cf. S̸^{txt} *wlḥptk* ※θʹ *btkltʾ wbʾrgwnʾ* [+ ※ B] *w*⋎*bzhwrytʾ* ※ *dmštgnyʾ* ⋎*wbbwṣʾ*)] OG και (+ τα AFMbd-jlpqs-wy-b$_2$) ποικιλτα υφαναι τω κοκκινω και τη βυσσω] MT *wrqm btklt wbʾrgmn btwlʿt hšny wbšš*.

The apparent expansion (και before εν τω κοκκινω) is discussed under item 18 in chapter three. In the hexaplaric manuscripts (ckmA̸E̸ᶜS̸), which insert the same plus found in Theodotion (but without τω αλλοιουμενω in k), υφαναι is shifted after τη βυσσω to reflect MT *wʾrg*. The only exception is Ɇ^c, which retains υφαναι after ποικιλτα and before εν τω υακινθω.

Presumably Theodotion is responsible for this shift, as well as for the insertion of εν τη υακινθω και εν τη πορφυρα και εν and τω αλλοιουμενω to represent elements of the MT not reflected in the OG. The agreements with the OG, especially ποικιλτα to represent MT *rqm* and the lack of a preposition before τη βυσσω, again make it likely that Theodotion depended on the OG at this point. Note that, as in the previous number, k omits τω αλλοιουμενω from the Theodotionic expression.

56. Exod. 37:10-15 (LXX 38:9-11): *ϑ' mn qys' l' ṁblṭ' dtṙtyn 'ṁ' 'wrk' dylh wd'mt' pty' dylh wd'mt' wplg rwm' dylh wqrmh bdhb' dky' w'bd lh spt' ddhb' kd ḥdr w'bd lh klyl' dzrt' kd ḥdr w'bd spt' ddhb' lkyl' dylh kd ḥdr w'bd lh 'rb' zqzqt' ddhb' wsm 'nyn lzqzqt' 'l 'rb'' yb' hlyn d'ytyhyn d'ṙb'tyhyn ṙgl' dylh ltḥt mn klyl' whwy hnyn zqzqt' ltyq' lqwp' 'yk dlmšqlh lptwr' w'bd lqwp' mn qys' l' ṁblṭ' wqrm 'nwn bdhb' 'yk dlmšqlh lptwr'* (S^{txt}; cf. GcɅɆ^c)] OG εκ χρυσιου καθαρου και εχωνευσεν αυτη τεσσαρας δακτυλιους χρυσους (om Bab$_2$) δυο (+ δακτυλιους AFMdlpqs^{mg}tuv^{mg}yz^{mg}a$_2$ɃɆȽ^r) επι του κλιτους του ενος (του$^{(1)}$--ενος: το κλιτος το εν AFdfilps^{mg}tv^{mg}xyz^{mg}a$_2$b$_2$) και δυο (+ δακτυλιους AFMdlqs^{mg}tuv^{mg}yz^{mg}a$_2$b$_2$Ƀ) επι του κλιτους του δευτερου (του$^{(3)}$--δευτερου: το κλιτος το δευτερον AFdfilps^{mg}tv^{mg}xyz^{mg}a$_2$b$_2$) ευρεις ωστε αιρειν τοις διωστηρσιν εν αυτοις και τους διωστηρας της κιβωτου και της τραπεζης εποιησεν και κατεχρυσωσεν αυτους χρυσιω (cf. S^{txt} ÷*mn dhb' dky' wnsk lh 'rb' zqzqt' ddhb' tṙtyn 'l sṭr' ḥd wtṙtyn 'l sṭr' tryn' ptyt' 'yk dlmšqlh bhwn bḥzq' wlṭ'wn' dq'bwt' wdptwr' 'bd wqrm 'nwn bdhb'*⤙)] MT *'ṣy šṭym 'mtym 'rkw w'mh rḥbw w'mh wḥṣy qmtw wyṣp 'tw zhb ṭhwr wy'ś lw zr zhb sbyb wy'ś lw msgrt ṭpḥ sbyb wy'ś zr zhb lmsgrtw sbyb wyṣq lw 'rb' ṭb't zhb wytn 't hṭb't 'l 'rb' hp't 'šr l'rb' rglyw l'mt hmsgrt hyw hṭb't btym lbdym lś't 't hslḥn wy's 't hbdym 'ṣy šṭym wyṣp 'tm zhb lś't 't hšlḥn.*

Various aspects of this reading are discussed in chapter three under items 19, 20, 49, 50, 57, 73, and 74. The OG and the MT for this passage about the table differ substantially in length and in content. The OG is retained by GckɅS̸ (under ÷ in GS̸), while the Theodotionic version is added by G(under ※)cɅɆ^c. A variant approximation to the MT is found in F^b.

The points of contact between the OG and Theodotion are minimal, and cannot be used to demonstrate dependence by the latter on the former in this passage.

57. Exod. 38:31-39:1 (LXX 39:9, 13): σ'θ' *wlklhyn šk' dmškn' wlklhyn šk' ddrt' kd ḥdr' wtklt' hy dšrkt w'rgwn' wzḥwryt' ʿzylt' ʿbdw 'šṭl' dtšmšt' 'yk dlmšmšw byt qwdš'* ($\mathcal{S}^{txt}$) I OG και τους πασσαλους της σκηνης και τους πασσαλους της αυλης κυκλω ... και την καταλειφθεισαν υακινθον και πορφυραν και το κοκκινον (+ και [+ την 64] βυσσον Ay, 64) εποιησαν στολας λειτουργικας ααρων ωστε λειτουργειν εν αυταις εν τω αγιω I MT *w't kl ytdt hmškn w't kl ytdt hḥṣr sbyb wmn htklt wh'rgmn wtwlʿt hšny ʿśw bgdy śrd lšrt bqdš.*

The σ'θ' reading of $\mathcal{S}^{txt}$ is in basic agreement with the OG of LXX Exod. 39:9, 13, but omits any reflection of LXX vv. 10-12. This is in conformity with MT Exod. 38:31-39:1, which corresponds to LXX Exod. 39:9, 13, without any support for the intervening LXX verses at this point. Theodotion and Symmachus twice insert *klhyn* (= παντας of km, and once also of G) to represent MT *kl* before each occurrence of MT *ytdt*. They also insert *ʿzylt'* (= το νενησμενον of Gckm) after *wzḥwryt'* (= OG και το κοκκινον) to reflect explicitly MT *hšny* after MT *wtwlʿt*, and they omit OG ααρων and OG εν αυταις that are not supported by the MT. The remaining agreements with the OG, especially the free translation *wtklt' hy dšrkt* (= OG και την καταλειφθεισαν υακινθον) to represent MT *wmn htklt*, discussed under item 135 of chapter three, are strong evidence for genuine Theodotionic dependence on the OG at this point. This is an important example, since the changes Theodotion had to make in the OG were far from minor.

Of the nineteen Theodotionic expansions partially agreeing with the OG that were considered under the present heading, nine provide additional firm evidence for genuine Theodotionic dependence on the OG: items 39, 40, 42, 45, 49, 53-55, and 57. In items 39, 54, and 57, the dependence is almost certain. In item 54, it is a revised form of the OG that is the basis for Theodotion's further revision. Compare items 29, 30, 35, 37, and 38.

Theodotionic Expansions of the OG that Require Special Comment

58. Exod. 3:11: $\mathcal{S}^{txt}$ ※ α'θ' *'n'ʾ'yty* I OG ειμι (after εγω ck; om 74, $\mathcal{B}^{vid}\mathcal{E}^{vid}$) εγω (om A*^{vid}F*Mdefijlqrtuvyzb$_2$c$_2$$^{a?}$) I MT *'nky.*

This item is discussed in connection with the fourth reading of chapter one. The Theodotionic variant could be viewed as an expansion of the reading found in A*F*M, or as a re-arrangement of that found in B, or as an independent translation to reflect MT *ʾnky*. This item cannot be used to prove or support Theodotionic dependence on the OG, although of course it does not contradict such dependence.

59. Exod. 9:25: ϑʹ *lklhwn hnwn dbḥqlʾ* (Ṡ^{mg}) I OG om. I MT *ʾt kl ʾšr bśdh*.

A variant reflection of the MT plus is found in B$^{b\ mg}$M^{mg}a-dhkmnptw xc$_2$^{mg}ȺP̸ (compare B̸^{w} and Ł^{z}) and under ⁜ in Ṡ^{txt}: παντα (om p) οσα ην εν τω πεδιω (παιδ- B$^{b\ mg}$) = Ṡ^{txt} ⁜ *lkl dʾyt hwʾ bpqʿtʾ* ⸔. Further variants are attributed to Aquila and Symmachus by Ṡ^{mg}. The partial agreement between Theodotion's expression and that found in B$^{b\ mg}$M^{mg}a-dhkmnptwxc$_2$^{mg} is not sufficient to prove that he knew or depended upon the latter reading.

60. Exod. 11:7: ϑʹ *(w)bmṣʿt* (Ṡ^{txt}--only B includes *w-* in the ϑʹ citation) I= OG και (Bbfioqrsw; + ανα μεσον AMacdeghj-nptvx-c$_2$ȺB̸ŁŁ^{v}P̸) I MT *wbyn*.

The OG uses ανα μεσον to represent MT *byn* earlier in the verse, but fails to reflect the preposition on its second occurrence. This oversight is corrected in most LXX manuscripts. The Theodotionic reading in Ṡ^{txt} presumably agrees with the LXX majority. This agreement need not imply direct dependence by Theodotion on the revised OG at this point, since Theodotion's phrase could just as easily be due to an independent translation of the MT preposition.

61. Exod. 12:32: σʹϑʹ *ʾyk mʾ dmlltwn* (Ṡ^{mg}) I OG om. I MT *kʾšr dbrtm*.

The MT phrase is left totally unreflected only in ABF^{txt}efgijloqrsy Ł. In F$^{a?\ mg}$Mbdhnptvwz-c$_2$ȺB̸Ł^{z}, Or-Lat, the following reflection is added out of place: καθαπερ (καθα h) ειρηκατε (+ προς ... F$^{a?\ mg}$). In ackmx Ṡ^{txt}, however, καθαπερ ειρηκατε or its Syriac equivalent *ʾyk mʾ dʾmrtwn* is found in the position corresponding to the location of the phrase in the MT. The σʹϑʹ reading of Ṡ^{mg} has a different verb. The new verb is shared by Aquila, who also has *ʾyknʾ* in place of *ʾyk mʾ*. If the different Syriac verb *mlltwn* reflects a different Greek verb, as is likely, then the agreement between σʹϑʹ and the expansion found in F$^{a?\ mg}$Ma-dhkmnptvw xz-c$_2$Ṡ^{txt} is minimal. It cannot be used to prove any direct relationship between Theodotion and a revised OG, but only their common dependence on Hebrew texts here equivalent to the MT and SP.

62. Exod. 27:6: α'σ'θ' *šqwl'* ($\mathcal{S}^{mg}$--marked as a variant to the second *qwp'* of $\mathcal{S}^{txt}$) I OG (+ φορεις AF*Mbefgijlmsvwz$\mathcal{A}$; + αναφορεις F^{b}ac dknpt$b_2\mathcal{B}$) τω θυσιαστηριω φορεις (B*h; αναφορεις B^{ab}acoqrux; om AFMbd-gi-npstvwz$\mathcal{AB}$) εκ ξυλων ασηπτων I $\mathcal{S}^{txt}$ *qwp' lmdbḥ' qwp' mn qys' l' mblṭ'* I MT *bdym lmzbḥ bdy ʿṣy šṭym.*

MT *bdym* and *bdy*, also found in SP, are both reflected only in ac $\mathcal{S}^{txt}$. The OG apparently reflected *bdy* and not *bdym*, while an early revision, presumably the Proto-Lucianic or Palestinian revision, shifted the noun earlier in the verse to reflect *bdym* and left *bdy* unrepresented. The Syriac variant for the second *qwp'*, corresponding to MT *bdy*, attributed to α'σ'θ' by $\mathcal{S}^{mg}$ may represent αναβασταζοντας of $F^{b\ mg}$. There is no way to tell what form of the OG Theodotion depended on here.

None of the five Theodotionic expansions considered in items 58-62 were found to provide solid evidence in support of Theodotionic dependence on the OG or on an early revision of the OG. They do not provide any evidence disproving such dependence either.

63. Exod. 28:23-28 (LXX v.22)--see chapter two.

Various aspects of this reading are included under items 29, 39, 40, 71, 84, and 85 in chapter three as well. It is clear from the discussions of chapter two that the Theodotionic version agrees in general with the version inserted into $F^{a?\ mg}$Mcdegjkmnpstvz$\mathcal{AE}^{c}$ (under ※ in svz). This extensive agreement reveals a genuine dependence of Theodotion on the revised form of the OG. The few variants attributed to Theodotion show that he made minor changes in the text available to him, at least some of which were revisions made in order to reflect the MT more exactly.

64. Exod. 31:8-9 (LXX v.8): α'σ'θ' και το θυσιαστηριον του θυμιαματος και το θυσιαστηριον της ολοκαυτωσεως και παντα τα σκευη αυτου (sv [under ※]; cf. cmz$^{mg}\mathcal{A}$ and $F^{c?\ mg}$; cf. also θ' *wlmdbḥ' dbsm' wlmdbḥ' dyqd' šlm' wlklhwn m'n' dylh* in $\mathcal{S}^{txt}$) I OG (out of place) και τα (το egj$\mathcal{BE}$) θυσιαστηρια (-ριον egj$\mathcal{BE}$) I $\mathcal{S}^{txt}$ (out of place) ⌐*wlmdbḥ'*˂ I MT *w't mzbḥ hqṭrt w't mzbḥ hʿlh w't kl klyw.*

There is virtually no agreement between Theodotion and the OG at this point, and certainly no further evidence that Theodotion had the OG as the basis of his version.

65. Exod. 33:7: σ'θ' *dshdwt' hw d-* (Ṡ^txt) ‖ OG την (BabkowxȻ^m; om AF Me-jlrsuvyzb$_2$ȾȻ; του μαρτυριου την cdmnpȺȽ^r, Luc [om την ȺȽ^r, Luc]; + του μαρτυριου την t) ‖ MT *mw'd 'šr*.

Even if σ'θ' *hw d-* represents την, there is no reason to say that Theodotion or Symmachus retained την from BabkowxȻ^m. The reading is best understood as an independent translation of MT *mw'd 'šr*, which presumably had no reflection in the OG text available to Theodotion. Its presence in cdmnptȺȽ^r, Luc, is probably the result of hexaplaric influence. This reading provides no evidence relating to Theodotionic dependence on any form of the OG.

66. Exod. 38:1-2 (LXX 38:22)--see the eighth reading in chapter one.

Theodotion's failure to represent MT *w-* is treated under item 32 in chapter three. This reading provides no evidence that Theodotion had the different OG available to him and hence cannot be used to support Theodotionic dependence on the OG.

Thirty-one Theodotionic readings have been found to point with at least reasonable certainty to Theodotion's genuine dependence on the OG or on a revision of the OG: items 1, 2, 4-8, 12, 16, 18, 21-25, 27, 29, 30, 35, 37-40, 42, 45, 49, 53-55, 57, and 63. Seven of these provide good evidence for a revised OG as the basis for Theodotion's version: items 29, 30, 35, 37, 38, 54, and 63. Many of the other readings discussed or referred to in this chapter have minor agreements with the OG or with a significant number of LXX manuscripts. While these could be due to coincidence, the readings that point clearly to genuine Theodotionic dependence on a form of the OG make it reasonable to regard most or all of the minor agreements between Theodotion and a form of the OG as due to similar dependence.

Theodotionic Readings that Agree with the OG, with the Shortened or Rearranged OG, or with One Strand of LXX Witnesses

67. Exod. 1:11: θ' and α'σ' *lpytw* (Ṡ^mg; cf. α'σ' φιθωμ in *b*) ‖ OG την τε πειθω (Bb'kqruwxȻ; πειθωμ Mcvy* vid$_z$; πιθωμ As; φιθωμ ah*b$_2$; πιθων n; φιθωθ dpt; etc.) ‖ Ṡ^txt *wlpytwm* ‖ MT *'t ptm* ‖ SP *'t pytwm*.

While the Syriac form attributed to θ' and to α'σ' could reflect OG την (τε) πειθω, a variant is attributed to α'σ' by *b*[mg]. The Syriac form in Ꞩ[txt] could be due to the reading of PS (*lpytwm*) rather than to a Greek variant. Since the Syriac reading attributed to θ' cannot be interpreted with certainty, it can provide no evidence about Theodotion's relation to the OG. This reading is also included under item 105 in chapter three.

68. Exod. 1:11: Ꞩ[txt] ※ α'σ'θ' *w*⸔*lr*ʿ*ms*ʾ I OG και (om k; + την ackx) ραμεσση (etc.) I MT *w*ʾ*t r*ʿ*mss*.

The agreement of α'σ'θ' with the OG on the use of και/*w*- to represent MT *w*- cannot be used to prove any sort of dependence by Theodotion on the OG. It is not clear why this unimportant reading was attributed to α'σ'θ' in Ꞩ. Perhaps the attribution is misplaced from the following element, Syriac -*l*-, which would represent την of ackx.

69. Exod. 7:19: θ' *hw*ʾ (Ꞩ[mg]) I OG και εγενετο (γενησεται F[b]dnpꞨ; εσται y) I MT *whyh*.

This variant is discussed under item 113 of chapter three, where it is argued that Theodotion's use of the past tense may be due to an uncritical acceptance of the OG reading or to the presence in his Hebrew text of SP *wyhy* rather than MT *whyh*. The second possibility makes it unwise to appeal to this reading as a proof of Theodotion's dependence on the OG.

70. Exod. 8:2 (LXX v.6): σ'θ' ʿ*l my*ʾ *dmṣryn* (Ꞩ[txt vid]) I OG επι τα υδατα αιγυπτου I MT ʿ*l mymy mṣrym*.

Field takes Ꞩ[txt] ※ *g' dylh* ⸔ σ'θ' ʿ*l* as an error for ※ ʿ'σ'θ' *dylh* ⸔ʿ*l*, so that ʿ'σ'θ' would be credited with the expansion αυτου, also found in acmxAꞨ[l] and in kꞨ[w], to represent the suffix on MT *ydw*. If Ꞩ is taken at face value, however, σ'θ' and OG agree on their translation of MT ʿ*l mymy mṣrym*. The equivalents are not unexpected, and the agreement does not prove Theodotionic dependence on the OG.

71. Exod. 10:12: α'θ' *wnsq* (Ꞩ[mg]--marker at *nsq* of Ꞩ[txt]; cf. also α'σ'θ' *bqmṣ*ʾ of Ꞩ[mg], with the marker at *wqmṣ*ʾ of Ꞩ[txt]) I OG και αναβητω (after ακρις acx) ακρις I Ꞩ[txt] *wqmṣ*ʾ *nsq* I MT *b*ʾ*rbh wy*ʿ*l*.

Apparently α'θ' and perhaps σ' reflect the MT order and structure exactly. A partial revision of the different OG order is found in acx

$\mathcal{S}^{txt}$, but with no change in structure. While a Theodotionic revision of the OG is not unlikely, an independent translation of the MT might well exhibit such partial agreement with the OG. Once again the Theodotionic reading cannot be used to prove genuine dependence on the OG.

72. Exod. 16:18: σ'θ' *gwmwr* ($\mathcal{S}^{mg}$; cf. also σ' *bgwmwr* in $\mathcal{S}^{mg}$)] OG τω (εν τω aca$_2$; το A^{a}bdegi-lnpqtwb$_2$$^{a?}$, Cyr; τον m) γομορ (γομωρ al; γομερ F$^{b?}$k)] $\mathcal{S}^{txt}$ *bgwmwr*] MT *bʿmr*.

The Syriac noun attributed to σ'θ' probably agrees with OG γομορ, but certainty is impossible. Agreement on an isolated noun, even if it is a transliteration of the Hebrew, is not sufficient to prove genuine dependence by Theodotion on the OG.

73. Exod. 17:9: α'σ'ο'θ' του βουνου ("one Regius" according to Montef. as cited by Field)] OG του βουνου] MT *hgbʿh*.

Agreement on του βουνου to represent MT *hgbʿh* is not surprising and cannot be used to prove genuine dependence by Theodotion on the OG.

74. Exod. 18:18: α'σ'θ' *wʿmʾ hnʾ* ($\mathcal{S}^{mg}$)] OG και πας (om cx) ο λαος (+ σου Aqu) ουτος (ουτως πας c; om B*[hab B$^{ab\ mg}$]opa$_2$b$_2$ÆE)] $\mathcal{S}^{txt}$ *wklh ʿmʾ hnʾ*] MT *gm hʿm hzh*.

This reading is discussed under item 122 of chapter three. Theodotion's failure to use καιγε rather than *w*- (= OG και) to represent MT *gm* may point toward Theodotionic inadvertence in retaining part of the OG reading. The remaining agreements with the OG (minus πας) need not imply genuine dependence, however, since none of the correspondences is at all unusual or unexpected. While the reading as a whole suggests Theodotionic dependence on the OG, it cannot be said to offer real proof of such dependence.

75. Exod. 19:4: θ'α' επι πτερυγων (v)] OG ωσει (ως bmnqu; οιονει Hip) επι πτερυγων] MT *ʿl knpy*.

The use of πτερυγες to represent MT *knpym* is not unusual, and so the agreement between θ'α' and the shortened OG may be the result of independent translations of the same Hebrew. It need not imply Theodotionic dependence on the OG.

76. Exod. 20:21 ($\mathcal{S}$ v.18): ο' and α' and θ' γνοφον (Dionys. Areop. as quoted by Field)] OG τον γνοφον] MT *hʿrpl*.

This agreement with the OG on the use of γνοφος to represent MT *ʿrpl* is too minor to serve as a proof of genuine Theodotionic dependence on the OG.

77. Exod. 22:19 (LXX v.20): α'σ'θ' *bh bdmwtʾ dmdbḥ lʾlhʾ* (Ṡ^mg) I OG ο (om egjln) θυσιαζων (+ εν d; + τοις ου F^b) θεοις (+ ετεροις Abf i^a? rwxBC^m L^w vid, Or-gr, Eus, Cyr 2/3) I Ṡ^txt *dmdbḥ lʾlhʾ* I MT *zbḥ lʾlhym*.

Once again the agreement with the OG concerns a phrase that would be expected as the translation of the MT phrase. This reading thus cannot be used to prove Theodotionic dependence on the OG.

78. Exod. 26:5: σ'θ' *dpgʿn* (Ṡ^mg) I OG αντιπροσωποι αντιπιπτουσαι (αντιτυπτουσαι ma_2; + αι αγκυλαι acmx[om αι]) I Ṡ^txt *lwqbl pṣwpʾ dpgʿn nhwyn hnyn* ※ *ʾlqlʾ*⋎ I MT *mqbylt hllʾt*.

The σ'θ' variant in Ṡ^mg may reflect OG αντιπιπτουσαι, one part of the long OG reflection of MT *mqbylt* with no OG reflection for MT *hllʾt*. While this agreement could point to Theodotionic dependence on the OG, the fact that the reading is a single word and is in Syriac makes it difficult to use it as proof for such dependence.

79. Exod. 26:32: α'σ'θ' *bh bdmwtʾ ʿmwdʾ ʾmrw hrkʾ* (Ṡ^mg) I OG στυλων I Ṡ^txt *ʿmwdʾ* I MT *ʿmwdy*.

This agreement with the OG on *ʿmwdʾ*/στυλοι to represent MT *ʿmwdym* is not surprising, since στυλος is a normal equivalent for MT *ʿmwd*. This reading cannot be used to prove genuine Theodotionic dependence on the OG.

80. Exod. 28:41 (LXX v.37): α'θ' *wtmlʾ* (Ṡ^mg) I OG και εμπλησεις (πλησεις xb_2) I Ṡ^txt *wtmlʾ* I MT *wmlʾt*.

The Syriac form attributed to α'θ' and also found in Ṡ^txt could reflect either the OG or its variant in xb_2. These translations for MT *mlʾ* are not unusual, and no conclusions about Theodotionic dependence on the OG can be based on them.

81. Exod. 31:13: σ'θ' υμιν (130--according to Field) I OG και εν υμιν I MT *wbynykm*.

This one-word reading is discussed under item 30 in chapter three. It is impossible to use it as proof of Theodotionic dependence on the OG.

82. Exod. 31:14: σ'θ'ο' οτι αγιον εστιν υμιν (v; cf. σ'θ' υμιν in s) I OG οτι αγιον (αγια x; + τουτο Baeg[-τω]hjorsv^{txt}z$\mathcal{B}$) εστιν (εσται Abhw; om qu$\mathcal{C}^{m}$; + τουτο F^{b}dinpqtua$_2$b$_2$$\mathcal{A}\mathcal{C}^{m}$) κυριου (BMa; κω και F^{b}degijo-suv^{txt}xza$_2$b$_2$$\mathcal{A}\mathcal{B}\mathcal{C}^{m}\mathcal{L}^{rz}$[om και ox$\mathcal{B}^{w}$]; τω κω και ft; υμιν κω n; om Abchklmwy$\mathcal{E}$) υμιν (εν υμιν d-gijpstv^{txt}za$_2$b$_2$$\mathcal{B}$; om mn; + τουτο M) I $\mathcal{S}^{txt}$ *mṭwl dqdyšt' 'ytyh lkwn* I MT *ky qdš hw' lkm*.

Theodotion's version translates the MT accurately and in a normal way. He has none of the expansions variously found in all OG witnesses except Abcklmwy$\mathcal{E}\mathcal{S}^{txt}$. The elements found in his version also appear in most OG witnesses, but this is not sufficient to prove Theodotionic dependence on the OG at this point. An independent translation of the MT would be expected to coincide with Theodotion's version more or less exactly.

83. Exod. 32:29: $\mathcal{S}^{txt}$ *bbr'* ※ α'θ' *dylh*↙ ※α'θ' *w*↙*b'ḥ'* ※ ʿ' *dylh*↙ I OG εν τω υιω (+ αυτου cmqux$\mathcal{A}\mathcal{B}\mathcal{C}^{m}$) και (η Babnw$\mathcal{L}^{rw}$, Phil, Luc; om F$^{b?}$; + εν AFMcdeghj-vy-b$_2$$\mathcal{B}^{l}\mathcal{E}\mathcal{L}^{r}$; + εκαστος εν x$\mathcal{A}$) τω αδελφω (+ αυτου F^{b}cmx$\mathcal{A}\mathcal{B}\mathcal{C}^{m}$) I MT *bbnw wb'ḥyw*.

The agreement between α'θ' *w-* and και, found in all OG witnesses except Babnw$\mathcal{L}^{rw}$, Phil, Luc, cannot be used to prove Theodotionic dependence on the OG, since και/*w-* is the obvious translation for MT *w-*. The α'θ' expansion *dylh* (= αυτου) does not enter into question here. It is one of the many minor expansions summarized in the first section of this chapter.

84. Exod. 34:35: σ'θ' *lṭhpyt'* ($\mathcal{S}^{txt}$) I OG το (om Babhknqruwx) καλυμμα (κατακαλυμμα bow) I MT *'t hmswh*.

The Syriac reading attributed to σ'θ' probably represents OG καλυμμα with the article (found in most LXX manuscripts). This presumed agreement between Theodotion and a slightly revised OG is not unusual enough, nor even certain enough, to serve as a proof of Theodotionic dependence on the OG here.

85. Exod. 35:3: θ' *d̈šb'* ($\mathcal{S}^{mg}$) I OG των σαββατων I $\mathcal{S}^{txt}$ *d̈šb'* I MT *hšbt*.

This reading is discussed briefly under item 86 in chapter three. The agreement between Theodotion and the OG on plural number is probably due to dependence by the former on the latter, but an independent use of the plural by Theodotion is not impossible.

86. Exod. 35:12 (LXX v.11): ϑ' και την κιβωτον και τους αναφορεις (v)] OG και την κιβωτον του μαρτυριου και τους αναφορεις] MT *'t h'rn w't bdy-*.

The first και in this reading is discussed under item 17 in chapter three. The exact agreement between Theodotion and the shortened OG is probably due to dependence by Theodotion on the OG, but a coincidental convergence of independent translations is not impossible. If Theodotion used the OG here, he simply omitted OG του μαρτυριου which had no support in the Hebrew text.

87. Exod. 36:4: α'σ'ϑ' *w'tw* (Ꞩ^{mg})] OG και παρεγινοντο (BhkqruȺ; παρεγενοντο F^bbcmnowxꞴȽ^r; παραγενομενοι AMd-gijlpstvy-b_2Ɇ^{vid}; παρετεινοντο a)] Ꞩ^{txt} *w'tw*] MT *wyb'w*.

The Syriac form found in Ꞩ^{txt} and attributed to α'σ'ϑ' in Ꞩ^{mg} could reflect either the imperfect or the aorist of the Greek verb, but not the participle. It could also reflect some other Greek verb. Even if Theodotion agreed with BhkqruȺ or with F^bbcmnowxꞴȽ^r against AMd-gijlpstvy-b_2, this would not prove his direct dependence on one of these forms of the OG. The ambiguity of the Syriac verb makes any firm conclusion impossible.

88. Exod. 36:38 (LXX 37:6): ϑ' και αι βασεις αυτων πεντε χαλκαι (v; and apparently α'ϑ' in sz)] OG (= Babhnqruwxa_2 and F^bGckmȺɆ^c) και αι (om F^b) βασεις αυτων (αι B*) πεντε χαλκαι] AMd-gilops^{txt}tyz^{txt}b_2 και τας βασεις αυτων πεντε χαλκας] v^{txt} και τας βασεις αυτων πεντε χαλκαι] MT *w'dnyhm ḥmšh nḥšt*.

Theodotion's agreement with the nominative construction of Babhnqru wxa_2 and the hexaplaric manuscripts against the accusative construction in AMd-gilopstyzb_2 does not prove that he had before him a form of the OG with the nominative construction. The complete agreement in vocabulary is not unexpected, since all the correspondences are customary ones. In spite of initial appearances to the contrary, this Theodotionic variant cannot be used to prove anything about Theodotion's relationship to the OG or to a revision of the OG.

89. Exod. 38;30 (LXX 39:8); σ'ϑ' *bšys* (Ꞩ^{mg})] OG (and F^bGckmȺɆ^c) τας βασεις] Ꞩ^{txt} *lhlyn bšys*] MT *'t 'dny*.

This agreement on βασεις/*bšys* as the translation for MT *'dnym* is not unusual, and cannot be used to prove Theodotionic dependence on the OG.

90. Exod. 40:2: α'θ' *dyrḥ'* (S̸^{txt}) I OG του μηνος I MT *ḥdš*.

This apparent agreement between α'θ' and the OG on μην/*yrḥ'* to translate MT *ḥdš* (חֹדֶשׁ) is not unusual and cannot be used to prove Theodotionic dependence on the OG here.

91. Exod. 40:10 (LXX v.9): α'σ'θ' *wnhw' hw mdbḥ'* (S̸^{txt}) I OG και εσται το θυσιαστηριον I MT *whyh hmzbḥ*.

The OG phrase is omitted by haplography in F*bdpqtx, Cyr-cod, and is found twice in g*. Even if α'σ'θ' agree exactly with the OG, this would not prove Theodotionic dependence on the OG here. The phrase in question is the most likely translation of the Hebrew words and could have been arrived at independently by Theodotion.

92. Exod. 40:26 (LXX v.24): ο'θ'σ' εν τη σκηνη (svz) I OG εν τη σκηνη (but εις την σκηνην in ejs^{txt}v^{txt}z^{txt}) I MT *b'hl*.

This agreement with the OG is not surprising, since the Greek phrase is the expected equivalent for MT *b'hl*.

93. Exod. 40:35 (LXX v.29); θ' ουκ ηδυνασθη (v) I OG ουκ ηδυνασθη (Bbhr; εδυνασθη Gak; ηδυνηθη AFMcefgijlnoqs-b_2d_2, Cyr; εδυνηθη dp) I MT *(w)l' ykl*.

The agreement between Theodotion and Bbhr need not be interpreted to mean that Theodotion found ουκ ηδυνασθη in the Greek text available to him and retained it. He could also have arrived at it independently as a translation for the Hebrew expression, or its presence in Bbhr could be due to hexaplaric influence. Compare ουκ εδυνασθη in Gak and in ο' of v.

In addition to the twenty-seven Theodotionic readings discussed above, of which only items 85 and 86 provide even moderately strong evidence for genuine Theodotionic dependence on the OG, two further Theodotionic variants remain to be considered.

94. Exod. 19:13: θ' εν τη απελευσει του ιωβηλ αυτοι αναβησονται εις το ορος (v; cf. θ' *bm'zlt' dywbl* in S̸^{mg}) I OG οταν (+ δε acfhijnptw xd$_2$A̸, Cyr-ed) αι φωναι και αι σαλπιγγες και η νεφελη απελθη απο του ορους εκεινοι αναβησονται επι (εις bh) το ορος I MT *bmšk hybl hmh y'lw bhr*.

This variant is discussed under the sixth reading in chapter one. Note the reflection of OG απελθη in Theodotion's εν τη απελευσει. While the lexical similarity is not overwhelming, the fact that it links such different modes of expression is suggestive. It is at least possible to argue from this variant that Theodotion retained the OG as the basis for his extensive revision of this verse. The remaining similarities, especially the agreement on αναβησονται to translate MT *y'lw*, strengthen the force of this example, although it probably remains less than compelling.

95. Exod. 30:13: θ' τουτο δωσουσιν πας ο παραπορευομενος επι τας επισκοπας (svz) ‖ OG και τουτο εστιν ο δωσουσιν οσοι (om afi, Cyr-cod$\frac{1}{2}$) αν (εαν cfis^{txt}v^{txt}z^{txt}) παραπορευωνται (παραπορευονται bcd giklnops^{txt}v*^{txt}w; etc.) την επισκεψιν ‖ MT *zh ytnw kl h'br 'l hpqdym*.

The resemblances between Theodotion and the OG are suggestive, especially their common choice of forms of παραπορευεσθαι to represent MT *'br*. While Theodotion could have arrived at this translation of the MT independently of the OG, it seems more likely that he depended on the OG here.

While most or all of the Theodotionic readings assembled under this last heading can be understood as due to Theodotionic retention of readings present in the form of the OG available to him, although sometimes with the omission of superfluous items, only items 85, 86, 94 and 95 provide additional evidence in support of such dependence by Theodotion on the OG.

There are sixteen places in which Theodotion is simply said to agree with ο' or to be *'yk šb'yn*. The full textual evidence for these readings is given in items 137-152 in chapter three. Since the exact form of the Theodotionic readings in these sixteen places is not available, detailed discussion would not be useful. Obviously all these instances of agreement with some form of the OG are in harmony with the theory that Theodotion used a form of the OG as the basis for his version, and that he then revised it to reflect a Hebrew text virtually identical with the present MT. This revision, while complete and thorough, occasionally left discrepancies between the OG and the MT uncorrected. These are attributable to inadvertence on Theodotion's part rather than to deliberate intent.

Evaluation

Theodotion's dependence on the OG extends to many more than the thirty-five items singled out in the course of this chapter.[14] The clear evidence found in these items supports the assumption that most other instances of partial or minor agreement between Theodotion and the OG, or the presumed proto-Lucianic or Palestinian revision of the OG, are also due to such dependence rather than to chance or similar factors.[15] Since hexaplaric variants tended to be preserved when they differed from the OG or when they were of interest for some other reason, it may be presumed that the incidence of agreement with the OG was higher in Theodotion's version of Exodus than appears from the readings that have been preserved for study. Even the material that was preserved provides sufficient and unambiguous evidence for the conclusion that Theodotion's version is properly regarded as a systematic revision of the OG and not as an independent translation of the Hebrew text. The form of the OG on which Theodotion based his revision contained a translation of MT Exod. 28:23-28, but there is no evidence that it differed from the OG on the order and content of cc. 36-40. In these chapters as elsewhere in Exodus, Theodotion's revision followed the MT very closely, even where this meant extensive departures from and expansions of the OG text that he was using as the basis for his revision.

---

[14] Items 1, 2, 4-8, 12, 16, 18, 21-25, 27, 29, 30, 35, 37-40, 42, 45, 49, 53-55, 57, 63, 85, 86, 94, and 95. Of these, items 1, 6, 16, 21-23, 27, 37-39, 54, 57, and 63 provide the best evidence; items 29, 30, 35, 37, 38, 54, and 63 show that Theodotion knew the OG in a slightly revised form.

[15] Other indications of Theodotionic dependence on the OG may be seen in his attempts to systematize his treatment of Hebrew words by using one of several OG equivalents as his normal correspondent for a particular Hebrew word. See, for example, Theodotion's use of Greek διασκεδαζειν to represent MT *pr'*, discussed in connection with the second reading of chapter one.

V Aquila's Agreement with Theodotion in Exodus

The nature and chief characteristics of Aquila's version and its close relation to the MT are well known, and need not be detailed here.[1] This chapter investigates the relationship between Theodotion's version in Exodus and Aquila's version in the same book. The investigation is limited to the establishment of a genuine affinity between the two versions. The precise nature of the relationship is the subject of chapter six.

Of the 398 Theodotionic readings in Exodus, all but 88 have partial or complete equivalents preserved from Aquila.[2] In some ten cases separate Aquilan readings correspond to different parts of a single Theodotionic reading. There are 154 instances in which Aquila is cited separately from Theodotion, as well as 166 instances in which Aquila and

---

[1]For a convenient collection of Aquila's readings throughout the OT, see RT. For a detailed discussion of Aquila's version and its characteristics, see J. Reider, *Prolegomena to a Greek-Hebrew and Hebrew-Greek Index to Aquila* (Philadelphia, 1916). Compare also Field, Vol. I, pp. xvi-xxvii; F. C. Burkitt, ed., *Fragments of the Books of Kings According to the Translation of Aquila* (Cambridge, 1897), pp. 12-16; H. B. Swete, *An Introduction to the Old Testament in Greek*, rev. ed. (Cambridge, 1914), pp. 31-42. Relevant observations may also be found in *DA*, pp. 3-30, 81-88.

[2]The Aquila-Theodotion readings in Exodus cover 920 separate MT items. This is well over half of the 1600 separate MT items covered by the extant Theodotionic material in Exodus. While this measurement is only approximate, it shows clearly that there is sufficient evidence on which to base an investigation of the relationship between Aquila and Theodotion.

Theodotion are simply cited together (as α'θ' or α'σ'θ').[3] All the Aquila-Theodotion readings are listed below under four headings. The first three headings group readings according to the degree of agreement between Aquila and Theodotion. The fourth heading is for the fifteen instances in which Theodotion is merely said to agree with Origen's standard text, while variant readings are explicitly attributed to Aquila. Under the first three headings the readings are grouped in terms of the relationship between the OG and the versions of Aquila and Theodotion. The working hypothesis is that Aquila knew the OG for Exodus in a version practically identical with Theodotion's revision, and that he further revised this Theodotionic version into more exact conformity with the MT. This hypothesis is tested in chapter six.

Complete Agreement between Aquila and Theodotion (177 Readings)

Of the 166 readings in which Aquila and Theodotion are cited together, there are sixteen readings in which they apparently agree fully with the OG or with the majority of LXX manuscripts:

1:11: α'σ'θ' w- (𝔖^{txt})] OG και$^{(3)}$] MT w-$^{(3)}$.

9:8: α'σ'θ' sbw lkwn (𝔖^{mg})] OG λαβετε (λαβε g) υμεις (Bab'cfh ikmnoqrsux𝔄𝔓; υμιν AM*b*degjlptvwyzb_2c_2𝔅𝔈; υμιν αυτοις a_2)] 𝔖^{txt} sbw ʼntwn] MT qḥw lkm.

17:9: α'σ'ο'θ' του βουνου ("one Regius" according to Montef. as cited by Field)] OG του τουνου] MT hgbʻh.

19:4: θ'α' επι πτερυγων σ' ως επι τερυγων (v)] OG ωσει (ως bmn qu; οιονει Hip; ܐܝܟ *ʼyk d-* 𝔖) επι πτερυγων] MT ʻl knpy.[4]

20:21: ο', α', θ' γνοφον (Dionys. Areop. as quoted by Field)]

---

[3]The α'θ' reading found in B-McL at MT Exod. 37:25 (α' *cubitus* α'θ' *duorum* ... 𝔖) is an error. Lagarde's 𝔖^{mg} actually has: α' *ʼmtʼ*· σ'θ' *dtrtyn*. While the interpretation of this citation remains uncertain, the α' and σ'θ' readings cannot really be said to overlap. For this reason, the citation has been included among the eighty-eight Theodotionic variants that have no equivalents preserved from Aquila.

[4]The format of the citation implies that θ'α' omitted OG ωσει, a word not supported by the MT. In general, separate readings from Symmachus are not included in these lists.

OG (τον) γνοφον ǀ MT (h)ʻrpl.[5]

21:18: α'σ'θ' wnmḥ' 'nš (𝔖mg) ǀ OG και παταξωσιν (Bbmqu; καταπαταξη c; παταξη afb$_2$𝔈; παταξη τις AF^{I}Mdeh-lnoprstv-a$_2$𝔄ℭ^{m}𝔏^r, Eus, Cyr, Spec [+ *ex eis* 𝔄; + *ex his* Spec]; παταξη ο εις F*; παταξη ανηρ F^b; *percusserit unus eorum* 𝔅) ǀ 𝔖txt wnmḥwn ǀ MT whkh 'yš.

22:19 (LXX v.20): α'σ'θ' bh bdmwt' dmdbḥ l'lh' (𝔖mg) ǀ OG (+ *et* 𝔅𝔏^w) ο (om egjln) θυσιαζων (θυων Or-gr; + εν d; + τοις ου F^b) θεοις (+ ετεροις Abfi$^{a?}$rwx𝔅ℭ^m, Or-gr, Eus, Cyr$\frac{2}{3}$; + *ali..* 𝔏^w) ǀ 𝔖txt dmdbḥ l'lh' ǀ MT zbḥ l'lhym.

23:31: α'θ' bdmwt' dhnwn šbʻyn· σ' dplšty' (𝔖mg) ǀ OG της (των 32, 𝔅; om h) φυλιστιειμ (φιλιστιειμ b'filnpa$_2$) ǀ 𝔖txt dplšt ǀ MT plštym.[6]

26:32: α'σ'θ' bh bdmwt' ʻmwd' 'mrw hrk' (𝔖mg) ǀ OG στυλων ǀ 𝔖txt ʻmwd' ǀ MT ʻmwdy.

28:41 (LXX v.37): σ' wtšml'· α'θ' wtml' (𝔖mg) ǀ OG και εμπλησεις (πλησεις xb$_2$; ευλογησεις h) ǀ 𝔖txt wtml' ǀ MT wml't.[7]

32:4: α'θ' w'mrw (𝔖mg) ǀ OG και ειπεν (BF*^{vid}defhmpqtua$_2$𝔅𝔈^{c}𝔏^z [+ *popul[o]*]; ειπαν AF$^{a?}$Mabcgi-lorsvwyzb$_2$, Cyr-ed; ειπον F^{b}n; *dixerunt* ℭ^{m}𝔈^f; *dicunt* 𝔄) ǀ 𝔖txt w'mrw ǀ MT wy'mrw.[8]

---

[5]The entire citation is as follows: χρη δε ειδεναι, ως εν τω εξοδω, ενθα γεγραπται οτι εισηλθε μωυσης εις τον γνοφον ου ην ο θεος, το μεν εβραικον εχει αραφελ· οι δε ο' και ακ. και θεοδ. το αραφελ γνοφον εξεδωκαν· συμ. μεντοι ομιχλην το αραφελ ηρμηνευσεν. This is taken from Field, p. 116, fn. 15, where Montfaucon's erroneous interpretation is also discussed and rejected.

[6]Presumably *plšt* of 𝔖txt was intended to represent OG φυλιστιειμ. Lagarde indicates that the marker for the variants of 𝔖mg was actually placed at the preceding *lym'* of 𝔖txt (𝔖txt *ʻdm' lym'* = OG εως της θαλασσης), rather than at *dplšt*. Perhaps the α'θ' agreement is with OG (εως) της θαλασσης, rather than with the OG proper noun. Whatever the explanation, α'θ' share a reading that is also found in the OG.

[7]The α'θ' reading could reflect OG εμπλησεις or perhaps xb$_2$ πλησεις.

[8]The α'θ' reading could reflect ειπον as well as ειπαν. The interpretation that α'θ' and 𝔖txt agree with the majority ειπαν is more likely to be correct. The σ' variant from 𝔖mg, *hnwn dyn 'mrw*, may include a

32:27: α'σ'θ' διελθετε (v) I OG και (om. fA̸) διελθατε (ABF^{*vid} iklov^{txt}xya$_2$b$_2$; διελθετε F$^{a?}$Ma-hjmnp-uwz) I MT ʿbrw.

32:29: α'θ' w- (𝔖^{txt}) I OG και$^{(2)}$ (n BabnwL̸^{rwz}, Phil, Luc) I MT w-$^{(2)}$.

34:22: α'θ' wʿʾdʾ (𝔖^{mg}) I OG και αρχην (BahrC̸^{m}; αρχη u; εορτην AFMb-gi[-τη i*]jptv-b$_2$A̸B̸E̸L̸^{rw}; εορτην και εορτην s; ... + εορτην h) I 𝔖^{txt} wryšʾ I MT wḥg$^{(2)}$.[9]

40:2: α'θ' dyrḥʾ (𝔖^{txt}) I OG του μηνος I MT hḥdš.

40:10 (LXX v.9): α'σ'θ' wnhwʾ hw mdbḥʾ (𝔖^{txt}) I OG και εσται (εστη F^{b}) το (om m) θυσιαστηριον (om και-θυσιαστηριον F* [hab F^{I}]bdpqtx, Cyr-cod) I MT whyh hmzbḥ.

There are thirty-three readings in which Theodotion and Aquila are cited together and apparently agree partially with the OG or with the majority of LXX manuscripts:

1:5: α'θ' εκ μηρων ιακωβ (64 according to Holmes as cited by Field) I OG εξ ιακωβ I MT yrk yʿqb.[10]

4:13: α'θ' εν εμοι $\overline{κε}$ (Mvz) I OG δεομαι κυριε I MT by ʾdny.

4:25: α'θ' wgšpt bṙglʾ dylh wʾmrt mṭl dḥtnʾ ddmʾ ʾyt (*read* ʾnt) ly (𝔖^{mg}; cf. θ' και ηψατο των ποδων αυτου και ειπεν οτι νυμφιος αιματων συ μοι... in vz and και ειπεν in the fragmentary α'

---

misplaced variant for 𝔖^{txt} *hlyn* (= OG αυτοι) to represent MT *ʾlh* (which occurs after MT *wʾmrw*, and is not to be taken as the subject of the verb but rather as the first word of the sentence *ʾlh ʾlhyk yśrʾl*, etc.).

[9]That α'θ' *wʿʾdʾ* and 𝔖^{txt} *wryšʾ* correspond to και εορτην and και αρχην, respectively, may be seen from the following sets of correspondences from the same verse:

MT *wḥg*$^{(1)}$ II OG και εορτην I 𝔖^{txt} *wʿʾdʾ*.

MT *bkwry* I OG αρχην$^{(1)}$ I 𝔖^{txt} *ryšʾ*.

Only BahrC̸^{m}𝔖^{txt} have the wrong noun to represent the second occurrence of *ḥg* in the MT. The σ' variant *wḥgʾ* presumably reflects a different Greek noun.

[10]For a more extensive collection of the textual evidence for this problematic reading, see item 104 in chapter three. Compare also the reading in the fragment from 4QEx^{a}, published by F. M. Cross, Jr., *The Ancient Library of Qumran and Modern Biblical Studies*, rev. ed. (Garden City, N.Y., 1961), p. 185, n. 31.

reading of vz)] OG και προσεπεσεν προς τους ποδας (ABafiq ru; + αυτου FMb-eghj-pstv-c_2 ꭿ𝔅𝔈^{vid}𝔏^r, Cyr) και ειπεν εστη το αιμα της περιτομης του παιδιου μου] 𝔖^{txt} wnplt lwt ʾrgl' dylh w'mrt qm dm' dgzwrt' dbr' dyly] MT wtgʿ lrglyw wt'mr ky ḥtn dmym 'th ly.[11]

10:12: α'σ'θ' bqmṣ' (𝔖^{mg}) *and* α'θ' wnsq (𝔖^{mg})] OG και αναβητω (after ακρις acx) ακρις] 𝔖^{txt} wqmṣ' nsq] MT b'rbh wyʿl.[12]

12:29: α'θ' bbyt' dgwb' (𝔖^{mg})] OG εν τω λακκω] 𝔖^{txt} (d)bgwb'] MT bbyt hbwr.

12:41: α'σ'θ' klhwn (𝔖^{mg})] OG πασα] 𝔖^{txt} kwlh] MT kl.

12:48: α'θ' lmry' (𝔖^{txt})] OG (+ τω ackx) κυριω (κυ efgijmnqsv za_2𝔈𝔏^z, Or-gr)] MT lyhwh.

16:14: α'θ' dqyq' qlyp' dqyq' 'yk 'glyd' (𝔖^{mg})] OG λεπτον (λευκον w; λευκη dp) ωσει κοριον (κηριον a_2; εριον dp) λευκον (λεπτον F[πτον sup ras F^b]w; om n) ωσει παγος (παχνη F[χνη sup ras F^b]M^{mg}j^{mg}z^{mg})] 𝔖^{txt} dqyq' 'yk kwsbrt' ḥwr' 'yk glyd'] MT dq mḥsps dq kkpr.

18:2: α'θ' btr šwdʾ' dylh (𝔖^{mg})] OG μετα την αφεσιν αυτης] 𝔖^{txt} btr šbyqwth] MT 'ḥr šlwḥyh.

18:18: α'σ'θ' wʿm' hn' (𝔖^{mg})] OG και πας (om cx) ο λαος (+ σου Aqu) ουτος (om B*[hab B$^{ab\ mg}$]opa_2b_2ꭿ𝔈; ουτως πας c)] 𝔖^{txt} wklh ʿm' hn'] MT gm hʿm hzh.

25.2: α'θ' wnsbwn (𝔖^{mg})] OG και λαβετε] 𝔖^{txt} wsbw] MT wyqḥw.

26:17: α'θ' δυο χειρας (M)] OG δυο αγκωνισκους] MT sty ydwt.

27:4: α'σ'θ' mṣydt' (𝔖^{mg})] OG δικτυωτω] 𝔖^{txt} dmṣydt'] MT ršt.[13]

27:14: α'σ'θ' dktp' ḥd' (𝔖^{mg}; cf. α'σ' τη ωμια in Ms[om σ']vz)] OG τω κλιτει τω ενι] 𝔖^{txt} lsṭr' ḥd] MT lktp.

28:3: α'σ'θ' πνς σοφιας (v)] OG πνευματος (πνευμα Mkmnr, Clem, Cyr) αισθησεως (συνεσεως fiy; σοφιας και αισθησεως r; σοφιας

---

[11]Compare οι λ̥ οτι νυμφιος αιματων συ μοι in Mz (and without name in v^{mg}) and το εβρ. νυμφιος αιματος συ μοι in F$^{b\ mg}$.

[12]Because they are intimately connected, these separate α'σ'θ' and α'θ' readings have been listed together.

[13]Since there is no marker in 𝔖^{txt} for this α'σ'θ' reading, it may also pertain to a different noun in the verse. See fn. 36.

s^{mg}Ⱥ^{vid}Ꞩ^{mg})] MT rwḥ ḥkmh.

28:4: ο'α'σ'θ' ααρων τω αδελφω σου (v: cf. $s^{mg}z^{mg}$)] OG ααρων (+ τω αδελφω σου cmȺꞨ)] MT l'hrn 'ḥyk.

28:16: α'σ'θ' σπιθαμης το μηκος αυτου (v; cf. α'θ' *dylh*(1) in Ꞩ^{txt})] OG σπιθαμης το μηκος (+ αυτου B^aF^bcm)] Ꞩ^{txt} dzrt' 'wrk' ※α'θ' dylh↙] MT zrt 'rkw.

28:21: α'θ'σ'ο' κατα το ονομα αυτου (v)] OG κατα (κατ brw; om a_2) το (τα fhikn, Cyr; om brw) ονομα (ονοματα fhikn, Cyr [+ αυτων hn, Cyr]; + αυτου cȺɃ; + ※'' *dylh*↙ Ꞩ)] MT ʿl šmw.

28:37 (LXX v.33): α'θ' επι της κινδαρεως (jsv, Nobil.; cf. 130 [130 and Nobil. cited from Field])] OG επι της μιτρας] MT ʿl hmṣnpt.

28:37 (LXX v.33): α'θ' κατα προσωπον της κινδαρεως (v)] OG κατα προσωπον της μιτρας] MT 'l mwl pny hmṣnpt.

28:43 (LXX v.39): α'ο'(?)θ' αιωνιον αυτου (v; cf. α' αιωνιον αυτ. in s)] OG αιωνιον (εις τον αιωνα $ns^{txt}v^{txt}z$) αυτω (αυτων F^bs^{txt})] MT ʿwlm lw.

29:1: α'θ' lmqdšw (Ꞩ^{mg}; cf. θ' εις το αγιασαι in *b*)] OG αγιασεις (BchoquxɃ^{w}; *et sanctificabis* Ⱥ; αγιασας r; αγιασαι AFMabdgi-lnpstvwy-b_2Ƀ^{l}Ȼ^{c}ɆŁ^{r}, Cyr)] Ꞩ^{txt} tqdš] MT lqdš.

29:16: ο'θ'σ'α' το αιμ[α] αυτου (v)] OG το αιμα (+ αυτου cegjk mȺ; + ※'' *dylh*↙ Ꞩ)] MT 't dmw.

29:18: α'θ' οσμη ευαρεστησεως πυρον κυριω αυτο ("one Regius" acc. to Montef. as cited by Field)] OG εις (om kmxꞨ) οσμην (οσμη mꞨ^{vid}) ευωδιας θυσιασμα (θυμιαμα B*f, Cyr-ed; ολοκαυτωμα a_2; + τω Axy^aa_2) κυριω (κ̄ῡ nsvz; + ο x) εστιν (εσται B, Cyr-cod; om εις-εσται c; om εις-κυριω g; om θυσιασμα-εσται eȺ-cod)] MT ryḥ nyḥwḥ 'šh lyhwh hw'.

30:3: α'σ'θ' δωμα αυτου (v)] OG εσχαραν (εσχαριδα AM^{mg}degjnps v^{txt}yz; εσχιδα qu) αυτου (om Cyr-cod)] MT ggw.

30:18: α'σ'θ' wtʿbd ((Ꞩ^{mg})] OG ποιησον (ποιησεις cŁ^{r}; και ποιησεις m)] Ꞩ^{txt} tʿbd] MT wʿśyt.

30:38: α'θ' ※ ανηρ ος αν (v; cf. α'θ' *gbr'* in Ꞩ^{txt})] OG (+ ανηρ $F^{c?}c^{smg}z^{mg}$Ⱥ; + ανηρ ... m) ος (ως o) αν (εαν k; om d; ... + ανηρ egj)] Ꞩ^{txt} ※α'θ' gbr'↙ hw d'n] MT 'yš 'šr.

31:6: α'σ'θ'·※· και εγω ιδου (v; cf. α'σ' ιδου in s, α'θ' *h'* in $\mathcal{S}^{txt}$)] OG και (+ ιδου cegjm) εγω (om efgjx; + *ecce* $\mathcal{A}$)] $\mathcal{S}^{txt}$ w'n' ※α'θ' h'⋎] MT w'ny hnh.

32:6: α'θ' wqdm ($\mathcal{S}^{mg}$)] OG και ορθρισας] $\mathcal{S}^{txt}$ wkd qdm] MT wyškymw.

32:31: θ'α'ο' επεστρεψεν δε μωσης (v)] OG (+ και egjns^{txt}v^{txt}z^{txt}, 25) υπεστρεψεν (Bafhioqu; επεστρεψεν AFMbcdklmprs^{mg}twy z^{mg}a$_2$b$_2$; απεστρεψεν n[-ψε]x; απεστραφη egjs^{txt}v^{txt}z^{txt}, 32; ανεστραφη 25) δε (om egjns^{txt}v^{txt}z^{txt}, 25) μωυσης (μωσης kmn)] MT wyšb mšh.

36:1: α'σ'θ' lmd' lm'bd ($\mathcal{S}^{mg}$)] OG (+ του qu) συνιεναι (after ποιειν g; om b$\mathcal{E}$; + και n$\mathcal{L}$: + ωστε bcmqu) ποιειν] $\mathcal{S}^{txt}$ lmstklw (+ ※ Lagarde) 'yk⋎ dlm'bd ('yk d⋎lm'bd Lagarde)] MT ld't l'śt.

38:17 (LXX 37:15): α'σ'θ' wdwbq' dylhwn ($\mathcal{S}^{mg}$)] OG και αι (om dpst) αγκυλαι αυτων] $\mathcal{S}^{txt}$ w'nqwl's dylhwn] MT wḥšwqyhm.

There are fifty-four readings in which Aquila and Theodotion are cited together with simple expansions of the OG:

3:11: α'θ' 'n' ($\mathcal{S}^{txt}$)] OG ειμι (εγω ειμι ck; εγω 74, $\mathcal{B}^{vid}$ $\mathcal{E}^{vid}$; + εγω Babghmnoswxa$_2$c$_2$*^{vid} [perhaps also A^{1}F^1]$\mathcal{A}\mathcal{C}^m\mathcal{L}^r$)] $\mathcal{S}^{txt}$ ※α'θ' 'n'⋎ 'yty] MT 'nky.[14]

4:23: α'θ' 'yty ($\mathcal{S}^{txt}$)] OG εγω (+ ειμι ckx$\mathcal{A}$)] $\mathcal{S}^{txt}$ 'n' ※α'θ' 'yty⋎] MT 'nky.

5:23: α'θ' mprq ($\mathcal{S}^{txt}$; B includes the preceding *w-* in the α'θ' citation)] OG om.] MT (w)hṣl.[15]

9:20: α'σ'θ' τους δουλους αυτου (*b*; cf. α'σ'θ' *l'bd' dylh* in $\mathcal{S}^{mg}$)] OG om.] MT 't bdyw.

10:9: α'θ' dyln(1) ($\mathcal{S}^{txt}$)] OG om.] MT (wbzqny)nw.

10:9: α'θ' dyln(2) ($\mathcal{S}^{txt}$)] OG om.] MT (bbny)nw.

10:29: α'θ' hkn' ($\mathcal{S}^{txt}$)] OG om.] MT kn.

---

[14]See item 58 in chapter four and the further references given there.

[15]MT *whṣl l' hṣlt* is translated by OT και (+ ρυομενος ck$\mathcal{A}$) ουκ ερρυσω and by $\mathcal{S}^{txt}$ *w* ※α'θ' *mprq*⋎ (※α'θ' *wmprq*⋎ B) *l' prqtyhy*. Aquila and Theodotion share the use of the cognate participle ρυομενος/*mprq* to represent the cognate infinitive absolute *(w)hṣl*.

11:1: α′θ′ mn hrk’ ($\mathcal{S}^{txt}$)] OG om.] MT mzh.

11:3: α′θ′ wb‘ẙn’ d‘m’ ($\mathcal{S}^{txt}$)] OG om.] MT wb‘yny h‘m.

12:6: α′σ′θ′ ywm’ ($\mathcal{S}^{mg}$)] OG om.] MT ywm.

14:17: α′θ′ dylh ($\mathcal{S}^{txt}$)] OG om.] MT (brkb)w.

14:29: α′θ′ dylhwn ($\mathcal{S}^{txt}$)] OG om.] MT (wmśm’l)m.

21:6: α′θ′ dylh ($\mathcal{S}^{txt}$)] OG om.] MT (’zn)w.

21:30: α′θ′ ’yk klhyn ($\mathcal{S}^{txt}$)] OG om.] MT kkl.

21:33: α′θ′ ’nš ($\mathcal{S}^{txt}$)] OG om.] MT ’yš$^{(2)}$.

22:26 (LXX v.27): α′θ′ ’p ($\mathcal{S}^{txt}$)] OG om.] MT w-$^{(2)}$.[16]

25:6: α′σ′θ′ hẙwm’ ($\mathcal{S}^{mg}$; B has *hrwm’*, however)] OG om.] MT bśmym.

25:23 (LXX v.22): α′θ′ dylh$^{(1)}$ ($\mathcal{S}^{txt}$)] OG om.] MT (’rk)w.

25:23 (LXX v.22): α′θ′ dylh$^{(2)}$ ($\mathcal{S}^{txt}$)] OG om.] MT (rḥb)w.

25:23 (LXX v.22): α′θ′ dylh$^{(3)}$ ($\mathcal{S}^{txt}$)] OG om.] MT (qmt)w.

25:36: α′θ′ dylhwn$^{(1)}$ ($\mathcal{S}^{txt}$)] OG om.] MT (kptry)hm.

25:36: α′θ′ dylhwn$^{(2)}$ ($\mathcal{S}^{txt}$)] OG om.] MT (wqnt)m.

26:15: α′θ′ dqymyn ($\mathcal{S}^{txt}$)] OG om.] MT ‘mdym.

27:13: α′θ′ lsṭr’ ($\mathcal{S}^{mg}$)] OG om.] MT lp’t.

28:16: α′θ′ dylh$^{(2)}$ ($\mathcal{S}^{txt}$)] OG om.] MT (rḥb)w.

29:14: α′θ′ b- ($\mathcal{S}^{txt}$)] OG om.] MT b-.[17]

29:28: α′θ′ dylhwn ($\mathcal{S}^{txt}$)] OG om.] MT (šlmy)hm.[18]

30:2: α′θ′ dylh$^{(1)}$ ($\mathcal{S}^{txt}$)] OG om.] MT (’rk)w.

30:2: α′θ′ dylh$^{(2)}$ ($\mathcal{S}^{txt}$)] OG om.] MT (rḥb)w.

30:37: α′θ′ w- ($\mathcal{S}^{txt}$)] OG om.] MT w-.

30:37: α′σ′θ′ hw dt‘bd (($\mathcal{S}^{txt}$)] OG om.] MT ’šr t‘śh.

31:8-9: α′σ′θ′ και το θυσιαστηριον του θυμιαματος και το θυσιαστηριον της ολοκαυτωσεως και παντα τα σκευη αυτου (sv[under ⋇]; cf. cmz^{mg}𝔄 and F$^{c?\ mg}$; cf. also θ′ *wlmdbḥ’ dbšm’ wlmdbḥ’*.

---

[16]Syriac *’p* probably corresponds to Greek και (inserted in ack).

[17]MT *b’š* is translated by OG (+ εν *b*ckw) πυρι (om aeghj𝔄𝔈^{f}) and by $\mathcal{S}^{txt}$ ⋇α′θ′ *bnwr’*. Thus Aquila and Theodotion both presumably insert the preposition εν/*b*- to represent the MT preposition *b*-.

[18]The suffix is not reflected by most LXX manuscripts (A*FM^{txt}abegj klqsu-b_2𝔅𝔏^{r}), while αυτων (= α′θ′ *dylhwn*) is found in M^{mg}cdmnpt𝔄𝔈^{vid} and των υιων ισραηλ is inserted in A$^{c\ mg}$Bfhior, Cyr. The latter is almost certainly a secondary expansion in the OG, rather than the original OG reading.

dyqdʾ šlmʾ wlklhwn mʾnʾ dylh in $\mathcal{S}^{txt}$)] OG om.] MT wʾt mzbḥ hqṭrt wʾt mzbḥ hʿlh wʾt kl klyw.

32:24: α'σ'θ' ʾnwn ($\mathcal{S}^{mg}$)] OG om.] MT (wʾšlk)hw.[19]

32:29: α'θ' dylh ($\mathcal{S}^{txt}$)] OG om.] MT (bbn)w.

34:7: α'θ' wʿl ($\mathcal{S}^{txt}$)] OG και$^{(7)}$] MT wʿl$^{(2)}$.[20]

34:12: α'θ' ʾnt ($\mathcal{S}^{txt}$)] OG om.] MT ʾth.

34:35: α'θ' hw ($\mathcal{S}^{txt}$)] OG om.] MT (bʾ)w.

35:22: α'θ' gbrʾ ($\mathcal{S}^{txt}$)] OG om.] MT ʾyš.[21]

36:2: α'θ' blbʾ ($\mathcal{S}^{txt}$)] OG om.] MT lb.

36:2: α'θ' dylhwn ($\mathcal{S}^{txt}$)] OG om.] MT (blb)w.[22]

36:21 (MT): α'θ' ddpʾ ($\mathcal{S}^{mg}$)] OG om.] MT hqrš$^{(1)}$.

36:23 (MT): α'θ' dtymnʾ ($\mathcal{S}^{mg}$)] OG om.] MT ngb.

36:25 (MT): α'σ'θ' grbyʾ ($\mathcal{S}^{mg}$)] OG om.] MT ṣpwn.

37:25 (MT): α'σ'θ' wdʾmtʾ$^{(1)}$ ($\mathcal{S}^{mg}$)] OG om.] MT ʾmh.

37:25 (MT): α'σ'θ' wdʾmtʾ$^{(2)}$ ($\mathcal{S}^{mg}$)] OG om.] MT wʾmh.

37:26 (MT): α'σ'θ' bh bdmwtʾ lʾgrʾ dylh ($\mathcal{S}^{mg}$; cf. $\mathcal{S}^{txt}$[under ※] *lʾgrʾ dylh* and ckAE^{c} [+ *et* A] το δωμα [δομα k] αυτου)] OG om.] MT ʾt ggw.

38:23 (LXX 37:21): α'θ' btkltʾ w- ($\mathcal{S}^{txt}$; B removes *w-* from the α'θ' citation)] OG om.] MT btklt w-.

39:9 (LXX 36:16): α'θ' ʾytyh hwt ($\mathcal{S}^{txt}$)] OG om.] MT hyh.

39:41 (MT): α'σ'θ' lḥḥtʾ dtšmštʾ ($\mathcal{S}^{mg}$)] OG om.] MT ʾt bgdy hśrd.

40:2: α'σ'θ' dstrʾ ($\mathcal{S}^{txt}$)] OG om.] MT ʾhl.

40:6: α'σ'θ' dstrʾ ($\mathcal{S}^{txt}$)] OG om.] MT ʾhl.

40:20 (LXX v.18): α'θ' wyhb ($\mathcal{S}^{mg}$)] OG om.] MT wytn$^{(2)}$.

40:30 (LXX v.26): α'σ'θ' wsm ($\mathcal{S}^{mg}$)] OG om.] MT wyśm.

40:33 (LXX v.27): α'θ' wyhb ($\mathcal{S}^{mg}$)] OG om.] MT wytn.

---

[19]See item 78 in chapter three.

[20]The sharing of και/*w-* by α'θ' and the OG need not prevent one from listing this reading among the simple expansions of the OG, rather than among the α'θ' readings that partially agree with the OG. Agreement on και/*w-*, especially where the MT also has *w-*, is completely insignificant in itself.

[21]See item 92 in chapter three.

[22]See item 79 in chapter three.

There are sixty-three readings in which Aquila and Theodotion are cited together with simple or expanded variants to the OG;

1:18: α'θ' παιδια (Regius 1871, according to Holmes' scribe as cited by Field) I OG αρσενα I MT (h)yldym.

2:3: α'θ' κιβωτον παπυρου (v; cf. α'σ' κιβωτον παπυρου in Mz) I OG θιβιν (+ παπυρου acxA𝔖[under ※]) I MT tbt gm'.

2:25; α'θ' wḥz' (𝔖^{mg}; cf. θ' ειδεν in *b*) I OG και επιδεν (επειδεν B^{ab}; εισιδεν AMegi*jvwy-c_2, Cyr-ed$\frac{1}{2}$; εισειδεν F; ειδεν 1; ως ειδεν 25) I 𝔖^{txt} wḥr I MT wyr'.

3:4: α'θ' ιδου εγω (64, according to Field) I OG τι εστιν (+ $\overline{κε}$ qsuB^{c}) I MT hnny.

3:14: α'θ' εσομαι εσομαι (64, according to Field; cf. εσ. ος εσ. in Graeco-Ven., according to Field) I OG εγω ειμι ο ων I MT 'hyh 'šr 'hyh.

4:11: α'σ'θ' μογιλαλον (Mjvzc_2; cf. *b*^{mg}; cf. also α'σ'θ' *l'g mmll'* in 𝔖^{mg}) I OG δυσκωφον I 𝔖^{txt} p'q' I MT 'lm.

4:21: α'θ' ενισχυσω (Mvz; cf. α' ενισχυσω in j and in Nobil. according to Field) I OG σκληρυνω I MT 'ḥzq.

5:7: α'σ'θ' καλαμασθωσαν (Mv; cf. j^{mg}z^{mg}c_2^{mg}; cf. also θ' καλαμασθωσαν and σ' καλαμασθωσαν in jvz) I OG συναγαγετωσαν (συναγετωσαν d-gj^{txt}z^{txt}; συναγαγετω b') I MT (w)qššw.

8:6 (LXX v.10): α'σ'θ' 'yk pypy 'lh' dyln (𝔖^{mg}) I OG αλλος (αγιος e; + $\overline{θς}$ fA-coddB^{w}; + $\overline{κς}$ ο $\overline{θς}$ ημων 128) πλην κυριου $\overline{κς}$ AFe ghjlwb_2; $\overline{κς}$ ο $\overline{θς}$ ημων ackmxA) I 𝔖^{txt} 'ḥrn' lbr mn mry' ※ 'lh' dyln↙ I MT kyhwh 'lhynw.

10:14: α'θ' ddm' lh (𝔖^{mg}) I OG τοιαυτη (out of place ackmx) I 𝔖^{txt} ※ d'yk hn'↙ I MT kn$^{(1)}$.[23]

12:7: α'σ'θ' w'l (𝔖^{mg}) I OG (+ και bcdk-nptwzd_2, Chr) εν$^{(1)}$ (επι abwx; om A^{vid}B^{vid}) I 𝔖^{txt} b-$^{(1)}$ I MT 'l$^{(2)}$.

12:11: α'θ' εν θαμβω (*b*; cf. α'θ' *btwht'* in 𝔖^{mg}, α' εν θαμβω in M jv and in c_2, and also α' εν βαθμω in z) I OG μετα σπουδης I 𝔖^{txt} 'm swrhb' I MT bḥpzwn.[24]

---

[23]The entire MT phrase *kn 'rbh kmhw* is translated by OG τοιαυτη (after ακρις ackmx; ουδεποτε f) ακρις (om fB) and by 𝔖^{txt} ※ *d'yk hn'*↙ (α'θ' *ddm' lh* 𝔖^{mg}) *qmṣ' 'kwth*

[24]The α' reading in z^{mg} is obviously a scribal error.

12:21: α'σ'θ' 'ntwn lkwn (Ѕ^mg)] OG υμιν (after εαυτοις 71; υμων 1; om Ѕ) εαυτοις (Bhi; out of place egj; αυτοι b_2*; αυτοις AMdfk-oqrst^a? vxyzb$_2$^a? c_2, Cyr; om abcpt*wa$_2$Ѧ^vid Ѕ)] Ѕ^txt 'ntwn lkwn] MT lkm.[25]

13:16: α'σ'θ' wdmttzy' ((Ѕ^mg; cf. α' και εισενεκτα in j, α' και εισιν ακτα in z[cf. also v^mg], and α' εις νακτα in M)] OG και (om d_2) ασαλευτον (σαλευτον a*)] Ѕ^txt wmttzy'n'] MT wlṭwṭpt.[26]

13:20: α'σ'θ' εν ηθαν την ερημοτατην (M)] OG εν οθομ παρα την ερημον] MT b'tm bqṣh hmdbr.[27]

14:2: α'σ'θ' φιεθρω (M; but compare α'σ' *py'yrwt'* θ' *p'yrwt* in Ѕ^mg)] OG της επαυλεως] Ѕ^txt dyr'] MT py hḥyrt.[28]

14:9: α'θ' επι φιεθρων (M; but compare α'θ' *lqwbl p'y'yrwt* in Ѕ^mg)] OG απεναντι της επαυλεως] Ѕ^txt qdm dyr'] MT 'l py hḥyrt.[29]

14:15: α'σ'θ' wnrymwn (Ѕ^mg)] OG και αναζευξατωσαν] Ѕ^txt wnšqlwn] MT wys'w.

15:5: α'σ'θ' thWm' (Ѕ^mg)] OG ποντω (ποντο M^mg fhnsxa$_2$; ποντος F^b? cj^mg v^mg z^mg ѦЕ, Cyr$\frac{1}{2}$-ed$\frac{1}{2}$; *aqua* Ѕ)] Ѕ^txt ym'] MT thmt.

---

[25]The Syriac phrase *'ntwn lkwn*, found in Ѕ^txt and also attributed to α'σ'θ' in Ѕ^mg, does not seem to reflect the LXX majority reading (υμιν αυτοις) or any of the preserved Greek variants.

[26]See item 65 in chapter three. While the original Greek α' reading cannot be recovered, the fact that Ѕ^mg attributes a common equivalent for the rare Hebrew word to α'σ'θ' is significant.

[27]The agreement on εν to represent MT *b-* and the slight lexical similarity between OG ερημον and α'σ'θ' ερημοτατην are not sufficient to place this α'σ'θ' variant among those that partially agree with the OG.

[28]The variation in Syriac forms need not contradict the α'σ'θ' reading of M^mg. The different Syriac forms could be due to inner-Syriac influences or to scribal error.

[29]The different Greek and Syriac forms of the proper name here provide further support for the suggestion made in the previous note. It is impossible to be sure which form most accurately reflects the one actually used by Theodotion and Aquila.

15:8: α'σ'θ' εσωρευθη (Mjvz) ‖ OG διεστη ‖ MT nʿrmw.

15:16: α'θ' nštqwn ($\mathcal{S}^{mg}$) ‖ OG απολιθωθητωσαν ‖ $\mathcal{S}^{txt}$ ntqšwn 'yk k'p' ‖ MT ydmw k'bn.[30]

16:5: α'θ' ywm' ywm' ($\mathcal{S}^{mg}$) ‖ OG το (τω c; om x) καθ ημεραν εις (om F*1) ημεραν (ημερας q; om F*1) ‖ $\mathcal{S}^{txt}$ kl ywm' lywmh ‖ MT ywm ywm.

16:10: α'θ' whpkw ($\mathcal{S}^{mg}$) ‖ OG και (om $\mathcal{A}\mathcal{L}^{z}$) επεστραφησαν (απεστραφησαν hm; εστραφησαν 18) ‖ $\mathcal{S}^{txt}$ 'p 'tpnyw ‖ MT wypnw.

19:11: α'σ'θ' bh bdmwt' dsyny ($\mathcal{S}^{mg}$) ‖ OG το (του 83, 132; om Adefi*jkmpd$_2$, Cyr$\frac{1}{4}$-ed$\frac{2}{4}$) σεινα (σινα AB^{b}F; σιναι n) ‖ $\mathcal{S}^{txt}$ dsyny ‖ MT syny.[31]

20:25 ($\mathcal{S}$ v.22): α'σ'θ' και εβεβηλωσας αυτο (v; cf. z^{mg}; cf. also α'σ'θ' *wsybtyhy* in $\mathcal{S}^{mg}$) ‖ OG και μεμιανται ‖ $\mathcal{S}^{txt}$ wmsyb hw ‖ MT wtḥllh.

22:9 (LXX v.10): α'σ'θ' dḥz' ($\mathcal{S}^{mg}$) ‖ OG γνω (ειδη cxv; ιδη anwz) ‖ $\mathcal{S}^{mg}$ ndʿ (= OG γνω) ‖ $\mathcal{S}^{txt}$ nḥz' ‖ MT r'h.

22:10 (LXX v.11): α'σ'θ' pypy ($\mathcal{S}^{mg}$) ‖ OG του θεου ‖ $\mathcal{S}^{txt}$ d'lh' ‖ MT yhwh.

22:27 (LXX v.28): α'σ'θ' ουκ ατιμασεις (jvz; cf. α'σ'θ' ου καταμασεις in s) ‖ OG ου κακολογησεις ‖ MT l' tqll.[32]

23:21: α'θ' bh bdmwt' bh ($\mathcal{S}^{mg}$) ‖ OG (+ εν ack, Eus$\frac{2}{4}$) αυτω (αυτου f; om mb$_2$, Phil-arm, Cyp-codd) ‖ $\mathcal{S}^{txt}$ lh ‖ MT bw.[33]

---

[30] The reading attributed to α'θ', *nštqwn* (= "they are quiet"), presumably represents only MT *ydmw*, while OG απολιθωθητωσαν (= $\mathcal{S}^{txt}$ *ntqšwn 'yk k'p'*) represents the entire MT phrase, *ydmw k'bn*.

[31] The Syriac form *syny* appears to reflect σιναι (of n), or the like, rather than OG σεινα. However, the change could be due to Syriac usage rather than to the presence of a Greek form different from that found in the OG.

[32] See the discussion under item 38 in chapter three for the reason why the α', σ', and θ' variants of $\mathcal{S}^{mg}$ are to be associated with $\mathcal{S}^{txt}$ *l' t'mr byš'yt*(2) (= OG ουκ ερεις κακως), rather than with $\mathcal{S}^{txt}$ *l' t'mr byš'yt*(1) (and hence with OG ου κακολογησεις) as marked.

[33] Since $\mathcal{S}^{txt}$ and the OG have *lh*/αυτω in place of α'θ' *bh* (= εν αυτω), the precise import of the formula *bh bdmwt'* in the α'θ' citation of $\mathcal{S}^{mg}$ remains uncertain.

24:12: α'σ'θ' τας πλακας (Mvz; cf. F^b mg and α'σ' τας πλακας in s)] OG τα πυξια] MT 't lḥt.

24:13: α'σ'θ' ο (om Mvz) λειτουργος αυτου (Msvz; cf. α'σ' ο λειτουργος αυτου in j and α'σ'θ' ο λειτουργος αυτω in F^b mg)] OG ο παρεστηκως αυτω] MT mšrtw.[34]

25:7 (LXX v.6): α'σ'θ' επενδυμα (85, according to Montef. as cited by Field)] OG την επωμιδα] Ꞩ^txt (l)kbynt'] MT (l)'pd.[35]

25:7 (LXX v.6): α'θ' εις το λογιον (M; cf. οι λ̥ το λογειον in svz)] OG τον ποδηρη] MMT (w)lḥšn.

26:15: α'σ'θ' τας σανιδας (*b*; cf. α'σ'θ' *dp'* in Ꞩ^mg)] OG (+ τους ack) στυλους] Ꞩ^txt 'mwd'] MT 't hqršym.

26:18: α'σ'θ' ldp' (Ꞩ^mg)] OG (+ τους F*acfhinqux) στυλους^(1)] Ꞩ^txt l'mwd'] MT 't hqršym.

27:4: α'σ'θ' 'yk d'rbl' (Ꞩ^mg; cf. σ'θ' κοσκηνου in *b* and οι λ̥ κοσκινωμα in M)] OG εσχαραν] Ꞩ^txt ṭrṭql' (ṭrṭql' B)] MT mkbr.[36]

27:6: α'σ'θ' šqwl' (Ꞩ^mg)] OG φορεις (B*h; αναφορεις B^ab acoqr ux; om AFM rell ȺꞨ)] Ꞩ^txt qwp'^(2)] MT bdy.[37]

---

[34]The replacement of αυτου with αυτω in the α'σ'θ' reading of F^b mg is probably a secondary scribal error under the influence of OG αυτω . The agreement between α'σ'θ' and the OG on the definite article is too minor to warrant listing this variant among those α'θ' readings that partially agree with the OG.

[35]This reading is of doubtful validity for two reasons. First, 85 = z, and no α'σ'θ' reading is here cited from z by B-McL. Second, following common OG usage, Theodotion regularly uses επωμις to represent MT *'pd*, while επενδυμα is used by Aquila and sometimes also by Symmachus. This matter has been discussed thoroughly under item 22 in chapter two.

[36]Lagarde notes that the marker for this reading was added at Ꞩ^txt *ṭrṭql'*, but he does not say by whom the addition was made. This α'σ'θ' reading of Ꞩ^mg is immediately followed by α'σ'θ' *mṣydt'*, listed above among the α'θ' readings that partially agree with the OG. See the comment in fn. 13 in this chapter.

[37]The complete evidence for the total phrase is; MT *bdym lmzbḥ bdy 'ṣy šṭym*] OG (+ φορεις AF*Mbefgijlmsvwz Ⱥ; + αναφορεις F^b acdknptb$_2$Ꞩ) τω (om a$_2$) θυσιαστηριω (om a$_2$) φορεις (B*h; αναφορεις B^ab acoqrux; om

27:19: α'θ' δουλεια αυτης (v)] OG τα εργαλεια (εργα c; + αυτης ckm𝔄)] MT ʿbdtw.

28:30 (LXX v.26): α'σ'θ' lnwhrʾ wlšwmlyʾ (𝔖^mg; cf. οι λ̥ τους φωτισμους και τας τελειοτητας in sv and without name in k^mg z^mg)] OG την δηλωσιν και την αληθειαν] 𝔖^txt lglynʾ wlšrrʾ] MT ʾt hʾwrym wʾt htmym.[38]

28:32 (LXX v.28): α'θ' ... της κεφαλης αυτου εν μεσω αυτου (v; cf. also z^mg and α' ... της κεφαλης αυτου εν μεσω αυτου in s)] OG (+ της αρχης cegjm [+ αυτου cm]) εξ (om k) αυτου (om k) μεσον (+ αυτου cm)] MT rʾšw btwkw.

28:32 (LXX v.28): α'θ' ... προσπλοκην σ' ... σειρωτον (M; but cf. α' ... προσπλοκην [-πλοκης v; -πλοις s] σ'θ' ... σειρωτον in svz)] OG συνυφασμενην] MT tḥrʾ.[39]

29:13: α'θ' το περιττον (M)] OG τον λοβον] MT (w)ʾt hytrt.

29:36: α'σ'θ' εξιλασμου (Mjvz; cf. k^mg n)] OG καθαρισμου] MT (h)kprym.

29:42: α'θ' lyqdʾ šlmʾ (𝔖^mg)] OG θυσιαν (θυσιας x)] 𝔖^mg dbḥʾ (= OG θυσιαν)] 𝔖^txt yqdʾ šlmʾ] MT ʿlt.[40]

30:4: α'σ'θ' τοις αναφορευσιν (*b*; cf. F^b mg, s^mg, θ'σ' τοις αναφορευσιν in M, and θ' τοις αναφορευσιν in vz)] OG ταις σκυταλαις] MT lbdym.

30:5: α'σ'θ' lqwpʾ (𝔖^mg)] OG σκυταλας] 𝔖^txt tʿwnʾ] MT ʾt hbdym.

AFMbd-gi-npstvwza$_2$b$_2$𝔄𝔅; λοστους i^mg; αναβασταζοντας F^b mg) εκ ξυλων ασηπτων] 𝔖^txt *qwpʾ lmdbḥʾ qwpʾ* (α'σ'θ' *šqwlʾ* 𝔖^mg) *mn qysʾ lʾ mblṭʾ*. Perhaps α'σ'θ' *šqwlʾ* represents αναβασταζοντας of F^b mg.

[38]For possible evidence of dependence by α'σ'θ' on the OG here, see items 99-100 in chapter three.

[39]It is impossible to decide whether Theodotion agreed with Aquila or with Symmachus. In the former alternative, the agreement on προσπλοκην would imply a genuine relationship between Aquila and Theodotion. In the latter case, there would be no evidence for such a relationship, while Symmachus and Theodotion would be related in some way.

[40]On the basis of normal correspondences, Syriac *yqdʾ šlmʾ* should reflect Greek ολοκαυτωσις rather than Greek θυσια, which would be represented accurately by Syriac *dbḥʾ*.

30:16: α'θ' επι την δουλειαν (*b*; cf. α'θ' *ʿl ʿbdwtʾ* in S^{mg}) I OG εις (om flnx^{vid}; + το AFMb-egijkpqs-wy-b_2) κατεργον I S^{txt} lpwlḥn ʿbdʾ I MT ʿl ʿbdt.

30:20: α'θ' πυρρον (Montef., no source given, as cited by Field, who corrects to πυρον) I OG τα (om ikn) ολοκαυτωματα (ολοκαρπωματα F*gjlsvz; καρπωματα nxL^{r}; καρπωμα k) I MT ʾšh.

32:1: α'θ' και εκκλησιασθη (*b*; cf. α'θ' *wʾtknšw* in S^{mg}) I OG (+ και Cyr-cod) συνεστη (συνεστησαν cdkm; συνεπεστη a; συνηθροισθη Cyr-cod; *surrexit* C^{m}; *consurrexit* L^{r}) *conuersus est* L^{z}) I S^{txt} wqm I MT wyqhl.

33:12: α'θ' bšmʾ (S^{mg}) I OG παρα παντας I S^{txt} ytyr mn kl ʾnš I MT bšm.

33:22: α'σ'θ' qywlnʾ (S^{mg} vid; cf. α' εν τω κολαματ... in *b*) I OG οπην I S^{txt} (b)ḥrwrʾ I MT (b)nqrt.[41]

35:9 (LXX v.8): α'θ' το (om vz) λογιον (Mvz; cf. α' λογιον in s) I OG τον ποδηρη I MT (wl)ḥšn.

35:11 (LXX v.10): α'σ'θ' wltksytʾ dylh (S^{mg}; cf. οι γ̷ και την σκεπην αυτης in Msv and without name in z^{mg}) I OG και τα (om egj) παραρυματα (etc.; + αυτης F^{b}ckmA) I S^{txt} wlzqwřy ṣbtʾ ※ ʿʾ dylh↙ I MT ʾt ʾhlw.

35:23: α'σ'θ' πεπυρωμενα (v) I OG ηρυθροδανωμενα I MT mʾdmym.

35:29: α'θ' ṣbynyʾ (S^{mg}) I OG αφαιρεμα I S^{txt} pwršnʾ I MT ndbh.

36:4: α'σ'θ' wʾtw (S^{mg}) I OG και παρεγινοντο (BhkqruA; παρεγενοντο F^{b}bcmnowxBL^{r}; παραγενομενοι AMd-gijlpstv^{txt}y-b_2E^{vid}) I S^{txt} wʾtw I MT wybʾw.[42]

36:7: α'σ'θ' lklh ʿbdʾ (S^{mg}) I OG εις (+ πασαν ckmA) την κατασκευην I S^{txt} lklh twqnh I MT lkl hmlʾkh.

37:17 (LXX 38:14): α'σ'θ' lʿṭmʾ dylh (S^{mg}) I OG τον καυλον (+ αυτης F^{b}GckE^{c}) I S^{txt}(under ※) lšwyʾ dylh I MT yrkh.[43]

---

[41] For more extensive textual evidence and a brief evaluation of this obscure α'σ'θ' reading, see item 132 in chapter three.

[42] See item 87 in chapter four for a brief discussion of the difficulties connected with the interpretation of this reading. The reading could also be listed among those apparently in partial or full agreement with the OG (but not with the majority of LXX manuscripts).

[43] The OG version and the longer version are found as doublets in GckAS^{txt}, with the former under ÷ and the latter under ※ in GS.

38:4 (LXX 38:24): α'σ'θ' ṭhyt ṭrṭql' dylh ($\mathcal{S}^{mg}$) ‖ OG κατωθεν (υπ αυτου ck[-το]) του πυρειου ‖ $\mathcal{S}^{txt}$ tḥwtwhy dpyrm' ‖ MT tḥt krkbw.

38:12 (LXX 37:10): α'σ'θ' w'ȳls ($\mathcal{S}^{mg}$) ‖ OG αυλαιαι ‖ $\mathcal{S}^{txt}$ yȳy't' ‖ MT ql'ym.

39:6 (LXX 36:13): α'σ'θ' του ονυχος (Montef., no source given, as cited by Field) ‖ OG της σμαραγδου ‖ MT hšhm.[44]

39:39 (LXX 39:10): α'σ'θ' wlmḥwlt' ($\mathcal{S}^{mg}$) ‖ OG και το παραθεμα ‖ $\mathcal{S}^{txt}$(under ※) wlṭrṭql' ‖ MT w't mkbr.[45]

40:20 (LXX v.18): α'σ'θ' lšqẅl' ($\mathcal{S}^{mg}$) ‖ OG τους (τας d) διωστηρας (διασζωστηρας G) ‖ $\mathcal{S}^{txt}$ lqwp' ‖ MT 't hbdym.

There are eleven additional readings in which Aquila and Theodotion agree, although they are cited separately. Once they apparently agree with the OG:

1:11: θ' lpytw' α'σ' lpytw ($\mathcal{S}^{mg}$) ‖ OG την τε(om 132) πειθω (Bb' kqruwxE; etc.) ‖ $\mathcal{S}^{txt}$ wlpytwm ‖ MT 't ptm.[46]

There are three readings shared by Aquila and Theodotion in which they apparently agree partially with the OG:

4:6: α' και ιδου (+ η z) χειρ αυτου λεπρωσα ωσει χιων (vz) ‖ θ' και ιδου η χειρ αυτου λεπρωσα ωσει χιων (vz) ‖ OG και εγενηθη (εγεννηθη w; εγενετο b'c-gijkmnsx, Or-gr) η χειρ αυτου (μωυσεως A; + λεπρωσα cfipstxa$_2$, Or-gr, Cyr; + λεπρος 83; + λεπρη F$^{b\ mg}$; + *leprosa* AB; + ※ *mgrb'* ⋌ $\mathcal{S}$; + λευκη km o^a) ωσει (ως x, Cyr) χιων ‖ MT whnh ydw mṣr't kšlg.[47]

---

[44]This α'σ'θ' reading is supported by Jerome in *Epist. 64 ad Fabiolam*, 15, as quoted by Field, vol. 1, fn. 2, pp. 157-158: "In utroque humero habet singulos lapides clausos et astrictos auro, qui Hebraice dicuntur SOOM; ab Aquila et Symmacho et Theodotione *onychini*, a LXX *smaragdi* transferuntur. Josephus *sardonychas* vocat, cum Hebraeo Aquilaque consentiens." Field suggests that the latter comment may depend on a second edition of Aquila.

[45]The OG reading is also under ※ in G.

[46]The Syriac forms attributed to θ' and α'σ' could reflect at least the noun in Greek την (τε) πειθω, but the great fluctuations in spelling for this name make any conclusion tentative.

[47]It is impossible to be sure that the article before χειρ was

4:26: α' αιματων εις περιτομας (vz) I θ' αιματων εις περιτομας (vz) I OG το αιμα της περιτομης του παιδιου μου (om Abmv $\mathfrak{B}^1\mathfrak{L}^r$, Cyr-codd$\frac{1}{3}$) I MT dmym lmwlt.

29:14; σ'θ' περι αμαρτιας εστιν (v; cf. θ' περι αμαρτιας in z) I α' περι αμαρτιας εστιν (s; cf. α' περι αμαρτιας in z and α' αμαρτιας [?] εστιν in v) I OG αμαρτιας (-τια $ckrv^{txt}z^{txt}$) γαρ (χαριν f) εστιν (om f) I MT ḥṭ't hw'.

There are two simple expansions of the OG shared by Aquila and Theodotion:

16:14: α' wslq mškb' ($𝔖^{mg}$) I θ' wslq mškb' ($𝔖^{mg}$) I OG om. I MT wt'l škbt.

34:29: α'σ' dshdwt'· θ' dshdwt' ($𝔖^{mg}$) I OG om. I MT h'dt.

There are five simple variants to the OG or to many LXX manuscripts that are shared by Aquila and Theodotion:

8:10 (LXX v.14): θ' κορους κορους (*b*) I α' κορους κορους (vzc_2; cf. α' σωρους σωρους in M, α'σ' *kwṭy' kwṭy'*· θ' *'yk šb'yn* in $𝔖^{mg}$, σαμ. σωρους σωρους βωμους βωμους in c_2, and κορους κορους in j^{mg}) I OG θιμωνιας (σωρηδιον 32) θιμωνιας (om $fjkma_2$. 32) I $𝔖^{txt}$ kšyt' kšyt' I MT ḥmrm ḥmrm.[48]

9:32: α'σ' kWnt'· θ' kWnt' ($𝔖^{mg}$; cf. α'σ' η ζεα in *b*) I OG η ολυρα I $𝔖^{txt}$ (w)kWnt' I MT (w)hksmt.[49]

---

omitted by Aquila. If it was, then Aquila was bringing greater precision to the Greek phrase. If its omission was secondary, then Aquila and Theodotion were in perfect agreement here. In view of Aquila's general tendency to omit unsupported articles, perhaps the former interpretation is to be preferred.

[48]The conflicting evidence cannot be reconciled. Greek κορους (from Hebrew כֹּר, a dry measure) is probably a variant translation for MT *ḥmrym*, while the enigmatic *kwṭy'* could be a corruption of *kwry' (= κορους). The forms θημωνια (note spelling), σωρος, and *kšyt'* all mean "heap." If Aquila and Theodotion did agree here (perhaps with κορους κορους), then this would be a clear indication of dependence by one on the other.

[49]There is no way to tell whether Theodotion's *kWnt'* represents OG η ολυρα (presumably reflected by $𝔖^{txt}$ [*w*]*kWnt'*) or α'σ' η ζεα (compare α' σ' *kWnt'*). It could also presumably represent some other Greek equivalent

25:12 (LXX v.11); α'σ' μερη (s) I σ'θ' μερη (v; cf. also z^{mg}) I σ' πλευρας θ' μερη (M) I OG κλιτη I MT p‘mty-.

28:4: σ'θ' pdt' ($S̸^{mg}$) I α' το (om Mv) λογιον (Msvz; cf. $F^{b\ mg}$ and αλλος φησι λογιον in j^{mg}) I OG το περιστηθιον I $S̸^{txt}$ br ḥdy' I MT ḥšn.[50]

28:25 (MT): θ' ḥy̆ṣt' ($S̸^{txt}$) I α' ḥy̆ṣt'' σ' ḥy̆ṣt (ḥyṣt B) 'kḥd' ($S̸^{mg}$) I OG om. I $F^{a?}$McdegjkmnpstvzA̸$E̸^{c}$ συσφιγκτων (σφιγκτων m) I MT hmšbṣwt.[51]

Partial Agreement Between Aquila and Theodotion (77 Readings)

There are forty-two readings in which Aquila and Theodotion agree partially, and in which Theodotion appears closer to the OG or to a large number of LXX manuscripts than Aquila does:

2:14: α' μητι του αποκτειναι με συ λεγεις καθα απεκτεινας συν τον αιγυπτιον (v) I θ' η ανελειν με συ λεγεις ον τροπον ανειλες τον αιγυπτιον (v) I OG μη (η AF*Mceg-jrsv^{txt}xz-c_2E̸S̸, Cyr; *si* A̸) ανελειν με (after συ $L̸^{r}$) συ (om defg*xA̸$E̸^{c}$S̸, Chr$\frac{1}{3}$) θελεις (θελης *b*cikd_2; λεγεις 64^{mg}S̸) ον τροπον (+ τη χθες a_2; + *heri* A̸) ανειλες (*occidisti* A̸; + εχθες B*lru; + χθες B^{ab}bdfhnpqxd_2) τον αιγυπτιον (+ εχθες FMaiotb_2c_2; + χθες Aceg jkmsv^{txt}wyzB̸$C̸^{m}$E̸$L̸^{r}$, Cyr$\frac{1}{2}$-codd$\frac{1}{2}$; + ÷ '*tmly*⸔ S̸) I MT hlhrgny 'th 'mr k'šr hrgt 't hmṣry.

5:3: α' npg‘ bn bmwt' 'w bsyp' ($S̸^{mg}$; cf. α'σ' λοιμος [λιμος F^{I}] η μαχαιρα in F^{I}[σ' $F^{?}$]Mv and without names in z^{mg}; cf. also

---

for MT *(w)hksmt*, although this is less likely. The Syriac evidence is ambiguous, and this reading could also be listed among those in which there is no agreement between Aquila and Theodotion.

[50]Syriac *pdt'* is the regular equivalent for Greek το λογιον. To represent Hebrew *ḥšn*, the Greek form is attributed to Theodotion (and also to Aquila) in Exod. 25:7 (LXX v.6); 35:9 (LXX v.8). The Syriac form is similarly attributed to Theodotion in Exod. 28:4, 23 (MT) *bis*, 24 (MT), 26 (MT), 28 (MT) *bis*. No other equivalent for MT *ḥšn* is attributed to Theodotion or Aquila (so Reider, *s.v.*) in Exodus.

[51]See the extended discussion of these variants under item 20 in chapter two.

α′ λοιμου σ′ η μαχαιρα ϑ′ η ρομφαια in *b*)][ϑ′ npgʿ bn mwtʾ ʾw sypʾ ($\mathcal{S}^{mg}$)][OG συναντηση (-σει AFMbʹginopa$_2$) ημιν (υμιν 1; ημων s; + ο Cyr-codd$\frac{1}{2}$) θανατος η φονος (φοβος A*^{vid}m)][$\mathcal{S}^{txt}$ nʾrwʿ ln mwtʾ ʾw qṭlʾ][MT ypgʿnw bdbr ʾw bḥrb.[52]

5:7: α′ καθα (κατα z) εχθες τριτην αυτοι πορευεσθωσαν (jvz)][ϑ′ καθαπερ εχθες και της τριτης αυτοι πορευεσθωσαν (j[πορευθεντες]vz)][OG καθαπερ (καθα bw) εχθες (χθες B^{b}cdfghlmn px) και (+ την x) τριτην ημεραν (+ και το της σημερον AMd j^{mg}n[της ημερου]pqtuv^{txt}z^{mg}a$_2$b$_2$c$_2$) αυτοι πορευεσθωσαν (-σεσθοσαν 71; -ετωσαν i*n)][$\mathcal{S}^{txt}$ ʾyk mʾ dʾtmly wd ÷ bywmʾ↙ tlytyʾ α′ϑ′ hnwn nʾzlwn (no ※ or ↙)][MT ktml šlšm hm ylkw.[53]

5:16: α′ και ιδου δουλοι σου πεπληγμενοι και αμαρτια λαω σου (jvz)][ϑ′ και ιδου οι δουλοι σου μεμαστιγωνται και η αμαρτια εις τον λαον σου (jvz)][OG και ιδου οι παιδες σου μεμαστιγωνται αδικησεις (μη αδικησης f; αδικεις c[-κης]mA) ουν (om A) τον (om a$_2$)λαον σου][MT whnh ʿbdyk mkym wḥṭʾt ʿmk.

6:1: α′ bʾydʾ dmṣyʾ ḥylʾ nšdr ʾnwn wbʾydʾ ḥyltnytʾ ($\mathcal{S}^{mg}$)][ϑ′ bʾydʾ ʾḥydtʾ nšdr ʾnwn wbʾydʾ ʾḥydtʾ ($\mathcal{S}^{mg}$)][OG εν ... χειρι κραταια εξαποστελει (-στελω a$^{a?}$1; -στελλω f) αυτους και εν βραχιονι υψηλω][$\mathcal{S}^{txt}$ bʾydʾ ... ʾḥydtʾ nšdr ʾnwn wbdrʿʾ rmʾ][MT byd ḥzqh yšlḥm wbyd ḥzqh.

7:1: α′ ιδε δεδωκα σε θν̄ τω φαραω (jvz)][σ′ϑ′ ιδε κατεστησα σε θν̄ φαραω (jvz[ϑ′ after σε jz])][OG ιδου δεδωκα σε θεον (+

---

[52]There is some confusion in the preserved α′ readings (see the remarks under item 26 in chapter three). $\mathcal{S}^{mg}$ alone indicates that Aquila inserted a reflection of the MT preposition *b-* on its two occurrences, but $\mathcal{S}^{mg}$ then fails to reflect Aquila's use of λοιμος (λιμος is an itacistic corruption) in place of OG θανατος to represent MT *(b)dbr*. Furthermore, $\mathcal{S}^{mg}$ uses *sypʾ* to represent α′ μαχαιρα (and σ′ μαχαιρα), as well as ϑ′ ρομφαια. If the Syriac can be trusted, Theodotion and Aquila agreed on their translation of MT *ypgʿnw* against the OG and against Symmachus.

[53]The replacement of καθα by κατα in α′ of z^{mg} is a secondary scribal corruption, as is the replacement of πορευεσθωσαν by πορευθεντες in ϑ′ of j^{mg} (see the remarks made under item 34 in chapter three).

τω dnpt, etc.) φαραω ‖ MT r'h nttyk 'lhym lpr'h.[54]

7:11: α' καιγε αυτοι κρυφιασται αιγυπτου (+ και j) εν ηρεμαιοις αυτων ουτως (jvz; cf. α' κρυφιασται in jvz, α' τρυφιασται in M, and α' εν [om vz] ηρεμαιοις in Mvz and without name in j^mg) ‖ θ' καιγε αυτοι οι επαοιδοι των αιγυπτιων εν ταις φαρμακειαις (!) αυτων ωσαυτως (vz; cf. j^mg) ‖ OG και (ʾp 𝔖; om f*bdegjnpwa$_2$𝔄𝔈, Thdt) οι επαοιδοι των (om 𝔅^1) αιγυπτιων (*Aegypti* 𝔅^1) ταις (τας fm) φαρμακιαις (-κιας fm) αυτων (om 130) ωσαυτως ‖ MT gm hm ḥrṭmy mṣrym blhṭyhm kn.[55]

7:24: α' και ωρυξεν πασα η αιγυπτος κυκλοθεν του ρειθρου υδωρ του πιειν οτι ουκ ηδυναντο πιειν εκ του υδατος του ποταμου (jvz c$_2$; cf. α' *myʾ lmšṭʾ mṭl dlʾ mṣyn hww mn myʾ myʾ dʿdyʾ lmšṭʾ* in 𝔖^mg) ‖ θ' και ωρυξαν παντες οι αιγυπτιοι (+ οι z) κυκλω του ποταμου υδωρ εις το πιειν οτι ουκ ηδυναντο πιειν (om οτι-πιειν$^{(2)}$ c$_2$) εκ του υδατος του ποταμου (vzc$_2$; cf. θ' *myʾ lmšṭʾ mṭl dlʾ mṣyn hww lmšṭʾ myʾ mn dnhrʾ*) ‖ OG ωρυξαν δε παντες οι αιγυπτιοι (+ οι 18) κυκλω του ποταμου (ρειθρου F^b) ωστε πιειν (ευρειν 32; after υδωρ$^{(1)}$ bw𝔄; ωστε πιειν after υδωρ$^{(1)}$ kx) υδωρ (+ απο [εκ 30] του ποταμου B*h, 30) και ουκ ηδυναντο (+ οι αιγυπτιοι i^a ry) πιειν υδωρ (om και-υδωρ$^{(2)}$ qtub$_2$) απο (εκ Fcegj^txt v^txt z^txt) του ποταμου (ρειθρου F^b; om πιειν$^{(2)}$-ποταμου$^{(2)}$ fn) ‖ 𝔖^txt ḥprw dyn klhwn mṣʿyʾ ḥdʿwhy dnhrʾ ʾyknʾ dlmštʾ myʾ wlʾ mškḥyn hww lmštʾ myʾ mn nhrʾ ‖ MT wyḥprw kl mṣrym sbybt hyʾr mym lštwt ky lʾ yklw lštt mmymy hyʾr.[56]

---

[54] See the discussion of this reading, especially the problematic attribution of ιδε κατεστησα σε to Theodotion, under item 63 in chapter three.

[55] See item 39 in chapter four for the correction of B-McL's φαρμακειας to φαρμακειαις in the Theodotionic reading. The insertion of και into the α' reading of j^mg and also α' τρυφιασται (for κρυφιασται) in M^mg are secondary scribal errors.

[56] For a discussion of the discrepancies between the Greek and Syriac versions for the last part of the α' and θ' citations, see item 35 in chapter three; see also item 23 in chapter four. The insertion of οι by z^mg and the omission of οτι-πιειν$^{(2)}$ by c$_2$^mg in their respective

8:3 (LXX v.7); α' οι κρυφιασται εν τοις ηρεμαιοις αυτων (85, cited from Montef. by Field) | ϑ' οι επαοιδοι εν ταις φαρμακειαις αυτων (85, cited from Montef. by Field) | OG και (om Ɇ) οι επαοιδοι των (om M1yɆ^{f}Ꞩ) αιγυπτιων (om M1yɆ^{f}Ꞩ; + εν AB^{ab}a moqu) ταις φαρμακιαις (επαοιδαις AM^{mg}qu[-διαις qu]) αυτων | MT hḥrṭmym blṭyhm.[57]

8:22 (LXX v.26): α' mṭl dṭnpwt' dmṣryn mdbḥynn lmry' 'lh' dyln 'n dbḥyn ḥnn lṭnpwt' dmṣryn l'ʿyn' dylhwn wl' nrgmwnn (Ꞩ^{mg}) | ϑ' mṭl dlṭḥpwt' dmṣryn ndbḥ lmry' 'lh' dyln wdbḥynn lṭnpwt' dmṣryn qdm 'ʿyn' dylhwn wl' rgmyn ln (Ꞩ^{mg}) | OG τα (το a_2) γαρ βδελυγματα (βδελυγμα a_2) των (om b, Phil) αιγυπτιων (αιγυπτου b, Phil; + ου bfmsw, Cyr-cod) ϑυσομεν (Baejk^{a}opsu xyc_2; ϑυσωμεν AMbcdf-ilmnqrtvwza_2b_2Ⱥ, Cyr-cod, Phil-cod [+ ημεις fir]) κυριω (after τω x; om acɆ, Phil$\frac{1}{2}$) τω ϑεω ημων (om Phil) εαν (+ τε s) γαρ (δε c_2Ɇ; om i*) ϑυσωμεν (after αιγυπτιων$^{(2)}$ egj; γαρ ϑυσωμεν after αιγυπτιων$^{(2)}$ 25; + κω̅ τω ϑω̅ ημων M^{mg}k^{b}, Cyr) τα βδελυγματα των αιγυπτιων (om ϑυσομεν-αιγυπτιων$^{(2)}$ k*, Cyr-cod) εναντιον αυτων (αυτου mȺ) λιϑοβοληϑησομεϑα (-λησομεϑα i*s, Cyr-cod; -λησωμεϑα b'dn; -λησουσιν ημας 71, Ɇ; *lapidant nos* Ⱥ) | Ꞩ^{txt} ḥdydwt' gyr dmṣry' ndbḥ lmry' 'lh' dyln 'n gyr ndbḥ ṭnpwt' dmṣry' qdmyhwn mtrgmynn | MT ky twʿbt mṣrym nzbḥ lyhwh 'lhnw hn nzbḥ 't twʿbt mṣrym lʿynyhm wl' ysqlnw.

8:25 (LXX v.29): α' και ειπεν μωσης ιδου εγω ειμι εξερχομαι παρα σου και ικετευσω προς (v) | ϑ' και ειπεν μωσης ιδου εγω ειμι εκπορευομαι απο σου και ευξομαι προς (v) | OG ειπεν δε μωυσης (μωσης amnxc_2; om 25) οδε (ωδε bcdfhnpsyz; οτι Or-gr; ιδου egjkmc_2, 77, ɃɆᵽꞨ; om w, 71, Ⱥ) εγω (om 71, 77) εξελευσομαι απο (προς b') σου (σε b') και (om af) ευξομαι (προσευξομαι w; om af) προς (om f) | MT wy'mr mšh hnh 'nky ywṣ' mʿmk whʿtrty 'l.

9:8: α' mwly' dzwʿ' dylkwn (Ꞩ^{mg}) | ϑ' ml' 'ydʿ' dylkwn (Ꞩ^{mg}) |

Theodotionic versions are both secondary scribal errors (the latter is a clear case of haplography; πιειν . . . πιειν).

[57]Since 85 = z, this set of variants should have been cited by B-McL if it is genuine (see item 40 in chapter four).

OG πληρεις (+ εις d) τας χειρας (+ υμων ackmx𝔄^vid𝔅) ‖ 𝔖^txt mwly' d'yd' dylkwn ‖ MT ml' ḥpnykm.[58]

12:32: α' 'ykn' dmlltwn' σ'θ' 'yk m' dmlltwn (𝔖^mg) ‖ OG om. ‖ F^a? mgMa-dhkmnptvwxz-c_2𝔄𝔅𝔏^z𝔓, Or-lat (out of place in all but ackmx𝔓) καθαπερ (καθα h) ειρηκατε (+ προς ... F^a? mg) ‖ 𝔖^txt 'yk m' d'mrtwn ‖ MT k'šr dbrtm.[59]

14:2: α' tryṣ'yt lqwblh tšr' (𝔖^mg) ‖ θ' qdmwhy tšrwn (𝔖^mg) ‖ OG ενωπιον (εναντιον c_2) αυτων (αυτου F^b; αυτης a_2) στρατοπεδευσεις (-σης beghipqt; *castra ponite* 𝔈; *iter faciens* 𝔏^z) ‖ 𝔖^txt qdmyhwn tšr' ‖ MT nkḥw tḥnw.

15:18: α' pypy nmlk (𝔖^mg) ‖ θ' pypy dmmlk (𝔖^mg) ‖ OG κυριος (κε AF*^vidMa*i*oa_2𝔅^vid, Or-lat) βασιλευων (-λεων *b*; -λευει 𝔄-codd, Phil-codd½) ‖ 𝔖^txt mry' hw dmmlk ‖ MT yhwh ymlk.[60]

16:16: α' gbr' lpwm' dm'kwlt' dylh 'mwr (𝔖^mg) ‖ θ' gbr' lm'kwlt' dylh gwmwr (𝔖^mg) ‖ OG εκαστος εις τους καθηκοντας (+ παρ αυτω acmx𝔄) γομορ (γομωρ al; γομερ F^b?k) ‖ 𝔖^txt kl ḥd lhnwn dzdqyn ※ lwth ⋖ gwmwr ‖ MT 'yš lpy 'klw 'mr.

18:5: α' και ηλθεν ιεθρω (-ρο js) νυμφευτης μωυση (jsv[-σει]z) ‖ θ' και ηλθεν ιοθορ γαμβρος μωυσει (v) ‖ OG και (om 128, ℭ^c) ηλθεν (εξηλθεν Bfioqru; *tulit autem* ℭ^c; + δε 128) ιοθορ (ιοθωρ ab'ijl; ιωθορ n; ιωθωρ qu, Cyr-cod) ο γαμβρος (πενθερος F^b mgdlw^b) μωυση (μωση aknx; om ο γαμβρος μωυση p; om ιοθορ-μωυση m) ‖ MT wyb' ytrw ḥtn mšh.[61]

---

[58]It is not likely that 𝔖^txt *mwly'* represents OG πληρεις. Hence it is not necessary to assume that Aquila shared the OG translation for MT *ml'*. The Greek forms underlying α' *mwly'* and θ' *ml'* remain uncertain.

[59]The phrase is added after OG πορευεσθε, rather than before it, in F^a? mgMbdhnptvwz-c_2𝔄𝔅, Or-lat, while 𝔏^z omits OG πορευεσθε. The phrase is omitted entirely by ABF^txtefgijloqrsy𝔈. It is assumed that Syriac *'yk m'* represents καθαπερ and that Syriac *'ykn'* represents καθα, but the reverse is also possible.

[60]It is not clear what difference in Greek forms, if any, is reflected by the difference between 𝔖^txt *hw dmmlk* and θ' *dmmlk*. Perhaps one of them represents the finite present tense (βασιλευει) rather than the OG participle, but this is undertain (see item 5 in chapter four).

[61]Note that Aquila and Theodotion agree on μωυσει according to v^mg

19:13: α' εν ελκυσμω του παραφεροντος (v; cf. α' *bngd' dhw dm'br* in 𝔖^{mg}) I θ' εν τη απελευσει του ιωβηλ (v; cf. b^{mg} and θ' *bm'zlt' dywbl* [*dywbb* B^{1}] in 𝔖^{mg}) I OG οταν (+ δε abcfhijnp twxd$_2$𝔄, Cyr-ed) και αι σαλπιγγες (*tuba* 𝔄; + παυσονται 71) και (om b) η (om b) νεφελη (om b; η νεφελη after απελθη c*) απελθη (απελθοι i; παρελθη a$_2$; om w) απο του ορους I 𝔖^{txt} 'mty dyn d ÷ ḳl' w↗ šypwr' n'zlwn ÷ wt'zl 'nn' mn ṭwr'↙ I MT bmšk hybl.[62]

19:13: α' αυτοι αναβησονται εν ορει (v) I θ' αυτοι αναβησονται εις το ορος (v) I OG εκεινοι (εκεινου s; εκει dpt; om 𝔈) αναβησονται (αναβητωσαν 37, 𝔅; ανεβησαν c) επι (εις bh) το (του F*f) ορος (ορου a$_2$; ορους F*f) I MT hmh y'lw bhr.

19:18: α' απο προσωπου ου κατεβη επ αυτου $\overline{κς}$ θ' δια το καταβηναι επ αυτο $\overline{κν}$ (v) I OG δια το καταβεβηκεναι τον (om o, 37, Cyr$\frac{1}{4}$, Cyr-codd$\frac{2}{4}$, Cyr-ed$\frac{1}{4}$) $\overline{θν}$ ($\overline{κν}$ F, Cyr$\frac{1}{4}$, Cyr-codd$\frac{2}{4}$, Cyr-ed$\frac{1}{4}$; om 37; τον $\overline{θν}$ after επ αυτο Ba[pr. $\overline{κν}$]kmrx, Eus) επ αυτο (αυτω bdep, Phil-codd; αυτου akqu, Cyr$\frac{1}{4}$, Cyr-ed$\frac{1}{4}$, Eus, Phil-codd; αυτον x, Cyr$\frac{1}{4}$; $\overline{κν}$ επ αυτο M^{mg}s^{mg}; επ αυτο out of place in A) I 𝔖^{txt} mtwl dnḥt 'lwhy 'lh' I MT mpny 'šr yrd 'lyw yhwh (cf. SP mpny 'šr yrd yhwh 'lyw).

20:25:(𝔖 v.22): α' οτι μαχαιραν σου εξηρες επ αυτο (js[αυτον]vz; cf. α' *mṭl dsyp' dylk 'rymt 'lwhy* in 𝔖^{mg}) I θ' οτι την ρομφαιαν σου επιβεβληκας επ αυτο (js[αυτον] vz; cf. θ' *mṭl dlsyp' dylk 'rmyt 'lwhy* in 𝔖^{mg}) I OG το γαρ ενχειριδιον σου (μου A; om Fejlqruℭ^{m}𝔈^{f}, Phil-arm) επιβεβληκας (εισβεβληκας l; καταβεβληκας f) επ (εις a$_2$𝔄^{vid}) αυτο (αυτω ch*j, Cyr-cod$\frac{1}{2}$; αυτων el; αυτου i*q*ux; αυτους Bfi$^{a?}$mq^{b}r; αυτ n) I

(the only one to cite θ'), while OG μωυση is found in the α' readings of j^{mg}s^{mg}z^{mg}. Such an itacistic change is insignificant, however.

[62]In item 94 in chapter four, these two consecutive readings from Exod. 19:13 are treated as a single reading. This was done under the influence of the unified treatment as the sixth reading in chapter one and the assumption that B-McL had divided the longer v^{mg} readings for ease in notation. Here, the division found in B-McL is followed. Because the totals of readings are already conditioned by the arbitrary choices of scribes, this minor divergence is of no importance. The θ' variant in B^{1} of 𝔖^{mg} is presumably an inner-Syriac scribal error.

$\mathcal{S}^{txt}$ br 'yd' gyr ※ dylk↙ 'rmyt 'lwhy ‖ MT ky hrbk hnpt 'lyh.[63]

21:7-8: α' ουκ εξελευσεται ως εξοδος των δουλων εαν κακισθη εν οφθαλμοις κυ αυτης ος ου καθωμολογησατο αυτην (vz; cf. s^{mg}; cf. also α' *l' tpwq 'yk mpqt' d'bd' 'n dyn ttmkk b'yn' dmr' dylh hw dl' 'štwdyh* in $\mathcal{S}^{mg}$) ‖ θ' ουκ εξελευσεται ωσπερ εκπορευονται οι δουλοι ει πονηρα εστιν εν οφθαλμοις κυ αυτης (+ ουν s) ην ου καθωμολογησατο αυτην (jsvz; cf. θ' *l' tpwq 'kn' dnpqyn 'bd' 'n byst' 'ytyh b'yn' dmr' dylh hy dl' 'štwdyh* in $\mathcal{S}^{mg}$) ‖ OG ουκ απελευσεται ωσπερ αποτρεχουσιν (-σαι 30) αι δουλαι εαν (+ δε $AF^{a}bej^{txt}ptwxa_{2}b_{2}\mathcal{B}\mathcal{C}^{m}\mathcal{E}$; + space of 2 or 3 letters o) μη (om w) ευαρεστηση (+ εν qu; + εν οφθαλμοις $F^{b\ mg}ack\mathcal{A}$) τω κυριω αυτης (εαυτης ik) ην (η $Bfb_{2}a^{?}\mathcal{E}^{vid}$; om $a\mathcal{A}\mathcal{C}^{m}$) αυτω (Bnqux$\mathcal{E}$; *cui* $\mathcal{A}\mathcal{C}^{m}$; εαυτω $F^{a?}$; αυτος bw; ου $AF^{*}M^{txt}acdehj^{txt}klmops^{txt}tv^{txt}y\text{-}b_{2}\mathcal{B}^{vid}$; om f $i^{a?}r$) καθωμολογησατο (καθομολογησατο $fi^{a?}r$; *desponsata est* $\mathcal{A}$; *confessus est dare eam* $\mathcal{C}^{m}$; + αυτω Aacm; + εαυτω k; + αυτην $F^{*}dhi^{a?}loprs^{txt}tv^{txt}y\text{-}b_{2}\mathcal{B}^{vid}$; + εαυτην f; + αυτη εν οφθαλμοις ej^{txt}) ‖ $\mathcal{S}^{txt}$ l' tpwq 'yk m' dnpqn 'mht' 'n l' tšpr ※ '' b'yn'↙ dmr' ※ dylh↙ hy dl' 'štwdy lh ‖ MT l' tṣ' kṣ't h'bdym 'm r'h b'yny 'dnyh 'šr l' y'dh (cf. SP l' tṣ' kṣ't h'bdym 'm r'h hy' b'yny 'dnyh 'šr l' h'dh [*h'ydh* many manuscripts]).[64]

28:1: α' του ιερατευειν αυτον εμοι (vz) ‖ θ' εις ιερατευειν αυτον μοι (vz) ‖ OG ιερατευειν (-σειν Cyr-cod$\frac{1}{2}$; + αυτον cm) μοι (εμοι $egjsv^{txt}$; om k; + ※ '' *hw*↙ $\mathcal{S}$) ‖ MT lkhnw ly.

28:3: α' του ιερατευειν αυτον εμοι s; cf. j^{mg}) ‖ θ' εις ιερατευειν αυτον μοι (s; cf. j^{mg}) ‖ OG εν (om f) η (om f) ιερατευσει (-ση b; -σεις 16; -ει t; -ειν fgil; *sacerdotium*

---

[63]The replacement of αυτο with αυτον in the α' and θ' readings of s^{mg} is presumably due to scribal error.

[64]Contrary to the format adopted in B-McL, the α' and θ' readings are continuous units in $\mathcal{S}^{mg}$, and hence may also be continuous in vz and jsvz, respectively. The insertion of ουν into θ' by s^{mg} and of *dyn* (= δε) into α' by $\mathcal{S}^{mg}$ are presumably secondary scribal errors.

agant L^r; *sanctificabit* E; + αυτος cm; + ※ ʿʾ *hw*↙ S; + αυτον 130) μοι (εμοι ckm; *me* E)] MT lkhnw ly.

28:5: αʹ και συν σκωληκος το διαφορον v; cf. s^mg z^mg)] θʹ και το κοκκινον το διαφορον v; cf. s^mg z^mg; cf. also αʹθʹ *mšḥlpt*ʾ in S^mg)] OG και το κοκκινον (+ κεκλωσμενον ckmA)] S^txt wlzḥwrytʾ ※ dmpšlʾ↙] MT wʾt twlʿt hšny.

28:25 (MT): αʹ εναντιον προσωπου αυτου (v)] θʹ lwqbl byt ʿynʾ dprṣwpʾ dylh (S^txt; cf. οʹθʹ του προσωπου αυτης in v)] OG om.] F^a?Mcdegjkmnpstv^txt zAE^c επι το μετωπον του προσωπου αυτου (αυτης F^a?ckm)] MT ʾl mwl pnyw.[65]

28:26 (MT): αʹ ο προς περαν του επενδυματος and αʹ οικονδε (vz; cf. s^mg)] θʹ (οʹθʹ v) ο εστιν εις το αντικρυς της επωμιδος (vz; cf. οʹθʹ αντικρυς της επωμιδος εσωθεν in s; cf. also θʹ *hw dʾytwhy mn lqwblh dkbyntʾ mn lgw* in S^txt) and οʹθʹ (+ σʹ v) εσωθεν (sv)] OG om.] F^a?Mcdegjkmns^txt tv^txt z^txt AE^c ο εστιν εις το μερος (αντικρυς F^a?cm[-κρυ]A; + αντικρυ k) της επωμιδος (του εφουδ F^b) εσωθεν] MT ʾšr ʾl ʿbr hʾpd byth (cf. SP ʾšr ʿl ʿbr [*ḥbr* many manuscripts] hʾpwd byth).[66]

28:27 (MT): αʹ απο εναντιον προσωπου αυτου συμφωνως επι συμβολη αυτου (v)] οʹθʹ εκ του κατα προσωπον συμφωνως κατα την συμβολην αυτου (v; θʹ *mn lwqbl prṣwpʾ* ↖*lmʾyt wrmyʾ dʾkḥdʾ dylh* in S^txt)] OG om.] F^a?Mcdegjkmnstv^txt zAE^c εκ του κατα προσωπον (-που n; + αυτ.. συμφωνως F^b; + συμφωνως F^a?ckms^mg [-ως]z^mg A) κατα (και ckmA) την (τη n^a?) συμβολην (συμβουλην ds; συμβολη n^a?) αυτων (αυτου F^a?dkmtAE^vid; om c)] MT mmwl pnyw lʿmt mḥbrtw.[67]

---

[65]This phrase is discussed thoroughly under item 23 in chapter two.

[66]Because the citations partially overlap, these readings have been taken together as a unit. Problems connected with the interpretation and evaluation of these readings are discussed under items 29-30 in chapter two. See also item 39 in chapter three. The agreement between Aquila and Theodotion is minimal here (only the relative pronoun, ο, to represent MT ʾ*šr*).

[67]Problems and aspects of these readings are discussed under items 36-37 in chapter two. See also item 40 in chapter three.

28:28 (MT): α' (α'ο' s) και ου σαλευθησεται (sv; cf. z^{mg})] θ' wl' thw' mtplṭ' (S^{txt}; cf. θ' [ο'θ' v] ου μη αποσπασθη in sv and without names in z^{mg})] OG om.] $F^{a?}$Mcdegjknps^{txt} tv^{txt}z^{txt}AEc και ου μη αποσπασης (αποσπασ... $F^{a?}$; αποσπασθη ckAE^{c})] MT wl' yzḥ.

29:9: α' διαζωνη ααρων (jsvz)] θ' ζωνη ααρων (jsvz)] OG ταις (τας fn^{vid}) ζωναις (ζωνας fn^{vid}; + ααρων cmA[pr ※] S[under ※])] MT 'bnṭ 'hrn.

30:13: α' τουτο δωσουσι πας ο παρερχομενος επι τους επισκεμμενους (v)] θ' τουτο δωσουσιν πας ο παραπορευομενος επι τας επισκοπας (svz)] OG και (om E) τουτο εστιν (εσται Cyr$\frac{1}{2}$; under ÷ S; om k) ο δωσουσιν (δωσωσιν s^{txt} vid$_x$; + μοι f; + σοι ai, Cyr$\frac{1}{2}$-cod$\frac{1}{2}$) οσοι (om afi, Cyr-cod$\frac{1}{2}$; *quodquod* L^{r}) αν (εαν cfis^{txt}v^{txt}z^{txt}; om L^{r}) παραπορευωνται (παραπορευονται bcd giklnops^{txt}v$_*$^{txt}w; προσπορευονται h; προπορευσονται m; πορευωνται Cyr-ed$\frac{1}{2}$; *incendent* L^{r}) την επισκεψιν] MT zh ytnw kl h'br '1 hpqdym.

31:14: α' οτι αγιασμενον εστιν υμιν (v)] σ'θ'ο' οτι αγιον εστιν υμιν (v; cf. σ'θ' υμιν in s)] OG οτι (το 71) αγιον (αγια x) τουτο (after υμιν M; after εστιν F^{b}dinpta$_2$b$_2$A; τουτω g; om Abcfklmwxy EL^{r}S) εστιν (εσται Abhw; om quC^{m}) κυριου (B Ma; τω $\overline{κω}$ ft; $\overline{κω}$ F^{b}degijo-suv^{txt}xza$_2$b$_2$B^{vid}C^{m}L^{r}; om Abchkl mnwyES; + και [om B^{w}] εν d-gijps^{txt}tv^{txt}za$_2$b$_2$B + και F^{b}qru AC^{m}L^{r}) υμιν (om m; + $\overline{κω}$ n)] MT ky qdš hw' 1km.

32:25: α' ειδεν δε μωυσης τον λαον οτι αποπετασμενος αυτος (om s) οτι απεπετασεν αυτον ααρων εις ονομα ρυπου εν ανθεστηκοσιν αυτων (sv[μωσης]z)] θ' και ειδεν μωυσης τον λαον οτι διεσκεδασμενος εστιν (om s) οτι διεσκεδασεν αυτον ααρων επιχαρμα τοις ανθεστηκοσιν αυτων (s[αυτον]v[αυτοις ^{vid}]z)] OG και ιδων (ειδεν xAL^{rw}S; + ο g) μωυσης (after λαον h; μωσης kmn) τον (om 73, AE) λαον (om 73, AE) οτι διεσκεδασται (*d' tplhdw* S^{txt}; + ο λαος 73, AE) διεσκεδασεν γαρ αυτους (αυτον z^{mg}) ααρων επιχαρμα τοις υπεναντιοις αυτων (αυτω 18)] MT wyr' mšh 't h'm ky pr' (cf. SP prw') hw' ky pr'h (cf. SP pr'w) 'hrn lšmṣh (cf. SP lšmṣw) bqmyhm (cf. SP bqwmyhm).[68]

---

[68]This set of variants is discussed as the second reading in chapter one. See also item 41 in chapter three. The θ' variations αυτον in s^{mg}

35:3: α'σ' dšbt'· θ' dšb' ($\not{S}^{mg}$) I OG των (του h) σαββατων (σαββατου h) I $\not{S}^{txt}$ dšb' I MT hšbt.

35:11 (LXX v.10): α' τους στυλους αυτης και τας βασεις αυτης (v) I θ' ※ και τους στυλους και τας βασεις αυτης (v) I OG και τους στυλους (*vectes earum* $\not{E}^{c}$; + και τας βασεις k; + αυτης και τας βασεις αυτης F^{b}cm[αυτης(2) written twice]$\not{A}$) I $\not{S}^{txt}$ ÷ wl'mwd'↙ ※ g' dylh↙ wlbsys ※ dylh↙ I MT 't 'mdyw w't 'dnyw.

35:12 (LXX v.11); α' συν το γλωσσοκομον και τους αναφορεις (v) I θ' και την κιβωτον και τους αναφορεις (v) I OG και την κιβωτον (+ την p) του (om $F^{b?}$k) μαρτυριου (*testamenti* $\not{L}^{r}$; om $F^{b?}$k) και τους (τας b'; της g) αναφορεις (-ριεις g; om και(2)-αναφορεις [also om αυτης] $\not{E}^{f}$) I MT 't h'rn w't bdy-.

35:23: α' και πας ανηρ ω ευρεθη συν αυτω υακινθος και πορφυρα και σκωληκος διαφορον και βυσσος και αιγεια και δερματα (svz) I θ' (+ ※ v) και πας ανηρ ω ευρεθη παρ αυτω υακινθος και πορφυρα και κοκκινον αλλοιουμενον και βυσσος και αιγεια και δερματα (svz) I OG (= Bafhinqrux, 71) και παρ (παντι n) ω (ο n) ευρεθη βυσσος (+ παρ αυτων n; + εν αυτω 71) και δερματα I MT wkl 'yš 'šr nmṣ' 'tw tklt w'rgmn wtwl't šny wšš w'zym w'rt.[69]

35:29: α' του ενεγκειν εις παν το εργον (sv) I θ' του ενεγκαι εις παντα τα εργα (v) I OG εισελθοντα (B*ar; εισελθοντες F*fix; εισελθοντας AF^{I}Mbcdkn-qtuwy$b_2\not{E}^{vid}\not{L}^{r(vid)}$w; εισελθοντων 1; εισηλθον του $B^{a?b}$; εισελθων γαρ a_2; εισελθειν eghj

---

and $αυτοις^{vid}$ in v^{mg} for αυτων of z^{mg}, and the α' variation μωσης in v^{mg} for μωυσης of $s^{mg}z^{mg}$, are of little significance. The omission of α' αυτος and θ' εστιν by s^{mg} is discussed in both places indicated above.

[69]See item 54 in chapter four for the remaining textual evidence bearing on these variants and for a discussion of the special nature of this verse. Note also α'θ' *gbr'* in $\not{S}^{txt}$, θ' *ṣby't'* in $\not{S}^{mg}$, and α' *wtwl't'* in $\not{S}^{mg}$. The reason for the apparent discrepancy between θ' αλλοιουμενον (= "altered, changed") and θ' *ṣby't'* (= "dyed") for MT *šny* is not clear, though it may be merely a translational deviation by the Syriac scribe. Compare fn. 13 in chapter four.

$s^{txt}v^{txt}z$; *lmʿl w-* 𝔖) ποιειν παντα (om eghjsvz) τα (om F*) εργα ‖ MT lhby' lkl hml'kh.

35:35: α' εν υακινθω και πορφυρα εν σκωληκος τω διαφορω και εν βυσσω (svz) ‖ θ' (+ ※ v) . . . εν τη υακινθω και εν τη πορφυρα και εν τω κοκκινω τω αλλοιουμενω (+ ⸔ v) και τη βυσσω (svz) ‖ OG (+ εν τη υακινθω και εν τη πορφυρα και εν ckmAE^c) τω κοκκινω (προκοκκινω a_2; + τω αλλοιουμενω cmAE^c) και τη (της s^{txt}; om ao) βυσσω ‖ $𝔖^{txt}$ ※θ' btklt' wb'rgwn' (+ ※ B) w⸔ bzḥwryt' ※ dmštgny'⸔ wbbwṣ' ‖ MT btklt wb'rgmn btwl'ʿt hšny wbšš.

36:38 (LXX 37:6): α' και αι βασεις αυτων πεντε χαλκου (v) ‖ θ' (α'θ'vid sz) και αι βασεις αυτων πεντε χαλκαι (svz) ‖ OG και αι (BGabchkmnqruwxa_2; τας AMa-gilops^{txt}tv^{txt}y$z^{txt}$$b_2$; om F^b) βασεις αυτων (αι B*) πεντε χαλκαι (BF^bGabchkmnqruv^{txt}wx a_2; χαλκας AMd-gilops^{txt}ty$z^{txt}$$b_2$) ‖ MT w'dnyhm ḥmšh nḥšt.[70]

40:26 (LXX v.24): α' εν σκεπη (vz; cf. s^{mg}) ‖ ο'θ'σ' εν τη σκηνη (svz) ‖ OG εν (εις ejs^{txt}$v^{txt}$$z^{txt}$) τη (την ejs^{txt}$v^{txt}$$z^{txt}$) σκηνη (-νην ejs^{txt}$v^{txt}$$z^{txt}$) ‖ MT b'hl.

40:35 (LXX v.29): σ'α' ουκ ηδυνατο (v) ‖ θ' ουκ ηδυνασθη (v) ‖ OG ουκ ηδυνασθη (Bbhr; εδυνασθη Gak; ηδυνηθη AFMcefgijlnoq s-$b_2$$d_2$, Cyr; εδυνηθη dp; *'tmṣy* 𝔖; *poterat* AL^{z} vid) ‖ MT (w)l' ykl.

There are thirty-five readings in which Aquila and Theodotion agree partially, and in which Theodotion does not appear closer to the OG or to a large number of LXX manuscripts than Aquila does:

1:7: α' (α'θ' Mv) εξηρποσαν (Mjvz; cf. α' εχεοντο in Procop., as cited by Field) ‖ θ' εξειρπον (*b*) ‖ α'σ' wrḥšw· θ' wršpyn hww ($𝔖^{mg}$) ‖ OG και επληθυνθησαν *or* και χυδαιοι εγενοντο (the two verbs are interchanged in akmx) ‖ $𝔖^{txt}$ wšpyʿ' hww ‖ MT wyšrṣw.[71]

---

[70]After the θ' reading, said to be in svz, B-McL adds "(α'θ' pro α' sz)." Since only θ' figures in the preceding citation, α' must be a misprint for θ' here. In any case, the α'θ' citation is probably an error in $s^{mg}z^{mg}$, since v^{mg} preserves a distinction between the two versions.

[71]The confusion is partly due to B-McL's notation. This relates the set of variants to OG χυδαιοι εγενοντο. The latter is the third verb in

1:19: α' mṭl dy̆ldt' hlyn (Ƨ^mg)] θ' οτι ζωογονουσιν αυται (Nobil., as cited by Field; cf. θ' *hnyn mḥy̆n* in Ƨ^mg)] OG τικτουσιν γαρ] Ƨ^txt yldn gyr] MT ky ḥywt hnh.[72]

6:12: α' ακροβυστος χειλεσιν (Mjvz; cf. F^b mg)] θ' απεριτμητος τοις χειλεσιν (Mjvz)] OG αλογος ειμι] MT ʿrl śptym.

8:17 (LXX v.21): α' lḥlwṭ' (Ƨ^mg)] θ' ḥlṭ' (Ƨ^mg)] OG (+ την kx) κυνομυιαν] Ƨ^txt ※ l⋎ dbb klb'] MT 't hʿrb.[73]

---

the series in all LXX witnesses except akmxƧ, where it is the second and OG επληθυνθησαν, the second verb in the OG, has become the third. In Ƨ, however, the variants are marked for the second verb, *wšpy*ʿʾ *hww*, which is equal to third-place OG και χυδαιοι εγενοντο, even though appearing in second place. The problem is whether these variants pertain to MT *wyšrṣw*, the second MT verb, as implied by Ƨ, in which case they should be compared with OG επληθυνθησαν (and χυδαιοι εγενοντο in akmx), or whether they should pertain to MT *wyrbw*, the third MT verb, as implied by B-McL. Following Ƨ and the meaning of the various α' and θ' forms (εξερπειν = "to creep out"; *rḥš* = "to creep, swarm"; *ršp* = "to crawl, creep"; and χεεσθαι = "to gush forth"), it is suggested that they belong with MT *wyšrṣw*, the second verb in the MT sequence. Obviously the OG reverses the MT order: while OG και χυδαιοι εγενοντο corresponds in sense to MT *wyšrṣw*, in position OG και επληθυνθησαν does so. Only akmxƧ invert the OG order into conformity with the MT. It is impossible to recover the two distinct Greek readings presupposed by the α'σ' and θ' citations of Ƨ^mg, but εχεοντο is probably not one of them.

72 Note the following Greek doublets. Before OG αι εβραιαι (= MT *hʿbryt*): τικτουσιν in b'. Between OG αι εβραιαι and OG τικτουσιν: τικτουσαι in *b* and τικτουσι in w. The reading in *b* probably agrees with α' *(d)y̆ldt'*, while b'w have suffered assimilation toward the OG form (and b' is out of place). If this interpretation is correct, then Aquila employed the participle of the OG verb to reflect the MT adjective, while Theodotion used a different verb. This reading and the others that make Aquila appear closer to the OG than Theodotion are discussed in the next chapter.

73 The θ' citation of Ƨ^mg need not imply that Theodotion did not have the article (often reflected by *l-*) before his noun, but it may do so.

8:18 (LXX v.22): α′ bgwh d'r'' ($\mathcal{S}^{mg}$) ‖ θ′ bmṣ'th d'r'' ($\mathcal{S}^{mg}$) ‖ OG πασης (εν[om k*] μεσω kx; om m) της γης ‖ $\mathcal{S}^{txt}$ d'r'' ‖ MT bqrb h'rṣ.

9:25: α′ lklhwn hlyn db'tr' ($\mathcal{S}^{mg}$) ‖ θ′ lklhwn hnwn dbḥql' ($\mathcal{S}^{mg}$) ‖ OG om. ‖ $B^{b\ mg}M^{mg}$a-dhkmnptwx$c_2^{mg}$$\mathcal{A}\mathcal{P}$ παντα (om p) οσα ην εν τω πεδιω (παιδ- $B^{b\ mg}$) ‖ $\mathcal{S}^{txt}$ ※ lkl d'yt hw' bpq't'↙ ‖ MT 't kl 'šr bśdh.[74]

12:42: α′σ′ hn' lly' hn' lpypy dmṭrt' ($\mathcal{S}^{mg}$; cf. α′ παρατηρησεων [-σεως c_2] σ′ παρατετηρημενη [-μενον c_2] in vzc_2) ‖ θ′ dmṭrt' hw llly' lpypy dnṭwrt' ($\mathcal{S}^{mg}$) ‖ OG εκεινη (αυτη m; om 71) η νυξ αυτη (om m) προφυλακη (after κυριω bkw; προς φυλακην m; προσφυλακη εστι d; φυλαγματων $F^{b\ mg}$; + εστιν τω [om $\mathcal{L}^{z}$] nptx$\mathcal{L}^{z\ vid}$; + τω Fdl$v^{txt}z^{txt}c_2^{txt}$) κυριω ($\overline{κυ}$ cefg j$\mathcal{B}^{vid}\mathcal{E}^{vid}\mathcal{L}^{z}$; om a) ‖ $\mathcal{S}^{txt}$ hw lly' hw mṭrt' lmry' ‖ MT hw' hlylh hzh lyhwh šmrym.[75]

13:13: α′ tprqywhy bbr mr'yt' 'n l' tprwq tqṭw' qdlh ($\mathcal{S}^{mg}$; cf. α′ τενοντωσεις in Mjvz[τενεντ-]c_2[-σης]) ‖ θ′ tprwq mn mr'yt' w'n l' tprqywhy tpswq ḥṣh ($\mathcal{S}^{mg}$; cf. θ′ νωτοκοπησεις in Mj[+ αυτο]vzc_2[-σης]) ‖ OG αλλαξεις (-ξης eho^{a}b_2, Phil-cod$\frac{1}{2}$) προβατω (-του am, Phil-codd; -των l; -τον c_2) εαν δε (om o*) μη (om Phil-cod$\frac{1}{2}$) αλλαξης (μεταλλαξης Phil-cod$\frac{1}{2}$; απολυτρω[σης] F^{b}; + λυτρω ac) λυτρωση (εξαγορασης F^{b}) αυτο (αυτον c*) ‖ $\mathcal{S}^{txt}$ tḥlpywhy b'rb' 'n dyn l' tḥlpywhy tprqywhy ‖ MT tpdh bśh w'm l' tpdh (cf. SP tpdnw) w'rptw.[76]

---

[74]The version in $B^{b\ mg}M^{mg}$a-dhkmnptwx$c_2^{mg}$$\mathcal{A}\mathcal{P}$ and under ※ in $\mathcal{S}$ is an independent translation of the MT plus. There is no reason to suppose that it was present in the OG text used by Theodotion (see item 59 in chapter four), or that it was known by Aquila.

[75]The Theodotionic doublet and omission are discussed in items 37 and 27, respectively, of chapter three. The α′ and σ′ variants in c_2^{mg} may be secondary corruptions. Note that $\mathcal{S}^{mg}$ fails to preserve the distinction between α′ and σ′ that is reflected by both $v^{mg}z^{mg}$ and c_2^{mg}.

[76]Aspects of this reading are discussed in items 3, 28, and 116 of chapter three. The minor variants in the form of the α′ reading in z^{mg} and c_2^{mg}, and of the θ′ reading in c_2^{mg}, are secondary scribal errors. The failure of Aquila to reflect MT *w-* in *w'm* may be due to a minor

17:6: α′ bprṣwp' dylk ($\mathcal{S}^{mg}$) I σ′θ′ εμπροσθεν σου (*b*; cf. σ′θ′ *qdmyk* in $\mathcal{S}^{mg}$) I OG προ (προς w, Phil-cod$\frac{1}{5}$) του (om w) σε (σου w; ελθειν Cyr-ed$\frac{1}{2}$-codd$\frac{1}{2}$; + ελθειν AFb-gijnprsty$^{a?}$z$\mathcal{L}^{v}$, Cyr-ed$\frac{1}{2}$-codd$\frac{1}{2}$; + ηκειν k) I $\mathcal{S}^{txt}$ qdm d'nt I MT lpnyk.[77]

17:7: α′ bgw' dyln ($\mathcal{S}^{mg}$) I θ′ bmṣʿt' dyln ($\mathcal{S}^{mg}$) I OG εν ημιν I $\mathcal{S}^{txt}$ bn I MT bqrbnw.

19:6: α′ mlkwt' dkhn̈' ($\mathcal{S}^{mg}$) I σ′θ′ βασιλει[α] ιερεων (*b*; cf. σ′θ′ *mlkwt' khn̈'* in $\mathcal{S}^{mg}$) I OG βασιλειον ιερατευμα I $\mathcal{S}^{txt}$ kwhn' mlky' I MT mmlkt khnym.[78]

22:8 (LXX v.9): α′ (d)mḥybyn 'ln̈' ($\mathcal{S}^{mg}$) I θ′ nḥybwn 'ln̈' ($\mathcal{S}^{mg}$) I OG αλους δια (απο x) του θεου I $\mathcal{S}^{txt}$ (d)mttṣyd byd 'lh' I MT yršyʿn 'lhym.

25:33:(LXX v.32): α′ ʿl̈b' d'yt ʿlyhyn dmŴt' dlŴz' ($\mathcal{S}^{mg}$) I θ′ 'g̈n' d'yt ʿlyhyn dmŴt' dlŴz' ($\mathcal{S}^{mg}$) I OG om. I $\mathcal{S}^{txt}$ 'g̈n' dmṭpsn gŴz'$^{(2)}$ I MT gbʿym mšqdym$^{(2)}$.[79]

---

variant in his Hebrew text or to scribal error, but his failure to represent MT *w-* in *wʿrptw* is probably due to simple inadvertence. Neither the OG nor Theodotion reflected the conjunction either. If $\mathcal{S}$ correctly represents a pronominal object after Aquila's first verb, then Aquila may have misinterpreted MT *tpdh*$^{(1)}$, even though he omitted the similar object introduced by Theodotion after MT *tpdh*$^{(2)}$. The ambiguities of the Syriac make it difficult to be more precise about the relations between Theodotion and Aquila in this verse.

[77]The OG reading is out of place in A^{a}BF^{a}bfikqrw$\mathcal{A}\mathcal{B}\mathcal{L}^{v}$, Cyr, Phil, because a reflection of MT *šm* has been inserted before the phrase rather than after it. The expansion ελθειν is obviously secondary.

[78]The precise nature of the difference between α′ and α′θ′, as reflected in $\mathcal{S}^{mg}$, remains obscure. Syriac *mlkwt' khn̈'* is at best an ungrammatical rendition of Greek βασιλεια ιερεων.

[79]Compare MT *gbʿym mšqdym*$^{(1)}$ I OG κρατηρες εκτετυπωμενοι καρυισκους I $\mathcal{S}^{txt}$ *'g̈n' dmṭpsn g̈wz'*$^{(1)}$ I and α′ εξημυγδαλισμενοι (Msvz) for the second and third OG words. See also item 62 in chapter three, and note that the entire $\mathcal{S}^{txt}$ supplement is under ※. Theodotion and $\mathcal{S}^{txt}$ have repeated OG κρατηρες/*'g̈n'* to represent MT *gbʿym* on its second occurrence in the verse. While $\mathcal{S}^{txt}$ also repeats the OG equivalent for MT *mšqdym*, Theodotion introduces a new translation that is shared by Aquila

25:38: α'σ' wmzmk' dylh' ϑ' wmlqṭ' dylh ($𝕾^{mg}$; cf. οι λ̥ λαβιδας in M^{mg} and και λαβιδας αυτου in b^{mg})] OG και τον (την f; τους F^b; om d*) επαρυστηρα (*suffusorium* $𝕷^v$; επαρυστηρας F^b; *emunctoria* 𝕬) αυτης (om k)] $𝕾^{txt}$ wlnšwk' dylh] MT wmlqḥyh.

28:6: α' w'rgwn' wtwl't' mšḥlpt' ($𝕾^{mg}$)] ϑ' και πορφυρας και κοκκινου νενησμενου (vz; cf. $j^{mg}s^{mg}$ and ck𝕬$𝕰^c$; cf. also ϑ' *mšḥlp'* in $𝕾^{mg}$)] OG om.] $𝕾^{txt}$ w'rgwn' wzḥwryt' d'zyl'] MT w'rgmn twl't šny.[80]

28:11: α' εσφιγμενους (sv; cf. α' *mḥzqt'* in $𝕾^{mg}$)] ϑ' και συνεσφιγμενους (svz[-σφραγισ- sz])] OG om.] $𝕾^{txt}$ wḥzyqn 'kḥd'] MT mšbṣwt.[81]

28:26 (MT): α'σ' και θησεις αυτους (v)] ο'ϑ' και δωσεις αυτους svz; cf. ϑ' *wttl 'nyn* in $𝕾^{txt}$] OG om.] $F^{a?}$Mcdegjkmnp $s^{txt}v^{txt}z^{txt}$𝕬$𝕰^c$ και θησεις (δωσεις $F^{a?}$ckm𝕬; ποιησεις j) αυτους] MT wśmt 'tm.[82]

28:35 (LXX v.31): α'σ' (σ'σ' s) επι του (τω v) ααρων (jsvz)] ο'ϑ' επι ααρων (jsvz)] OG (+ επι ck𝕬; + ※ g' 'lχ 𝕾) ααρων] MT 'l 'hrn.[83]

29:5: α' τον χιτωνα και το ενδυμα του επενδυματος (v; cf. α'

---

and that presumably equals α' εξημυγδαλισμενοι for MT *mšqdym*(1). Aquila, however, introduces a new equivalent for MT *gb'ym* as well (compare α' σκυφοι in v^{mg} for OG κρατηρες, MT *gb'ym*, in Exod. 25:34 [LXX v.33]). Thus it is also possible to understand Theodotion as closer to OG usage here, even though there is no OG translation for this second occurrence of the MT phrase.

[80]On the conflict between ϑ' νενησμενου and ϑ' *mšḥlp'* (which should = διαφορου, or the like), see fn. 13 in chapter four where there is further evidence of inconsistency in the treatment of MT *šny* by Theodotion and by his Syriac translators.

[81]See item 10 in chapter three for the remaining textual evidence bearing on these variants. On the Theodotionic corruption, συνεσφραγισμενους for συνεσφιγμενους, see p. 127.

[82]See item 71 in chapter three for a discussion of this reading and its problems.

[83]The variant τω (for του) in the α'σ' reading of v^{mg} is secondary. The reason for the insertion of the article by Aquila is not clear.

lkwtyn' wllbwš' dhw dl'l mn lbwš in $\mathcal{S}^{mg}$) ‖ θ' τον χιτωνα και τον επενδυτην (επιδ- v) της επωμιδος (jsvz; cf. θ' *lkwtyn' wll'l mn lbwšh dkbynt'* in $\mathcal{S}^{mg}$) ‖ OG και τον χιτωνα (+ και $F^{b}ck\mathcal{E}^{c}$) τον ποδηρη (*varium* $\mathcal{C}^{c}$; + και τον [την 128] υποδυτην [εποδ- c; επενδ- 128] της επωμιδος ck, 128; + του επενδυματος egj^{txt}; + *super subuculas* $\mathcal{A}$) ‖ $\mathcal{S}^{txt}$ wlkwtyn' wlpwdr' ※ dl'l mn lbwš'↙ ‖ MT 't ktnt w't m'yl h'pd.[84]

29:22: α' το στεαρ και την κερκον σ'θ' το στεαρ και το κερκιον (v) ‖ OG το στεαρ (+ και την κερκον m; + ※ '' *wl'lyt'*↙ $\mathcal{S}$) αυτου (under ÷ $\mathcal{S}$; *et caudam* $\mathcal{A}$; + και την κερκον cj^{mg} $s^{mg}z^{mg}$) ‖ MT hḥlb wh'lyh.

30:7: α'σ' (om α' s) θυμιαμα ηδυσματων (svz) ‖ θ' θυμιαμα αρωματων (svz) ‖ OG θυμιαμα συνθετον (συνθεσεως blwx; *compositionis* $\mathcal{L}^{r}$; + το 1) λεπτον (λεπτης bwx; *comminutum parvum tanquam pulverem* $\mathcal{A}$) ‖ MT qṭrt smym.

30:32: α' κατα την συμμετριαν (v; cf. α' συμμετριαν in M and without name in z^{mg}) ‖ σ'θ' κατα την συνταξιν (v) ‖ OG κατα την (το $k^{mg}n$) συνθεσιν (ειδος $k^{mg}n$) ‖ MT (w)bmtknt-.

31:17: α' bynt ly wbynt bnÿ' d'ysr'yl ($\mathcal{S}^{mg}$) ‖ θ' bmṣ't ly wbmṣ't bnÿ' d'ysr'yl ($\mathcal{S}^{mg}$) ‖ OG εν (*inter* $\mathcal{L}^{z}$; om $efgijksvxz\mathcal{C}^{m}\mathcal{E}$ $\mathcal{L}^{r}$) εμοι (*me* $\mathcal{L}^{z}$; om $\mathcal{L}^{r}$) και (+ εν $cm\mathcal{A}^{vid}$) τοις (+ οι f) υιοις (*filios* $\mathcal{L}^{z}$) ισραηλ ‖ $\mathcal{S}^{txt}$ by wbbÿy' d'ysr'yl ‖ MT byny wbyn bny yśr'l.[85]

32:8: α' μοσχον χωνευσεως (v) ‖ σ'θ' μοσχον χωνευτον (v) ‖ OG μοσχον (+ χωνευτον cm$\mathcal{A}$; + ※ '' *nsyk'*↙ $\mathcal{S}$) ‖ MT 'gl mskh.

---

[84] The substitution of επιδυτην for επενδυτην in the θ' reading of v^{mg} is probably a secondary scribal error. A similar variation in the θ' equivalents for MT *m'yl* occurs at 1 Sam. 2:19.

[85] Since Syriac *bmṣ't* could represent Greek ανα μεσον (compare $\mathcal{S}^{txt}$ *bmṣ't* twice for Exod. 11:7, each time to represent MT *byn*, the second explicitly attributed to θ' by $\mathcal{S}^{txt}$) as well as Greek εν μεσω or the like, Theodotion cannot here be said to be closer to the OG than Aquila is. No mutually exclusive pattern of correspondences for Syriac *bynt* and *bmṣ't* has been discovered in Exodus. The Syriac translator does not seem to have been completely consistent on this point.

32:9: α′ σκληροτερων εστ[ιν] (v) I σ′θ′ σκληροτραχηλος εστιν (s[om εστιν]vz; cf. cmp$^{b?}$$b_2$, 128, A̸S̸[under ※]) I OG om. I MT qšh ʿrp hwʾ.

32:18: α′ lʾ ʾytwhy qlʾ dhlyn dmʿnyn bḥylʾ (!) wlʾ ʾytwhy qlʾ dhnwn dmʿnyn mn zkwtʾ ʾlʾ qlʾ dmʿnyn ʾnʾ šmʿ ʾnʾ (S̸^{mg}) I θ′ lʾ ʾytwhy qlʾ dqrbʾ dmʿnyn bḥylʾ (!) wlʾ ʾytwhy qlʾ dmʿnyntʾ dzkwtʾ qlʾ dhnyn dmʿnyn ʾnʾ ʾyty dšmʿ ʾnʾ (S̸^{mg}) I OG ουκ εστιν φωνη (om L̸^{r}) εξαρχοντων (κατισχυωντων αρχοντων x) κατ (om a^{b}dx) ισχυν (κατισχειν d; εις παραταξιν a^{b}; om x) ουδε φωνη (-νης x; -νην a) εξαρχοντων (om κατ-εξαρχοντων(2) h) τροπης (*pugnae* B̸^{1}) αλλα φωνην (φωνης z^{mg}; φωνη m; φωνη ην gj) εξαρχοντων (om τροπης-εξαρχοντων(3) dpt) οινου (ην x; + ως m) εγω (after ακουω A̸E̸) ακουω I S̸^{txt} lʾ ʾytwhy qlʾ dhnwn dmʿnyn bḥylʾ ʾp lʾ qlʾ dhnwn dmʿnyn bzkwtʾ ʾlʾ bqlʾ dhnwn mʿnyn ÷ dḥmrʾ ↙ ʾnʾ šmʿ ʾnʾ I MT ʾyn qwl ʿnwt gbwrh wʾyn qwl ʿnwt ḥlwšh qwl ʿnwt ʾnky šmʿ.[86]

33:5: α′ mnʾ ʾʿbd lk· θ′ mṭl dʾʿbd lk (S̸^{mg}) I OG α ποιησω (-σει h; -σεις Mdlpt; -σετε f) σοι (υμιν 130^{mg}, B̸E̸L̸^{rz}, Luc; om F$^{corr\ vid}$Mdflpt) I S̸^{txt} hlyn dʾʿbd lk I MT mh ʾʿśh lk.[87]

33:15: α′ ʾn prṣwpʾ dylk lʾ ʾzlyn (S̸^{mg}) I σ′θ′ ʾn prṣwpʾ dylk lʾ ʾzl (S̸^{mg}) I OG ει μη αυτος συ (or συ αυτος) πορευη (or συμπορευη; etc.; + μεθ ημων AFMb-gi-lnopstvwy-$b_2d_2(\frac{1}{2})$, 130, A̸B̸ C̸^{m}L̸^{r}; etc.) I S̸^{txt} ʾn ʾnt lʾ ʾzl ʾnt ʿmn I MT ʾm ʾyn pnyk hlkym.

34:9: α′ bgwn· σ′θ′ bmṣʿtn (S̸^{mg}) I OG μεθ (εν n) ημων (υμων gh; ημιν n) I S̸^{txt} ʿmn I MT bqrbnw.

34:20: α′ τενοντοκοπησεις (-ναντ- svz) αυτο (Ms[-τον]vz; cf. α′ *tpswq ṣwrʾ dylh* in S̸^{mg}) I θ′ tpswq ḥṣʾ dylh (S̸^{mg}) I OG τιμην (τιμη 71; τομην c; + αυτου nA̸B̸C̸^{m}) δωσεις (-σης fix; + αυτου AFMbd-gijloprstvyzb_2; + αυτω a_2) I S̸^{txt} ṭymʾ ttl dylh I MT (w)ʿrptw.[88]

---

[86]These variants are discussed under the seventh reading in chapter one. See also item 12 in chapter three.

[87]See item 42 in chapter three.

[88]The variants in the spelling of the α′ verb in s^{mg}v^{mg}z^{mg} and in the α′ pronoun in s^{mg} are presumably secondary scribal corruptions. Compare the α′ and θ′ equivalents for the same MT verb listed above under Exod. 13:13.

35:11 (LXX v.10): α' και τους κρικους αυτης και τας σανιδας (v; cf. α' κρικους in Msvz and without name in b^{mg}; cf. also α'σ'θ' *wlqwfqs' dylh* in $\mathcal{S}^{mg}$) ‖ σ'θ' και τας περονας αυτης και τας σανιδας (v; cf. σ'θ' *'bf'* in $\mathcal{S}^{mg}$; cf. also θ' και τας σανιδας out of place in 130, as cited by Field) ‖ OG και τα διατονια (-να n; + αυτης και τας σανιδας F^bck[om αυτης]m A; + και τας σανιδας $s^{mg}z^{mg}$[cf. v^{mg}]) ‖ $\mathcal{S}^{txt}$ wlṭwfb' ※g' dylh⋎ wldp' ‖ MT 't qrsyw w't qršy-.[89]

35:24: α' και πας ω ευρεθη παρ αυτω (v) ‖ θ' και πας ος ευρεθη παρ αυτω (v) ‖ OG και παρ (πας c; παντι km; *omnis apud* A) οις (ως c; οσοις km; *quem* A, Or-lat) ευρεθη (*inveniebatur* A; + παρ αυτοις Mcdegi*j-npstv^{txt}z$a_2$$b_2$) ‖ $\mathcal{S}^{txt}$ wklhwn 'ylyn d'štkḥw lwthwn ‖ MT wkl 'šr nmṣ' 'tw.

38:10 (LXX 37:8): α' wqplyd' d'mwd' wdwbq' dylhwn ($\mathcal{S}^{mg}$) ‖ θ' wšbt' d'mwd' wps'lyds dylhwn ($\mathcal{S}^{txt}$; cf. και οι κοσμοι των στυλων και αι ψαλιδες αυτων in ckAE^c) ‖ OG om. ‖ MT wwy h'mdym whšqyhm.

38:23 (LXX 37:21): α'σ' w'mh ($\mathcal{S}^{mg}$; cf. και μετ αυτου in F^bkE^c) ‖ θ' wbtrkn ($\mathcal{S}^{txt}$; cf. και μετα [+ τα c] ταυτα in cmA) ‖ OG και ‖ MT w'tw.[90]

39:16 (LXX 36:23): α'σ' σφιγκτηρας (M; cf. α' *hyst'* σ' *hyst 'khd'* in $\mathcal{S}^{mg}$) ‖ θ' hywst' ($\mathcal{S}^{mg}$) ‖ OG ασπιδισκας ‖ $\mathcal{S}^{txt}$ skr' ‖ MT mšbṣt.[91]

No Significant Agreement Between Aquila and Theodotion (51 Readings)

There are sixteen readings in which Theodotion's variant appears closer to the OG or to a large number of LXX manuscripts than Aquila's variant does:

---

[89]The α'σ'θ' attribution of *wlqwfqs' dylh* in $\mathcal{S}^{mg}$ is an error for α' (unless σ'θ' refer only to *wl-* and *dylh*), since σ'θ' have *'bf'* (= περονας).

[90]See the discussion of these readings under item 44 in chapter three. The presumed original agreement of θ' and α'σ' on και μετ αυτου to translate MT *w'tw* is not of great significance.

[91]The conflated attribution in M^{mg} should simply be α' (since σ' should have a singular noun with a συν- prefix, for example, συσφιγκτηρα, if $\mathcal{S}^{mg}$ is correct).

5:4: α' αποπεταζετε (Mvz)] θ' διασκεδαζετε (Mvz; cf. θ' διασωζετε in c_2)] OG διαστρεφετε (διαστρεφεται A; αποστρεφετε p; *avertistis* $\mathcal{L}^r$)] MT tpry'w.[92]

7:19: α'σ' nhw' ($\mathcal{S}^{mg}$)] θ' hw' ($\mathcal{S}^{mg}$)] OG εγενετο (γενησεται F^bdnp$\mathcal{B}$; εσται y; om M$\mathcal{E}^c$)] $\mathcal{S}^{txt}$ (w)hw'] MT (w)hyh.[93]

12:41: α'σ' στρατεια (*b*; cf. στρατια in i^{mg} and α'σ' *pl̈ḥwt'* in $\mathcal{S}^{mg}$)] θ' ḥyl̈wt' ($\mathcal{S}^{mg}$)] OG η δυναμις] $\mathcal{S}^{txt}$ ḥylh] MT ṣb'wt.[94]

13:18: α'σ' καθωπλισμενοι (jvz; cf. α' ενωπλισμενοι σ' οπλιται in M and ενωπλισμενοι in $F^{b\ mg\ vid}$)] θ' πεμπταιζοντες (Mjv z)] OG πεμπτη...γενεα] MT (w)ḥmšym.[95]

16:18: α' (b)'mwr ($\mathcal{S}^{mg}$)] σ'θ' gwmwr ($\mathcal{S}^{mg}$; cf. σ' [*b*]*gwmwr* in $\mathcal{S}^{mg}$)] OG γομορ (γομωρ al; γωμερ $F^{b?}$k)] $\mathcal{S}^{txt}$ (b)gwmwr] MT (b)'mr.

16:21: α' 'yk pwm' dm'kwlt' dylh ($\mathcal{S}^{mg}$)] θ' bhlyn d'klyn lh ($\mathcal{S}^{mg}$)] OG (om B) το καθηκον αυτω (αυτο q)] $\mathcal{S}^{txt}$ hw m' dzdq lh] MT kpy 'klw.

---

[92]For a discussion of the Theodotionic corruption in c_2^{mg}, see item 33 in chapter three and also item 5 of the second reading in chapter one. While Theodotion's variant here is primarily conditioned by his acceptance of OG usage in Exod. 32:25, it also shares the prefix δια- with OG διαστρεφετε; Aquila's variant has no connection, however slight, with the OG.

[93]See item 113 in chapter three.

[94]The Syriac plural *pl̈ḥwt'* may mean that α'σ' στρατεια is to be taken as the plural of στρατιον (-ειον), rather than the singular στρατεια. Theodotion presumably substituted the plural of δυναμις for the OG singular. These correspondences are discussed in chapter seven, since they conform to καιγε and α' categories established by Barthélemy.

[95]Since only ενωπλισμενοι is attributed to α' in Josh. 4:12 for MT *ḥmšym* and since only ενοπλισμος is (mistakenly) used by Aquila in 2 Sam. 2:23 and 3:27 to represent MT *ḥmš* (חֹמֶשׁ = "belly"), the α' reading of M^{mg} is here to be preferred to the α'σ' reading of $j^{mg}v^{mg}z^{mg}$. The difference in meaning between the two forms is not too great. M^{mg} also preserves a different variant for Symmachus, and this is presumably also to be accepted.

20:24 (𝔖 v.21): α′ d'r'' (𝔖^{mg})] ϑ′ mn 'dmt' (𝔖^{mg})] OG εκ γης] 𝔖^{txt} mn 'r''] MT 'dmh.

22:10 (LXX v.11): α′ šdr 'yd' (𝔖^{mg})] σ′ϑ′ mtḥ 'b'š (𝔖^{mg}; cf. σ′ μετεσχηκεναι in sv and without names in M^{mg}z^{mg})] OG πεπονηρευσθαι καθολου] 𝔖^{txt} 'štwtp ͞ kl klhy] MT šlḥ yd-.[96]

22:27 (LXX v.28): α′ lmšql'' σ′ϑ′ lryšn' (𝔖^{mg})] OG αρχοντας (BacovzA-coddC^{m}, etc.; -ντα AFMbd-np-ywxa$_2$b$_2$A-edBE, etc.)] 𝔖^{txt} (w)lršn'] MT (w)nśy'.

25:2: α′ αφαιρεμα (*b*svz; cf. α′ *pwršn'* in 𝔖^{mg}; cf. also α′ αφαιρεματα in M and without name in k^{mg})] σ′ϑ′ ršyt' (𝔖^{mg})] OG απαρχας] 𝔖^{txt} ršyt'] MT trwmh.[97]

25:18 (LXX v.17): α′ ελατους (*b*; cf. α′ *ršyš'* [*dšyš'* B] in 𝔖^{mg})] σ′ϑ′ ngydy bṭwrnws (𝔖^{mg})] OG τορευτα (τορνευτα F$^{b?}$fl mna$_2$)] 𝔖^{txt} ngydy bṭwrnwn] MT mqšh.[98]

28:27 (MT): α′ διαζωσματος (v; cf. α′ *dhmyn'* in 𝔖^{mg})] ϑ′ mtqnwt' (𝔖^{txt})] OG om.] F$^{a?}$Mcdegjkmnpstv^{txt}zAE^{c} μηχανωματος (-νηματος F$^{a?}$degkp)] MT (l)ḥšb.

28:28 (MT): α′ διαζωσματος (s)] ϑ′ mtqnwt' (𝔖^{txt})] OG om.]

---

[96]For the remaining textual evidence and a tentative evaluation of the obscure σ′ϑ′ reading in 𝔖^{mg}, see item 125 in chapter three. If Syriac *'b'š* represents OG πεπονηρευσθαι (while Syriac *mtḥ* means "to stretch out"), and if the Syriac expression *mtḥ 'b'š* is correctly attributed at least to ϑ′, then Theodotion may have attempted to insert a translation of MT *šlḥ* before the OG verb. The verb in 𝔖^{txt} would better reflect σ′ μετεσχηκεναι or ack^{mg} μετασχειν than the OG reading. While the Syriac expression attributed to σ′ϑ′ remains obscure, α′ *šdr 'yd' dylh* is obviously a literal translation of MT *šlḥ ydw*.

[97]The plural form attributed to α′ by M^{mg} is presumably a secondary scribal error, perhaps under the influence of the OG plural.

[98]The variant α′ reading in B of 𝔖^{mg} is an inner-Syriac scribal error. Both 𝔖^{txt} and the σ′ϑ′ reading of 𝔖^{mg} could apparently represent the variant τορνευτα, and perhaps also OG τορευτα (τορνευτος = "turned on a lathe"; τορευτος = "worked in relief, chased"; *ngydy* = "drawn, chased, embossed, engraved"; *ṭwrnws* = "lathe-chisel"; *ṭwrnwn* may be another form of *ṭwrnws*).

$F^{a?}$Mcdegjkmns^{txt}tvzAE^{c} του μηχανωματος (-νηματος $F^{a?}$cek)][MT ḥšb.

29:26: α' dmwly'' σ'θ' dšwmly' (S^{mg})][OG της τελειωσεως][S^{txt} dšwmly'][MT hml'ym.

39:22 (LXX 36:30): α' lbwš' ddl'l mn lbwš' (S^{mg})][θ' lbwš' 'ly' dkbynt' (S^{mg})][OG τον υποδυτην (+ υποδυτην ποδηρη dpt; + ποδηρη M^{mg}hn) υπο (επι bckmAE^{c}L^{r}; om b_2) την (om b_2) επωμιδα][S^{txt} lprzwm' 'l kbynt'][MT 't m'yl h'pd.

40:5: α' το παρατανυσμα του ανοιγματος (v)][θ' το επισπαστρον της θυρας (v; cf. θ' επι in z)][OG το (om Bafhirx, Cyr$\frac{1}{2}$-ed$\frac{1}{2}$) καλυμμα (καταλυμμα go; κατακαλυμμα Fbcejlnpstv^{txt}wy z^{txt}; *velum* E) του (om BafhirxE, Cyr$\frac{1}{2}$-ed$\frac{1}{2}$) καταπετασματος (κατασκεπασματος e; παραπετασματος cm; πετασματος 128; om E) επι (εις egjs^{txt}v^{txt}z^{txt}; παρα s^{mg}z^{mg}; *in* AL^{z}; *ad* L^{rw}) την (της fi) θυραν (θυρας fi; *ianua* A)][S^{txt} ltḥpyth dprs' 'l tr''][MT 't msk hpth.[99]

There are thirty-five readings in which Theodotion's variant does not appear closer to the OG or to a large number of LXX manuscripts than Aquila's variant does:

1:8: α' αλλος σ' δευτερος θ' καινος (c_2; cf. οι λ̥ καινος in M, α'σ'θ' [om σ' j; om θ' z] καινος in jvz, and *g' ḥdt'* in S^{mg})][OG ετερος][S^{txt} 'ḥrn'][MT ḥdš.[100]

1:13: α' εντρυφηματι (Montef., no source given, as cited by Field; cf. α' εντρυ... in 64, according to Field)][θ' εμπεγμω (M; cf. θ' εμπαιγμοι in v; cf. also σ'θ' εμπαιγματι according to Montef., no source given, as cited by Field, and σ' εντρυφωντες in Mv)][OG βια][MT bprk.[101]

4:24: α' ο (om jvz) θ̅ς̅ (Mjvz; cf. α' *'lh'* in S^{mg})][σ'θ' κ̅ς̅ (M jvz; cf. $F^{b\ mg}$; cf. also σ'θ' *mry'* in S^{mg})][OG αγγελος

---

[99]The apparently erroneous or misplaced θ' επι of z^{mg} is discussed under item 45 in chapter three.

[100]The various conflate attributions are secondary to the separate attributions of c_2^{mg}.

[101]The original θ' reading is difficult to determine. In any event, the α', θ', and OG variants are clearly different and unrelated.

κυριου (om FM^txt egj^txt lya$_2$b$_2$c$_2$Ƀ, Cyr$\frac{1}{3}$)][Ꞩ^txt ml'k'][MT yhwh.

4:25: α' πετρον (jvz; cf. α' πετρα in M)][ϑ' ακροτομον (Mvz)][OG ψηφον (+ πετρινον n)][MT ṣr.[102]

6:23: α'σ' bh bdmwt' ʿmyndbʾ ϑ' ʿnmyddb (Ꞩ^mg)][OG αμειναδαβ (etc.)][Ꞩ^txt (d) ʿmyndb][MT ʿmyndb.[103]

9:22: α'σ' d'tr'ʾ ϑ' dḥql' (Ꞩ^mg)][OG om. (+ εν τω πεδιω ackmx Ⱥᵽ)][Ꞩ^txt ※ dpq'tʾ↙][MT hśdh.

12:26: α'σ' lkwn (Ꞩ^txt)][ϑ' ln (Ꞩ^mg)][OG om. (+ υμιν acegj kmxȺ, Or-gr$\frac{1}{2}$)][MT lkm.[104]

18:26: α'σ' (+ ϑ' M) σκληρον ϑ' (om Ms) δυσχερες (Mjsz)][OG υπερογκον][MT (h)qšh.[105]

19:13: α' ροιζησει (Mjsvz)][ϑ' τοξευομενος (Mjvz; cf. s^mg)][OG βολιδι][MT yrh.[106]

19:22: α' διακοφη (Mjsz; cf. α' *npsq* in Ꞩ^mg)][ϑ' ngmr (Ꞩ^mg)][OG απαλλαξη (απαλλαξει b; απολεση ȺɃ, Cyr-cod$\frac{1}{5}$)][Ꞩ^txt ngmr][MT yprṣ.[107]

---

[102]The α' variant in M^mg is probably secondary to that found in j^mg v^mg z^mg, since it would be either plural where the MT is singular, or nominative where the syntax demands accusative.

[103]The Theodotionic variant is undoubtedly the result of a secondary scribal error.

[104]The Theodotionic variant is again due to secondary scribal error. See item 36 in chapter three.

[105]The conflate attribution in M^mg is obviously secondary. Compare the omission of ϑ' in s^mg.

[106]Since the following MT *yyrh* is translated by OG κατατοξευθησεται, the ϑ' variant (τοξευομενος for MT *yrh*) is actually closer to OG usage in the verse than is Aquila's ροιζησει. See item 7 under the sixth reading in chapter one for more extensive discussion of these variants and the patterns of usage to which they belong.

[107]Ꞩ^txt *ngmr* (ܢܓܡܪ) means "he will destroy" and presumably represents απολεση, or the like, rather than OG απαλλαξη ("he will set free, escape"). It is not clear what Greek verb is reflected by ϑ' *ngmr* (ܢܓܡܪ). The form is either Aphel ("he will accomplish, do away with, destroy") or Pael (agreeing with Ꞩ^txt). Note that the σ' attribution of

19:24: α' διακοψη διαφθειρη (k; cf. α' *npsq·* σ' *nḥbl* in $\mathcal{S}^{mg}$)]
        θ' npswq ($\mathcal{S}^{mg}$)] OG απολεση (απολεσει fn; απαλλαξη ac
        k^{txt}mxb₂)] $\mathcal{S}^{txt}$ nwbd] MT yprṣ.[108]

25:23 (LXX v.22): α' dqys' dsṭym ($\mathcal{S}^{mg}$)] θ' mn qẏs' l' ḿblṭ'
        ($\mathcal{S}^{txt}$)] OG (+ εκ F*ntz^{mg}a₂) χρυσιου (om ackmA$\cancel{E}^{c}$) καθαρου
        (εκ ξυλων ασηπτων F^{b} mgacmA$\cancel{E}^{c}$; om k; + και ξυλων ασηπτων
        b)] $\mathcal{S}^{mg}$ dḋhb' dky'] MT 'ṣy šṭym.

25:30 (LXX v.29): α' προσωπου (F^{b}Mjsvz; cf. k^{mg} and σ' προσωπου
        in M)] θ' προθεσεως (M; cf. j^{mg}km gs^{mg}, σ' προθεσεως in
        F^{b}vz, and σ' *dsymwt qdn'* in $\mathcal{S}^{mg}$)] OG ενωπιους] $\mathcal{S}^{txt}$ dqdm
        'ḅ'] MT pnym.[109]

26:37: α' dsṭym ($\mathcal{S}^{mg}$)] θ' l' ḿblṭ' ($\mathcal{S}^{txt}$)] OG om. (+ ασηπ-
        τους F^{b}acmxA$\cancel{E}^{c}$)] MT šṭym.

28:14: α'σ' αλυσεις (M*b*[-οις]; cf. α'σ' *ššlt'* in $\mathcal{S}^{mg}$; cf. also
        εν αλλω βιβλιω ευρον α'σ' συσφιγκτα in M and σ' συσφιγμα in
        vz)] θ' χαλαστα (M; cf. θ' *nẏpt'* in $\mathcal{S}^{mg}$)] OG κροσωτα *or*
        κροσσωτα] $\mathcal{S}^{txt}$ ḥWṭ'] MT šršrt.[110]

28:14: α'σ' βροχωτον (Mvz)] θ' dššlṭ' ($\mathcal{S}^{mg}$)] OG πλοκης]

Mjz is missing in s^{mg}, so that α' would appear to have διακοψη διαφθειρη
attributed to him in s^{mg}.

[108]The α' citation from k^{mg} is presumably a conflation of the α'
and σ' variants. See the previous example and the last sentence in the
preceding note, as well as α' and σ' in $\mathcal{S}^{mg}$. It is not clear what Greek
reading is presupposed by the Theodotionic *npswq*.

[109]See item 98 in chapter three.

[110]The conflicting variants, α'σ' συσφιγκτα of M^{mg} and σ' συσφιγμα
of v^{mg}z^{mg}, are probably misplaced. General Aquilan usage suggests that
they should be associated with an occurrence of MT *mšbṣt*. The word occurs
once in this verse and once in the preceding one. In the preceding verse,
α'σ' (om σ' sv) σφιγκτηρας is found in Msv for MT *mšbṣt*. In the present
verse, α' σφιγκτηρας is found in z for MT *(h)mšbṣt*, while the same noun
is associated with OG κροσσωτα by k^{mg}. See the discussion of hexaplaric
equivalents for MT *mšbṣt* and related forms in chapter two under item 20.
The α'σ' variant αλυσις in *b*^{mg} is an itacistic corruption of the correct
α'σ' αλυσεις in M^{mg}. Compare the α'σ' and θ' readings cited below for MT
šršt in Exod. 28:22.

Ṡ^txt dgdwl'][MT ʿbt.

28:22: α'σ' s̈šlt' (Ṡ^mg; cf. οι λ̥ αλυσεις in Msz and without name in v^mg)][θ' nÿpt' (Ṡ^mg)][OG κροσους *or* κροσσους][Ṡ^txt ḥẄṭ'][MT šršt.[111]

28:33 (LXX v.29): α' αποληγμα (svz; cf. α' αποπλεγμα in M)][σ'θ' lwt ẗgl' (Ṡ^mg; cf. σ' προς ποδων in Msvz)][OG το λωμα (δωμα m) του υποδυτου (υποδηματος m; *tunicae talaris* L^r) κατωθεν (κυκλοθεν A)][Ṡ^txt šp̈wlwhy dlbwš' mn lthṭ][MT šwly-.[112]

28:33 (LXX v.29): α' διαφορου διβαφου (*b*; cf. α' *mšḥlpt'* [*mšḥlp̈t'* B]˙ σ' *byd ṣwbʿ'* in Ṡ^mg)][θ' dmštgnynyt' (Ṡ^mg)][OG διανενησμενου (-νενιγμενου s; -νενησμενης 30)][Ṡ^txt dʿzyl'][MT šny.[113]

28:39 (LXX v.35) α'σ' μιτραν θ' υφωμα (M)][OG κινδαριν][MT mṣnpt.[114]

28:40 (LXX v.36): α'σ' μιτρας θ' υφωματα (v)][OG κινδαρεις][

---

[111]MT *šršt* is presumably an error for *šršrt*. See item 3 in chapter two.

[112]The α' reading in M^mg is a secondary corruption for the more correct αποληγμα. The σ'θ' variant is a descriptive rendition of the Hebrew noun, but acceptable. See item 128 in chapter three and also compare RT, p. 202. RT argues that τα προς ποδων is an unacceptable α' rendition of MT *šlym* in Nah. 3:5; Isa. 6:1; Jer. 13:22. It is possible, however, that in each case Aquila simply neglected to revise the reading present in his Greek text as a result of the earlier Theodotionic/ΚΑΙΓΕ revision. In the present instance, however, Aquila did notice the inadequacy of the phrase and replaced it with a more literal equivalent.

[113]The α' reading of *b*^mg is a conflation of α' διαφορου and σ' διβαφου; compare Exod. 28:5, 6; 35:23, 35. Ṡ^mg supports this interpretation, although σ' *byd ṣwbʿ'* represents a corrupt form (*δια βαφου, or the like). The correct Syriac equivalent would be *trynt ṣwbʿ'*, as in Exod. 28:5, 6; 35:23. The addition of plural marks to the α' reading in B of Ṡ^mg is obviously an error. The variations in Theodotion's equivalents for MT *šny* and also in the Syriac translations of the Theodotionic equivalents have been mentioned previously. The evidence is collected in fn. 13 in chapter four.

[114]For this reading and the following one, see fn. 17 in chapter three.

I MT (w)mgbʻwt.

29:2: α′ αναμεμιγμενα (s[-μενους]vz; cf. j^{mg}) I θ′ αναπεποιημενους (svz) I OG πεφυραμενους (-μενας m; -μενα c) I MT blwlt.[115]

29:24: α′ ʼnwnˑ σ′θ′ ʼnyn (Ꞩ^{mg}) I OG αυτοις (BF*^{vid}b$_2$; αυτα bckmnps^{txt}tvwz^{txt}ȺɃȽ^{r}, Cyr; αυτους AF^{I}Mae-jloqrs^{mg}uxyz^{mg}a$_2$ Ɇ^{vid}) I Ꞩ^{txt} ʼnwn I MT ʼtm.[116]

29:41: θ′ dylhˑ α′σ′ ʼyk šbʻyn (Ꞩ^{mg}) I OG αυτου (αυτης Mls^{mg}x; om B*) I Ꞩ^{txt} dylh I MT 3 f.s. suffix on *wknskh*.[117]

---

[115]Presumably the neuter is more correct for Aquila's variant, since the masculine could be the result of assimilation to the OG and Theodotionic readings by a careless scribe. The question could only be settled if the α′ variant for OG αρτους$^{(2)}$ to represent MT *(w)ḥlt* were known.

[116]The form αυτους (Syriac *ʼnwn*) refers to Aaron and his sons, and makes them the object of the offering or presentation before Yahweh (MT *whnpt . . . lpny yhwh*). The noun αφορισμα, corresponding to MT *tnwph*, would then be in apposition to αυτους (MT *ʼtm*). This is the interpretation of Aquila. The form αυτα (Syriac *ʼnyn*) refers back to OG τα παντα (Syriac *lklhyn*), representing MT *hkl* and summarizing the various offerings described in vv. 22-23. It makes these offerings, rather than Aaron and his sons, the object of the presentation before Yahweh. Once again αφορισμα (= MT *tnwph*) would be in apposition to the pronoun. This is Theodotion's interpretation. Either interpretation can be supported by the present MT, although their theological value clearly differs. The minority reading αυτοις also avoids taking Aaron and his sons as the object of the presentation before Yahweh, but does so at the expense of fidelity to the Hebrew text. It makes αφορισμα (= MT *tnwph*) the object of the verb, and transforms MT *ʼtm* into a dative of advantage.

[117]OG αυτου has OG τον αμνον (= MT *[w]ʼt hkbś*) as its antecedent. This is presumably reflected in Ꞩ^{txt} *dylh* (ܕܝܠܗ), and consequently in α′σ′, although the α′σ′ Greek reflection of the antecedent could be different. The variant αυτης, presumably reflected by θ′ *dylh* (ܕܝܠܗܿ), apparently takes the nearer OG την θυσιαν την πρωινην (= MT *[k]mnḥt hbqr*) as the antecedent. The latter is in conformity with the normal interpretation and the vocalization of the suffix on MT *wknskh* (וּכְנִסְכָּהּ), but the unvocalized suffix could also be interpreted as masculine and as

30:1: α' d'ṭr' (Ꞩmg) I σ'θ' pyrm' (Ꞩtxt) I OG om. (+ θυμιατηριον Mmgv[entire verse under ※]z[pr ※]a₂A; + θυμηιαματηριον c) I MT mqṭr.[118]

30:4: α'σ' (om α' vz) εισοδοι (Mvz; cf. smg) I θ'σ' (om σ' vz) εις θηκας (Mvz; cf. *b*mgsmg; cf. also σ' *ltÿq'* in Ꞩmg) I OG ψαλιδες I Ꞩtxt ṗs'lydys I MT lbtym.[119]

32:6: α'σ' 'sqw (Ꞩmg) I θ' (w)'ytyw (Ꞩmg) I OG ανεβιβασεν (ανεβιβασαν g; ανηνεγκεν cka; προσηνεγκεν x) I Ꞩtxt 'sq I MT (w)y'lw.[120]

34:35: α' δερμα (v) I θ' ḥzt' d- (Ꞩtxt) I OG om. (+ η οψις egjsz; + η οψις του χρωτος cvmg[under ※]; + η οψις του χρωματος m; + *visus coloris* A) I Ꞩtxt ※ θ' ḥzt' d⋖ pgr' I MT 'wr.[121]

35:24: σ'θ' ršyt'˙ α' bdmwt' dhnwn šb'yn (Ꞩmg) I OG το (om AFM

---

written in archaic orthography (compare SP *wknskw*). If Theodotion actually had αυτης, then his consonantal text must have agreed with the MT. If Aquila had αυτου, however, his consonantal text could have agreed either with the MT or with the SP. His agreement with the OG on the interpretation of the suffix could be independent of the OG and the result of a rejection of Theodotion's reading. He could also, of course, be understood as retaining an OG reading against Theodotion, but this is less likely.

[118]The α' reading of Ꞩmg is marked as a variant for the σ'θ' expansion in Ꞩtxt, and hence as an equivalent for MT *mqṭr*. It could also be interpreted as a translation for MT *qṭrt* (so B-McL), but this would be at once unnecessary and in conflict with the evidence. Syriac *d'ṭr'* can be understood as the participle of *'ṭr* ("to steam, smoke, rise up as steam or smoke"), and not just as the noun ("vapor, fume, steam, incense"). Note that θυμιατηριον (+ αγιον m) replaces the preceding OG θυσιαστηριον (= MT *mzbḥ*) in mn.

[119]If Ꞩmg can be trusted, then the α'σ' citation of Mmg is an error for α' alone (but cf. vmgzmg).

[120]The α'σ' citation of Ꞩmg need not be interpreted to mean that Aquila failed to represent the MT conjunction *w*- explicitly, though this is possible.

[121]See item 133 in chapter three for a brief discussion of these readings.

b-egjklnpqs-wy-b$_2$) αφαιρεμα ‖ S^{txt} pwršn' ‖ MT trwmt.[122]

38:3 (LXX 38:23): α' 'wqynʾ' (S^{mg}) ‖ θ' (w)lšqwl' (S^{mg}) ‖ OG om. (+ το γεισιον ckA; + τας σουβλας αυτου F^b; + *lebetes* E^c) ‖ S^{txt} (w)lgys' ‖ MT (w)'t hy'ym.[123]

38:28 (LXX 39:6): α'σ' qplyd'' θ' šbt' (S^{mg}) ‖ OG εις (om F^b) τας (om F^b) αγκυλας (κεφαλιδας F^b) ‖ S^{txt} b'nqwl's ‖ MT wwym.

39:2 (LXX 36:9): α'σ' το επενδυμα θ' το εφωδ (Montef., from his manuscripts, as cited by Field) ‖ OG την επωμιδα ‖ MT 't h'pd.[124]

39:15 (LXX 36:22): α'σ' gdyl'' θ' dššlt' (S^{mg}) ‖ OG εμπλοκιου (ενπλοκιου A^{vid}; εμπλοκιον b$_2$; εκπλοκιου q; *tortile* L^r) ‖ S^{txt} dgdwl' ‖ MT 'bt.

39:17 (LXX 36:25): α'σ' αλυσεις θ' χαλαστα (M) ‖ OG εμπλοκια (-κιον begjnsvzL^r) ‖ S^{txt} lgdylt' ‖ MT (h)'btt.[125]

39:28 (LXX 36:36): α'σ' dgby' (S^{mg}[B only]) ‖ θ' db'd (S^{txt}) ‖ OG om. (+ του εξαιρετου ck; + *lintea* A) ‖ MT hbd.

---

[122] Apparently Theodotion generalized one OG equivalent, απαρχη/*ršyt'*, and Aquila a second, αφαιρεμα/*pwršn'*, for MT *trwmh*. Compare Exod. 25:2. This suggestion is discussed in the following chapter.

[123] BabdfhinoqruxL^z and AFMegjlpstvwy-b$_2$BE^f have four items where the MT has five. The items are in different order in the two groups. Only F^{b}ckAE^{c}S^{txt} have five items, with the original four (at least in ckA and S) rearranged again and the new item inserted in second place. The second-place items in F^b and E^c are cited as well, although at least E^c may have a different order. The α', σ', and θ' variants of S^{mg} are to this new second item.

[124] This reading is suspect, because θ' εφωδ is at variance with the normal and well-attested use of επωμις/*kbynt'* by Theodotion to represent MT *'pd*. The α'σ' variant is not unexpected, since επενδυμα is Aquila's normal equivalent for MT *'pd*. See the discussion under item 22 in chapter two.

[125] Under item 14 in chapter two, it is explained why these α'σ' and θ' readings are probably incorrectly associated with OG εμπλοκια and MT *(h)'btt*. Perhaps they should be associated with OG κροσους/κροσσους (LXX Exod. 36:22), which stands for MT *šršrt* (MT Exod. 39:15).

Theodotionic ομοιως τοις ο'/*'yk šb'yn* Readings and Similar Readings for Which an Aquilan Reading is Separately Cited (15 Readings)

There are five readings in which Aquila's variant is in partial agreement with the presumed Theodotionic reading:

3:9: α' καιγε εωρακα συν τον αποθλιμμον ον οι αιγυπτιοι αποθλιβουσιν αυτους (jvz)] θ' (ο' j) ομοιως τοις ο' (jvz)] OG καγω (Bafikmoqrsu; και εγω AFMb-eghj^{txt}lnptv^{txt}wxyz^{txt}$a_2b_2c_2$) εωρακα τον (την 32) θλιμμον (θλιψιν 32; + αυτων a$\mathcal{B}\mathcal{C}^m$) ον (ην 32) οι (om df) αιγυπτιοι θλιβουσιν (εκθλιβουσιν bw) αυτους] MT wgm r'yty 't hlḥṣ 'šr mṣrym lḥṣym 'tm.[126]

12:42 (LXX vv. 41-42): α' lly' dmṭrt' 'ytwhy hw' lpypy ($\mathcal{S}^{mg}$; cf. α' νυξ παρατηρησεως τω πιπι in *b* and α' παρατηρησεων in M)] θ' 'yk šb'yn ($\mathcal{S}^{mg}$)] OG νυκτος (om A*y*c_2, Ath, Thdt; out of place Mvz; + νυκτα F$^{b?}$; + [*h*]*aec* $\mathcal{L}^z$) προφυλακη (προφυλακης abx; προσφυλακη dp) εστιν (*erat* $\mathcal{A}$; *enim erat* $\mathcal{P}$) τω (om egjnprw$\mathcal{B}^{l\ vid}\mathcal{E}^{vid}$) κυριω ($\overline{κυ}$ egjn$\mathcal{B}^{l\ vid}\mathcal{E}^{vid}$)] $\mathcal{S}^{txt}$ blly' dmṭrt' 'ytyh hwt dmry'] MT lyl šmrym hw' lyhwh.[127]

14:7: α' wtlyty' ($\mathcal{S}^{mg}$)] θ' bdmwt' dhnwn šb'yn ($\mathcal{S}^{mg}$)] OG και τριστατας] $\mathcal{S}^{txt}$ wtlyty' dqymyn] MT wšlšm.[128]

15:15: α' twht' wdḥlt'' θ' 'yk šb'yn ($\mathcal{S}^{mg}$)] OG τρομος (Balsw$\mathcal{B}$; φοβος AFMb-km-rtvx-$b_2d_2$$\mathcal{E}\mathcal{P}$, Or-lat, Cyr, Luc) και (om w) φοβος (Bals$\mathcal{B}$; τρομος AFMb-km-rtvx-$b_2d_2$$\mathcal{E}\mathcal{P}$, Or-lat, Cyr, Luc)

---

[126]See item 137 in chapter three. Theodotion presumably agreed with the OG here, except that he probably had και εγω rather than καγω. Note that he failed to introduce καιγε to represent MT *wgm*.

[127]See item 140 in chapter three. If Theodotion agreed with the text reflected by $\mathcal{S}^{txt}$, then he presumably had νυκτος προφυλακης (or παρατηρησεως) *ην κυριου, or the like. Syriac *mṭrt'* could easily represent προφυλακη. The equation with παρατηρησις is less accurate, but the various α' readings show that it too is possible. The α' plural in M^{mg} would reflect MT *šmrym* more exactly, and may be the correct reading (against $b^{mg}\mathcal{S}^{mg}$). The α' verb (Syriac *'ytwhy hw'*), representing MT *hw'*, has been secondarily omitted by b^{mg}. There was some agreement between Aquila and Theodotion here, but the preserved evidence does not permit specification of its extent.

[128]See item 141 in chapter three. The short α' reading may reflect a Greek variant such as *τρισσους (so RT, *s.v.*, following a suggestion by Field). Theodotion's agreement with the OG is clear.

I $\mathcal{S}^{txt}$ r'lt' wdḥlt' I MT 'ymth wpḥd.[129]

20:17 ($\mathcal{S}$ v.14): α' dbyt' dḥbr' dylk· σ'θ' 'yk šb'yn ($\mathcal{S}^{mg}$) I OG την οικιαν του πλησιον σου ουδε (ουτε BFMh; ου f) τον αγρον αυτου I $\mathcal{S}^{txt}$ byth dqryb' dylk ÷wl' ḥql' dylh↙ I MT byt r'k (cf. SP byt r'k ... śdhw).[130]

There are ten readings in which there is no agreement between Aquila's variant and the presumed Theodotionic reading:

12:11: α' υπερβασις (Mj[bis][-σιν once]vz; cf. α' *m'brt'* in $\mathcal{S}^{mg}$; cf. also α' και σ' φασιν in j^{mg}) I θ' 'yk šb'yn ($\mathcal{S}^{mg}$) I OG πασχα I $\mathcal{S}^{txt}$ pṣḥ' I MT psḥ.[131]

12:27: α' dm'brt' 'ytwh ($\mathcal{S}^{mg}$) I θ' 'yk šb'yn ($\mathcal{S}^{mg}$) I OG το πασχα τουτο I $\mathcal{S}^{txt}$ pṣḥ' hn' I MT psḥ hw'.[132]

15:21: α' και κατελεγεν (M; cf. $j^{mg}z^{mg}$ and $F^{b\ mg}$; cf. also α' *m'ny' hwt* in $\mathcal{S}^{mg}$) I θ' 'yk šb'yn ($\mathcal{S}^{mg}$) I OG εξηρχεν δε I $\mathcal{S}^{txt}$ mšry' hwt ... dyn I MT wt'n.[133]

---

[129]Theodotion appears to have agreed with Bals$\mathcal{B}\mathcal{S}^{txt}$ against the majority of LXX manuscripts. If this is correct, it is probable that the reading in Bals$\mathcal{B}\mathcal{S}^{txt}$ is a revision of the OG, or actually only a rearrangement of terms, drawn from Theodotion. It is this rearranged OG text that Aquila further revised by providing a new equivalent for MT *'ymth*.

[130]See item 146 in chapter three. The citations from $\mathcal{S}^{mg}$ need not imply that Theodotion's text contained the phrase under ÷ in $\mathcal{S}^{txt}$ and corresponding to SP *śdhw*. Presumably Theodotion had the part of the OG not under ÷ in $\mathcal{S}$ (την οικιαν του πλησιον σου), while Aquila made a grammatical change and inserted a replacement for OG του πλησιον. Aquila's grammatical change was probably conditioned by a change in the verb that governed the phrase (i.e., in the equivalent for MT *tḥmd*$^{(1)}$).

[131]See item 138 in chapter three. The apparent attribution of φασιν to α' by j^{mg} is undoubtedly erroneous. Theodotion's agreement with the OG is clear.

[132]See item 139 in chapter three. Theodotion's agreement with the OG is clear.

[133]See item 143 in chapter three. See also item 4 of the seventh reading in chapter one. The association of σ' *m'ny' hwt dyn* with θ' *'yk šb'yn* in $\mathcal{S}^{mg}$ makes it likely, though not certain, that Theodotion retained

18:1: α′ ytrw' σ′θ′ 'yk šb'yn ($\mathcal{S}^{mg}$) I OG ιοθορ (ιοθωρ ab′gijl$^{a?}$; ιωθορ fn; ιωθωρ qu, Cyr-cod; ιαθωρ m; ιορθορ a_2) I $\mathcal{S}^{txt}$ ytrwn I MT ytrw.[134]

18:1: α′ ḥtn' ($\mathcal{S}^{mg}$) I θ′ 'yk šb'yn ($\mathcal{S}^{mg}$) I OG ο (οτι h) γαμβρος (πενθερος $F^{b\ mg}dlp^bw^b$) I $\mathcal{S}^{txt}$ hw ḥmwhy I MT ḥtn.[135]

22:27 (LXX v.28): α′ l' tlwṭ ($\mathcal{S}^{mg}$) I θ′ 'yk šb'yn ($\mathcal{S}^{mg}$) I OG ουκ (ου Bkmo) ερεις (after κακως Bkmo) κακως I $\mathcal{S}^{txt}$ l' t'mr byš'yt$^{(2)}$ I MT l' t'r.[136]

24:6: α′ εθηκεν (Mz; cf. s^{mg}) I σ′θ′ bdmwt' dhnwn šb'yn ($\mathcal{S}^{mg}$) I OG ενεχεεν I $\mathcal{S}^{txt}$ nsk I MT wyśm.[137]

25:31 (LXX v.30): α′ ελατην (*b*; cf. $F^{b\ mg}$; cf. also α′ *ršyšt* in $\mathcal{S}^{mg}$) I θ′ 'yk šb'yn ($\mathcal{S}^{mg}$) I OG τορευτην (τορνευτην f,

---

OG εξηρχεν δε unchanged. He apparently failed to make his usual substitution of και for OG δε. Compare Exod. 32:31 (listed above on p. 207) for a similar failure by θ′α′. That reading was discussed under item 35 in chapter four.

[134]See item 144 in chapter three. The form in $\mathcal{S}^{txt}$ is probably influenced by PS *ytrwn*, so that σ′θ′ can be understood as agreeing with OG ιοθορ here. Compare θ′ and σ′ ιοθορ and α′ ιεθρω/ιεθρο in Exod. 18:5 (listed above on p. 222; see also item 121 in chapter three).

[135]See item 145 in chapter three. Since the σ′ reading cited with α′ and θ′ by $\mathcal{S}^{mg}$ has $\mathcal{S}^{txt}$ *ḥmwhy*, but does not have $\mathcal{S}^{txt}$ *hw* (= OG ο), it is likely that α′ and σ′ omitted the OG article which was not supported by the MT, while θ′ retained it together with the OG noun. If Exod. 18:5 is any indication, Aquila's new noun for MT חֹתֵן was probably νυμφευτης, while he and Theodotion both used the related νυμφιος for MT חָתָן. The only apparent exception to this latter usage, according to RT, is actually an οι λ citation from Judg. 15:6, where one major strand of witnesses to the LXX has νυμφιος and the other has γαμβρος. No exception to the use of νυμφευτης for MT חֹתֵן is attributed to Aquila by RT.

[136]See items 147 and 38 in chapter three. Theodotion's agreement with the majority of LXX manuscripts is clear.

[137]See item 149 in chapter three. Since there is no indication in $\mathcal{S}$ as to the extent of the σ′θ′ agreement with the OG or $\mathcal{S}^{txt}$, it cannot be assumed to extend beyond $\mathcal{S}^{txt}$ *nsk* (= OG ενεχεεν) for MT *wyśm*.

Cyr-ed; *tornatum* 𝔄𝔈𝔏^{rv}, Phil-arm)] 𝔖^{txt} ngydt bṭwrnwn] MT mqšh.[138]

25:33 (LXX v.32): α' pr'' (𝔖^{mg})] θ' 'yk šb'yn (𝔖^{mg})] OG om.] 𝔖^{txt} (under ※) (w)šwšnt'$^{(2)}$] MT (w)prḥ$^{(2)}$.[139]

28:15: α' λογιστικου (*b*; cf. α'σ' *dmtṭ'nn'* [*dmtṭknn'* C^{corr}] in 𝔖^{mg})] θ' bdmwt' dhnwn šb'yn (𝔖^{mg})] OG ποικιλτου] 𝔖^{txt} dmptkn'] MT ḥšb.[140]

Evaluation

Unless there is genuine evidence to the contrary, joint α'θ' citations should be taken at face value, as evidence that the given reading occurred in both Aquila and Theodotion. If Aquila based his revision of Exodus on a copy of the Theodotionic text, then the presence of identical readings in the two versions is no surprise. This would happen whenever Aquila saw no need to revise the Theodotionic text or when he neglected to do so.

Over half of the readings for which Aquila and Theodotion are both cited are joint α'θ' readings. Sixteen times the joint α'θ' citation agrees with the OG or with the majority of LXX manuscripts, and thirty-three times there is partial agreement between α'θ' and the OG or the majority of LXX manuscripts. These areas of agreement reveal nothing about the relationship between Aquila and Theodotion, since each could have drawn the readings independently from texts of the OG available to him. The areas of disagreement between α'θ' and the OG or between α'θ' and the majority of LXX manuscripts are more important. While many could

---

[138]See item 150 in chapter three. If, as seems at least possible, 𝔖^{txt} reflects τορνευτην rather then OG τορευτην, then Theodotion probably also had that variant in place of the OG noun.

[139]See item 151 in chapter three. Since 𝔖^{txt} *(w)šwšnt'*$^{(1)}$ represents OG κρινον, to translate MT *(w)prḥ*$^{(1)}$, Theodotion here presumably repeats the OG noun to translate the second occurrence of the Hebrew noun.

[140]See item 152 in chapter three. Theodotion's agreement with the OG is clear. The Syriac form attributed to α'σ' by C^{corr} of 𝔖^{mg} is a closer reflection of λογιστικου than is the form found in the remaining witnesses for 𝔖^{mg}. The latter is presumably a secondary error, perhaps inner-Syriac.

be coincidental, the following are more significant: Exod. 4:25; 16:14; 18:2; 28:37 (LXX v.33) *bis*; 29:18; 30:3; 32:6; 38:17 (LXX 37:15).

There are fifty-four joint α'ϑ' citations that contain simple expansions of the OG. Many of the common readings could be due to coincidence and the fact that the two revisors were each attempting to reflect the MT more accurately. The following readings contain more significant agreements between Aquila and Theodotion: Exod. 3:11; 4:23; 5:23; 21:30, 33; 26:15; 27:13; 32:24; 35:22; 36:2, 21 (MT); 37:26 (MT); 39:41 (MT); 40:2, 6. The remaining sixty-three joint α'ϑ' citations are simple or expanded variants to the OG. Here too, many of the common readings could easily have arisen in the course of independent revision of the OG toward the MT. Those that seem to provide relatively clear evidence of genuine affinity between Aquila and Theodotion include: Exod. 1:18; 2:3; 4:11, 21; 5:7; 10:14; 12:11, 21; 13:16, 20; 14:2, 9, 15; 15:5, 8, 16; 16:10; 20:25 (Ꞩ v.22); 22:27 (LXX v.28); 24:12, 13; 25:7 (LXX v.6)[(2)]; 26:15, 18; 27:4, 6, 19; 28:30 (LXX v.26), 32 (LXX v.28)[(1)]; 29:13, 36, 42; 30:4, 5, 16, 20; 32:1; 33:22; 35:9 (LXX v.8), 11 (LXX v.10), 23, 29; 36:7; 37:17 (LXX 38:14); 38:4 (LXX 38:24), 12 (LXX 37:10); 39:6 (LXX 36:13), 39 (LXX 39:10); 40:20 (LXX v.18).[141]

There are eleven additional readings in which Aquila and Theodotion agree exactly (with the possible omission of an article by Aquila once), even though they are cited separately. Significant agreements between Aquila and Theodotion against the OG occur in Exod. 4:6; 16:14; 25:12 (LXX v.11); 28:4; 29:14; 34:29. Three other readings apparently have similar significance, but the textual evidence or the interpretation of Syriac forms remains uncertain: Exod. 8:10 (LXX v.14); 9:32; 28:25 (MT).

The second main classification in the foregoing lists includes all instances of partial agreement between Theodotion and Aquila. Frequently this partial agreement is in contrast to the OG or the majority of LXX

---

[141]The α'σ'ϑ' reading of Exod. 25:7 (LXX v.6)[(1)] was not included among the significant agreements because the evidence is of doubtful validity. It should be noted that the reading conflicts with normal Theodotionic usage. See the discussion in chapter two, pp. 85-87. The evidence for Exod. 28:32 (LXX v.28)[(2)] is ambiguous. If Theodotion agreed with Aquila on the translation of MT *ṭhr'*, this would provide further evidence for genuine affinity between the two versions.

manuscripts. Among the forty-two readings in which Theodotion appears closer to the OG or to the majority of LXX manuscripts than Aquila does, the following contain significant partial agreements between Theodotion and Aquila against the OG or against many LXX manuscripts: Exod. 5:3, 16; 7:11; 8:25 (LXX v.29); 12:32; 16:16; 19:13(2); 21:7-8; 28:5, 27 (MT); 32:25; 35:11 (LXX v.10), 23, 35. Among the thirty-five readings in which Theodotion does not appear closer to the OG or to the majority of LXX manuscripts, the following contain significant partial agreements between Aquila and Theodotion against the OG or many LXX manuscripts: Exod. 6:12; 13:13; 19:6; 22:8 (LXX v.9); 25:33 (LXX v.32); 28:6; 35:11 (LXX v.10).

The third main classification in the foregoing lists contains all instances of complete lack of agreement between Aquila and Theodotion. There are fifty-one readings in this group. Almost all concern only one or two words.

Finally there are fifteen Theodotionic ομοιως τοις ο'/*'yk šb'yn* readings for which a separate reading from Aquila has been preserved. Five times there is partial agreement between the Aquilan reading and the presumed Theodotionic reading. In two of these cases, Exod. 12:42 (LXX vv.41-42) and 15:16, Theodotion's text may actually have agreed with the revision of the OG found in $\mathfrak{S}^{txt}$ and a few other witnesses. In other words, the text used by Origen and taken up by $\mathfrak{S}^{txt}$ would have been equivalent to Theodotion's revision, but not marked as such. In both cases, there is a significant degree of partial agreement between Aquila and $\mathfrak{S}^{txt}$ against the OG, and hence presumably between Aquila and Theodotion independent of the OG.

While there may be some question about a few of the instances listed above, the majority are significant and provide firm evidence for a genuine affinity between Aquila and Theodotion that is independent of the OG. For the most part, significant agreement exists where Aquila and Theodotion replace an acceptable OG translation of the Hebrew with a different one, where they choose one of several possible equivalents for a Hebrew word or phrase that is not reflected in the OG, or where they differ from the MT in some way that is not a mere repetition of the OG. This last category is rather infrequent.

The evidence summarized justifies the attribution of most or all of the many minor agreements between Aquila and Theodotion to their common affinity independent of the OG. Additional similarities between Aquila and

Theodotion that are not conditioned by the OG include variant forms of a noun or verb not used by the OG, as well as similar or identical constructions with different words where the OG had a variant mode of expression.

VI Aquila's Dependence on Theodotion in Exodus

Some readings partially shared by Theodotion and Aquila are particularly important, because they show that Theodotion's version of Exodus was prior to Aquila's and that Aquila based his version on the Greek text produced by Theodotion rather than on the OG directly. Approximately seventy-five readings seem to show that Theodotion is closer to the OG, or to an earlier revision of the OG, than Aquila is. These readings are not all equally probative. Some involve relatively minor points or conjectural interpretations and would not suffice of themselves for any firm conclusions about Theodotion's relationship to Aquila. Other readings are very instructive. Charts are provided of the most important. In the charts the OG, the revised OG and/or g^{txt} where necessary, Theodotion, Aquila, and the MT are arranged one below the other. Where any version agrees on a word with the one above it, "id" is listed. Where any member lacks a word found in any other, "om" occurs. The resultant pattern indicates clearly that Aquila revises Theodotion's text, itself a revision of the OG, rather than the original OG.

There are also seventeen readings, almost all involving only minor points or single items, that seem to show Aquila closer to the OG than Theodotion is.[1] These readings, discussed briefly at the end of the chapter, provide little solid evidence to conflict with Theodotion's priority to Aquila in Exodus.

---

[1]In several cases, the relevant comparison constitutes only a small part of a longer reading in which Theodotion may otherwise appear closer to the OG than Aqula does.

Evidence for Aquila's Use of the Theodotionic Text

Exod. 5:16:	OG	και	ιδου	οι	παιδες	σου	μεμαστιγωνται	om.
	ϑ′	id.	id.	id.	δουλοι	id.	id.	και
	α′	id.	id.	om.	id.	id.	πεπληγμενοι	id.
	MT	*w-*	*-hnh*	om.	*ʿbdy-*	*-k*	*mkym*	*w-*

OG	om.	αδικησεις	ουν	om.	τον	λαον	σου
ϑ′	η	αμαρτια	om.	εις	id.	id.	id.
α′	om.	id.	om.	om.	om.	λαω	id.
MT	om.	*-ḥṭʾt*	om.	om.	om.	*ʿm-*	*-k*

Theodotion agrees with the OG against Aquila on μεμαστιγωνται. He agrees with Aquila against the OG on δουλοι and on the general interpretation of MT *wḥṭʾt ʿmk*. Aquila omits superfluous elements and uses a participle to represent the MT participle *mkym*, but he never agrees with the OG against Theodotion.

Exod. 7:11:	OG	και	om.	οι	επαοιδοι	των	αιγυπτιων
	ϑ′	καιγε	αυτοι	id.	id.	id.	id.
	α′	id.	id.	om.	κρυφιασται	om.	αιγυπτου
	MT	*gm*	*hm*	om.	*ḥrṭmy*	om.	*mṣrym*

OG	om.	ταις	φαρμακιαις	αυτων	ωσαυτως
ϑ′	εν	id.	φαρμακειαις	id.	id.
α′	id.	om.	ηρεμαιοις	id.	ουτως
MT	*b-*	om.	*-lhṭy-*	*-hm*	*kn*

Aquila and Theodotion agree on καιγε αυτοι for MT *gm hm*, where the OG merely has και. Except for the insertion of εν to represent MT *b-* and a minor itacism, Theodotion agrees with the OG for the remainder of the reading. Aquila, however, differs from the OG completely for the remainder of the reading. He omits superfluous elements and shares the use of εν for MT *b-* with Theodotion. See also Exod. 8:3 (LXX v.7) for a similar but less probative example.

Exod. 7:24:	OG	om.	ωρυξαν	δε	παντες	οι	αιγυπτιοι
	ϑ′	και	id.	om.	id.	id.	id.
	α′	id.	ωρυξεν	om.	πασα	η	αιγυπτος
	MT	*w-*	*-yḥprw*	om.	*kl*	om.	*mṣrym*

OG	κυκλω	του	ποταμου	om.	ωστε	om.	πιειν
θ′	id.	id.	id.	υδωρ	εις	το	id.
α′	κυκλοθεν	id.	ρειθρου	id.	του	om.	id.
MT	*sbybt*	*h-*	*-yʾr*	*mym*	*l-*	om.	*-štwt*

OG	υδωρ	και	ουκ	ηδυναντο
θ′	om.	οτι	id.	id.
α′	om.	id.	id.	id.
MT	om.	*ky*	*lʾ*	*yklw*

a)

OG	πιειν	om.	om.	υδωρ	απο	του	ποταμου
θ′	id.	εκ	του	υδατος	om.	id.	id.
α′	id.	id.	id.	id.	om.	id.	id.
MT	*lštt*	*m-*	om.	*-mymy*	om.	*h-*	*-yʾr*

b)

$\mathcal{S}^{txt}$	*lmštʾ*	om.	*myʾ*	*mn*	om.	*nhrʾ*	om.
θ′	id.	om.	id.	id.	*d-*	id.	om.
α′	om.	*mn*	*myʾ myʾ*	om.	id.	*-rdyʾ*	*lmštʾ*
MT	*lštt*	*m-*	*-mymy*	om.	*h-*	*-yʾr*	om.

The Greek witnesses and $\mathcal{S}^{mg}$ disagree on the readings of Aquila, Symmachus, and Theodotion for the last part of this selection. It was suggested in item 35 of chapter three that $\mathcal{S}^{mg}$ has preserved the proper distinctions, while the Greek witnesses have lost the distinction between the various versions and have apparently attributed Symmachus' version to Aquila and Theodotion as well. For the last part of the selection, then, the Syriac readings have been cited after the Greek ones and are regarded as more probably authentic.

Theodotion retains the initial OG plurals, while Aquila takes MT *mṣrym* as singular and ignores the plural ending on MT *wyḥprw*. Aquila has a new equivalent for MT *sbybt*, perhaps to distinguish it from Hebrew *sbyb*. He has a variant for MT *hyʾr* twice, the second one only indicated in the $\mathcal{S}^{mg}$ citation, and introduces a double expression to represent MT *mymy*, if the Syriac *myʾ myʾ* is correct. Each time Theodotion retains the OG reading. Theodotion and Aquila agree against the OG on their approach to MT *mym lštwt*, though Aquila's version omits one superfluous element. They also agree on και for OG δε (= MT *w-*) and on οτι for OG και (= MT *ky*). Nowhere does Aquila agree with the OG against Theodotion.

Exod. 8:22 (LXX v.26):

OG	om.	τα	γαρ	βδελυγματα	om.	των
$\mathfrak{s}^{txt}$	om.	om.	om.	*ndÿdwt’*	*gyr*	*d-*
ϑ′	*mṭl d-*	*-l-*	om.	*-ṭnpẅt’*	om.	*d-*
α′	id.	om.	om.	*-ṭnpwt’*	om.	id.
MT	*ky*	om.	om.	*twʿbt*	om.	om.

OG	αιγυπτιων	θυσομεν	κυριω	τω	θεω	ημων	εαν
$\mathfrak{s}^{txt}$	*-mṣrÿ’*	*ndbḥ*	*lmry’*	om.	*’lh’*	*dyln*	*’n*
ϑ′	*-mṣryn*	id.	id.	om.	id.	id.	*w-*
α′	id.	*mdbḥynn*	id.	om.	id.	id.	*’n*
MT	*mṣrym*	*nzbḥ*	*lyhwh*	om.	*’lh-*	*-nw*	*hn*

OG	γαρ	θυσωμεν	τα	βδελυγματα	των	αιγυπτιων
$\mathfrak{s}^{txt}$	*gyr*	*ndbḥ*	om.	*ṭnpẅt’*	*d-*	*-mṣrÿ’*
ϑ′	om.	*-dbḥynn*	*l-*	id.	*d-*	*-mṣryn*
α′	om.	*dbḥyn ḥnn*	*l-*	*ṭnpwt’*	id.	id.
MT	om.	*nzbḥ*	*’t*	*twʿbt*	om.	*mṣrym*

OG	εναντιον	om.	αυτων	om.	om.	λιθοβοληθησομεθα	om.
$\mathfrak{s}^{txt}$	*qdmy-*	om.	*-hwn*	om.	om.	*mtrgmynn*	om.
ϑ′	*qdm*	*ʿÿn’*	*dylhwn*	*w-*	*-l’*	*rgmyn*	*ln*
α′	*l-*	id.	id.	id.	id.	*nrgmwn-*	*-n*
MT	*l-*	*-ʿyny-*	*-hm*	*w-*	*-l’*	*ysql-*	*-nw*

Here Theodotion agrees with Aquila against the OG on the treatment of MT *mṣrym* twice. They also share the use of *mṭl d-* (= *οτι) instead of OG γαρ for MT *ky*. In spite of $\mathfrak{s}^{txt}$ *ndÿdwt’* the first time, Theodotion probably retains OG βδελυγματα twice, while Aquila changes it to the singular each time. This is in conformity with the tradition reflected in the MT vocalization. Theodotion apparently retains OG θυσομεν for MT *nzbḥ*(1), while Aquila replaces it with the present tense. The second time MT *nzbḥ* occurs, Theodotion and Aquila both replace OG θυσωμεν with present tense constructions. The differences, if any, in the Greek forms represented by α′ *mdbḥynn*, α′ *dbḥyn ḥnn*, and ϑ′ *dbḥynn* can no longer be recovered.

The reason for Theodotion's unusual treatment of MT *hn* is obscure, but it may be the result of secondary scribal error. Compare item 64 in chapter three for another possible explanation. Aquila's *ʾn* need not imply a knowledge of the OG independent of Theodotion, since it would be the natural correction of the erroneous Theodotionic *w*- for MT *hn*. Aquila and Theodotion both omit OG γαρ(2), which is not supported by the MT. Both Aquila and Theodotion insert *ʿyn*ʾ (= *οφθαλμοι) to represent MT *ʿyny* explicitly. While Theodotion inserts it into the OG phrase, Aquila replaces OG εναντιον with *l*- (=*εις) to reflect MT *l*- more closely. Finally Aquila and Theodotion agree on a new approach to MT *wlʾ ysqlnw*. They differ only in the tense of the active verb that they substitute for the OG passive.

While the pattern is complicated by its preservation only in Syriac, Theodotion clearly occupies a position midway between the OG and Aquila, just as in the preceding three examples.

Exod. 8:25 (LXX v.29):

OG	om.	ειπεν	δε	μωυσης	οδε	εγω
ϑ'	και	id.	om.	μωσης	ιδου	εγω ειμι
α'	id.	id.	om.	id.	id.	id.
MT	*w*-	-*yʾmr*	om.	*mšh*	*hnh*	*ʾnky*

OG	εξελευσομαι	απο	σου	και	ευξομαι	προς
ϑ'	εκπορευομαι	id.	id.	id.	id.	id.
α'	εξερχομαι	παρα	id.	id.	ικετευσω	id.
MT	*ywṣʾ*	*mʿm*-	-*k*	*w*-	-*hʿtrty*	*ʾl*

Theodotion and Aquila agree against the OG especially on the use of εγω ειμι plus the finite verb to represent MT *ʾnky*. They also share και in place of OG δε, a variant spelling for Moses' name, and ιδου rather than OG οδε. Theodotion agrees with the OG against Aquila on απο for MT *mʿm* and on ευξομαι for MT *hʿtrty*. Aquila never agrees with the OG against Theodotion.

Exod. 16:16:

OG	εκαστος	εις	τους	καθηκοντας	om.	γομορ
𝔰txt	*kl ḥd*	*l*-	-*hnwn*	*dzdqyn*	※*lwth*↙	*gwmwr*
ϑ'	*gbrʾ*	id.	om.	-*mʾkwltʾ*	*dylh*	id.
α'	id.	id.	-*pwmʾ*	*dmʾkwltʾ*	id.	*ʾmwr*
MT	*ʾyš*	*l*-	-*py*	*ʾkl*-	-*w*	*ʿmr*

Theodotion revises the rather free OG, but retains the OG equivalent for MT *ʿmr*. Aquila inserts an explicit reflection of MT *py* into the Theodotionic version, but otherwise he agrees with Theodotion against the OG.

Aquila introduces a new equivalent for MT *ʿmr* against the OG and Theodotion, but nowhere does he agree with the OG against Theodotion. In Exod. 16:21 Aquila has a similar translation for MT *kpy ʾklw*, but Theodotion has a rather free rendition. In Exod. 16:18 Theodotion again agrees with the OG on the equivalent for MT *ʿmr*, while Aquila introduces the same variant as here.[2]

Exod. 19:13:					
OG	εκεινοι	αναβησονται	επι	το	ορος
ϑ'	αυτοι	id.	εις	id.	id.
α'	id.	id.	εν	om.	ορει
MT	*hmh*	*yʿlw*	*b-*	om.	*-hr*

Theodotion and Aquila agree on αυτοι in place of OG εκεινοι to represent MT *hmh*. Theodotion replaces OG επι with εις, but retains OG το ορος. Aquila uses εν as a more accurate equivalent for MT *b-*, and therefore has to replace OG ορος with ορει. He omits the article retained by Theodotion, since there is no separate consonantal element in the MT to support it. He has no agreements with the OG against Theodotion.

In the previous phrase in this verse, Aquila and Theodotion replace the OG οταν clause with different prepositional phrases (each introduced by εν to represent MT *b-*).[3] Theodotion's use of τη απελευσει to represent MT *mšk* may have been influenced by OG απελθη. No such influence of the OG can be detected in Aquila's phrase or in the remainder of Theodotion's phrase.

Exod. 21:7-8:					
OG	ουκ	απελευσεται	ωσπερ	αποτρεχουσιν	αι
ϑ'	id.	εξελευσεται	id.	εκπορευονται	οι
α'	id.	id.	ως	εξοδος	των
MT	*lʾ*	*tṣʾ*	*k-*	*-ṣʾt*	*h-*

OG	δουλαι	εαν	μη ευαρεστηση	om.	om.	om.
ϑ'	δουλοι	ει	πονηρα	εστιν	εν	οφθαλμοις
α'	δουλων	εαν	κακισθη	om.	id.	id.
MT	*-ʿbdym*	*ʾm*	*rʿh*	om.	*b-*	*-ʿyny*

[2] Both readings are given in chapter five, p. 236.

[3] The reading is given in chapter five, p. 223.

OG	τω	κυριω	αυτης	ην	ου	καθωμολογησατο	om.
θ'	om.	$\overline{\text{κυ}}$	id.	id.	id.	id.	αυτην
α'	om.	id.	id.	ος	id.	id.	id.
MT	om.	*ʾdny-*	*-h*	*ʾšr*	*lʾ*	*yʿd-*	*-h*

Note that BnquxƐ have αυτω in place of ου in the OG row. Theodotion agrees with Aquila against the OG on εξελευσεται for MT *tṣʾ*, on the insertion of εν οφθαλμοις for MT *bʿyny* and the subsequent change of κυριω to $\overline{\text{κυ}}$, with the omission of the unsupported article, and on the insertion of αυτην after καθωμολογησατο to represent the suffix on MT *yʿdh*. Theodotion agrees with the OG against Aquila on the use of ωσπερ and a finite verb rather than ως plus a noun to represent MT *kṣʾt*. Theodotion does replace OG αποτρεχουσιν with the more accurate εκπορευονται, however, Theodotion also agrees with OG ην against Aquila's ος as an equivalent for MT *ʾšr*.

The only agreement between Aquila and the OG against Theodotion is on the use of εαν rather than ει to represent MT *ʾm*. Aquila's use of εαν could be independent of OG εαν, however, and need not mean that Aquila knew the OG independently of Theodotion. The other elements in this selection have been discussed in earlier chapters.

Exod. 28:1:	OG	om.	ιερατευειν	om.	μοι
	θ'	εις	id.	αυτον	id.
	α'	του	id.	id.	εμοι
	MT	*l-*	*-khn-*	*-w*	*ly*

Exod. 28:3:	OG	εν	η	ιερατευσει	om.	μοι
	θ'	εις	om.	ιερατευειν	αυτον	id.
	α'	του	om.	id.	id.	εμοι
	MT	*l-*	om.	*-khn-*	*-w*	*ly*

These two readings provide additional slight indications of Theodotion's position between the OG and Aquila. Each time Aquila and Theodotion agree on the insertion of αυτον, while Theodotion agrees with OT μοι against Aquila's εμοι. Aquila and Theodotion are also both consistent in their approaches to the two occurrences of the MT phrase, while the OG treatment of the second differs slightly from that of the first.

Exod. 28:5:	OG	και	το	κοκκινον	om.	om.
	θ'	id.	id.	id.	το	διαφορον
	α'	id.	συν	σκωληκος	id.	id.
	MT	*w-*	*-ʾt*	*twlʿt*	*h-*	*-šny*

Theodotion adds το διαφορον to the OG reading, so as to reflect MT *hšny* explicitly, while retaining OG και το κοκκινον to represent MT *wʾt twlʿt*. Aquila agrees with Theodotion's expansion, το διαφορον, but replaces OG and Theodotionic το κοκκινον with συν σκωληκος. Since Theodotion's treatment of MT *hšny* is inconsistent, there is no reason to deny that he introduced το διαφορον here. Aquila adopted it as his normal equivalent of the MT noun, perhaps as a result of its use by Theodotion here, just as he regularly used σκωληκος to represent MT *twlʿt*.

Exod. 28:27 (MT):

OG	om.	om.	om.	om.	om.
LXX^2	εκ	του	κατα	προσωπον	om.
ϑ'	id.	id.	id.	id.	om.
α'	απο	om.	εναντιον	προσωπου	αυτου
MT	*m-*	om.	*-mwl*	*pny-*	*-w*

OG	om.	om.	om.	om.	om.
LXX^2	om.	κατα	την	συμβολην	αυτων
ϑ'	συμφωνως	id.	id.	id.	αυτου
α'	id.	επι	om.	συμβολη	id.
MT	*lʿmt*	om.	om.	*mḥbrt-*	*-w*

Theodotion accepts the reading found in LXX^2 with only two changes, the insertion of συμφωνως before κατα and the substitution of αυτου for αυτων. The phrase συμφωνως κατα thus comes to represent MT *lʿmt* in Theodotion. Aquila provides a more literal reflection of MT *mmwl pnyw* than that common to LXX^2 and Theodotion, and inserts αυτου to represent the suffix which is not reflected in LXX^2 or Theodotion. Aquila agrees with Theodotion on the insertion of συμφωνως, but replaces κατα with επι so that συμφωνως επι represents MT *lʿmt*. This leads him to put the following noun in the dative, while also omitting the superfluous article. Aquila also agrees with Theodotion on the replacement of LXX^2 αυτων with αυτου. Aquila nowhere agrees with LXX^2 against Theodotion, but Theodotion agrees with LXX^2 against Aquila and with Aquila against LXX^2.

Exod. 32:25:

OG	και	ιδων	om.	μωυσης	τον	λαον	οτι
ϑ'	id.	ειδεν	om.	id.	id.	id.	id.
α'	om.	id.	δε	id.	id.	id.	id.
MT	*w-*	*-yrʾ*	om.	*mšh*	*ʾt h-*	*-ʿm*	*ky*

OG	διεσκεδασται	om.	om.	διεσκεδασεν	γαρ
θ'	διεσκεδασμενος	εστιν	οτι	id.	om.
α'	αποπετασμενος	αυτος	id.	απεπετασεν	om.
MT	*prʿ*	*hwʾ*	*ky*	*prʿ-*	om.

OG	αυτους	ααρων	επιχαρμα	τοις
θ'	αυτον	id.	id.	id.
α'	id.	id.	εις ονομα ρυπου	εν
MT	*-h*	*ʾhrn*	*lšmṣh*	*b-*

OG	υπεναντιοις	αυτων
θ'	ανθεστηκοσιν	id.
α'	id.	id.
MT	*-qmy-*	*-hm*

Theodotion agrees with the OG against Aquila on διεσκεδασεν, on επιχαρμα, on τοις rather than εν, and on και against Aquila's unexpected δε. He agrees with Aquila against the OG on ανθεστηκοσιν, on οτι(2), on αυτον, and on ειδεν. His treatment of MT *prʿ hwʾ* is influenced by the OG, while Aquila's is not. Nowhere in this reading does Aquila agree with the OG against Theodotion. This selection is one of the best examples of Theodotion's intermediary relationship between the OG and Aquila.

Exod. 35:11 (LXX v.10):

OG	και	τους	στυλους	om.
θ'	id.	id.	id.	om.
α'	om.	id.	id.	αυτης
MT	om.	*ʾt*	*ʿmdy-*	*-w*

OG	om.	om.	om.	om.
θ'	και	τας	βασεις	αυτης
α'	id.	id.	id.	id.
MT	*w-*	*-ʾt*	*ʾdny-*	*-w*

Theodotion adds a translation of MT *wʾt ʾdnyw* to the OG reading, but he fails to notice that the OG did not translate the suffix on MT *ʿmdyw* either. Aquila agrees with Theodotion's expansion, but also inserts αυτης after OG στυλους and omits the unsupported και that is common to the OG and to Theodotion.

Exod. 35:29:						
OG	εισελθοντα	ποιειν	om.	παντα	τα	εργα
θ'	του	ενεγκαι	εις	id.	id.	id.
α'	id.	ενεγκειν	id.	παν	το	εργον
MT	*l-*	*-hby'*	*l-*	*-kl*	*h-*	*-ml'kh*

Theodotion agrees with the OG against Aquila on the plural translation of the MT singular *kl hml'kh*. He agrees with Aquila on the insertion of εις to represent the preposition in MT *lkl*, and on the replacement of OG εισελθοντα ποιειν with του plus an aorist infinitive of φερειν. They differ only on the form of the infinitive, Theodotion using the Hellenistic ενεγκαι and Aquila the more classical ενεγκειν. Nowhere in this reading does Aquila agree with the OG against Theodotion.

The fifteen examples just presented provide clear evidence that Theodotion's revision of the OG was the basis of Aquila's further revision. Theodotion's agreements with the OG against Aquila show that he knew the OG independently of Aquila. His agreements with Aquila against the OG and the absence of significant contrary agreements between Aquila and the OG against Theodotion show that Aquila knew the OG through Theodotion rather than directly. The best examples from the foregoing group are Exod. 8:25 (LXX v.29); 21:7-8; 32:25; together with Exod. 28:27 (MT), which shows that the OG used by Theodotion and mediated to Aquila had already undergone some revision. Important examples are also found in Exod. 5:16; 7:11; 16:16; 35:11 (LXX v.10); 35:29. The other six examples--Exod. 7:24; 8:22 (LXX v.26); 19:13; 28:1, 3, 5--are also helpful, although they are of themselves somewhat less probative.

Further Evidence for Aquila's Use of the Theodotionic Version

While other readings do not provide such clear evidence for Aquila's dependence on Theodotion, many illustrate the relationship to some degree.

Exod. 2:14:						
OG	μη	om.	ανελειν	με	συ	θελεις
θ'	η	om.	id.	id.	id.	λεγεις
α'	μητι	του	αποκτειναι	id.	id.	id.
MT	*h-*	*-l-*	*-hrg-*	*-ny*	*'th*	*'mr*

OG	ον τροπον	ανειλες	om.	τον	αιγυπτιον
θ'	id.	id.	om.	id.	id.
α'	καθα	απεκτεινας	συν	id.	id.
MT	*k'šr*	*hrgt*	*'t*	*h-*	*-mṣry*

Note that OG μη is replaced by η in AF*Mceg-jrsvxz-c_2Ɇ$, Cyr, and that the plus εχθες/χθες is added before or after OG τον αιγυπτιον in virtually all LXX manuscripts. Theodotion shares λεγεις with Aquila against the OG. Otherwise he agrees with the OG or, in the case of η for μη, with AF*Mceg-jrsvxz-c_2Ɇ$, Cyr against Aquila. Nowhere in this reading does Aquila agree with the OG against Theodotion.

Exod. 5:3:	OG	συναντησει	ημιν	om.	θανατος	η	om.	φονος
	$^{txt}	*nʾrwʿ*	*ln*	om.	*mwtʾ*	*ʾw*	om.	*qṭlʾ*
	θʹ	*npgʿ*	*bn*	om.	id.	id.	om.	*sypʾ* (= ρομφαια)
	αʹ	id.	id.	*b-*	id.	id.	*b-*	*sypʾ* (= μαχαιρα)
	MT	*ypgʿ-*	*-nw*	*b-*	*-dbr*	*ʾw*	*b-*	*-ḥrb*

While $^{mg} does not preserve all the distinctions between the versions (see especially αʹ λοιμος, λιμος, or λοιμου in FM*b*v, where $^{mg} repeats *mwtʾ*), Theodotion apparently agrees with Aquila against the OG on the treatment of MT *ypgʿnw*, and with the OG against Aquila on the failure to reflect the MT prepositions in *bdbr ʾw bḥrb*. There is no evidence of agreement between Aquila and the OG against Theodotion in this reading.

Exod. 5:7:	OG	καθαπερ	εχθες	και	om.	τριτην	ημεραν	αυτοι	πορευεσθωσαν
	θʹ	id.	id.	id.	της	τριτης	om.	id.	id.
	αʹ	καθα	id.	om.	om.	τριτην	om.	id.	id.
	MT	*k-*	*-tml*	om.	om.	*šlšm*	om.	*hm*	*ylkw*

Theodotion agrees with OG καθαπερ against αʹ καθα. He replaces OG και τριτην ημεραν with και της τριτης, to represent MT *šlšm*, while Aquila has simply τριτην. Theodotion's reading omits the superfluous OG ημεραν, but retains the unsupported OG και and introduces an article. The change from accusative case to genitive is interpretational, and would not need to be mentioned except that Aquila's accusative τριτην agrees with the OG against Theodotion's genitive. Aquila omits OG και and has no article. The agreement between Aquila and the OG on the accusative case need not mean that Aquila here knew the OG independently of Theodotion, since Aquila might just as well have chosen the accusative case as more appropriate than Theodotion's genitive.

Exod. 6:1:

OG	εν	γαρ	χειρι	om.	κραταια	εξαποστελει
$\mathfrak{S}^{txt}$	*b-*	om.	*-ʾydʾ*	*gyr*	*ʾḥydtʾ*	*nšdr*
ϑ'	id.	om.	id.	om.	id.	id.
α'	id.	om.	id.	om.	*dmṣyʾ ḥylʾ*	id.
MT	*b-*	om.	*-yd*	om.	*ḥzqh*	*yšlḥ-*

OG	αυτους	και	εν	βραχιονι	υψηλω
$\mathfrak{S}^{txt}$	*ʾnwn*	*w-*	*-b-*	*-drʿʾ*	*rmʾ*
ϑ'	id.	id.	id.	*-ʾydʾ*	*ʾḥydtʾ*
α'	id.	id.	id.	id.	*ḥyltnytʾ*
MT	*-m*	*w-*	*-b-*	*-yd*	*ḥzqh*

Theodotion uses the OG translation of the first MT *byd ḥzqh* for the second as well, and also omits OG γαρ, presumably introducing the clause with οτι to represent MT *ky*. Aquila agrees with Theodotion on the omission of OG γαρ and on the use of εν χειρι for the second MT *byd* as well as for the first. Aquila rejects the OG and Theodotionic treatments of MT *ḥzqh*, however, and substitutes two different but related translations. Perhaps his replacements were forms of ισχυειν and ισχυρος, respectively. According to RT, these words and the related ισχυς are all used by Aquila for forms of MT *ḥzq* (as well as for other MT words, for example, *ʿwz*, *ʿṣm*, *ʾl*), while κραταιος and κραταιουν are used less frequently. Nowhere in this reading does Aquila agree with the OG against Theodotion.

Exod. 9:8:

OG	πληρεις	τας χειρας	om.
ϑ'	*mlʾ*	*ʾydÿʾ*	*dylkwn*
$\mathfrak{S}^{txt}$	*mwlyʾ*	*dʾydʾ*	id.
α'	id.	*dzẅrʾ*	id.
MT	*mlʾ*	*ḥpny-*	*-km*

There are obscurities in this selection. None of the Syriac renditions represents the OG accurately. Theodotion apparently replaced OG πληρεις with a singular noun, the better to represent MT *mlʾ*, while retaining OG τας χειρας unchanged and adding *dylkwn* (= υμων) to represent the suffix on MT *ḥpnykm*. Aquila has a different noun to represent MT *mlʾ* and introduces a more accurate equivalent for MT *ḥpny-* in place of OG and Theodotionic τας χειρας. He puts this new noun in the genitive case. Aquila agrees with Theodotion on the translation of the suffix.

The changes made by $\mathfrak{S}^{txt}$ are not relevant here, since $\mathfrak{S}^{txt}$ does not represent the OG at this point. Hence the agreement between Aquila and $\mathfrak{S}^{txt}$ on *mwly'* to represent MT *ml'* does not mean that Aquila is closer to the OG than Theodotion is. Aquila has no agreements with the OG against Theodotion here.

Exod. 18:5:	OG	και	εξηλθεν	ιοθορ	ο	γαμβρος	μωυση
	θ'	id.	ηλθεν	id.	om.	id.	μωυσει
	α'	id.	id.	ιεθρω	om.	νυμφευτης	id.
	MT	*w-*	*-yb'*	*ytrw*	om.	*ḥtn*	*mšh*

Theodotion and Aquila share ηλθεν, found in all LXX manuscripts except Bfioqru. The replacement of εξηλθεν with ηλθεν may have been due to the pre-Theodotionic revision of the OG. Theodotion and Aquila also agree against the OG on the omission of the article and, if v^{mg} is correct, on the spelling of Moses' name. Aquila's reading is preserved with the OG spelling in $j^{mg}s^{mg}z^{mg}$, but no Theodotionic reading is found in these manuscripts. Theodotion agrees with the OG against Aquila on the noun chosen to translate MT *ḥtn* and on the form of Jethro's name. Aquila's ιεθρω/ιεθρο is a more accurate transliteration of MT *ytrw*. Nowhere in this reading does Aquila agree with the OG against Theodotion.

Exod. 19:18:	OG	δια	το	καταβεβηκεναι
	θ'	id.	id.	καταβηναι
	α'	απο προσωπου	ου	κατεβη
	MT	*mpny*	*'šr*	*yrd*

OG	τον	θεον	επ	αυτο	om.
θ'	om.	om.	id.	id.	$\overline{\kappa\nu}$
α'	om.	om.	id.	αυτου	$\overline{\kappa\varsigma}$
MT	om.	om.	*'ly-*	*-w*	*yhwh*

Theodotion modifies the OG translation of MT *mpny 'šr yrd* only slightly, while Aquila substitutes a more literal translation of the Hebrew. Theodotion and Aquila agree on replacing OG τον θεον with $\overline{\kappa\nu}$/$\overline{\kappa\varsigma}$, and in putting the replacement after the prepositional phrase rather than before it. Aquila's use of $\overline{\kappa\varsigma}$ rather than $\overline{\kappa\nu}$ is due to the different syntax of his new translation for the entire phrase. He also replaces OG and Theodotionic αυτο with αυτου, but he never agrees with the OG against Theodotion in this reading.

Exod. 20:25 (Ꞩ v.22):

OG	om.	το	γαρ	ενχειριδιον	σου
ϑ'	οτι	την	om.	ρομφαιαν	id.
α'	id.	om.	om.	μαχαιραν	id.
MT	*ky*	om.	om.	*ḥrb-*	*-k*

OG	επιβεβληκας	επ	αυτο
ϑ'	id.	id.	id.
α'	εξηρες	id.	id.
MT	*hnpt*	*ʿly-*	*-h*

Theodotion agrees with the OG against Aquila on the use of επιβεβληκας to translate MT *hnpt* and also on the use of an article with the translation for MT *ḥrbk*. He agrees with Aquila against the OG on the use of οτι rather than γαρ to represent MT *ky*. There are no agreements between Aquila and the OG against Theodotion in this reading.

Exod. 28:28 (MT):

OG	om.	om.	om.
LXX^2	και	ου μη	αποσπασης
ϑ'	*w-*	id.	αποσπασθη
α'	και	ου	σαλευθησεται
MT	*w-*	*-lʾ*	*yzḥ*

Theodotion modifies the LXX^2 verb only slightly, while Aquila introduces a new verb and also simplifies the compound negative by the omission of μη. Nowhere in this reading does Aquila agree with the OG against Theodotion.

Exod. 30:13:

OG	και	τουτο	εστιν	ο	δωσουσιν	οσοι	αν
ϑ'	om.	id.	om.	om.	id.	πας	ο
α'	om.	id.	om.	om.	δωσουσι	id.	id.
MT	om.	*zh*	om.	om.	*ytnw*	*kl*	*h-*

OG	παραπορευωνται	om.	την	επισκεψιν
ϑ'	παραπορευομενος	επι	τας	επισκοπας
α'	παρερχομενος	id.	τους	επισκεμμενους
MT	*-ʿbr*	*ʿl*	*h-*	*-pqdym*

Theodotion and Aquila both omit the unsupported OG elements και and εστιν ο. They both replace OG οσοι αν παραπορευωνται with more literal participial constructions, but Theodotion uses a participle from the OG verb while Aquila introduces a new verb. They both insert επι to represent MT *ʿl*, and replace the OG singular equivalent for MT *hpqdym* with different plural equivalents. Aquila has no agreements with the OG against Theodotion in this reading.

Exod. 31:14:						
OG	οτι	αγιον	τουτο	εστιν	κυριου/$\overline{κω}$	υμιν
ϑʹ	id.	id.	om.	id.	om.	id.
αʹ	id.	αγιασμενον	om.	id.	om.	id.
MT	*ky*	*qdš*	om.	*hwʾ*	om.	*lkm*

The OG appears differently in various manuscripts: τουτο is not found in AbcfklmwxyE̸L̸^{r}S̸, and is after εστιν in F^{b}dinpta$_2$b$_2$A̸, while εστιν is itself missing in quC̸^{m}; κυριου of BMa is replaced by $\overline{κω}$, sometimes followed by και or και εν, in many manuscripts; it is omitted in AbchklmnwyE̸S̸.

Theodotion agrees exactly with the shortened OG, but Aquila replaces OG and Theodotionic αγιον with αγιασμενον to represent MT *qdš*. There are no agreements between Aquila and the OG against Theodotion in this reading.

Exod. 35:12 (LXX v.11):					
OG	και	om.	την	κιβωτον	του
ϑʹ	id.	om.	id.	id.	om.
αʹ	om.	συν	το	γλωσσοκομον	om.
MT	om.	*ʾt*	*h-*	*-ʾrn*	om.

OG	μαρτυριου	και	τους	αναφορεις
ϑʹ	om.	id.	id.	id.
αʹ	om.	id.	id.	id.
MT	om.	*w-*	*-ʾt*	*bdy-*

Theodotion and Aquila both omit the unsupported OG του μαρτυριου. While Theodotion otherwise agrees exactly with the OG, Aquila replaces την κιβωτον with συν το γλωσσοκομον to represent MT *ʾt hʾrn* and also omits the initial και (not supported by the MT). Nowhere in this reading does Aquila agree with the OG against Theodotion.

Exod. 35:23:					
OG (=Bafhinqrux,71)	και	παρ	om.	ω	ευρεϑη
FMdegjlpstvza$_2$b$_2$B̸	id.	πας	om.	id.	id.
Abowy	id.	id.	om.	id.	id.
ϑʹ	id.	id.	ανηρ	id.	id.
αʹ	id.	id.	id.	id.	id.
MT	*w-*	*-kl*	*ʾyš*	*ʾšr*	*nmṣʾ*

OG

OG	om.	om.	om.	om.	om.
FM . . .	(om.)	(om.)	om.	om.	om.
Abowy	παρ	αυτω	υακινθος	και	πορφυρα
ϑ′	id.	id.	id.	id.	id.
α′	συν	id.	id.	id.	id.
MT	*ʾt-*	*-w*	*tklt*	*w-*	*-ʾrgmn*

OG	om.	om.	om.	om.
FM . . .	om.	om.	om.	om.
Abowy	και	κοκκινον	om.	και
ϑ′	id.	id.	αλλοιουμενον	id.
α′	id.	σκωληκος	διαφορον	id.
MT	*w-*	*-twlʿt*	*šny*	*w-*

OG	βυσσος	om.	om.	και	δερματα
FM . . .	id.	om.	om.	id.	id.
Abowy	id.	om.	om.	id.	id.
ϑ′	id.	και	αιγεια	id.	id.
α′	id.	id.	id.	id.	id.
MT	*-šš*	*w-*	*-ʿzym*	*w-*	*-ʿrt*

The textual evidence for this selection is quite complex. Further material is found under item 54 in chapter four, where it is suggested that FMdegjlpstvza$_2$b$_2$Ƀ represent a pre-Theodotionic revision of the OG. The precise affinities of Abowy are not clear. For the FMdegjlpstvza$_2$b$_2$Ƀ reading, note that the phrase παρ αυτω is found after βυσσος in $F^{a?}$Megj, before βυσσος in dpt, and in place of βυσσος in F*la$_2$b$_2$Ƀ.

Theodotion and Aquila share the expansions ανηρ, υακινθος και πορφυρα, and και αιγεια against the major LXX strands. They also share πας (for MT *kl*), an early revision of the OG. Theodotion shares the expansion παρ αυτω with a number of LXX manuscripts, while Aquila has the variant συν αυτω. Aquila and Theodotion have different expansions to represent MT *wtwlʿt šny*. Note that Abowy share Theodotion's equivalents for MT *ʾtw tklt wʾrgmn wtwlʿt*, but fail to have his equivalent or any other separate equivalent for MT *šny*.

An apparent variant for ϑ′ αλλοιουμενον (*ṣbyʿtʾ*, "dyed," where *mšgnytʾ* or the like would be more expected) is attributed to Theodotion by 𝔖^{mg}, but this does not affect the evaluation here. Aquila has no agreements with the OG against Theodotion in this reading.

Exod. 35:35:								
OG	om.	om.	om.	om.	om.	om.	om.	om.
θ′	εν	τη	υακινθω	και	εν	τη	πορφυρα	και
α′	id.	om.	id.	id.	om.	om.	id.	om.
MT	*b-*	om.	*-tklt*	*w-*	*-b-*	om.	*-ʾrgmn*	om.

OG	om.	τω	κοκκινω	om.	om.	και	τη	βυσσω
θ′	εν	id.	id.	τω	αλλοιουμενω	id.	id.	id.
α′	id.	om.	σκωληκος	id.	διαφορω	id.	εν	id.
MT	*b-*	om.	*-twlʿt*	*h-*	*-šny*	*w-*	*-b-*	*-šš*

Theodotion inserts εν τη υακινθω και εν τη πορφυρα και εν before OG τω κοκκινω, and τω αλλοιουμενω between it and OG και τη βυσσω. He makes no changes in the OG readings and inserts no preposition before OG τη βυσσω. Aquila omits the unsupported Theodotionic articles before υακινθω and πορφυρα, the unsupported Theodotionic και after πορφυρα, and also the Theodotionic preposition before (τη) πορφυρα. This last omission may have been inadvertent, perhaps due to the omission of the following article. Aquila replaces OG τω κοκκινω (also in Theodotion) with σκωληκος, taking the occasion to omit the unsupported article. Aquila again differs from Theodotion in his expansion to represent MT *hšny*. Finally Aquila replaces τη, found before βυσσω in both the OG and Theodotion's version, with εν, to represent MT *-b-* more literally.

Other readings partially support the placement of Theodotion as an intermediary between the OG and Aquila. There are cases in which Theodotion agrees with the OG, while Aquila has a variant.[4] There are also cases in which neither Theodotion nor Aquila appears closer to the OG, but in which Aquila can be understood as revising Theodotion by omitting superfluous elements or by providing new equivalents for particular Hebrew words.[5] Few, if any, of these readings could be used to prove the hypothesis, but they become more intelligible in its light.

Readings that Conflict with Theodotionic Priority to Aquila

Along with the strong evidence for Aquila's dependence on the

---

[4]E.g., Exod. 7:1 (if jz are correct, rather than v); 35:3; 40:26 (LXX v.24); and perhaps Exod. 36:38 (LXX 37:6).

[5]E.g., Exod. 6:12; 8:18 (LXX v.22); 9:25; 13:13; 17:7; 25:33 (LXX v.32); 28:11; 33:15; 34:9; 35:11 (LXX v.10), 24.

Theodotionic revision of the OG, there are a few readings that appear to contradict this thesis. These readings are all included under the second and third headings in the lists of chapter five. The textual evidence given there is presupposed in the following comments.

Exod. 1:19. Aquila's *(d)yldt'* apparently reflects a participle of OG τικτουσιν (compare the *b* doublet τικτουσαι) to represent MT *ḥywt*, while Theodotion introduces a new finite verb. Both Aquila and Theodotion replace OG γαρ with οτι to represent MT *ky*, and insert pronouns to represent MT *hnh*. If the interpretation of α' *(d)yldt'* is correct, then Aquila either knew the OG here or accidentally replaced Theodotion's verb with the participle from the OG verb. The latter explanation is not too convincing, and so this example remains a problem.

Exod. 5:7. The partial agreement between Aquila's τριτην and OG και τριτην ημεραν for MT *šlšm* was discussed earlier in this chapter. Their agreement on the accusative case against Theodotion's genitive (και της τριτης) is not very impressive, especially when it is noted that Theodotion shares the unsupported conjunction και with the OG against Aquila and that he also has another agreement with the OG against Aquila in the same clause.

Exod. 6:23. The corrupt Syriac form *'nmyddb*, attributed to Theodotion for MT *'myndb*, could easily be due to secondary scribal error. Even if it had been present in the Theodotionic text available to Aquila, comparison with the MT would have enabled him to restore the correct Greek equivalent.

Exod. 7:1. The attribution of ιδε κατεστησα σε to σ'θ' by v^{mg}, rather than just to σ' (so $j^{mg}z^{mg}$), may be erroneous. There is no reason why Theodotion should replace OG δεδωκα with κατεστησα to represent MT *ntty-*. If he did so, Aquila would naturally replace κατεστησα with δεδωκα, whether he knew the OG or not.

Exod. 8:22 (LXX v.26). Theodotion's unexpected replacement of OG εαν ($\mathcal{S}^{txt}$ *'n*) with *w-* to represent MT *hn* has been discussed earlier in this chapter, as well as in item 64 in chapter three. While puzzling, the variant may have been present in the Theodotionic text available to Aquila. If so, a replacement with ει or εαν (Syriac *'n* can equal either one) would naturally be expected. Since Theodotion is otherwise closer to the OG than Aquila is in this verse, the minor agreement between Aquila and the OG is of little significance, and should not be regarded as a sign that Aquila had some knowledge of the OG independently of Theodotion.

Exod. 12:42. Since the Theodotionic reading has suffered major corruption, Aquila's agreement with OG η νυξ--as reflected in $\mathcal{S}^{txt}$ *lly*ʾ--for MT *hlylh*, against Theodotion's *llly*ʾ, is of little importance. The Greek reading represented by ϑ' *llly*ʾ (perhaps *εις νυκτα or *τω νυκτι) could be due to the secondary corruption rather than to Theodotion himself. If it were present in the Theodotionic text available to Aquila, he would be expected to replace it with η νυξ anyway.

Exod. 14:2:	OG	ενωπιον	αυτων	στρατοπεδευσεις
	$\mathcal{S}^{txt}$	*qdmy-*	*-hwn*	*tšr*ʾ
	ϑ'	*qdmw-*	*-hy*	*tšrwn*
	α'	*tryṣ*ʾ*yt lqwbl-*	*-h*	*tšr*ʾ
	MT	*nkḥ-*	*-w*	*tḥnw*

Theodotion apparently agrees with OG ενωπιον against Aquila, while Aquila and Theodotion both replace OG αυτων with a singular pronoun. Theodotion pluralizes OG στρατοπεδευσεις to represent the plural MT verb, but Aquila has the singular with the OG. The unexpected singular verb in Aquila, in opposition to the MT, may be due to scribal error in the transmission of the Aquilan version, perhaps under the influence of the OG column in the hexapla. If it is a genuine Aquilan reading, it is hard to deny that the Greek text used by Aquila agreed with the OG verb against Theodotion here. Perhaps Theodotion's plural verb is due to a slight further revision toward the MT, although there is very little evidence for such a secondary revision of the Theodotionic material itself.

Exod. 20:24 ($\mathcal{S}$ v.21). Theodotion's *mn* ʾ*dmt*ʾ retains the structure of OG εκ γης (= $\mathcal{S}^{txt}$ *mn* ʾ*r*ʿʾ), but substitutes a new noun. Aquila rejects the periphrastic structure, not supported by MT ʾ*dmh*, but apparently uses the noun found in the OG. This partial agreement between Aquila and the OG independently of Theodotion could mean that Aquila knew the OG directly here, but it could as easily be due to an independent revision of Theodotion's reading by Aquila.

Exod. 21:7-8. The agreement between Aquila and the OG on εαν against Theodotion's ει, to represent MT ʾ*m*, was discussed earlier in this chapter. The point is too minor to serve as proof that Aquila knew the OG independently of Theodotion here, especially in view of the other clear indications of Theodotionic priority to Aquila and the partial agreement with him in this verse.

Exod. 28:25 (MT). Theodotion agrees with LXX^2 on the translation of MT *ʾl mwl pnyw*, except that he has αυτης for the suffix rather than LXX^2 αυτου. Aquila's revision departs from LXX^2 considerably but agrees on the use of αυτου to represent the suffix. In chapter two, item 23 and fn. 46, it was suggested that Aquila's use of αυτου might be independent of LXX^2. The pronoun may have referred to Aquila's presumed antecedent, του επενδυματος, rather than LXX^2 and Theodotionic της επωμιδος, for MT *hʾpd*. Theodotion's replacement of LXX^2 αυτου with αυτης would have made the LXX^2 pronoun conform with its proper antecedent, της επωμιδος. LXX^2 may have misinterpreted the suffix on MT *pnyw* as referring to Aaron, rather than to the ephod, but this is less faithful to the Hebrew text, since Aaron is last mentioned in v. 12.

Exod. 28:26 (MT). While LXX^2 and Aquila both have θησεις to represent MT *(w)śmt*, Theodotion has the unexpected variant δωσεις. In item 71 of chapter three, it was suggested that Theodotion's variant was an inadvertent one, due to the sequence of δωσεις forms in the immediate context. If the Theodotionic variant were present in the Greek text used by Aquila, he would be expected to replace it with θησεις to represent the MT verb. There is no reason to conclude that Aquila knew LXX^2 independently of Theodotion here.

Exod. 29:24. The interpretations underlying majority αυτους (= α' *ʾnwn*) and the variant αυτα (= σ'θ' *ʾnyn*) were explained in footnote 116 in chapter five. Since neither interpretation is self-evidently correct, Theodotion could have replaced majority αυτους with αυτα, and then Aquila could have replaced αυτα with αυτους without knowing that it was the reading of most LXX manuscripts. This set of variants cannot be used to prove that Aquila knew the OG independently of Theodotion.

Exod. 29:41. The interpretation of these variants was discussed in footnote 117 in chapter five. As in the previous example, Aquila's apparent agreement with the OG against Theodotion could be coincidental, that is, independent of the OG and the result of a rejection of Theodotion's reading. It cannot be used to prove that Aquila knew the OG independently of Theodotion.

Exod. 32:6. Apparently Aquila has the plural of the OG singular verb, while Theodotion has a different verb. The Greek verb αναβιβαζειν is the most accurate translation of the MT verb *ʿlh* (Hiphil). The RT index lists several other instances of this correspondence in Aquila, as well as many instances of the related αναβαινειν used for MT *ʿlh* (Qal). If Theodotion had replaced the OG singular with the plural of a somewhat less accurate verb (perhaps προσφερειν or αναφερειν--compare x and ck[a]), Aquila would have been expected to replace it with the plural of αναβιβαζειν.

Exod. 32:18. Aquila retains the unsupported OG αλλα against Theodotion and fails to reflect either Theodotion's *ʾyty d-* (= *ειμι) after OG εγω (to represent MT *ʾnky*) or the unsupported Theodotionic expansion *dqrbʾ*, presumably based on the previous verse. If *dqrbʾ* were present in the text used by Aquila, he would be expected to omit it. The omission of Theodotionic ειμι is less expected, since Aquila elsewhere agrees with Theodotion on the use of εγω ειμι to represent MT *ʾnky*. Perhaps its omission is due to scribal error in the transmission of Aquila's text. The presence of OG αλλα in Aquila, but not in Theodotion, must mean that the Greek text available to Aquila also had OG αλλα. Perhaps its omission in Theodotion's text is another trace of the hypothetical minor revision of the Theodotionic material after Aquila had made use of it. Another possible explanation is offered in fn. 48 in chapter one. This set of readings is clearly in opposition to the main hypothesis, and its two important items cannot be brushed aside.

Exod. 35:24. Here Aquila agrees with the OG in using αφαιρεμα to represent MT *trwmh*, while Theodotion has the variant *ršytʾ* (= *απαρχη). According to RT, αφαιρεμα is Aquila's only equivalent for MT *trwmh*. Four citations are given: Exod. 25:2; 35:24; 2 Sam. 1:21; Prov. 29:4, the last an α'θ' citation. RT lists no instances of απαρχη in Aquila. Both αφαιρεμα and απαρχη are used fairly often by the OG for MT *trwmh*. There are two places in Exodus where Theodotion's equivalent for MT *trwmh* is preserved--here and in Exod. 25:2. In the latter verse Theodotion replaces the OG plural απαρχας with the corresponding singular, while Aquila has αφαιρεμα. Since RT lists no instances of απαρχη in Aquila, it is not known whether Aquila avoided using it altogether for some reason or whether he used it to represent some other MT word, perhaps MT *tnwph* which is occasionally represented by both απαρχη and αφαιρεμα in the OG and for which no Aquilan equivalent is noted by RT.

The evidence is clear that Theodotion, presumably influenced by one OG pattern of usage, employed απαρχη to represent MT *trwmh*. Aquila, however, used αφαιρεμα, thus putting himself in conformity with another OG pattern of usage. Since Aquila sometimes introduced words not found anywhere in the OG, it is possible that his choice of αφαιρεμα was totally independent of the OG and that he found Theodotion's απαρχη representing MT *trwmh* everywhere it appeared. The α'θ' reading of Prov. 29:4 (cited from Nobil. by Field) suggests another more likely possibility. Theodotion may sometimes have followed the other OG pattern, and thus have retained or, as in Prov. 29:4, introduced αφαιρεμα to represent MT *trwmh*. Aquila, finding both equivalents used in his presumably Theodotionic Greek text, decided to use αφαιρεμα exclusively. While these suggestions may be too ingenious to be adopted, they indicate that this reading does not prove that Aquila knew the OG independently of Theodotion here, though the latter alternative cannot be excluded.

Exod. 39:15 (LXX 36:22). If $\mathcal{S}^{mg}$ can be trusted, Theodotion replaces OG εμπλοκιου with a different noun in the genitive (perhaps *αλυσεως), while Aquila uses an adjective whose Syriac equivalent is related to the $\mathcal{S}^{txt}$ reflection of the OG. However, α'σ' βροχωτον for MT *'bt* in Exod. 28:14 leads one to expect Aquila to use a similar form here, especially since Syriac *gdyl'* could easily represent Greek βροχωτος. The apparent similarity here between Aquila and the OG is probably illusory.

All the cases in which Aquila appears to have known the OG independently of Theodotion in Exodus are included among the preceding seventeen examples. At best, only six of the examples were found to have Aquilan agreements with the OG against Theodotion that are at all significant.[6] Even here the agreements need not all imply that Aquila knew the OG rather than Theodotion's revision. All seventeen examples together are much less impressive than the more extensive, firm evidence that Aquila knew Theodotion's version and used it as the basis for his further revisional activity.

---

[6] Exod. 1:19; 14:2; 20:24 ($\mathcal{S}$ v.21); 32:6, 18; 35:24.

VII The Relationship Between Theodotion in Exodus and the KAIΓE Recension Elsewhere

The Theodotionic material in Exodus constitutes a systematic revision of the OG or, at times, of a revised form of the OG to reflect the present MT. This revision was prior to Aquila, and was known and used by him as the basis of his further revisional activity. The Theodotionic revision in Exodus thus occupies a position analogous to that of Barthélemy's KAIΓE recension in the Minor Prophets and in Samuel-Kings, even though the Hebrew text presupposed by the KAIΓE recension in those books differs significantly from the present MT.[1] This merely means that the Pentateuchal text preserved in the Masoretic recension was also available to the KAIΓE revisor(s), while the texts of the Former and Latter Prophets were still subject to further recensional activity.[2]

This chapter examines separately the characteristics or distinctive features of the KAIΓE recension proposed by Barthélemy,[3] as well as additional KAIΓE features suggested by Shenkel.[4] The purpose of the examination is to determine how applicable these features are to the Theodotionic material in Exodus and thus to establish whether Theodotion in Exodus and KAIΓE in Samuel-Kings and in the Minor Prophets form a single unified recension.

---

[1]For Aquila's dependence on KAIΓE in the Minor Prophets, see *DA*, pp. 246-252.

[2]See p. 163.

[3]*DA*, pp. 31-87.

[4]J. D. Shenkel, *Chronology and Recensional Development in the Greek Text of Kings* (Cambridge, 1968), pp. 13-18, 113-116. He also pointed out (pp. 12-13, and n. 45, p. 127) that many of Barthélemy's criteria are actually drawn from H. St.J. Thackeray, *The Septuagint in Jewish Worship* (London, 1921), where they are arranged in tables on pp. 114-115.

Characteristics of the KAIΓE Recension Identified by Barthélemy

The use of καιγε to represent MT *gm* is the primary feature of the KAIΓE recension, from which the recension takes its name. The usage is retained by Aquila.[5] In Exodus, MT *gm* and *wgm* occur forty times.[6] Thirty-five times no reading is cited from Theodotion or Aquila in B-McL, although in Exod. 12:32 F^b has καιγε in place of OG και to represent MT $gm^{(1)}$.

For the remaining five occurrences of MT *gm* or *wgm*, the following hexaplaric readings are preserved:

Exod. 3:9: MT *wgm*] OG καγω/και εγω] α′ καιγε, σ′ και, θ′ ομοιως τοις ο′ (vz and, with ο′ for θ′, j).
Exod. 4:10: MG $gm^{(3)}$] OG ουδε] α′ καιγε (vz).
Exod. 7:11: MT $gm^{(2)}$] OG και] α′ καιγε, σ′ και, θ′ καιγε (vz and, with no names for the σ′ and θ′ readings, j).
Exod. 18:18: MT $gm^{(2)}$] OG και] $\not{s}^{txt}$ *w*-] α′σ′θ′ *w*- ($\not{s}^{mg}$).
Exod. 19:22: MT *wgm*] OG και] α′ και (v).

Both Aquila and Theodotion sometimes introduce καιγε to represent MT *gm/wgm*, but not always. The inconsistency could be due to inadvertence. It is also possible that καιγε was present in the versions of Theodotion and/or Aquila, but that the scribe who cited the readings overlooked it while concentrating on other aspects of the readings in question.[7]

Both KAIΓE and Aquila use ανηρ rather than OG εκαστος to translate MT *ʾyš*, even when the Hebrew word is used idiomatically to mean "each."[8] The MT noun *ʾyš* occurs eighty-three times in Exodus.[9] It is used in a

---

[5]*DA*, pp. 31-47.

[6]MT *gm*: Exod. 1:10; 4:9 *ter*, 10; 5:14 *bis*; 7:11 *bis*, 23; 8:28; 10:24, 25; 11:3; 12:31 *bis*, 32 *ter*; 18:18 *bis*; 33:17; 34:3. MT *wgm*: Exod. 2:19; 3:9; 4:14; 5:2; 6:4, 5; 8:17; 10:26; 12:38, 39; 18:23; 19:9, 22; 21:29, 35; 33:12; 34:3.

[7]Barthélemy relates the use of καιγε to translate MT *gm/wgm* with the rabbinic exegesis of *gm* as an inclusive particle (*DA*, p. 31) and observes that this exegesis was more commonly accepted than Akiba's similar exegesis of the accusative particle *ʾt* (*DA*, pp. 11-12).

[8]*DA*, pp. 48-54.

[9]MT *ʾyš*: Exod. 1:1; 2:1, 11 *bis*, 12, 19; 4:10; 7:12; 10:23 *bis*;

distributive sense (= "each") approximately thirty-three times,[10] in an indefinite sense (= "someone, anyone") approximately twenty-six times,[11] and with MT *kl* (= "everyone") seven times.[12] The remaining seventeen times it has various other uses.

The OG has ανηρ for MT *ʾyš* only five times,[13] but has εκαστος for MT *ʾyš* twenty-four times[14] and τις for MT *ʾyš* seventeen times.[15] The latter correspondence occurs twice more in the majority of LXX manuscripts.[16]

Equivalents from Theodotion and/or Aquila to represent MT *ʾyš* are preserved only eight times in Exodus:

4:10: MT *lʾ ʾyš dbrym*] OG ουχ ικανος] α' ουκ ανηρ ρηματων σ'

11:2; 12:3, 4, 22, 44; 15:3; 16:15, 16 *bis*, 18, 19, 21, 29 *bis*; 18:7, 16; 19:13; 21:7, 12, 14, 16, 18, 20, 26, 28, 29, 33 *bis*, 35, 37; 22:4, 6, 9, 13, 15; 25:2, 20; 28:21; 30:12, 33, 38; 32:27 *quater*, 28, 29; 33:4, 8, 10, 11; 34:3, 24; 35:21, 22, 23, 29; 36:1, 2, 4 *bis*, 6; 37:9; 39:14. MT *wʾyš*: Exod. 34:3. MT *hʾyš*: Exod. 2:20, 21; 11:3; 22:6; 32:1, 23. MT *lʾyš*: Exod. 2:14. MT *lmʾyš*: Exod. 11:7.

[10] Exod. 1:1, 11 *bis*; 7:12; 10:23 *bis*; 11:2; 12:3, 4, 22; 16:15, 16 *bis*, 18, 21, 29a; 18:7, 16 (?); 25:20; 28:21; 30:12; 32:27 *quater*, 29; 33:4, 8, 10; 36:4 *bis*; 37:9; 39:14.

[11] Exod. 16:19, 29b; 21:7, 12, 14, 16, 18, 20, 26, 28, 29, 33 *bis*, 35, 37; 22:4, 6, 9, 13, 15; 30:33, 38; 34:3 *bis*, 24; 36:6.

[12] Exod. 25:2; 35:21, 22, 23, 29; 36:1, 2.

[13] Exod. 21:28, 29; 32:28 (ανδρας); 35:29; 36:6. Compare OG ανδρες for MT *ʾnšym* in Exod. 2:13; 17:9; 18:21 *bis*, 25; 21:18, 22; 22:31 (MT v. 30); 35:22.

[14] Exod. 1:1; 7:12; 11:2; 12:3, 4, 22; 16:16 *bis*, 18, 21 (om. B), 29; 18:16 (OG εκαστον = MT *byn ʾyš wbyn rʿhw*); 28:21; 30:12; 32:27 *quater* (the phrase with the third is omitted by haplography in B), 29; 33:8, 10; 35:21 (OG εκαστος = MT *kl ʾyš*); 36:4 (OG εκαστος = MT *ʾyš ʾyš*), 21 (MT 39:14).

[15] OG τις = MT *ʾyš* in Exod. 2:1, 11; 21:7, 12, 14, 17 (MT v.16), 20, 26, 33, 35; 22:1 (MT 21:37), 5 (MT v.4), 7 (MT v.6), 10 (MT v.9), 14 (MT v.13), 16 (MT v.15); 33:11.

[16] MT *ʾyš* is represented by τις in all but Bb for Exod. 12:44 and in all but Babcfmqub$_2$ȻS̶ and F* for Exod. 21:18.

ουκ ευλαλος (Mjvzc$_2$) ‖ F$^{b\ mg}$ ουκ ανηρ λογιος.

16:16: MT *ʾyš*(1) ‖ OG εκαστος ‖ 𝔖^{txt} *kl ḥd* ‖ α′ *gbrʾ*, σ′ *kl ḥd*, ϑ′ *gbrʾ* (𝔖^{mg}).

21:7: MT *ʾyš* ‖ OG τις ‖ α′ ανηρ (vz; cf. j^{mg}s^{mg}) ‖ α′ *gbrʾ* (𝔖^{mg}) ‖ F$^{b\ mg}$ τις.

21:18: MT *ʾyš* ‖ Babcfmqub$_2$𝔈𝔖^{txt} om. ‖ AF^{I}Mdeh-lnoprstv-a$_2$𝔄(+ *ex eis*)ℭ^{m}𝔏^{r}, Eus, Cyr, Spec (+ *ex his*) τις ‖ α′σ′ϑ′ *ʾnš* (𝔖^{mg}) ‖ F* ο εις ‖ 𝔅 *unus eorum* ‖ F^{b} ανηρ.

21:33: MT *ʾyš*(2) ‖ OG om. ‖ ac τις ‖ α′ϑ′ *ʾnš* (𝔖^{txt}).

30:38: MT *ʾyš* ‖ OG om. ‖ F$^{c?}$cms^{mg}z^{mg}𝔄 (and out of place in egj) ανηρ ‖ α′ϑ′※ ανηρ, σ′ α̅ν̅ο̅ς̅ (v) ‖ α′ϑ′ *gbrʾ* (𝔖^{txt}).

35:22: MT *wkl ʾyš* ‖ OG και παντες (om F^{b}nx𝔏^{r}; + οι ανδρες c𝔄) ‖ 𝔖^{txt} *wklhwn* ※ α′ϑ′ *g̈brʾ*↙.

35:23: MT *ʾyš* ‖ OG om. ‖ ck𝔄 ανηρ ‖ ϑ′ ανηρ, α′ ανηρ, σ′ ανηρ (svz) ‖ α′ϑ′ *gbrʾ* (𝔖^{txt}).

Once, in Exod. 16:16, Aquila and Theodotion replace OG εκαστος with Syriac *gbrʾ* (= *ανηρ). This is a perfect example of the KAIΓE and Aquilan characteristic as described by Barthélemy. Symmachus does not follow the two revisions on this point. Twice, once opposed by Symmachus (Exod. 30:38) and once joined by him (Exod. 35:23), Aquila and Theodotion agree on ανηρ/*gbrʾ* to represent MT *ʾyš*, where the latter was not reflected in the OG. Because the OG is plural in Exod. 35:22, Aquila and Theodotion both have *g̈brʾ* (= *οι ανδρες) to represent MT *ʾyš*, again not represented in the OG. Two additional instances of this usage are attributed to Aquila in Exod. 4:10 and 21:7, each time replacing a variant rendition in the OG and with no Theodotionic reading cited. These examples are all in agreement with expected KAIΓE and Aquilan usage.

Twice (Exod. 21:18, 33), however, both Aquila and Theodotion, joined once by Symmachus, use Syriac *ʾnš* (= *τις) rather than *gbrʾ*/ανηρ to represent MT *ʾyš*. The first time, α′σ′ϑ′ merely retain a revision of the OG that is present in most LXX witnesses. The second time, α′ϑ′ follow the OG usage of the immediate context and insert Syriac *ʾnš* (= *τις) to represent MT *ʾyš*(2), which is not reflected in the OG.[17] These two deviations from the normal KAIΓE pattern, common to Aquila and Theodotion, and in conformity with one strand of OG usage, were deliberately allowed by

[17] See the discussion under item 30 in chapter four.

Theodotion; the second was introduced by him. Aquila's retention of them may have been inadvertent rather than deliberate, however (compare Aquila's rejection of OG τις in Exod. 21:7 and also F^b ανηρ in Exod. 21:18).[18]

There are ten more places in Exodus where one or more witnesses preserve a form of ανηρ to represent MT *'yš*.[19] These may all be traces of the KAIΓE/Theodotionic revision and its general tendency to use ανηρ for MT *'yš*.

The use of επανωθεν or απανωθεν, rather than απο or επανω, to translate MT *m'l* (מֵעַל) is a development within the Palestinian or KAIΓE recension. It becomes widespread in some books, but is apparently not so regular as the use of καιγε and the avoidance of εκαστος for MT *'yš*.[20] That is the evaluation given by Barthélemy to his third proposed KAIΓE characteristic. Since it is really a tendency rather than a genuine characteristic, it is not surprising that there is no evidence of its use in Exodus by Theodotion or by anyone else.[21]

---

[18]With reference to this failure to use ανηρ/*gbr'* as the equivalent for MT *'yš* in Exod. 21:18, 33, attention is drawn to Barthelemy's interesting comments on MT *'yš* in rabbinic exegesis. In general, laws and statements concerning *'yš* were said to refer only to male persons (*DA*, p. 53, with a supporting citation from the *Mekhilta* concerning Exod. 12:4). It was at Exod. 21:18, according to the *Mekhilta* as cited by Barthélemy (*DA*, p. 54), that R. Ishmael and his disciples R. Josiah and R. Jonathan found the law difficult to interpret according to the narrow exegesis of *'yš*. Does such difficulty account for the retention or introduction of τις by Theodotion and Aquila in this verse and in v.33?

[19]Exod. 2:11, 14, 20, 21; 15:3; 32:1, 23; 33:4; 36:1; 38:8 (LXX 37:9).

[20]*DA*, pp. 54-59.

[21]The compound preposition occurs nine times in Exodus, five times governing a noun (Exod. 3:5; 25:22; 28:28; 39:21; 40:36) and four times with a pronominal suffix (Exod. 10:17, 28; 18:22; 33:5). Apart from OG εκ in Exod. 3:5 and OG ανωθεν in Exod. 25:22 (LXX v.21), the constant translation in the OG or in supplements to the OG is απο. There is no evidence for επανωθεν or απανωθεν in any LXX witnesses. The only Theodotionic reading is in Exod. 28:28 (MT), where θ' *mn* reflects απο of

The KAIΓE recension extends the OG translation of MT *mṣbh* with στηλη, and uses the verb στηλουν rather than ισταναι and derivatives to translate MT verbs from the root *nṣb-yṣb*.[22] There is no evidence bearing on this practice in the Theodotionic material that has survived for Exodus.[23]

While the OG used σαλπιγξ to represent both MT words for trumpet (*šwpr* and *ḥṣṣrh*), the KAIΓE recension restricted σαλπιγξ to MT *ḥṣṣrh* and introduced κερατινη to represent MT *šwpr*.[24] There is no evidence for Theodotionic practice in Exodus on this point either. The noun *ḥṣṣrh* never occurs in the MT for Exodus, while the noun *šwpr* occurs only three times.[25] Each time the OG equivalent is σαλπιγξ, with no significant variants and no hexaplaric readings recorded.[26]

LXX². Note that there is no evidence in B-McL or in Field of a σ'θ' citation for Exod. 39:21 (referred to by Barthélemy, *DA*, p. 57).

Note further that Barthélemy's KAIΓE scroll of the Minor Prophets overlaps MT *m‘lyk* in Zech. 3:4, and has απο σου in agreement with Ziegler's Lucianic witnesses against the OG omission. This is noted in *DA*, p. 199. There is no other occurrence of the compound Hebrew preposition in those parts of the MT represented by the extant fragments of the scroll.

[22] *DA*, pp. 59-60; but note the exception in 2 Sam. 21:5: MT *mhtyṣb* I majority recension (= KAIΓE) του μη εσταναι αυτον I boc_2e_2 του μη αντικαθιστασθαι (αντικαθησασθαι o; καθιστασθαι αυτον b'). This exception is included in Barthélemy's list on p. 100, and is discussed by him on pp. 108-109.

[23] The noun *mṣbh* occurs three times in the MT for Exodus, twice translated by OG στηλη (Exod. 23:24; 34:13) and once by OG λιθος (Exod. 24:4). There are fourteen occurrences of the verb *nṣb-yṣb* in Exodus: 2:4; 5:20; 7:15; 8:16; 9:13; 14:13; 15:8; 17:9; 18:14; 19:17; 33:8, 21; 34:2, 5. The OG equivalents vary, but nowhere does στηλουν occur in any witness. There are no Theodotionic or Aquilan readings cited at any of these points. See *DA*, p. 199, which notes that there is no positive evidence for this usage in the KAIΓE scroll of the Minor Prophets either.

[24] *DA*, pp. 60-63. This usage was retained by Symmachus as well as Aquila.

[25] Exod. 19:16, 19; 20:18.

[26] One instance of κερατινη replacing OG σαλπιγξ for MT *šwpr* is preserved in the KAIΓE scroll of the Minor Prophets at Zeph. 1:16. See *DA*, p.200.

The KAIΓE recension of Samuel-Kings systematically eliminated the rather frequent OG occurrences of the historical present to represent the MT converted imperfect.[27] Since the OG for Exodus does not normally use the historical present for the MT converted imperfect but rather the imperfect or the aorist, and since most of the Theodotionic readings are preserved in Syriac, where no distinction is made between Greek aorists and imperfects, there is no clear evidence for Theodotion's practice in this matter. Nowhere is a present tense (Greek or Syriac) or even a Greek imperfect tense attributed to him as a translation for an MT converted imperfect.[28]

The KAIΓE recension underlined the a-temporal character of MT *ʾyn* by translating it with ουκ εστιν in the midst of a series of aorist verbs. This practice is followed by Aquila, but not by Symmachus.[29] The particle of negation, *ʾyn*, occurs twenty-two times in the MT for Exodus.[30] Readings from Theodotion, Aquila, and Symmachus are cited for only three of these occurrences, twice (Exod. 32:18 *bis*) when the particle is followed by a noun (and hence is used in place of a verb) and once (Exod. 33:15) when the particle is followed by a noun and participle (and hence functions as a simple negative). All three are preserved only in Syriac, and the relevant texts are given in the seventh reading of chapter one and in item 97 of chapter three.

In Exod. 32:18, all three versions preserve OG ουκ εστιν for MT *ʾyn*. Theodotion and Aquila replace OG ουδε with *wlʾ ʾytwhy* (= *και ουκ εστιν) to represent MT *wʾyn* further along in the same verse, while Symmachus has only *wlʾ* (perhaps = *και ουκ). Thus Theodotion and Aquila bring consistency into the translation of the entire verse, but their uses of ουκ εστιν are not within a sequence of aorist verbs and hence do not fit into the special category described by Barthélemy.

---

[27] *DA*, pp. 63-65.

[28] *DA*, p. 200, notes that the KAIΓE scroll for the Minor Prophets similarly cannot eliminate OG historical presents, since there are none in the corresponding sections of the OG.

[29] *DA*, pp. 65-68.

[30] Exod. 2:12; 3:2; 5:10, 11, 16; 8:6, 17; 9:14; 12:30 *bis*; 14:11; 17;1, 7; 21:11; 22:1, 2, 9, 13; 32:18 *bis*, 32; 33:15. Three occurrences are with suffixes (Exod. 3:2; 5:10; 8:17), while the rest are without suffixes.

In Exod. 33:15, α′ and σ′θ′ provide much more exact translations of MT *'m 'yn pnyk hlkym* than the OG does. The only difference between σ′θ′ and α′ is that the latter violates Greek usage to represent the plural number of the MT noun and participle. All agree with the OG in having a simple negative to represent MT *'yn*. The Syriac form (*l'*) of α′ and σ′θ′ could represent either μη with the OG or ου. In any case, this example does not fit into Barthélemy's special category either, since the clause is not found within a series of aorist verbs. Once again a characteristic of the KAIΓE recension delineated by Barthélemy is neither confirmed nor denied by the extant Theodotionic material in Exodus.[31]

The KAIΓE recension uses εγω ειμι rather than εγω to represent MT *'nky* (as opposed to simple *'ny*), and regards the phrase as a unit that can be used as the subject of a finite verb.[32] Theodotion's adherence to this striking usage in Exodus, and Aquila's similar tendency, are discussed thoroughly under item 4 of the fourth reading in chapter one. Theodotion and Aquila clearly know and accept this characteristic usage.[33]

The KAIΓE recension replaces OG εις απαντησιν with εις συναντησιν in Judges and with εις απαντην in Samuel-Kings to represent MT *lqr't*.[34] The MT expression occurs seven times in Exodus, with a suffix in Exod. 4:14; 5:20; 7:15; 14:27 and followed by a noun in Exod. 4:27; 18:7; 19:17. The

---

[31]Barthélemy notes one instance in which the KAIΓE scroll of the Minor Prophets introduces ουκ εστιν into a context where OG ουκ εσται fit more smoothly (Mic. 4:4), and one instance in which the criterion is not applicable (Hab. 2:19) because the scroll retains the OG present tense demanded by the context (*DA*, p. 200).

[32]*DA*, pp. 69-78.

[33]Barthélemy overlooked two instances of Aquila's retention of Theodotion's εγω ειμι, so that he doubted Aquila's adherence to the pattern of usage (see fn. 9 in chapter one). Aquila's one failure to retain the usage may be due to secondary scribal error (see pp. 45-46, 272). Barthélemy found no opportunities for this usage in the extant fragments of the KAIΓE scroll of the Minor Prophets. See *DA*, p. 200.

[34]*DA*, pp. 78-80. Note that Barthélemy's identification of the KAIΓE recension in Judges (*DA*, pp. 34-35) has not been proven as yet, and should not be adopted without reservation.

OG has εις συναντησιν in Exod. 4:14, 27; 5:20; 18:7; 19:17 and has the related συναντων in Exod. 7:15. Only in Exod. 14:27 does the OG have a different equivalent, υπο το υδωρ, which is either a very free rendition of the MT or the reflection of a different Hebrew text. No evidence of a replacement with εις συναντησιν or εις απαντην has survived.

Apart from the last example, the OG offered no opportunity for Theodotion to employ the supposed ΚΑΙΓΕ revision. Indeed the OG in Exodus may have been the inspiration for the ΚΑΙΓΕ revision of the OG in Judges. No readings from Theodotion, Aquila, or Symmachus are preserved for any of the seven occurrences of MT *lqr't* in Exodus, so there is no way to tell what Theodotion's practice on this point was in Exodus.[35]

Barthélemy calls attention to a number of additional features in the ΚΑΙΓΕ recension that are modified or rejected by Aquila.[36] Only one of these features has application to the preserved Theodotionic material in Exodus. In all the other cases, either the Hebrew expression that ΚΑΙΓΕ attempted to reflect more precisely is not present in the MT of Exodus or no Theodotionic reading survives to reflect the expression that does occur there. The one applicable feature concerns the treatment of MT *yhwh ṣb'wt*. The ΚΑΙΓΕ recension generalizes κυριος των δυναμεων (OG of Psalms), rather than κυριος παντοκρατωρ (OG generally) or κυριος σαβαωθ (OG of Isaiah), to represent the MT phrase. Aquila restricted δυναμις and its derivatives for forms of MT *gbr*. Therefore, outside of Jeremiah and, according to Reider's index, Isaiah, Aquila replaces των δυναμεων with στρατειων. Both ΚΑΙΓΕ and Aquila use the tetragrammaton for MT *yhwh*, though later copyists sometimes write κ̅ς̅ in place of πιπι.[37]

While the phrase *yhwh ṣb'wt* never occurs in Exodus, the noun *ṣb'wt* appears five times, in construct with *yhwh* in Exod. 12:41 and with a pronominal suffix in Exod. 6:26; 7:4; 12:17, 51. Every time the OG equivalent is δυναμις in the singular. Only in Exod. 12:41 are readings from Theodotion and Aquila cited: MT *ṣb'wt* I OG η δυναμις I α'σ' *plḥwt'* θ' *ḥylwt'* (ꞩ^{mg}) I α'σ' στρατεια (*b*) I i^{mg} στρατια.

---

[35]*DA*, p. 200, indicates a similar lack of evidence in the ΚΑΙΓΕ scroll of the Minor Prophets.

[36]*DA*, pp. 81-87.

[37]*DA*, pp. 82-83. The treatment of the MT tetragrammaton by Theodotion and Aquila in Exodus was discussed in chapter three.

As suggested in chapter five, α'σ' *plḥwt'* of S^{mg} presumably means that α'σ' στρατεια is to be taken as the plural of στρατιον (compare i^{mg}), rather than as the singular στρατεια. Theodotion's Syriac reading almost certainly represents the plural of OG δυναμις. Thus Theodotion and Aquila agree with normal KAIΓE and Aquilan usages, respectively, in their treatment of MT *ṣb'wt* in Exodus.[38]

KAIΓE Characteristics Proposed by Shenkel

The OG avoided εν οφθαλμοις as a translation for MT *b'yny* when the object of the phrase was Yahweh. When the object was not Yahweh, the OG frequently used εν οφθαλμοις, although other translations also occur. The KAIΓE recension in Samuel-Kings uses the phrase εν οφθαλμοις almost exclusively to translate MT *b'yny*, even when the object of the phrase is Yahweh. This is a striking difference between the OG and the KAIΓE recention, whose validity Shenkel has demonstrated conclusively.[39]

The MT expression *b'yny* occurs fifteen times in Exodus: with a noun object referring to someone other than Yahweh in Exod. 3:21; 5:21 *bis*; 11:3 *ter*; 12:36; 21:8 and with a pronominal suffix referring to Yahweh in Exod. 15:26; 33:12, 13 *bis*, 16, 17; 34:9. The OG uses a variety of equivalents for these occurrences of MT *b'yny*, but never εν οφθαλμοις. No Theodotionic readings are cited for any of the seven instances of *b'yny* plus a pronoun that equals Yahweh, and there is no trace of εν οφθαλμοις in any other witnesses. These are the only cases in which Shenkel's characteristic could have been fully verified, since these are the only places in which the expression refers to Yahweh.

Shenkel's criterion finds partial application in two of the instances of MT *b'yny* plus a noun that refers to someone other than Yahweh, however. The one in Exod. 21:8 is discussed under item 10 of the fifth reading in chapter one. There Theodotion, Aquila, and Symmachus all insert εν οφθαλμοις (Syriac *b'yn'*) to represent MT *b'yny* explicitly. The OG merely has the following noun in the dative.[40] The same insertion is found in $F^{b\ mg}$ack$A\mathit{S}^{txt}$ (under ※ϵ') and out of place in ej^{txt}.

---

[38]Note that Symmachus agrees with Aquila here, though Barthélemy, *DA*, p. 82, says that elsewhere Symmachus agrees with KAIΓE on this point.

[39]Shenkel, *Chronology*, pp. 13-17.

[40]Theodotion and Aquila, but not Symmachus, replace the OG dative with a genitive and omit the unsupported OG article.

The other instance is more complex, and will be better understood if the relevant textual evidence is presented in full:

Exod. 11:3: MT *bʿyny mṣrym . . . bʾrṣ mṣrym bʿyny ʿbdy prʿh wbʿyny hʿm* I SP = MT, but with a long expansion inserted as well I OG εναντιον των αιγυπτιων . . . εναντιον των αιγυπτιων και εναντιον (om. d) φαραω και εναντιον (om. dp) παντων (om. A cdmpxyẞE) των θεραποντων αυτου (φαραω akmP; + και εν οφθαλμοις του [om. 128] λαου [αυτου 128; + αυτου c(αυτων c*)] ackmx, 128, AP) I $\mathcal{S}^{txt}$ *qdm mṣryʾ . . . qdm mṣryʾ* ⸗*wqdm prʿwn* ⸔ *wqdm klhwn mnyhnʾ* (*dylh* $\mathcal{S}^{mg}$) *dprʿwn* ※α'θ' *wbʿynʾ dʿmʾ*⸔.

The OG does not reflect the MT as a whole accurately, and εναντιον (Syriac *qdm*) is used to represent MT *bʿyny* on each of its three occurrences.[41] When Origen began revising the OG to reflect the MT more accurately, he discovered that nothing in the OG corresponds to MT *wbʿyny hʿm*. Instead of making a new translation in the style of the OG with εναντιον for MT *bʿyny*, he took the phrase already present in the versions of Theodotion and Aquila (so $\mathcal{S}^{txt}$). This phrase had the more literal rendition εν οφθαλμοις, reflected by Syriac *bʿÿnʾ*, rather than εναντιον (Syriac *qdm*). The hexaplaric addition, marked as such in $\mathcal{S}^{txt}$, is also found in akmxAP and with minor changes in c and in 128. This reading from α'θ' clearly conforms to Shenkel's pattern of ΚΑΙΓΕ usage, even though the object of the phrase is MT *hʿm* rather than Yahweh. Shenkel's criterion may be broadened to say that the ΚΑΙΓΕ/Theodotionic revision and the Aquilan revision always use εν οφθαλμοις to translate MT *bʿyny*, even where the OG would have avoided the literal translation.

There is no trace of a revision to εν οφθαλμοις in any of the other instances of *bʿyny* plus a noun object that refers to someone other than Yahweh in Exodus, nor are Theodotionic readings cited for these passages. In Exodus at least, both Aquila and Symmachus share this ΚΑΙΓΕ feature with Theodotion.

Shenkel has identified ten additional stylistic features of the ΚΑΙΓΕ recension in Samuel-Kings.[42] Eight of the ten find no application

---

[41]The use of OG εναντιον των αιγυπτιων for MT *bʾrṣ mṣrym* may be due to the influence of the previous MT *bʿyny mṣrym* or its OG translation.

[42]Shenkel, *Chronology*, pp. 17-18, 113-116.

to the Theodotionic material in Exodus, because the extant material does not overlap any occurrences of the various Hebrew words in question. The other two find some support and no opposition in the Theodotionic material for Exodus.

The first feature is the use of θυσιαζειν, rather than any other Greek verb, to represent MT *zbḥ*. In Samuel-Kings, it is OG θυειν that is replaced by θυσιαζειν in the KAIΓE recension. Theodotionic equivalents are preserved, all in Syriac, for three instances of the MT verb *zbḥ* in Exodus. In Exod. 22:19 (LXX v.20), α'σ'θ' are said by 𝔖mg to agree with 𝔖txt *dmdbḥ*, which presumably represents OG ο θυσιαζων, to translate the MT participle *zbḥ*. In Exod. 8:22 (LXX v.26), MT *nzbḥ* is twice represented by forms of θυειν in the OG. The various Syriac readings attributed to Aquila, Symmachus, and Theodotion each time could represent forms of θυειν or of θυσιαζειν:

MT *nzbḥ*] OG θυσομεν/θυσωμεν] 𝔖txt *ndbḥ*] θ' *ndbḥ* α' *mdbḥynn*, σ' *dbḥynn* (𝔖mg).

MT *nzbḥ*] OG θυσωμεν] 𝔖txt *ndbḥ*] θ' *(w)dbḥynn*, α' *dbḥyn ḥnn*, σ' *dbḥynn* (𝔖mg).

The second feature is the use of Greek words from the root σοφ- to represent MT words derived from the root *ḥkm*. Only one instance is preserved in Exodus:

28:3: MT *ḥkmh*] OG αισθησεως] fiy συνεσεως] 𝔏r *intellectui*] r σοφιας και αισθησεως] α'σ'θ' σοφιας (v)] smg𝔄vid𝔖mg σοφιας.

These are the only places in which Shenkel's new criteria are applicable to the Theodotionic material in Exodus. There is obviously no conflict between Theodotion and KAIΓE on these points.

While only a few of the KAIΓE characteristics or stylistic features assembled by Barthélemy and Shenkel are applicable to the extant Theodotionic material in Exodus, there is no evidence of real conflict between the Theodotionic material in Exodus and the KAIΓE material in Samuel-Kings and in the Minor Prophets on any of these characteristics. The correlation between the Theodotionic revision in Exodus and the KAIΓE recension generally, established on other grounds in the previous chapters, receives added confirmation here.

VIII Additional Suggested Characteristics of the Theodotionic Revision in Exodus

In Appendix B there is a complete list of all the Hebrew words in Exodus for which Theodotionic equivalents are preserved. Apart from a few very common items such as the definite article, the accusative particle, the relative *ʾšr*, and pronominal suffixes, each Theodotionic equivalent has been listed together with verse references for all occurrences. In the case of the very common words, only the verse references have been given.

The entire list provides much useful data, and will deserve detailed examination in the future. This chapter merely draws attention to some thirty-six Hebrew words whose Theodotionic equivalents are particularly significant. It does not include those Theodotionic variants that merely extend normative OG usage in Exodus to places in which the OG had either no equivalent or an unexpected one, nor does it include the KAIΓE characteristics discussed in the previous chapter. All the information found in Appendix B and, for Aquila, that found in RT is presupposed. Descriptions of OG usage are based on H-R.

ʾdm (Pual part.). ϑʹ πεπυρωμενος (error for πεπυρρωμενος). The same variant is attributed to οι λ̥ in Exod. 25:5, and is an extension to the Pual participle of the normal OG equivalent for MT *ʾdm* (אָדֹם), πυρρος.

ʾhl. ϑʹ *strʾ* (= *σκεπη), σκηνη, *mškn*ʾ (= *σκηνη). The OG used σκηνη frequently for both MT *ʾhl* and MT *mškn*. When there is a contrast between the two terms in Exodus, Theodotion restricts σκηνη to MT *mškn* and introduces σκεπη for MT *ʾhl*. When no such contrast is necessary, he is content to follow OG practice and use σκηνη for MT *ʾhl* too. In Exod. 40:26 (LXX v.24), where no contrast is found, Aquila replaces OG and οʹϑʹσʹ σκηνη with σκεπη for MT *ʾhl*, thus extending the tendency begun by Theodotion.

ʾwrym. ϑ' *nwhrʾ* (= *φωτισμοι ?). See the discussion in chapter two, items 71-72. Note the possible relationship between Theodotion's equivalents for MT *ʾwrym* and for MT *ʾwr* if Syriac *nhr*, Aphel, stands for φωτιζειν, rather than for φαινειν.

ʾlyh. ϑ' κερκιον. The OG uses οσφυς for MT *ʾlyh* on its four occurrences in Leviticus. In Lev. 8:25, α' την κερκον and σ'ϑ' το κερκειον follow the pattern represented by the single set of readings in Exodus. Lev. 3:9 and 7:3 (LXX 6:33) have κερκον and/or κερκιον attributed to οι λ̥. There are no instances of OG κερκος/κερκιον being used for MT *ʾlyh* according to H-R.

ʾlm. ϑ' μογιλαλον (*lʿg mmllʾ*). There is no constant OG equivalent for MT *ʾlm*. The α'σ'ϑ' variant in Exod. 4:11 agrees with OG usage in Isa. 35:6.

ʾšh. ϑ' πυρον, πυρρον (error for πυρον). To the two α'ϑ' readings in Exodus, add α'ϑ' (and α'σ') πυρον in Lev. 2:9, α'ϑ' πυρρον in Lev. 2:16, and α' πυρον in Lev. 3:9, all for MT *ʾšh*, as well as ϑ' απο των του πυρος and α' απο πυρων for MT *mʾšy* in Lev. 2:3 and 24:9. There are also anonymous variants πυρον/πυρρον in the margins of hexaplaric manuscripts for other occurrences of MT *ʾšh* in Leviticus. The OG never uses πυρον or the less accurate πυρρον as an equivalent for MT *ʾšh* according to H-R.

byn. ϑ' *bmṣʿtʾ*, *bynt*. While the Syriac translations of Theodotion's variants include both *bmṣʿtʾ* and *bynt*, it appears that Theodotion differs from both the OG and Aquila in his treatment of MT *byn* in Exodus. His equivalent may have been *ανα μεσον each time, though this is not certain. Aquila twice has Syriac *bynt* where Theodotion has Syriac *bmṣʿtʾ* (Exod. 31:17 *bis*), but the difference between their Greek readings is not known.

bqrb. ϑ' *bmṣʿtʾ* (= *εν μεσω ?). Theodotion differs from the OG, while Aquila has another variant (*bgwʾ*), each time. Once again, the precise difference between Aquila's Greek form and Theodotion's is not known. RT, following Field, suggests εντος for Aquila's *bgwʾ* at Exod. 17:7 (Field also has this interpretation at Exod. 34:9), but no justification of the equivalent is presented by either RT or Field.

bśmym. ϑ' αρωματα (*hrẅm'*), *hrẅm'* (= *αρωματα) or *hrwm'*. The distribution of OG equivalents for MT *bśmym* is uneven. All instances of αρωματα, corresponding to MT *bśmym*, are in 2 Kings (one), 1 Chronicles (two), 2 Chronicles (five), Esther (one), and Song of Solomon (six). It is never used by the OG in Exodus, for MT *bśmym* or for anything else. In addition to the two Theodotionic instances listed in Appendix B, αρωματα (for MT *bśmym*) occurs anonymously and attributed to αλλος in Exod. 30:23.

btym. ϑ' ϑηκαι, *ltÿq'* (= *εις ϑηκας). Theodotion twice introduces an expression used for MT *btym* by the OG only in Exod. 25:27 (LXX v. 26), once substituting it for a different OG expression (φαλιδες in Exod. 30:4). In the latter case, Aquila has a different variant (εισοδοι).

wwym. ϑ' *wṣ̈bt'* (= *και οι κοσμοι), *ṣ̈bt'* (= *κοσμοι ?). Four times Theodotion apparently uses an equivalent for MT *wwym* that is never so used by the OG. Aquila has a different reading, Syriac *q̈plyd'* (= *κεφαλιδες), in Exod. 38:10 (LXX 37:8) and in Exod. 38:28 (LXX 39:6). The latter is an α'σ' citation.

ḥzq (Piel). ϑ' ενισχυειν. This one α'ϑ' variant in Exodus may be part of a concerted effort at reinterpretation. RT lists twelve instances in which Aquila (once α' ϑ', twice α' σ' ϑ') has the same Greek word for some form of MT *ḥzq*.

ḥrb. ϑ' ρομφαια (*syp'*). At least in Exodus, Theodotion uses ρομφαια, while Aquila and Symmachus use μαχαιρα, to represent MT *ḥrb*. Both equivalents are commonly used by the OG, but other translations are found in the OG for the two instances involved here.

ḥšb (noun). ϑ' *mtqnwt'* (= *μηχανωματος or *μηχανηματος). See the discussion of the equivalents for this word in chapter two under item 38.

ḥšn. ϑ' λογιον, *pdt'* (= *λογιον). Theodotion and Aquila are consistent in using λογιον for MT *ḥšn*, a frequent but not exclusive pattern in the OG.

ḥtn. ϑ' νυμφιος (*ḥtn'*) and ϑ' γαμβρος. The OG tends to use γαμβρος for both MT חֹתֵן and MT חָתָן. Theodotion restricts γαμβρος to MT חֹתֵן, and introduces νυμφιος for MT חָתָן. For Aquila's further introduction of νυμφευτης to represent MT חֹתֵן, see fn. 135 to chapter five.

yldym. ϑ′ παιδαρια, παιδια. RT lists additional instances of these related equivalents being used for MT *yldym* by Aquila. Perhaps Theodotion also used these words more frequently for MT *yldym*, even though their use by the OG in this way is rare.

yrh. ϑ′ τοξευεσθαι. See the discussion of the equivalents for MT *yrh* in the sixth reading in chapter one.

ytrt. ϑ′ περιττον. The α′ ϑ′ variant in Exod. 29:13 is an extension of OG usage for derivatives of the verbal root *ytr* to the noun *ytrt*. The normal OG equivalent for MT *ytrt* is λοβος.

kprym. ϑ′ εξιλασμος. The α′ σ′ ϑ′ variant in Exod. 29:36 is more in conformity with the OG treatment of words from the root *kpr* (compare εξιλασκειν and related nouns, as well as ιλαστηριον, in H-R), than is OG καθαρισμος.

mʿyl. ϑ′ επενδυτης or επιδυτης (*lʿl mn lbwšʾ*), *lbwšʾ ʿlyʾ*. Theodotion's equivalent was probably επενδυτης, against the more common OG equivalents (e.g., υποδυτης, διπλοις, ποδηρης) and against Aquila's normal equivalent (ενδυμα).

mšbṣwt/mšbṣt. ϑ′ συνεσφιγμενοι or συνεσφραγισμενοι, *ḥ̈yṣtʾ* (= *σφιγκτοι ?), *ḥ̈ywṣtʾ*. See the discussion in chapter two, item 20.

nyḥwḥ. ϑ′ ευαρεστησις. Theodotion has the same variant to represent MT *nyḥwḥ* in Lev. 1:9, with another variant attributed to α′ σ′. The word ευαρεστησις never occurs in the OG, according to H-R.

ʿbdh and *ʿbdym*. ϑ′ δουλεια (*ʿbdwtʾ*), δουλεια, *pwlḥn ʿbdwtʾ* (= *δουλια) and ϑ′ δουλοι (*ʿb̈dʾ*), δουλοι. Theodotion apparently uses only forms from the Greek root δουλ- for MT words from the Hebrew root *ʿbd*. While this is a common pattern in the OG, there are many exceptions, including several of the places in which Theodotionic readings are cited for these words in Exodus.

ʿbt and *ʿbtt*. ϑ′ *š̈šltʾ*, *ššltʾ* and ϑ′ *š̈šltʾ* (= *αλυσιδωτα and/or *αλυσεις), χαλαστα (?). See the discussion in chapter two, item 14.

ʿrp (verb). ϑ′ νωτοκοπειν (*psq ḥṣʾ*), *psq ḥṣʾ* (= *νωτοκοπειν). Theodotion's variant is not shared by the OG or by Aquila. Note that Greek νωτος is used for MT *ʿrp* (עֹ֫רֶף) three times in the ΚΑΙΓΕ sections of Samuel-Kings according to H-R, and only two other times in the rest of the Greek OT.

pr'. ϑ' διασκεδαζειν, διασκεδαζειν or διασωζειν. See the discussion under item 5 in the second reading of chapter one.

qrsym. ϑ' περοναι (*'bḥ'*, or erroneously *qwrqs'* [= *κρικοι]), *'bḥ'* (= *περοναι). The Theodotionic equivalent, περοναι, is independent of OG usage (where περοναι never occurs) and of Aquila's κρικοι.

qrš. ϑ' σανις (*dp'*), σανις, *dp'* (= *σανις). Theodotion's equivalent is shared by Aquila and Symmachus, but it is never used by the OG for MT *qrš*.

šhm. ϑ' ονυξ. The α'σ'ϑ' variant for MT *šhm*, given by Montef. for Exod. 39:6 (LXX 36:13), is also attributed to οι λ̥ for MT *šhm* three times in Exodus: 25:7 (LXX v.6); 28:9; 35:9 (LXX v.8). Each time the OG has a different equivalent.

šwlym. ϑ' *lwt rgl'* (= *προς ποδων). See the comments in footnote 112 of chapter five.

šlm (Piel). ϑ' *pr'* (= *αποτιννυειν). While the OG often uses αποτινειν to represent the MT Piel of *šlm* (thirteen times in Exodus according to H-R), Theodotion's apparent equivalent *αποτιννυειν is never so used by the OG (where it occurs only three times).

šrṣ. ϑ' εξερπειν (*ršp*). The verb εξερπειν for MT *šrṣ* is also attributed to Aquila, Symmachus, and Theodotion in Gen. 1:20 (against OG εξαγειν) by Field (citing Philop.).

šršrt/šršt. ϑ' χαλαστα (*nšpt'*), *nšpt'* (= *χαλαστα). See the discussion under item 3 of chapter two.

tmym. ϑ' *šwmly'* (= *τελειοτητες ?). See the discussion in chapter two, items 71-72.

trwmh. ϑ' *ršyt'* (= *απαρχη). See the discussion in chapter six, pp. 272-273.

The foregoing list is presented for further study. At least some of the Theodotionic usages in Exodus will be found to characterize the ΚΑΙΓΕ material generally. Because Theodotion did not exercise complete consistency in his approach to all Hebrew words, and also because Aquila frequently retained distinctive readings introduced by Theodotion, the presence of one or another equivalent from the foregoing list would not be sufficient to mark a text as Theodotionic or KAIΓE. However, the presence of such equivalents as variants to the OG correspondents could indicate that a Theodotionic/KAIΓE text, or a derivative therefrom, has left its mark. The best way to identify KAIΓE material is to show its intermediary position between the OG and Aquila, its tendency to revise the OG toward the Hebrew text (whether MT or proto-MT), and its sharing of known KAIΓE stylistic or translational characteristics.

CONCLUSION

The foregoing investigations have established conclusively that the Theodotionic material in Exodus comes from a systematic revision of the OG to reflect the present MT. Theodotionic readings that might represent Hebrew variants amount to less than two and a half percent of the extant material, and most of the differences involve minor points. Many of the Theodotionic readings in Exodus have little or no agreement with the OG, because hexaplaric readings were generally preserved only when they varied from the OG or expanded it. Other readings are in total or partial agreement with the OG, and some thirty-five solidly support the conclusion that Theodotion's version in Exodus depended on a form of the OG that had already undergone partial revision towards a Hebrew text. This form of the OG contained a translation of MT Exod. 28:23-28, but apparently did not differ from the original OG on the form and general content of chapters 36-40.

There is a genuine relationship between the versions of Theodotion and Aquila in Exodus that cannot be explained by common familiarity with the OG tradition. There is limited but adequate evidence that Aquila's revision in Exodus was based, not upon the OG directly, but upon a Greek text that had already undergone the revision represented by the Theodotionic material. In other words, Aquila knew and used Theodotion's recension as the basis for his own further revision to the MT. Readings at variance with this conclusion are few and generally involve minor points. If these readings were the result of a secondary revision of the Theodotionic material in Exodus independently of or after Aquila, then that secondary revision was neither extensive nor significant. The Theodotionic version of Exodus existed in substantially its final form at least by the late first century A.D. There is thus no reason to attribute any decisive role in its formation to the traditional author, second-century

Theodotion of Ephesus, although he may well have made use of the revision and may have been responsible for the few minor changes noted above. The main author of this revision can be referred to as Theodotion, since the material is marked with a ϑ′, but the person so designated cannot be identified with any precision. He can only be said to have lived and worked prior to Aquila, and hence in the late first century A.D. or earlier.

Theodotion's version in Exodus shares those stylistic and lexical characteristics of the general ΚΑΙΓΕ recension for which any firm evidence is available. There is no evidence of real conflict between the Theodotionic material in Exodus and the ΚΑΙΓΕ material in Samuel-Kings and in the Minor Prophets on any of the characteristics. Because Theodotion's version in Exodus occupies a position in the textual tradition analogous to that of the ΚΑΙΓΕ recension in other books and because his version shares the distinctive features identifying that recension, it can be concluded that Theodotion's version in Exodus is an integral part of the general ΚΑΙΓΕ recension identified by Barthélemy, and that Barthélemy's original suggestion to this effect is amply proven.

This conclusion has an important corollary. The ΚΑΙΓΕ recension generally depends on the proto-MT, a version of the Hebrew text directly related to the present MT but with significant divergences from the MT as well, while Theodotion's version in Exodus presupposes a Hebrew text that diverged only very slightly from the MT. This means that the proto-MT and the MT for Exodus, and presumably for the rest of the Pentateuch, were virtually identical. In other words, the ΚΑΙΓΕ revisor(s) of Exodus already had available the excellent Pentateuchal text that is preserved in the Masoretic recension. In Samuel-Kings and in the Minor Prophets, however, there is evidence of greater recensional activity, presumably because the proto-MT was less satisfactory in those books.

APPENDIX A

A CLASSIFIED LIST OF THEODOTIONIC READINGS IN EXODUS[1]

Readings that have nothing, or only *και/w-*, in common with the OG.

Simple expansions.

4:9: σʹ θʹ wnhwwn.

4:23: αʹ θʹ ’yty.

5:20: σʹ θʹ b-.

5:23: αʹ θʹ (w)mprq.

6:13: σʹ θʹ lwt bny’ d’ysr’yl w-.

9:20: αʹ σʹ θʹ τους δουλους αυτου] αʹ σʹ θʹ l‘bd’ dylh.

9:22: θʹ dḥql’.

10:9: αʹ θʹ dyln$^{(1)}$.

10:9: αʹ θʹ dyln$^{(2)}$.

10:15: θʹ dklh.

10:29: αʹ θʹ hkn’.

11:1: αʹ θʹ mn hrk’.

11:3: αʹ θʹ wb‘yn’ d‘m’.

12:6: αʹ σʹ θʹ ywm’.

12:26: θʹ ln.

13:21: σʹ θʹ lmnhrw lhwn lmḥzq b’ymm’ wblly’.

14:17: αʹ θʹ dylh.

14:29: αʹ θʹ dylhwn.

16:2: σʹ θʹ bmdbr’.

16:14: θʹ wslq mškb’.

18:10: θʹ hw.

21:6: αʹ θʹ dylh.

21:30: αʹ θʹ ’yk klhyn.

21:33: αʹ θʹ ’nš.

---

[1]See pp. 164-167.

21:36: ϑ´ mr’ dylh.

22:3 (LXX v.4): ϑ´ twr’ w-.

22:5 (LXX v.6): σ´ϑ´ mpr‘.

22:11 (LXX v.12): ϑ´ mtgnbw.

22:13 (LXX v.14): σ´ϑ´ dylh.

22:13 (LXX v.14): ϑ´ mpr‘.

22:14 (LXX v.15): ϑ´ dylh.

22:25 (LXX v.26): ttl ※ϑ´ywhy↙.

22:26 (LXX v.27): α´ϑ´ ’p.

22:30 (LXX v.31): σ´ϑ´ bḥql’.

25:6: α´σ´ϑ´ hr̈wm’ (hrwm’ B).

25:10 (LXX v.9): ϑ´ dylh$^{(1)}$.

25:10 (LXX v.9): ϑ´ dylh$^{(2)}$.

25:10 (LXX v.9): ϑ´ dylh$^{(3)}$.

25:12 (LXX v.11): σ´ϑ´ dylh$^{(1)}$.

25:12 (LXX v.11): σ´ϑ´ dylh$^{(2)}$.

25:15 (LXX v.14): σ´ϑ´ mnh.

25:17 (LXX v.16): ϑ´ dylh.

25:19 (LXX v.18): σ´ϑ´ dylh.

25:20 (LXX v.19): σ´ϑ´ dylhwn.

25:23 (LXX v.22): α´ϑ´ dylh$^{(1)}$.

25:23 (LXX v.22): α´ϑ´ dylh$^{(2)}$.

25:23 (LXX v.22): α´ϑ´ dylh$^{(3)}$:

25:25 (LXX v.24): σ´ϑ´ ddhb’.

25:33 (LXX v.32): ϑ´ ’g̈n’ d’yt ‘lyhyn dmẅt’ dlẅz’.

25:36: α´ϑ´ dylhwn$^{(1)}$.

25:36: α´ϑ´ dylhwn$^{(2)}$.

26:13: ϑ´ w-.

26:15: α´ϑ´ dqymyn.

26:37: ϑ´ l’ M̈blṭ’.

27:13: α´ϑ´ lsṭr’.

28:1: ϑ´ ‘mh.

28:11: ϑ´ και συνεσφιγμενους (*or* συνεσφραγισμενους).

28:16: α´ϑ´ dylh$^{(2)}$.

28:29: σ´ϑ´ bkl zbn.

29:14: α´ϑ´ b-.

29:28: α´ϑ´ dylhwn.

30:1: σ'ϑ' pyrm'.

30:2: α'ϑ' dylh(1).

30:2: α'ϑ' dylh(2).

30:12: σ'ϑ' bmnyn' dylhwn.

30:37: α'ϑ' w-.

30:37: α'σ'ϑ' hw dt'bd.

31:5: ϑ' dmwly'.

31:10: ϑ' wllbw̵š' dqwdš'.

31:18: ϑ' hw.

32:2: ϑ' wdbh̵y' dylkwn.

32:9: σ'ϑ' και ειπεν $\overline{\text{κς}}$ (*or* pypy) προς μωυσην (*or* μωσην) εωρακα τον λαον τουτον και ιδου λαος σκληροτραχηλος εστιν (*or om.*).

32:24: α'σ'ϑ' 'nwn.

32:29: α'ϑ' dylh.

34:12: α'ϑ' 'nt.

34:19: ϑ' wdklhwn b'yr̵' dylk.

34:29: ϑ' dshdwt'.

34:35: ϑ' ḥzt' d-.

34:35: α'ϑ' hw.

35:14-15 (LXX vv.16-17): ϑ' wlšr̵g' dylh wlmšḥ' dnhyr' wlmdbḥ' dbs̵m' wlqwp̵' dylh.

35:16 (LXX v.17): σ'ϑ' dyq̵d' šlm̵' wlṭrṭql' dnḥš' dylh lqwp̵' dylh.

35:22: α'ϑ' gbr̵'.

35:28: ϑ' wmšḥ' lnhyr'.

36:2: α'ϑ' blb'.

36:2: α'ϑ' dylhwn.

36:3: ϑ' dpwlḥn 'bdwt'.

36:4: σ'ϑ' klhwn.

36:5: σ'ϑ' kd 'mryn.

36:8: ϑ' blb'.

36:21 (MT): α'ϑ' ddp'.

36:22 (MT): ϑ' ldp'.

36:23 (MT): α'ϑ' dtymn'.

36:25 (MT): α'σ'ϑ' grby'.

37:1 (LXX 38:1): ϑ' mn qys̵' l' m̵blṭ' dtr̵tyn 'm̵' wplg 'wrk' dylh w'mt' wplg pty' dylh w'mt' wplg rwm' dylh.

37:4-5 (LXX 38:4): ϑ´ wʻbd ꝗwp' mn qy̆s' l' M̵blṭ' wqrm 'nwn bdhb'
w'ʻl lqwꝑ' bzqz̈qt' ʻl dꝑnth dq'bwt'.

37:25 (MT): α´σ´ϑ´ wd'mt'(1).

37:25 (MT): α´σ´ϑ´ wd'mt'(2).

37:25 (MT): σ´ϑ´ dtr̈tyn.

37:26 (MT): α´σ´ϑ´ bh bdmwt' l'gr' dylh.

38:3 (LXX 38:23): ϑ´ wlšqW̵l'.

38:6 (LXX 38:24): ϑ´ wʻbd qwꝑ' qys̈' l' M̵blṭ' wḥpy 'nwn bnḥš'.

38:10 (LXX 37:8): ϑ´ wṣ̈bt' dʻM̵wd' wꝑs'lyds dylhwn ds'm'.

38:11 (LXX 37:9): ϑ´ wṣ̈bt' dʻM̵wd' wdwbꝗ' dylhwn ds'm'.

38:12 (LXX 37:10): ϑ´ wṣ̈bt' dʻM̵wd' W̵dwbq' dylhwn ds'm'.

38:23 (LXX 37:21): α´ϑ´ btklt' w-.

38:25 (LXX 39:2): ϑ´ bsyqlwn dqwdš'.

39:9 (LXX 36:16): α´ϑ´ 'ytyh hwt.

39:28 (LXX 36:36): ϑ´ db'd'.

39:33 (LXX 39:14): ϑ´ ʻbr̈' dylh wdꝑ' dylh.

39:37 (LXX 39:17): σ´ϑ´ wklhwn m'H̵' dylh.

39:39 (MT): σ´ϑ´ lmšgt' wlbsys dylh.

39:41 (MT): α´σ´ϑ´ lH̵ḥt' dtšmšt'.

40:2: α´σ´ϑ´ dstr'.

40:6: α´σ´ϑ´ dstr'.

40:20 (LXX v.18): α´ϑ´ wyhb.

40:24 (LXX v.22): σ´ϑ´ lwqbl ptwr'.

40:28 (LXX v.25): ϑ´ wsm lprs' dtrʻ' dmškn'.

40:29 (LXX v.26): ϑ´ dstr'.

40:29 (LXX v.26): ϑ´ w'sq ʻlwhy lyqd' šlm' wldbḥ'.

40:30 (LXX v.26): α´σ´ϑ´ wsm.

40:30 (LXX v.26): ϑ´ bynt mškn' dshdwt' lbynt mdbḥ' wyhb tmn my̆'.

40:33 (LXX v.27): α´ϑ´ wyhb.

Simple variants, some of which may agree with an OG definite article

1:8: ϑ´ καινος (*also conflate attributions*).

1:13: ϑ´ εμπαιγμοι *or* ϑ´ εμπεγμω *or* σ´ϑ´ εμπαιγματι.

1:17: ϑ´ τα παιδαρια.

1:18: α´ϑ´ παιδια.

1:20: ϑ´ ...ηθυνεν.

3:4: α´ϑ´ ιδου εγω.

3:14: α´ϑ´ εσομσι εσομαι.

4:11: α'σ'ϑ' μογιλαλον I α'σ'ϑ' l‘g mmll’.

4:21: α'ϑ' ενισχυσω.

4:25: ϑ' ακροτομον.

5:4: ϑ' διασκεδαζετε (*or* διασωζετε).

6:12: ϑ' απεριτμητος τοις χειλεσιν.

6:23: ϑ' ‘nmyddb.

8:10 (LXX v.14): ϑ' κορους κορους *or* ϑ' ’yk šb‘yn (*cf.* $\mathcal{S}^{txt}$ kš̈yt’ kš̈yt’).

8:17 (LXX v.21): ϑ' ḥlṭ’.

8:18 (LXX v.22): ϑ' ωστε μη γενεσθαι.

12:11: α'ϑ' εν θαμβω I α'ϑ' btwht’.

14:2: α'σ'ϑ' φιεθρω *or* ϑ' p’yrwt.

14:9: α'σ'ϑ' επι φιεθρων *or* α'ϑ' lqwbl p’y’yrwt.

15:5: α'σ'ϑ' thẄm’.

15:8: α'σ'ϑ' εσωρευθη.

15:16: α'ϑ' nštqwn.

15:16: ο'ϑ' ελυτρωσω.

17:6: σ'ϑ' εμπροσθεν σου I σ'ϑ' qdmyk.

18:22: σ'ϑ' συμβαστασουσιν.

18:26: ϑ' δυσχερες (α'σ'ϑ' σκληρον δυσχερες *is a conflation of the* α'σ' *and* ϑ' *variants*).

19:13: ϑ' τοξευομενος.

22:8 (LXX v.9): ϑ' nḥybwn ’lH'’.

22:9 (LXX v.10): α'σ'ϑ' dḥz’.

22:10 (LXX v.11): α'σ'ϑ' pypy.

24:12: α'σ'ϑ' τας πλακας.

25:7 (LXX v.6): α'σ'ϑ' επενδυμα (*doubtful*).

25:12 (LXX v.11): ϑ' (*or* σ'ϑ') μερη.

25:23 (LXX v.22): ϑ' mn qÿs’ l’ Mblṭ’.

25:30 (LXX v.29): ϑ' προθεσεως.

26:15: α'σ'ϑ' τας σανιδας I α'σ'ϑ' dꝑ’.

26:18: α'σ'ϑ' ldꝑ’.

27:14: σ'ϑ' κοσκηνομ. *or* α'σ'ϑ' ’yk d‘rbl’ (*no marker in* $\mathcal{S}^{txt}$).

28:4: σ'ϑ' pdt’.

28:14: ϑ' χαλαστα I ϑ' nÿpt’.

28:22: ϑ' nÿpt’.

28:32 (LXX v.28): α'ϑ' ...προσπλοκην *or* σ'ϑ' ...σειρωτον.

28:33 (LXX v.29): σ´ϑ´ lwt ʿgl'.

28:33 (LXX v.29): ϑ´ dmštgnynyt'.

28:39 (LXX v.35): ϑ´ υψωμα.

28:40 (LXX v.36): ϑ´ υψωματα.

29:2: ϑ´ αναπεποιημενους.

29:13: α´ϑ´ το περιττον.

29:36: α´σ´ϑ´ εξιλασμου.

29:42: α´ϑ´ lyqd' šlm'.

30:5: α´σ´ϑ´ lqẘp'.

30:16: α´ϑ´ επι την δουλειαν I α´ϑ´ 'l 'bdwt'.

30:20: α´ϑ´ πυρρον.

33:12: α´ϑ´ bšm'.

33:22: α´σ´ϑ´ qywln' (*so Lagarde, who remarks that Field corrected* bḥwln' *from* 'wṣr 'ʿz').

35:9 (LXX v.8): α´ϑ´ το λογιον (*or* α´ϑ´ λογιον).

35:23: α´σ´ϑ´ πεπυρωμενα.

35:24: σ´ϑ´ ršyt' (*no marker in* $\mathcal{S}^{txt}$)

35:29: α´ϑ´ ṣbyny'.

38:12 (LXX 37:10): α´σ´ϑ´ w'ẙls.

38:28 (LXX 39:6): ϑ´ ỵ̈bt'.

39:2 (LXX 36:9): ϑ´ εφωδ (*doubtful*).

39:6 (LXX 36:13): α´σ´ϑ´ του ονυχος.

39:6 (LXX 36:13): σ´ϑ´ dḥdyʿn bpšl' (*no marker in* $\mathcal{S}^{txt}$)

39:15 (LXX 36:22): ϑ´ dššlt'.

39:16 (LXX 36:23): ϑ´ ḥẙwṣt'.

39:17 (LXX 36:25): ϑ´ χαλαστα (*perhaps out of place*).

40:20 (LXX v.18): α´σ´ϑ´ lšqẘl'.

Short variants that share και/*w*- with the OG

1:7: ϑ´ wršpyn hww *or* α´ϑ´ εξηρποσαν *or* ϑ´ εξειρπον.

2:25: α´ϑ´ wḥz' *or* ϑ´ ειδεν.

14:15: α´σ´ϑ´ wnrymwn.

16:10: α´ϑ´ whpkw.

25:29 (LXX v.28): σ´ϑ´ wpẙ'lys.

28:30 (LXX v.26): α´σ´ϑ´ lnwhr' wlšwmly'.

39:33 (LXX v.14): ϑ´ wlstr'.

39:34 (LXX v.21): ϑ´ wlprs' hw dmṭll.

39:39 (LXX v.10): α´σ´ϑ´ wlmḥwlt'.

Short variants that contain items not present in the OG

2:3: α΄θ΄ κιβωτον παπυρου.

2:21: θ΄ και ηρξατο μ.....τοικει...

8:6 (LXX v.10): α΄σ΄θ΄ 'yk pypy 'lh' dyln.

12:7: α΄σ΄θ΄ w'l.

25:7 (LXX v.6): α΄θ΄ εις το λογιον.

27:19: α΄θ΄ δουλεια αυτης.

30:4: θ΄ (*or* θ΄σ΄) εις θηκας τοις αναφορευσιν (*also* α΄σ΄θ΄ τοις αναφορευσιν).

32:1: α΄θ΄ και εκκλησιασθη ‖ α΄θ΄ w'tknšw.

32:6: θ΄ w'ytyw.

34:20: θ΄ tpswq ḥṣ' dylh.

37:17 (LXX 38:14): α΄σ΄θ΄ l'ṭm' dylh.

38:4 (LXX 38:24): α΄σ΄θ΄ tḥyt ṭrṭql' dylh.

Short variants that share και/*w*- with the OG and that also contain items not present in the OG

20:25 ($ v.22): α΄σ΄θ΄ και εβεβηλωσας αυτο ‖ α΄σ΄θ΄ wsybtyhy.

35:11 (LXX v.10): α΄σ΄θ΄ wltksyt' dylh.

Readings that appear to have some minor agreement or connection with the OG

Short expansions that share a proper name, the conjunction και/*w*-, or apparently the definite article with the OG

1:5: θ΄ αι εκ μηρου (ιακωβ) *or* θ΄ αι εκ μηρων *or* α΄θ΄ εκ μηρων ιακωβ.

25:26 (LXX v.25): θ΄ hlyn d'ytyhyn d'rb'tyhyn.

28:4: ο΄α΄σ΄θ΄ ααρων τω αδελφω σου.

28:35 (LXX v.31): ο΄θ΄ επι ααρων.

34:7: α΄θ΄ w'l.

38:23 (LXX 37:21): θ΄ wbtrkn.

Variants that share minor points of agreement with the OG

4:13: α΄θ΄ εν εμοι κε.

4:25-26: θ΄ και ηψατο των ποδων αυτου και ειπεν οτι νυμφιος αιματων συ μοι και αφηκεν αυτον οτι ειπεν νυμφιος αιματων εις περιτομας (*also* α΄θ΄ wgšpt brgl' dylh w'mrt mṭl dḥtn' ddm' 'yt [*read* 'nt] ly).

13:13: θ΄ tprwq mn mr'yt' w'n l' tprqywhy tpswq ḥṣh.

13:20: α´σ´ϑ´ εν ηϑαν την ερημοτατην.

16:16: ϑ´ gbr' lm'kwlt' dylh gwmwr.

16:21: ϑ´ bhlyn d'klyn lh.

18:2: α´ϑ´ btr šwdʏ' dylh.

20:24 (Ꞩ v.21): ϑ´ mn 'dmt'.

22:27 (LXX v.28): α´σ´ϑ´ ουκ ατιμασεις (*or* ου καταμασεις).

24:13: α´σ´ϑ´ ο λειτουργος αυτου (*or* αυτω) *or* α´σ´ϑ´ λειτουργος αυτου.

25:38: ϑ´ wMlqṭ' dylh.

26:17: α´ϑ´ δυο χειρας.

28:14: ϑ´ gdẙly 'kḥd' nʿbd 'nwn ʿbd' dšš̈lt'.

28:37 (LXX v.33): α´ϑ´ επι της κινδαρεως.

30:3: α´σ´ϑ´ δωμα αυτου.

33:15: σ´ϑ´ 'n prṣwp' dylk l' 'zl.

38:17 (LXX 37:15): α´σ´ϑ´ wdwbʠ' dylhwn.

Syriac variants that might agree in part or totally with the OG

9:8: ϑ´ ml' 'ydẙ' dylkwn.

9:32: ϑ´ kẄnt'.

10:11: σ´ϑ´ mpysyn 'ntwn.

10:14: α´ϑ´ ddm' lh.

12:21: α´σ´ϑ´ 'ntwn lkwn.

12:48: α´ϑ´ lmry'.

13:16: α´σ´ϑ´ wdmttzyʿ.

15:23: ϑ´ 'yk šbʿyn lmwr'.

19:11: α´σ´ϑ´ bh bdmwt' dsyny.

19:22: ϑ´ ngmr.

19:24: ϑ´ npswq.

22:10 (LXX v.11): σ´ϑ´ mtḥ 'b'š.

23:21: α´ϑ´ bh bdmwt' bh.

25:18 (LXX v.17): σ´ϑ´ ngẙdy bṭwrnws.

27:4: α´σ´ϑ´ mṣydt'.

29:24: σ´ϑ´ 'nyn.

29:41: ϑ´ dylh.

Short variants that have lexical similarities to the OG, two of which also share και/*w*- with the OG

12:41: α´σ´ϑ´ klhwn.

12:41: ϑ′ ḥylWt’.

13:18: ϑ′ πεμπταιζοντες.

19:6: σ′ϑ′ βασιλει[α] ιερεων ‖ σ′ϑ′ mlkwt’ khH’.

25:2: α′ϑ′ wnsbwn.

25:2: σ′ϑ′ ršyt’.

32:6: α′ϑ′ wqdm.

Short variants that contain items not present in the OG and that also have minor agreements with the OG

4:6: ϑ′ και ιδου η χειρ αυτου λεπρωσα ωσει χιων.

8:18 (LXX v.22): ϑ′ bmṣ‘th d’r‘’.

12:29: α′ϑ′ bbyt’ dgwb’.

17:7: ϑ′ bmṣ‘t’ dyln.

28:3: ϑ′ εις ιερατευειν αυτον μοι.

29:5: ϑ′ τον χιτωνα και την επενδυτην (*or* επιδυτην) της επωμιδος ‖ ϑ′ lkwtyn’ wll‘l mn lbwšh dkbynt’.

31:17: ϑ′ bmṣ‘t ly wbmṣ‘t bnY’ d’ysr’yl.

34:9: σ′ϑ′ bmṣ‘tn.

35:11 (LXX v.10): σ′ϑ′ και τας περονας αυτης και τας σανιδας και τους μοχλους (*or* ϑ′ και τας σανιδας αυτης, *also* σ′ϑ′ ‘bY’ [*or* α′σ′ϑ′ wlqwYqs’ dylh - *with the noun at least improperly attributed to* ϑ′ *and* σ′] *and* σ′ϑ′ dylh *after the second noun*).

35:24: ϑ′ και πας ος ευρεθη παρ αυτω.

36:7: α′σ′ϑ′ lklh ‘bd’.

Short variants that contain items not present in the OG and that have lexical similarities to the OG

10:12: α′σ′ϑ′ bqmṣ’.

28:32 (LXX v.28): α′ϑ′ ... της κεφαλης αυτου εν μεσω αυτου.

29:9: ϑ′ ζωνη ααρων.

30:18: α′σ′ϑ′ wt‘bd.

38:3 (LXX 38:23): ϑ′ klhwn m’H’ dylh ‘bd dnḥš’.

Corrupt variant that has minor agreements or similarities with the OG

12:42: ϑ′ dmṭrt’ hw llly’ lpypy dnṭwrt’.

Short variants that omit OG items and that partially agree with the OG

16:14: α′ϑ′ dqyq’ qlyp’ dqyq’ ’yk ’glyd’.

24:10: σ′ϑ′ ’kwth dšmy’.

29:18: α′ϑ′ οσμη ευαρεστησεως πυρον κυριω αυτο.

29:20: ϑ´ wt'šwd ldm' 'l mdbḥ' lḥwdr'.

30:7: ϑ´ θυμιαμα αρωματων.

Short variants that omit OG items and that also have lexical similarities to the OG

4:24: σ´ϑ´ $\overline{\kappa\varsigma}$ I σ´ϑ´ mry'.

16:5: α´ϑ´ ywm' ywm'.

39:22 (LXX 36:30): ϑ´ lbwš' 'ly' dkbynt'.

40:5: ϑ´ το επισπαστρον της θυρας. Note the erroneous or misplaced ϑ´ επι listed below.

Problematic citations

26:24: α´ mt'myn˙ σ´ mn ltḥt˙ ϑ´.

40:5: ϑ´ επι either misplaced or an error for ο´ επι.

Theodotionic readings that have or may have significant agreements with the OG

1. Items 1-95 on pp. 167-199.
2. Items 137-152 on pp. 160-162.

APPENDIX B

AN INDEX TO HEBREW WORDS IN EXODUS WHOSE THEODOTIONIC EQUIVALENTS ARE PRESERVED

The readings included in this Index are found in B-McL, in Field, or in Lagarde's $. When a Theodotionic reading is preserved in both Greek and Syriac, the Syriac reading is given in parentheses after the Greek reading unless the two conflict. If the Greek and Syriac readings conflict, they are listed as alternatives, connected by "or". Conflicting Greek readings are listed as alternatives in the same way. When the Theodotionic reading is preserved only in Syriac, then the Syriac reading is listed. If the Greek original can be determined from other evidence, it is given in parentheses after the Syriac reading and is preceded by an asterisk. Such equivalents are suggested only if they appear probable, and they remain only suggestions. When the Theodotionic reading is ομοιως τοις ο′, Syr *ʾyk šbʿyn*, or the like, the Hebrew words are preceded by — and only the verse number of the reading is given.[1] Unless the contrary is indicated, Hebrew verbs are Qal and Syriac verbs are Peal. Joint citations (α′θ′, α′σ′θ′, etc.) are included, but are not distinguished from ordinary θ′ citations.

Index

ʾbnṭ. ζωνη 29:9.

ʾdm (Pual). πυρουσθαι (error for πυρρουσθαι) 35:23.

ʾdmh. Syr *mn ʾdmtʾ* 20:24 ($ v.21).

ʾdnym (אֲדָנִים). βασεις 35:11 (LXX v.10); 36:38 (LXX 37:6). Syr *bsys* (= *βασεις) 38:30 (LXX 39:8).

ʾdnym (אֲדֹנִים). κ̅ς̅ (Syr *mrʾ*) 21:8. κ̅ς̅ 4:13.

ʾhl. Syr *strʾ* (= *σκεπη) 39:33 (LXX v.14); 40:2, 6, 29 (LXX v.26). Syr *tksytʾ* (= *σκεπη) 35:11 (LXX v.10). σκηνη 40:26 (LXX v.

[1]These readings are listed in chapter three, items 137-152.

24). Syr *mškn'* (= *σκηνη) 40:30 (LXX v.26).

'hrn. ααρων 28:4, 35 (LXX v.31); 29:9; 32:25.

'w. η (Syr *'w*) 5:3.

'wr (Hiphil). Syr *nhr* (Aphel) (= *φαινειν or *φωτιζειν) 13:21.

'wrym. Syr *nwhr'* (= *φωτισμοι ?) 28:30 (LXX v.26).

'z. οτι 4:26.

'zn. Syr *'dn'* (= *ους) 29:20.

'ḥ. αδελφος 28:4.

'ḥr. Syr *btr* (= *μετα with acc.) 18:2.

'ylm. κριοι 35:23.

— *'ymth.* 15:16.

'yn. Syr *l' 'ytwhy* (= *ουκ εστιν) 32:18 *bis*. Syr *l'* 33:15.

'yš. ανηρ (Syr *gbr'*) 30:38; 35:23. Syr *gbr'* (= *ανηρ) 16:16; 35:22 (plural). Syr *'nš* (= *τις) 21:18, 33.

'kl. See *lpy 'klw* and *kpy 'klw* under *ph*.

'l. προς 1:19; 8:25 (LXX v.29); 32:9. Syr *lwt* (= *προς) 6:13; 28:24 (MT). Syr *l-* (= *εις) 28:28 (MT).

'l mwl. Syr *lwqbl byt 'yn'* (= *επι το μετωπον) 28:25(MT).

'l 'br. εις το αντικρυς (Syr *mn lqwbl'*) 28:26(MT).

'lhym. θ̅ς̅ 7:1. Syr *'lh'* (= *θ̅ς̅ or *θεος) 8:6 (LXX v.10), 22 (LXX v.26). Syr *'lḧ'* (= *θεοι) 22:8 (LXX v.9), 19 (LXX v.20).

'lyh.(אַלְיָה). κερκιον 29:22.

'lm (אִלֵּם). μογιλαλον (Syr *l'g mmll'*) 4:11.

'm. ει (Syr *'n*) 21:8. Syr *'n* 13:13; 33:15.

'mh. Syr *'mt'*, plur *'m̈'* (= *πηχυς) 37:1 (LXX 38:1) *ter*, 10 (LXX 38:9) *ter*, 25 (MT) *bis*; 38:1 (LXX 38:22) *ter*.

'mr. ειπειν (Syr *'mr*) 4:25. ειπειν 4:26; 8:25 (LXX v.29); 32:9. Syr *'mr* (= *ειπειν) 32:4. λεγειν 2:14. Syr *'mr* (= *λεγειν) 36:5.

'ny. εγω 31:6.

'nky. εγω ειμι 8:25 (LXX v.29). Syr *'n' 'yty d-* (= *εγω ειμι) 32:18. Syr *'n'* (= *εγω) added before Syr *'yty* (= *ειμι) 3:11. Syr *'yty* (= *ειμι) added after Syr *'n'* (= *εγω) 4:23.

'pd/'pwd. επωμις (Syr *kbynt'*) 28:26 (MT); 29:5. επωμις 28:6. Syr *kbynt'* (= *επωμις) 28:25 (MT), 27 (MT) *bis*, 28 (MT) *ter*; 39:22 (LXX 36:20). επενδυμα (?) 25:7 (LXX v.6). εφωδ (?) 39:2 (LXX 36:9).

ʾrbh. Syr *qmṣʾ* (= *ακρις) 10:12.

ʾrbʿ. Syr *ʾrbʿ*, etc. (= *τεσσαρες, -ρα) 25:26 (LXX v.25); 37:13 (LXX 38:10) *ter*; 38:2 (LXX 38:22).

ʾrgmn. πορφυρα (Syr *ʾrgwnʾ*) 35:25. πορφυρα 28:6; 35:23. Syr *ʾrgwnʾ* (= *πορφυρα) 39:1 (LXX 39:13).

ʾrk. μηκος 28:16. Syr *ʾwrkʾ* (= *μηκος) 37:1 (LXX 38:1), 10 (LXX 38:9); 38:1 (LXX 38:22).

ʾrn. κιβωτος 35:12 (LXX v.11). Syr *qʾbwtʾ* (= *κιβωτος) 37:5 (LXX 38:4)

ʾrṣ. Syr *ʾrʿʾ* (= *γη) 8:18 (LXX v.22).

— *ʾrr.* 22:27 (LXX v.28). See items 38 and 147 in chapter three.

ʾšh (אִשֶּׁה). πυρον 29:18. πυρρον (error for πυρον) 30:20.

ʾšr. 9:25; 18:10; 21:8; 25:26 (LXX v.25); 28:26 (MT); 30:37, 38; 33:7; 35:23, 24; 37:13 (LXX 38:10).

ʾšr lw. Syr *dylh* (= *το αυτου) 35:16 (LXX v.17).

kʾšr. ον τροπον 2:14. Syr *ʾyk mʾ d-* (= *καθαπερ or *καθα) 12:32.

mpny ʾšr. δια το 19:18.

Untranslated. 3:14. See *ʾhyh ʾšr ʾhyh* under *hyh*.

— *ʾšr.* 3:9.

ʾt (accusative particle). Before nouns: 1:11, 17; 2:14; 5:20; 8:17, 22 (LXX v.26); 9:20, 25; 24:12; 26:15, 18; 28:5, 6, 23 (MT) *bis*, 24 (MT), 25 (MT), 28 (MT), 30 (LXX v.26) *bis*; 29:5 *bis*, 13, 16, 20; 30:5; 31:8, 9 *bis*, 10; 32:9, 25; 34:35; 35:11 (LXX v.10) *sexies*, 12 (LXX v.11) *bis*, 14 (LXX v.16) *bis*, 15 (LXX v. 16) *bis*, 16 (LXX v.17) *bis*, 28; 37:5 (LXX 38:4), 13 (LXX 38:10), 14 (LXX 38:10), 15 (LXX 38:11) *bis*, 26 (MT); 38:3 (LXX 38:23), 6 (LXX 38:24), 31 (LXX 39:9) *bis*; 39:22 (LXX 36:30), 33 (LXX 39:14), 34 (LXX 39:21), 37 (LXX 39:17), 39 (LXX 39:10) *ter*, 41 (MT); 40:5, 20 (LXX v.18), 28 (LXX v.25), 29 (LXX v.26) *bis*. With pronominal suffixes: 28:14, 26 (MT), 27 (MT); 29:24; 30:12; 37:4 (LXX 38:4), 11 (LXX 38:9), 15 (LXX 38:11); 38:2 (LXX 38:22), 6 (LXX 38:24).

— *ʾt* (accusative particle). Before nouns: 3:9. With pronominal suffixes: 3:9.

ʾt (preposition). παρ 35:23, 24. Syr *ʿm* (= *μετα with gen.) 28:1. Syr *btr* (= *μετα with acc.; error for *μετα with gen.) 38:23 (LXX 37:21).

ʾth. σu (Syr *ʾyt*; error for Syr *ʾnt*) 4:25. σu 2:14. Syr *ʾnt* (= *σu) 34:12.

ʾtm (אַתֶּם). ηθαν 13:20.

b- (preposition). εν (Syr *b-*) 12:11; 19:13; 21:8; 35:35 *bis*. εν 7:11; 8:3 (LXX v.7); 13:20; 35:35; 40:26 (LXX v.24). Syr *b-* (= *εν) 6:1 *bis*; 9:25; 11:3; 12:29; 16:2; 22:30 (LXX v.31); 23:21; 28:28 (MT); 29:14; 30:12; 38:23 (LXX 37:21), 25 (LXX 39:2). Syr *b-* 10:12; 33:12. Syr *b-* (= *εις) 37:5 (LXX 38:4). εις 19:13. κατα 30:32. Dative case of article 32:25; 35:35.

bṭrm. διοτι πριν 1:19.

bprk. εμπαιγμοι or εμπεγμω or εμπαιγματι 1:13.

bqdš. Syr *byt qwdšʾ* (= *εν τω αγιω) 39:1 (LXX 39:13).

bqṣh hmdbr. την ερημοτατην 13:20.

bqrb. Syr *bmṣʿtʾ* (= *εν μεσω ?) 8:18 (LXX v.22); 17:7; 34:9.

bśh. Syr *mn mrʿytʾ* 13:13.

btwk. εν μεσω 28:32 (LXX v.28).

Untranslated. 5:3 *bis*.

See *by* (particle of entreaty).

bgdym. Syr *lbwšʾ* (= *ιματια) 31:10. Syr *ʾsṭlʾ* (= *στολαι) 39:1 (LXX 39:13). Syr *ḥlṭtʾ* 39:41 (MT).

bd. Syr *bʾd* 39:28 (LXX 36:36).

bdym. αναφορεις 30:4; 35:12 (LXX v.11).– Syr *qwpʾ* (= *αναφορεις) 30:5; 35:15 (LXX v.16), 16 (LXX v.17); 37:4 (LXX 38:4), 5 (LXX 38:4), 14 (LXX 38:10), 15 (LXX 38:11); 38:6 (LXX 38:24). Syr *šqwlʾ* (= *αναβασταζοντες ?) 27:6; 40:20 (LXX v.18).

bhmh. κτηνος 22:18 (LXX v.19).

bwʾ. Qal: ερχεσθαι 18:5. εισερχεσθαι 1:19. Syr *ʾtʾ* (= *παραγινεσθαι) 36:4.

Hiphil: φερειν 35:29. Syr *ʿl* (Aphel) (= *εισφερειν) 37:5 (LXX 38:4).

bwr. Syr *gwbʾ* (= *λακκος) 12:29.

bṭrm. διοτι πριν 1:19.

by (particle of entreaty). εν εμοι 4:13.

byn (preposition). Syr *bmṣʿtʾ* (= *ανα μεσον) 11:7. Syr *bmṣʿtʾ* 31:17 *bis*. Syr *bynt* (= *ανα μεσον) 40:30 (LXX v.26) *bis*.

bynykm. υμιν 31:13. This one-word reading may refer only to the suffix.

byt. Syr *byt'* 12:29. See *btym* below.

— *byt*. 20:17 ($ v.14).

byth. εσωθεν (Syr *mn lgw*) 28:26 (MT).

bll. αναποιειν 29:2.

blt. See *lblty*.

bnym. Syr *bny'* (= *υιοι) 6:13; 29:20; 31:17; 32:2.

b'lym. Syr *mr'* (= *κς) 21:36.

bprk. εμπαιγμοι or εμπεγμω or εμπαιγματι 1:13.

bqrb. Syr *bmṣ't'* (= *εν μεσω ?) 8:18 (LXX v.22); 17:7; 34:9.

bqš (Piel). Syr *pys* (Aphel) 10:11.

bryḥym. μοχλοι 35:11 (LXX v.10).

bśmym. αρωματα (Syr *ḥlwm'*) 35:8 (LXX v.7). Syr *ḥlwm'* (= *αρωματα) or Syr *ḥrwm'* 25:6.

btwk. εν μεσω 28:32 (LXX v.28).

btym. θηκαι 30:4. Syr *ltyq'* (= *εις θηκας) 37:14 (LXX 38:10). See *byt* above.

gbwrh. Syr *bḥyl'* 32:18.

gb'h. βουνος 17:9.

gb'ym. Syr *'gn'* (= *κρατηρες) 25:33 (LXX v.32).

gg. δωμα 30:3. Syr *'gr'* (= *δωμα) 37:26 (MT).

gm. καιγε 7:11. Syr *w-* (= *και) 18:18.

— *wgm*. 3:9.

gm'. παπυρου 2:3.

gnb (infinitive absolute). Syr *gnb* (Ethpeel infinitive) (= *κλοπη) 22:11 (LXX v.12).

dbr (דֶּבֶר). Syr *mwt'* (= *θανατος ?) 5:3.

dbr (Piel). Syr *mll* (Pael) 12:32.

dm. αιμα (Syr *dm'*) 4:25. αιμα 4:26; 29:16. Syr *dm'* (= *αιμα) 29:20.

dmm. Syr *štq* 15:16.

dq. Syr *dqyq'* (= *λεπτος, -η, -ον) 16:14 *bis*.

h- (definite article). 1:17, 19; 2:14; 7:24 *bis*; 8:3 (LXX v.7), 17 (LXX v.21), 18 (LXX v.22); 9:22, 32; 11:3; 12:29, 42 *bis*; 13:20; 14:2, 9; 17:9; 18:18 *bis*; 19:13; 21:7; 24:10; 26:15, 18; 27:15; 28:5, 6, 23 (MT) *ter*, 24 (MT) *ter*, 25 (MT) *ter*, 26 (MT) *bis*, 27 (MT) *bis*, 28 (MT) *quinquies*, 30 (LXX v.26) *bis*, 37 (LXX v.33) *bis*; 29:5, 13, 20 *bis*, 22 *bis*, 26; 30:5,

13 *bis*, 37 (?); 31:8, 9, 10; 32:9 *bis*, 25; 34:29, 35; 35:3, 8 (LXX v.7) *bis*, 12 (LXX v.11), 14 (LXX v.16), 15 (LXX v.16), 16 (LXX v.17) *bis*, 28, 29, 35; 36:7, 21 (MT); 37:5 (LXX 38:4) *bis*, 13 (LXX 38:10) *bis*, 14 (LXX 38:10) *ter*, 15 (LXX 38:11) *bis*; 38:3 (LXX 38:23), 6 (LXX 38:24), 10 (LXX 37:8), 11 (LXX 37:9), 12 (LXX 37:10), 25 (LXX 39:2), 31 (LXX 39:9) *bis*; 39:1 (LXX 39:13) *ter*, 6 (LXX 36:13), 22 (LXX 36:20), 28 (LXX 36:36), 33 (LXX 39:14), 34 (LXX 39:21), 39 (MT), 41 (MT); 40:2, 5, 10 (LXX v.9), 20 (LXX v.18), 24 (LXX v.22), 28 (LXX v.25), 29 (LXX v.26) *bis*, 30 (LXX v.26).

— *h*- (definite article). 3:9.

h- (interrogative particle). η 2:14.

-*h* (directional). See *byth* under *byt* and *mrth* under *mrh*.

hwʾ. εστιν 29:14; 31:14; 32:9, 25. αυτο 29:18. Syr *hw* (= *αυτη ?) 12:42.

— *hwʾ*. 12:27, 42.

hyh. γινεσθαι 8:18 (LXX v.22). Syr *hwʾ* (= *γινεσθαι) 7:19; 37:14 (LXX 38:10); 38:2 (LXX 38:22). Syr *hwʾ* (= *ειναι) 4:9; 28:28 (MT); 39:9 (LXX 36:16); 40:10 (LXX v.9).

ʾhyh ʾšr ʾhyh. εσομαι εσομαι 3:14.

hlk. πορευεσθαι 5:7. Syr *ʾzl* (= *πορευεσθαι) 33:15. Syr *ḥzq* (= *οδευειν) 13:21.

hm. αυτοι (Syr *hnwn*) 5:7. αυτοι 7:11.

hmh. αυτοι 19:13.

hn (הֵן). Syr *w*- (= *και) 8:22 (LXX v.26).

hnh (הִנֵּה). ιδου (Syr *hʾ*) 31:6. ιδου 3:4; 4:6; 5:16; 8:25 (LXX v.9); 32:9.

hnh (הֵנָּה). αυται (Syr *hnyn*) 1:19.

hr. ορος 19:13.

hrg. αναιρειν 2:14 *bis*.

w- (conjunction). και (Syr *w*-) 4:25 *bis*; 20:25 (Ꞩ v.22); 28:26 (MT); 29:5; 31:8, 9 *bis*; 32:1; 35:8 (LXX v.7) *ter*, 35. και 2:21; 4:6, 26; 5:7, 16 *bis*; 7:24; 8:25 (LXX v.29) *bis*; 18:5; 28:5, 6 *ter*; 29:22; 31:6; 32:9 *bis*, 25; 35:7, 11 (LXX v.10) *bis*, 12 (LXX v.11), 23 *sexies*, 24, 35 *bis*; 36:38 (LXX 37:6). Syr *w*- (= *και) 1:7, 11; 2:25; 4:9; 5:23; 6:1, 13; 8:22 (LXX v.26); 10:12; 11:3; 13:13, 16, 21; 14:15; 16:10, 14; 21:18; 25:2, 29

(LXX v.28), 38; 27:15; 28:23 (MT) *bis*, 24 (MT), 25 (MT) *bis*, 26 (MT), 27 (MT) *bis*, 28 (MT) *bis*, 30 (LXX v.26), 41 (LXX v. 37); 29:20 *bis*; 30:18, 37; 31:10, 17; 32:4, 6 *bis*, 18, 29; 34:7, 19, 22; 35:14 (LXX v.16) *bis*, 15 (LXX v.16) *bis*, 16 (LXX v.17), 28; 36:4; 37:1 (LXX 38:1) *quinquies*, 4 (LXX 38:4) *bis*, 5 (LXX 38:4), 10 (LXX 38:9) *ter*, 11 (LXX 38:9) *bis*, 12 (LXX 38:9) *bis*, 13 (LXX 38:10) *bis*, 15 (LXX 38:11) *bis*, 25 (MT); 38:1 (LXX 38:22) *bis*, 2 (LXX 38:22), 3 (LXX 38:23), 6 (LXX 38:24) *bis*, 10 (LXX 37:8), 11 (LXX 37:9), 12 (LXX 37:10), 17 (LXX 37:15), 23 (LXX 37:21) *bis*, 31 (LXX 39:9) *bis*; 39:1 (LXX 39:13) *ter*, 34 (LXX 39:21), 37 (LXX 39:17), 39 (LXX 39:10) *bis*; 40:10 (LXX v.9), 20 (LXX v.18), 28 (LXX v.25), 29 (LXX v.26) *bis*, 30 (LXX v.26) *bis*, 33 (LXX v.27). Syr *ʾp* (= *και) 22:26 (LXX v.27). Syr *l-* (= *και) 40:30 (LXX v.26). δε 32:31. See *wwym* below.

Untranslated. 1:19; 13:13; 38:2 (LXX v.22).

— *w-* (conjunction). 14:7; 15:16, 21; 24:6.

— *wgm*. 3:9.

wwym. Syr *wšbtʾ* (= *και οι κοσμοι) 38:10 (LXX 37:8), 11 (LXX 37:9), 12 (LXX 37:10). Syr *šbtʾ* (= *κοσμοι ?) 38:28 (LXX 39:6).

zbḥ. Syr *dbḥ* (Pael) (= *θυσιαζειν) 22:19 (LXX v.20). Syr *dbḥ* (Peal or Pael) 8:22 (LXX v.26). Syr *dbḥ* (Peal) 8:22 (LXX v. 26).

zh. ουτος, αυτη, τουτο 30:13; 32:9. Syr *hnʾ* (= *ουτος, etc.) 18:18.

Untranslated. 12:42.

mzh. Syr *mn hrkʾ* (= *εντευθεν) 11:1.

zhb. χρυσιον 28:6. Syr *dhbʾ* (= *χρυσιον) 37:4 (LXX 38:4), 11 (LXX 38:9), 15 (LXX 38:10). Syr *dhbʾ* (= *χρυσους, -η, -ουν) 25:25 (LXX v.24); 28:23 (MT), 24 (MT), 26 (MT), 27 (MT); 37:11 (LXX 38:9), 12 (LXX 38:9), 13 (LXX 38:10).

ẓḥḥ (Niphal). αποσπασθαι (Syr *plṭ*, Ethpeel or Ethpaal) 28:28 (MT).

zr (זֵר). Syr *sptʾ* (= *κυματιον) 37:11 (LXX 38:9), 12 (LXX 38:9).

zrq. Syr *ʾšd* (= *προσχειν) 29:20.

zrt. σπιθαμη 28:6.

ḥg. Syr *ʿʾdʾ* (= *εορτη) 34:22.

ḥdš (חָדָשׁ). καινος (Syr *ḥdtʾ*) 1:8.

ḥdš (חֹדֶשׁ). Syr *yrḥ'* (= *μην) 40:2.

ḥzq (Piel). ενισχυειν 4:21.

ḥzq (חָזָק). Syr *'ḥyd'* (= *κραταιος, -α, -ον) 6:1 *bis*.

ḥṭ't (חַטָּאת). αμαρτια 5:16.

ḥṭ't (חַטָּאת). περι αμαρτιας 29:14.

ḥyh (adjective). ζωογονειν (Syr *ḥy'*, apparently Aphel) 1:19.

ḥyrt. See *py hḥyrt* under *ph*.

ḥkmh. σοφια 28:3.

ḥlb. στεαρ 29:22.

ḥlwšh. Syr *zkwt'* 32:18.

ḥll (Piel). βεβηλουν (Syr *swb*, Pael) 20:25 (*$* v.22).

ḥmrm. κοροι 8:10 (LXX v.14) *bis*. Note ϑ' *'yk šb'yn* in *$* at this point.

ḥmš, *ḥmšh*. πεντε 36:38 (LXX 37:6). Syr *ḥmš* (= *πεντε) 38:1 (LXX 38:22) *bis*.

ḥmšym (חֲמֻשִׁים). πεμπταιζοντες 13:18.

ḥnh. Syr *šr'* (= *στρατοπεδευειν) 14:2.

ḥsps. See *mḥsps*.

ḥpzwn. θαμβος (Syr *twht'*) 12:11.

ḥpnym. Syr *'ydy'* (= *χειρες) 9:8.

ḥpr. ορυσσειν 7:24.

ḥṣy. Syr *plg'* (= *ημισυς) 37:1 (LXX 38:1) *ter*, 10 (LXX 38:9).

ḥṣr. Syr *drt'* (= *αυλη) 38:31 (LXX 39:9).

ḥrb. ρομφαια (Syr *syp'*) 5:3; 20:25 (*$* v.22).

ḥrṭmym. επαοιδοι 7:11; 8:3 (LXX v.7).

— *ḥšb* (participle). 28:15.

ḥšb (חֵשֶׁב). Syr *mtqnwt'* (= *μηχανωματος or *μηχανηματος) 28:27 (MT), 28 (MT).

ḥšn. λογιον 25:7 (LXX v.6); 35:9 (LXX v.8). Syr *pdt'* (= *λογιον) 28:4, 23 (MT) *bis*, 24 (MT), 26 (MT), 28 (MT) *bis*.

ḥšqym/ḥšwqym. Syr *dwbq'* (= *κατακολλησεις ?) 38:11 (LXX 37:9). Syr *dwbq'* (= *κολλησεις ?) 38:12 (LXX 37:10). Syr *dwbq'* 38:17 (LXX 37:15). Syr *ps'lyds* (= *φαλιδες) 38:10 (LXX 37:8).

ḥtn (חָתָן). νυμφιος (Syr *ḥtn'*) 4:25, 26.

ḥtn (חֹתֵן). γαμβρος 18:5.

— *ḥtn* (חֹתֵן). 18:1.

ṭb't/ṭb'wt. Syr *'zqt'* (= *δακτυλιος) 28:28 (MT) *bis*. Syr *'zqt'* (=

*δακτυλιοι) 28:23 (MT) *bis*, 24 (MT), 26 (MT), 27 (MT). Syr *zqzqt'* (= *δακτυλιοι) 37:5 (LXX 38:4), 13 (LXX 38:10) *bis*, 14 (LXX 38:10). The MT always has plural vocalization, even in 28:28.

ṭhwr. Syr *dky'* (= *καθαρος, -α, -ον) 37:11 (LXX 38:9).

ṭwṭpt (plural vocalization). Syr *dmttzy'* (Ethpeel participle of *zw'*) 13:16.

ṭpḥ. Syr *zrt'* (= *παλαιστης) 37:12 (LXX 38:9).

ṭrm. See *bṭrm*.

y'l (Hiphil). αρχεσθαι 2:21.

y'r. ποταμος (Syr *nhr'*) 7:24. ποταμος 7:24.

ybl. ιωβηλ (Syr *ywbl* or Syr *ywbb*) 19:13.

yd. χειρ 4:6; 26:17. Syr *'yd'* (= *χειρ) 6:1 *bis*.

šlḥ yd-. Syr *mtḥ 'b'š* 22:10 (LXX v.11).

yd'. Syr *yd'* 36:1.

yhwh. $\overline{\kappa\varsigma}$ (Syr *mry'*) 4:24. $\overline{\kappa\varsigma}$ 19:18. κυριος 29:18. Syr *mry'* (= *κυριος) 8:22 (LXX v.26); 12:48. $\overline{\kappa\varsigma}$ or Syr *pypy* (= *πιπι) 32:9. Syr *pypy* (= *πιπι) 8:6 (LXX v.10); 12:42; 15:18; 22:10 (LXX v.11).

—*yhwh*. 12:42.

ywm. Syr *ywm'* (= *ημερα) 12:6; 16:5 *bis*.

ywmm. Syr *b'ymm'* (= *ημερας) 13:21.

ykl. δυνασθαι (Syr *mṣ'*) 7:24. δυνασθαι 40:35 (LXX v.29).

yld. Qal: τικτειν 1:19.

Piel (participle); Untranslated. 1:19.

yldym. παιδαρια 1:17. παιδια 1:18.

y'd. καθομολογεισθαι (Syr *yd'*, Eshtaphal) 21:8.

y'ym. Syr *šqšl'* 38:3 (LXX 38:23).

y'qb. ιακωβ 1:5.

yṣ'. εξερχεσθαι (Syr *npq*) 21:7. εκπορευεσθαι (Syr *npq*) 21:7. εκπορευεσθαι 8:25 (LXX v.29).

yṣq. Syr *'bd* (= *ποιειν) 37:13 (LXX 38:10).

yrd. καταβαινειν 19:18.

yrh (infinitive absolute). τοξευεσθαι (participle) 19:13.

yrk. μηρος or μηροι 1:5. Syr *'ṭm'* (= *μηρος ?) 37:17 (LXX 38:14).

yśr'l. Syr *'ysr'yl* (= *$\overline{\iota\eta\lambda}$ or *ισραηλ) 6:13; 31:17.

ytdt. Syr *šk'* (= *πασσαλοι) 38:31 (LXX 39:9) *bis*.

ytrw. ιοθορ 18:5.

— *ytrw*. 18:1.

ytrt. περιττον 29:13.

k- (preposition). ωσει 4:6. ωσπερ (Syr *'ykn' d-*) 21:7. καθαπερ
     4:7. Syr *'yk* (= *ωσει) 16:14. Syr *'yk* (= *κατα) 21:30. Syr
     'yk 8:6 (LXX v.10). See *kpy 'klw* under *ph*.

    k'šr. ον τροπον 2:14. Syr *'yk m' d-* (= *καθαπερ or *καθα)
        12:32.

    k'ṣm. Syr *'kwth* 24:10.

khn (Piel). ιερατευειν 28:1, 3.

khnym. ιερεις (Syr *khn̈'*) 19:6.

ky (conjunction). οτι (Syr *mṭl d-*) 4:25; 7:24; 20:25 (𝔖 v.22). οτι
        1:19; 31:14; 32:25 *bis*. Syr *mṭl d-* (= *οτι) 8:22 (LXX v.26).

kyr. Syr *mšgt'* (= *λουτηρ) 39:39 (MT).

kl. πας, πασα, παν 7:24; 22:18 (LXX v.19); 30:13; 31:9; 35:23, 24,
        29. Syr *kl* (= *πας, etc.) 9:25; 10:15; 12:41; 21:30; 34:19;
        36:4, 7; 38:3 (LXX 38:23), 31 (LXX 39:9) *bis*; 39:37 (LXX 39:17).

klym. σκευη (Syr *m'n̈'*) 31:9. Syr *m'n̈'* (= *σκευη) 38:3 (LXX 38:23);
        39:37 (LXX 39:17).

kmhw. See the last item under *kn* (adverb).

kn (noun). Syr *bsys* (= *βασις) 39:39 (MT).

kn (adverb). ωσαυτως 7:11. Syr *hkn'* (= *ουτως ?) 10:29. Syr *ddm'*
     lh 10:14 (This could also be interpreted as a misplaced
     equivalent for MT *kmhw*.).

knpym. πτερυγες 19:4.

ksmt. Syr *kûnt'* (= *ολυρα or *ζεα) 9:32.

ksp. Syr *s'm'* (= *αργυραι) 38:10 (LXX 37:8), 11 (LXX 37:9), 12
        (LXX 37:10).

kpy. See under *ph*.

kpr. Syr *'glyd'* (= *παγος ?) 16:14.

kprym. εξιλασμος 29:36.

krkb. Syr *trṭql'* 38:4 (LXX 38:24).

ktnt. χιτων (Syr *kwtyn'*) 29:5.

ktp. Syr *ktp'* (= *ωμια) 27:14. Syr *ktp'* 27:15.

    ktpwt. Syr *ktp̈t'* (= *ωμοι) 28:25 (MT), 27 (MT).

l- (preposition). Before nouns, verbs, other words: εις (Syr *l-*)
        7:24; 35:8 (LXX v.7) *ter*. εις 4:26; 25:7 (LXX v.6); 28:1, 3;

29:1; 30:4; 35:29. των (Syr *b-*) 4:25. τοις 30:4. του 35:29. Syr *'yk d-* (= *ωστε) 37:14 (LXX 38:10), 15 (LXX 38:11); 39:1 (LXX 39:13). Syr *qdm* (= *εναντιον) 8:22 (LXX v.26). Syr *l-* (= *εις) 35:28; 36:7. Syr *l-* (= *ινα) 28:28 (MT). Syr *l-* (may = *definite article or dative case) 8:22 (LXX v.26); 12:42, 48; 13:21 *bis*; 22:19 (LXX v.20); 27:13, 15; 36:1 *bis*, 22 (MT); 37:12 (LXX 38:9), 14 (LXX 38:10). Syr *d-* (may = *definite article) 25:26 (LXX v.25); 27:14; 31:5; 37:13 (LXX 38:10); 40:28 (LXX v.25). With pronominal suffixes: Greek dative (Syr *l-*) 4:26. Greek dative 5:7; 28:1, 3; 31:14. Greek genitive 28:43 (LXX v.39). Syr *l-* (= *dative case) 9:8; 12:21, 26; 13:21; 33:5; 37:11 (LXX 38:9), 12 (LXX 38:9), 13 (LXX 38:10).

'šr lw. Syr *dylh* (= *το αυτου) 35:16 (LXX v.17).

lblty. ωστε μη 8:18 (LXX v.22).

l'mt. συμφωνως κατα or Syr *šlm'yt w-* (= *συμφωνως και) 28:27 (MT). Syr *lṭḥt mn* (= *υπο) 37:14 (LXX 38:10).

lpy 'klw. See under *ph.*

lpnyk. εμπροσθεν σου (Syr *qdmyk*) 17:6.

mlmṭh. Syr *mn lṭḥt* (= *κατωθεν) 28:27 (MT).

Untranslated. 2:14; 7:1, 24; 13:16; 28:4, 27 (MT); 29:18; 32:25; 36:5.

— *l-* (preposition). 12:42.

l'. ου, ουκ (Syr *l'*) 7:24, 21:7, 8. ου μη (Syr *l'*) 28:28 (MT). ου, ουκ 22:27 (LXX v.28); 40:35. Syr *l'* (= *μη) 13:13. Syr *l'* 8:22 (LXX v.26).

— *l'.* 22:27 (LXX v.28). See items 38 and 147 in chapter three.

lb. Syr *lb'* (= *καρδια) 36:2, 8.

lblty. ωστε μη 8:18 (LXX v.22).

lhṭym. φαρμακειαι 7:11. See *lṭym.*

— *lḥṣ* (verb). 3:9.

— *lḥṣ* (noun). 3:9.

lḥt (plural of *lwḥ*). πλακες 24:12.

lṭym. φαρμακειαι 8:3 (LXX v.7). See *lhṭym.*

lylh. Syr *lly'* (= *νυξ) 12:42; 13:21.

— *lylh.* 12:42 (LXX v.41).

l'mt. συμφωνως κατα or Syr *šlm'yt w-* (= *συμφωνως και) 28:27 (MT).

Syr *ltḥt mn* (= *υπο) 37:14 (LXX 38:10).

lpy. See under *ph*.

lpnyk. εμπροσθεν σου (Syr *qdmyk*) 17:6.

lqḥ. Syr *nsb* (= *λαμβανειν) 9:8; 25:2.

m- (preposition). εκ (Syr *mn*) 7:24. Syr *mn* (= *εκ) 28:28 (MT).

mn (preposition). Syr *šrk* (verb) (= *καταλειπειν, passive participle) 39:1 (LXX 39:13).

mmn- (preposition). Syr *mn*(= *εξ) 25:15 (LXX v.14); 38:2 (LXX 38:22).

mmnw. αυτον 4:26.

mzh. Syr *mn hrkʾ* (= *εντευθεν) 11:1.

mlmṭh. Syr *mn ltḥt*. (= *κατωθεν) 28:27 (MT).

mmwl. εκ του κατα (Syr *mn lwqbl*) 28:27 (MT).

mmʿl. Syr *lʿl mn* (= *επανω) 28:27 (MT).

mʿl. Syr *mn* (= *απο) 28:28 (MT).

mʿm. απο 8:25 (LXX v.29).

mpny ʾšr. δια το 19:18.

mʾwr. φως (Syr *nhyrʾ*) 35:8 (LXX v.7). Syr *nhyrʾ* (= *φως) 35:14 (LXX v.16), 28.

mgblt. Syr *gdy̆ly ʾkḥdʾ* 28:14.

mgbʿwt. υφωματα 28:40 (LXX v.26).

mdbr. Syr *mdbrʾ* (= *ερημος) 16:2.

bqṣh hmdbr. την ερημοτατην 13:20.

mh. Syr *mṭl d*- (= *οτι ?) 33:5.

mwl. See *ʾl mwl* under *ʾl* (preposition) and *mmwl* under *m*- (preposition).

mwlt. περιτομαι 4:26.

mwʿd. Syr *shdwtʾ* (= *μαρτυριον) 33:7; 40:30 (LXX v.26).

mwt (verb). Only:

mwt ywmt. αναθεματισθησεται 22:18 (LXX v.19).

mzbḥ. θυσιαστηριον (Syr *mdbḥʾ*) 31:8, 9. Syr *mdbḥʾ* (= *θυσιαστηριον) 29:20; 35:15 (LXX v.16); 40:10 (LXX v.9), 30 (LXX v.26).

mzh. Syr *mn hrkʾ* (= *εντευθεν) 11:1.

mḥbrt. συμβολη (Syr *rmyʾ dʾkḥdʾ*) 28:27 (MT).

mḥsps. Syr *qlp* (passive participle) (= *ανασυρεσθαι, participle) 16:14.

mṭh. See *mlmṭh*.

mym. υδωρ (Syr *myꞌ*) 7:24. Syr *myꞌ* (= *υδωρ) 40:30 (LXX v.26).

mymy. υδωρ (Syr *myꞌ*) 7:24. Syr *myꞌ* (= *υδατα) 8:2 (LXX v.6).

mkbr. κοσκηνομ̲. or Syr *ꞌyk dʿrblꞌ* 27:4. Syr *ṭrṭqlꞌ* (= *κοσκινωμα) 35:16 (LXX v.17). Syr *mḥwltꞌ* 39:39 (LXX 39:10).

mlꞌ (Piel). Syr *mlꞌ* (= *πιμπλαναι or *εμπιμπλαναι) 28:41 (LXX v. 37).

mlꞌt (infinitive construct). Syr *mwlyꞌ* (= *πληρωσις) 31:5.

mlꞌ (מְלֹא). Syr *mlꞌ* 9:8.

mlꞌym. Syr *šwmlyꞌ* (= *τελειωσεις) 29:26.

mlꞌkh. εργα 35:29. Syr *ʿbdꞌ* (= *εργον) 36:7.

mlk. Syr *mlk* (Aphel) (= *βασιλευειν) 15:18.

mlmṭh. Syr *mn ltḥt* (= *κατωθεν) 28:27 (MT).

mlqḥym. Syr *mlqṭꞌ* (= *λαβιδες) 25:38.

mmlkt. βασιλει[α] (Syr *mlkwtꞌ*) 19:6.

mmn- (preposition). See under *m-* (preposition).

mn (preposition). See under *m-* (preposition).

mnḥh. Syr *dbḥꞌ* (= *θυσια) 40:29 (LXX v.26).

msbt. Syr *ḥdyln bpslꞌ* 39:6 (LXX 36:13).

msgrt. Syr *klylꞌ* (= *στεφανη) 37:12 (LXX 38:9) *bis*, 14 (LXX 38:10).

mswh. Syr *tḥpytꞌ* (= *καλυμμα) 34:35.

msk. επισπαστρον 40:5. Syr *prsꞌ* (= *επισπαστρον) 40:28 (LXX v.25). Syr *ṭll* (Pael participle) (= *συσκιαζειν, participle) 39:34 (LXX 39:21).

mskh. χωνευτος, -η, -ον 32:8.

mʿyl. επενδυτης or επιδυτης (Syr *lʿl mn lbwšꞌ*) 29:5. Syr *lbwšꞌ ʿlyꞌ* 39:22 (LXX 36:30).

mʿl (מַעַל). See *mmʿl* under *m-* (preposition).

mʿl (מֵעַל). See under *m-* (preposition).

mʿm. See under *m-* (preposition).

mʿśh. Syr *ʿbdꞌ* (= *εργον) 28:14.

mṣꞌ (Niphal). ευρισκειν (passive) 35:23, 24.

mpny. See under *pnym*.

mṣnpt. κιναρις 28:37 (LXX v.33) *bis*. υφωμα 28:39 (LXX v.35).

mṣry. αιγυπτιος, -α, -ον 2:14.

mṣrym (מִצְרַיִם). αιγυπτιοι 7:11, 24. Syr *mṣryn* (= *αιγυπτος) 8:2 (LXX v.6), 22 (LXX v.26).

— *mṣrym* (מִצְרַיְם). 3:9.

mqṭr. Syr *pyrm'* (= *θυσιαστηριον) 30:1.

mqnh. Syr *bʿyr'* (= *κτηνη) 34:19.

mqšh. Syr *ngydy bṭwrnws* 25:18 (LXX v.17).

— *mqšh*. 25:31 (LXX v.30).

mrh (מָרָה). Only:

mrth. Syr *lmwr'* 15:23.

mšbṣt/mšbṣwt. συνεσφιγμενοι or συνεσφραγισμενοι 28:11. Syr *ḥyṣṭ'* (= *σφιγκτοι ?) 28:25 (MT). Syr *ḥywṣṭ'* 39:16 (LXX 36:23).

mšh. μωυσης 18:5; 32:25. μωυσης or μωσης 32:9. μωσης 8:25 (LXX v.29); 32:31.

mšḥh. χρισις (Syr *mšyḥwt'*) 35:8 (LXX v.7).

mšk (infinitive construct). απελευσις (Syr *m'zlt'*) 19:13.

mškn. Syr *mškn'* (= *σκηνη) 38:31 (LXX 39:9); 40:28 (LXX v.25).

mtknt. συνταξις 30:22.

ngb. Syr *tymn'* (= *νοτος) 36:23 (MT).

ngʿ (Hiphil). απτειν (Syr *gšp*) 4:25.

ndbh. Syr *ṣbyny'* 35:29.

nwp (Hiphil). επιβαλλειν (Syr *rm'*, Aphel) 20:25 (Ꞩ v.22).

nḥšt. χαλκαι 36:38 (LXX 37:6). Syr *nḥs'* (= *χαλκος or *χαλκους, -α, -ουν) 35:16 (LXX v.17); 38:2 (LXX 38:22), 3 (LXX 38:23), 6 (LXX 38:24).

nyḥwḥ. ευαραστησις 29:18.

nkh. Hiphil: Syr *mḥ'* (= *πατασσειν) 21:18.

Hophal: μαστιγουσθαι 5:16.

nkḥ. Syr *qdm* (= *ενωπιον) 14:2. Syr *lwqbl* (= *απεναντι) 40:24 (LXX v.22).

nsʿ. Syr *rwm* (Aphel) 14:15.

nṣl (Hiphil infinitive absolute). Syr *prq* (infinitive) (= *ρυεσθαι, participle) 5:23.

nqrh. Syr *qywln'* (?) 33:22.

nrt. Syr *šrg'* (= *λυχνοι) 35:14 (LXX v.16).

nś'. συμβασταζειν 18:22. Syr *šql* (= *αιριεν) 37:14 (LXX 38:10), 15 (LXX 38:11).

nśy'. Syr *ryšn'* (= *αρχων) 22:27 (LXX v.28).

ntn. διδοναι 30:13. Syr *yhb* (= *διδοναι) 40:20 (LXX v.18), 30 (LXX v.26), 33 (LXX v.27). Syr *ntl* (= *διδοναι) 28:23 (MT), 24 (MT), 25 (MT) *bis*, 27 (MT). καθισταναι 7:1. Syr *swm* (= *επιτιθεναι) 37:13 (LXX 38:10).

sbb (Pual). See *msbt*.

sbyb. Syr *lḥwdr'* (= *κυκλω) 29:20. Syr *kd ḥdr* (= *κυκλω) 37:11 (LXX 38:9), 12 (LXX 38:9) *bis*; 38:31 (LXX 39:9).

sbybt. κυκλω 7:24.

syny. Syr *syny* 19:11.

smym. αρωματα 30:7. συνθεσις (Syr *rwkb'*) 35:8 (LXX v.7).

sql. Syr *rgm* (= *λιθοβολειν) 8:22 (LXX v.26).

'bdh. δουλεια (Syr *'bdwt'*) 30:16. δουλεια 27:19. Syr *pwlḥn 'bdwt'* (= *δουλια) 36:3.

'bdym. δουλοι (Syr *'bd'*) 9:20; 21:7. δουλοι 5:16.

'br (verb). διερχεσθαι 32:27. παραπορευεσθαι 30:13.

'br (עֵבֶר). Only:

'l 'br. εις το αντικρυς or Syr *mn lqwbl'* 28:26 (MT).

'bt. Syr *ššlt'* 28:14. Syr *ššlt'* 39:15 (LXX 36:22).

'btt. Syr *ššlt'* (= *αλυσιδωτα) 28:24 (MT). Syr *ššlt'* (= *αλυσεις or *αλυσιδωτα) 28:25 (MT). χαλαστα (perhaps misplaced, see pp. 73-74, 79) 39:17 (LXX 36:25).

'gl. μοσχος 32:8.

'd (preposition). Syr *w-* (= *και) 22:3 (LXX v.4).

'dt. Syr *shdwt'* (= *μαρτυριον ?) 34:29.

'wlm. αιωνιος, -ον 28:43 (LXX v.39).

'wr. Syr *ḥzt'* (=*οφις) 34:35. See *'rt* below.

'zym. αιγεια 35:23.

'ynym. οφθαλμοι (Syr *'yn'*) 21:8. Syr *'yn'* (= *οφθαλμοι) 8:22 (LXX v.26); 11:3.

'l (preposition). επι or Syr *lqwbl* 14:9. επι (Syr *'l*) 20:25 (Ꞩ v. 22); 30:16. επι 19:4; 28:35 (LXX v.31), 37 (LXX v.33); 30:13. Syr *'l* (= *επι) 8:2 (LXX v.6); 12:7; 19:18; 28:23 (MT) *bis*, 24 (MT), 25 (MT) *bis*, 26 (MT) *bis*, 27 (MT), 28 (MT); 29:20 *bis*; 34:7; 37:5 (LXX 38:4), 13 (LXX 38:10); 38:2 (LXX 38:22); 40:29 (LXX v.26). κατα 28:21.

m'l. Syr *mn* (= *απο) 28:28 (MT).

'lh (verb). Qal: αναβαινειν 19:13. Syr *slq* (= *αναβαινειν) 10:12; 16:14.

Hiphil: Syr *'t'* (Aphel) 32:6. Syr *slq* (Aphel) (= *αναφερειν) 40:29 (LXX v.26).

'lh (noun). ολοκαυτωσις (Syr *yqd' šlm'*) 31:9. Syr *yqd' šlm'* (=

*ολοκαυτωσις) 35:16 (LXX v.17). Syr *yqd' šlm'* (= *ολοκαυτωσις) 29:42; 40:29 (LXX v.26).

ʿm (preposition). μετα 22:18 (LXX v.19).

mʿm. απο 8:25 (LXX v.29).

ʿm (noun). λαος 5:16; 32:9 *bis*, 25. Syr *ʿm'* (= *λαος) 11:3; 18:18.

ʿmd (participle). Syr *qwm* (participle) (= *ισταναι, participle) 26:15. (Syr *dqymyn* could = *εστωτας or *εστηκοτας or *ισταμενους).

ʿmdym/ʿmwdym. στυλοι 35:11 (LXX v.10). Syr *ʿmwd'* (= *στυλοι) 26:32; 38:10 (LXX 37:8), 11 (LXX 37:9), 12 (LXX 37:10).

ʿmyndb. Syr *ʿmyddb*. 6:23.

ʿmr. Syr *gwmwr* (= *γομορ) 16:16, 18.

ʿmt. See *lʿmt*.

ʿnh. Qal (infinitive construct): Syr *mʿnyn* 32:18. Syr *mʿnynwt'* 32:18.

Piel (infinitive construct): Syr *mʿnyn* 32:18.

— *ʿnh*. 15:21.

ʿṣym. ξυλα 35:7. Syr *qys'* (= *ξυλα) 25:23 (LXX v.22); 37:1 (LXX 38:1), 4 (LXX 38:4), 10 (LXX 38:9), 15 (LXX 38:11); 38:1 (LXX 38:22), 6 (LXX 38:24).

ʿṣm. See *kʿṣm* under *k-* (preposition).

ʿrb. Syr *ḥlṭ'* 8:17 (LXX v.21).

ʿrl. απεριτμητος 6:12.

ʿrm (Niphal). σωρευεσθαι 15:8.

ʿrp (verb). νωτοκοπειν (Syr *psq ḥṣ'*) 13:13. Syr *psq ḥṣ'* (= *νωτοκοπειν) 34:20.

ʿrp (noun). Only:

qšh ʿrp. σκληροτραχηλος, -ον 32:9.

ʿrpl. γνοφος 20:21 (₰ v.18).

ʿrt (plural of *ʿwr*). δερματα 35:23. See *ʿwr* above.

ʿśh. ποιειν 28:6. Syr *ʿbd* (= *ποιειν) 28:14, 23 (MT), 26 (MT), 27 (MT); 30:18, 37; 33:5; 36:1; 37:4 (LXX 38:4), 11 (LXX 38:9), 12 (LXX 38:9) *bis*, 15 (LXX 38:11); 38:2 (LXX 38:22), 3 (LXX 38:23), 6 (LXX 38:24); 39:1 (LXX 39:13).

ʿtr (Hiphil). ευχεσθαι 8:25 (LXX v.29).

p'h. Syr *ṣtr'* 27:13.

p't (plural). Syr *gb'* (= *μερη) 37:13 (LXX 38:10).

pg'. Syr *pg'* 5:3.

pdh. Syr *prq* (= *λυτρουσθαι ?) 13:13 *bis*.

ph. Only in phrases:

py hḥyrt. φιεθρω or Syr *p'yrwt* 14:2. φιεθρων or Syr *p'y'yrwt* 14:9.

kpy 'klw. Syr *bhlyn d'klyn lh* 16:21.

lpy 'klw. Syr *lm'kwlt' dylh* 16:16.

— *pḥd*. 15:16.

— *plštym*. 23:31.

pnh. Syr *hpk* 16:10.

pnym. προσωπον (Syr *prṣwp'*) 28:25 (MT), 27 (MT). προσωπον 28:37 (LXX v.33). Syr *prṣwp'* (= *προσωπον) 33:15. προθεσις 25:30 (LXX v.29).

lpnyk. εμπροσθεν σου (Syr *qdmyk*) 17:6.

mpny 'šr. δια το 19:18.

pnt (plural). Syr *ẓwnwt'* (= *γωνιαι) 38:2 (LXX v.22).

— *psḥ*. 12:11, 27.

p'mt. μερη 25:12 (LXX v.11).

pqd (infinitive construct). Syr *mnyn'* (= *επισκοπη) 30:12.

pqdym (פְּקֻדִים). επισκοπαι 30:13.

— *prḥ*. 25:33 (LXX v.32).

prk. Only:

bprk. εμπαιγμοι or εμπεγμω or εμπαιγματι 1:13.

prkt. Syr *prs'* (= *καταπετασμα) 39:34 (LXX 39:21).

pr'. διασκεδαζειν 32:25 *bis*. διασκεδαζειν or διασωζειν 5:4.

pr'h. φαραω 7:1.

prṣ. Syr *gmr* (Aphel or perhaps Pael) 19:22. Syr *psq* 19:24.

ptḥ. θυρα 40:5. Syr *tr''* (= *θυρα) 40:28 (LXX v.25).

ptyl. Syr *pšl'* (= *κλωσμα) 28:28 (MT).

ptm (פִּתֹם). Syr *pytw* 1:11.

ṣb'wt. Syr *ḥylwt'* (= *δυναμεις ?) 12:41.

ṣl't. Syr *dpnt'* (= *πλευρα) 37:5 (LXX 38:4).

ṣph (Piel). Syr *qrm* (= *καταχρυσουν) 37:4 (LXX 38:4), 11 (LXX 38:9), 15 (LXX 38:11). Syr *ḥpy* (= *καλυπτειν) 38:2 (LXX 38:22), 6 (LXX 38:24).

ṣpwn. Syr *grby'* (= *βορρας) 36:25 (MT).

ṣr. ακροτομος, -ον 4:25.

ṣrʿ (Pual participle). λεπραν (participle) 4:6.

qbl (Hiphil participle). Syr *pgʿ* (participle) (= *αντιπιπτειν, participle ?) 36:5.

qdš (Piel). αγιαζειν (Syr *qdš*, Pael) 29:1.

qdš (קָדֹשׁ). αγιος, -α, -ον 31:14. Syr *qwdšʾ* (=*αγιον or *αγιος, -α, -ον) 31:10; 38:25 (LXX 39:2); 39:1 (LXX 39:13).

qhl (Niphal). εκκλησιαζεσθαι (Syr *knš*, Ethpeel or Ethpaal) 32:1.

qwl Syr *qlʾ* (= *φωνη) 32:18 *ter*. The first is followed by the expansion Syr *dqrbʾ* (= *πολεμου).

qwm (participle). ανθισταναι (perfect participle) 32:25.

qṭrt. θυμιαμα (Syr *bsmʾ*) 35:8 (LXX v.7). θυμιαμα (Syr *bšmʾ*) 31:8. θυμιαμα 30:7. Syr *bšmʾ* (= *θυμιαμα) 35:15 (LXX v.16).

qll. ατιμαζειν or καταμαν (?) 28:27 (LXX v.28). See items 38 and 147 in chapter three.

qlʿym. Syr *wʾlls* (= *ιστια) 38:12 (LXX 37:10).

qmh. Syr *rwmʾ* (= *υψος) 37:1 (LXX 38:1), 10 (LXX 38:9); 38:1 (LXX 38:22).

qnh. λυτρουσθαι 15:16.

qṣh. See *bqṣh hmdbr* under *mdbr*.

qṣwt. Syr *ryšʾ* (= *ακρα) 28:24 (MT), 25 (MT), 26 (MT). Syr *ršʾ* (= *ακρα) 28:23 (MT).

qrb. Only:

bqrb. Syr *bmṣʿtʾ* (= *εν μεσω) 8:18 (LXX v.22); 17:7; 34:9.

qrnt. Syr *qrntʾ* (= *κερατα) 38:2 (LXX 38:22) *bis*.

qrsym. περοναι (Syr *ʿbrʾ*) or Syr *qwrqsʾ* (= *κρικοι) 35:11 (LXX v. 10). The second alternative is the α′ reading, erroneously attributed to α′σ′θ′ by $. Syr *ʿbrʾ* (= *περοναι) 39:33 (LXX 39:14).

qrš. σανις (Syr *dpʾ*) 26:15. σανις 35:11 (LXX v.10). Syr *dpʾ* (= *σανις) 26:18; 36:21 (MT), 22 (MT); 39:33 (LXX 39:14).

qśwt. Syr *pylʾlys* (= *φιαλαι) 25:29 (LXX v.28).

qšh. δυσχερης, -ες 18:20. α′σ′θ′ σκληρον δυσχερες of M is a conflation of the α′σ′ and θ′ variants.

qšh ʿrp. σκληροτραχηλος, -ον 32:9.

qšš (Polel). καλαμασθαι 5:7.

rʾh. ιδειν (Syr *ḥzʾ*) 2:25. ιδειν 7:1; 32:25. οραν 32:9. Syr *ḥzʾ* (= *ιδειν or *οραν) 22:9 (LXX v.10).

— *rʾh*. 3:9.

r'š. κεφαλη 28:32 (LXX v.28).

rbw'. Syr *ṭṭrgwnwn* (= *τετραγωνος, -ον) 38:1 (LXX 38:22).

rglym. ποδες (Syr *rgl'*) 4:25. Syr *rgl'* (= *ποδες) 37:13 (LXX 38:10).

rwḥ. πνευμα (abbreviated genitive: πνς) 28:3.

rḥb. Syr *pty'* (= *ευρος) 37:10 (LXX 38:9); 38:1 (LXX 38:22). Syr *pty'* (= *πλατος ?) 37:1 (LXX 38:1).

ryḥ. οσμη 29:18.

rks. Syr *ḥwṣ* (= *συσφιγγειν) 28:28 (MT).

— *r'* (רֵעַ). 20:17 (*S* v.14).

r'h (feminine of *r'*, רַע). πονηρα (Syr *byšt'*) 21:8.

rph. αφιειν, αφιεναι 4:26.

rqm (participle). ποικιλτα (neuter plural) 35:35.

rš' (Hiphil). Syr *ḥwb* (Pael). 22:8 (LXX v.9).

ršt. Syr *mṣydt'* (= *δικτυον ?) 27:4. There is no marker in the text, and so the reading could pertain to another MT word.

śdh. Syr *ḥql'* (= *αγρος) 9:22, 25; 22:30 (LXX v.31).

śh. Only:

bśh. Syr *mn mr'yt'* 13:13.

śwm, śym. Syr *swm* (= *τιθεναι) 40:28 (LXX v.25), 30 (LXX v.26). διδοναι (Syr *ntl*) 28:26 (MT).

— *śwm, śym*. 24:6.

śph. χειλος 6:12. Syr *spt'* (= *χειλος) 28:26 (MT).

śrd. Syr *tšmšt'* (= *λειτουργικος, -η, -ον) 39:1 (LXX 39:13), 41 (MT).

šbt (שַׁבָּת). Syr *šb'* (= *σαββατα) 35:3.

šhm. ονυξ 39:6 (LXX 36:13).

šwb. επιστρεφειν 32:31.

šwlym. Syr *lwt rgl'* (= *προς ποδων) 28:33 (LXX v.29).

šwr. Syr *twr'* (= *μοσχος) 22:3 (LXX v.4).

šzr (Hophal participle). κλωθεσθαι (perfect participle) 28:6.

šṭym. ασηπτοι, -α 35:7. Syr **l' mblṭ'* (= *ασηπτοι, -α) 25:23 (LXX v.22); 26:37; 37:1 (LXX 38:1), 4 (LXX 38:4), 10 (LXX 38:9), 15 (LXX 38:11); 38:1 (LXX 38:22), 6 (LXX 38:24).

škb. κοιμασθαι 22:18 (LXX v.19).

škbh. Syr *mškb'* 16:14.

škm (Hiphil). Syr *qdm* (Pael) (= *ορθριζειν) 32:6.

šlg. χιων 4:6.

šlwḥym. Syr *šwdḥ'* (= *εξαποστολαι) 18:2.

šlḥ (Piel). Syr *šdr* (Pael) (= *εξαποστελλειν) 6:1.

šlḥ yd-. Syr *mtḥ 'b'š* 22:10 (LXX v.11). This time *šlḥ* is Qal.

šlḥn. Syr *ptwr'* (= *τραπεζη) 37:14 (LXX 38:10), 15 (LXX 38:11); 40:24 (LXX v.22).

šlm (Piel infinitive absolute). Syr *pr'* (infinitive) (= *αποτινυειν, participle) 22:5 (LXX v.6), 13 (LXX v.14).

šlš (שָׁלֹשׁ). Syr *tlt* (= *τρεις, τρια) 38:1 (LXX 38:22).

šlšm (שִׁלְשֹׁם). τριτος, -η, -ον 5:7.

— *šlšm* (שְׁלֹשָׁם). 14:7.

šm. ονομα 28:21. Syr *šm'* (= *ονομα ?) 33:12.

šmh. Syr *tmn* (= *εκει) 40:30 (LXX v.26).

šmym. Syr *šmy'* (= *ουρανος) 24:10.

šmn. ελαιον (Syr *mšḥ'*) 35:8 (LXX v.7) *bis*. Syr *mšḥ'* (= *ελαιον) 35:14 (LXX v.16), 28.

šm'. Syr *šm'* (= *ακουειν) 32:18.

šmṣh. Only:

lšmṣh. επιχαρμα 32:25.

šmrym. Syr *nṭwrt'* and Syr *mṭrt'* (a doublet, out of place) (may = *παρατετηρημενος, -η, -ον and/or *παρατηρησις) 12:42. The clause is corrupt in ϑ'.

— *šmrym*. 12:42.

šny (שָׁנִי). διαφορος, -ον (Syr *mšḥlpt'*) 28:5. νενησμενος, -α, -ον or Syr *mšḥlp'* 28:6. αλλοιουμενος, -α, -ον or Syr *ṣby't'* 35:23. αλλοιουμενος, -α, -ον 35:35. Syr *mštgnynyt'* 28:33 (LXX v.29). Syr *'zylt'* (= *νενησμενος, etc. ?) 39:1 (LXX 39:13).

šnym, *štym*. δυο 26:17. Syr *tṛyn*, *tṛtyn* (= *δυο) 28:23 (MT) *ter*, 24 (MT) *bis*, 25 (MT) *ter*, 26 (MT) *bis*, 27 (MT) *bis*.

šnyt. Syr *trynyt'* 27:15.

šqd (Pual participle). Syr *d'yt 'lyhyn dmṭt' dlwz'* (= *εξαμυγδαλιζεσθαι, perfect participle) 25:33 (LXX v.32).

šql. Syr *syqlwn* (= *σικλος) 38:25 (LXX 39:2).

šrṣ. εξερπειν (Syr *ršp*) 1:7.

šršrt. χαλαστα (Syr *nṛpt'*) 28:14.

šršt. Syr *nṛpt'* (= *χαλαστα) 28:22.

šrt (Piel). Syr *šmš* (Pael) (= *λειτουργειν) 39:1 (LXX 39:13).

Piel participle. λειτουργος 24:13.

šš. βυσσος 28:6; 35:23, 35.

šth. πιειν (Syr *št'*) 7:24 *bis*.

štym. See *šnym*, *štym*.

tbh. κιβωτος 2:3.

tbn. αχυρον 5:7.

thmt. Syr *thwm'* 15:5.

twk. Only:

btwk. εν μεσω 28:32 (LXX v.28).

twl't. κοκκινον 28:5, 6; 35:23, 35. Syr *zhwryt'* (= *κοκκινον) 39:1 (LXX 39:13).

tw'bt (vocalized as construct singular of *tw'bh*). Syr *ṭnpwt'* (= *βδελυγματα) 8:22 (LXX v.26) *bis*

tḥr'. προσπλοκη or σειρωτος, -η, -ον 28:32 (LXX v.28).

tḥt. Syr *tḥyt* 38:4 (LXX 38:24).

tklt. υακινθος (Syr *tklt'*) 35:35. υακινθος 28:6; 35:23. Syr *tklt'* (= *υακινθος) 38:23 (LXX 37:21); 39:1 (LXX 39:13). Syr *tklt'* (= *υακινθινος) 28:28 (MT).

tmwl. εχθες 5:7.

tmyd. Syr *bkl zbn* (= *δια παντος) 28:29 (LXX v.25).

tmym (תֻּמִּים). Syr *šwmly'* (= *τελειοτητες ?) 28:30 (LXX v.26).

tnwk. Syr *ṭrp'* (= *λοβος) 29:20.

trwmh. Syr *ršyt'* (= *απαρχη) 25:2; 35:24.

Pronominal suffixes.

Object-suffixes on verbs: 2:14; 5:3; 6:1; 7:1; 8:22 (LXX v.26); 13:13; 20:25 (Ꞩ v.22); 21:8; 22:25 (LXX v.26); 32:24, 25; 34:20.

Subject-suffixes on infinitives construct: 28:1, 3; 31:18; 34:35.

Suffixes on prepositions:

On *'l*. 1:19.

On *'t*. 28:1; 35:23, 24; 28:23 (LXX 37:21).

On *b-*. 23:21. Cf. the treatment of MT *by* (the particle of entreaty) in 4:13.

On *byn*. 31:13, 17.

On *mmn-*. 25:15 (LXX v.14); 38:2 (LXX 38:22).

On *nkḥ*. 14:2.

On *'l*. 19:18; 20:25 (Ꞩ v.22); 40:29 (LXX v.26).

On *m'm*. 8:25 (LXX v.29).

Suffixes on *hnh*: 3:4.

Suffixes on the accusative particle (*'t*): 28:14, 26 (MT), 27 (MT); 29:24; 30:12; 37:4 (LXX 38:4), 11 (LXX 38:9), 15 (LXX 38:11); 38:2 (LXX 38:22), 6 (LXX 38:24).

Suffixes on substantives: 4:6, 25; 5:16 *bis*; 7:11; 8:3 (LXX v. 7), 6 (LXX v.10), 22 (LXX v.26) *bis*; 9:8, 20; 10:9 *bis*; 14:17, 29; 16:16, 21; 17:6, 7; 18:2; 20:25 (S̸ v.22); 21:6, 8, 36; 22:13 (LXX v.14), 14 (LXX v.15); 24:13; 25:10 (LXX v.9) *ter*, 12 (LXX v.11) *bis*, 17 (LXX v.16), 19 (LXX v.18), 20 (LXX v. 19), 23 (LXX v.22) *ter*, 36 *bis*, 38; 27:19; 28:4, 16 *bis*, 21, 25 (MT), 26 (MT), 27 (MT), 28 (MT), 32 (LXX v.28) *bis*; 29:16, 20, 28, 41; 30:2 *bis*, 3; 31:9; 32:2, 25, 29; 33:15; 34:9, 19; 35:11 (LXX v.10) *quater*, 14 (LXX v.15), 15 (LXX v.16), 16 (LXX v.17); 36:2, 38 (LXX 37:6); 37:1 (LXX 38:1) *ter*, 10 (LXX 38:9) *ter*, 12 (LXX 38:9), 13 (LXX 38:10), 17 (LXX 38:14), 26 (MT); 38:1 (LXX 38:22) *ter*, 2 (LXX 38:22) *ter*, 3 (LXX 38:23), 4 (LXX 38:24), 10 (LXX 37:8), 11 (LXX 37:9), 12 (LXX 37:10), 17 (LXX 37:15); 39:33 (LXX 39:14) *bis*, 37 (LXX 39:17), 39 (MT).

Untranslated: Suffixes on *pnyw* in 28:27 (MT) and on *'mdyw* in 35:11 (LXX v.10).

Doubtful: suffix on *kmhw* in 10:14. The variant is probably for MT *kn*, as marked, rather than for MT *kmhw*.

Suffix on *wbmtkntw*: ταυτην 30:32.

— Pronominal suffixes. On the accusative particle (*'t*) in 3:9 and on a substantive in 20:17 (S̸ v.14).

Dual ending on *'mtym*. Syr *tr̈tyn* (= *δυο) 37:1 (LXX 38:1), 10 (LXX 38:9), 25 (MT). Elsewhere the dual is treated as a plural, and receives no special translation.

"*He*-Directional." See -*h* (directional) after *h*- (definite article) and *h*- (interrogative particle).

BIBLIOGRAPHY

Barnes, William Emery, *et al.*, eds. *Pentateuchus syriace post Samuelem Lee*. London, 1914.

Barthélemy, Dominique. *Les devanciers d'Aquila: Première publication intégrale du texte des fragments du dodécaprophéton trouvés dans le désert de Juda, précédée d'une étude sur les traductions et recensions grecques de la Bible réalisées au premier siècle de notre ère sous l'influence du rabbinat palestinien*. Supplements to *VT*, 10. Leiden, 1963.

________ "Redécouverte d'un chaînon manquant de l'histoire de la Septante," *RB* 60 (1953), 18-29.

Bickerman, Elias J. "Some Notes on the Transmission of the Septuagint," in *Alexander Marx Jubilee Volume on the Occasion of His Seventieth Birthday*. New York, 1950, pp. 149-178.

Brooke, Alan England, and Norman McLean, with Henry St. John Thackeray for Vols. II and III, eds. *The Old Testament in Greek According to the Text of Codex Vaticanus, Supplemented from Other Uncial Manuscripts, with a Critical Apparatus Containing the Variants of the Chief Ancient Authorities for the Text of the Septuagint*. Vol. I: *The Octateuch*. Vol. II: *The Later Historical Books*. Vol. III, Part 1: *Esther, Judith, Tobit*. Cambridge, 1906-1940.

Brown, Francis, S. R. Driver, and Charles A. Briggs, eds. *A Hebrew and English Lexicon of the Old Testament with an Appendix Containing the Biblical Aramaic*. Corrected reprint of 1907 ed. Oxford, 1966.

Burkitt, F. Crawford, ed. *Fragments of the Books of Kings According to the Translation of Aquila*. Cambridge, 1897.

Burrows, Millar, *et al.*, eds. *The Dead Sea Scrolls of St. Mark's Monastery*. Vol. I: *The Isaiah Manuscript and the Habakkuk Commentary*. New Haven, 1950.

Ceriani, Antonio Maria, ed. *Codex Syro-Hexaplaris Ambrosianus photolithographice editus.* Monumenta sacra et profana, Vol. VII. Milan, 1874.

Cross, Frank Moore, Jr. *The Ancient Library of Qumran and Modern Biblical Studies.* Rev. ed. Garden City, New York, 1961.

________ "The History of the Biblical Text in the Light of Discoveries in the Judean Desert," *HTR* 57 (1964), 281-299.

DeRossi, Johannis Bern., ed. *Variae lectiones Veteris Testamenti ex immensa mss. editorumq. codicum congerie haustae et ad Samar. textum, ad vetustiss. versiones, ad accuratiores sacrae criticae fontes ac leges examinatae.* Reprint of the 1784-1798 Parma ed. 4 vols. and supp. in 2. Amsterdam, 1969-1970.

Field, Frederick, ed. *Origenis Hexaplorum quae supersunt sive veterum interpretum Graecorum in totum Vetus Testamentum fragmenta.* 2 vols. Oxford, 1875.

Hatch, Edwin, and Henry A. Redpath. *A Concordance to the Septuagint and the Other Greek Versions of the Old Testament (Including the Apocryphal Books).* Photomechanical reprint of the 1897 Oxford ed. 3 vols. in 2. Graz, Austria, 1954.

Holmes, Robert, and James Parsons, ed. *Vetus Testamentum graecum cum variis lectionibus.* 5 vols. in 4. Oxford, 1798-1827.

Kennicott, B., ed. *Vetus Testamentum Hebraicum cum variis lectionibus.* 2 vols. Oxford, 1776-1780.

Kittel, Rud., *et al.*, eds. *Biblia Hebraica.* 11th ed., emended printing of 7th ed., a revised and expanded version of 3d ed. Stuttgart, n.d.

Klein, Ralph W. "Studies in the Greek Texts of the Chronicler." Th.D. diss., Harvard University, 1966.

Lagarde, Paul de. *Bibliothecae Syriacae a Paulo de Lagarde collectae quae ad philologiam sacram pertinent.* Ed. Alfred Rahlfs. Göttingen, 1892.

Lisowsky, Gerhard. *Konkordanz zum hebräischen Alten Testament nach dem von Paul Kahle in der Biblia Hebraica edidit Rudolf Kittel besorgten Masoretischen Text.* Stuttgart, 1958.

Mandelkern, Solomon. *Veteris Testamenti Concordantiae Hebraicae atque Chaldaicae.* 5th expanded and rev. ed. Jerusalem—Tel-Aviv, 1962.

Orlinsky, Harry M. "The Columnar Order of the Hexapla," *JQR* n.s. 27 (1936-1937), 137-149.

Rahlfs, Alfred, ed. *Septuaginta: Id est Vetus Testamentum graece iuxta LXX interpretes.* 2 vols. 7th ed. Stuttgart, 1962.

Reider, Joseph. *An Index to Aquila, Greek-Hebrew·Hebrew-Greek·Latin-Hebrew, with the Syriac and Armenian Evidence.* Completed and revised by Nigel Turner. Supplements to *VT*, 12. Leiden, 1966.

Sanders, J. A., ed. *The Psalms Scroll of Qumrân Cave 11 (11Q Ps^{a}).* Discoveries in the Judean Desert of Jordan, IV. Oxford, 1965.

Shenkel, James Donald. *Chronology and Recensional Development in the Greek Text of Kings.* Harvard Semitic Monographs, 1. Cambridge, 1968.

Skehan, Patrick W. "The Qumran Manuscripts and Textual Criticism," *Volume du Congrès Strasbourg 1956.* Supplements to *VT*, 4. Leiden, 1957, pp. 148-158.

Sperber, Alexander, ed. *The Bible in Aramaic Based on Old Manuscripts and Printed Texts.* Vol. I: *The Pentateuch According to Targum Onkelos.* Leiden, 1959.

Swete, Henry Barclay. *An Introduction to the Old Testament in Greek.* Rev. ed. Cambridge, 1914.

Taylor, Charles, ed. *Hebrew-Greek Cairo Genizah Palimpsests from the Taylor-Schechter Collection.* Cambridge, 1900.

Thackeray, H. St. John. *The Septuagint and Jewish Worship: A Study in Origins.* The Schweich Lectures 1920. London, 1921.

Von Gall, August, ed. *Der hebräische Pentateuch der Samaritaner.* Photomechanical reprint of 1914-1918 Giessen ed. 5 vols. in one. Berlin, 1966.

Waltke, Bruce K. "Prolegomena to the Samaritan Pentateuch." Ph.D. diss., Harvard University, 1965.

Ziegler, Joseph, ed. *Septuaginta: Vetus Testamentum Graecum Auctoritate Academiae Litterarum Gottingensis editum.* Vol. XII, 1: *Sapientia Salomonis.* Vol. XII, 2: *Sapientia Iesu Filii Sirach.* Vol. XIII: *Duodecim Prophetae.* Vol. XIV: *Isaias.* Vol. XV: *Ieremias, Baruch, Threni, Epistula Ieremiae.* Vol. XVI, 1: *Ezechiel.* Vol. XVI, 2: *Susanna, Daniel, Bel et Draco.* Göttingen, 1939-1965.